V&R

Lutherjahrbuch

Organ der internationalen Lutherforschung

Im Auftrag der Luther-Gesellschaft herausgegeben von
Christopher Spehr

80. Jahrgang 2013

Luther als Lehrer und Reformer der Universität
Luther as Teacher and Reformer of the University

Hauptvorträge und Seminarberichte
des Zwölften Internationalen Kongresses für Lutherforschung
Helsinki / Finnland 5.–11. August 2012

Vandenhoeck & Ruprecht

Gedruckt mit freundlicher Unterstützung der VELKD.

Mit drei Abbildungen

Bibliografische Information der Deutschen Nationalbibliothek
Die Deutsche Nationalbibliothek verzeichnet diese Publikation in der
Deutschen Nationalbibliografie; detaillierte bibliografische Daten sind
im Internet über http://dnb.d-nb.de abrufbar.

ISBN 978-3-525-87445-5
ISBN 978-3-647-87445-6 (E-Book)

Anschriften

der Mitarbeiter:

Ass. Priest Phillip Anderas, St. Michael's Anglican Church, 34245 Nasho-tah Rd., USA-53058 Nashotah, WI; phillip.anderas@gmail.com; Prof. Dr. Albrecht Beutel, Erich-Greffin-Weg 37, D-48167 Münster, beutel@uni-muenster.de; Ass. Prof. Dr. Christopher B. Brown, Boston University School of Theology, 745 Commonwealth Ave., USA-02215 Boston, MA, cbbrown@bu.edu; Prof. Dr. Christoph Burger, Sonderholm 67, NL-2133 JB Hoofddorp, info@christophburger.nl; Prof. Dr. Kirsten Busch Nielsen, Det Teologiske Fakultet, Københavns Universitet, Købmagergade 44–46, DK-1150 København K, kbn@teol.ku.dk; PD Dr. Matthias Deuschle, Stefanusstraße 6, D-71083 Herrenberg, Matthias.Deuschle@elkw.de; Prof. Dr. Theodor Dieter, Institut für Ökumenische Forschung, 8, rue Gustave-Klotz, F-67000 Strasbourg, theodor_dieter@yahoo.de; Prof. Dr. Irene Dingel, Leibniz-Institut für Europäische Geschichte, Alte Universitätsstr. 19, D-55116 Mainz, dingel@ieg-mainz.de; Ass. Prof. Dr. Mary Jane Haemig, Luther Seminary, 2481 Como Avenue, USA-55108 Saint Paul, MN, mhaemig@luthersem.edu; Ass. Prof. Ph.D. Rev. H. Ashley Hall, Creighton University, 2500 California Plaza, USA-68102 Omaha, NE, h.hall@creigh-ton.edu; Prof. Dr. Christine Helmer, Northwestern University, Depart-ment of Religious Studies, Crowe Hall 5–179, 1860 Campus Drive, USA-60208 Evanston, IL, c-helmer@northwestern.edu; Prof. Dr. Bo Kristian Holm, Aarhus University, Jens Chr. Skous Vej 3, DK-8000 Aarhus C, BH@teo.au.dk; Bishop Eero Huovinen, Suonionkatu 7 C 40, FI-00530 Hel-sinki, eero.huovinen@helsinki.fi; Director Dr. Roger Jensen, Pilegrimssen-ter Oslo, Akersbakken 30, N-0172 Oslo, roger.jensen@teologi.uio.no; Ass.

Prof. Ph. D. Anna Marie Johnson, Garrett Evangelical Theological Seminary, 2121 Sheridan Rd., USA-60201 Evanston, IL, anna.johnson@garrett.edu; Adj. Prof. Dr. Pekka Kärkkäinen, University of Helsinki, Faculty of Theology, PO Box 4, FI-00014 University of Helsinki, pekka.karkkainen@helsinki.fi; Prof. Dr. Ulrich Köpf, Liststr. 24/1, D-72074 Tübingen; Pfr. Dr. Roland M. Lehmann, August-Bebel-Str. 30, D-06618 Naumburg, roland.lehmann@uni-jena.de; Rev. Prof. Dr. Pilgrim W. K. Lo, Lutheran Theological Seminary, Hong Kong, 50 To Fung Shan Road, Shatin, Hong Kong China, pilgrimlo@yahoo.co.uk; Ass. Prof. Dr. Mark Mattes, Grand View College, 1200 Grandview Ave., USA-50316 Des Moines, IA, mmattes@grandview.edu; Dr. Stefan Michel, Lutherstraße 18, D-07743 Jena, s.michel@uni-jena.de; Pfr. Dr. Matthias Mikoteit, Im Wiesengrund 44, D-46342 Velen-Ramsdorf, matthias.mikoteit@t-online.de; Prof. James Arne Nestingen, St. Paul Lutheran Seminary, 2216 Ferris Lane, USA-55113 St. Paul, MN, nesjim@gmail.com; Vikar Dr. Christoph T. Nooke, Kettelerstraße 22, D-48147 Münster, ctnooke@gmx.de; Prof. Dr. Friederike Nüssel, Ruprechts-Karls-Universität Heidelberg, Ökumenisches Institut, Plankengasse 1, D-69117 Heidelberg, Friederike.Nuessel@oek.uni-heidelberg.de; Ass. Prof. Ph. D. Else Marie Wiberg Pedersen, Aarhus University, Jens Chr. Skous Vej 3, DK-8000 Aarhus C, EWP@teo.au.dk; Prof. Dr. Michael Plathow, Beintweg 41, D-69181 Leimen, michael@plathow.de; Prof. Dr. Tarald Rasmussen, University of Oslo, Faculty of Theology, PO Box 1023, Blindern, N-0315 Oslo, tarald.rasmussen@teologi.uio.no; Prof. Dr. Ricardo Willy Rieht, Universidade lutherana do Brasil, Rua Borges de Medeiros, 495, BR-93030–200 São Leopoldo, RS, ricardo.rieth@gmail.com; Prof. Dr. Miikka Ruokanen, University of Helsinki, Faculty of Theology, PO Box 33, FI-00014 Helsinki, miikka.ruokanen@helsinki.fi; Prof. Dr. Dr. Risto Saarinen, University of Helsinki, Faculty of Theology, PO Box 33, FI-00014 Helsinki, risto.saarinen@helsinki.fi; Spiritual Pater Dr. Augustinus Sander OSB, Abtei vom Hl. Kreuz zu Herstelle, Carolus-Magnus-Str. 9, D-37688 Beverungen, p.augustinus@web.de; Prof. Dr. Dr. Johannes Schilling, Esmarckstraße 64, D-24105 Kiel, jschilling@kg.uni-kiel.de; Prof. Dr. Brooks Schramm, Lutheran Theological Seminary at Gettysburg, 61 Seminary Ridge, USA-17325 Gettysburg, PA, bschramm@ltsg.edu; Prof. Dr. Jens Schröter, Humboldt-Universität zu Berlin, Theologische Fakultät, Burgstr. 26, D-10178 Berlin, schroetj@cms.hu-berlin.de; Prof. Dr. Notger Slenczka, Humboldt-Universität zu Berlin, Theologische Fakultät, Burgstr. 26, D-10178 Berlin, notger.slenczka@theologie.hu-berlin.de; Prof. Dr. Christopher Spehr, Fritz-Krieger-Straße 1, D-07743 Jena, christopher.spehr@uni-jena.de; Prof. Dr. Kirsi I. Stjerna, Lutheran Theological Seminary at Gettysburg, 61 Seminary Ridge, USA-17325 Gettysburg, PA, kstjerna@ltsg.edu; Prof. Dr. Wolfgang Thönissen, Johann-Adam-Möhler-Institut für Ökumenik, Leostr. 19a, D-33098 Paderborn, A.Pollmann@moehlerinstitut.de; Ass. Prof. Dr. Anna Vind, University of Copenhagen, Faculty of Theology, Købmagergade 44–46, DK-1150 København K, av@teol.ku.dk; Dr. Andrew Wilson, 10, quai Kléber, F-67000 Strasbourg, alarswilson@gmail.com; Prof. Dr. Markus Wriedt, Goethe-Universität Frankfurt, Fachbereich Ev. Theologie, Grüneburgplatz 1, D-60323 Frankfurt am Main, m.wriedt@em.uni-frankfurt.de

Vorwort des Präsidenten der Luther-Gesellschaft

Das Lutherjahrbuch erscheint in diesem Jahr als Berichtsband des 12. Internationalen Kongresses für Lutherforschung, der vom 5. bis 11. August 2012 in Helsinki stattfand. Er bezeugt Reichtum und Vielfalt der Vorträge und Diskussionen und berichtet über die Seminare, die in Helsinki gehalten wurden und in denen die Lutherforschung in großer thematischer Breite und vielfältigen Aspekten zur Darstellung kam.

Seit dem 6. Internationalen Kongress für Lutherforschung in Erfurt 1983 dient das Lutherjahrbuch als Publikationsort für die Veröffentlichung der Vorträge und Berichte dieses bedeutenden Symposiums. Die gute Verbindung zwischen dem Continuation Committee des Kongresses für Lutherforschung und der Luther-Gesellschaft ist durch Helmar Junghans gestiftet und über Jahrzehnte gepflegt worden, der als Herausgeber des Lutherjahrbuchs Mitglied des Vorstands der Luther-Gesellschaft war und zugleich dem Continuation Committee angehörte. Während des Schlussbanketts in Helsinki am 10. August 2012 hat seine Witwe, Frau Thekla Junghans, Leidenschaft und Leistung ihres Mannes für die Lutherforschung noch einmal beeindruckend zur Sprache gebracht.

Das vorliegende Jahrbuch ist zugleich das erste unter der Herausgeberschaft von Christopher Spehr. Herr Spehr, Professor für Kirchengeschichte an der Friedrich-Schiller-Universität Jena, gehört dem Vorstand der Luther-Gesellschaft seit 2010 an. Dass er Herausgeber des Lutherjahrbuchs werden würde, war zunächst nicht abzusehen. Nach dem Willen des Vorstands der Luther-Gesellschaft und dem Wunsch von Helmar Junghans hatte Professor Dr. Albrecht Beutel 2010 die Herausgeberschaft des

Jahrbuchs übernommen. Er hat die unter seiner Herausgeberschaft erschienenen Bände vorbildlich betreut. Als ihm die Herausgeberschaft der Zeitschrift für Theologie und Kirche angetragen wurde, mochte er sich dieser ehrenvollen Verpflichtung nicht entziehen, sah sich aber nicht in der Lage, auch das Lutherjahrbuch weiterhin als Herausgeber zu betreuen.

Dass Christopher Spehr, sein ehemaliger Assistent, seinem Lehrer in diesem Amt nachfolgt, mag als ein gutes Zeichen für Kontinuität wie für Qualität gelten. Der Vorstand der Luther-Gesellschaft dankt seinem Mitglied Albrecht Beutel für die geleistete Arbeit während seiner Herausgeberschaft und er begrüßt sein Mitglied Christopher Spehr in seinem neuen Amt des Herausgebers des Jahrbuchs mit guten Wünschen. Auf seine Weise wird das Lutherjahrbuch Organ der internationalen Lutherforschung bleiben. Der vorliegende Band ist dafür der schönste Beweis.

Weil der neue Herausgeber anstrebt, das Lutherjahrbuch jährlich im Herbst erscheinen zu lassen, fällt die von Dr. Michael Beyer mit großer Umsicht zusammengestellte Lutherbibliographie dieses Jahr ein wenig schmaler aus. Für die redaktionelle Arbeit an dem vorliegenden 80. Jahrgangsband sei den Jenaer Mitarbeiterinnen und Mitarbeitern Frau Ute Jakob, Frau Johanna Hilpert, Herrn Markus Löffler, Frau Ulrike Löffler und Frau Susann Häßelbarth sowie allen, die am Zustandekommen dieses Buchs tatkräftig mitgewirkt haben, herzlich gedankt.

Kiel, den 31. Mai 2013   Johannes Schilling

Doctor communis?

The ecumenical significance of Martin Luther's theology

Eero Huovinen

Distinguished participants of the 12th International Congress for Luther Research, sisters and brothers in Christ.

It is a great joy and honour to welcome you to Helsinki, and especially to the Lutheran Cathedral of Helsinki. As you entered the sanctuary, you noticed the statues of three Reformers, Martin Luther, Philip Melanchthon, as well as our own, namely, Bishop Michael Agricola. This Cathedral was built with money granted by the Russian Orthodox Czar in the 19th century. Yet, we Finns, and now you, our honoured guests, are solidly situated in the midst of the Reformation tradition. The altar painting truly depicts the person central to our Christian faith, Jesus Christ.

The nature of scholarly research is that it is analytical and critical. The objective is to find the specific characteristics of the subject under scrutiny, that is, its exceptionality. In the study of history, we aim to put emphases on the uniqueness of each era, every ideological trend, each individual thinker.

In addition, when we study the Reformation we frequently ask how Martin Luther stands out from his own environment and background, from his contemporaries. What is Luther *specificus*? What relation does he have to the Medieval Roman Catholic Church and its theology?

This issue can be approached from different angles. For a good while, we looked for »the real« Luther by emphasising the differences and disputes that he had in regard to the mainstream of his time. Many researchers maintained that it was either Luther's fault or to his credit that the western part of Christendom was divided in the 16th century.

The viewpoint of this research shifted as late as the middle of last century. While nonetheless admitting the differences, both Catholic and Lutheran scholars now aim to assess how Luther connects with the preceding age and with the classic interpretation of Christianity. This has no doubt happened because of the rise of the Ecumenical Movement since World War II. As 2017 draws nearer, we find it appropriate to ask what the ecumenical significance is of Martin Luther and his theology, what they mean a half a millennium after the Reformation.

I Martin Luther as ecumenical »problem«

In the Fifth Assembly of the Lutheran World Federation at Evian, France, 1970, Cardinal Jan Willebrands applied the classic Roman Catholic title of *doctor communis* to Martin Luther. Cardinal Willebrands referred to the well-known thought of Luther that justification is the doctrine upon which the church stands or falls. In speaking of this matter, Luther can also be a »common teacher« for the Roman Catholic Church, because Luther desires that »God will remain our Lord and that our most important human response is unconditional trust and respect for God.«[1]

The title Cardinal used of Luther, *doctor communis*, is one of the honorifics of St Thomas Aquinas. According to Willebrands, St Thomas and Luther, the Middle Ages and the Reformation, belong together. Luther represents and continues a common tradition. Nevertheless, *doctor communis* is not simply a historical title, pointing to the past. With this title, the Cardinal wishes to show us that Luther has something to say jointly to the Roman Catholic and Lutheran Churches.

Cardinal Willebrands' thoughts are continued by Karl Lehmann, then Roman Catholic Bishop of Mainz. Cardinal Lehmann writes of the ecumenical significance of Luther's *Small Catechism*. Lehmann states that the *Small* and *Large Catechisms* – in contrast to certain other writings of Luther – are an excellent example of the linkage of the Reformer with earlier tradition.

Within the history of the church Luther's *Catechisms* are neither new nor the random contrivance of a single theologian. Rather, they are closely

---

1 J. WILLEBRANDS, Mandatum unitatis. Beiträge zur Ökumene, 1989, 124.

related, both in their structure and their content, to the classical theology of the early church and the medieval church. According to Lehmann, Luther is a »Teacher of the Faith« (*Lehrer des Glaubens*).[2]

Although the churches' evaluations of Luther have throughout history differed greatly as to content and estimation, both sides have long held certain features to be common. Just as Luther's valuation as *doctor communis* has not been self-apparent to Roman Catholics, it has not been that clear to Protestants either. Luther has been interpreted as an individual, a person who started something new – whether that was negative or positive. Luther created a new »protestant« Christian belief – or at least he presented an interpretation of the original belief which differed radically from the faith of earlier centuries.

According to Roman Catholics, Luther departed from the one, catholic tradition – which was his downfall. In the assessment of Protestants, Luther departed from tradition, and that was his accomplishment. Overstating the case only slightly, we can say that Luther was not *doctor communis* for either side.

For Roman Catholics Luther has been one of those deviating from the main tide, in other words, a heretic, while for the Protestants he has been a guiding light whose significance is emphasized against an otherwise dark firmament overshadowing the church. And even when Luther has been studied in relation to his background of ecclesiastical and general history, his qualities, uniqueness and digression from the norm, that is to say, his significance as an individual has come to the fore. So it is rather understandable that there has not been enough motivation for scrutinizing Luther as *doctor communis*, as a representative of the one, classical Christendom.[3]

---

2 K. Lehmann, Luther als Lehrer des Glaubens? Die ökumenische Bedeutung seiner Katechismen (LKW 45, 1998, 131–146).

3 »Die Bedeutung des überkommenen Dogmas für Luther kann schwerlich überschätzt werden; sie ist in der Forschung weithin zu gering veranschlagt worden.« B. Lohse, Martin Luther. Eine Einführung in sein Leben und sein Werk, 1981, 171. On the history of Luther research, see 207–246.

II Luther, individualist destroying the Church?

During the Reformation, Roman Catholics depicted Luther as an arch-heretic and as a destroyer of the unity of the church. Even at the beginning of the 20th century Luther was seen in dark colours, not only to be avoided in doctrine but also to be studied under the typology of a personal pathology. For example Heinrich Denifle claimed that Luther had created his doctrine of justification simply in order to be able to live a carefree, libertarian life himself. From these viewpoints, we could say that both Luther the person and Luther the theologian were viewed as a sum of individual flaws and biases.

On the eve of the Second World War, there was a new breakthrough both academically and ecumenically in the publication of Joseph Lortz's book: *Die Reformation in Deutschland*. Lortz critiqued the errors of the medieval church. He strove to understand Luther's own spiritual intentions. He appreciated Luther as a »religious personality«. Nonetheless, he concluded that as a theologian Luther was a »subjectivist«. In Lortz's view Luther represents a catholicity without being catholic in an authentic sense. In a unique way Luther had stressed the significance of the Apostle Paul. Yet, Luther did not attend fully (*Vollhörer*) to the Holy Bible. The revolutionary Luther was entirely a prisoner of his own deliberations.[4]

The theory of Luther's subjectivism was soon re-evaluated by Roman Catholic scholars. Lortz's own students, in particular Erwin Iserloh and Peter Manns, held that the thesis of subjectivism was overly superficial and denigrating. Manns used the name »Father in Faith« (*Vater im Glauben*) for Luther. Manns examined Luther with special reference to the devotional life of the medieval and early churches. The title »Father in Faith« arises from that spiritual tradition.

In his broad-ranging study of St Thomas Aquinas and Martin Luther, Otto Hermann Pesch asserted that their understanding of the doctrine of justification was not mutually exclusive. Thus, Luther's theology is to be

---

4 J. LORTZ, Die Reformation in Deutschland, Bd. 1–2, 1941. See also: E. HUOVINEN, Die ökumenische Bedeutung des Luther-Verständnisses von Joseph Lortz für die Luther-forschung in Finnland (in: Zum Gedenken an Joseph Lortz. Beiträge zur Reformations-geschichte und Ökumene [VIEG.B 30], hg. v. R. DECOT/R. VINKE, 1989, 262–292).

properly situated among the common traditions of Christendom, regardless of the denomination of the person doing the evaluation.[5]

In official Roman Catholic evaluations after Vatican II, the position afforded to Luther is substantially different from those given at the beginning of the 20th century. In addition to Cardinal Willebrands and other ecumenics, Pope John Paul II in several instances quoted Luther's spiritual texts, e.g. the *Commentary on Romans*. Furthermore, he spoke positively of Luther's significance for all of Christendom.

III A precursor of individual freedom?

Mutatis mutandum, Protestant Luther research has followed the same channels as Roman Catholic scholarship. Protestant studies either historically or systematically tended to support a view of Luther as »the Reformer«. Indirectly, this research setting quite possibly led to an emphasis on Luther's distinctiveness and exceptionality.

In examining the history of Protestant Luther studies[6], it is rather amazing how radically Luther is emphatically viewed as extraordinary and original. During the period of Lutheran Orthodoxy, Luther was held by many to be unique, even infallible, as a teacher of correct doctrine. Luther was considered to correspond to the angel in Revelation: »having an eternal gospel to preach to those who dwell on the earth, and to every nation and tribe and tongue and people« (Rev 14:6). Pietism regarded Luther's theology as an expression of individual piety, i.e. from the point of view of regenerated, living faith and sanctification. In such a view, the significance of the Christian faith lies in the internal and personal experience of belief.

---

5 Martin Luther »Reformator und Vater im Glauben«. Referate aus der Vortragsreihe des Instituts für Europäische Geschichte Mainz, hg. v. P. MANNS (VIEG.B 18), 1985; P. MANNS, Vater im Glauben. Studien zur Theologie Martin Luthers, Festgabe zum 65. Geburtstag am 10. März 1988, hg. v. R. DECOT (VIEG 131), 1988; O.H. PESCH, Theologie der Rechtfertigung bei Martin Luther und Thomas von Aquin, 1967; O.H. PESCH, Martin Luther, Thomas von Aquin und die reformatorische Kritik an der Scholastik. Zur Geschichte und Wirkungsgeschichte eines Missverständnisses mit weltgeschichtlichen Folgen, 1994.

6 See LOHSE (see n. 3), 213–240.

During the Enlightenment, Luther was construed as the precursor of the freedom of reason and the conscience, the one who freed the Christian faith from the dark disbelief of the Middle Ages. The general anthropological mode of thought, characteristic of the era, led to a delineation of Luther as a situation-bound thinker whose thoughts could not claim normativeness. Luther was esteemed as a great person and fighter, but he too was to be critically evaluated on the basis of reason and the ethical demands of the conscience.

Gotthold Ephraim Lessing boasted of Luther that he set people free from the bondage of tradition. The task of the Enlightenment was only to carry this liberation to its fruition. Frederick the Great was not satisfied even with this, but rejoiced that Luther, the »poor, damn devil«, freed the people from the yoke of the priests and thus increased the income of the state. Lutheranism began to change into Protestantism, which turned into enlightened subjectivism.

Albert Ritschl strove to place Luther into his own historical framework. Nevertheless, Ritschl was of the opinion that Luther's value was primarily in the overturning of old speculative metaphysics and mysticism. Ultimately, Luther proclaimed freedom and independence of the soul.

More recent Luther research has been deeply influenced by the same Protestant theological models. In popular church discussions Luther is often held to be a situation-bound dilettante, or an otherwise unrestrained exception in the history of theology, one to whom Christians following current trends should not be too committed. Such comments often reflect, in their background, the same setting of the question: Was Luther a private sage or *doctor communis*?

Contrary to the previously used paradigm emphasizing the differences between the Catholic Middle Ages and Luther, we find that, for example, in the United States, Profs. Robert Jenson and Carl Braaten's theological interpretation of the »Catholicity of the Reformation« has brought up new points of view.[7] In Finland, similar new thoughts were also intro-

---

7 See C. E. BRAATEN/R. W. JENSON (ed.), Catholicity of the Reformation, 1996.

duced by Prof. Tuomo Mannermaa and his students.[8] Both of these parties delineated the philosophical, theological, and spiritual nature of the Middle Ages, thus attempting to understand the era preceding Luther. Furthermore, they focused their attention on how the modern image of Luther has been influenced by various philosophical preconceptions and trends.

So, back to our fundamental question: Was Luther exceptional, unique, i.e. in some manner a *novum*, or was he rather one link, one witness on the chain of the shared classic Christian faith? Without a doubt, this question is, to the observant academic researcher, quite a generalised one. Nonetheless, answering it may be a justifiable attempt to understand heuristically what is at stake in Luther's theology and, shall we dare to say, the whole of Christian belief. Was Luther simply the father of Lutheranism or was he also, for all of Christendom, »*Vater im Glauben*«? *Doctor privatus* or *doctor communis*?

IV *The ecumenical significance of Luther's* Catechisms

In attempting an incipient answer to the question above, I want to adapt the interpretation of Karl Lehmann. According to Lehmann's view, particularly the *Catechisms* of Luther can, for their part, shed light on both Luther's relationship to the tradition preceding him and on his significance for the church today. Lehmann says he is astonished how little Luther's *Catechisms* have undergone ecumenical evaluation.[9] There appear to be at least six well-founded reasons for giving the *Catechisms* an ecumenical reading.

(1) First, the *Small* and *Large Catechisms* are examples of Luther's deepest desire to be *doctor communis*. In the *Catechisms*, if anywhere, Luther

---

8 On Finnish Luther research, see J. Forsberg, Die finnische Lutherforschung seit 1979 (LuJ 72, 2005, 147–182).

9 Lehmann (see n. 2), 142. In 1999 the Finnish Evangelical Lutheran Church approved a new official *Catechism*. Its base text was written by Eero Huovinen. Due to its historical and ecumenical significance, the *Catechism* included the entire text of Luther's *Small Catechism*. This new *Catechism* has been translated, e.g., into English, Swedish, Latin, Arabic, Russian, Chinese, Hungarian, German, Spanish, Croatian, and French.

was *doctor*, a teacher of the ordinary people and a guide of priests in need of theological knowledge and training. Among Luther's writings, the *Catechisms* emphasize most visibly what is common to the classic Christian faith.

In accord with the basic idea of a catechism, Luther wanted to teach what is necessary in being and living as a Christian. As *doctor*, Luther, the catechete, was primarily a spiritual teacher. His goals of teaching and learning were not just to increase knowledge for its own sake, but to foster faith in God and to strengthen love for one's fellow human being.

(2) Secondly, in his *Catechisms* Luther was *doctor communis* in the sense that he structured his catechetical teaching on the foundation of a long tradition. That is to say, Luther's *Small* and *Large Catechisms* were firmly, knowingly built on the framework of the tradition of the Jews and of the early church (the Decalogue, the Creed, the Lord's Prayer, and the Sacraments). Even in its own time Luther's catechetical ideas were neither original nor a new plan. The Commandments, Creed, and Lord's Prayer were the didactic heritage of the Middle Ages.

Although catechetic-type books of this form had not been written down, the three primary points mentioned above were the main body of Christian upbringing. Peter Abelard prepared his famous *Commentary on the Apostles' Creed and the Lord's Prayer*, which all Christians were to study together and learn by heart. Erasmus of Rotterdam wrote a catechism soon after 1510. This is the structure Luther developed and deepened.

The very framework of the catechism emphasizes continuity with the tradition of the faith. The Ten Commandments are the foundation of the Judeo-Christian way of life. The Apostles' Creed has its roots in the first Christian century. The Lord's Prayer is the model prayer taught by Jesus. The solutions of Luther's *Catechism* are more those coming from the Jews, the New Testament and Early Christianity than they are innovations of the Reformation.

(3) Thirdly, Luther's *Catechisms*, especially the explanation of the Third Article of the Creed, are constructed on two classic dogmas of Christianity, i.e. the doctrines of the trinity and the two natures of Christ.

Although justification is not mentioned as a term in the catechisms, it is implicitly a central theme and is firmly based on trinitarian doctrine and christology: Salvation is the work of the triune God, which is grounded in the person and work of Jesus Christ. Currently, the Roman Catholic Church, the World Council of Churches, the Lutheran World Federation, as well as the constitutions of many other ecumenical organizations are built upon these *dogmata*.

(4) Fourthly, Luther's *Catechisms* are also witness to the common faith in the sense that, in them, controversial theology aimed at either Rome or the radical Reformation remains only in a subordinate role. The *Small Catechism* does not include any direct polemic. The *Large Catechism*, intended for pastors, has some critical comments on the »church of the Pope« and on spiritualistic baptismal concepts, but in comparison to Luther's other writings, it does not have anti-ecumenical, controversialist traits.

(5) Fifthly, in line with Karl Lehmann's thoughts, in Luther's *Large Catechism* one can discern a spiritual self-critical ethos, which may also have ecumenical significance.

The *Large Catechism* is a good example of what an honest and open-minded analysis of the church and Christendom could be. At the same time the *Catechism* boasts of the breakthrough of the Gospel, it appraises not only the problems of its theological opponents but also, in the same measure, the pitiful mediocrity of the Christian life of its own camp.

In the Preface, for example, we read that it is expressly its own »shepherds«, i.e. the priests who had migrated to the Reformation camp, who were afforded an earful as »lazy bellies« (*faule Wänste, ignavos vetres*) and »presumptuous saints« (*vermessene Heiligen, praesumptuosos sanctos*). They are depicted as being more interested in the perquisites of their office than in the duties of the office, or in such matters as prayer, study and serving the parishioners: »These shameful gluttons and servants of their bellies are better suited to be swineherds or keepers of dogs than guardians of souls and pastors.« Self-criticism in regard to one's own Church and one's own state of Christianity is a precondition for genuine ecumenical relations.

(6) Sixthly, in the explanations of the Sacraments at the end of the *Large Catechism*, Luther attempts to link up with the teaching of his predecessors. This too has positive ecumenical significance. Sacramental teaching of Martin Luther is characterized by a strong theological realism and an understanding of the effectiveness of the Word of God. Baptism, confession, and Holy Communion do not simply refer to things external to themselves, but they include and give Christ and all his works. They are the efficacious signs (*signa efficacia*) of Christ's presence, God's grace and the communion of Christians.[10]

V *The central place of the Sacraments*

The Holy Sacraments have central standing in the *Catechisms* of Luther as well as in his other texts. Baptism joins one both to Christ and to his church. In accord with the strong words of the *Catechism*, in baptism God donates to the believer »victory over death and the devil, forgiveness of sin, God's grace, the entire Christ and all his Works, and the Holy Spirit with his gifts.«[11] Simultaneously, it is made clear that the one who is baptized every single day needs teaching, prayer, exhortation, and the support of other Christians in order to prevail over troubles, to persevere in faith, and to be strengthened in love.

In addition to Baptism, there is a link established to theological realism in the explanation of Holy Communion in the *Catechism*. The Eucharist is the meal of Christ's presence, which joins to other Christians and donates »the forgiveness of sins and everlasting life«.

Currently, the doctrine and praxis of Holy Communion remain a central ecumenical issue between Lutherans and Roman Catholics as well as other churches. Holy Communion includes nearly all theological *loci* from creation to redemption and eschatology. The bottleneck choking off the visible unity of the Churches is the theology of the ministry, which reaches its culmination in Holy Communion.

---

10 On the effective character of the sacraments in the theology of Luther, see E. HUOVINEN, Fides infantium. Martin Luthers Lehre vom Kinderglauben (VIEG 159), 1997, 45–74.
11 Large Catechism, Baptism, 41 f.

Thus, it is interesting to ask what Martin Luther's concept of Holy Communion could bring to the rapprochement between the churches in our day. Could he also be *doctor communis* for the theology of the Eucharist?[12]

VI The Sacrament of Christ's presence

To Martin Luther, the Eucharist was the sacrament of Christ's real presence. Thus it is not only a feast of remembrance where we recall Jesus' teachings and deeds. Neither is it a mere symbolic feast where the bread and the wine might remind us of Christ's body, absent and distant in heaven.

Luther frequently repeated the words of institution, that is, »this is my body«, *hoc est corpus meum*. These words are to be interpreted simply and realistically. The host does not merely signify the body of the Lord, referring only to a Christ dwelling elsewhere. The words of institution include and effect what they promise.

The concept of the real presence, naturally enough, is not the sole content of Holy Communion in the Bible and tradition. Luther, too, links other motifs to Communion: grace and the forgiveness of sins, the communion of Christians, the remembrance of Christ, the meal of gratitude to and confession of faith in God. It is at one and the same time the representation of the sacrifice given by Christ on Golgatha and the foretaste of the heavenly feast.

According to Luther the essence of the Eucharist is, however, the real presence of Christ's body and blood in the bread and the wine. To Luther this faith was no abstract theological theory or philosophical idea. He wanted to rely on the simple Word of God, on the New Testament instituted by Christ himself. Christ gave his own body »for us for the forgiveness of sins« (Mt 26: 28).

Faith in the real presence of Christ at the Eucharist has always united Lutherans and Catholics. We have always wanted to have confidence that

---

12 See, e.g.: Justification in the Life of the Church: A Report from the Roman Catholic – Lutheran Dialogue Group for Sweden and Finland, 2010.

Christ himself is present at the Holy Eucharist in the bread and the wine »truly and in substance«, *vere et substantialiter*, giving the baptized believer the reality of all of salvation. As a community the church lives in the true meaning of the words *de eucharistia*, out of the mystery and gift of the Eucharist.

In accordance with the Lutheran theology of the Eucharist, Christ's real presence is based on the doctrine of God, on Christology and on the doctrine of justification. To Luther God is in his essence the Giver and the Donor.

According to the Creed, the Triune God is not a jealous judge or a merchant demanding compensation, but rather self-sacrificing Love, who loves us and wants good things for us. Luther summed up the message of the Creed by using the metaphor of giving gifts:

> We see here in the Creed how God gives himself completely to us, with all his gifts and power [...] the Father gives us all creation, Christ all his works and the Holy Spirit all his gifts.[13]

God's love is the reason for Christ's incarnation and the basis for the Sacrament of the Eucharist. Out of love for us God became man in Christ, making peace with us. Out of love for us Christ instituted the Eucharist so that he might continue to be present among us and to bring the gifts of reconciliation to our lives.

Christ's real presence at the Eucharist is thus in inseparable union with the gift of the Sacrament, its efficacy. The Eucharist is the feast of Christ's death and resurrection, where we partake of the reconciliation on

---

13 M. LUTHER, The Large Catechism (in: The Book of Concord: The Confessions of the Evangelical Lutheran Church, ed. by R. KOLB/T.J. WENGERT, 2000, 440). »Here in the Creed you have the entire essence, will, and work of God exquisitely depicted in very brief but rich words [...]. For in all three articles God himself has revealed and opened to us the most profound depths of his fatherly heart and his pure, unutterable love [...]. We see here in the Creed how God gives himself completely to us, with all his gifts and power, to help us keep the Ten Commandments: the Father gives us all creation, Christ all his works and the Holy Spirit all his gifts.« Large Catechism, II, 63–69. On the theology of the Eucharist in Luther, see e.g.: J. JOLKKONEN, Eucharist (in: Engaging Luther: A [New] Theological Assessment, ed. by O.-P. VAINIO, 2010, 108–137).

the cross, the forgiveness of sins, life eternal – all in all, we partake of Christ himself.

Trust in Christ's real presence in the Sacrament of the Eucharist is such a treasure of faith which could bring Lutherans ever closer to Roman Catholics, the Orthodox, and to other Christians who confess this faith in doctrine and practice.

It is this mystery of faith that Pope John Paul II wrote about in his encyclical *Ecclesia de Eucharistia*. Christ, the true man and the true God is present in the bread and the wine of the Eucharist really, wholly and entirely.[14] We Lutherans can also wholeheartedly join in the words of the encyclical concerning Christ's presence and the gift of the Eucharist. Christ's presence is true »in objective reality«, *in ipsa rerum natura*, and »independently of our minds«, *a nostro scilicet spiritu disiuncta*. The Sacrament of the Eucharist, apart from bringing Christ's person and work into the present, also donates them to us personally. »The Eucharist thus applies (*applicat*) to men and women today the reconciliation won once for all by Christ for mankind in every age.«[15]

VII *The Eucharist and Christ's sacrifice*

As a feast of the presence of Christ crucified and resurrected, the Eucharist is also a feast of sacrifice. During the Lutheran Reformation a dispute arose as to how the Eucharist could be understood as a sacrifice in the genuine sense so that the sacrifice would not cancel out the gift. In describing Christ's sacrifice on the cross, the New Testament uses the Greek word *ephapax*, meaning something sufficient, perfect, unique, something not repeatable (Heb 10:10). What is the relation of this sacrifice given by Christ on the cross to the sacrifice of the Eucharist?

In ecumenical dialogues with the Roman Catholic Church we Lutherans have been concerned about the sufficiency of Christ's cross, asking: If the Eucharist is understood as being an independent propitiatory sacrifice, does that not render the sacrifice on the cross insufficient, questioning

---

14 Ecclesia de Eucharistia, §15.
15 Ibd., §12.

Christ as the only mediator?[16] And, Catholics have been concerned about the efficacy of the Eucharist. They ask: If the connection between the Eucharist and Christ's sacrifice were to be severed, would the benefit of the cross and its fruit be left in the past, in which case also the Eucharist might lose its significance?

In the light of both Luther studies and of ecumenical dialogues, we can state that despite the differences in emphases we Lutherans are of one accord with Roman Catholics in two vital issues. United we can say that 1) Christ's sacrifice is unique and sufficient and 2) it is truly and efficaciously present in the celebration of the Eucharist.

The commission on the Lutheran-Catholic dialogues in 1980 stated:

> Catholic and Lutheran Christians together recognize that in the Lord's Supper Jesus Christ ›is present as the Crucified who died for our sins and who rose again for our justification, as the once-for-all sacrifice for the sins of the world‹. This sacrifice can neither be continued, nor repeated, nor replaced nor complemented; but rather, it can and should become effective ever anew in the midst of the congregation.[17]

For us Lutherans it is important that Christ's sacrifice need not be repeated or complemented. Without the perfect and sufficient propitiatory work performed by Christ, we lack the strength to live. Our faith and sacrifice arise out of joy and gratitude that our reconciliation is perfect and that we can talk about it in the past: Sin *was* reconcil*ed*, victory acquir*ed* and final peace achiev*ed*. Is this not actually the entire core and content of the Gospel?

Nevertheless, in a great many meanings we can, together with Luther, call the Eucharist a sacrifice. First, at the beginning of the liturgy of the Eucharist, we carry bread and wine to the altar as an offering and as a symbol of thanksgiving for creation.[18] Second, in Holy Communion Christ is present as the sacrificed and crucified Lord. Third, the Eucharist is the commemoration in word and deed of Christ's sacrifice (*memoria passio-*

---

16 The Eucharist, §59, Lutheran/Roman Catholic Joint Commission, LWF 1980.

17 The Eucharist, §56, Lutheran/Roman Catholic Joint Commission, LWF 1980. Quotation from the US dialogue document.

18 »Panis enim et vinum antea offeruntur ad benedicendum, ut per verbum et orationem santificentur. Postquam autem benedictus et consecratus est, iam non offertur sed accipitur dono a deo.« WA 6; 525,1–3.

nis). Fourth, Christ's sacrifice is currently present at the Eucharist (*repraesentatio passionis*). Fifth, the fruit, benefit and gift of Christ's cross are applied (*applicat*) to the believing recipients. Sixth, we sacrifice to God thanksgiving when we confess our sins, give thanks, pray and celebrate the Eucharist in accord with the First Commandment, the institution of Christ and the apostolic admonition (Rm 12:1). Seventh, the Eucharist constrains us to sacrifice ourselves to one another as an offering in mutual love.

Eighth – and maybe most importantly – Christ offers himself as a sacrifice prior to us, together with us and after us. He is not only the food and drink of the Holy Supper but also the host of the feast and the celebrant. The Catechism of the Catholic Church names Christ the real subject of the liturgy[19] and Martin Luther expresses the same thought in a different manner: »Christ is the chef, the waiter, as well as the food and drink of the Eucharist«.[20]

The Holy Communion can well be termed a sacrifice, above all because »Christ appeared as a high priest of the good things to come« (Heb 9:11), giving himself to the Father and to us. Luther writes:

> From these words we learn that we do not offer Christ as a sacrifice, but that Christ offers us. And in this way it is permissible, yes, profitable, to call the mass a sacrifice; not on its own account, but because we offer ourselves as a sacrifice along with Christ.[21]

---

19 »Liturgy is an ›action‹ of the whole Christ (*Christus totus*).« Catechism of the Catholic Church, §1136. See also §1084–1090.

20 »Denn der herr hatts nicht alleine eingesetzt, sondern machts vnd hellts auch selbs, vnd ist der koch, kelner, speise vnd tranck selbs«. WA 23; 270,9–11.

21 LW 35,99. »Auß welchen worten wir lernen das wir nit Christum, sondern Christus vns opffert, vnd nach der weyß, ist es leydlich, yha nuetzlich, das wir die meß ein opffer heyssen, nit vmb yret willen, sondern das wir vns mit Christo opffern«. StA 1; 303,11–15.

VIII The Holy Eucharist as a communal feast

On the basis of its name (*synaksis, communio*) the Holy Eucharist is a communal feast. St Paul writes: »Is not the bread which we break a sharing [*koinonia*] in the body of Christ?« (I Cor 10: 16–17)

The Holy Eucharist connects Christ and sinner, and a Christian to other Christians. Communion is not only a matter between God and the individual but a communal event with an ecclesiological and ethical dimension. Those who share the consecrated bread and wine also share all joy and sorrow, victory and suffering, concern and comfort. Those who are joined to Christ in the consecrated bread and wine are also joined to one another in faith and love.

The communal nature of this Holy Supper is brought out forcefully in the theology of the Holy Communion of Martin Luther:

> Besides all this, Christ did not institute these two forms solitary and alone, but he gave his true natural flesh in the bread, and his natural true blood in the wine, that he might give a really perfect sacrament or sign. For just as the bread is changed (*vorwandelt*) into his true natural body and the wine into his natural true blood, so truly are we also drawn and changed (*als so warhaftig werden wir vorwandelt*) into the spiritual body, that is, into the fellowship of Christ and all saints and by this sacrament put into possession of all the virtues and mercies of Christ and his saints.[22]
>
> Again through this same love, we are to be changed and to make the infirmities of all other Christians our own; we are to take upon ourselves their form and their necessity, and all the good that is within our power we are to make theirs, that they may profit from it. That is real fellowship, and that is the true significance of this sacrament. In this way we are changed into one another and are made into a community by love. Without love there can be no such change.[23]

As the Eucharist is a *communio* in Christ, so also the sacrament unites us with other Christians and the whole *Gemeinschaft* of the *commmunio sanctorum*. Participation in Christ through word and sacrament is, in fact, sharing in the body of Christ, in the community of all saints. The interchange of the love of Christ takes place between all the members of this community.

---

22 LW 35,59 (StA 1; 279,31–280,4).
23 LW 35,58 (StA 1; 278,34–279,12).

The manner in which Martin Luther here speaks about the communal nature of the Eucharist and faith can open possibilities for new ecumenical convergence in the field of ecclesiology.[24]

In the *Large Catechism*, Luther strongly emphasises the role of the Christian church. In creating new spiritual life, the Holy Spirit accomplishes this »through the Christian church.« Luther states that: »In the first place he [the Holy Spirit] has a unique community in the world. It is the mother that begets and bears every Christian through the Word of God.« When the Holy Spirit sanctifies us, »he first leads us into his holy community, placing us upon the bosom of the church, where he preaches to us and brings us to Christ.«[25]

On the above bases where Luther speaks of the presence of Christ, the communal nature of the Holy Eucharist and the role of the church, we Lutherans may join in with the words of Pope John Paul II that the Holy Eucharist has a »unifying power«.[26] »Our union with Christ, which is a gift and grace for each of us, makes it possible for us, in him, to share in the unity of his body which is the Church.« Communion not only joins Christ and sinner, it also joins together Christians within the same church, young and old, women and men, priests and parishioners. It joins together dioceses and finally also local churches ministering to various parts of the world, churches confessing the same faith.

---

24 S. PEURA, The Church as a Spiritual Communion in Luther (in: The Church as Communion: Lutheran Contributions to Ecclesiology, ed. by H. HOLZE, LWF Documentation 42, 1997, 93–131).

25 The Book of Concord, T. G. TAPPERT, Large Catechism, Creed, the Third Article, 415 f.

26 »Eucharistic communion also confirms the Church in her unity as the body of Christ. Saint Paul refers to this *unifying power* of participation in the banquet of the Eucharist [...]. The argument is compelling: our union with Christ, which is a gift and grace for each of us, makes it possible for us, in him, to share in the unity of his body which is the Church. The Eucharist reinforces the incorporation into Christ which took place in Baptism though the gift of the Spirit (cf. I Cor 12: 13.27) [...]. The seeds of disunity, which daily experience shows to be so deeply rooted in humanity as a result of sin, are countered by the *unifying power* of the body of Christ. The Eucharist, precisely by building up the Church, creates human community.« Ecclesia de Eucharistia, § 23 f.

It is my fervent wish that we Lutherans could come together with our Roman Catholic and other Christian sisters and brothers at the common Communion table. We yearn for a common table because the Holy Eucharist is the feast of Christ's presence and *communio sanctorum*.

On the basis of Luther's theology we have no difficulty in joining with those words which Benedict XIV, Bishop of Rome, stated in his inaugural homily:

> All of us belong to the communion of Saints, we who have been baptized in the name of the Father, and of the Son and of the Holy Spirit, we who draw life from the gift of Christ's Body and Blood, through which he transforms us and makes us like himself.[27]

There is, however, no shortcut to a joint Holy Eucharist. Unity does not endure without truth, we require »the truth in love«, *veritas in caritate*. The goal of visible unity and of a common Communion demand that we dig deeper into the foundation of our common Christian faith. We need patience to delve into revealed truth and we need the courage then to take decisive steps when adequate consensus is achieved.

In summary, may I dare to contend that Martin Luther, in his *Catechisms* and his writings on Holy Communion, speaks as *doctor communis*, not attempting to develop new doctrine but rather striving to express and interpret the common faith of the undivided Christendom. Thus his writings still bear ecumenical fruit.

27 Omelia del Santo Padre per il solenne inizio del Ministerio Petrino, Domenica, 24 April 2005.

Martin Luthers Beitrag zur Universitätsreform

Ulrich Köpf

An den Beginn unseres Kongresses über »Luther als Lehrer und Reformer der Universität« wurde mit guten Gründen ein Referat über Martin Luthers Beitrag zur Universitätsreform gestellt.[1] Doch denken wir bei diesem Thema[2] tatsächlich zuerst an Luther und nicht vielmehr an den anderen großen Reformator, der in seiner Wittenberger Antrittsvorlesung 1518 ein Programm zur Erneuerung der Studien vorgelegt, der später mehrfach neue Ordnungen für die Artisten, für die Theologen und für die gesamte Universität erarbeitet, der wiederholt Studienpläne für einzelne Studenten entworfen und zahlreiche vielgelesene Lehrbücher verfasst hat?

In der Tat erscheint Philipp Melanchthon heute als *der* große Reformer der Universität, der auch weit über Wittenberg hinaus gewirkt hat.[3]

---

1 Vortrag gehalten am 6. August 2013 beim 12. Internationalen Kongress für Lutherforschung in Helsinki. Für die Veröffentlichung wurde der Vortragstext nur geringfügig überarbeitet und mit ausgewählten Nachweisen – vor allem aus den Quellen – versehen.

2 Zum weiteren Kontext vgl. U. Köpf, The Reformation as an Epoch of the History of Theological Education (in: Hebrew Bible, Old Testament: The History of Its Interpretation. Vol. II From the Renaissance to the Enlightenment, ed. by M. Sæbø, 2008, 347–362).

3 Noch immer grundlegend: K. Hartfelder, Philipp Melanchthon als Praeceptor Germaniae (MGP 7), 1889. Die neuere Forschung wird zusammengefasst und fortgeführt von H. Scheible, Melanchthon. Eine Biographie, 1997, mit Nachweisen in: Ders., Art. Melanchthon, Philipp (TRE 22, 1992, 371–410). Scheible hat auch mehrere wichtige Beiträge zur Universitätsreform verfasst. Sie sind gesammelt in: Ders., Melanchthon und die Reformation. Forschungsbeiträge (VIEG. Beiheft 41), hg. v. G. May/R. Decot, 1996; Ders., Aufsätze zu Melanchthon (SMHR 49), 2010.

Doch war Melanchthon keineswegs der Erfinder aller Reformideen, die er so wirkungsvoll vorzutragen und umzusetzen verstanden hat. Er gehörte in den Zusammenhang einer umfassenden Bildungsbewegung, die im 14. Jahrhundert in Italien aufgekommen war und sich im 15. Jahrhundert zunehmend über Europa ausbreitete, wobei sie viele Neuerungen am abendländischen Bildungssystem hervorbrachte, zumal an den Universitäten. Melanchthon nahm diese Gedanken und Anregungen auf, bündelte sie im Rahmen der reformatorischen Bestrebungen und entwickelte sie durchaus selbständig weiter. Dabei kam ihm zugute, dass er von Beginn seines eigenen Bildungswegs an mit den neuen Ideen und Entwicklungen vertraut war. Schon in der Pforzheimer Lateinschule Georg Simlers hatte er Griechisch gelernt, und in Tübingen, wo er nach seinen Heidelberger Anfängen Ende 1512 das artistische Studium fortsetzte, traf er seine Pforzheimer Lehrer Simler und Johannes Hiltebrant wieder.[4] Zum Hebräischen vermittelte ihm sein älterer Verwandter Johannes Reuchlin früh einen Zugang – vor allem durch sein Lehrbuch *De rudimentis Hebraicis* von 1506, aber auch durch die Entleihung hebräischer Handschriften.[5] Melanchthon beherrschte diese Sprache so gut, dass er als Wittenberger Griechischprofessor nach dem Ausfall des Hebräischprofessors Bernhard Böschenstein länger als ein Jahr (vom 24. Januar 1519 bis Ostern 1520) vertretungsweise über den hebräischen Psalter las. Sein enges Verhältnis zu den antiken Sprachen und Texten war durch und durch von humanistischem Geist geprägt. Die Philosophie lernte er in Heidelberg zwar noch nach der scholastischen *via antiqua* kennen und wirkte in Tübingen als Lehrer an der Burse der Realisten. Doch führte ihn das Studium des Aristoteles im Urtext, zu dem ihn sein Lehrer Georg Simler in Tübingen anleitete, rasch von der scholastischen Gestalt der Wissenschaft weg. Seine Art, Philosophie zu treiben, nahm bald einen entschieden philologisch-

---

4 Vgl. H. Scheible, Melanchthons Pforzheimer Schulzeit. Studien zur humanistischen Bildungselite (in: Melanchthon und die Reformation [s. Anm. 3], 29–70); S. Lorenz, Melanchthon in Tübingen (1512–1518) (in: Vom Schüler der Burse zum »Lehrer Deutschlands«. Philipp Melanchthon in Tübingen [Tübinger Kataloge 88], hg. v. S. Lorenz u. a., 2010, 83–103).

5 Vgl. H. Scheible, Reuchlins Einfluß auf Melanchthon (in: Melanchthon und die Reformation [s. Anm. 3], 71–97).

humanistischen Charakter an. Von einem seelischen Ringen auf diesem Weg und von einem Umbruch in seinem Denken ist uns so wenig bekannt wie von religiösen Anfechtungen. Melanchthon ist offenbar problemlos in seine humanistische Haltung hineingewachsen. Was er in Tübingen an traditioneller Theologie kennenlernte, das wirkte wenig anziehend auf ihn. Dagegen öffnete er sich in Wittenberg von Anfang an dem neuen Geist, der hier 1518 bereits kräftig wehte – vor allem unter dem Einfluss Martin Luthers. Reformideen, die Melanchthon aus Tübingen mitbrachte, ließen sich mühelos in die Gedanken der Wittenberger Bewegung einfügen.

Anders als der gut 13 Jahre jüngere Melanchthon hatte Luther eine religiöse, schulische und wissenschaftliche Bildung durchlaufen, die noch im Herkömmlichen verhaftet war – angefangen beim Lateinunterricht. Diese Feststellung wird nicht dadurch entwertet, dass Luther – wie Helmar Junghans gezeigt hat[6] – spätestens während seines Studiums in Erfurt mit humanistisch gesinnten Lehrern in Berührung kam. Während er sich allmählich den neuen Gedankengängen und Bestrebungen annäherte, hat er sein Studium doch noch ganz im Rahmen der traditionellen Bildungsinstitutionen absolviert und hat die Geltung dieser Institutionen zunächst verinnerlicht. Sein artistisches Studium in Erfurt stand im Zeichen der dort allein herrschenden *via moderna*, und seine sprachlich-dialektische Ausbildung folgte noch ganz den bekannten spätantiken und mittelalterlichen Lehrbüchern. Auch durch die Lektüre Gabriel Biels bei seiner Vorbereitung auf die Priesterweihe und im Unterricht der theologischen Fakultäten von Erfurt und Wittenberg lernte Luther noch die ungebrochene Wirklichkeit des mittelalterlichen Studiensystems kennen, wie es im frühen 13. Jahrhundert an der Universität Paris begründet worden war.[7] In der kurzen Zeit, während der er an der juristischen Fakultät eingeschrieben

---

6 H. JUNGHANS, Der junge Luther und die Humanisten, 1985, besonders Kapitel 2.
7 Überblick bei U. KÖPF, The Institutional Framework of Christian Exegesis in the Middle Ages (in: Hebrew Bible, Old Testament: The History of Its Interpretation. Vol. I From the Beginnings to the Middle Ages [Until 1300], part 2: The Middle Ages, ed. by M. SÆBØ, 2000, 148–179); DERS., The Institutional Framework of Theological Studies in the Late Middle Ages (in: Hebrew Bible, Old Testament: The History of Its Interpretation. Vol. II, [s. Anm. 2], 123–153).

33

war, gewann er sogar erste Eindrücke von deren Studienbetrieb, die ihn freilich nicht für die Rechtswissenschaften gewinnen konnten. Im Unterschied zu Melanchthon hat Luther also das scholastische Bildungssystem noch in seiner klassischen Ausprägung gründlich kennengelernt – mit all seinen Problemen, mit denen er sich bald selbständig auseinandersetzen musste. Bevor wir fragen können, was sein konkreter Beitrag zur Universitätsreform war, müssen wir uns klarmachen, wie er sich im Laufe seiner Entwicklung aus dem traditionellen System herausgearbeitet hat.

Eine wichtige Rolle spielte dabei seine Beschäftigung mit den biblischen Sprachen weit über alles hinaus, was bisher in der Schulwissenschaft üblich gewesen war. Die ersten Belege dafür liegen in seinen Randbemerkungen zu den Sentenzen des Petrus Lombardus vor, die er als theologischer *Baccalaureus* 1509/10 erklärte.[8] Luther zeigte damals Anfangskenntnisse im Griechischen und vor allem im Hebräischen, an dem er auch später immer das größere Interesse hatte. Allerdings war er zur Zeit der Sentenzenvorlesung noch weit davon entfernt, auch nur einfache griechische oder hebräische Sätze zu verstehen. Er begnügte sich damit, die Schreibweise einzelner Wörter zu korrigieren oder ihren Sinn laienhaft aus ihrer sprachlichen Bildung zu erklären. Gelegentlich ging er auch darüber hinaus. Als der Lombarde den hebräischen Plural *Elohim* als Beweis für die Mehrzahl der göttlichen Personen nennt, trägt Luther aus einer *Quaestio quodlibetica* des Nikolaus von Lyra Belege für die alttestamentliche Redeweise zusammen.[9] Da Luther sich hier[10] und öfter auf Reuchlins *Rudimenta* beruft, meinte er zweifellos dieses Werk, als er später sagte, er habe einst in Erfurt ein hebräisches Lexikon gekauft.[11] Die erwähnten und andere Zeugnisse zeigen, wie sehr sich Luthers Situation

---

8 Die frühen Randbemerkungen sind jetzt in der vorzüglichen Neuedition durch den japanischen Germanisten Jun Matsuura zu benutzen: M. LUTHER, Erfurter Annotationen 1509–1510/11, hg. v. J. MATSUURA (AWA 9), 2009; die Anmerkungen zu den Sentenzen: 251–560.

9 AaO., 270–272.

10 AaO., 272,2: »Jo. Reuchlin in vocabulo«.

11 Brief an Johann Lang vom 29. Mai 1522 (WAB 2; 547,2 f): »Lexicon Hebraicon remitto, sed illud primum, quod olim Erfordiae emeram ab initio«.

von der Melanchthons unterschied. War jener schon als ganz junger Mensch in die Kenntnis der biblischen Sprachen hineingewachsen und beherrschte er sie bereits in seiner Tübinger Zeit souverän, so begann Luther erst mit etwa 25 Jahren, sich ihnen allmählich autodidaktisch zu nähern. Siegfried Raeder hat in sorgfältigster Analyse gezeigt, wie Luther sich über Jahre hin langsam und mühsam in das Hebräische einarbeitete.[12]

Gleichzeitig rang er mit religiösen Problemen, die im Leben Melanchthons keine Rolle spielten: Wie er vielfältig bezeugt hat, bereitete ihm das Leben als Mendikant, das er 1505 hoch motiviert begonnen hatte, bald innere Schwierigkeiten. Während er eine erfolgreiche Karriere im Augustinereremitenorden durchlief und sich aufrichtig um die Erfüllung des Ordensideals bemühte, weckten seine persönlichen Erfahrungen wachsende Zweifel an der Möglichkeit, die Forderungen dieses Ideals zu erfüllen. Auch sein Verhältnis zu der Bildungsinstitution, in der er seit Oktober 1512 ganz selbständig, als Inhaber des von seinem Orden zu besetzenden Wittenberger Lehrstuhls für Theologie, wirkte, war von vornherein durch seine Zugehörigkeit zum Stand des Religiosen mitbestimmt. Der Theologieprofessor Martin Luther war zugleich Mönch mit allen Chancen, aber auch mit allen Problemen dieser Lebensform.

Die Luther-Biographen haben sich angewöhnt, Luthers Wittenberger Lehrstuhl als etwas Besonderes zu betrachten:[13] als eine neuartige »Bibelprofessur«, eine »exegetische« oder gar eine »alttestamentliche« Professur, die nach Meinung mancher sogar für Luther neu geschaffen worden sein soll. Doch alle Vermutungen gehen in die Irre, die meinen, aus den in den frühen Quellen gelegentlich begegnenden Formulierungen *ordinaria*

---

12 S. RAEDER, Das Hebräische bei Luther, untersucht bis zum Ende der ersten Psalmenvorlesung (BHTh 31), 1961; DERS., Die Benutzung des masoretischen Textes bei Luther in der Zeit zwischen der ersten und zweiten Psalmenvorlesung (1515–1518) (BHTh 38), 1967; DERS., Grammatica Theologica. Studien zu Luthers Operationes in Psalmos (BHTh 51), 1977.

13 Zum Folgenden vgl. U. KÖPF, Martin Luthers theologischer Lehrstuhl (in: Die Theologische Fakultät Wittenberg 1502 bis 1602. Beiträge zur 500. Wiederkehr des Gründungsjahres der Leucorea [Leucorea-Studien zur Geschichte der Reformation und der Lutherischen Orthodoxie 5], hg. v. I. DINGEL/G. WARTENBERG, 2002, 71–86).

in biblia[14] oder *biblia auf das closter gestift*[15] eine Sonderrolle dieses »biblischen« Lehrstuhls neben zwei angeblich »scholastischen« oder gar »dogmatischen« Professuren herauslesen zu können.[16] Wie die Wittenberger Statuten zeigen, bedeutete die Bezeichnung *biblia* oder *sacra scriptura* im Zusammenhang der universitären Ordnungen noch zu Luthers Zeit wie während des ganzen Mittelalters nichts anderes als *theologia*. Luther übernahm von seinem Vorgänger Johann von Staupitz die vom Augustinereremitenorden zu besetzende Professor an der theologischen Fakultät: eine ganz normale Professur der Theologie, deren Inhaber – wie seit dem 13. Jahrhundert üblich – drei Aufgaben hatte:

1. die gründliche Vorlesung über Bücher der Bibel,
2. die Disputation über einzelne Themen und Themenkomplexe,
3. die Predigt vor Studenten der Theologie und anderen Universitätsangehörigen.

Seit jeher war es Aufgabe des Lehrstuhlinhabers (des *magister regens*) der Theologie gewesen, in seinen Vorlesungen die Heilige Schrift eingehend auszulegen. Zu sachlich-systematischen Erörterungen hatte er vor allem in den Disputationen Gelegenheit. Die Sentenzenvorlesung war und blieb dagegen die Aufgabe des Baccalars, nachdem er kursorisch über biblische Bücher gelesen hatte. Abweichungen von dieser Verteilung der Pflichten hatten sich erst im späten Mittelalter eingeschlichen – selten sind sie und ihre Gründe genauer bekannt. Fehlerhafte Interpretationen dieser Phänomene bestehen oft darin, dass man Abweichungen von der herkömmlichen Ordnung irrtümlich als lokal geltende Regeln zu erklären versucht. Solche Irrtümer haben ihren Grund einerseits in den meist sehr lücken-

---

14 Urkundenbuch der Universität Wittenberg. Teil 1 (1502–1611) (Geschichtsquellen der Provinz Sachsen und des Freistaates Anhalt N. R. Bd. 3), bearb. v. W. Friedensburg, 1926, 13 (Nr. 14). Oft beruft man sich auf einen gar nicht in den Wittenberger Statuten bezeugten Begriff *lectura in biblia*.
15 AaO., 77 (Nr. 57).
16 So z. B. noch M. Nieden, Die Erfindung des Theologen. Wittenberger Anweisungen zum Theologiestudium im Zeitalter von Reformation und Konfessionalisierung (SMHR 28), 2006, 41.47.49.

haften Quellen, andererseits in missverständlichen Formulierungen dieser spärlichen Quellen. Während die Statuten in der Regel ausführlich auf die Zeiten der Lehrveranstaltungen, auf die Besoldung und die Arbeitsmoral der Professoren, auf die Disziplin der Studenten und andere Äußerlichkeiten eingehen, geben sie über die Lehrinhalte gewöhnlich nur unzureichend Auskunft – wohl deshalb, weil sie das Selbstverständliche des herkömmlichen Lehrbetriebs einfach voraussetzen. Daher ist es sinnvoll, bei ihrer Erklärung zunächst immer von den überkommenen Strukturen des Lehrbetriebs auszugehen.

Martin Luther hat die reguläre Laufbahn des Theologen absolviert, wenn auch zuweilen aus äußeren Gründen rascher als die meisten seiner Kollegen. Bereits als er mit 29 Jahren den Wittenberger Lehrstuhl der Theologie übernommen hatte, zeigte sich seine Selbständigkeit in der Sorgfalt, mit der er seine Aufgabe in Angriff nahm. Monatelang bereitete er sich auf seine erste Vorlesung über das von ihm gewählte Textbuch, den Psalter, vor. Gerhard Ebeling hat gezeigt, mit welcher Gründlichkeit er für seine Vorlesung einen eigenen Psalterdruck herstellen ließ, der einen Gesamttitel mit Erklärungen, eine *Praefatio* mit hermeneutischem Programm, Summarien zu den einzelnen Psalmen, *Tituli* und einen gründlich überarbeiteten, mit mancherlei erläuternden Zusätzen versehenen Text enthielt.[17] In all diesen Beigaben spiegelt sich Luthers wachsende Bekanntschaft mit der hebräischen Sprache und dem hebräischen Urtext des Alten Testaments wider. Für die Vorbereitung seiner Vorlesung zog er die neuesten Hilfsmittel heran, die ihm die humanistische Hebraistik bot. Bereits indem er für diese durchaus noch im Rahmen des scholastischen Lehrsystems gehaltene Vorlesung ein Textbuch mit humanistischen Elementen bereitstellte, entfernte er sich vom hergebrachten Vorgehen.

Nun war Luther natürlich nicht der erste Theologe, der im scholastischen Rahmen humanistische Anregungen aufgriff. Im Philologischen blieb er trotz aller Bemühungen auch weit hinter dem zurück, was humanistische Gelehrte seiner Zeit leisteten. Man merkt, wie schwerfällig er mit den vom Humanismus gebotenen Methoden und Werkzeugen noch

---

17 G. EBELING, Luthers Psalterdruck vom Jahre 1513 (ZThK 50, 1953, 43–99); wieder abgedruckt in: DERS., Lutherstudien Bd. 1, 1971, 69–131.

zu einer Zeit umging, als der jugendliche Melanchthon sie auf dem Gebiet des Lateinischen und Griechischen bereits meisterhaft handhabe. Die Stärke Luthers lag nicht eigentlich im Philologisch-Handwerklichen, so sehr er sich darum bemühte, sondern im Inhaltlichen. Dabei verzichtete er allerdings weitgehend auf die in der mittelalterlichen Exegese so beliebten systematischen Exkurse und Quaestionen, die im Schulbetrieb diskutierte Anliegen und Ansichten an den Text heran- und in ihn hineintrugen. Ihm ging es allein darum, die Aussagen des biblischen Texts mit allen Mitteln zur Geltung zu bringen. Allerdings scheute er sich auch nicht vor Folgerungen aus dem Text, die sich auf aktuelle Verhältnisse bezogen – etwa, wenn er im Anschluss an Röm 13,1 auf Schäden im deutschen Episkopat wie an der Römischen Kurie hinwies[18] oder anlässlich von Röm 14,1 die Frage erörterte, ob es in der Gegenwart gut sei, in den Stand des Religiosen zu treten.[19]

Ein Sachverhalt hatte bereits in seiner ersten Psalmenvorlesung weit mehr Gewicht als in der scholastischen und auch in der humanistischen Auslegung: Bei der Erschließung des Texts, den Luther ja seit Jahren regelmäßig gebetet hatte, brachte er in unerhörter Intensität seine eigenen Erfahrungen und Probleme ein. Damit stand er in der Tradition der monastischen Schriftauslegung, aus der ihn seit seiner ersten Psalmenvorlesung vor allem Bernhard von Clairvaux beeinflusst hat.[20] *Ein* Begriff, der in den Psalmen eine wichtige Rolle spielt, bewegte ihn bereits während der ersten Vorlesung spürbar: der Begriff der *iustitia*, der in verschiedenen Verbindungen begegnet – besonders bewegend, wenn der Psalmist zu Gott von *iustitia tua* und *iustitia mea* spricht.[21] Den herkömmlichen Sinn dieses Begriffes hatte Luther bereits in seinem artistischen Studium aus der Nikomachischen Ethik des Aristoteles und anderer philosophischer Literatur kennengelernt. Im Kloster und beim Theologiestudium war er ihm

18 Römerbriefvorlesung 1515/16 (WA 56; 476,27–480,16).

19 AaO., 497,18–498,12.

20 Der Einfluss Bernhards wurde ausführlich nachgewiesen durch T. BELL, Divus Bernhardus. Bernhard von Clairvaux in Martin Luthers Schriften (VIEG 148), 1993, und F. POSSET, Pater Bernhardus: Martin Luther and Bernard of Clairvaux (CistSS 168), 1999.

21 Z.B. »Iudica me, Domine, secundum iustitiam meam« (Ps 7,9); »Iudica me secundum iustitiam tuam, Domine Deus meus« (Ps 34 [35], 24).

im Psalter wie bei Paulus immer wieder begegnet, jetzt aber in anderen Kontexten und mit ganz neuem Gewicht, in einer ihn selbst betreffenden existentiellen Tiefe. Noch in seiner letzten, großen Vorlesung über das Buch Genesis erinnerte er sich ganz genau des Schauders, den er einst empfunden hatte, wenn er im Stundengebet das Psalmwort »Durch deine Gerechtigkeit errette mich!« (Ps 30 [31],2; 70 [71],2) las und betete.[22] Wie tief die Erinnerung daran saß, zeigt sich auch daran, dass der Bericht in den Tischreden der späten dreißiger und frühen vierziger Jahre mehrfach überliefert ist.[23]

Während seiner ersten Psalmenvorlesung begann Luther ein bisher unbekannter Sinn des Begriffes aufzugehen, der ihn – wie er nicht lange vor seinem Tode berichten sollte – mit ungeheurer Wucht innerlich berührte und den er als eine Erfahrung höchsten religiösen Glücks empfand.[24] Schon in seiner Sentenzenvorlesung hatte er Kritik am aristotelischen *habitus*-Begriff als Grundlage der scholastischen Tugendlehre geübt: *habitus* als eine seelische Verfassung *(qualitas animae)*, die das Seelenvermögen beim Handeln bestimmt.[25] Jetzt, im Verlauf der ersten Psalmenvorlesung, erkannte er, wie fragwürdig das übliche theologische Reden von der im aristotelischen Sinne aufgefassten zentralen Tugend der »Gerechtigkeit« war. In der folgenden Römerbriefvorlesung vertiefte er in der Exegese von Röm 1,17 das seit der ersten Psalmenvorlesung Erkannte. Im Gegensatz zur Lehre der Nikomachischen Ethik, nach der die Gerechtigkeit aus gerechten Handlungen hervorgeht und dementsprechend beurteilt wird,[26] also im Gegensatz zum philosophischen Verständnis der *iusti-*

22 WA 44; 485,41–486,2: »Olim ego cum legendum et orandum esset illud Psalmi: ›In iusticia tua libera me‹, totus exhorrescebam et ex toto corde vocem illam oderam: Ne me liberes, cogitabam, tua iusticia, qua tu iustus es, active.«

23 WATR 4; 72,27–73,1 (Nr. 4007); 5; 26,18–26 (Nr. 5247). 234,36–235,13 (Nr. 5553).

24 Vorrede zu Band 1 seiner *Opera latina* (WA 54; 186,8f): »Hic me prorsus renatum esse sensi, et apertis portis in ipsam paradisum intrasse.« (aaO., 14–16): »Iam quanto odio vocabulum ›iustitia Dei‹ oderam ante, tanto amore dulcissimum mihi vocabulum extollebam, ita mihi iste locus Pauli fuit vere porta paradisi.«

25 Zu Sent. I dist. 17 mit der Spitze: »Quia commentum illud de habitibus opinionem habet ex verbis Aristotelis rancidi philosophi.« (Luther, Erfurter Annotationen [s. Anm. 8], 320,6f).

26 WA 56; 172,8–10: [Iustitia Dei] »dicitur ad differentiam Iustitiae hominum, que ex operi-

tia Dei als einer *iustitia formalis, activa* oder *distributiva,* nahm er den biblischen Gedanken einer von Gott geschenkten Gerechtigkeit, einer *iustitia passiva,* für die Theologie in Anspruch.[27] Dadurch gewann er einen festen Punkt seines Denkens, von dem aus er sich rasch von der traditionellen Schultheologie absetzte.

Luthers neues Verständnis von *iustitia Dei* im Gegensatz zu dem philosophischen des Aristoteles und der von diesem geprägten Scholastik führte ihn zugleich zu wachsender grundsätzlicher Kritik an der Verwendung aristotelischer Elemente in der scholastischen Theologie. Man hat Luther immer wieder eine pauschale Ablehnung der Philosophie unterstellt, wofür es auch gewisse Anhaltspunkte unter seinen Äußerungen geben mag. Aber in seiner Undifferenziertheit ist der Vorwurf unangemessen. Luthers Kritik richtete sich im wesentlichen gegen einen *bestimmten* Gebrauch der Philosophie in der Theologie. Bereits seine Römerbrief-Auslegung von 1515/16 war eine klare Absage an die scholastische Sünden-, Tugend- und Rechtfertigungslehre, die auf der Grundlage aristotelischer Auffassungen entworfen worden war. Im Fortgang seiner Paulusvorlesungen und durch die gleichzeitige Beschäftigung mit Augustinus, besonders mit dessen antipelagianischen Schriften, vertiefte Luther seine Antipathie gegen die aristotelische Scholastik. Im Laufe der Jahre formulierte er zahlreiche negative, geradezu respektlose Äußerungen über den Philosophen,[28] die freilich in ihrem jeweiligen Kontext gesehen werden müssen.[29]

Ich habe mich deshalb so lange bei Luthers religiöser und theologischer Entwicklung aufgehalten, weil hier sein Beitrag zur Reform der Uni-

---

bus fit. Sicut Aristoteles 3. Ethicorum manifeste determinat, secundum quem Iustitia sequitur et fit ex actibus.« Luther bezieht sich hier auf Aristoteles, Ethica Nicomachea 1105a16; b9; 1103a30ff.

27 Begrifflich ausformuliert erscheint der Gegensatz erst später: vor allem im großen Galaterkommentar von 1535 (besonders in dessen *Argumentum*: WA 40,1; 40–52).

28 Belege für seine Urteile über Aristoteles bei G. ROKITA, Aristoteles, Aristotelicus, Aristotelicotatos, Aristoteleskunst (in: Zum Sachregister der Weimarer Lutherausgabe, in: ABG 15, 1971, 51–93), 56–60.

29 Über die Sachfragen gründlich und differenziert: T. DIETER, Der junge Luther und Aristoteles. Eine historisch-systematische Untersuchung zum Verhältnis von Theologie und Philosophie (TBT 105), 2001.

versität seine sachlichen, theologischen Wurzeln hat. Wenn wir Luther im Ganzen der Universitätsreformen seiner Zeit sehen, dann wird deutlich, dass die Veränderungen der Unterrichtsformen und Unterrichtsmethoden im frühen 16. Jahrhundert auf den Humanismus zurückgehen. Luther selbst hat dazu kaum etwas Neues beigetragen; aber er hat humanistische Anregungen und Forderungen in seine Exegese wie in seine programmatischen Äußerungen aufgenommen. Sein eigener Beitrag bezog sich nicht so sehr auf die Verwendung oder gar Schaffung neuer didaktischer Elemente und neuer Arbeitsformen als auf die inhaltliche, d. h. auf die religiöse und theologische Begründung von Änderungen am Überkommenen. Er entwickelte seine Reformideen also nicht wie die humanistischen Erneuerer der Universitätspädagogik auf einer formalen, methodischen Ebene. Ihn bewegten in erster Linie solche inhaltlichen Einsichten, die ihm halfen, auch seine eigene religiöse Situation besser zu verstehen und angemessen, in heilsamer Weise, mit ihr umzugehen. Aus ihnen ging das hervor, was wir als seinen eigentlichen Beitrag zur Universitätsreform bezeichnen können.

Was Luther in den frühen Vorlesungen vor seinen Hörern entwickelte, das drängte zu Konsequenzen in der Praxis des Lehrbetriebs. Bereits Anfang 1517 versuchte er durch Vermittlung seines Mitbruders Johann Lang, damals Prior des Erfurter Augustinerkonvents, seine ehemaligen Lehrer Jodokus Trutfetter und Bartholomäus Arnoldi von Usingen für eine Änderung der Erfurter Studienordnung zu gewinnen, die in der Artistenfakultät vor allem im Verzicht auf Aristoteles und Porphyrius,[30] in der theologischen Fakultät aber in der Weglassung der Sentenzenvorlesung bestehen sollte.[31] Bezeichnenderweise hat ja Luther selbst, der noch regulär über die Sentenzen gelesen hatte, bewusst auf die Veröffentlichung eines

---

30 Damit ist die Isagoge des Porphyrius gemeint: seine Einleitung in die Kategorienschrift des Aristoteles – ein Grundtext der mittelalterlichen Logik.

31 Brief vom 8. Febr. 1517 (WAB 1; 88,4–8; 89,27–29): »Mitto has literas, mi Pater, ad eximium Dominum Iodocum Isennacensem, plenas quaestionum adversus logicam et philosophiam et theologiam, id est, blasphemiarum et maledictionum contra Aristotelem, Porphyrium, Sententiarios, perdita scilicet studia nostri saeculi. […] Vellem, quod et M. Usingen una cum Isennach abstinerent, imo continerent aliquando ab istis laboribus. Plena sunt mihi omnia armaria contra eorum editiones, quas video esse prorsus inutiles«.

eigenen Sentenzenkommentars verzichtet, also gerade jenes Typus einer Gesamtdarstellung der Theologie, der seit dem 14. Jahrhundert das Hauptwerk vieler großer Theologen (Duns Scotus, Wilhelm von Ockham und anderer) gewesen war. Seine Bemühungen um eine Reform in Erfurt blieben erfolglos. Doch bereits ein Vierteljahr später berichtete er Lang über die Wittenberger Verhältnisse reichlich optimistisch: »Durch Gottes Wirken machen unsere Theologie und der hl. Augustinus die erwünschten Fortschritte und herrschen an unserer Universität.« Mit Aristoteles gehe es abwärts, die Sentenzenvorlesungen würden verschmäht und nur derjenige könne auf Hörer hoffen, der über die Bibel, Augustinus oder einen anderen Kirchenlehrer vortrage.[32] »Bibel« bedeutet hier in Übereinstimmung mit der humanistischen Forderung nach Rückgang auf die Quellen den Bibeltext ohne kirchliche und scholastische Interpretationen, und Augustin (gemeint sind seine Schriften gegen die Pelagianer) las Luther jetzt in erster Linie als Hilfe bei seiner Auseinandersetzung mit der Schultheologie.[33] Nach seinem Zeugnis von 1545 hat ihm die Lektüre der Schrift *De spiritu et litera* sein neues Verständnis von *iustitia Dei* bekräftigt.[34] Es gelang ihm auch, seinen theologischen Kollegen Andreas Bodenstein von Karlstadt gegen anfängliches Widerstreben von der Bedeutung Augustins zu überzeugen. Karlstadt hielt im Sommersemester 1517 eine Vorlesung über *De spiritu et litera*, die er von 1517 bis 1519 veröffentlichte. In der ersten Lieferung des Werks weist er darauf hin, dass neben Luther, der den Hebräerbrief auslege, die Kollegen Petrus Lupinus über Ambrosius und Johannes Rhagius Aesticampianus über Hieronymus läsen, wodurch er Luthers Äußerung über die Rolle weiterer Kirchenväter in der Wittenberger Lehre bestätigt.[35]

---

32 Brief vom 18. Mai 1517 (WAB 1; 99,8–13): »Theologia nostra et S. Augustinus prospere procedunt et regnant in nostra universitate Deo operante. Aristoteles descendit paulatim inclinatus ad ruinam prope futuram sempiternam. Mire fastidiuntur lectiones sententiariae, nec est, ut quis sibi auditores sperare possit, nisi theologiam hanc, id est bibliam aut S. Augustinum aliumve ecclesiasticae autoritatis doctorem velit profiteri.«
33 Vgl. L. GRANE, Modus loquendi theologicus. Luthers Kampf um die Erneuerung der Theologie (1515–1518) (AThD), 1975.
34 WA 54; 186,16–18.
35 Karlstadt und Augustin. Der Kommentar des Andreas Bodenstein von Karlstadt zu

An die weitere Öffentlichkeit trat Luther mit seiner Aristoteleskritik am 4. September 1517 in 97 Thesen für die Disputation zur Promotion des Franz Günther aus Nordhausen zum *Baccalaureus biblicus*[36] – Thesen, die er an Johann Lang in Erfurt[37] und außerdem nach Nürnberg an Christoph Scheurl mit der Bitte um Weitergabe sandte.[38] Luther behauptet hier unter anderem, fast die ganze Ethik des Aristoteles sei die schlimmste Feindin der Gnade[39] – eine Konsequenz aus seiner grundlegenden Einsicht in die verheerende Wirkung des aristotelischen Gerechtigkeitsbegriffs auf die religiöse Auffassung von Lohn und Verdienst. Deshalb kann er formulieren, Aristoteles verhalte sich zur Theologie wie die Finsternis zum Licht.[40] In geradem Widerspruch gegen die verbreitete Meinung,[41] es sei ein Irrtum, zu sagen, ohne Aristoteles werde man nicht zum Theologen,[42] betont er: Richtig sei vielmehr, dass man zum Theologen nur unter Verzicht auf Aristoteles werde.[43]

Den Teilnehmern an dieser Disputation müssen die Ohren geklungen haben. Nie zuvor hatte Luther die Bedeutung des Aristoteles für die Theologie öffentlich so radikal verneint. Mit seinen Thesen richtete er geradezu einen Generalangriff auf das gesamte Studiensystem der mittelalterlichen Universität. Seit der umfassenden Aristoteles-Rezeption des 12. und 13. Jahrhunderts, die sich Hand in Hand mit der Ausbildung der Universität vollzogen hatte, waren die Werke des Philosophen rasch zum beherrschenden Lerninhalt der Artistenfakultät geworden. Durch die Rezeption des vollständigen Organons war die Logik ins Zentrum des Tri-

---

Augustins Schrift De spiritu et litera. Einführung und Text v. E. Kähler (HM 19), 1952, 10.

36 WA 1; 221–227.

37 Brief vom 4. September 1517 (WAB 1; 103 f).

38 Brief vom 11. September 1517 (WAB 1; 105 f).

39 These 41 (WA 1; 226,10): »Tota fere Aristotelis Ethica pessima est gratiae inimica.«

40 These 50 (aaO., 226,26): »Breviter, Totus Aristoteles ad theologiam est tenebrae ad lucem.«

41 Luther schreibt später seinem Weihbischof Johannes Bonemilch von Lasphe die Aussage zu: »Sine Aristotele nemo fit Doctor theologiae.« (WATR 5; 512,34 f [Nr. 5967]).

42 These 43 (WA 1; 226,14 f): »Error est, sine Aristotele non fit theologus. Contra dictum commune.«

43 These 44 (aaO., 226,16): »Immo theologus non fit nisi id fiat sine Aristotele.«

viums gerückt und hatte Grammatik und Rhetorik an den Rand gedrängt. Die Werke zur Physik, zur Naturkunde und zur Ethik hatten den Kreis der *Artes liberales* gesprengt, und mit der Auslegung der Metaphysik war eine philosophische Theologie entstanden, die der kirchlichen Theologie an den theologischen Fakultäten Konkurrenz machte. Die Theologen, die durchweg nicht nur ein artistisches Studium durchlaufen, sondern in der Regel anschließend noch ein paar Jahre an der Artistenfakultät gelehrt hatten, arbeiteten zugleich sehr produktiv mit den Begriffen und Theorien, die ihnen Aristoteles auch für die Behandlung der meisten religiösen Themen bot. Dabei wirkten freilich einzelne seiner Lehren störend, wie die von der Ewigkeit der Welt und von der Vergänglichkeit der individuellen Seele. Sie boten auch schon im 13. Jahrhundert Ansatzpunkte zu einer theologischen und kirchlichen Aristoteleskritik.

Bei der Disputation am 26. April 1518, die Luther auf dem Kapitel der Reformkongregation seines Ordens in Heidelberg leitete, verzichtete er auf pauschale Angriffe und ließ sich dafür stärker auf inhaltliche Aspekte ein, aus denen die Unbrauchbarkeit des Aristoteles für die Theologie hervorgehen sollte.[44] So verband er etwa die beiden traditionellen Kritikpunkte miteinander, indem er betonte, Aristoteles habe leicht an die Ewigkeit der Welt glauben können, da nach seiner Meinung die menschliche Seele sterblich sei,[45] und leugnete die Qualifikation zum Theologen durch die Erkenntnis der unsichtbaren Eigenschaften Gottes aus der Schöpfung.[46] Hier betonte er auch die Überlegenheit der platonischen Ideenlehre gegenüber dem aristotelischen Denken,[47] ohne freilich einen Weg aufzuweisen, wie Platon für das Studium fruchtbar gemacht werden könnte.

Wenn Luther mit solcher Radikalität, wie sie sich besonders in der Disputation für Franz Günther zeigte, gegen den Gebrauch des Aristoteles

---

44 WA 1; 353–355.

45 These 31 ex philosophia (aaO., 355,6f): »Facile fuit Aristoteli mundum aeternum opinari, quando anima humana mortalis est eius sententia.«

46 These 19 ex theologia (aaO., 354,17f): »Non ille digne Theologus dicitur, qui invisibilia Dei per ea, quae facta sunt, intellecta conspicit.«

47 These 36 ex philosophia (aaO., 355,16f): »Aristoteles male reprehendit ac ridet Platonicarum Idearum meliorem sua Philosophiam.«

in der Theologie auftrat, dann drohte er dem gesamten traditionellen Universitätsbetrieb seine bewährten Grundlagen zu nehmen. Doch die Realität der über Hunderte von Jahren gewachsenen Wissenschaftspraxis war zunächst stärker als die Reformforderungen selbst eines damals schon so einflussreichen Professors wie Luther. Konkrete Reformen an diesem Betrieb ließen sich nur in kleinen Schritten verwirklichen. Blicken wir deshalb von Luthers Ideen kurz auf die Geschichte der jungen Universität Wittenberg zurück, besonders auf die Entwicklung ihrer Artistenfakultät!

Die 1502 gegründete Universität Wittenberg hatte für ihre Artistenfakultät die Statuten von Tübingen übernommen.[48] Die ältesten Wittenberger Statuten setzten wie ihre Tübinger Vorlage das Vorhandensein von zwei »Wegen« voraus.[49] Während in Tübingen darunter *via antiqua* und *via moderna* verstanden wurden, änderte sich in Wittenberg allerdings unter der Hand der Sinn dieser Begriffe. Zwar ist in den neuen Statuten von 1508 von drei Wegen die Rede.[50] Aber die dort als dritte erwähnte *via Gregorii* – wenn dieser singuläre Begriff tatsächlich so gemeint war und nicht versehentlich gebraucht wurde – diese allein auf die Artistenfakultät bezogene *via Gregorii* wurde in Wittenberg nie mit Leben erfüllt, so dass alle Spekulationen der letzten Jahrzehnte[51] über sie haltlos sind. Selbst eine *via moderna*, in welcher Nachfolge auch immer, kann in Wittenberg nur während der kurzen und wenig einflussreichen Tätigkeit Trutfetters 1507–1510 bestanden haben. In diese Zeit (von Herbst 1508 bis Herbst 1509) fällt auch Luthers Vertretung der Wittenberger artistischen

---

48 Vgl. T. MUTHER, Die ersten Statuten der Wittenberger Artistenfacultät v. J. 1504 (NMHAF 11 [1874], 177–208), mit der Quelle in: Urkunden zur Geschichte der Universität Tübingen aus den Jahren 1476 bis 1550 [hg. v. R. ROTH], 1877, 322–375.

49 MUTHER (s. Anm. 48), 182: »vnus Decanus antiquus […], alter vero alterius viae«.

50 Urkundenbuch (s. Anm. 14), Nr. 26, 56: »indifferenter profiteatur via Thome, Scoti, Gregorii«, daneben 53 (zur Wahl des Dekans): »[…] quicumque ille fuerit, seu religiosus seu secularis, Thome, Scotho sive Gregorio mancipatus«.

51 Vgl. besonders H. A. OBERMAN, Werden und Wertung der Reformation. Vom Wegestreit zum Glaubenskampf, 1977, 90f; DERS., Vorwort, in: Gregorii Ariminiensis OESA Lectura super primum et secundum Sententiarum. Tomus IV Super secundum (Dist 1–5) (SuR 9), hg. v. A. D. TRAPP, 1979, VIII; M. SCHULZE, ›Via Gregorii‹ in Forschung und Quellen, in: Gregor von Rimini. Werk und Wirkung bis zur Reformation (SuR 20), hg. v. H. A. OBERMAN, 1981, 1–126.

Professur, die sein Orden zu besetzen hatte. Soll man etwa annehmen, er habe über die Nikomachische Ethik im Sinne der *via moderna* gelesen?

Im übrigen meinen die Wittenberger Dokumente, die von »zwei Wegen« sprechen, damit stets die *via Scoti* und die *via Thomae*. Doch bezeichnenderweise war in Wittenberg der anderswo vorhandene Gegensatz zwischen diesen beiden Richtungen der *via antiqua* nie stark ausgeprägt, und schon früh näherten sich beide einander an. Es gab Professoren wie Johannes Dölsch und Andreas Karlstadt, die bereits wenige Jahre nach der Universitätsgründung über aristotelische Werke sowohl an Hand thomistischer als auch scotistischer Kommentare lasen.[52] Der vom Humanismus getragene Wunsch, die Werke des Aristoteles ohne Benutzung scholastischer Kommentare auszulegen, der in Erfurt schon zwei Jahre zuvor Erfolge gezeitigt hatte,[53] führte dazu, dass in Wittenberg seit Wintersemester 1517/18 Vorlesungen über die aristotelische Logik, Physik, Metaphysik und Zoologie *textualiter* gehalten werden sollten – allerdings noch nicht auf der Grundlage des griechischen Texts, zu dessen Lektüre den Studenten noch die Sprachkenntnisse fehlten, sondern unter Benutzung einer neuen, humanistischen Übersetzung.[54] Außerdem wurden Vorlesungen über Plinius, Quintilian und Priscian neu eingeführt.[55] Nach monate-

---

52 J. DOELSCH, Contra doctrinalem quorundam Magistrorum nostrorum damnationem, Louaniensis & Coloniensis studii, e sacris literis petita defensio, pro Christianissimo praeceptore suo Martino Luthero, Wittenberg s. a. [1520], f. Fij[r]: »Egi iam Vuittenbergae supra quindecim annos, atque in iis, amplius quam duodecim. Physica Aristotelis publice docui, non tantum in secta Thomae, sed ex maxima parte in secta Scoti.« Zu Karlstadt: J. J. MADER, Scriptorum insignium, qui in celeberrimis, praesertim Lipsiensi, Wittenbergensi, Franfordiana ad Oderam Academiis, A fundatione ipsarum, usque ad annum Christi 1515. floruerunt, Centuria, ab avctore eivs temporis anonymo concinnata, nunc vero in Lucem edita, Helmstedt 1609, Nr. LXXXIV.

53 E. KLEINEIDAM, Universitas Studii Erffordensis. Überblick über die Geschichte der Universität Erfurt. Teil II: Spätscholastik, Humanismus und Reformation 1461–1521 (EthSt 22), [2]1992, 205 f.

54 Urkundenbuch (s. Anm. 14) 85 (Nr. 64): »Logica Aristotelis textualiter secundum novam translationem durch einen sonderlichen magistrum. Physicam und metaphysicam Aristotelis textualiter secundum novam translationem. Aristotelem de animalibus.«

55 Die Matrikel schreibt zum Rektorat des Balthasar Fabricius (Phachus) im Wintersemester 1517/18: »Sub cuius Rectoratu [...] respublica literaria aucta est Lectione Plyniana, Quintiliani, Prisciani et pedagogis duobus publicis, ac ceptus est legi textus Aristotelis

langen Verhandlungen mit Spalatin stellte Luther am 23. Februar 1519 zusammen mit vier Kollegen beim Kurfürsten den Antrag, unter anderem den thomistischen Kommentar zur Physik durch die Auslegung des aristotelischen Texts und die thomistische Logik durch eine Vorlesung über Ovids Metamorphosen zu ersetzen. Außerdem sollte für Wittenberg ein Drucker gewonnen werden, um den Text für die Vorlesung über Aristoteles und für andere Vorlesungen herzustellen.[56] Erst seit 1520 war in den Quellen nicht mehr von »Wegen« die Rede, sondern nur noch von Disziplinen und von Textbüchern, wobei Aristoteles bei den Artisten anscheinend weiterhin eine wichtige Rolle spielte.[57]

Die Realität des Lehrbetriebs stand also noch längere Zeit weit hinter dem zurück, was Luther schon Anfang 1517 gefordert hatte. Am 9. Mai 1518 schrieb er noch grundsätzlicher und radikaler an Trutfetter, die Kirche könne seiner Meinung nach nicht reformiert werden, wenn nicht die

in Physicis et logicis« (Album Academiae Vitebergensis ab a. Ch. MDII usque ad a. MDLX, hg. v. K. E. FÖRSTEMANN, 1841, 69).

56 WAB 1; 349,13–350,36: »Es ist eine Thomistische Lection, nämlich in Physica, weliche itzo Magister Johannes Gunckel liest, dieselben als ein unnötige ganz abetun uns vor gut ansicht, also daß derselb Magister Johannes Gunckel *textum Aristotelis* fur die abgetane Lection lese, bei ihrem Sold, wie bisher unser Rector, Magister Bartholomäus Bernhardt dieselben gelesen. Und daß der Sold abgetaner Lection zugegeben wurd dem Magistro Philippo umb seines getreuen ubirtrefflichen [vorzüglichen, U. K.] Fleißes [...]. Ubir das ist noch ein Lection *Thomistica in Logica*, die do liest Magister Jacobus Premßel für 20 fl. Sold. Wäre unser Gutdunken, das solich Sold und Stund fruchtbarlicher angelegt wurd und dieselb Lection gewandelt in *Ovidium Metamorphoseon* 1^a angesehen, daß an der schotistichen und Textualis Logica und Physica gnug were und die Jugend mit soviel einerlei Lection nit ubirladen und im Bessern vorhindert wurde, sunderlich so doch wenig *auditores* und Studenten dozu gehen. [...] Auch ist's bei Vielen fur gut angesehen, so wir mochten einen redlichen Drucker hie zu Wittenberg haben, dann das sollt nit wenig der Universität Furderung und E[urer] K[urfürstlichen] Gn[aden] Ehr einlegen. Den Text *Aristotelis* und ander Lection künnt man damit furdern, die sonst an [ohne, U. K.] Bucher gehort nit so begreiflich und nutzlich sein mögen.«

57 Liste der besoldeten Dozenten und Lektionen (nach 31. Mai) 1520 (Urkundenbuch [s. Anm. 14], 99 f [Nr. 82]): z. B. »magister Johans Juncklin von der lection naturalis philosophie. [...] magister Joannes Doelsch von der lection philosophia libros de anima. [...] magistro Jodoco Morlin von der lection metaphisices. [...] magister Augustino Schurff von der lection in Aristotelem.«

kirchenrechtlichen *canones* und Dekretalen sowie die scholastische Theologie, Philosophie und Logik, wie sie jetzt vorhanden seien, mit der Wurzel ausgerissen und dafür andere Studien – nämlich über die Bibel und die Kirchenväter – eingerichtet würden.[58] Auch die fulminante, aber sehr blumig formulierte Antrittsvorlesung Melanchthons *De corrigendis adolescentiae studiis* vom 28. August 1518[59] bestärkte zwar die damals in Wittenberg ohnehin schon vorhandenen humanistischen Bestrebungen, bot aber keine konkreten Vorschläge zu einer Reform der Ordnungen. Nachdem sich die Veränderungen in Wittenberg bisher nur langsam entwickelt hatten, trat Luther im Sommer 1520 mit einer Reformschrift auf, die auch seine Forderungen für die Universitäten an die größtmögliche Öffentlichkeit trug: mit der am 23. Juni vollendeten und Mitte August gedruckt vorliegenden Schrift *An den christlichen Adel deutscher Nation von des christlichen Standes Besserung.*[60] Binnen weniger Tage hatte der Drucker alle 4000 Exemplare der 1. Auflage ausgegeben.[61]

Diese Schrift bietet erstmals umfassend Luthers Vorschläge zur Reform der Universitäten. Sie ist dreigeteilt: Nach einer Beschreibung und Kritik der drei »Mauern«, welche die Anhänger Roms zu ihrem Schutz um sich errichtet haben – der Unterscheidung zwischen geistlichem und weltlichem oder Laien-Stand, dem Alleinanspruch auf Auslegung der Heiligen Schrift und der Behauptung, allein der Papst könne ein Konzil einberufen –, nach der Auseinandersetzung mit diesen römischen Abwehrstrategien[62] nennt Luther die kurialen Missstände und Missbräuche, die durch ein Konzil beseitigt werden sollten,[63] und fügt ihnen eine lange Reihe konkreter Reformmaßnahmen an, die teils durch die weltli-

---

58 WAB 1; 170,33–38: »Atque ut me etiam resolvam, ego simpliciter credo, quod impossibile sit ecclesiam reformari, nisi funditus canones, decretales, scholastica theologia, philosophia, logica, ut nunc habentur, eradicentur et alia studia instituantur; atque in ea sententia adeo procedo, ut cotidie Dominum rogem, quatenus id statim fiat, ut rursum Bibliae et S. Patrum purissima studia revocentur.«

59 P. Melanchthon, Werke in Auswahl, hg. v. R. Stupperich. Bd. 3, hg. v. R. Nürnberger, 1961, 29–42.

60 WA 6; (381–403) 404–469.

61 Brief Luthers an Johann Lang vom 18. August 1520 (WAB 2; 167,9–11).

62 AaO., 406,21–415,6.

63 AaO., 415,7–427,29.

chen Obrigkeiten, teils durch ein allgemeines Konzil durchgeführt werden sollten.[64] Der 25. und vorletzte Punkt[65] seiner Aufzählung betrifft die Universitäten, für die er ein umstürzendes, allerdings auf wenige Punkte beschränktes Reformprogramm vorträgt. Dabei beschränkt er sich auf die Artisten, Juristen und Theologen, während er die Mediziner übergeht.

In einem ersten Angriff auf die Universitäten, der sachlich auf die Artisten zielt, behauptet Luther, »der blind heydnischer meyster Aristoteles«,[66] »der vordampter, hochmutiger, schalckhafftiger heide«,[67] »der elend mensch«,[68] habe viele Christen verführt und getäuscht und die Heilige Schrift beinahe verdrängt. Konkret verlangt er die Beseitigung der aristotelischen Physik, Metaphysik, Psychologie und Ethik aus dem Unterricht, was er mit der Lehre von der Unsterblichkeit der Seele in *De anima* und dem problematischen Einfluss der Ethik auf die Auffassung der Gnade und der Tugenden begründet.[69] Beibehalten möchte er dagegen die »bucher von der Logica, Rhetorica, Poetica«, also die inhaltlich ungefährlichen Schriften, die den humanistischen Interessen am ehesten entsprachen, am besten in der Kurzfassung von Lehrbüchern, allerdings ohne die scholastischen Kommentare mit ihren Schulmeinungen, d.h. mit ihren Festlegungen auf die *viae*.[70] Daneben empfiehlt er aus dem humanistischen Programm die Sprachen Latein, Griechisch und Hebräisch, dazu die mathematischen Disziplinen, die bisher im Rahmen des Quadriviums gelehrt worden waren, sowie die Geschichte.[71]

Ausführlich geht Luther sodann auf die Rechtswissenschaft ein. Die Kanonistik solle ganz wegfallen; denn er möchte, dass »das geistlich recht von dem ersten buchstaben bisz an den letzten wurd zugrund auszgetilget, sonderlich die Decretalen«, da der Papst mit den Seinen dieses Recht

---

64 AaO., 427,30–468,27.
65 AaO., 457,28–462,11. Der aaO., 462,12–465,21 abgedruckte Abschnitt »Zum xxvi« wurde in der zweiten Ausgabe, von Luther »selbs gemehret vnd corrigit«, hinzugefügt.
66 AaO., 457,34f.
67 AaO., 458,4f.
68 AaO., 458,7.
69 AaO., 457,35–458,17.
70 AaO., 458,26–31.
71 AaO., 458,32–34.

durch seinen Missbrauch und vor allem durch die Lehre vom Vorbehalt »in seynis hertzen kasten« *(scrinium pectoris)* ohnehin aufgehoben habe, während den Christen doch die Weisungen der Bibel genügten.[72] Aber auch das weltliche Recht, das an sich viel »besser, kunstlicher, redlicher« sei als das geistliche, verdiene Kritik: offenbar wegen der Rezeption des Römischen Rechts, das Luther als ein fremdes, weit hergeholtes Recht betrachtet. Da jedes Land »seine eygen art und gaben« habe, müsse es »auch mit eygenenn kurtzen rechten geregiert« werden; deshalb sollte »das landrecht und land sitten den keyserlichen gemeynen rechten« vorgezogen und jene »nur zur not« gebraucht werden.[73]

Zuletzt setzt er sich mit der Theologie und dem religiösen Unterricht im allgemeinen auseinander.[74] Er beginnt mit einer kritischen Darstellung der bestehenden Lage:

> Meine lieben Theologen haben sich ausz der muhe und erbeit gesetzt, lassen die Biblien wol rugen und leszen sententias. Ich meynet, die sententie solten der anfang sein der jungen Theologen, und die Biblia den doctoribus bleyben, szo ists umbkeret, die Biblien ist das erst, die feret mit dem Baccalariat dahin, und sententie sein das letzt, die bleyben mit dem doctorat ewiglich.[75]

Der zweite Satz soll die Norm darstellen, der erste und dritte kritisch die Verhältnisse in der Gegenwart schildern. Viele Luther-Biographen haben diese Aussagen für bare Münze genommen. Sie haben daraus – in Verbindung mit anderen Äußerungen Luthers – auf die Vernachlässigung der Bibel und auf die Vorherrschaft der Sentenzenvorlesung im Theologiestudium seiner Zeit geschlossen. Doch das Bild, das Luther hier entwirft, ist polemisch verzerrt. Die Ausnahmen von der Norm im Lehrbetrieb des späten 15. und frühen 16. Jahrhunderts rechtfertigen seine Behauptungen

---

72 AaO., 459,2–16.
73 AaO., 459,30–460,5. Zwar hat Luther an der Überzeugung festgehalten, das Recht müsse sich nach den Verhältnissen des Landes richten, für das es bestimmt ist (noch: Von Ehesachen, 1530 [WA 30,3; 225,25–29]); doch hatte er inzwischen auch das Römische (»kaiserliche«) Recht schätzen gelernt (z.B. Eine Predigt, daß man Kinder zur Schulen halten solle, 1530 [WA 30,2; 557,14–16]); Auslegung des 101. Psalms, 1534/35 [WA 51; 242,20–24.36–243,5]).
74 WA 6; 460,6–462,11.
75 AaO., 460,6–10.

nicht. Die Aussage, dass »die Sentenzen allein herrschen«, ist eine über-treibende Verallgemeinerung, vielleicht im Blick auf das Luther wohlbe-kannte Sentenzenwerk Gabriel Biels. Soviel wir aus den Vorbemerkungen des Herausgebers[76] wissen, hat Biel – vom Üblichen abweichend – in hohem Alter an der Universität Tübingen und im dortigen Universitäts-stift der Brüder vom gemeinsamen Leben Vorlesungen über den Messka-non und die Sentenzen gehalten, dagegen nicht über biblische Bücher, während von seinem Mitbruder und Schüler, dem Herausgeber seiner Werke und Tübinger Professor Wendelin Steinbach nur reguläre biblische Vorlesungen überliefert sind. Luther mag bei seiner Aussage auch an berühmte ältere scholastische Lehrer wie Duns Scotus oder Wilhelm von Ockham gedacht haben, deren umfangreiche, immer wieder redigierte und seit dem späten 15. Jahrhundert gedruckt vorliegende Sentenzenkom-mentare ein lebenslanges Arbeiten an dieser typisch scholastischen Werk-gattung bezeugen. Er lässt bei seinem Urteil aber die viel zahlreicheren Bibelkommentare außer Acht, die von den Theologieprofessoren auf Grund ihrer Vorlesungen verfasst worden waren.

Luthers Forderung an die Theologen geht vom Herkommen insofern ab, als er unter Berufung auf den theologischen Doktortitel die Heilige Schrift exklusiv in den Mittelpunkt des gesamten Theologiestudiums stellen möchte.[77] Diesem Ziel dient auch sein Wunsch, die Zahl der beim Studium der Schrift benutzten Bücher solle verringert werden.[78] Zwar mag er die Kirchenväter nicht ganz verwerfen. Sie sollen aber nur eine Zeitlang als Einführung in die Schrift gelesen und danach beiseite getan werden. Gegenstand und Norm des Theologiestudiums solle allein die

---

76 G. BIEL, Collectorium circa quattuor libros Sententiarum. Prologus et Liber primus, hg. v. W. WERBECK/U. HOFMANN, 1973, 3,32–34; 6,3–5; DERS., Canonis missae expositio, Pars I (VIEG 31), hg. v. H. A. OBERMAN/W. J. COURTENAY, 1963, 2.

77 WA 6; 460,20–22: »Szo wir den haben den namen und titel, das wir lerer der heyligen schrifft heyssenn, solten wir warlich gezwungen sein dem namen nach, die heyligen schrifft und kein andere leren«.

78 AaO., 461,1–4: »Die Theologische bucher must man auch wenigern und erleszen die besten, dan viel bucher machen nit geleret, vil leszen auch nit, szondern gut ding unnd offt leszenn, wie wenig sein ist, das macht geleret in der schrifft und frum datzu.«

Schrift sein.[79] Über die Methode des Studiums verliert Luther in diesem Zusammenhang freilich kein Wort. Er begnügt sich mit dem Rat, Gott demütig um »Doctores Theologie« zu bitten; denn »eynen Doctorn der heyligenn schrifft« könne »niemandt machenn, denn allein der heylig geyst vom hymel« gemäß dem Wort Christi Joh 6,45: »Sie mussen alle von got selber geleret sein.«[80] Er kann so argumentieren, weil er hier und anderswo die im Mittelalter übliche[81] Gleichsetzung von *theologia* mit *sacra scriptura* beibehält und deshalb die Inspiriertheit der Heiligen Schrift einfach auf die Theologen überträgt.

Was Luther in seiner Adelsschrift vortrug, das war teilweise durchaus realistisch gedacht, teilweise aber stellte es eine von Emotionen getragene Utopie dar. Die Vorschläge für die Artisten entsprachen den in Wittenberg bereits eingeschlagenen Maßnahmen. Ohne Ausbildung in gewissen philosophischen Disziplinen ließ sich keine Wissenschaft treiben. Auf Aristoteles konnte dabei nicht gänzlich verzichtet werden. Man muss ja fragen, wodurch seine Werke hätten ersetzt werden können. Der von Luther bevorzugte Platon stand bei der Universitätsreform nicht ernsthaft zur Wahl. Auch die Humanisten konnten gewisse aristotelische Werke gebrauchen; Melanchthon hatte in seiner Tübinger Zeit sogar eine neue Aristoteles-Ausgabe geplant.[82] Es lag aber in der Konsequenz der reformatorischen Erkenntnisse, jene Werke auszuschließen, die inhaltlich mit dem biblischen Gottes-, Welt- und Menschenbild unvereinbar schienen; das waren die von Luther genannten. Dass das aristotelische Werk in Wittenberg bereits durch Melanchthon wieder in großer Breite rezipiert wurde, das steht auf einem anderen Blatt.

Auf die Kanonistik zu verzichten, lag nahe, nachdem Luther das kirchliche Recht im Laufe seines römischen Prozesses mit wachsendem Nachdruck als päpstliches, antichristliches Recht zu verstehen und zu verwerfen gelernt hatte; die Verbrennung des *Corpus iuris canonici* am 10.

---

79 AaO., 461,4–10.
80 AaO., 460,27–32.
81 Dazu U. Köpf, Die Anfänge der theologischen Wissenschaftstheorie im 13. Jahrhundert (BHTh 49), 1974, bes. 262–264.
82 G. Frank, Melanchthons Tübinger Plan einer neuen Aristoteles-Ausgabe (in: Vom Schüler der Burse zum »Lehrer Deutschlands« [s. Anm. 4], 105–115).

Dezember 1520 und ihre anschließende öffentliche Begründung[83] machten diese Verwerfung unumkehrbar. Konsequenterweise wurde bei der Gründung der ersten evangelischen Universität in Marburg 1527 die Kanonistik kategorisch aus dem Kreis der Fakultäten ausgeschlossen.

Die Vorschläge für die Theologische Fakultät stellten freilich eine Kapitulation vor der wissenschaftsorganisatorischen und didaktischen Aufgabe dar. Luther erhielt die Quittung dafür von seinen radikalen Schülern, vor allem von Thomas Müntzer, für den die Erfahrung des Glaubens aus dem heiligen Geist zu einer Quelle theologischer Erkenntnis wurde, die nicht nur jede wissenschaftliche Beschäftigung mit der Schrift, sondern am Ende die Schrift selbst hinter sich ließ.[84] Das war natürlich nicht in Luthers Sinn, der uneingeschränkt an der Schrift als Grundlage der Theologie festhielt. Ein reiner Biblizismus konnte jedoch nicht die Grundlage einer wissenschaftlichen Theologie sein, und die Kirchenväter, die Luther zum Bibelverständnis heranziehen wollte, leisteten nur begrenzt, was er von ihnen erwartete. Vor allem eigneten sie sich kaum als Lehrbücher für den akademischen Unterricht. Die Lösung konnte nur auf jenem Weg gesucht werden, den Luther schon selbst eingeschlagen und damit vorgezeichnet hatte: auf dem Weg einer philologisch-theologischen Exegese, die alle Werkzeuge der humanistischen Philologie, aber auch die bewährten und unanstößigen Erkenntnisse der Philosophie für die Auslegung und Auswertung der Heiligen Schrift gebrauchte. Damit war er frei-

---

83 Warum des Papsts und seiner Jünger Bücher von Doct. Martino Luther verbrannt sind (WA 7; 161–182).

84 Vgl. z. B. T. MÜNTZER, Ausgedrückte Entblößung des falschen Glaubens, 1524 (in: DERS., Schriften und Briefe. Kritische Gesamtausgabe [QFRG 33], hg. v. G. FRANZ, 1968), 277a7–33: »Darumb muß die verhaltene warheyt eynmal gantz küne an den tag kummen, welche also gantz lange geschlaffen hat; in solcher maß, wenn eyn christ unter dem armen hauffen sprech, das er den christenglauben von Gott selber gelernet het, würde man im nit glauben […], wenn er mit der schrifft durch seyn berechen nicht übereynstympte, wie alle außerwelten sollen von Got gelert werden, Joannis 6, Isaie 54, Jeremie 31, Job 35, Psal. 17, 24, 33, 70, 93, und vil ander schrifft dreybt alle drauff, von Got alleyn gelert werden. Wenn eyner nu seyn leben lang die biblien wider gehöret noch gesehen het, kündt er woll für sich durch die gerechten lere des geystes eynen unbetrieglichen christenglauben haben, wie alle die gehabt, die one alle bücher die heylige schrifft beschriben haben.«

lich noch weit von einer historisch-kritischen Schriftauslegung entfernt, wie sie erst im 19. Jahrhundert voll entwickelt wurde.

Immerhin rückte unter Luthers Einfluss die Auslegung der Bibel in den Mittelpunkt der Wittenberger Theologie. Der Reformator selbst hat ja als Professor sein Leben lang nur über Texte aus der Heiligen Schrift Vorlesungen gehalten. Die Zentralstellung der Bibel drückte sich auch darin aus, dass die Bedeutung der Sentenzen im Lehrbetrieb rasch sank. Melanchthon, der am 19. September 1519 den Grad des *Baccalaureus biblicus* erworben hatte, verzichtete bereits bewusst darauf, den Grad eines *Sententiarius* zu erwerben. Jedoch hatte er es schon früh aus didaktischen Gründen als zweckmäßig erkannt, den Studenten wenigstens einen Überblick über die christliche Lehre zu bieten. Nach einigen Überlegungen über den Ersatz der Sentenzen durch eine von der Rhetorik angeregte alternative Darstellungsweise[85] verfasste er auf Grund seiner Römerbrief-Vorlesung mit den *Loci communes rerum theologicarum seu hypotyposes theologicae*[86] bereits 1521 eine erste Darstellung der evangelischen Dogmatik.[87] In den von ihm verfassten neuen Statuten der Theologischen Fakultät von 1533 konzentriert sich die Lehre jedoch ganz auf das, was sich an theologischen Erkenntnissen aus der Bibel gewinnen lässt. Die scholastischen Grade eines *Biblicus*, *Sententiarius* und *Formatus*[88] blieben zwar vorerst erhalten; aber die Aufgabe ihrer Inhaber sollten jetzt die Darstellung des *integrum corpus doctrinae christianae* aus dem Römerbrief und dem Johannesevangelium (Trinitätslehre) sowie die Auslegung ausgewählter Psalmen und Stücke aus den Propheten sein.[89] Die Professo-

---

85 Vgl. dazu Melanchthons Brief an J. Heß vom 27.4.1520 (MELANCHTHONS Briefwechsel hg. v. H. SCHEIBLE, Bd. T1, bearb. v. R. WETZEL, 1991, 191–197 [Nr. 84], bes. 193,30f. 195,69–74).

86 MELANCHTHONS Werke in Auswahl (wie Anm. 59), Bd. 2/1, hg. v. H. ENGELLAND/R. STUPPERICH, ²1978, 15–185.

87 Vgl. U. KÖPF, Melanchthons »Loci« und ihre Bedeutung für die Entstehung einer evangelischen Dogmatik (in: Philipp Melanchthon. Lehrer Deutschlands, Reformator Europas [Leucorea-Studien zur Geschichte der Reformation und der Lutherischen Orthodoxie 13], hg. v. I. DINGEL/A. KOHNLE, Leipzig 2011, 129–152).

88 Der Titel eines *Formatus* wurde im scholastischen Studiensystem dem *Baccalaureus sententiarius* zu Beginn seiner Vorlesung über das dritte Buch der Sentenzen verliehen.

89 Urkundenbuch (s. Anm. 14), 156 (Nr. 171, Absatz 7).

ren sollten sich dagegen ganz der Auslegung biblischer Bücher widmen, unter denen Römerbrief, Johannesevangelium, Psalmen, Genesis und Jesaja hervorgehoben wurden. Gelegentlich sollte einer von ihnen auch Augustins *De spiritu et littera* kommentieren, um die Übereinstimmung der reformatorischen Lehre mit der Lehre der Väter darzulegen.[90] Die *Loci* wurden nach wiederholter Umarbeitung erst 1588 endgültig in den Wittenberger Statuten zur Grundlage regelmäßiger dogmatischer Vorlesungen gemacht, nachdem Melanchthon selbst und mehrere jüngere Magistri längst darüber gelesen und andere Universitäten sie bereits als theologisches Lehrbuch in ihren Ordnungen verankert hatten.[91] Daneben gab es auch Überlegungen, die Summe der christlichen Lehre nach anderen Texten zu entwickeln, vor allem nach dem *Nicaenum*, dessen gelegentliche Auslegung Melanchthon in seinen Satzungen von 1545 vorsah.[92] Luther überließ Melanchthon die Ausarbeitung der universitären Ordnungen und wirkte auch an der Entwicklung einer evangelischen Disziplin »Dogmatik« nicht mehr aktiv mit. Doch hat er Melanchthons *Loci* gelobt und war zweifellos zumindest an den Überlegungen beteiligt, die sich in Melanchthons Ordnungen für die Theologische Fakultät niederschlugen. Gewiss ist es auch seinem Einfluss zuzuschreiben, dass die biblischen Grundlagen dieses Faches im nachreformatorischen Protestantismus dauerhaft bewahrt blieben.

Anders als die Vorlesung stand die zweite traditionelle Form der Lehre, die seit jeher der eigentliche Ort systematischer Erörterung von Problemen gewesen war, in den Anfängen der Wittenberger Reformation zur Disposition: die Disputation.[93] Sie wurde von den humanistischen

---

90 AaO., 155 (Nr. 171, Absatz 3).

91 Vgl. U. Köpf, Die Anfänge einer evangelischen Dogmatik in Tübingen. Zugleich ein Beitrag zur Wirkungsgeschichte der theologischen *Loci* Philipp Melanchthons (in: Die Universität Tübingen zwischen Scholastik und Humanismus [Tübinger Bausteine zur Landesgeschichte 20], hg. v. S. Lorenz u. a., 2012, 191–219), 198 f.

92 Urkundenbuch (s. Anm. 14), 263 (Nr. 272). Dazu P. Melanchthon, Enarratio secundae tertiaeque partis Symboli Nicaeni (1550) (QFRG 64), hg. v. H.-P. Hasse, 1996, 14–23: Die Auslegung des Nizänischen Glaubensbekenntnisses an der Universität Wittenberg 1546 bis 1557.

93 Über Luthers Disputationen jetzt grundlegend der Überblick von R. Schwarz, Disputationen (in: Luther Handbuch, hg. v. A. Beutel, 2005, 328–340).

Kritikern seit langem als besonders fragwürdiger Teil des scholastischen Lehrbetriebs betrachtet. Melanchthon ersetzte gegen Ende 1523 als Rektor die scholastischen Disputationen der Artisten in neuen Statuten durch »Deklamationen«, d.h. durch Reden nach den Regeln der humanistischen Rhetorik, die zweimal im Monat bald von den Professoren der Rhetorik und Grammatik, bald von den Studenten gehalten werden sollten.[94] Die theologische Fakultät beschloss unter dem Dekanat Karlstadts schon im Sommer 1521, also während Luthers Abwesenheit von Wittenberg, die Beschränkung auf eine reguläre Disputation in der Woche (»Zirkulardisputation«) und auf die Disputationen anlässlich der Promotionen.[95] Karlstadt drängte aber weiter. Aus seiner mit Mt 23,8ff begründeten Ablehnung des Magistertitels zog er als Dekan am 3. Februar 1523 anlässlich der Promotion zweier Augustinereremiten die Konsequenz und erklärte seine Absicht, künftig niemand mehr einen Grad zu verleihen.[96] Luther fügte im Dekansbuch eigenhändig seinen scharfen Widerspruch gegen Karlstadts Eintrag und die dahinter stehende Theologie hinzu.[97] Immerhin hatte Karlstadts Vorgehen die einschneidende Folge, dass die theologischen Promotionen und damit die dafür nötigen Disputationen ins Stocken gerieten und nach der Promotion am 26. Juni 1525 für acht Jahre vollständig unterblieben.[98] Die Unterbrechung der Promotionen und der

94 Urkundenbuch (s. Anm. 14), 129 (Nr. 131, Absatz 3) mit der Begründung: »frigere coeperunt philosophicae disputationes«.

95 AaO., 110 (Nr. 101): »Duo sunt disputacionis ordines: unus hebdomatim suis vestigiis vadit; alter est presidencia eorum qui pro gradibus nanciscendis respondent propriumque cursum hic facit.«

96 Liber decanorum facultatis theologiae academiae Vitebergensis, hg. v. C.E. FÖRSTEMANN, 1838, 28: »is tum palam testabatur post hoc se ne vllum in quemvis gradum subuerturum«.

97 Ebd. Anm. 1: »Et ego testor hac mea manu, me in eodem actu affuisse Et etiam has sacrilegas voces ex ore eius blasphemo audisse (Sed quibus tunc palam reclamare non licuit): Ego prudens facio impie, quod propter ij flor. promoueo. Et contendebat ex Matth. 23 neminem esse vocandum patrem aut Magistrum in terra, Sed vnum esse Magistrum & patrem in caelis etc. Ex quibus intelligitur, quo spiritu ceperit suam Theologiam. Mart. Luther m: propria.«

98 Nach Karlstadts Weigerung wurden unter dem Dekanat von Justus Jonas 1523 und 1524 noch jeweils zwei Theologen zu *magistri* und am 26. Juni 1525 als letzter Ambrosius

dadurch bedingte Ausfall von Nachwuchs führten allmählich zu Schwierigkeiten im theologischen Lehrbetrieb. Erst 1533 führten die Theologen auf Wunsch des Kurfürsten Johann Friedrich wieder eine Promotion durch.[99] Melanchthon sah in den Statuten der theologischen Fakultät von 1533 erneut reguläre theologische Disputationen und Promotionen vor.[100] Gerne benutzte jetzt auch Luther wieder diese Gelegenheit, um im Rahmen der traditionellen Unterrichtsform zentrale Themen seiner Theologie systematisch zu erörtern: zum Beispiel die Auffassung des Menschen in seiner Beziehung zu Gott,[101] die Rechtfertigungslehre im Anschluss an Röm 3,28[102] und die Rolle des Gesetzes.[103]

Der Blick auf Luthers Beitrag zur Universitätsreform wirkt ernüchternd. Weder auf dem Gebiet der Didaktik noch auf dem der Wissenschaftsorganisation hat der Reformator schöpferisch gewirkt. Hier hat er vielmehr zunächst humanistische Vorschläge aufgegriffen und später Melanchthon die Gestaltung der Ordnungen überlassen. Luthers wichtigster Beitrag zur Universitätsreform der Wittenberger Reformation waren seine inhaltlichen, theologischen Erkenntnisse, die zu einer Neuorientierung der reformierten Universität führten. Grundlegend für die gesamte Universität – nicht nur für ihre theologische Fakultät – wurde die Anerkennung der Heiligen Schrift als einzige geistliche Autorität. Ihr fiel vor allem die Kanonistik zum Opfer. In der Theologie mussten die an Aussagen der kirchlichen Tradition reichen Sentenzen weichen. Im Mittelpunkt

---

Moibanus aus Breslau zum *magister Theologiae* promoviert. Der nächste Eintrag im *Liber decanorum* stammt vom 16. Juni 1533 (AaO., 28).

99 Zu den Umständen vgl. SCHEIBLE, Melanchthon (s. Anm. 3), 51–54.

100 Urkundenbuch (s. Anm. 14), 155 f (Nr. 171, Absatz V, VII).

101 Disputation *De homine* 1536 (WA 39,1; 175–180). Vgl. dazu die umfassende und tiefschürfende Untersuchung von G. EBELING, Lutherstudien II: Disputatio de homine, 1. Teil: Text und Traditionshintergrund, 1977; 2. Teil: Die philosophische Definition des Menschen. Kommentar zu These 1–19, 1982; 3. Teil: Die theologische Definition des Menschen. Kommentar zu These 20–40, 1989.

102 Zwei Disputationen 1535 (WA 39,1; 44–62); zwei 1536 (aaO., 82–126); eine 1537 (aaO., 202–257; 260–263).

103 Sechs Disputatinen in der Auseinandersetzung mit den Antinomern 1537–1540 (WA 39,1; 342–358; 360–417; 419–485; 489–584; 39,2; 124–144).

der theologischen Fakultät stand jetzt die Auslegung der Bibel, und es war nicht Luthers Einfluss, der allmählich zu einer systematischen Darstellung der christlichen Lehre auch im Studienbetrieb hinführte. Seine inhaltlich begründete radikale Aristoteleskritik nahm Luther bereits in der Adelsschrift so weit zurück, dass er den Gebrauch der vom Humanismus geschätzten sprachlich-logischen Werke des Philosophen akzeptierte. Doch hat er kräftig darauf hingewirkt, dass die vom Wegestreit geprägten scholastischen Kommentare endgültig wegfielen und neue Übersetzungen oder gar die griechischen Originaltexte benutzt wurden. Die humanistische Forderung nach dem Erlernen der drei alten Sprachen hat er tatkräftig unterstützt, aber auch schon auf die Beachtung bisher vernachlässigter Gebiete wie der mathematischen Disziplinen und der Historie gedrängt. Die weitere Entwicklung der reformatorischen Theologie, die zur altprotestantischen Orthodoxie hinführte, ließ seine breite Aristoteleskritik allerdings zunehmend in Vergessenheit geraten, während die von ihm geforderte Zentralstellung der Schrift sowie seine inhaltlichen Einsichten bewahrt blieben und den reformierten theologischen Unterricht durchdrangen – allen voran sein neues Verständnis der Gerechtigkeit Gottes, aus dem bald eine richtiggehende Rechtfertigungslehre werden sollte. Luther hat später auch Anweisungen für »eine rechte weise in der Theologia zu studirn« hinterlassen,[104] die im Luthertum stark fortwirkten,[105] ohne freilich die institutionelle Ausgestaltung des Theologiestudiums an der Universität Wittenberg zu beeinflussen.[106] Doch seine *persönliche*

---

104 In der Vorrede zu Band 1 der Wittenberger Ausgabe seiner deutschen Schriften 1539 (WA 50; 657–661); das Zitat aaO., 658,29 f.

105 Vgl. O. Bayer, Lutherischer Pietismus. Oratio, Meditatio, Tentatio bei August Hermann Francke (in: Religiöse Erfahrung und wissenschaftliche Theologie. Festschrift für Ulrich Köpf zum 70. Geburtstag, hg. v. A. Beutel/R. Rieger, 2011, 1–12).

106 Luther nennt »drey Regel« für die Beschäftigung mit der Heiligen Schrift: »Oratio, Meditatio, Tentatio« (WA 50; 659,3 f). Wenn er hier das Gebet um den Heiligen Geist empfiehlt, »der dich erleuchte, leite und verstand gebe« (659,12), so meint er konkret das Verstehen der Schrift durch den einzelnen Theologen und nicht, wie in der Schrift »An den christlichen Adel« (WA 6; 460,27 f: »ein demuttig gepet zu got, das uns der selb Doctores Theologie gebe«), die Theologenausbildung. – Zu den drei Regeln vgl. R. Schäfer, Oratio, meditatio, tentatio. Drei Hinweise Luthers auf den Gebrauch der Bibel (in: Ders., Gotteslehre und kirchliche Praxis. Ausgewählte Aufsätze, hg. v. U. Köpf/R.

Art, unter ständigem Bezug auf religiöse Erfahrung und mit einem prägnanten Erfahrungsbegriff Theologie zu treiben, die an die monastische Theologie des 12. Jahrhunderts erinnert und von deren bedeutendstem Vertreter Bernhard von Clairvaux beeinflusst ist,[107] war unnachahmlich.

Rittner, 1991, 245–251); O. Bayer, Theologie (HST 1), 1994, 55–106; M. Nieden (s. Anm. 16), 80–87.

107 Vgl. z.B. U. Köpf, Zwei große monastische Theologen: Bernhard von Clairvaux und Martin Luther (rhs 42, 1999, 355–361).

Luther, Theology, and the University

Christine Helmer[1]

Now is a good time to be a Luther scholar. The five years since the last Luther Congress have seen extraordinary changes in the international community of Luther scholars and we see their effects in the present Congress. Participants from all academic ranks are welcome at this congress, from undergraduate students excited by Luther studies and graduate students who will open up new areas of scholarship for us to consider to scholars of both genders and from many different ethnic and national backgrounds, each with the gift of a distinct perspective that they bring to this conference. This International Luther Congress claims a few important firsts: it is the first congress to have placed a public »call for papers« on the internet, thereby changing the procedure on how invitations to speak were issued; it is the first congress to have a seminar in feminist theology (hopefully in future congresses, this seminar will also attract more male participants); and this congress has attracted the highest number of attendees in its history. The 12th International Luther Congress has issued a new and clear welcome to study Luther and there is no going back now!

This is as it should be, for the questions emerging for the study of Martin Luther today require the imaginative energies of many scholars whose diverse experiences shape their research and its political consequences. Luther is contextualized very differently today than he was only five years

1 I thank the Helsinki Collegium for Advanced Studies and particularly the EURIAS (European Institutes for Advanced Study) Fellowship Programme for generous funding that made possible the revision of this essay.

ago. The world is more precarious financially now than it was in 2007. An unprecedented economic situation challenges politicians who cannot seem to balance fiscal responsibility with the global reach of multinational corporations. The ever starker discrepancy between rich and poor is the product of a cruel neoliberal economic hegemony that offers no vision of a common life, tolerates no regulation of business, and elevates the unfettered individual as the hero of our times. The real face of the neighbor that obliges a response of ethical care has disappeared into the screen of potentially infinite friends of the web's social network. Human personhood, in turn, has become fragmented by the distraction characterizing modern life, the self's reality is virtual in its self-performance on the screen for any and every viewer, perpetually hammered with sound-bites of information that cannot be integrated into coherent knowledge, its desires projecting infinite possibilities onto the virtual screen.

It is this world that contextualizes our discussion of Luther this year in Helsinki, specifically the topic of Luther and the university. My aim is to talk about Luther, theology, and the university in sight of contemporary reality. My scholarly commitment as a theologian is to orient the intellectual practice of producing theological knowledge to think about the self in the reality of its being in this world as well as the reality of being whole and cared for as is Christ's promise of a redeemed life.

Luther is a powerful resource for this task. As a theologian in the university, he invested energy in changing the curriculum to fit the new emerging fields of textual studies. His vocation as a scholar was practiced in his study, the classroom lecture, and the disputation forum, three locations of academic subjectivity and activity that shaped his thoughts and changed the world. In this talk I will sketch out a few points that I think are helpful in engaging Luther in the university today, in view of the questions pressed upon us by the world's new situation.

I make my points in reference to my own academic situation as a theologian in a religious studies department in a secular U.S. American private university. This is not always the most hospitable context for doing theology! Religious Studies in the United States sees itself as (mostly) freed from its Christian-theological (German) father. Theology's conceptual abstract methods place it at odds, or so it is said, with the empirical-historical and ethnographic methods privileged by the modern study of religion. Christianity is usually twinned with the eurocentric bias of Western modernity, and both theology and Christianity are the objects of critical deconstruction, with the result that theology's fate is displacement from the university to the denominationally-run seminary. Furthermore, theology is reckoning today with declining administrative support for the humanities – the study of German in particular, which is so crucial to the history of the humanities –, the developing field of religious studies and a new and growing interest in Islam, and the institutional challenges facing the enterprise scholarly thinking from the concrete institutional concern with utility and economics. But lest you despair at the very outset of my talk by this grim accounting, my contention is that the current crisis of the humanities and more broadly of the university offer a unique opportunity for theology to revive its critical voice, to challenge the domination of all inquiry by function and utility, and to help restore a public voice to humane scholarship, just when we need it. But it will take me a while to get there!

I begin with the popular picture of Luther, the hagiography, and show how theologians can address this topic in order to open it to more interesting and creative critical thinking and action.

I Hagiography

Who is Martin Luther? There needs to be at least two answers to this: Luther in the popular imagination and the Luther of scholars. First the popular Luther: like Paul the Apostle and Aristotle the Philosopher, Luther is identified with a movement that transcends its and his historical particularity. He is the Reformer who comes to us in a story of freedom that has inspired different people struggling to speak truth to power long after his death and way beyond his native Saxony. This Luther has wide public salience. He is identified with the personal, religious, and political breakthrough to freedom; he has become synonymous with a dramatic rupture from the past to be free for the future. »For freedom Christ has set you free,« is the Galatians' motto (Gal 5:1) that has become the global trope for liberation. Whether as the Iranian Luther or as the Buddhist or Muslim »Luther,« or the »Luther« of contemporary Catholic survivors of clerical sexual abuse who see him as the prophet of a church that might have been, the 16th century Luther is in the popular imagination a legend of fearless commitment to the truth of freedom.

The smaller circle of Luther scholars and Lutheran theologians seem a bit less excited. Five hundred years of footnotes have tamed the man. If footnotes were a climate event, Luther footnotes would be a tsunami. The scholarly obeisance that defers to his authority has flattened him into a one-dimensional hero. Luther has become the imprimatur for authorizing theological positions articulated centuries after his death; his name is invoked to underwrite supposedly pure doctrine (or even the idea of the possibility of pure doctrine). Where the world looks to him as a hope for freedom and truth, Luther scholars have rendered him into an insipid theological cliché.

So here we come to a pass: Would Luther scholars rather see justification as a language game than experience the contagious power of God's grace? Do they prefer to preserve the predictable epistemic trope of law and gospel rather than be open to the unpredictable *mysterium tremendum et fascinans*? – to refer to the term that one Luther scholar applied to Luther's volatile God at the turn of the 20th century.

The only answer to these questions is that Luther must be set free from his parochial domestication and brought up to speed in a changing world that requires more critical, intuitive, and prophetic voices to guide clear thinking and responsible action. The university has historically been the place where thought is set free for innovation that moves history. It was the place where Luther wrestled with scripture using the new critical product of Erasmus' study; it has been the place where theologians have engaged Luther to ask the question of how God is related to the world such as it is. In fact the history of academic Luther scholarship is such a powerful intellectual legacy that it can write the intellectual history of the West. Lutheran Pietists appropriated the mystical Luther in the late 17th century and constructed the dialectic between the inner and outer aspects of modern subjectivity. The Luther who had focused hermeneutical attention on the literal sense of the Bible conveyed a nominalist and humanist preoccupation with language that can be traced through the 20th century's »linguistic turn.« Luther's holy God was used by early 20th century Luther scholar Rudolf Otto as the template for a comparative concept of religion. Each generation of academic reflection on Luther has generated religious and theological creativity by asking pressing questions from epistemology to piety. And if the university resists promoting provocative intellectual struggle, then theologians should take on this historical leadership role.

Luther's gift to the university is that questions should be asked in a way that causes thinking to take place. When theologians highlight the question of God in the university, they remind their academic conversation partners that there is another perspective, a theological perspective, which situates human reality »under the species of eternity« (*sub specie aeternitate*). In the next section I will address the problem of the academic disciplinary reduction of questions to historical causality. Suffice to say at this point that contemporary academic discussions tend to mute the question of God, even while the student in the middle row, who has grown up in an entirely secular household, all of a sudden realizes that the concept of God's love gives her a compelling angle on a concept she thought she already knew, or when the literary critic in the German Department analyzes a text by Heine and is not quite sure what to make of the allusion to God. Where God is not given a place, there the academic theologian can gently inspire her colleagues to open the questions that have been closed by the alleged prescriptions of what it means to be a modern academic discipline. In the university where evangelical students sit together with secular kids and non-Christians, it is the theologian's responsibility to invite the voicing of questions and fears about evil and eternity. In the university where reality is studied from its many perspectives, the theologian should keep alive the question about the ultimate reality, the *ens realissimum*, the living God. Luther's hagiography holds open these questions – the talk of God who is dangerous in his wrath and even more dangerous in his love.

II Reductionism

Luther's hagiography has raised one particular issue of perennial interest to academics, namely the relation of the old to the new. The study of Luther over the past one hundred years has been particularly taken with this relation. The interest was inspired by the historicist turn that began to dominate academic methodologies at the beginning of the 20th century. Karl Holl, who is credited with the original *Lutherrenaissance*, first saw Luther's *Lectures on Romans* as the hermeneutical key to dating the shift in Luther's religious biography from a terrified conscience to grace. Holl raised the historical question concerning the reformation breakthrough, the novelty of dramatic conversion that preoccupied the bulk of Luther studies through the 1980s. There were admittedly ideological reasons why this search for the reformation breakthrough was so intense. Protestant identity was asserted as distinct from Roman Catholic identity (and vice versa); early modernism introduced the values of enlightenment over and against a slavish Middle Ages.

Yet a quick survey of contemporary themes in Luther studies finds that one hundred years after Holl the search for a breakthrough in Luther's religion does not excite scholars. In fact, the interest in Luther seems to be of development rather than discontinuity. In part this has to do with ecumenical interests, which have driven the search for the Catholic Luther over the past twenty years, as I will talk about in the next section. Another reason for the shift in interest from the young to the old Luther, from the date of the reformation breakthrough to the continuity of Luther's thought with his predecessors, is the psychological model of development that has taken hold in the humanities and social sciences. As studies in human development show, change is difficult for humans; grace requires unflinching habituation in order for change to be sustained over time.

Deconstructionist philosophy has also mounted a successful campaign against the conceptuality assumed by discontinuity. The binary opposites of the discontinuity between old and new are no longer viewed as dangerous metaphysical truths. Binaries have been unveiled as fictitious signifiers that gesture infinitely towards a logos, desirous of but never finally attaining it. Infinite movement, rather than one heroic leap to the infinite, characterizes the contemporary scholarly bias. Luther, the master of discontinuous binary thinking, is completely out of touch here. Finally, Luther has fallen victim to new models of human subjectivity (the word that has come to replace »personhood« in academic discourse). As psychologist of religion Jim Jones argues, Luther's thought on justification might no longer be relevant to the modern self because Luther presupposes a strong coherent subjectivity,[2] contemporary accounts assume multiple epistemologies and argue that porous hybrid identities are constructed by culture and shaped by bodily practices. The discourse on the »technology of the self« has squeezed agency out of consciousness, and into the realm of social and political instruments of power. Luther and his God who creates the self with the radical actuality of a new subjectivity is not welcome in this discussion.

But Luther scholarship need not react to this situation by rigidly holding onto the opposing paradigm of a strong self who makes unwavering assertions based on binary thinking and a dualist conception of ontological principles (God and devil). Nor is a complete surrender to the paradigm an option, thereby eliminating the particular idiosyncrasy that our subject matter offers. Rather, we can use this opportunity to think critically about the academic consensus in psychology and deconstruction, to make fruitful use of our distinct theological perspectives in order to diagnose intellectual blindspots, and make creative use of theological rationality to point out new paths for academic discussion.

Such an opportunity is currently available, and badly needed, in the field of religious studies. The issue has to do with the historiography currently reigning in the academy, including the modern study of religion. The study of religion emerged at the turn of the 20th century from the turn to history as reigning paradigm in the humanities. While history has remained the science (*Wissenschaft*) responsible for explaining events and phenomena in the humanities, its focus has been narrowed – also under the influence of deconstructionism. Historical explanations are articulated as social, cultural, and political causes. Events are viewed as products of historical forces that have shaped them, while persons have lost their agency in an explanatory paradigm that has assigned responsibility for change to technologies of the body and community identity. Determinism rather than freedom has become the metaphysic of history.

---

2 See J. W. JONES, Luther and Contemporary Psychoanalysis: Living in the Midst of Horrors (in: The Global Luther: A Theologian for Modern Times, ed. by C. HELMER 2009, 67–81).

In a recent essay recently, for example, entitled *Thinking about religion, belief, and politics*, Talal Asad proposes that the five bodily senses should be the focus of the study of religion.[3] Religion shapes the way in which the body senses, tastes, touches, so that a study of the senses can be referred to interests and forces at stake in their production.[4] Asad proposes this move to the senses in view of a criticism that he and many other scholars of religion share about the domination of a Protestant notion of faith or belief that has illegitimately determined the definition of religion. Religion is not to be identified with faith, as this term imposes a Western Protestant theological bias in religion. Rather the subject of religion must be defined in ways that are freed from a Protestant Christian theological determination and open to historical and ethnographic investigation. The study of the body's senses eliminates religion's alleged task of interpreting its behaviors in terms of faith or belief, thereby freeing the study of the body from the vestiges of theological meaning imposed on it by a Western conceptuality.[5] Religion as the study of the senses then is connected directly to politics as its explanation.

This reduction of religion to politics seems to be the result of a direction taken in the study of religion that opposes (and more often than not, naïvely opposes) the Protestant identification of religion to faith and the Western philosophical understanding of the human subject as autonomous and free. But if modern critical scholarship is unable to address the

3 T. ASAD, Thinking about religion, belief, and politics (in: The Cambridge Companion to Religious Studies, ed. by R. A. ORSI, 2012, 36–57).
4 Asad writes, »To explore how religion, belief, and politics are linked to one another, we need to enquire not only into institutional landscapes but also ask a number of questions about the body, its senses, and its attitudes. For this, we need ethnographies of the human body – its attitudes toward pain, physical damage, decay and health, as well as toward bodily integrity, growth and enjoyment, and the conditions that isolate persons and things from or connect them strongly with others. What architecture of the senses – hearing, seeing, smelling, touching and tasting – do particular embodiments and sensibilities depend on?« ASAD (see n. 3), 51.
5 Asad again: »I suggest, therefore, that instead of approaching such behavior in terms of belief […] one might enquire into how the bodily senses are cultivated or how they take shape in a world that cannot be humanly controlled, and hence in what politics these formations make possible or difficult.« ASAD (see n. 3), 54.

most elementary phenomena of religious nature except by reducing them to politics, then it needs to be criticized, not uncritically followed.

Scholar of religion and American religious historian Robert A. Orsi has recently proposed taking again seriously the concept of the »holy« to study the reality that religion opens up – humans as agents, but also agents in the supernatural realm, the realm of religion: the saints, the gods, the angels and devils.

> Holiness describes something real in culture and history, with real, if ambivalent effects [...] I mean something that is more than the sum of its social parts and that comes to have a life of its own independent of the humans out of whose imaginations, inheritances and circumstances it emerged.[6]

In a move that decisively opposes Asad, Orsi asks scholars of religion to consider the terms of religion established at the foundation of the discipline, for example, »the holy,« that in spite of their problematic Western Protestant inheritances, point to something »more« beyond the reductionism by the modern historical study of religion.[7]

It looks as though we have come full circle, back to the origin of the study of religion precipitated in the first place by the historicist turn in Christian theology. Yet there is a difference. We have come to this point chastened by deconstructionist philosophy and historicist reductionism. The influence of theology in the field of religion has been substantially truncated, if not excised altogether. So the fate of Luther in the university is bound up with the fate of religion and theology in contemporary departments of religious studies. If the study of Luther has any aspirations in the university, then Luther scholars must acknowledge this current chastened situation. Yet because there are intimations towards the full circle that might be moving beyond deconstructionism, Luther studies can join in

---

6 R. A. Orsi, The problem of the holy (in: The Cambridge Companion to Religious Studies, ed. by R. A. Orsi, 2012, 84–108), 91.

7 »But we can acknowledge the problems with it and still recognize that the theoreticians were embarked on an important and necessary project, which we understand more fully now. They wanted to account for the really realness of religion in such a way that complicated and called into question the absolute authority of naturalistic explanations, and they did so in a comparative frame that brought a vast array of events and experiences from around the world and across time to the theoretical table.« Orsi (see n. 6), 99.

these glimpses of construction. The way forward would be to account adequately for human subjectivity beyond determinism by social-political forces. Luther can be called upon as an exciting resource. His thought includes some of the funkiest reflections on the supernatural – the naked God, God's bottom, the reality of »this is my body.« His cosmology is bursting with angels and devils, and his account of subjectivity veers into the mystical posture of »I, not I, but Christ who lives in me« (cf. Gal 2:20) that overtly challenges naïve caricatures about the West's alleged commitment to the autonomous self. Luther's »vibrant materiality« may just be a timely and welcome conversation partner to the new discussion emerging in religious studies today.

III Ecumenism

Theology has, as Schleiermacher has taught us, a twofold interest.[8] Theology is committed to the production of theological knowledge in conversation with the intellectual resources available to it in the university. Yet theology has an equal interest in promoting healthy spiritualities as these are formed in the churches. Theologians, as Schleiermacher has also taught us, tend to one or the other interest in their intellectual commitments, although each theologian embodies both interests in a unique proportion.[9] If Luther studies takes one lead from the university, then its relation to the church invokes other considerations that may or may not dovetail with the former's concerns. However, the context for studying church interests is academic, so that even ecclesial interests are couched in the terms of intellectual-academic discussion.

8 F. SCHLEIERMACHER, Brief Outline of Theology as a Field of Study, 3rd edn., revised translation of 1811 and 1830 editions by T.N. TICE 2011, § 9 (p. 4): »If one were to conceive religious interest and scientific spirit to be conjoined in the highest degree and with the finest balance for the purpose of theoretical and practical activity alike, that would be the idea of a ›prince of the church‹.«

9 SCHLEIERMACHER (see n. 8), § 13 (p. 7): »Every person who finds oneself called to exercise leadership in the church discovers the primary function one is to perform according to the measure in which one or the other of these two elements is dominant within that person.«

The ecumenical context has provided the ecclesial stimulus for Luther scholarship for the last three decades. Particularly the ecumenical conversations between Lutherans and Roman Catholics have significantly shaped the research trajectory in Luther studies. Ever since German Catholic Luther scholar Peter Manns began publishing his research on the Catholic Luther in the 1980's, scholarly effort has been expended to situate Luther's thought in proximity to the Middle Ages, to late medieval philosophy, and to Catholic doctrine. Debunked is the hagiography that the Protestant Reformation sprang from Luther's head like Minerva from Zeus. Rather, Luther's reformation theology had precursors and forerunners. The resulting consensus is that Luther's thought is deeply Catholic, rooted in late medieval mystical and biblically-based piety, shaped by his education in the *via moderna* at the University of Erfurt, and quite orthodox in its Christological and Trinitarian commitments. Rather than breaking with Rome, Luther regarded his reformation as a temporary exile from mother church. His theology was not constructive, but prophetic, calling for a refocusing on Christ's sacrifice for the forgiveness of human sin.

Many of the major publications of the last three decades in Luther scholarship reflect an honest ecumenical attempt to conceive Luther in broader continuity with Western Catholicism. Great credit is owed American theologian George A. Lindbeck for the »cultural-linguist« model of religion that facilitated the mutual recognition between Lutherans and Roman Catholics of their respective understandings of justification. Lindbeck's academic context was a university divinity school (Yale), a university location mediating academic and ecclesial interests. Although Lindbeck's cultural-linguist model can be criticized for an inherent Lutheran word-oriented bias, its theological theory concerned the construction of doctrine by intramural systems of meaning that were »not necessarily incompatible« with other systems within the broad fold of Christianity.[10]

---

10 For example, when discussing the papacy as topic of ecumenical dialogue, Lindbeck writes, »In any case, the purpose of a classificatory scheme such as this is not to settle material questions about the nature or location of particular doctrines, but rather to indicate the formal possibilities and thereby to enhance the changes of meaningful dis-

The application of Lindbeck's theory to church politics put an end to 500 years of animosity between Lutherans and Roman Catholics, and with the mediation of one of the most competent Luther scholars in the world today, Theodor Dieter, the *Joint Declaration on Justification between the Lutheran World Federation and the Roman Catholic Church* was signed in Augsburg Germany on October 31, 1999.[11]

If 1999 was carried by the spirit of Vatican II, the situation today is very different. The contemporary papacy has become entrenched in positions that are oddly similar to the 16th century church that Luther saw it as his duty to reform. Recent decisions, campaigns of repression and self-inflicted crises fly in the face of Protestant ecumenical optimism. These include the return to the Latin mass (and its English translation) that reinstates the Good Friday prayers for the Jews who killed Jesus[12]; the pope's ecclesiological distinction between the true Catholic Church and renegade Protestant »ecclesial communities«[13]; the legacy from Pope John Paul II concerning the non-discussability of women's ordination[14]; the Vatican's sad silence on the issue of divorced – meaning excommunicated – Catholics; the church's failure to accept full responsibility for the scandal of the sexual abuse of children and youth by priests and its pernicious cover-up[15]; the current assault against women religious in the U.S, which has targeted among others Lindbeck's colleague, emeritus Professor Mar-

cussion and debate.« G. A. LINDBECK, The Nature of Doctrine: Religion and Theology in a Postliberal Age, 1984, 86.

11 The Lutheran World Federation and The Roman Catholic Church, Joint Declaration on the Doctrine of Justification, English-language edn., 2000.

12 See J. BURKE, Pope's move on Latin mass a ›blow to Jews‹, July 8, 2007; online (accessed January 16, 2013) at: http://www.guardian.co.uk/world/2007/jul/08/religion.catholicism.

13 Pope BENEDICT XVI, Responses to Some Questions Regarding Certain Aspects of the Doctrine of the Church, June 29, 2007; online (accessed Dec. 19, 2012) at: www.vatican.va/roman_curia/congregations/cfaith/documents/rc_con_cfaith_doc_20070629_responsa-quaestiones_en.html.

14 Pope JOHN PAUL II, Ordinatio sacerdotalis, May 22, 1994; online (accessed Dec. 19, 2012) at: www.vatican.va/holy_father/john_paul_ii/apost_letters/documents/hf_jp-ii_apl_22051994_ordinatio-sacerdotalis_en.html.

15 See the website devoted to »documenting the abuse crisis in the Roman Catholic Church«: www.bishopaccountability.org.

garet Farley, who has written on sexual ethics[16]; the bishops' investigation of the U.S. Girl Scouts,[17] and the threat to apply the office of the keys to withhold the mass from progressive American Catholic politicians, like John Kerry, Illinois governor Pat Quinn, and New York governor Andrew Cuomo. These developments in the Roman Catholic Church are provocations not invitations to ecumenism.

At this point in my talk I admit the political incorrectness in my position as a Protestant theologian pointing to problems I see within the Roman Catholic Church, when my own denomination is rife with its own controversies. But political incorrectness regarding ecumenism is appropriate today given the uncanny similarity of issues prompting Luther to speak 500 years ago. Luther's pastoral concerns for those excommunicated by human traditions, the distinction between church power and divine grace, the criticism of the false piety that leads to abusive actions and theology: in short, Luther's distinction between law that would mete judgment on those that church power makes comfortable and grace distributed to the afflicted, terrified and oppressed. Luther's reformation theology still holds out the possibility of reform pertinent to contemporary Roman Catholicism, while conversely Lutheran theology continues to require the Christ-focused truths of its shared Catholic theological commitments.

We are perhaps entering into a time of vigorous ecclesial differentiation, rather than one of ecclesial unity.[18] Looking around to mainline Protestant Churches, differentiation seems to be playing itself out in for example the split in the ELCA brought about by the progressive consensus

16 M. A. FARLEY, Just Love: A Framework for Christian Sexual Ethics, 2006.
17 The United States Conference of Catholic Bishops are inquiring into the Girl Scouts' association with programs that support »family planning or emergency contraception.« AP, Bishops Group to Investigate Girl Scouts, May 11, 2012; online (accessed Dec. 19, 2012) at: www.nytimes.com/2012/05/11/us/bishops-group-to-investigate-girl-scouts.html?_r=0.
18 I am grateful to Professor Marilyn McCord Adams for making this distinction in a personal conversation, March 23, 2012; see also her article: M. McCORD ADAMS, Face to faith, March 25, 2006; online (accessed Dec. 19, 2012) at: www.guardian.co.uk/world/2006/mar/25/religion.uk.

on gays and lesbians in August of 2009[19] to the votes against the global Anglican covenant precipitated by the Episcopal Church in May of 2012.[20] The church interests recommending the agenda for Luther studies do not necessarily need to take unity as sole ecumenical mandate. Indeed, we might say the time for this has come to an end for the moment. Now it is time to reassert Luther's insight that God the Spirit creates the church. Perhaps we should recognize difference, not stifle it, and discern how the Spirit is creating the church today.

IV The Public Nature of Theology

Luther once credited his license to dispute in public to his academic doctorate. Early on in his career, Luther wrote to the pope that he had the right as a doctor of theology to dispute theological questions.[21] Neither the monastic vow nor his ordination, but the doctorate was the medieval license for challenging Rome in public debate. Luther's recourse to his academic title reminds us that the university is a public forum, and as such, the appropriate setting for theology as a form of public engagement, with its unique potential for social, political, and institutional change. To end this talk I want to mention one model of inspiration, a theologian who represents the public transformation of theology from the New World, a German émigré to Canada. He is a model for the sort of scholarship for change that I think can help us reflect together on how Luther, theology, and the university can present new opportunities for creative thinking and action.

The theologian I want to talk about here is Ulrich Siegfried Leupold. Some of you might recognize his name from the cover of volume 53 of the

---

19 See the ELCA's social statement on human sexuality that was adopted at a Churchwide Assembly meeting on Aug. 19, 2009; online (accessed January 16, 2013) at: http://www. elca.org/What-We-Believe/Social-Issues/Social-Statements/JTF-Human-Sexuality.aspx.

20 See the website providing up-to-date information on all national churches within the worldwide Anglican communion concerning their respective positions vis-à-vis the Anglican covenant online (accessed January 16, 2013) at: http://noanglicancovenant.org/background.html#tec.

21 WA 1; 528,27–31.

American Edition of Luther's Works.[22] Leupold edited and translated this volume dedicated to Luther's hymns and liturgies. But what you might not know is that he held a doctorate from the University of Berlin, earned at the age of 23 in musicology, and his *Staatsexamen* in theology, and that he came to Canada during the Second World War, was dean of Waterloo Lutheran Seminary, and helped found the music department of Waterloo Lutheran University (now institutionally distinct from the seminary and renamed Wilfrid Laurier University).

Leupold was educated in Berlin and Zürich during the 1920s and 1930s.[23] He studied with Germany's brightest in both fields of musicology and theology. His doctoral dissertation *Die liturgischen Gesänge der evangelischen Kirche im Zeitalter der Aufklärung und der Romantik* (*The Liturgical Chants of the Evangelical Church at the Time of the Enlightenment and Romantic Periods*), was a study of the organization of the Prussian musical establishment under King Frederick Wilhelm III, and was snapped up in 1933 by Bärenreiter in Kassel, one of Germany's most prestigious publishers.[24] But Leupold's mother was Jewish, and because of the Aryan race laws imposed on Protestant ordinations, Leupold joined the Confessing Church in order to be ordained (although it is not clear which of the Confessing Church seminaries he attended). He left Germany in 1938/39 for England because of his sister who had married an Englishman and then went to the United States, his emigration brokered by a pastor who sponsored Leupold as a church musician at Augsburg Lutheran Church in Toledo, Ohio. On March 29, 1939 Leupold moved to Canada as assistant pastor to St. Matthew's Lutheran Church in Kitchener (former

22 Philadelphia: Fortress Press, 1965.
23 Substantive research to date on Ulrich Leupold has been published by Canadian musicologist (and my father) Paul Helmer. My remarks on Leupold are summaries of the following two articles by P. HELMER: Ulrich Siegfried Leupold (1909–70) (Consensus: A Canadian Lutheran Journal of Theology 34, no. 1, 2012); online (accessed December 21, 2012) at: http://www.consensusjournal.ca/Current%20Issue/Article%2001-Ulrich%20Siegfried%20Leupold.pdf and Ulrich Siegfried Leupold (in: Canterbury Dictionary of Hymnology, ed. by J. R. WATSON/E. HORNBY, 2013); online (accessed January 16, 2013) at: http://hymnology.org.uk/dictionary/Ulrich_Siegfried_Leupold.
24 This sentence is taken from Helmer's formulation in HELMER (see n. 23), 3 f.

name Berlin). This emigration did not come a moment too soon. In 1940, his name and that of his mother appeared in Theophil Stengel's *Lexikon der Juden in der Musik*, equivalent to a death sentence.[25]

Leupold would give to his new country of Canada his extraordinary gifts as musicologist, organist, pastor, theologian, and university administrator. After a short time as pastor of a parish in Maynooth, Ontario, a small northern Canadian town near Lake Huron, Leupold moved to Waterloo in southern Ontario where he became dean of Waterloo Lutheran Seminary, along with appointments as Assistant Professor of Music and Professor of New Testament Studies and Church Music. There he regularly taught Greek and offered the seminary's first course in music, inaugurated a master's degree in sacred music, and through his administrative efforts, was the driving force behind the creation of the music department at Waterloo Lutheran University. His academic publication record in both musicology and theology was phenomenal, and in addition, he edited 200 motets and anthems by American and Canadian composers, served on the task forces for the preparation of two Lutheran worship books, the *Service Book and Hymnal* (»The Red Book«) from 1958, and the Inter-Lutheran Commission on Worship begun in 1966, which resulted in the *Lutheran Book of Worship* (»The Green Book«), published after his early death in 1970 of Lou Gehrig's disease. On the liturgical committee, he »proposed that liturgies be commissioned from the leading American and European composers such as Igor Stravinsky, Roger Sessions, Walter Piston, Benjamin Britten, Luigi Dallapiccola and Hans Werner Henze, among others,« a proposal that unfortunately was not accepted by the general committee.[26] He was a pioneer in Lutheran world music, working on projects to collect hymn materials for Spanish-speaking Lutheran congregations in the Americas and putting together the list of global hymns for the 1970 assembly of the Lutheran World Federation.

What we see with Leupold is the best of the Lutheran tradition, fine music, a sense to the present needs of the church, and an intellectual legacy that if it had taken place in Germany would be lauded, though in

25 See HELMER (see n. 23), 6, n. 5.
26 Loc. cit., 14f.

Canada forgotten, even to Canadians.[27] Although the intellectual agenda opened up by deconstructionism has been remarkably pertinent to global pluralism, its accompanying critical edge has resulted in a naïveté concerning the intellectual legacy that has to a large extent been shaped by the German academy since Schleiermacher. The current situation offers a huge opportunity for Luther studies to reengage with the related fields of theology and religious studies – by reconnecting both with the history of German thought as a source of innovation in many modern disciplines and by reconnecting theology with the broader humanities and sciences of the university. What we can also acknowledge in Leupold is his inspiration to academics to follow new paths of creative vision that would continue to establish the values of academic freedom and research in the modern university.

V Conclusion

Leupold's life and work demonstrate the power of Luther's thought, the intellectual vision it may inspire, and the capacity to contextualize theology in an academic setting so that it can benefit other disciplines beyond theology and the study of religion (like musicology). Leupold was not content to worship Luther from afar, but courageously and resourcefully put Luther's legacy to work on behalf of social, institutional, and intellectual change. This is just one example of many appeals to Luther as a global trope for freedom, innovation, and resistance to the status quo. Luther scholars should pay attention to these representatives of Luther's own commitments to witness to truth in public and to stubbornly insist on grace and the incarnation, on justification and justice, on the capacity for love to change – even beyond death. This is the legacy of Luther today in the global context.

---

27 Helmer concludes his article on Leupold in *Consensus* with the following desideratum. »A systematic study of the Leupold *fonds* in the Laurier archives is a must. I am augmenting their holdings by donating a transcript of the interview I had with Gertrude Leupold on 5 Oct. 2002. I have only barely scratched the surface here, and that only in the musical realm. What about all the materials in the pastoral-theological area?« HELMER (see n. 23), 18.

Luther und humanistische Philosophie

Risto Saarinen

I Das Erbe von Junghans und seine Weiterführung

Vor einer Generation unternahm Helmar Junghans in seinem Buch *Der junge Luther und die Humanisten* eine neue Gesamtwertung des Humanismus in seiner Bedeutung für das Denken Martin Luthers.[1] Während die ältere Forschung vor allem den Gegensatz zwischen Luther und Erasmus von Rotterdam betonte, richtet Junghans seine Aufmerksamkeit auf die vielen Beziehungen Luthers zu den humanistischen Strömungen in Erfurt und Wittenberg sowie auf die humanistischen Interessen seiner Studienfreunde.

Junghans hebt die große Bedeutung der Rhetorik und der humanistischen Auffassung von Sprache und Stil hervor. Die literarische und pädagogische Form der Schriften Luthers zeuge von einem positiven Einfluss des Humanismus auf den Reformator. Die Arbeitsweise Luthers sowie sein methodisches Vorgehen folgten oft der humanistischen Wissenschaftsmethode, die durch einen programmatischen Gegensatz zur herkömmlichen Scholastik gekennzeichnet sei.[2] Beim Aufzeigen dieser Ähnlichkeiten will Junghans sorgfältig vorgehen: Einerseits konstatiert er, dass auch Luthers inhaltliche Erkenntnisse einen Zusammenhang mit der humanistischen Denkrichtung aufweisen, andererseits will er die refor-

---

1 H. JUNGHANS, Der junge Luther und die Humanisten, 1985.
2 AaO., 269–273.319–323.

matorischen Einsichten nicht auf eine Geistesströmung reduzieren, sondern betont die Eigenart der theologischen Sprache und deren Inhalte.[3]

In den letzten 30 Jahren hat die Humanismusforschung beträchtliche Fortschritte genommen. Viele Forscher haben Spezialstudien veröffentlicht, in denen das Verhältnis zwischen Reformation und Humanismus detailliert untersucht wird.[4] In meinem heutigen Vortrag werde ich einige Züge der humanistischen Philosophie sowie ihre Bedeutung für das Denken Luthers erläutern. Philosophiegeschichtliche Studien haben zu beweisen versucht, dass Renaissance und Humanismus als philosophisch eigenständige und kreative Perioden aufgefasst werden könnten.[5] Mit deren Hilfe könnte behauptet werden, dass der Humanismus nicht nur wegen seines literarischen Stils und seiner antischolastischen Methode, sondern auch wegen seines philosophischen Gehalts für die Reformation bedeutsam war.

Zuerst sollen die neueren Anschauungen über die Eigenart von Renaissancephilosophie bzw. Philosophie im Humanismus präziser erläutert werden. Es ist heute unbestreitbar, dass die Erneuerung von Sprache und Methode ein zentrales Anliegen der Renaissancephilosophie war. Von den neuen Büchern kann Lodi Nautas Studie zur humanistischen Kritik der scholastischen Philosophie erwähnt werden.[6] Durch eine sorgfältige Analyse von Lorenzo Vallas *Repastinatio dialectice et philosophie* weist Nauta nach, wie die Humanisten das technische Vokabular der Scholastik durch eine allgemein verständliche Sprache ersetzen. Auf diese Weise werden zum Beispiel viele aristotelische Kategorien einfach als Qualitäten interpretiert. Des Weiteren werden die Tugenden nicht anhand der Habi-

---

3 AaO., 323–325.
4 An dieser Stelle kann z.B. die Buchreihe »Spätmittelalter, Humanismus, Reformation« (Tübingen: Mohr Siebeck) erwähnt werden, die seit 2008 die ältere Reihe »Spätmittelalter und Reformation« ersetzt. Siehe auch E. RUMMELS zahlreiche Veröffentlichungen sowie das neue Buch von W. WRIGHT, Martin Luther's Understanding of God's Two Kingdoms, 2010.
5 Siehe z.B. B.P. COPENHAVER/C.B. SCHMITT, Renaissance Philosophy, 2003; J. HANKINS (ed.), The Cambridge Companion to Renaissance Philosophy, 2007 und R. SAARINEN, Weakness of Will in Renaissance and Reformation Thought, 2011.
6 L. NAUTA, In Defense of Common Sense: Lorenzo Valla's Humanist Critique of Scholastic Philosophy, 2009.

tuslehre, sondern im Rahmen der Emotionstheorie als Affekte behandelt. Auch in der Trinitätslehre lehnt Valla manche aristotelische Kategorien ab, so dass die Trinität eher als Mysterium, denn als ein logisch-philosophisches Denkgebäude erscheint.[7] Solchen im Grunde genommen sprachlichen und methodischen Erneuerungen begegnen wir auch bei den Reformatoren; so beweist Nautas neue Studie, dass die Beobachtungen von Junghans hinsichtlich der humanistischen Sprache und Methode treffend und aktuell geblieben sind. Die neue Studie von William Wright zeigt im Weiteren, dass der Einfluss von Lorenzo Valla auf Luther erneut brisant geworden ist.[8]

Die große Frage der Renaissancephilosophie ist aber, ob die Erneuerung in Sprache und Methode auch neue inhaltliche Schwerpunkte und philosophische Fragestellungen mit sich bringt. Viele Studien beantworten diese Frage eher negativ und zeigen, wie der mittelalterliche Aristotelismus trotz des eleganten Lateins und der neuen Griechischkenntnisse relativ unverändert bleibt. Die von Quentin Skinner und Charles Schmitt herausgegebene umfassende Geschichte der Renaissancephilosophie zeigt die ungebrochene Kontinuität des Aristotelismus vom Mittelalter bis zum Zeitalter des Descartes. Die im Grunde genommen thomistischen philosophischen und theologischen Positionen werden in der Renaissance zwar mit elegantem Latein vertreten, aber neue inhaltliche Gesichtspunkte kommen eher selten zum Vorschein.[9]

Auf der anderen Seite werden in der neueren Forschung auch Positionen vertreten, die in der Renaissancephilosophie grundlegende inhaltliche Erneuerungen feststellen. Der französische Philosoph Pierre Hadot hat eine große Diskussion ausgelöst mit seiner Darstellung der Philosophie als Lebenskunst oder Lebensform.[10] In seinen Studien vertritt Hadot die These, dass seit der Antike neben der theoretischen akademischen Philo-

---

7 AaO., 82–128.152–210.

8 WRIGHT (s. Anm. 4).

9 C. SCHMITT/Q. SKINNER (ed.), The Cambridge History of Renaissance Philosophy, 1988. Ähnlich auch D. LINES, Aristotle's Ethics in the Italian Renaissance (ca. 1300–1650), 2002.

10 Besonders die englische Ausgabe: Philosophy as a Way of Life, 1995 (französische Texte teilweise schon früher).

79

sophie eine andere Art von Philosophie existiert, die die Weisheit als praktischen Lebensweg oder eine Lebenskunst betrachtet. Diese andere Philosophie kann die Form von Therapie oder geistiger Übung annehmen; oft hat sie die Kontrolle oder Mäßigung der Emotionen zum Zweck. Hadot folgend haben viele Philosophiehistoriker mit unterschiedlichem Erfolg nach Spuren der therapeutischen Philosophie in verschiedenen Perioden der Ideengeschichte gesucht.[11] Die Renaissance und der Humanismus eignen sich besonders gut für die Suche nach Philosophie als Lebenskunst. Weit verbreitete und viel gelesene Werke wie Petrarcas *De remediis utriusque fortunae*, die blühende *Ars moriendi*-Literatur[12] oder viele Schriften von Erasmus von Rotterdam können im Rahmen des Programms »Philosophie als Lebenskunst« interpretiert werden, da sie von der Wirkungskraft der philosophischen Gedanken außerhalb des akademischen Vorlesungsraums zeugen. Im Prinzip könnte man die Eigenart der Philosophie in der Renaissance bzw. im Humanismus als neue Popularität der Philosophie als Lebensform definieren.[13]

Näher betrachtet eignet sich Hadots Ansatz allerdings kaum als alternative Gesamterklärung der Philosophiegeschichte. Sein Ansatz kann zwar zeigen, wie die Populärphilosophie am Rande der akademischen Philosophie existiert, aber die therapeutischen Alternativerklärungen folgen letzten Endes weitgehend den Ansätzen der akademischen Philosophie.[14] Obwohl der Ansatz von »Philosophie als Lebensform« deswegen keine grundlegend neue Perspektive bietet, kann er als heuristische Einsicht in

---

11 Zu den ersten Versuchen gehört M. Nussbaum, The Therapy of Desire: Theory and Practice in Hellenistic Ethics, 1994. Siehe auch R. Sorabji, Emotion and Peace of Mind, 2000.

12 Zu Petrarca z.B. Saarinen, Weakness (s. Anm. 5), 43–54; zu Ars moriendi B. Hamm, Luthers Anleitung zum seligen Sterben vor dem Hintergrund der spätmittelalterlichen Ars moriendi (in: ders., Der frühe Luther. Etappen reformatorischer Neuorientierung, 2010, 115–163).

13 So z.B. S. Ebbersmeyer, Philosophie als Lebensform: eine Einführung in die Philosophie der Renaissance, www.phil-hum-ren.uni-muenchen.de/LV/EinfWise99.htm (gelesen am 19.12.2012).

14 Mein eigenes Urteil folgt an dieser Stelle den materialreichen Studien von Sorabji (s. Anm. 11) sowie Ders., Self: Ancient and Modern Insights about Individuality, Life, and Death, 2006.

gewissen Themen hilfreich sein. Im Folgenden werde ich eine solche Einsicht auf den Bereich der Lutherforschung verwenden, um gewisse Themen von humanistischer Philosophie sichtbar zu machen.

Luthers antischolastischer Ansatz trägt bisweilen populärphilosophische Züge, die durch den Humanismus geprägt sind. Die historischen Quellen solcher Populärphilosophie sind vor allem Ciceros *De officiis* und Senecas *De beneficiis*, die zu Luthers Zeiten weit über die Universitäten hinaus verbreitet waren und als Lehrbücher des angemessenen Verhaltens gelesen wurden.[15] Wahrscheinlich erscheint die Populärphilosophie von Cicero und Seneca für Luther in erster Linie als allgemeines Kulturerbe und soziales Verhaltensmuster, das in den gebildeten Kreisen in Luthers Umgebung[16] bekannt war. Wenn Luther Motive aus dieser Tradition gebraucht, geht es für ihn vor allem um die Kommunikation theologischer Sachverhalte: Wenn er seine Theologie anhand der populären Verhaltensmuster beleuchtet, verstehen seine Leser und Zuhörer seine Botschaft besser mit Hilfe dieses Sprachgebrauchs. Luthers Botschaft ist aber an sich eine theologische.

Im Folgenden werde ich die über Junghans hinausführende These vertreten, dass Luther vom Humanismus nicht nur Sprache und Methode, sondern darüber hinaus gewisse populärphilosophische Inhalte übernimmt, die bei Cicero und Seneca vorhanden sind und Luthers Publikum allgemein bekannt waren. Wenn ich diesen Schritt wage, behaupte ich nicht, es hätte zu Luthers Zeiten so etwas wie eine »Philosophie als Lebenskunst« im Sinne von Pierre Hadot gegeben. Ich kann im Folgenden keinen systematischen Vergleich zwischen Luther einerseits und Cicero und Seneca andererseits anstellen; ich gehe davon aus, dass es sich bei den festgestellten Ähnlichkeiten eher um ein gemeinsames Kulturerbe des

---

15 Siehe z.B. J. Kraye, Moral Philosophy (in: Cambridge History [s. Anm. 9], 301–386). Zu Senecas theologische Bedeutung vgl. T. Engberg-Pedersen, Gift-Giving and Friendship: Seneca and Paul in Romans 1–8 on the Logic of God's Charis and Human Response (HTR 101, 2008, 15–44) sowie M. Hénaff, Der Preis der Wahrheit, 2009, 393–409 (franz. Original 2002).

16 Hilfreich für die Identifizierung dieser Kreise ist L. Grane, Martinus noster: Luther in the German Reform Movement 1518–1521, 1994.

Humanismus handelt als um eine unmittelbare literarische Abhängigkeit.[17]

Zu dieser Auffassung haben mich zwei neue Studien geleitet, die dieses gemeinsame Kulturerbe sowohl sozialgeschichtlich als auch philosophiegeschichtlich beleuchten. In ihrem Buch *The Gift in Sixteenth-Century France* untersucht Natalie Zemon Davis die mannigfaltigen Gabenbeziehungen im frühneuzeitlichen Europa. Nach ihr konnten die Menschen im 16. Jahrhundert sehr scharfsinnig und nuanciert zwischen Gabenbeziehungen einerseits und Handelsbeziehungen andererseits unterscheiden. Das angemessene Geben und Empfangen von Gaben war in allen sozialen Klassen ausgesprochen wichtig, da Ehre, Rang und soziale Wertschätzung nicht in erster Linie gekauft und verkauft, sondern mit gegenseitigen Gaben manifestiert werden konnten.[18] Für die oberen Klassen wurden die bestehenden Rangordnungen deswegen anhand von Gaben konkretisiert; Seneca und Cicero hatten die Natur solcher Gaben philosophisch bestimmt. Auch für die armen Menschen waren Gaben belangvoll, weil sie ihre sozialen Beziehungen nur relativ selten mit Geld und Handel regulieren konnten; oft waren es eher gegenseitige Wohltaten und Geschenke, aus denen das soziale Leben in der Gesellschaft bestand.

Auch für das Gottesverhältnis und die Religion war das rechte Unterscheiden zwischen Gabenbeziehungen und Handelsbeziehungen ausschlaggebend. Die Reformation hat zielgerichtet gegen die Irrlehre gepre-

---

17 Trotz einiger positiver Äußerungen Luthers über *De officiis* (e.g WATR 2; 456,29–457,3) bietet das WA-Sachregister kaum ein informatives Bild von Luthers Gebrauch von Cicero und Seneca. Man sollte vor allem die Begrifflichkeit wie *honestum, beneficium, gratitudo, gratias agere, consuetudo, dignus* usw. sowie die bei Cicero und Seneca vorhandenen Argumente über das rechte Geben und Empfangen von Wohltaten, Gaben usw. sorgfältig mit Luther vergleichen. Z.B. diskutieren Cicero (off 1, 49) und Seneca (ben 1, 5–7, 2, 18–25, 31–35) ausführlich die Natur von »accepta beneficia«. Diese Wendung kommt auch bei Luther häufig und an theologisch prägnanten Stellen vor, z.B. WA 3; 89,12; 276,17; 5; 181,18; 6; 364,20; 13; 355,23; 20; 33,29; 29; 452,2; 454,9–13. Die Rede von einem gemeinsamen »Kulturerbe« soll also die literarische Abhängigkeit nicht allzu schnell ausschließen.

18 Z. Davis, The Gift in Sixteenth-Century France, 2000, 56–73 (auf S. 59–61 diskutiert sie das Verhalten von Erasmus).

digt, dass Gottes Gunst anhand von menschlichen Verdiensten gekauft werden könnte. Zemon Davis konstatiert wie folgt:

> the religious reformations of the sixteenth century were a quarrel about the gifts, that is, about whether humans can reciprocate to God, about whether humans can put God under obligation, and about what this means for what people should give to each other. The religious quarrel stands on its own and is argued in its own terms, but is parallel to the quarrel about the king's obligation to his subjects.[19]

In seiner Studie *Der Preis der Wahrheit* erläutert Marcel Hénaff die Ideengeschichte des Gedankens, dass die Wahrheit und die rechte Lehre keinen Preis haben, da sie nicht zum Privatbesitz des Individuums gehören und deswegen nicht gekauft oder verkauft werden können. Wahrheit, Lehre und Unterweisung gehören darum eher in den Bereich der Gabenbeziehungen als in den der Handelsbeziehungen. Die Gegenseitigkeit, die für das historische Weitergeben von Lehre und Wahrheit notwendig ist, ist darum eine Gegenseitigkeit der Anerkennung, Ehre und Dankbarkeit, die durch die angemessene Gabenbeziehung entsteht.[20] Auch für Hénaff erscheint die Reformation als Kampf um die rechte religiöse Bestimmung von Gabe, Dankbarkeit, Leistung und Preis. Er schreibt: »Wahrscheinlich ist es letztlich die Frage der Gabe, die die beiden im christlichen Abendland herrschenden Konfessionen trennt«.[21]

Hénaff geht es grundsätzlich darum, dass »der vertraglich geregelte Handelsaustausch« und die dazu gehörende Rationalität erst mit der Reformation zur herrschenden Norm des alltäglichen, weltlichen Lebens werden. Im mittelalterlichen Christentum manifestierte die Mildtätigkeit der guten Werke teils die Gabenbeziehungen, teils die Handelsbeziehungen, die stets als miteinander gemischt erschienen. Der theozentrische Protestantismus hat eine klare Trennung zwischen den beiden etabliert, indem er die Gabe auf Gottes Wirksamkeit zurückführte und die Möglichkeit der menschlichen guten Werke bestritt. So wurden im Protestantismus die Gabenbeziehungen rein innerlich und theologisch verstanden,

---

19 AaO., 167–168.
20 HÉNAFF (s. Anm. 15), 36–40. Wie er auf S. 539–552 erläutert, hatte die Entdeckung des Buchdrucks und der entstehende Beruf des Buchhändlers diese Einsicht von Lehre und Wahrheit verändert.
21 AaO., 411.

während die entzauberte, äußerliche Welt anhand der Handelsbeziehungen reguliert wurde.[22]

Weder Hénaff noch Zemon Davis interpretieren Luthers eigene Texte, aber sie behandeln ausführlich Luthers geistige Umgebung. Im Folgenden werde ich einige Texte Luthers zu theologischen Gabenbeziehungen interpretieren. Drei Themenbereiche kommen vor, erstens die Natur der Wohltaten, zweitens die Art der rechten Lehre und Unterweisung und drittens die Kunst des rechten Empfangens. Die angemessene Ehre und Dankbarkeit sowie das Vermeiden von Hochmut und die angemessene Demut werden stets im Kontext dieser Themen diskutiert. Parallelen aus Ciceros *De officiis* und Senecas *De beneficiis* werden erwähnt. Wir werden einerseits sehen, dass für Martin Luther die Unterscheidung von Gabenbeziehungen und Handelsbeziehungen durchaus belangvoll ist. Insofern bestätigt meine Diskussion die Thesen von Zemon Davis und Hénaff. Andererseits zeigt Luther eine tiefere Sensibilität für diese Unterscheidung, als was Hénaffs schematische Zweiteilung zwischen Protestantismus und Katholizismus annimmt.

II Beneficia – die Wohltaten Gottes

Zuerst sollen drei Begriffe kurz erläutert werden: Gabe, Geschenk und Wohltat. Für Luther gehören die Gaben mit dem Glauben und der Gnade zusammen, während Verdienste und Werke eine Handelsbeziehung ausdrücken. So ist für Luther das Maß des Glaubens ein anderes als das Maß der Verdienste. Das antike Prinzip »jedem das Seine« kann aber auch als Prinzip der Gabenbeziehungen erscheinen, und so nehmen die Gabenbeziehungen an einer ihrem Maß entsprechenden Reziprozität teil.[23]

---

22 AaO., 428f.

23 Z.B. WA 17,1; 38,12–23: »Das der glaube mit sich bringe als ein heubt gutt die andern gaben, das es darumb heysse glaubens mas und nicht unsers willens odder verdiensts mas, das wyr solche gaben nicht verdienet haben, sondern wo glaube ist, da ehret Gott den selben glauben mit ettlichen gaben als zur mitgabe odder ubergabe wie viel er will, als er spricht 1. Cor. 12.: ›Er teylet eynem iglichen aus nach seynem willen‹. Eph. 4.: ›eyn iglich gelied ynn seyner mas‹. Eben darumb spricht er auch, es seyen mancherley gaben, nicht nach unserm verdienst, sondern nach der gnaden, die uns geben ist, Das also die gnade gleich wie der glaube mit sich bringe solch edle kleynot und geschencke,

Den Grundbegriffen der Handelsbeziehung, also kaufen und verkaufen, entsprechen in der reziproken Gabenbeziehung das Geben und Empfangen von Wohltaten. Luther übersetzt den lateinischen Begriff *beneficium* stets mit »Wohltat« (in Luthers Rechtschreibung: *Wolthat*). Als Substantivform des Gebens umfasst der Begriff »Gabe« (*donum*) alle Primärobjekte des Gebensaktes. Die Gabe unterscheidet sich vom Handelsobjekt dadurch, dass sie keinen Preis hat und darum in der Reziprozität, die ihrem Maß entspricht, nur Dankbarkeit oder gar nichts als Gegenleistung verlangt. Im Akt des Gebens wird die Gabe allerdings nicht notwendigerweise zum Privatbesitz des Empfängers; zum Beispiel als Leihgabe kann die Gabe im Besitz des Gebers bleiben.

In Luthers Sprache implizieren Wendungen wie »Gnade geben« somit keinen notwendigen Transfer in den Eigentumsverhältnissen: Auch im Menschen kann die Gnade immer noch Gottes Gnade bleiben. Analog dazu können Luthers Wendungen wie »Gottes Gabe«, »hohe« bzw. »köstliche Gabe«[24] so verstanden werden, dass die Gabe ein Eigentum des Gebers oder zumindest unbestimmt oder unverfügbar bleibt – semantische Möglichkeiten, die für die nähere Bestimmung von einigen theologischen Gaben höchst bedeutsam sind. Wenn der Eigentumstransfer oder zumindest ein Verwaltungstransfer im Akt des Gebens unterstrichen wird, kommt das Wort »ubergeben« in Luthers Sprache oft vor.[25]

Der Begriff Geschenk, der bei Luther ebenfalls oft vorkommt, häufig in der doppelten Wendung »Gabe und Geschenk«, ist bisweilen mit Gabe synonym. Im Begriff Geschenk ist allerdings das Eigentumsverhältnis stärker mit dem Empfänger verbunden.[26] Wenn Luther zum Beispiel sagt:

---

eym iglichen seyne mas, Das ia also allenthalben die werck und verdienst ausgeschlossen und wyr mit den wercken nuer zum nehisten geweyset werden.«

24 Z.B. Gottes Gabe: WA 16; 299,34–37; hohe Gabe: WA 51; 215,24; köstliche Gabe: WA 20; 392,3 (Anm.). In WA 50; 368,17–18 wird Musik als »koestliche Gabe Gottes« bezeichnet; diese Gabe bleibt offenbar nicht im Privatbesitz des Empfängers.

25 Wie z.B. WA 52; 620,1–16 im Anschluss an Mt 11,27 zeigt, ist »ubergeben« die Wiedergabe vom griechischen *paradidômi*, ein Wort, das viele theologische Bedeutungen trägt. Siehe dazu R. SAARINEN, God and the Gift: An ecumenical theology of giving, 2005, 37–44.

26 Auch im heutigen Deutsch wird darum z.B. »Leihgeschenk« viel seltener gebraucht als »Leihgabe«

»eyn gabe und geschenck, das dyr von Gott geben, und deyn eygen sey«[27], verbindet er durch den zitierten Relativsatz das Moment des Gebens mit »Gabe« und das Moment des Besitzes mit »Geschenk«. Ähnliches geschieht in Wendungen wie: »gabe und geschenck [...] von Gott mitgeteilt und verliehen« oder »gab und geschenck [...] Das du magst sagen: kom her, lieber herr, Du bist mein«.[28] In diesen Wendungen unterscheidet Luther zwischen der Dynamik des Gebens (von Gott geben, mitgeteilt, kom her: Gabe) einerseits und dem resultierenden Eigentumsverhältnis (deyn eigen, verliehen, bist mein: Geschenk) andererseits.

Wenn Luther das Wort »Geschenk« benutzt, fügt er auch häufig eine Eigentumsbezeichnung wie »zu eigen« oder »mein eigen« hinzu.[29] So hat im »Geschenk« der Transfer zum Privatbesitz des Empfängers deutlicher stattgefunden als in der allgemeinen »Gabe«. Alle Geschenke sind folglich auch Gaben, aber nicht alle Gaben sind Geschenke; zum Beispiel kann der Sonnenschein als Gabe bezeichnet werden, aber er kann kein solches Eigentum werden, das ihn zu einem Geschenk macht. Folglich ist die Wendung »ich erhielt es als Gabe und Geschenk« nicht tautologisch, sondern sie unterstreicht, dass der Gegenstand sowohl (a) mir gegeben als auch (b) zu meinem konkreten Eigentum geworden ist. Auf diese Weise entspricht »Geschenk« dem lateinischen Begriff *donatio*.[30]

Der Begriff der Wohltaten, *beneficia*, hat einen wichtigen Stellenwert für Humanisten wie Erasmus von Rotterdam und Philipp Melanchthon.

---

27 WA 10,1,1; 11,13–14.

28 WA 16; 353,31; WA 49; 661,41–662,23.

29 Zu diesem Phänomen siehe M. SEILS, Gabe und Geschenk: eine Zugabe (in: Denkraum Katechismus. Festgabe für Oswald Bayer zum 70. Geburtstag, hg. v. J. VON LÜPKE/E. THAIDIGSMANN, 2009, 87–103), 98 f.

30 Diese Beobachtungen möchte ich Martin Seils' äußerst wertvollen Studien zu Gabe und Geschenk in der Luthersprache hinzufügen. Es ist merkwürdig, dass Seils diese Unterscheidung zwischen Gabe und Geschenk schließlich nicht macht, obwohl schon seine allererste Belegstelle (WA 10,1,1; 11,12–18, 87) sie expliziert. SEILS (ebd.) spürt auch korrekt, dass bei Luther hinter »Geschenk« der rechtliche Begriff »donatio« steckt, vgl. z. B. WA 4; 596,13–14: »Quia donatio, dicunt Iuristae, constituit possessorem recipientem« – Schon in seinem Hauptvortrag auf dem Lutherforschungskongress in Erfurt 1983 hat Seils Luthers Theologie als Theologie des Gebens bezeichnet, s. M. SEILS, Die Sache Luthers (LuJ 52, 1985, 64–80).

Darum haben die Forscher völlig richtig den Hintergrund des Begriffs im Humanismus lokalisiert.[31] Auch Luther gebraucht diesen Begriff sehr häufig, aber die Lutherforscher haben merkwürdigerweise die Beziehungen zwischen Luther und humanistischer Philosophie nicht anhand dieses Begriffs untersucht. In einer längeren Studie habe ich neulich nachgewiesen, dass alle wichtigen Dimensionen von *beneficia* bei Luther schon in seiner ersten Psalmenvorlesung vorhanden sind.[32] Diese Beobachtung zeigt erstens, dass Luther den Begriff nicht erst von Melanchthon gelernt hat. Zweitens unterstützt sie die These von Helmar Junghans, der zufolge schon der junge Mönch Luther wichtige Anstöße vom Humanismus bekommen hat.

Im Folgenden werde ich nur einige Abschnitte aus der ersten Psalmenvorlesung hervorheben und sie mit dem wichtigsten humanistischen Quellentext, Senecas *De beneficiis*, kurz vergleichen. Der grundlegende Unterschied zwischen Gabenbeziehungen und Handelsbeziehungen prägt das Verständnis von Wohltaten bei Luther und Seneca. Für beide ist darüber hinaus der Unterschied zwischen göttlichen und menschlichen Wohltaten charakteristisch.

Ein gerechter Akt, konstatiert Luther, ist durch die angemessene Berücksichtigung von Verdiensten und Schulden charakterisiert. Dagegen berücksichtigt eine Wohltat die Verdienste des Empfängers nicht.[33] Unter den Menschen werden Wohltaten durch andere Wohltaten belohnt; auch die Heiden können Wohltaten auf diese Weise in den Kreislauf bringen. Gott kann allerdings Wohltaten auf eine radikalere Weise hervorbringen, nämlich so, dass er allen Menschen Wohltaten erweist, ohne Rücksicht auf Dankbarkeit. Gottes Sein ist im Geben, so dass er Gutes austeilt und somit sogar Böses mit Gutem vergilt. Gott erscheint als wahrer Gott, indem er ausschließlich gibt und die Menschen ausschließlich empfangen. Um dieses wahre Gott-Sein aufrechtzuerhalten, nimmt Gott keine

---

31 Siehe z. B. H. G. Pöhlmanns Anmerkungen in P. Melanchthon, Loci communes 1521, Lateinisch-Deutsch, 1993, 21 f.
32 R. Saarinen, Luther und Beneficia (in: The Reformation as Christianization [SMHR 66], ed. by A. M. Johnson/J. A. Maxfield, 2012, 169–188).
33 WA 55,2; 888,6–13.

Wohltaten von den Menschen entgegen.[34] Auf diese Weise bleibt Gott außerhalb des Kreislaufs der Wohltaten; zugleich ist er aber das Vorbild und der Ansatzpunkt aller menschlichen Wohltaten.

Ein Mensch soll die Wohltaten Gottes empfangen und Dank sagen. Im Akt des Empfangens erkennt der Mensch an, dass alles Gute im Leben von Gott gegeben ist.[35] Im Einklang mit diesem Gedanken konstatiert Luther, dass Gott schon im natürlichen Lauf des Lebens den Menschen täglich verschiedene Wohltaten erweist, wie Leben, Sein, Fühlen, Geist, Essen, Kleidung, Sonne, Himmel und Erde sowie alle Elemente. Darüber hinaus gibt Gott verschiedene geistliche Wohltaten, wie Essen und Kleidung in geistlichen Sachen, Sonne der Gerechtigkeit und alle Wohltaten der Kirche.[36]

Diese Grundzüge der Wohltaten werden von Luther theologisch begründet, aber sie sind zugleich auch in der philosophischen Tradition vorhanden. Sowohl Cicero (off 1, 45–60) als auch Seneca (ben 1, 6–15) unterscheiden deutlich zwischen ökonomischen Transaktionen und Pflichten einerseits und freiwilligen Wohltaten andererseits. Die Wohltaten sollen mit Dankbarkeit empfangen werden; die Dankbarkeit ist aber keine Bezahlung, und die Wohltat ist nicht durch Gegenleistung bestimmt, sondern durch die wohlwollende Intention des Gebers. Deswegen sind für Seneca (e.g. ben 4, 30–32) auch einseitige Wohltaten echte Wohltaten.[37]

In seiner Schrift *De beneficiis* diskutiert Seneca auch ausführlich die Rolle von Gott als Geber und als Vorbild aller menschlichen Wohltaten. Senecas Götter können Wohltaten allen Menschen spenden, auch solchen, die sich unwissend oder ablehnend zu den göttlichen Gaben verhalten:

> Was die Götter tun, aller Dinge vorzügliche Urheber, die einem Wohltat ohne dessen Wissen zu erweisen beginnen und auch, ohne Dank zu erhalten, damit fortfahren [...] Nichtsdestoweniger jedoch, nach Art wirklich guter Eltern, die zu den Schmähungen

---

34 WA 55,2; 883,100–103; 889,18–36.
35 WA 55,2; 105,10–14; 889,18–21; WA 55,1; 660–661.
36 WA 55,2; 401,508–525.
37 Siehe z.B. R. Saarinen, The Language of Giving in Theology (NZSTh 52, 2010, 268–301), 278–282, sowie Engberg-Pedersen (s. Anm. 15).

ihrer kleinen Kinder lachen, säumen die Götter nicht, Wohltaten denen zuzuwenden, die an dem Urheber der Wohltaten zweifeln (ben 7, 31).

Bemerkenswert ist auch, dass Seneca eine lange Liste von natürlichen Wohltaten Gottes anführt, die u. a. die folgenden Sachen umfasst: Bäume, Kräuter, Nahrungsmittel, Lebewesen aller Art, Flüsse, Heilwasserquellen, Landflächen, Metalle, Gold, Silber, Kupfer, Eisen, Himmel am Tag und Nacht, Atem, Licht, Blut, Delikatessen, Reizmittel des Genusses, Ruhe, Frieden, Tierherden, alle Künste und die verschiedenen Lebensalter des Menschen (ben 4, 4–6). Die Interpretation von Naturereignissen als Wohltaten Gottes unterstützt die These, dass Gott seine Wohltaten allen Menschen ohne Rücksicht auf deren Dankbarkeit erweist. Eine solche Interpretation hat Parallelen schon im Alten Testament (e. g. Psalm 104), aber es ist auffallend, wie Luther und Seneca die kosmischen Ereignisse und den Reichtum der Natur als göttliche Wohltaten auffassen. Auch in seinen späteren Schriften wiederholt Luther oft ähnliche Listen[38].

Darüber hinaus ist zu notieren, dass Luther in der ersten Psalmenvorlesung eine ähnliche Dreiteilung von Tauschbeziehungen wie Seneca verwendet. (1) Die Verdienste und deren Gerechtigkeit beziehen sich auf den ökonomischen Tausch, also auf Handel. (2) Die Gabenbeziehungen unter den Menschen vollziehen sich im Kreislauf von Wohltaten, bei dem die einzelnen Wohltaten mit angemessener Dankbarkeit empfangen werden. Darüber hinaus sollen (3) die Wohltaten Gottes als kosmischer Ausgangspunkt aller späteren Wohltaten und Dankbarkeit begriffen werden. Die göttlichen Wohltaten beziehen sich universal auf alle Menschen, und zwar dessen ungeachtet, wer sie identifiziert oder dankbar ist. Wenn Luther in der ersten Psalmenvorlesung konstatiert, dass Gottes Sein im Geben besteht, braucht er darum keine platonische Emanationslehre oder kein bestimmtes Partizipationsverständis zu vertreten[39], sondern der Kon-

---

38 Z. B. im Großen Katechismus: BSLK 648. In BSLK 649, 11–17 spricht der lateinische Text von empfangenen Wohltaten. Andere Belege in SAARINEN, Beneficia (s. Anm. 32), 178–181.

39 Einige positive Äußerungen des jungen Luthers zu Platon brauchen also keine generelle Annahme des Platonismus bedeuten. Vgl. T. DIETER, Der junge Luther und Aristoteles. Eine historisch-systematische Untersuchung zum Verhältnis von Theologie und Philosophie, 2001, 619–627.

text spricht eher von der herkömmlichen Dreiteilung zwischen Handelsbeziehungen, Gabenbeziehungen und den konstituierenden Wohltaten Gottes. Diese Dreiteilung konnten die Humanisten bei Seneca wiederfinden: Sie ist also ein genereller Topos oder ein Kulturgut, das bei den konkreten Tauschbeziehungen und Wohltaten vorausgesetzt wurde.

In der ersten Psalmenvorlesung verbindet Luther auch eigenständig die Wohltaten mit einem spezifischen theologischen Thema, nämlich mit Gottes Barmherzigkeit. Einen unmittelbaren Anlass für diese Verbindung bietet die Erklärung des Wortes *hesed* in Reuchlins hebräischem Wörterbuch: »Hesed – Wohltat, Gnade oder Gnadenhaftigkeit«. Die Septuaginta übersetzt das Wort mit *eleos*, deswegen benutzt die lateinische Übersetzung stets Barmherzigkeit.[40] Die *misericordia* war ein zentrales Thema der spätmittelalterlichen Frömmigkeit, und das häufige Vorkommen des lateinischen Wortes in den Psalmen motiviert Luther dazu, den Zusammenhang zwischen Wohltaten und Barmherzigkeit theologisch zu reflektieren.

So kann er zum Beispiel konstatieren, die Wohltaten Gottes auf uns seien lauter Barmherzigkeit, die Gott uns ohne Rücksicht auf unsere Verdienste gebe.[41] Das Wort Barmherzigkeit als Attribut von göttlichen Wohltaten bedeutet, dass Gott allein sie gibt und dass unser Dank nur an Gott gerichtet sein soll. Auch wenn eine undankbare Person eine solche Anerkennung nicht leistet, bekennen die barmherzigen Taten an sich schon den Herrn, so dass andere Menschen durch diese Taten Gott anerkennen können.[42] Die Verbindung zwischen Wohltaten und Barmherzigkeit prägt auch Luthers spätere Theologie.[43]

Die Tugend der Barmherzigkeit ist biblisch und bringt einen Aspekt in die Diskussion ein, der bei Seneca nicht als solcher vorhanden ist. Auch für Seneca ist aber die Wohltat vor allem durch den guten Willen und die rechte Intention gekennzeichnet. Ein göttlicher Geber betrachtet nach Seneca nicht die Gegenleistung des Empfängers, sondern ausschließlich seine *fides*, das heißt seine Rezeptivität (*solam accipientis fidem specta*,

---

40 J. Reuchlin, De rudimentis hebraicis libri III, Reprint 1974, 185.
41 WA 55,2; 832,94–96.
42 WA 55,2; 831,81–84.
43 Saarinen, Beneficia (s. Anm. 32), 181–184.

ben 3, 14, 2). Auf diese Weise sollen auch die Menschen in den Wohltaten vorgehen:

> Die meisten Wohltaten und bedeutendsten wendet uns der Gott wahrhaftig ohne eine Hoffnung zu, seinerseits etwas zu erhalten, da je weder er eine Zuwendung bedarf noch wir ihm irgendetwas zuwenden können; also ist eine Wohltat um ihrer selbst willen eine wünschenswerte Sache. Allein werde an ihr gewünscht des Empfangenden Nutzen; ihm wollen wir nahekommen und zugleich beiseite lassen unseren Vorteil. (ben 4, 9).

In ähnlicher Weise ist die göttliche Barmherzigkeit eine Gabenbeziehung, die nicht die Verdienste oder die Dankbarkeit des Empfängers betrachtet, sondern Gottes grundlegende Wohltat zum Ausdruck bringt. Der theologische Ort der Barmherzigkeit ist nicht im Humanismus, sondern in der heiligen Schrift sowie in der spätmittelalterlichen Frömmigkeit zu finden. Luthers Verbindung von Barmherzigkeit und Wohltaten in der ersten Psalmenvorlesung veranschaulicht gewissermaßen Senecas Einsicht, dass Gottes grundlegende Wohltat alle späteren *beneficia* vorbereitet.[44]

III Doctrina – die Autonomie der Lehre

Die Unterscheidung zwischen Gaben und Handelsobjekten spielt ebenfalls eine große Rolle in der begrifflichen Bestimmung von Lehre und Unterweisung, Themen, die auch für unseren Lutherkongress bedeutsam sind. Natalie Zemon Davis hebt die Wichtigkeit des mittelalterlichen Sprichwortes *Scientia est donum dei* in verschiedenen Lebensbereichen hervor.[45] Als Gaben Gottes können das Wissen und die Lehre nicht verkauft werden. Wissen und Lehre sind keine Handelsobjekte, die zum Privatbesitz werden könnten, sondern sie sollen als permanent freie Gaben verbreitet werden, wie die Statuten der Universität Paris im Jahre 1536 formulierten.[46]

---

44 Gegen HÉNAFF (s. Anm. 15), 428f sei bemerkt, dass eine solche Theologisierung der Gaben nicht nur eine protestantische Entwicklung, sondern schon ein antiker Gedanke ist.

45 DAVIS (s. Anm. 18), 75–81. Das Sprichwort kommt z.B. bei THOMAS VON AQUIN, Summa theol. 1/2 q112 a5 2, vor.

46 DAVIS (s. Anm. 18), 79f.

Wenn die Professoren in ihrem Unterricht eine Distribution der freien göttlichen Gaben praktizieren, können sie für diese Beschäftigung kein Gehalt und keine Bezahlung erhalten in der Weise, wie ein Handwerker einen Preis für sein Produkt verlangt. Das verbreitete Wissen ist kein Eigentum des Professors in dem Sinne, wie ein Handelsprodukt dem Hersteller oder dem Händler gehört. Das Wissen ist eine frei bleibende Gabe oder eine Leihgabe, die nicht zum Privateigentum des Lehrers wird und deswegen nicht verkauft werden kann. Auf der anderen Seite bleiben die Professoren nicht gänzlich ohne Belohnung für ihr Lehramt, da sie von dankbaren Studenten Honorare und Gaben erhalten können. Zemon Davis bestreitet, dass die Honorare nur maskierte Bezahlungen waren. Für die Akademiker des 16. Jahrhunderts war es wichtig, eine ordentliche Unterscheidung zwischen den Geschäftshandlungen einerseits und der Zirkulation der freien Gaben andererseits zu treffen.[47] Wenn die Professoren Honorare anstatt von Gehältern erhielten, könnten sie der Natur ihrer Lehre und ihres Wissens als freie göttliche Gabe Rechnung tragen.

Marcel Hénaff unternimmt eine philosophiegeschichtliche Vertiefung dieser Einsicht. Nach Hénaff entdeckt schon Platons Sokrates den Gedanken, dass die Wahrheit keinen Preis haben kann. »Wissen und Geld lassen sich nicht mit einem Maß messen«, konstatiert Aristoteles in seiner *Eudemischen Ethik*.[48] Aus diesem Grund sind die Beziehungen zwischen Wahrheit, Wissen und Belohnung im abendländischen Denken keine Handelsbeziehungen, sondern Gabenbeziehungen.[49] Es ist wichtig zu sehen, dass die Gabenbeziehungen auch zumeist reziprok sind: Der Empfänger des Wissens reagiert auf diese Gabe, obwohl er keinen Kaufakt leistet.

Der historische Grundmodus eines solchen Reagierens ist die Dankbarkeit, die auch konkrete Formen wie Honorar oder Gegengabe annehmen kann. Hénaff unterscheidet zwischen (1) reziproken zeremoniellen Gaben, die die gegenseitige Anerkennung der Partner zum Zweck haben, und (2) vorwiegend unilateralen Gaben, die die vielen Dimension des griechischen Wortes *charis* zum Ausdruck bringen: die Großmut, Gunst und

---

47 AaO., 81; HÉNAFF (s. Anm. 15), 36 f.
48 HÉNAFF (s. Anm. 15), 159–162. ARISTOTELES, Eudemische Ethik VII, 10; 1243b23.
49 HÉNAFF (s. Anm. 15), 36 f.479 f. Siehe auch DAVIS (s. Anm. 18), 73–109.

Gnade des Gebers, die Dankbarkeit und Freude des Empfängers. Die christliche Tradition des Abendlandes erörtert vor allem diese Aspekte der Gabenbeziehungen.[50]

Zum unmittelbaren Kontext der Dankbarkeit gehört auch der Begriff des Ehrenhaften (*honestas, honestum*), den Cicero (e. g. off 1, 60–61, 79, 93) und Seneca (e. g. ben 4, 1, 9–10, 16) ausführlich erläutern. Für die kalkulativen Handelsbeziehungen spielt die Ehre nur untergeordnete Rolle, während die Gabenbeziehungen ehrenhaft vorgehen und die Würde des Gebers sowie des Empfängers manifestieren sollen. Zugleich ist Ehre aber auch ambivalent, da der Geber falschen Stolz vermeiden und ohne Rücksicht auf Gegengaben großzügig agieren soll. Die Ehre des Empfängers kann leicht verletzt oder falsch verstanden werden. Ein angemessenes *honestum* soll sowohl problematische Arroganz als auch falsche Demut vermeiden.

Die wahrhafte Achtung, Dankbarkeit und Freude können nicht gekauft oder verkauft werden, sondern sie kommen durch angemessene Gabenbeziehungen zustande. Zemon Davis präsentiert eine große Zahl an konkreten Beispielen, wie angemessene Gunst, Würde und Ehre durch die sozialen Praktiken von Gabenbeziehungen im 16. Jahrhundert aufgebaut wurden. Die angemessene Ehrung und Würdigung eines akademischen Lehrers ist ein Beispiel für solche Gabenbeziehungen, denn einerseits verteilt der Lehrer besonders wertvolle göttliche Gaben, andererseits kommen diese Gaben nicht aus seinem Privatbesitz und können deswegen nicht verkauft werden.[51]

Luthers Texte zur Wahrhaftigkeit der Lehre und der christlichen Predigt nehmen teil an dieser großen Tradition des Wissens als Gabe, die keinen Preis hat. Die Spuren dieser Tradition sind nicht ohne weiteres offenbar, da Luther von der biblischen Sprache ausgehend seine Argumente präsentiert. Wenn ich im Folgenden diese Ähnlichkeiten näher erläutere, meine ich nicht, dass Luthers Argumente ausschließlich die sozialen Praktiken des 16. Jahrhunderts oder die philosophische Tradition des Wis-

---

50 HÉNAFF (s. Anm. 15), 406–409.
51 DAVIS (s. Anm. 18), 79–82. Auch ihr Kapitel »Gifts gone Wrong« (aaO., 110–141) beleuchtet das Wesen von Ehre bzw. *honestum*.

sens als Gabe manifestieren. Die theologischen Argumente haben durchaus ihren Eigenwert; es geht vor allem darum, dass diese Argumente gewisse Entsprechungen mit den philosophischen und sozialgeschichtlichen Traditionen der Gabenbeziehungen aufweisen und so der Kommunikation der theologischen Botschaft dienen.

In einer Predigt aus dem Jahre 1537 behandelt Luther das Predigtamt im Anschluss an Mt 21,14–16.[52] Ein Prediger soll nicht ehrgeizig sein, aber die Lehrer und Doktoren leiden häufig an diesem Übel. Weil zeitliche Ehre nur Gott gebührt, ist Ehrgeiz im Predigtamt ein besonders giftiges Laster.[53] Im Prediger wirken Ehrgeiz und falscher Stolz wie Gift, das sein Amt und seine Lehre unrein macht. Wer im Predigtamt nach Ehre und Weisheit strebt, ist ungläubig.[54] Ein ehrgeiziger Prediger will sich selbst als feinen Mann darstellen. Wenn die Zuhörer ihn loben, muss er auch sie loben, und das gegenseitige Loben bringt schließlich sowohl den Prediger als auch seine Gemeinde in die Hölle.[55] Die so beschriebene Reziprozität ist einer Handelsbeziehung ähnlich: Der ehrgeizige Prediger beweist seinen eigenen Wert und verkauft sich so an die eitlen Zuhörer, die als Gegenleistung ebenfalls den Preis des Lobes verlangen.

Gegen Stolz und Eitelkeit soll der Prediger mit den Worten von Joh 7,18 sagen: »Wer von ihm selbst redet, der sucht seine eigene Ehre. Wer aber sucht die Ehre des, der ihn gesandt hat, der ist wahrhaftig«. Der rechte Prediger soll ebenfalls Demut üben und sagen: »Geheiligt werde dein Name«.[56] Die Dialektik der angemessenen Ehre ist aber komplex, denn auf der anderen Seite soll der Prediger stolz die Ehre des Wortes Got-

---

52 WA 47; 397–408.

53 WA 47; 401,19–26: »ein Prediger sol nicht ehrgeitzig sein, wie sich den auch ein jeder Christ also halten sol. Dan ein Christ ist nicht drumb getaufft und zum ewigen leben beruffen, das ehr seine ehre suchete, viel weniger ein Prediger. Dennochs ists ein gemeine plage, das die Doctores und Lehrer der kirchen oben aus und nirgents an wollen, als am Muntzer und andern zu sehen ist. Es ist an einem Christen, jha viel mehr an einem Prediger kein grossere, ergere gifft, dan wen ehr in zeitlichen sachen ehre suchet, welche ehre doch Gott allein geburet.« – Der traditionelle Gegensatz zwischen »Gabe« und »Gift« prägt den gesamten hier referierten Abschnitt Luthers.

54 WA 47; 402,8–17.

55 WA 47; 402,25–29.

56 WA 47; 403,5–19.

tes verteidigen. Dann sagen aber die Gegner, dieser Prediger suche seine eigene Ehre. Die Frommen sind auch an sich lobenswert, obwohl ein Lob zu falschem Stolz verleiten kann. Angesichts dieser Komplexität vergleicht Luther die falsche Ehre mit einer Distel: Wo immer man sie hinwirft, bleibt sie irgendwo stecken.[57] Die Wahrhaftigkeit zu predigen, ohne den eigenen Wert und die eigene Ehre ins Bild zu bringen, ist also eine schwierige Tugend.[58]

Die Dialektik der angemessenen Ehre findet aber schließlich eine gelungene Synthese, wenn man das Wort und die damit verbundene Ehre nicht als Privatbesitz betrachtet:

> Kompts nun in den Punct, das ich soll gottes wort predigen und bekennen, da mus man getrost stehen und sagen: Alhier ist die warheit und dort die Lugen, und als dan sagen: O himlisscher vater, es ist dein wortt, du wilst, das ichs soll frej bekennen und sagen: ›Geheiliget werde dein name‹. So aber andere sagen, ich sej ehrgeitzig und stoltz, so liegen sie dran, den ich suche alsdan die ehre des, der mich gesanth hat, den das wortt ist nicht mein wortt, sondern gottes. Wens mein Wortt were, das ich predigte, so wolt ich meine ehre verfluchen. Aber es ist gottes wort, drumb so hebet man ahn und betet: ›Geheiliget werde dein name‹ &c.. und ist stoltz und hoffertig.[59]

In ähnlicher Weise wie ein Professor im 16. Jahrhundert seine Lehre weder selbst erfunden hat noch diese freie Gabe besitzen kann, stellt Luther vom Wort Gottes fest:

> Dieses wort hab ich nicht erdacht, ich habs auch nicht geschrieben, nemet brillen in die hand und thut die heilige schrifft auf [...] ihr sollet mir dieses Buchs schuler bleiben. Wenn der Papst fragt, willst Du mich lehren, antwortet der Prediger: Ich lehre dich nicht, sondern ich weise dir einen Lehrer [...] Gott hat mir das Wort gegeben.[60]

Wenn das Wort als gegeben verstanden wird, bleibt es Gabe und erzeugt nicht den giftigen Stolz, sondern manifestiert die Ehre Gottes.

Zusammenfassend kann Luther das Problem der angemessenen Ehre wie folgt lösen:

---

57 WA 47; 404,3–405,8.
58 »Der Wertbegriff ist eigentlich ein Gegenbegriff zum Begriff der Wahrheit«, wie E. Jüngel, Wertlose Wahrheit. Zur Identität und Relevanz des christlichen Glaubens. Theologische Erörterungen III (BEvTh 107), 1990, 92 konstatiert.
59 WA 47; 405,9–17.
60 WA 47; 405,22–406,26.

Man mus alhier von einander scheiden Gottes ehre und menschen ehre. Wens gottes ehre angehet, do sei du nicht demuttig. Hoere andere nicht, die grosser und gelertter sindt den du. Lass es geschehen, das sie dieselbigen gaben haben, aber dennochs sind sie nicht gelerter noch hoher den das Gottliche wortt, welches alleine gottes ist, den dasselbige ist ein meister aller meister. Du bist nicht grosser noch mechtiger den diess wortt. Du und ich sollen unter dem wort sein. Das Wort ist nicht mein und dein […].[61]

Diese Einsichten Luthers von der Lehre und dem Wort Gottes wenden also den alten Gedanken an, demgemäß das Wissen eine freie Gabe Gottes ist. Folglich kann der Lehrer seinen Unterricht nicht als eigenes Kapital betrachten oder für eigennützige Zwecke anwenden. Als freie Gabe oder Leihgabe kann die Lehre nicht im Rahmen der Handelsbeziehungen, sondern nur im Rahmen der Gabenbeziehungen angemessen verstanden und vermittelt werden.

Gerhard Ebeling hat Luthers Gedanken untersucht, demgemäß die »Lehre« zu Gott gehört, das »Leben« dagegen zu uns, wie der Reformator an einer berühmten Stelle des Galaterbriefkommentars konstatiert.[62] Im Rahmen unserer Fragestellung können die von Ebeling untersuchten Luthertexte so ausgelegt werden, dass das Leben aus messbaren ökonomischen Leistungen und Beiträgen besteht, während die Lehre eine himmlische Gabe manifestiert, die der Mensch nicht mit seinen eigenen Fähigkeiten erfinden oder ändern darf:

die lere ist Gotts wort und Gotteswarheit selbs, Aber das leben ist unsers thuns mit, Darumb mus die lere gantz rein bleiben, Und wer am leben feilet und gebrechlich ist, da kan Gott wol gedult haben und vergeben, Aber die lere selbs, darnach man leben sol, endern odder auff heben, das kan und wil er nicht leiden, sol es auch nicht leiden, Denn das trifft seine hohe Goettliche maiestet selbs an, Da gilt kein vergeben noch gedult haben.[63]

Nach Luther gehört unser Leben zu uns, aber die Lehre gehört allein zu Gott. Die Lehre betrifft die allerhöchsten Sachen und kann deswegen

---

61 WA 47; 407,18–24.
62 WA 40,2; 46,5–8. G. EBELING, Lehre und Leben in Luthers Theologie (in: DERS., Lutherstudien III, 1985, 3–43), 30. Die abendländische Ideengeschichte von *doctrina* ist erstaunlich wenig untersucht worden, siehe z.B. die Ausführungen im Band Vera Doctrina: zur Begriffsgeschichte der Lehre von Augustinus bis Descartes, hg. v. P. BÜTTGEN u.a., 2009.
63 WA 30; 343,30–344,20.

nicht unser Eigentum sein; die Reinheit dieser kostbaren Leihgabe soll besonders beachtet werden.[64]

Den biblischen Hintergrund dieses Gedankens bildet Joh 7,16: »Die Lehre ist nicht mein«. Wenn der Lehrer predigt, ist er letzten Endes nicht das Subjekt oder der Besitzer der Lehre, sondern Gott hat das Wort des Predigers gedacht und ihm gegeben.[65] Die Logik der Lehre folgt der Logik der Gabe und Leihgabe: Ein Christ soll Gott die Ehre geben für all die Gaben, die er erhalten hat. So soll auch ein gelehrter Mensch zugeben, dass seine Lehre nicht eigentlich die seine ist, sondern die Gottes.[66] Der Lehrer kann zwar zwischen Menschenwort und Gottes Wort unterscheiden und über menschliche Lehren urteilen, aber er kann nicht über Gottes Wort und die christliche Lehre verfügen, weil diese freien Gaben nicht zum Besitz des Predigers werden können. Als Vermittler der göttlichen Lehre ist der Lehrer darum schließlich ein Schüler Gottes, und sein Amt kann als »Schüleramt« begriffen werden.[67]

---

64 WA 18; 112,9–13. EBELING (s. Anm. 62), 30, verweist im Weiteren auf WA 51; 518,21–23; 520,21–24 und WA 37; 669,1–34.

65 WA 40,2; 255,25–31.

66 WA 23; 743,25–744,14: »Drum ist maxima res contemnere nostram gloriam. Nemo ita utitur donis a deo acceptis in commodum proximi, sed ut utilitas sequatur et habeat voluptatem dran. Ergo 1. geben sie die ehr got irem hern pro magno opere, quod deus dedit filium, quia est mera gratia et inexpressibilis, ergo honor non sit noster. [...] Quando ehr datur deo et hoc bene caneretur a nobis, so wuerde die 2. leise auch, wenn die Ehr von uns ist, non est discordia. Ubi humilitas, ibi concordia, Sol. Qui volunt domini esse ex paradiso, non potest pacem habere, quia quisque vult aliquid esse et alios contemnere. Sed si dicit pius: Ego sum doctier te, tu ditior, *mea doctrina non est mea* nec habeo gloriam inde, sed deo pertinet, si possum tibi cum ea servire, sie sol dir offen stehen semper et omnibus hominibus. Si sic ago cum eo, non fimus discordes, quia do donum meum da hin et dico domini mei esse, nach der ere, nach dem nutz proximi.« – Hervorhebungen hier und in der nächsten Anm. von mir.

67 WA 33; 365,35–366,40: »und ob ich schon kan scheiden die lehre, so von Gott ist oder von menschen hehrkommen, dennoch so hab ich die macht nicht uber das wort Gottes zu herrsschen oder gottes wortt zuverwerffen, sondern dieweil ich gottes Schuler bin, so werde ich mit meinem Schuler ampt ein Magister uber menschen satzung und lehre, aber nicht uber gottes wortt. [...] Also gehets auch mit einem Hausvatter zu, der knecht soll nicht fragen nach des herrn wortt und disputiren, sondern es heist: der Herr hats gesagt, darumb so schweige der knecht stille und thue, was der herr befohln hat. Also

Das mittelalterliche Sprichwort wurde häufig auch in der längeren Form: *Scientia est donum Dei, unde vendi non potest* wiedergegeben: »Das Wissen ist Gabe Gottes, deswegen kann es nicht verkauft werden«. Dieser Satz wurde in der mittelalterlichen Diskussion um kirchliche Ämter und Simonie benutzt[68]; zum Beispiel Pierre d'Ailly erläutert ihn ausführlich in seiner Abhandlung über die Lust.[69] Auch Luther erwähnt den Endteil des Sprichwortes einmal in seiner Genesisvorlesung, wenn er die Simonie und den Verkauf von geistlichen Gütern kritisiert.[70]

Auf der anderen Seite vertritt Luther bekanntlich die Meinung, dass der Pfarrer eine angemessene Belohnung verdient. Luthers kurze *Annotationes zu Matthäus* sind aufschlussreich, denn sie zeigen, wie er anhand einer leicht spiritualisierenden Auslegung die Unverfügbarkeit der Lehre mit der Bezahlung des Pfarrers verbinden kann. Obwohl Jesus in Mt 10,8 sagt, dass wir umsonst empfangen haben und darum umsonst geben sollen, verbietet dieser Satz nach Luther nicht eine Bezahlung des Predigers nach seinem konkreten Bedarf. Jesus verbietet nur die falsche Gier, aber der Prediger kann sich selbst und seine Familie mit angemessener Bezahlung ernähren. Am wichtigsten ist es zu verstehen, dass ein Lehrer in seinem Amt des Wortes keine innerliche Begierde nach Geld, Ruhm, Ehre oder Macht haben sollte; ein Prediger soll nichts sagen oder tun, um solche eigennützigen Ziele zu fördern. Als Träger des Wortes soll der Lehrer nackt auftreten, das heißt, als frei von bösen Affekten und so, dass seine Hörer nur das Wort und nicht die Person des Predigers wahrnehmen.[71]

Obwohl der Prediger auf diese Weise eine konkrete Bezahlung erhalten kann, bleibt die innere Natur der Lehre als Gabe unberührt. Die Bezahlung ist eine äußerliche Kostenerstattung für den Prediger, der seine eige-

---

ists alhier auch, es will der herr Christus sagen: Jch bin ein prediger und Gott redet selbst, es ist sein wortt, *Meine lehre ist nicht mein,* drumb gedenckt und horet, was ich rede.«

68 Siehe G. Post u. a., The medieval heritage of a humanistic ideal: ›scientia donum dei est, unde vendi non potest‹ (Traditio 11, 1955, 195–234).

69 Eine Edition dieses Textes (d'Ailly, Radix omnium malorum est cupiditas) bietet A. Bernstein, Pierre d'Ailly and the Blanchard Affair, 1978, 199.

70 WA 43; 281,22–33.

71 WA 38; 496,5–28.

nen Verdienste in keine Beziehung zu seiner Lehre setzen soll. Die Hingabe, die Jesus in Mt 10,8–10 verlangt, bedeutet für Luther letzten Endes die innere Ablehnung der falschen Affekte, die die Gabe zum Handelsobjekt machen. Der bezahlte Prediger soll aus seiner Person oder Lehre kein Handelsobjekt machen – modern ausgedrückt: er hat kein intellektuelles Recht auf seine Lehre. So bleibt die innerliche Gabenbeziehung zwischen dem Lehrer und seinen Zuhörern auch dann bestehen, wenn der Lehrer eine Entlohnung bekommt.

Eine wichtige systematisch-theologische Anwendung des Gedankens vom Wissen als Gabe besteht darin, dass die Offenbarung Gottes in einem solchen Kontext als unverfügbare Selbstoffenbarung verstanden wird. Christoph Schwöbel formuliert diesen Sachverhalt treffend:

> Die für die reformatorische Theologie grundlegende Unterscheidung und Beziehung zwischen Gottes Werk und menschlichem Handeln greift auch in Bezug auf das Verhältnis von Offenbarung und kirchlichem Amt [...] Die Autorität der Offenbarung kann nicht auf die Kirche übertragen werden. Sie ist Zeugin der Wahrheit, indem sie Auslegerin des Wortes ist und auf die nur von Gott selbst verliehene Gabe der inneren Klarheit hofft.[72]

Dabei ist allerdings wichtig zu sehen, dass auch das römisch-katholische Lehramt auf seine Weise dem mittelalterlichen Prinzip »scientia est donum dei« sowie dem biblischen Satz »die Lehre ist nicht mein« Rechnung trägt. Wenn der katholische Amtsträger konstatiert, dass er keine Befugnis hat, die für ihn als Leihgabe übertragene Lehre zu ändern, will er auch den Gabencharakter der Offenbarung bewahren. So ist der konfessionelle Unterschied nicht einfach in der Eigentumsbeziehung zwischen Amt und Offenbarung, sondern eher in den unterschiedlichen Interpretationen des gemeinsamen Satzes »Die Lehre ist nicht mein« feststellbar.

IV Accipere – die Passivität des Empfangens

Die Freiheit des Menschen im Empfangen des Evangeliums gehört zu den großen Streitfragen des abendländischen Christentums. Im Rahmen unse-

---

72 C. Schwöbel, Art. Offenbarung V. Christentum 2. Dogmatisch b) Evangelisches Verständnis (RGG⁴ 6, 2003, 479–481), 480.

res Themas können wir die folgende Frage stellen: Kann eine Unterscheidung zwischen Handelsbeziehungen und Gabenbeziehungen auch die Freiheit bzw. Unfreiheit des Christen neu gestalten und somit für die Lösung dieser Streitfrage hilfreich sein? Ich möchte im Folgenden eine vorsichtige bejahende Antwort geben. Zugleich ist eine Warnung nötig, denn die Frage ist sehr kompliziert, und unterschiedliche Spuren führen leicht zu unterschiedlichen Ergebnissen.

In der Lutherforschung der letzten Jahre hat vor allem Bo Kristian Holm[73] sehr wertvolle Anregungen zur Beantwortung dieser Frage gegeben. Holm will Luthers Theologie konsistent im Rahmen der Gabenbeziehungen analysieren. Er gebraucht sozialwissenschaftliche Studien, die die Gegenseitigkeit von Gaben hervorheben. Holm will zeigen, dass eine gewisse Reziprozität oder menschliche Mitwirkung auch in der Heilsaneignung bei Luther zu bemerken ist, obwohl diese Gegenseitigkeit deutlich von allerlei Selbstgerechtigkeit und Handelsbeziehungen unterschieden werden soll. Die Einsicht, dass Gaben ihrer eigenen Logik der Gegenseitigkeit folgen, motiviert Holm dazu, menschliche Mitwirkung im Rahmen der Gabenbeziehung theologisch zu explizieren.[74]

Die Sprache von Gaben, Dankbarkeit und Wohltaten, also von Gabenbeziehungen insgesamt, führt allerdings in Sachen Mitwirkung und Synergie m.E. eher zu einer antipelagianischen und monergistischen Heilslehre. Zwar ist es auch wichtig zu sehen, dass Geben und Empfangen stets einen intentionalen und personalen Empfänger voraussetzen; deswegen ist eine gewisse Reziprozität mit der Begrifflichkeit der Gabe semantisch verbunden. Aber das große Bild, nämlich der frühneuzeitliche Unterschied zwischen »Gifts and Sales«, Gabenbeziehungen und Handelsbeziehungen, führt zu einer angemessenen Minimalisierung der menschlichen Mitwirkung im Empfangen des Heils.

In Luthers unmittelbarer Umgebung herrschte die spätmittelalterliche Handlungstheorie, für die die Möglichkeit der willentlichen Zustimmung konstitutiv für die Entstehung der menschlichen Handlung ist. Ohne sol-

---

73 B.K. Holm, Gabe und Geben bei Luther. Das Verhältnis zwischen Reziprozität und reformatorischer Rechtfertigungslehre (TBT 134), 2006.

74 AaO., 104–131. Vgl. auch B.K. Holm, Rechtfertigung und Gabe. Ein Beitrag zur Resozialisierung der Rechtfertigungslehre (ÖR 60, 2011, 178–190).

che Zustimmung kann der Mensch seine Handlung nicht als die »seine« bezeichnen, sondern sie wird zu einem bloßen Geschehen oder kompulsiven Verhalten. Luthers Lehrer Usingen gebraucht die Handlungstheorie Johannes Buridans, um die herkömmliche Lehre von der menschlichen Handlung zu entfalten. Nach Usingen und Buridan ist die willentliche Zustimmung zu einer Handlung ein *actus acceptationis* oder *refutationis*, und der moralische Wert der Handlung wird normalerweise durch die Art dieser Zustimmung gemessen.[75]

Die buridanische Handlungstheorie weist auffallende Ähnlichkeiten mit einer Handelsbeziehung auf. Um *dominus actus sui*, Herr seiner Akte bzw. ein Moralagent zu sein, muss das Subjekt durch seine willentliche Zustimmung ein *dominium*, ein Machtverhältnis, zum entstehenden Akt aufweisen. Die in dieser Zustimmung entstehende *acceptatio* oder *refutatio* ist wie die Annahme oder Nicht-Annahme eines käuflichen Angebotes, das dem Subjekt bereitgestellt wird. Bei Buridan und Usingen geschieht diese Bereitstellung als ein vorausgehender, unfreier Akt der *complacentia* oder *displicentia*, die die Sympathie bzw. Antipathie des potentiellen »Käufers« erwecken soll. Das Subjekt hat aber eine freie Wahl darin, seine faktische Zustimmung zu bestimmten Akten unter vielen bereitgestellten Handlungsoptionen zu geben.[76]

Wichtig für unser Thema ist, dass die so dargestellte Handlungstheorie wie ein Kaufakt auf dem Marktplatz aussieht: Das Subjekt sieht eine Reihe von bereitgestellten Optionen, die ihm mehr oder weniger gefallen und so, wie die Spätscholastik formuliert, *sub ratione boni* erscheinen. Danach gibt das Subjekt seine willentliche Zustimmung zu bestimmten Optionen, die der freie Wille aus dem Gesamtangebot wählt. Die Zustimmung ist somit wie ein Kaufvertrag, und die moralische Natur der Person wird anhand dieses Kaufvertrags gemessen. Durch diese Theorie, die Usingen als »katholische« Handlungstheorie bezeichnet[77], ist der Zustimmungsakt und folglich das gesamte »Menschenwerk« einer Handelsbeziehung auffallend ähnlich.

---

75 Siehe ausführlicher SAARINEN, Weakness (s. Anm. 5), 36–41.106–108.

76 Ebd., in meinen früheren Veröffentlichungen spreche ich jedoch nicht von einer »Handelsbeziehung«.

77 AaO., 106f.

Wenn Martin Luther mit seiner theologischen Sprache von Gabe, Wohltat und Passivität eine bewusste Alternative zu dieser seines Erachtens pelagianisch klingenden Handlungstheorie entwerfen will, findet er wichtige Unterstützung aus einigen Aspekten der klassischen humanistischen Sprache des Gebens und Empfangens. Die entscheidenden lateinischen Wörter bei Cicero und Seneca sowie in der Vulgata sind bekanntermaßen *dare* und *accipere*. Dabei hat aber *accipere* im Kontext der Gabenbeziehungen einen grundlegend anderen Sinn als die Begriffe *consentire* (zustimmen), *acceptatio* und *refutatio* in der spätmittelalterlichen Handlungstheorie.

Für das abendländische Christentum sind vor allem Mt 10,8 und 1Kor 4,7 ausschlaggebende Belegstellen für das rechte Empfangen. *Gratis accepistis, gratis date*, »Umsonst habt ihr's empfangen, umsonst gebt es auch« formuliert Mt 10,8 prägnant; 1Kor 4,7 fragt rhetorisch: *Quid autem habes quod non accepisti*, »Was hast du, was du nicht empfangen hast?« Beide Verse betonen, dass die christliche Existenz sich im Rahmen der Gabenbeziehungen, als Geben und Empfangen vollzieht. Bekanntlich war 1Kor 4,7 für Augustin ein ganz wichtiger Vers bei der Bekämpfung des Pelagianismus.[78] Empfangen, *accipere*, signalisiert also ein Verhalten, das ohne eigene Leistung geschieht.

Sowohl Cicero als auch Seneca diskutieren das rechte Empfangen von Wohltaten. Während beide die Freiwilligkeit der Wohltaten hervorheben, betont Cicero die aktive Reziprozität und die gegenseitigen Pflichten (e. g. off 1, 47–48). Für Seneca ist aber auch ein passives Empfangen von Wohltaten durchaus möglich, weil eigentlich nur die zielgerichtete Intention des Gebers für die Wohltat konstitutiv ist. Die angemessene Reaktion des Empfängers ist zwar wichtig für die Wahrnehmung seiner Würde, aber das Wesen der Wohltat ist nicht an sich von dieser Reaktion abhängig. Im rechten Geben einer Wohltat soll ich Seneca zufolge beachten, »dass ich um dessentwillen handle, in dessen Hände ich die Wohltat gelangen lassen will, ihn für würdig halte, ihm das gerne schenke und aus meinem Geschenk Freude gewinne«. (ben 4, 29, 3). Im Idealfall reagiert der Empfänger mit Dankbarkeit und zeigt so die vorausgesetzte Würde.

---

78 So E. Mühlenberg, Art. Augustin (RGG⁴ 1, 1998, 959–967), 965.

Allerdings ist diese Würde ein komplexes Phänomen, das nicht notwendigerweise ein Danksagen oder sonstiges Reagieren des Empfängers bedeutet. Die Intentionalität des Gebers braucht nicht von einer ähnlichen Intentionalität und Willentlichkeit des Empfängers begegnet werden; bisweilen kann der Geber die Würde auch ohne Dankbarkeit oder sonstige Reaktion feststellen. »Eine Wohltat kann jemand empfangen, ohne es zu wissen«, konstatiert Seneca (ben 6, 8, 1). Es ist sogar möglich, gegen den ausgesprochenen Willen des Empfängers eine Wohltat zu erweisen: Eltern, die ihre Kinder bisweilen mit Zwang erziehen, sind ein Beispiel dafür. »Daher sind unter den Wohltaten am größten die, die wir von den Eltern empfangen haben, ohne es zu wissen oder zu wollen« (ben 6, 24, 2). Das Modell solcher Wohltaten ist für Seneca ein göttliches Wesen, das die Würde und den Bedarf der Empfänger besser als sie selbst feststellen kann. Unter den Wohltaten des göttlichen Wesens ist gerade die am bedeutendsten, die einem Menschen, der sich dagegen beklagt, erwiesen wird (ben 6, 23, 8). Die Götter säumen nicht, Wohltaten denen zuzuwenden, die an dem Urheber der Wohltaten zweifeln (ben 7, 31, 4).

Senecas Diskussion ist für uns relevant, weil er ein Modell des Empfangens entwirft, das sehr deutlich vom scholastischen Zustimmungsmodell der menschlichen Handlung abweicht. Das Zustimmungsmodell setzt voraus, dass der Mensch das präsentierte Angebot selber wählt. Das Wohltatenmodell Senecas lehrt aber, dass im Geben und Empfangen nur der Geber eigentlich willentlich und intentional tätig sein muss. Das Empfangen kann ohne oder sogar gegen den Willen des Empfängers stattfinden – auch in solchen Fällen kann man von *accipere* sprechen. Zugleich muss der Empfänger aber eine solche Würde haben, dass er als Person ein Adressat des Gebensaktes sein kann. Bisweilen konzipiert Seneca diese Einsicht anhand des Gedankens der Verzögerung: Der Empfänger soll zu einem späteren Zeitpunkt die Mündigkeit haben, dankbar zu sein (ben 7, 30–32). Wichtig ist aber, dass die in den Wohltaten ausgesprochene Gabenbeziehung eine ganz andere Art des Empfangens aufweist als die Handelsbeziehung, für die die willentliche Zustimmung beider Seiten konstitutiv ist. Für eine Wohltat ist es ausreichend, wenn nur der Geber einen zielgerichteten Willensakt zustande bringt.

Für Luthers Rede von Gottes Wohltaten ist bekanntermaßen die Passivität des menschlichen Empfangens, die sogenannte *mere passive*, von grundlegender Bedeutung. In einer Diskussion mit Bo Holm hat Ingolf Dalferth neulich Wörter wie »Passivitätsaktivität« und »Empfangenkönnen der Gabe« benutzt, wenn er *mere passive* interpretiert hat.[79] Philipp Stoellger hat gezeigt, dass die Kategorie der *passio* für Luther eine facettenreiche Wirklichkeit darstellt, die die gleichzeitige Möglichkeit von Ruhe und Offenheit durchaus erlaubt.[80] Mein Plädoyer für ein besonderes *accipere*, willenloses Empfangen, das in den Gabenbeziehungen zum Vorschein kommt, geht in die gleiche Richtung wie die wertvollen Studien von Dalferth und Stoellger.[81] Meine These ist, dass die humanistische Philosophie der Wohltaten, besonders wie sie in *De beneficiis* formuliert worden ist, eine bemerkenswerte Ähnlichkeit mit Luthers Einsicht von *mere passive* aufweist.

Wenn wir Luthers Gebrauch des Wortes *accipere* näher studieren, fällt sofort auf, dass dieses Empfangen nicht mit dem freien Willen oder mit Werken identifiziert wird, sondern im Gegenteil als glaubendes Empfangen der Wohltaten Gottes. Wer Glauben in Christus empfängt, ist gerecht und heilig.[82] Wenn wir im Glauben beten, verspricht Gott, dass wir alles empfangen.[83] Der Glaube empfängt die Sündenvergebung.[84]

Die humanistische Unterscheidung zwischen Handelsbeziehungen und Gabenbeziehungen kommt an den zahlreichen Stellen zu Vorschein, in denen Luther eine bewusste Unterscheidung zwischen *facere* und *accipere* vornimmt: »Lex gibt's *facere, fides accipere*«[85]. Unter den weltlichen Menschen wird derjenige gelobt, der viel tut, aber bei Gott derjenige, der vieles empfängt.[86] Im Feiern des Sakraments wird das Gute nicht von den Menschen gemacht, sondern von ihnen empfangen.[87] Die Gnade wird

---

79 I.U. Dalferth, Mere Passive. Die Passivität der Gabe bei Luther (in: Word-Gift-Being, hg. v. B.K. Holm/P. Widmann, 2009, 43–73), 57.64. Vgl. Holm, Gabe (s. Anm. 73).

80 P. Stoellger, Passivität aus Passion. Zur Problemgeschichte einer »categoria non grata« (HUTh 56), 2010, z.B. 298–308.

81 Vgl. Saarinen, Language (s. Anm. 37), 290–294.

82 WA 39,1; 221,15.

83 WA 14; 579,6.

84 WA 30,3; 489,10.

85 WA 40,1; 426,2.

86 WA 1; 78,21.

87 WA 6; 521,30–31.

nicht so gepredigt: »Mach dies, mach jenes«, sondern so: »Empfange dies, dann hast du es«.[88]

Typisch für diesen Kontrast ist im Weiteren, dass Luther *facere* als Handlung Gottes und *accipere* als Reaktion des Christen bezeichnet. »Was Christus lehrt und tut, wird von uns empfangen«.[89] Das Evangelium fordert nicht unser Tun, sondern unser Empfangen. Gott ist der Handelnde, nicht wir.[90] In der Nächstenliebe geht es um das Empfangen der für diese Person vollbrachten Liebestaten.[91] Das Wort Gottes, das Evangelium, wird nicht von uns gemacht, sondern empfangen.[92] »Wir sollen nichts anderes tun als alles umsonst empfangen«.[93] Im Neuen Testament werden wir nicht im Tun unterrichtet, sondern im Empfangen, so dass wir alles als Gabe erhalten.[94] Unser Hören des Evangeliums ist kein Werk, sondern ein Empfangen. »Wenn ich empfange, tue ich nichts. Wenn ich arbeite, empfange ich nicht«.[95] »Gott handelt und wir empfangen«.[96]

Die Belegstellen von *accipere* zeigen deutlich, dass das Empfangen kein Werk ist, sondern eine willenlose und zugleich personale Rezeption

---

88 WA 11; 215,31–32.

89 WA 9; 515,25.

90 WA 16; 586,4–6.

91 WA 20; 514,1–5.

92 WA 27; 136,3–5.

93 WA 31,2; 318,11.

94 WA 34,2; 164,24–26.

95 WA 36; 15,10–11. Der Kontext (WA 36; 14,11–16,11) erläutert die Dialektik von Handelsbeziehung und Gabenziehung: »Dilige proximum, benefac illi &c.. Das heyst das gesecz abgeczirckelt ab Euangelio. Das uns heyst thun, Euangelion nihil mandat et exigit, Es heyst nur nhemen und lassen geben, scilicet promissione dei. Das schencke ich dyr, do kan ich nichts zw thun, Ut baptizari aliquem non est opus meum, sed dei donum et opus, ders thut und schenckt. Summa: per legem exigitur, Durchs Euangelion werde ich zur spende geruffen. Illud discrimen ita notate. Euangelion est donum, do sol ich uffhalden. Den magna est differentia inter Nhemen und geben. Quando accipio, nihil facio. Quando laboro, tunc non accipio. Das eyne ist promissio, aliud praeceptum. Illud dat, illud exigit. Wie eyn lehenher gibt eynem edelman eyn gut, hoc est opus principis. Deinde cum ille ministraverit myt pferden, do thut er was. Das ist de caussa finali. Wens yns geystliche werk kumpt, das gesecz, tunc exigit, terret, si non fecerimus, habemus malam conscienciam. Econtra euangelion praedicat donum, do wyl das hercz nicht hinan.«

96 WA 36; 229,11.

der Wohltaten und Gaben. Der Begriff des Empfangens gehört mit der göttlichen Gabenbeziehung eng zusammen und wird häufig mit solchen Handelsbeziehungen kontrastiert, die *facere* benutzen. Auf diese Weise ist eine auffallende Ähnlichkeit zwischen Seneca und Luther im Gebrauch des Begriffs *accipere* zu bemerken. Übrigens wird der scholastische Begriff *acceptatio* von Luther ganz deutlich als Werk, als *facere*, verstanden; wie bei Buridan und Usingen setzt dieser Begriff bei Luther eine willentliche Zustimmung voraus. Deswegen kann Luther, anders als die Buridanisten, *acceptatio* eigentlich nur als göttlichen Akt bezeichnen.[97] Das Wort *consentire*, »zustimmen«, gehört bei Luther ebenfalls eng mit *facere* zusammen.[98]

Das Verständnis des menschlichen Empfangens als willenlose, personale Gabenbeziehung kann auch hilfreich für die Interpretation von *De servo arbitrio* sein. Zwar soll Luthers Position in dieser Schrift anhand anderer Begrifflichkeiten skizziert werden[99], aber sie manifestieren die gleiche Logik der Gabenbeziehungen wie der Kontrast zwischen *facere* und *accipere*. In seiner Debatte mit Erasmus nimmt Luther bekanntlich eine ganz eigenwillige Definition von Notwendigkeit als Unveränderlichkeit (*immutabilitas*) vor. Der Wille kann, so Luther, nicht autonom seine Grundrichtung verändern und ist in diesem Sinne gebunden bzw. unterliegt einer Notwendigkeit.[100] Allerdings gibt Luther zu, dass (1) der Mensch eine *aptitudo naturalis*, eine personale rezeptive Fähigkeit hat.[101] Die Aufgaben dieser Fähigkeit sind denjenigen Funktionen auffallend ähnlich, die bei Seneca sowie in vielen anderen Lutherschriften mit dem Verb *accipere* bezeichnet worden sind.[102]

---

97 Z. B. WA 39,1; 228,9; WA 40,1; 233,25.

98 Z. B. WA 1; 472,26; 2; 592,5; 8; 116,33 und 120,34–35; 12; 177,10; 40,3; 716,20; 43; 74,31.

99 Das Wort *accipere* bezieht sich in *De servo arbitrio* zumeist auf die philologische Frage, wie ein Wort »verstanden« (accipitur) wird.

100 WA 18; 634,14–29.

101 WA 18; 636,16–22.

102 Auch die rezeptive Fähigkeit ist letzten Endes von Gott gegeben, vgl. WA 18; 753,8–10 im Anschluss an Joh 3,27 Vulgata: »non potest homo accipere quicquam nisi fuerit ei datum de caelo«. Wichtig ist, dass diese Fähigkeit den Tieren, Pflanzen und leblosen Dingen nicht gegeben worden ist und dass der Mensch auf diese Weise eine Person ist. Die Gaben sowie die Akte von *dare* und *accipere* beziehen sich auf Personen.

Diese zwei Züge erlauben durchaus, dass der Mensch Eindrücke empfangen und diesen mit seinem Willen folgen kann. Luthers Definition von Notwendigkeit verbietet nur die autonome oder spontane Veränderung der Willensrichtung; eine heteronome Bestimmung kann aber bestehen und willentlich unterstützt werden. Im Weiteren gibt Luther zu, dass (2) der Gebrauch einiger unwichtiger Mittel im alltäglichen Leben frei bleibt und dass (3) der Christenmensch anhand der Gnade zu einer gewissen Kooperation mit Gott fähig ist.[103]

Aus diesen Grundzügen entsteht ein handlungstheoretisches Modell, in dem der Motivationsgrund bzw. das Herz des Menschen immer schon durch die empfangenen Eindrücke entweder vom Fleisch oder vom Geist heteronom bestimmt wird. Zugleich ist auch das endgültige Ziel seiner Handlungen durch diese heteronomen Kräfte vorbestimmt. Zwischen dem inneren Motivationsgrund und dem endgültigen Ziel kann der Mensch zwar gewisse unwichtige Mittel frei wählen, aber der Wille kann seine grundlegende Gesamtrichtung nicht autonom verändern. Zugleich ist aber auch wahr, dass der Mensch durchaus willentlich handelt, weil er seinen grundlegenden Eindrücken folgt und gewissermaßen eine Kooperation mit denen aufweist.[104]

Ein derartiges Gesamtbild kann zum beträchtlichen Teil als Gabenbeziehung verstanden werden. Für das Entstehen einer Gabenbeziehung braucht man keinen Willen, wohl aber die *aptitudo naturalis* bzw. die rezeptive Fähigkeit des personalen Empfangens. Die Gabe hat im Weiteren die Fähigkeit, den Empfänger zu verändern; Senecas Beispiel dafür ist die Erziehung als Gabe, die gegen den Widerstand der Kinder wirksam werden kann. Ingolf Dalferth spricht in diesem Kontext sogar von einer »Gabe zur Destruktion«, um zu zeigen, wie die Gabe der Annihilation die fleischliche Existenz vernichten kann.[105] Wichtig ist aber, dass bei einer solchen Zerstörung das Person-Sein des Menschen nicht gänzlich aufhört. Die Rolle von *aptitudo naturalis* sowie der alltäglichen Wahl der unwichtigen Mittel kann so interpretiert werden, dass sie die kontinuierliche

---

103 WA 18; 638,4–11; 753–754.
104 Siehe ausführlicher SAARINEN, Weakness (s. Anm. 5), 128–130.
105 DALFERTH (s. Anm. 79), 54.

Identität der Person auf dem heteronom bestimmten Wege vom Fleisch zum Geist durch Annihilation und Umwandlung bewahren.

So verstanden geht es Luther in *De servo arbitrio* nicht um metaphysische Notwendigkeiten, sondern um die bleibende Passivität des Menschen innerhalb der Gabenbeziehung. Für die Handelsbeziehung ist es konstitutiv, dass der Wille eine *mutabilitas*, eine autonome Veränderungspotenz, besitzt, damit er durch seine Zustimmung den Kaufvertrag schließen kann. In der Gabenbeziehung reicht es aber, dass das Empfangen als *aptitudo naturalis* gesichert ist und dass die Identität der Person durch diese Offenheit und die Wahl von unwichtigen Mitteln erhalten bleibt. In der Gabenbeziehung handelt der Mensch ohne autonome Entscheidungspotenz, aber durchaus willentlich, da sein Wille durch die fleischlichen oder geistlichen Gaben heteronom aktiviert wird. Zugleich erlaubt die rezeptive Fähigkeit, dass der empfangende Glaube[106] und die Affekte des Menschen »seine« personalen Eigenschaften bleiben, obwohl sie aus theologischer Sicht eher ein *accipere* als *facere* oder *liberum arbitrium* manifestieren.

Diese Vorschläge, Luthers *De servo arbitrio* im Rahmen der humanistischen Gabenbeziehung zu interpretieren, sind provisorischer Art, da Luthers Text eine philosophische Systematik eher vermeidet. In vielen anderen Schriften bietet jedoch Luthers explizite und systematische Kontrastierung zwischen *accipere* und *facere* eine starke Evidenz für die These, dass die humanistische Dialektik zwischen »gifts and sales«, Gabenbeziehungen und Handelsbeziehungen, in Luthers Theologie ein systematisches Deutungsmuster ist, das seine Auffassung von den menschlichen Werken tiefgreifend prägt.

V Fazit

Anhand der neuen Studien von Natalie Zemon Davis und Marcel Hénaff habe ich die These formuliert, dass die Unterscheidung zwischen Gaben-

---

106 Wegen seiner rezeptiven Fähigkeit ist der Glaube für Luther ein Ergreifen der theologischen Wirklichkeit. Zu dieser sog. *fides apprehensiva* siehe R. SAARINEN, Art. Glaube (in: Luther-Lexikon, hg. v. V. LEPPIN/G. SCHNEIDER-LUDORFF, erscheint 2013).

beziehungen und Handelsbeziehungen zu Luthers Zeit eine prominente geistesgeschichtliche Idee war. Diese Unterscheidung war vor allem durch die popularphilosophischen Werke Ciceros und Senecas den Gelehrten bekannt, aber sie prägte auch das kulturelle Verhalten der verschiedenen Klassen in der Gesellschaft. Ich habe nachgewiesen, dass Luther diese Unterscheidung in verschiedenen Variationen benutzt, um seine theologische Botschaft zu erhellen. Die Wohltaten Gottes, die Autonomie der christlichen Lehre und die Passivität des menschlichen Empfangens sind theologische Phänomene, die die grundlegende Figur der Gabenbeziehung manifestieren. Zugleich kritisiert Luther das Verstehen des Gottesverhältnisses als eine Handelsbeziehung.

Wenn Luther die Unterscheidung von »gifts and sales« benutzt, geht es ihm allerdings nicht primär um die Vertretung einer philosophischen oder sozialgeschichtlichen Position, sondern die Unterscheidung dient der theologischen Kommunikation: Luther will zeigen, wie seine reformatorische Theologie anhand von Gabenbeziehungen verstanden werden kann. Die von Luther gebrauchte Terminologie bietet starke Evidenz dafür, dass sein Gebrauch der Unterscheidung zur Wirkungsgeschichte von Ciceros *De officiis* und Senecas *De beneficiis* gehört. Allerdings ist eine direkte literarische Abhängigkeit schwierig nachzuweisen. Da wir aus anderen Studien wissen, dass diese Texte zu Luthers Zeit weit verbreitet waren und die Unterscheidung an sich zur sozialen und intellektuellen Kultur Europas gehörte, können wir Luther auch ohne direkte literarische Abhängigkeit dieser Wirkungsgeschichte zurechnen.

Dieser Befund vertieft die Einsicht von Helmar Junghans, der gemäß Luther viele positive Einflüsse aus dem Humanismus seiner Zeit erhalten hat. Er zeigt im Weiteren, dass Luthers philosophischer Hintergrund nicht nur im Aristotelismus der Spätscholastik zu lokalisieren ist. Auch die humanistische Rezeption von Cicero und Seneca spielt für den Reformator eine Rolle, die kultur- und sozialgeschichtlich beträchtlich sein kann. Durch die Begrifflichkeit von Lehre und Handel kann diese Rezeptionslinie auch die frühneuzeitlichen Auffassungen von Pädagogik und Ökonomie beleuchten.

Luther's Use of Philosophy

Mark Mattes

Anyone who assumes that Luther believed that philosophy had no positive contribution to make to theology simply fails to deal with Luther's corpus. Undoubtedly, Luther puts his finger on an irresolvable tension between philosophy and theology, especially as the latter is obliged to articulate faithfully the gospel as *promissio* (of which philosophy knows nothing). However, there is no question that Luther found philosophy, especially logic, to be a helpful tool by which to establish doctrinal clarity through the use of syllogisms when properly following the grammar of the new tongue (*nova lingua*) of theology.[1] As such, logic helps ward off heresy

---

1 However, we must keep in mind that »even the study of grammar that Luther praised so highly and gave pride of place to in the *trivium* is not something that theology can follow uncritically, for it also reflects certain biases and the linguistic conventions of the day. The way that key theological terms are used, such as the words ›God‹ and ›human being‹, ›creator‹ and ›creature‹, proves disastrous for theology. The world of sin, the old world, also has its own ›old language‹ [...]. In this sense the Holy Spirit, who makes the old world and its old language new, ›has his own grammar‹ [WA 39,2; 104,24]. Indeed, ›grammar operates in all fields, but when the subject is greater than can be comprehended by the rules of grammar and philosophy, it must be left behind‹ [WA 39,2; 104,24–26].« Indeed, »Grammar confirms and strengthens the ›philosophical argument‹, that ›there is no relation between the creature and the creator, between the finite and the infinite‹, between a beginning in time and eternity. ›We, on the other hand, assert not only a relation, but [even] the union of the finite and the infinite‹ [WA 39,2; 112,15–19].« See O. Bayer, Theology the Lutheran Way, trans. by J. Silcock/M. Mattes, 2007, 81. – Luther particularly employed syllogistic reasoning in Christology. See his comments on Hebrews 1 at WA 10,1,1; 151 or on the deity of Christ at WA 37; 44,10–14 or on the deity of Christ at WA 28; 92,29–36. See also S. Becker, The Foolishness of God: The Place of Reason in the Theology of Martin Luther, 2009, 82–87.

and clarifies true doctrine.[2] Secondly, however, at least early in his career, Luther could employ not merely the formalism of logic but also the substance of Platonic thinking in opposition to Aristotelian since he saw its apophaticism[3] as better able to honor God's hiddenness and more compatible with a theology of the cross (*theologia crucis*). Extending the *via negativa*, Luther claims that the theology of the cross enables us to distinguish appearance and reality with respect to God and our works since we become aware that while our works appear meritorious and God's appear evil, in fact just the opposite is the case. More generally, philosophical concepts – including metaphysical ones – must first be »bathed« before they can become useful in theology.[4] Thirdly, with respect to the divergent schools of Nominalism and Realism, Luther comes across as somewhat eclectic – borrowing ideas from and rejecting aspects of both – making it challenging to peg him under those categories. The overall shape of relating philosophy and theology in terms of »two spheres,«[5] (1) philoso-

---

2 »Reason is used to understand the object of faith in an area formed by the center and circumscribed by the boundary. When attacks from the boundary threaten to erode the center, or when the certainty of the center is shaken, the theological task begins.« See C. HELMER, The Trinity and Martin Luther: A Study on the Relationship between Genre, Language and the Trinity in Luther's Works (1523–1546), 1999, 3.

3 Knut Alfsvåg, who places Luther within the wider Platonic-Augustinian-Mystical apophatic tradition defines apophaticism as that path which systematically rejects all necessary predicates of God, and then again rejects the rejections, locating the presence of God in an area beyond all positive conceptualities including the concepts of being and not-being. See K. ALFSVÅG, What No Mind Has Conceived: On the Significance of Christological Apophaticism, 2010, 1.

4 See S. JUNTUNEN, Luther and Metaphysics: What it is the Structure of Being according to Luther? (in: Union with Christ: The New Finnish Interpretation of Luther, ed. by C. BRAATEN/R. JENSON, 1998, 129–160), 134. »Si tamen vultis uti vocabulis istis, prius quaeso illa bene purgate, füret sie mal zum Bade« in WA 39,1; 229,16–19.

5 Usually Luther distinguishes the sphere of philosophy as dealing with the temporal while theology deals with the eternal (WA 51; 243,10–18 = LW 13,199) but sometimes he distinguishes them as »present« (philosophy) and »future« (theology) (WA 56; 371,30 = LW 25,361). Oswald Bayer helpfully situates the relation between philosophy and theology as parallel to »humanity in general and Christians in particular«. »Luther's distinction between knowledge and certainty is along the same lines as that between ›holy‹ and ›saved‹ that we find in his *Confession* (1528). This distinction is highly illuminating

phy, aligned with temporal matters, and (2) theology, aligned with eternal ones, as well as his view of the inscrutability of God's will,[6] seems to be indebted to Nominalism. However, in theology, Luther is not averse to using a Realist approach to universals and in semantics. Luther's eclecticism is not inconsistent because his standard for evaluating philosophy is primarily the requirement of clarifying and advancing the gospel to which philosophy is called upon to serve. Fourthly, in Luther's view, when philosophy is applied to practical matters in the temporal realm, it can positively contribute to human flourishing. Just as the law is valuable for directing human conduct *coram mundo* but has no say as a way for self-justification *coram deo*, so philosophy works in tandem with the law to help people determine more productive ways to support the common good. Finally, philosophy needs to come with a warning label. It is not neutral turf but can be exploited by the purposes of the old Adam. If philosophy opts to encroach upon theology, Luther sets clear demarcations for it.[7] He will not allow it to be misused to bury the risen Christ who seeks

for his definition of the relationship between philosophy and theology. God orders his creation within three orders. The basic order of all human life is ›holy‹ because it is ›grounded in God's word and commandment‹. However, none of the orders is a way of salvation. There is only one way beyond all these, the way of faith in Jesus Christ. For to be holy and to be saved are two entirely different things. We are saved through Christ alone. But we become holy through this faith as well as through these divine institutions and orders. Even the godless can have much about them that is holy, but they are not for that reason saved inwardly.« Bayer refers to WA 26; 505,16–21 = LW 37,365. See BAYER (see n. 1), 75.

6 Against Erasmus, Luther writes, »I say that the righteous God does not deplore the death of His people which he Himself works in them, but He deplores the death which He finds in His people and desires to remove from them. God preached works to the end that sin and death may be taken away, and we may be saved. ›He sent His word and healed them‹ (Ps. 107.20). but God hidden in Majesty neither deplores nor takes away death, but works life, and death, and all in all; nor has He set bounds to Himself by His Word, but has kept Himself free over all things.« See WA 18; 685,18–24 = M. LUTHER, The Bondage of the Will, trans. by J. I. PACKER/O. R. JOHNSTON, 1957, 170.

7 »To be sure, theology encroaches upon the rules of philosophy, but, contrariwise, philosophy itself encroaches more often upon the rules of theology.« WA 39,2; 4,22–23 (Die Disputationen über Joh 1,14, 1539) = LW 38,240 (thesis 15).

to raise those dead in sin.[8] Indeed, this risen Christ renders all theoreticians guided by *ambitio divinitatis*[9] quite passive *coram deo*. It is Christ as the *novum* to whom every thought – including philosophical ones – must be taken captive. In so doing, *philosophia* can serve »not as mistress but as maidservant and bondwoman and most beautiful helper« for theology.[10]

I The Scope of Philosophy in the Late Medieval University

Philosophia in the Late Middle Ages was a demonstrative science based on Aristotle's *Posterior Analytics*, established through analytic deductions and syllogisms. It included those sub-disciplines present in contemporary philosophy, such as metaphysics and ethics, but was wider than the discipline as presently defined since it included what we would call the natural sciences.[11] The most important subject for the Bachelor's Degree was logic.[12] The Master's Degree continued the study of logic,

---

8 WA 39,2; 13,15 = LW 38,248.

9 In his letter to George Spalatin (June 30, 1530), Luther writes, »Be strong in the Lord, and on my behalf continuously admonish Philip [Melanchthon] not to become like God [Gen 3:5], but to fight that innate ambition to be like God, which was planted in us in paradise by the devil. This [ambition] doesn't do us any good. It drove Adam from paradise, and it alone also drives us away, and drives peace away from us. In summary: we are to be men and not God; it will not be otherwise, or eternal anxiety and affliction will be our reward.« (WAB 5; 415,41–46 = LW 49,337).

10 WA 39,2; 24,24 = LW 38,257. In general, Luther represents the view that philosophy is an *ancilla theologiae* or servant of faith. See WA 39,2; 24,20–26 and WA 1; 355,1–5. Luther says, »Theology shall be empress. Philosophy and other good arts shall be her servants. They are not to rule or to govern« (WATR 5; 616).

11 G. WHITE, Luther as Nominalist: A Study of the Logical Methods used in Martin Luther's Disputations in the Light of Their Medieval Background, 1994, 86 ff. As White and others note, philosophy in Luther's day was guided by semantic and ontological concerns, not epistemological ones as has been the case since Descartes and Hobbes.

12 The primary textbook on logic was the thirteenth-century compendium of Petrus Hispanus. However, the Neo-Platonist Porphyry's commentary on Aristotle (called the »old art« [*ars vetus*]) was studied, culminating in a reading of Aristotle's Prior Analytics and Posterior Analytics, and Aristotle's work dealing with fallacies. See M. BRECHT, Martin Luther: His Road to Reformation 1483–1521, trans. by J. SCHAAF, 1993, 32 ff.

investigating Aristotle's *Topics* and his philosophy of nature.[13] Martin Brecht notes that Luther's Erfurt philosophy teachers, Trutvetter and Usingen, following the *via moderna,* »did not question the superior authority of revelation and the Bible over against philosophy.«[14] Nevertheless, all *moderni* acknowledged that theology was not a science, a theoretical system of truth established via demonstration. Reason could work within theology but its fundamental axioms were accepted on the basis of authority.[15]

The foundation for all study in medieval universities was the *trivium,* i.e., grammar, logic, and rhetoric. For Scholastics, the study of grammar included semantical and logical analysis. Luther was grounded in these disciplines at Erfurt. However, Luther was also influenced by Humanism, best understood not as a philosophical system but as a cultural program.[16] Especially in Northern Europe, the Humanists' call was a return to the sources (*ad fontes*) of classical and biblical texts in their original languages. In contrast to Scholasticism, Humanists were primarily lexicographers, recounting matters within a text, and not analysts, who are better served by syllogistic reasoning.

The public exercise of logic in the university for the sake of establishing clarity and truth culminated in academic disputations, a dialectic between two people, a master and a respondent. »Disputations were a regular part of academic life, which occurred publicly at fixed points on the academic calendar, as part of graduation exercises, and in private between pupils and masters.«[17] The goal of such disputations, which all made

---

13 Aristotle's philosophy of nature included: »On the Heavens«, »On Generation and Corruption«, »Meteorology«, »On the Soul«, and »Parva Naturalia.«

14 BRECHT (see n. 12), 35.

15 Indeed, Luther regarded Trutvetter as the one »who first taught him that belief is to be accorded only to the biblical books, and all others are to be accepted with critical judgment«, a precursory formulation of the »scriptural principle«, as Brecht notes, making possible a kind of coexistence between philosophy and theology. See BRECHT (see n. 12), 35.

16 A.E. McGRATH, Luther's Theology of the Cross, 1985, 40.

17 R.S. CLARK, Iustitia Imputata Christi: Alien or Proper to Luther's Doctrine of Justification (CTQ 70, 2006, 269–310), 297. In an academic disputation, theses written by a professor were presented. In the course of the disputation opponents would provide arguments

extensive use of syllogistic reasoning, was to establish theological truth (though not the agenda or grounds for truth) in the face of heresies threatening the catholic faith or to clarify specific loci. Early in the Reformation, between the years 1522–1533, there were practically no disputations held at Wittenberg. However, when Luther was Dean of the Theological Faculty, after 1533, the practice was revived. It is likely that Luther, who had a reputation as a skillful interlocutor in disputations, valued them »because it was through them […] that he made his most important breakthroughs in 1518 (Heidelberg) and 1519 (Leipzig).«[18]

II Nominalism and Realism

Insofar as Luther's thinking is beholden (as he claims) to Ockham, Luther too takes a position that rejects a radical separation which would wholly isolate faith from reason but also rejects a synthesis of faith and reason. For Luther, the relation between philosophy and theology is not determined by the relation between nature and grace (as it was for Nominalists and Realists). Instead, it is guided by the distinction between law and gospel which construes philosophy as a suitable instrument for service in this world – including theology as an academic endeavor.[19] For Luther, in stark

---

attacking the theses while it was the responsibility of the *respondens*, usually a doctoral candidate, to reply to these arguments. The *respondens*' job was not to argue for the theses but instead to find fault with the opposing syllogisms of the *opponentes*. Given that the primary vocation of the Theological Faculty was the training of clergy, it is clear that what in contemporary parlance is called »critical thinking« was deemed requisite for successful pastoral leadership. It staggers the imagination to think if such public disputations would be required of today's pastoral and doctoral candidates. Additionally, disputation as a social practice indicates the high value that was placed on rigorous, clear thinking in the attempt to establish theological truth.

18 CLARK (see n. 17), 297.

19 Ingolf Dalferth notes, »The difference may be described as the transition from an additive co-ordination of the two perspectives of Faith and Reason to an internal reconstruction of the perspective of Reason within the perspective of Faith. What used to be an external contrast between Nature and Grace is now re-created as an internal differentiation of the perspective of Faith in terms of Law (*lex*) and Gospel (*evangelium*), viz. the knowledge of God, world and human existence *extra Christum* and *in Christo*. This is a

contrast to Aristotle's valuation of philosophy as contemplative, theology is a practical not a contemplative discipline. Early in his career he defined it as *sapientia experimentalis* which, as Oswald Bayer notes, means that, as wisdom, it includes science, unites theory and practice and grounds both in an experiential or receptive life (*vita passiva*). Again, as Bayer notes, experiential wisdom would be a contradiction in terms for Aristotle. Nothing historical or experiential can serve as a basis for knowledge in Aristotle's perspective.[20]

While the subject matter of philosophy in the medieval German university centered primarily (though not solely) on Aristotle's works, these writings were interpreted through the lens of two opposing perspectives, Realism and Nominalism. The heart of the philosophical debate between these schools was over the nature of universals. Realists held that universals like »whiteness« had their being either apart from their instantiations in white things (the Platonic view, as seen in William of Champaeux), or had their being not fully accounted for by their instantiations in white things, but not yet having their being apart from their instantiations (the Aristotelian view, as seen in Thomas Aquinas). In contrast, extreme Nominalists (like Roscelin) held that general terms like »whiteness« did not refer to universals, but simply were different names for the particulars of which they were predicated. For Nominalists like Ockham, all that exists are particular entities having particular qualities. As noted, Luther was educated in the Ockhamist (Nominalist) tradition.[21] However, his teachers were more eclectic in their approach to the status of universals than what they supposed. While the approach of Luther's teacher Trutvet-

---

purely theological distinction. But by relating two theological perspectives, not a theological and a non-theological one, the theological perspective is universalized and made independent on the philosophical perspective. Theology is seen strictly in the service of the explication of faith in Christ and its vision of reality [...]. Hence it constitutes the decisive point of reference for interpreting the totality of reality, and requires all theological thinking about God, the world, and human existence to be christologically determined.« See I. Dalferth: Theology and Philosophy, 1988, 76.

20 Bayer (see n. 1), 28 f.

21 See D. Bielfeldt, Clarity with Respect to Realism. *Disputationes* (http://disputationes.blogspot.com).

ter to logic and semantics was shaped by Nominalism, in metaphysics he assumed a theory of participation of creatures in God which is closer to a Realist position on the status of universals as objective realities.[22]

Luther referred to himself as a »terminist« (a Nominalist), and that Ockham was his teacher (*magister meus*).[23] It is likely, however, that his approach, similar to his teachers, is more fluid than his self-designation would indicate. When he calls himself a *modernus*, he is referring to semantic and logical skills he gained from disputational methodology. However, he is also indebted to the *via moderna* for its greater emphases on discontinuity between philosophy and theology than that of the *via antiqua*. In Luther's judgment, philosophy and theology constitute two quite different spheres whose boundaries must be properly honored if both philosophy and theology are to do their respective work.[24] Broadly construed, he rejected Aristotelian essentialism (that our duty in life is to realize our fixed potentials in a hierarchical scheme), but he thinks in terms of »natures« as sets of possibilities by which we generalize and classify

---

22 »Luther's teachers Jodocus Trutvetter and Bartholomaus Usingen, who wanted to renew teaching at the University of Erfurt and bring it into line with orthodox Ockhamist tradition, were actually themselves Ockhamist only in their logic. When they treated themes like creation or the existence of creatures in their natural philosophy, they could imply the concept of participation in a way that was contradictory to Ockham's basic intentions [...] that his teacher did not pay much attention to contradiction between the use of the supposition they and the ontological use of the concept of participation leads one to think that Luther might have understood created being as participation in God, though as a good ›terminist‹ he should not have done so.« See S. JUNTUNEN (see n. 4), 150.

23 See WA 38; 160,3; see also McGRATH (see n. 16), 36.

24 Bruce Marshall helpfully indicates that theology unlike philosophy deals with the *whole* of reality. »Theology and philosophy each has its own ›sphere‹; neither provides the content for the other's discourse, and each has its own rules for forming true sentences. But this distinction turns out to be a way of insisting that theology has to keep its epistemic priorities straight. Theology's ›sphere‹ ends up being the whole; theology puts philosophy in its place by defining philosophy's sphere, that is, by marking out the boundaries within which its rules for forming true sentences may apply (viz., wherever they do not conflict with the truth of Scripture and creed taken in their natural sense).« See B. MARSHALL, Faith and Reason Reconsidered: Aquinas and Luther on Deciding what is True (The Thomist 63, 1999, 1–48), 46.

objects in the world.[25] In theology, however, he could at times think in terms very similar to that of Realists. For instance, when he describes Christ as the *forma* of faith,[26] in which believers share the same form as

25 For this insight I am indebted to Paul Hinlicky, email correspondence of August 17, 2011.

26 See WA 40,1; 229,22–32 = LW 26,130 and T. MANNERMAA's discussion in Christ Present in Faith: Luther's View of Justification, trans. by K. STJERNA, 2005, 57f. With respect to the relation between God's favor and God's gift in justification, which is disputed between advocates of »forensic« justification and the Mannermaa school, Risto Saarinen makes headway, »While it is true that God's benevolence and God's gift appear together, one also needs to say that God's gift needs to be preconditioned by benevolence in order that it can be a gift [...]. In this very specific and limited sense, there is a conceptual priority of favor over the gift.« Saarinen goes on to caution »adherents to forensic justification readily affirm the primacy of merciful favor, but they fail to see the dynamics of one's being both recipient and beneficiary. Adherents of effective justification grasp this dynamic, but they do not see the fine differences between the concepts of favor and gift.« See R. SAARINEN, Finnish Luther Studies: A Story and a Program (in: Engaging Luther: A (New) Theological Assessment, ed. by O.-P. VAINIO, 2010, 1–27), 23f. However, for all Saarinen's protestations, I find his position here to be hardly different from my own (»Christ is so for us that he becomes one with us in this marriage of the conscience to Christ«) which he describes on pages 21f. For a thorough critique of the Finnish School, see W.W. SCHUMACHER, Who Do I Say That You Are? Anthropology and the Theology of Theosis in the Finnish School of Tuomo Mannermaa, 2010. Commenting on WA 31,1; 217,4–17 = LW 13,71 Schumacher writes (p. 113), »Here Luther construes the sense of ›deify‹ in a very different way than the ›real-ontic‹ union urged by the Finnish school. In a sense, Luther is more pragmatic, and more ›real‹, since he has here become anchored to the concrete realities of human existence as creatures. In this mature, evangelical view, such human existence is properly connected to God – ›deified‹ – precisely to the extent that it is concretely played out in the divinely ordered (divinely ›spoken‹) sphere of very *human* activity: parents, children, master, servants. The ›divine‹ character of such people has nothing to do with overcoming or transcending who they are as human creatures, but depends directly on what God says. God's word blesses, sanctifies – even *deifies* – precisely in the midst of created human life.« Simply said, united with Christ believers share in both natures of Christ – they are not only being »deified« but also »humanized.« Hence, in Two Kinds of Righteousness (WA 2; 148,33–149,16 = LW 31,302–303), Luther writes, »If one has wisdom, righteousness, or power with which one can excel others and boast in the ›form of God‹, so to speak, one should not keep all this to himself, but surrender it to God and become altogether as if he did not possess it [II Cor 6: 10], as one of those who lack it. Paul's meaning is that

the object of their knowledge, Christ, then Christ is the reality as such, the universal, and that believers as »little Christs,« have their reality as participating in Christ, as Christ's instantiations in the world.

The *via antiqua* hearkened back to Thomas Aquinas who as much as possible sought to harmonize the Christian faith and Aristotelian philosophy.

> Observing that in Christ grace and nature are combined, Aquinas argued that a commonality exists between God and the creature whereby grace perfects nature, and nature serves as a vehicle for grace. But this also means for the later Thomists that reason is a necessary starting point for theology, and that philosophy and theology are completely intertwined.[27]

In contrast, the *via moderna* left open »the question of the coherence of reality, of the commonality between the Creator and the creature.«[28] The *via moderna* held faith to be a separate realm of truth, though not a demonstrative science, and so »not subject to the same methods and standards of proof.«[29] For the Ockhamists, theology and philosophy do not dissolve into a unity of truth. When Ockham asserted that there were »many kings« governing a plurality of academic disciples, it would seem that he was opposing Aristotle's dictum that the »rule of many is not good; let one [reason] be the ruler.«[30] Hence, Ockham countenances the possibility

> when each person has forgotten himself and emptied himself of God's gifts, he should conduct himself as if he neighbor's weakness, sin, and foolishness were his very own. He should not boast or get puffed up. Nor should he despise or triumph over his neighbor as if he were his god or equal to God. Since God's prerogatives ought to be left to God alone, it becomes robbery when a man in haughty foolhardiness ignores this fact […]. And if we do not free desire to put off that form of God and take on the form of a servant, let us be compelled to do so against our will.«

27 R. BRADBURY, Cross Theology: The Classical Theologia Crucis and Karl Barth's Modern Theology of the Cross, 2010, 49. For an extensive discussion of the relation between Luther and Aquinas, see D. JANZ, Luther on Thomas Aquinas: The Angelic Doctor in the Thought of the Reformer, 1989.

28 BRADBURY (see n. 27), 50.

29 Ibd.

30 »Luther does not agree with this sole or absolute rule of reason, nor does William of Ockham whose philosophy of science Luther had become acquainted with through his Erfurt teacher and his own study of Biel's *Collectorium*, especially the prologue, which

of conflict between faith and reason that is irresolvable in this life. Such a distinction (though not separation) of philosophy and theology influenced Luther's view. Upping the ante, Luther's conviction that the gospel is a *promise* – a word which creates new life from the nothingness of sin and death and neither a directive nor a description of a state of affairs – further situates philosophy as belonging to the temporal and not the eternal realm.[31]

In general, the Realists affirmed a continuum between nature and grace, in which grace is able to perfect nature by healing the wound of sin and elevating finite, created being to the infinite, uncreated Being, God. For Realists, it was possible to establish a synthesis of all knowledge achieved through various gradations of reality as instantiating the triune life. By contrast, Nominalists felt that the analogical transparency of such gradations violated the very divinity of God, which for them was anchored in God's will and not God's intellect. Nominalists focused on the divine will as inscrutable while Realists focused on God's intellect whose intelligence is imprinted in the various gradations of order attested to in the world. Realism affirmed that the analogy of being (*analogia entis*) assumes a still greater difference in the midst of such great similarity between the uncreated God and his created world. By contrast, Nominalism focused not on the analogy of being but instead on »being« as a univocally shared

---

deals with the questions of the philosophy of science. Ockham is skeptical of the Aristotelian idea that science should rule supreme. His remark at the end of book 12 of Aristotle's Metaphysics, that there is not just one king but many kings, can no doubt be understood as a counter-metaphor.« See BAYER (see n. 1), 28 f.

31 Luther notes, »Gospel is and should be nothing else than a discourse or story about Christ, just as happens among men when one writes a book about a king or a prince, telling what he did, said, and suffered in his day. Such a story can be told in various ways; one spins it out, and the other is brief. Thus the gospel is and should be nothing else than a chronicle, a story, a narrative about Christ, telling who he is, what he did, said, and suffered – a subject which one describes briefly, another more fully, one this way, another that way.« See WA 10,1,1; 9,11–15 = LW 35,117 (Eyn kleyn unterricht, was man ynn den Evangelijs suchen und gewartten soll). Of course, the gospel as a creative word which creates out of nothing stands in contrast to the philosophical axiom that »out of nothing, nothing comes.«

concept between the infinite and the finite in the fact that both realities *are*.

For Nominalists, grace elevates nature by requiring humans to honor what God has enjoined humans to do via covenant (*pactum*) while, for Realists, grace perfects humans as they more and more conform to eternal law. For Luther, both views are criticized in that they fail to love God for his own sake because we eudaimonistically seek our own well being even in our quest for salvation.[32] Both views could appeal to the Aristotelian dictum, »reason pleads for the best.«[33] Hence, Luther was adverse to Aristotle's voice in matters pertaining to salvation, although he would find a place for Aristotle in logic and ethics for the good of worldly affairs (including theological inquiry). Likewise, for Luther, there is a sense in which nature as created good needs not perfection but liberation – from sin, death, and the accusations of the law. So, for Luther, theology does not perfect philosophy (Realism) nor does it do parallel play with philosophy (Nominalism); instead, it sets limits to philosophy which surreptitiously seeks to enter theology's arena (matters of infinitude and/or grace) but also exploits its logical tools for rigorous clarification of doctrine.

For some time there has been a tendency to »cast« Aquinas as a veritable »rationalist« in order to contrast his view of faith and reason in opposition to Ockham's alleged »fideism.« But as Alfred Freddoso notes, this opposition engenders »exaggerated estimates of the degree of confidence that Aquinas and Scotus repose in natural reason.«[34] All medieval theologians believed that »divine revelation is absolutely necessary« for humans to flourish and »that, as far as ultimate metaphysical and moral questions

---

32 See T. DIETER, Why Does Luther's Doctrine of Justification Matter Today? (in: The Global Luther: A Theologian for Modern Times, ed. by C. HELMER, 2009, 189–209), 194–196.

33 Luther was fond of criticizing this expropriation of Aristotle's thinking for late Medieval scholastic soteriology. See WA 42; 107,34–38 = LW 1,143 where Luther indicates that »when they say: ›Reason pleads for the best‹, you should say: ›For the best in a mundane sense that is, in things about which reason can judge‹. There it directs and leads to what is honorable and useful in respect to the body or the flesh.« Luther makes a sharp distinction between the temporal and the eternal and situates philosophy as appropriate in the former while theology alone is appropriate in the latter.

34 See A. FREDDOSO, Ockham on Faith and Reason, http://www.3nd.edu/-afreddos/papers/ f&rcam.htm, for all references in this paragraph.

are concerned, we remain in an utterly perilous state of ignorance without it.«[35] Even in Thomas's approach to reason and faith, philosophy and theology, »theological inquirers cannot have *scientia* with respect to the conclusions of theology. This is a point Ockham emphasizes repeatedly in his critique of the claim that ›our theology‹ counts as a science.«[36] Ockham offers an »irenic separatism« that rejects

> the prototypically Catholic intellectual project of unifying classical philosophy and the Christian faith in such a way as to exhibit the latter as the perfection of the former, and yet that stops short of disdaining the light of natural reason in the manner of radical intellectual separatism.

Overall, such an Ockhamist spirit seems to be operative in Luther's distinction between philosophy and theology as »two spheres.« If anything, Luther – less irenic than Ockham – accentuates the distinction between philosophy and theology since he will indulge no *mixing* between philosophy and theology,[37] providing no philosophical fuel that might aid the free

---

35 Freddoso notes that »Aquinas divides divinely revealed truths into what he elsewhere calls the mysteries [or: articles] of the faith, which ›altogether exceed the capability of human reason‹, and the preambles of the faith, which can at least in principle be established by the light of natural reason. Ockham draws a similar distinction between theological truths that we are naturally able to have evident cognition of and theological truths that we can have cognition of only supernaturally.«

36 Freddoso indicates that »Aquinas cites approvingly Aristotle's dictum that natural reason is as incapable of comprehending the most intelligible natures as the eye of an owl is of viewing the sun.« Hence, for both Thomas and Ockham, »philosophical inquiry unaided by divine revelation can help foster logical skills and intellectual habits that are required for the articulation of true wisdom within Christian theology; it can even provide Christian thinkers with new and useful conceptual resources. But it cannot on its own make any noteworthy progress toward providing us with the substance of absolute wisdom.«

37 Luther maintains that the Scholastics mistaken notion of seeing faith as a habit is due to the fact that they have obscured faith by mixing Aristotelian philosophy with theology. Hence, he notes, »Philosophy and theology must be carefully distinguished. Philosophy also speaks of a good will and of right reason, and the sophists are forced to admit that a work is not morally good unless a good will is present first. And yet they are such stupid asses when they proceed to theology. They want to prescribe a work before the good will, although in philosophy it is necessary for the person to be justified morally

will in its conviction that it can make progress in righteousness *coram deo* and so marginalize faith.

III *Luther's Divergences from Nominalism*

Nominalism's assumption of a *pactum de potentia ordinata* between God and humanity in which God will give his grace to those who do their very best (*facere quod in se est*), maintained by Gabriel Biel, was Luther's chief target in his early attempt to understand the true nature of human justification *coram deo*. In spite of Luther's self-identity as a »terminist« it is hard to imagine that his rejection of a Nominalist view of salvation would have no impact whatsoever on his reception of philosophy. Bengt Hägglund pointed out that, unlike Nominalist psychology which assumed reason's capacity to submit itself to the imperative to conform to the truth that God as the Supreme Being ought to be loved above all things, Luther affirmed instead that we rebel against grace and are unable to control our interior will.[38] Nor for Luther is grace to be understood as an infused new quality in the regenerate but instead is »the divine mercy that brings about the forgiveness of sins. As the Spirit of God gives life, so grace confers that eternal life which is given us in and with the forgiveness of sins.«[39] But given that the Nominalists held that God of his absolute power (*de potentia absoluta*) could declare humans »righteous only because God accepts« them »as such quite apart from any infusion of grace« (the doctrine of acceptance),[40] Luther was decisively anti-Nominalist. For Luther, »imputation is nothing else but the work of grace. And grace, instead of being the arbitrary will of God, works the justification of the sinner because of Jesus Christ.«[41] Nominalist views of justification as construed either through the lens of *de potentia ordinata* or *de potentia*

---

before the work. Thus the tree is prior to the fruit, both in essence and in nature.« See WA 40,1; 410,14–20 = LW 26,261.
38 B. HÄGGLUND, Was Luther a Nominalist? (Theology 59, 1956, 226–234), 227.
39 Loc. cit., 228.
40 Loc. cit., 229.
41 Ibd.

absoluta fail to acknowledge that our justification is *propter Christum* (for the sake of Christ).

Jettisoning any saving efficacy for the law, Luther heightens the distinction between faith and works. Works are crucial for the well-being of the neighbor, not for our salvation. Luther construes philosophy as parallel to works or law and theology as parallel to God's favor or grace. With respect to salvation Christ alone means that the law codified as the *pactum* offers nothing *coram deo*. No longer given the aura of a manual to salvation, the law is restored as a way to order life *coram mundo*. It is relegated to temporal matters and loses any potency in eternal matters. But Luther notes that the Nominalist perspective also appeals to philosophy as a way to affirm human activity *coram deo*. In so doing, such »sophist« mixing of philosophy with theology marginalizes the efficacious role of an active Christ. Speaking against the Faculty of the Sorbonne, Luther in 1539 writes:

> But here we especially oppose the men at the Sorbonne who allow such things as the forgiveness of sins and the mystery of the incarnation and eternal life to be deduced by logic. They have asserted that they are there and can be obtained by living according to the law and through philosophy. This we deny. For they speak thus and allege that whoever has done what he was able to do is justified and merits grace according to his fitness, and afterward even in strict justice. This we deny. What use would there be here for Christ? He would be set aside and buried completely. For when they want to be justified altogether without Christ, what else are they doing than consigning Christ to oblivion so that Christ might be completely useless for us and have died in vain? We admit that philosophy teaches and all men know by nature that theft is unlawful, as are many other things. But we cannot and ought not tolerate the fact that these chief theological articles – for whose sake alone Scripture was given – namely, those concerning justification, the forgiveness of sins, liberation from eternal death, are actually attributed to philosophy and human powers.[42]

In a word, philosophy knows nothing of grace – which is the most important thing to know.[43] Just as an active – unburied Christ – relativizes law and gives it its appropriate locus in temporal matters, so philosophy is similarly relativized by the gospel *promissio* – a move which, given their

---

42 WA 39,2; 13,10–14,6 (Die Disputationen über Joh 1,14) = LW 38,248.
43 Luther writes that philosophers know nothing of mercy and truth. See WA 43; 242,21–22 (Genesisvorlesung) = LW 4,148.

soteriology of human contribution to justification, Nominalists could not make. For Luther, philosophy has its full voice in temporal matters, not eternal matters. In the same disputation, he notes,

> we say that theology does not contradict philosophy because the latter speaks only about matrimony, obedience, chastity, liberality, and other virtues. But it is one thing to believe in the Son of God, to posses and to expect eternal life, and something else again to be chaste, to marry, to live honestly in the world, to be liberal, meek, obedient, kind, and peaceable.[44]

As noted above, for Aristotle, reason had a divine status in the theoretical, contemplative life. In contrast, Luther shifts the focus of the divine dimension of human reason to the »active life« of human beings where reason is capable of making sound decisions about the economy, politics, and natural sciences. Luther reverses the Augustinian and scholastic distinction between a superior part (*a portio superiore*) and an inferior part (*a portio inferiore*) of reason with respect to faith. In the traditional Augustinian scheme, the superior part of reason

> is directed toward the *aeterna*, or eternal things, and the inferior part is directed toward the *temporalia*, the temporal objects. This distinction also reflects two different acts of knowledge: the superior part of reason is intellectual (*intelligere*), knowing something in its simple wholeness, and the inferior part employs discursive thinking (*ratiocinari*). This distinction in other words is the distinction between wisdom and science. The Scholastics, like Augustine, distinguished between use (*uti*) and enjoyment (*frui*), which means that all *temporarlia* are meant to be used by us, and all *aeterna* are meant to be enjoyed by us – and not to be used.[45]

Luther rejects this classic distinction between the superior and inferior parts of reason and distinguishes instead between reason (*ratio*) and faith (*fides*).

> any relationship between human beings and God (and all eternal things) is not conceived by reason – not even by a superior part of reason. Faith alone is the vehicle and instrument by which the human person is related to the triune God [...]. Reason is, thereby, freed by faith from any illusions of attaining God on its own capacity.[46]

---

44 WA 39,2; 14,8–13 = LW 38,248.
45 H.-P. GROSSHANS, Luther on Faith and Reason: The Light of Reason at the Twilight of the World (in: The Global Luther, [see n. 32], 173–185), 181.
46 Ibd.

While demarcating philosophy as a demonstrable science in contradistinction to theology as grounded in revelation that is to be accepted on the basis of the authority, Hägglund noted that Nominalism also affirmed that

> not only are certain theological truths are accessible to reason and that those that rest on a supernatural revelation can, after the event, become the object of rational speculation. Theological knowledge is, so to speak, on the same level as rational knowledge. The chief difference between them is that the former presupposes revelation and faith, faith being conceived as the submission of the will to the authority of revealed truth.[47]

For Nominalists, humans are capable of producing saving faith on the basis of one's natural powers. »Free will is then capable of adhering to truths of faith which ecclesiastical authority proposes to it.«[48] When useful for theology, *recta ratio* is defined not from nature but from grace. Such reasoning will follow the narrative of the gospel as outlined and presented in scripture.

Repeatedly Luther cautions that when there is conflict between philosophy and theology – as invariably there must be since philosophy knows nothing of God's grace, nor can it encompass God's infinity which transcends all human conceptuality –, then »all thought (no doubt this also includes philosophy) is to be taken captive to the obedience of Christ (II Cor 10: 5)«[49] and following Ambrose he argues that »the dialecticians have to give way where the apostolic fishermen are to be trusted.«[50] Syllogistic reasoning is an excellent approach to academic inquiry, but it is useful only to the extent that it conveys the subject matter. And, the subject matter of theology – the sinful human needing justification and the God who justifies in Christ as promise – cannot be encompassed by reason. Rather, it is reason which must be subject to Christ.

The means by which Luther limits the scope of philosophy to temporal matters is nothing other than his distinction between law and gospel.

---

47 HÅGGLUND (see n. 38), 231.
48 Ibd.
49 WA 39,2; 4,6–7 (Die Disputationen über Joh 1,14, 1539) = LW 38,239 (thesis 8).
50 WA 39,2; 4,8–9 = LW 38,239 (thesis 9).

The meaning of the law is, under various circumstances, known to the philosophers. But the promises of God belong to theology, and the gospel is not known to every creature because it is a mystery hidden from the world.[51]

Philosophy is akin to law as theology is akin to gospel. Just like God's promise actually affirms the law by situating it within *temporarlia* where it properly belongs, indicating that antinomianism is inappropriate, so also there is no »antinomianism of philosophy.« Even as the law abides for sinners as an instructor and accuser, so philosophy abides as practical thinking about furthering human life, community, and service. It also, as we shall see, can provide theology useful logical tools to establish sound doctrine, once thinking is taken captive to Christ (and not vice versa).

IV Aristotle's Inadequacies and Adequacies

As is well known, Luther at times disparaged Aristotle (designated by medieval theologians as »the philosopher«) for Aristotle's discrepancies from scripture and the misuse of Aristotelian reasoning in Nominalist schemes of salvation.[52] Luther repeatedly noted that neither Aristotle's cosmology nor his psychology squares with scripture. For Aristotle, the world is eternal while the soul is mortal, a reversal of scriptural truth.[53] Even so, Luther appeals to Aristotle's conviction that the goal of life is happiness. Here, Aristotle has an inkling of the truth.[54] The problem is that Aristotle's God,

51 WA 39,2; 5,3–4 = LW 38,258 (argument 24).
52 For the most thorough recent studies of Luther on Aristotle, see T. DIETER, Der junge Luther und Aristoteles. Eine historisch-systematische Untersuchung zum Verhältnis von Theologie und Philosophie, 2001 and E. ANDREATTA, Lutero e Aristotele, 1996.
53 WA 42; 3,31–4,1 (Genesisvorlesung) = LW 1,3–4.
54 »Aristotle says something worthwhile when he declares that the goal of man is happiness, which consists in a virtuous life. But in view of the weakness of our nature who can reach this goal? Even those who are the most fortunate encounter discomforts of various kinds, which both misfortune and the ill will and meanness of men bring on. For such happiness peace of mind is necessary. But who can always preserve this amid the great changes of fortunate? It is vain, therefore, to point out this goal which no one reaches. The main goal, then, to which Scripture points is that man is created according to the likeness of God; in eternity, therefore, he is to live with God, and while he is here on earth, he is to preach God, thank Him, and patiently obey His Word. In this life we lay hold of this goal in ever so weak a manner; but in the future life we shall attain it

who cares nothing for the world but only for himself, can never be the *telos* of human life. Aristotle's God knows nothing of grace. While God exists for Aristotle, Aristotle's God simply does not communicate with humans, which is vital for Luther's understanding of God. Hence, Luther is quick to respond about this Aristotelian God, »He means nothing to us.«[55] However, Luther's rapport with Aristotle is far broader than this. As can be seen in *The Disputation Concerning Man* (1536), Luther does not reject Aristotle's theory of fourfold causality consisting of the efficient (from whence does the matter come?), material (in what does it consist?), formal (as what does it exist?), and final (toward what does it aim?) causes but does indicate its inadequacy for theological anthropology. What is problematic is the limited epistemological access which humans have about themselves with respect to ultimate matters. Here, philosophy offers only »fragmentary, fleeting, and exceedingly material« knowledge.[56] We scarcely perceive humanity's material cause sufficiently, and philosophy does not know the efficient nor final cause for certain.[57] Instead, it is through scriptural revelation that we learn that »man is a creature of God consisting of body and a living soul, made in the beginning after the image of God, without sin, so that he should procreate and rule over the created things, and never die.«[58] The problem is not with reason as such which is »most excellent,« indeed »a sun and a kind of god appointed to administer these things in this life.« (Indeed, after the fall, God did not »take away this majesty of reason, but rather confirmed it.«[59]) Rather, the problem is that we finite and sinful creatures are too distanced from these truths. It is through Paul that we properly understand that it is justification by faith alone which briefly sums up the definition of humanity.[60]

fully. This the philosophers do not know. Therefore the world with its greatest wisdom is most ignorant when it does not take advantage of Holy Scripture or of theology. Human beings know neither their beginning nor their end when they are without the Word.« See WA 42; 98,13–26 (Genesisvorlesung) = LW 1,131.
55 WA 43; 240,30 (Genesisvorlesung) = LW 4,145 (translation altered).
56 WA 39,1; 175,3–4 (Die Disputation de homine) = LW 34,138 (thesis 19).
57 WA 39,1; 175,26–29 = LW 34,138 (theses 12–13).
58 WA 39,1; 176,7–9 = LW 34,138 (thesis 21).
59 WA 39,1; 175,24–25 = LW 34,137–138 (thesis 11).
60 WA 39,1; 176,33–35 = LW 34,139 (thesis 32).

V Early Appropriation of Plato

In spite of Luther's rejection of a hierarchy between *a portio superior* and *a portio inferior*, we can discern an appropriation of aspects of Plato's thinking, especially in his early theology. This appropriation of Plato's thinking over Aristotle's is likely traced to his intense reading of Augustine as well as German mystics such as Tauler and the anonymous author of *Theologia Deutsch*, a book he edited early in his career. In his explanation of thesis eight of the philosophical theses of the *Heidelberg Disputation* (1518) Luther argued that Aristotle who »insists on the priority of the sensible« only *seems* to give knowledge of reality.[61] As Knut Alfsvåg notes, for Luther, Aristotle's epistemology arises from the senses. So, for Aristotle, if knowledge is to obtain, then (unlike Plato) form and matter cannot be separated. But for Luther, such an approach is tied to the »instability« and uncertainty of the senses and thus fails to convey the eternal. In fact, with Plato, we should affirm the »priority of the infinite and divine. True knowledge is according to Luther dependent on the acceptance of unkowability.«[62] There is no *proportio* between the Creator and created things, and thus no ladder between what we can perceive and the »invisible things of God« can be constructed for the *viator*. Hence, the »visible and manifest things of God« are to be seen only »through suffering and the cross.« So, in the following thesis (nine), Luther argues that Pythagorus and especially Plato, unlike Aristotle, appropriately integrate the infinite and the finite in the concept of participation.[63] Alfsvåg notes:

> As evidence for the latter, Luther explicitly refers to what he calls the most beautiful discussion of oneness in Parmenides, where the author first deprives oneness of every-

---

61 See K. Alfsvåg (see n. 3), 194. For a translation of the Heidelberg Disputation's philosophical theses into German, see H. Junghans, Die probationes zu den philosophischen Thesen der Heidelberger Disputation Luthers im Jahre 1518 (LuJ 46, 1979, 10–59). This article contains both Latin and German; however, the Latin text can also be found in WA 59; 409–425. Thesis 36 reads: »Aristotle wrongly finds fault with and derides the ideas of Plato, which actually are better than his own.« WA 1; 355.

62 Alfsvåg (see n. 3), 194.

63 Thesis 37 reads: »The mathematical order of material things is ingeniously maintained by Pythagoras, but more ingenious is the interaction of ideas maintained by Plato.« See WA 1; 355 (Disputatio Heidelbergae habita. 1518) = LW 31,42.

thing until it is reduced to nothing, and then gives everything back until there is nothing left in which oneness is not. There is thus nothing that does not exist through oneness, which in this way at the same time is outside of and in everything.[64]

Since God is incomprehensible and invisible, we simply cannot move, as Luther notes in the theological theses of the Heidelberg Disputation, from knowledge of creatures to their creator. This truth is decisive for his rejection of a »theology of glory« and his approval of a »theology of the cross.« As important as this move is for Luther's theological development in distinguishing law from gospel and associating the gospel with a word of promise, Luther would increasingly challenge the »speculation« inherent in Platonism and Christian Platonists' neglect of the word of God. Or, said differently, a consistent *via negativa* leads not only to negating divine attributes and then negating these negations, but also to the negation or death of the theologian himself or herself since such an apophatic approach gains us only the *deus absconditus* and thus functions as God's *opus alienum*. Only in the word does God wish to be found.[65]

Nevertheless, Luther's consistent perspective that God is a given for all people not especially needing demonstration seems to be grounded in a Platonic view of anamnesis as can be seen in Luther's description of the terrified sailors who flee to God in his *Commentary on Jonah* (1526). Luther perceives the general revelation of God less through the lens of inference on the basis of design in nature or the goal of human life and more through an anamnesis in which all people have a memory that there is a God.[66]

For Luther, the existence of God is never in doubt. But God's disposition toward humankind is.

> That there is a God, by whom all things were made, that you know from his works, [...] but God himself, who he is, what sort of divine Being he is, and how he is disposed toward you – this you can never discover nor experience from the outside.[67]

---

64 ALFSVÅG (see n. 3), 195.
65 See Alfsvåg's discussion in What No Mind Has Conceived, 197.
66 WA 19; 205,27–206,7 = LW 19,53.
67 WA 51; 150,42–151,3.

True knowledge of God must acknowledge awareness that God cares for his world. This divine love is foreign to philosophers, even the likes of Plato.

> Philosophers argue and ask speculative questions about God and arrive at some kind of knowledge, just as Plato looks at and acknowledges the government of God. But everything is merely objective; it is not yet that knowledge which Joseph has, that God cares, that He hears the afflicted and helps them. Plato cannot determine this; he remains in his metaphysical thinking, as a cow looks at a new door.[68]

If one is to have true knowledge of God, one cannot escape the forensic, *pro me* dimension if such knowledge is in fact true.

> You have the true knowledge of God when you believe and know that God and Christ are your God and your Christ. This the devil and the false Christians cannot believe. Thus this knowledge is nothing else than the true Christian faith; for when you know God and Christ in this way, you will rely on Him with all your heart and trust in Him in good fortune and misfortune, in life and death.[69]

To call Luther's view of knowledge of God »existentialist« would be anachronistic, but it is true to say that Luther's perspective is highly experiential without permitting experience to be a source or norm for theology. Of course, our experience with God is often quite painful for, as you remember, »it is by living – no, not living, but by dying and giving ourselves up to hell that we become theologians, not by understanding, reading, and speculating.«[70]

VI The Question of Double Truth

In his 1539 *Disputation Concerning the Passage: ›Word Was Made Flesh‹* Luther maintains that even though »every truth is in agreement with every other truth,« still »what is true in one field of learning is not always true in other fields of learning.«[71] His chief example is the Christological principle that in theology »it is true that the Word was made flesh« but in

---

68 WA 44; 591,34–39 = LW 8,17.
69 WA 14; 16 = LW 30,152.
70 WA 5; 163,28f.
71 WA 39,2; 3,1–2 (Die Disputationen über Joh 1,14) = LW 38,239 (thesis 1).

philosophy the »statement is simply impossible and absurd.«[72] Was Luther an advocate of the »double truth« theory, that what is true in philosophy may be false in theology and vice versa?

In this disputation, Luther takes the Scholastic axiom *nulla est proportio finite ad infiniti* (»there is no relationship between the finite and the infinite«) as a philosophical given. The infinite cannot be made finite and still remain infinite.[73] But this is exactly what has happened in the incarnation. Luther proceeds by developing a series of syllogisms which are formally sound philosophically but which result in false conclusions in theology. He also provides examples from the »other arts and sciences that the same thing is not true in all of them,« for instance, an incommensurability between the measurements of lines and weights.[74]

Luther rejects the position of the Sorbonne that the same is true in philosophy and theology. His point is that in their attempt to defend univocal truth between philosophy and theology, they equivocate on the nature of humanity as shared by all people and Christ. The Sorbonne's position represents a reaction against »double truth theory« of Latin Averroism (radical Aristotelianism), which had been championed by Siger of Brabant (c. 1235–c. 1282).[75] Following up on Parisian Bishop Stephen Tempier's gen-

---

72 WA 39,2; 3,3–4 = LW 38,239 (thesis 2).

73 The phrase as such can be traced to Scotus but it can be found through medieval scholasticism, including Thomas Aquinas and Bonaventure. The phrase was used by these earlier figures as »just one aspect of the *analogia entis*, to be complemented by the notion of a likeness or relation between God and humanity. The nominalists, in opposing Thomistic Christology, emphasize the distinction in a stronger way than their predecessors.« See D. W. CONGDON, Nova Lingua Dei: The Problem of Chalcedonian Metaphysics and the Promise of the Genus Tapeinoticon in Luther's Later Theology, unpublished paper, 2011, 42, n. 126.

74 WA 39,2; 5,19–20 = LW 38,242 (thesis 32). Theses 16–25 develop syllogism which are structurally sound philosophically but conclude with false beliefs theologically. Theses 29–37 offer examples of matters true in one discipline but not in another.

75 This position can be traced to the Muslim philosopher Averroes (1126–1198) known as the »Commentator« on Aristotle. Since Averroes judged Aristotle to be the pinnacle of human intellect but his views did not always correspond with the Quran, he proposed a double truth. »This does not mean that [...] a proposition can be true in philosophy and false in theology or vice versa: his theory is that one and the same truth is understood clearly in philosophy and expressed allegorically in theology. The scientific formulation

eral condemnation (219 condemnations) of Latin Averroism on March 7, 1277,[76] Edward Kilwardby, Archbishop of Canterbury, on March 18, 1277, published thirty prohibited propositions, known as the Oxford condemnation. The first two condemned theses read:

1. *Quod contraria simul possunt esse vera in aliqua materia* (that contraries can be simultaneously true in a certain subject-matter).
2. *Item quod syllogismus pecans in material non est sillogismus* (that the syllogism which is materially erroneous [with respect to a subject-matter] is not a syllogism).[77]

> By rejecting the first thesis, Kilwardby seems to affirm that truth is univocal; there can only be one kind of attribution of truth. In rejecting the second thesis, it is affirmed that as long as a syllogism is formally correct, it remains rational regardless of the subject-matter. These theses, along with the others, together imply a rejection of any contradiction between philosophy and theology; what is rational and true in one subject-matter must be rational and true in the other.[78]

Luther is no advocate of double truth theory, but he does maintain that philosophy and theology constitute two distinct spheres with their own distinct logics. The univocal approach to truth advocated by the Sorbonne would result in the »articles of faith« to be »subject to the judgment of human reason.«[79]

In their attempt to establish univocal truth in philosophy and theology the Sorbonne actually equivocates. The word »man« ends up meaning one thing in reference to humans generally and another in reference to the Word made flesh. Hence the syllogism:

of truth is achieved only in philosophy, but the same truth is expressed in theology, only in a different manner.« See CONGDON (see n.73), 29–30, quoting Frederick Copleston. While privileging philosophy over theology, Averroes still maintained the unity of truth. In contrast, Siger allowed philosophy to contradict theology in favor of philosophy.

76 Here Bishop Tempier rejected the view that »things are true according to philosophy, but not according to the catholic faith, as if there are two contrary truths.«
77 Denifle and Chatelain, Chartularium Universitatis Parisiensis, 1:558, as quoted by CONGDON (see n.73), 31.
78 Ibd.
79 WA 39,2; 4,2–3 = LW 38,239 (thesis 6).

1. Every man is a creature.
2. Christ is a man.
3. Therefore, Christ is a creature.[80]

Luther notes that this is a sound syllogism in philosophy but in theology has an erroneous conclusion. As Reijo Työrinoja notes,

> According to the philosophical argumentation, there is no proportion between the Creator and a creature, infinite and finite. But in theology, Luther states, there is not only a proportion, but in Christ the unity of finite and infinite (*unitas finiti et infiniti*). Therefore the predicates of God and man are the same.[81]

The point is that the above syllogism fails to follow theological grammar. Luther notes that with respect to such syllogistic reasoning the fault is not due to a

> defect of the syllogistic form but because of the lofty character and majesty of the matter which cannot be enclosed in the narrow confines of reason or syllogism. So the matter is not indeed something contrary to, but is outside, within, above, below, before, and beyond all logical truth.[82]

While the

> syllogism is a most excellent form [...] it is useless with regard to the matter itself. Therefore, in articles of faith one must have recourse to another dialectic and philosophy, which is called the word of God and faith.[83]

---

80 WA 39,2; 5,3–4 = LW 38,241 (thesis 24) translation altered.
81 R. Työrinoia, Nova Vocabula et Nova Lingua: Luther's Conception of Doctrinal Formulas (in: Thesaurus Lutheri. Auf der Suche nach neuen Paradigmen der Luther-Forschung, 1987, 221–236), 229. As a rule, Luther does not generalize expressions like unity of finite and infinite, but limits that very concretely to the incarnation and the person of Christ. Melanchthon, Chemnitz, and others make it more explicit perhaps, or emphasize it more, but Luther does not argue for a general unity of the finite and the infinite but limits it to the person of Christ.
82 WA 39,2; 4,34–35 = LW 38,241 (thesis 21).
83 WA 39,2; 5,9–10 = LW 38,241 (thesis 27).

VII Priority of Grammar over Logic

For Luther, philosophy, including logic, is beholden to grammar (semantical analysis). His view came to the fore in his debates with Zwingli and Oecolampadius over the nature of the Lord's Supper.[84] Following the Roman rhetorician Quintilian on the nature of metaphor or »transfers of words« (new words or tropes) produced according to the rules of comparison, Luther indicates that a word such as »vine« has both an old and a new meaning. In the old sense it means simply the stock in the vineyard. But »according to the new it means Christ, Jn 15[: 5]: ›I am the vine‹.«[85] Luther explains how Christ himself is the basis on which the comparison is made. »For Christ is not a likeness of the vine, but on the contrary the vine is a likeness of Christ.« Explaining the word »seed« in »the seed is the word of God« [Lk 8: 11], Luther says,

> here the word ›seed‹ does not indicate the grain, which is a simile of the gospel, but as a new word or trope should, signifies the gospel, the true, new seed itself, which is not a likeness. And so forth; all tropes in Scripture signify the true, new object, and not the simile of this new object.[86]

Luther agrees with his opponents that »it is undeniably true that two diverse substances cannot be one substance. For example, an ass cannot be an ox, a man cannot be a stone or a piece of wood.«[87] This, of course, follows the law of contradiction and it makes it problematic for reason to be able to affirm that bread simultaneously can be Christ's body. Luther notes that Wycliffe solved the problem by affirming that bread remains bread while Christ's body is literally absent, while Aquinas maintained that Christ's body is literally present but the bread is absent. Luther responds, »against all reason and hairsplitting logic I hold that two diverse

---

84 See WA 26; 437–445 (Vom Abendmahl Christi. Bekenntnis) = LW 37,294–303. For a sound commentary on this treatise, see J. Baur, Luther und die Philosophie (NZST 26, 1984, 13–28) and E. de Negri, Offenbarung und Dialektik. Luthers Realtheologie, 1973, 207–218.

85 WA 26; 379,27 = LW 37,252–253.

86 WA 26; 380,27–33 = LW 37,253.

87 WA 26; 439,6–7 = LW 37,295.

substances may well be, in reality and in name, one substance.«[88] Building his case, he provides examples of how two distinct beings can be one. The Trinity, for example, is a »natural union« of the three triune persons sharing the same essence. Likewise, Christ is one person with two natures, a »personal union.« There is also a »union of effect« when angels are described in scripture as winds and flames of fire. Similarly there is a »formal union« when the Holy Spirit is seen as a dove. All this makes plausible Luther's contention that there is a »sacramental union« in which bread can be Christ's body and wine can be Christ's blood. He chides Wycliffe's view of an absent Christ in the host for prematurely applying logic and not taking into account the rules of grammar or the science of words.

> Logic rightly teaches that bread and body, dove and Spirit, God and man are diverse beings. But it should first seek the aid of grammar, which lays down a rule of expression applicable to all languages: when two diverse beings become one being, grammar embraces these two things in a single expression, and as it views the union of the two beings, it refers to the two in one term.[89]

Grammatically, Luther maintains that his examples are expressions of synecdoche. Hence, Luther concludes,

> No *identical* predication is even there; Wycliffe and the sophists only dream that it is. For even though body and bread are two distinct substances, each one existing by itself, and though neither is mistaken for the other where they are separated from each other, nevertheless where they are united and become a new, entire substance, they lose their difference so far as this new, unique substances is concerned.[90]

Hence we can see why in the *Disputation on the Divinity and Humanity of Christ* (1541) that Luther maintained that »it is certain that with regard to Christ [*in Christo*] all words receive a new signification, though the thing signified is the same.«[91] He was building on his understanding of grammar as accountable to the narrative of Jesus Christ who is the truth.

---

88 WA 26; 439,29–31 = LW 37,296.
89 WA 26; 443,12–16 = LW 37,301.
90 WA 26; 445,1–6 = LW 37,303.
91 WA 39,2; 94 = Disputation on the Divinity and Humanity of Christ, trans. C.B. Brown (http://www.leaderu.com/philosophy/luther-humanitychrist.html), thesis 20, page 2.

In the old usage of language »creature« signifies (causes us to think[92]) »a thing separated from divinity by infinite degrees« while in the new usage creature »signifies a thing inseparably joined with divinity in the same person in an ineffable way.«[93] Indeed, words like »man, humanity, suffered« and »everything that is said of Christ, are new words.«[94] With Ingolf Dalferth, we can conclude that philosophy and theology deal not with different things but with the same things in different ways.[95]

92 See D. BIELFELDT, Luther's Late Trinitarian Disputations: Semantic Realism and the Trinity (in: The Substance of Faith: Luther's Doctrinal Theology for Today, ed. by D. BIELFELDT/M. MATTOX/P. HINLICKY 2008, 59–130), 109.

93 WA 39,2; 94,19–20 = Disputation on the Divinity and Humanity of Christ, thesis 21, page 2.

94 WA 39,2; 94,23–24 = Disputation on the Divinity and Humanity of Christ, thesis 23, page 2.

95 DALFERTH, Theology and Philosophy (see n. 19), 77, says »According to Luther, philosophy and theology are fundamentally different, yet they neither contradict nor complement each other (WA 39,2; 27,31–32). Philosophy has the world for its field and whatever it talks about, even in metaphysics, must make itself felt in the present and experienced world. Theology, on the other hand, has ›the invisible things as subject‹ (WA 39,2; 15,8–9), i.e., those ›which are believed, i.e., which are apprehended by faith‹ (WA 39,2; 6,26–28). This looks like the traditional distinction between the knowable and the merely credible. But it is not. Philosophy and theology are neither different stages in our knowledge of things nor knowledge about different sorts of things. They are different kinds of knowledge of the same things, placed in different perspectives and different frames of reference: viz. the *coram mundo-deo*-perspective of its relations to God. Both perspectives are necessary for an adequate understanding of reality; both allow for growth of knowledge and a perfecting of our understanding of God, world and human existence; but there is no transition from knowledge in the first perspective to knowledge in the second, and thus no direct combination of knowledge achieved in the one frame with knowledge achieved in the second. Confusion is bound to result from mixing philosophical discourse about things *coram mundo* with theological discourse about things *coram deo*; and precisely this mixing of discourses Luther diagnoses as having been the endemic evil of scholastic theology.« With respect to grammar, Risto Saarinen notes, »it can be observed that Luther distinguishes theological grammar from philosophical. However, theological grammar is for him by no means an esoteric code that has normal words and everyday phrases as its external manifestation. The difference between philosophical and theological grammar is, linguistically speaking, not primarily a syntactic but a *semantic* and a *pragmatic* difference. The specific art of theological grammar is determined by its subject matter, namely, by the *significata* of biblical language. The

Theology acknowledges a new signification for the same thing in Christ. In the old usage there can be no inclusion of the property of humanity in the property of God. But in the new, the property of the divine conjoins itself with the property of the human. Hence, the Sorbonne must be wrong in maintaining a univocal view of truth shared between philosophy and theology. It fails to acknowledge the newness of words transposed in Christ. This »eschatological« dimension[96] – for lack of a better term – of Christ the *novum* both constitutes the old as old, but does not eliminate or dismiss it but allows it to stand in its own unique temporality and likewise can incorporate it in theology with its own intelligibility. As Luther notes,

> We would act more correctly if we left dialectic and philosophy in their own area and learned to speak in a new language in the realm of faith apart from every sphere. Otherwise, it will turn out that, if we put the new wine in old wineskins, both of them will perish.[97]

VIII The Semantics of the New Tongue

But this raises the question about Luther's Christological syllogism outlined above: what semantic theory would allow (1) and (2) to be true, but (3) false? Is it the case that new meanings of terms emerge within theological contexts or is it the case that no real difference in meanings exists between the terms within the two languages but there is only a difference in the inferences permitted? It would seem that different rules govern theology and philosophy. Just as different rules apply in regions within philosophy, so too are there different rules operative between theology and philosophy. Dennis Bielfeldt has cogently argued that Luther should not be seen here as having employed standard Ockhamist supposition the-

---

presence of the unique subject matter, the new entity (*nova res*), implies that even the way of the understanding that new entity and the modes of speaking about its properties have to be unique, although these new ways and modes are, nevertheless, conveyed by normal, everyday words.« See R. SAARINEN, The Word of God in Luther's Theology (LuthQ 4, 1990, 31–44), 39f.

96 DALFERTH (see n. 19), 79.

97 WA 39,2; 5,35–38 (Die Disputationen über Joh 1,14) = LW 38,242 (theses 40–41).

ory. Supposition is a semantic relation between the terms in a proposition and the things to which those terms refer (their extension).[98] Since Ockham rejected the existence of real universals or common natures, written and spoken terms must »primarily« signify individuals, »the things they can be truly predicated of.« For example in the proposition »the cow is red« is true, the term »cow« supposits for the same individual for which the term »red« supposits. Late medieval supposition theory understood the truth conditions and the meaning of statements extensionally, that is, by whether or not they supposit for the same individual or individuals. By contrast, the *via antiqua* was more intensionalist. Bielfeldt argues:

> All men are rational is true if and only if ›man‹ signifies (causes the mind to think about) a property inexorably instanced only if the property signified by ›rational‹ is instanced. An intension of a predicate specifies all and only those properties a thing must have in order for the predicate truly to apply to it. An extension, on the other hand, is the class of things to which the predicate rightly applies. In an intensionalist semantics, the intension establishes the conditions by virtue of which extension is determined.[99]

Bielfeldt asks whether »God is man« is best understood in an nominalistic, extensional sense or in an intensionalist way. He answers that if »God is man« is construed intensionally, then the property of being God does not exclude the property of being a man. In theology, this is the truth of the incarnation. But this is impossible in philosophy. Here specification of the properties of God includes that of being infinite. But since human beings are not infinite, specification of God-making properties must include the property of not being a human being. Thus, the conceptual rules by which theology proceeds must differ from philosophy, because terms such as »God« and »mother« do not exclude predication by man and virgin respectively. Indeed, the terms »God« and »mother« have different significations in theology and philosophy respectively. They cause one to think about different things in philosophy and theology, as one would expect in signification theory.

The upshot of Bielfeldt's case is that theological truth cannot be reduced to that which can be said philosophically. Hence Luther refuses

---

98 Bielfeldt, Luther's Late Trinitarian Disputations (see n. 92), 111.
99 Loc. cit., 113.

the notion that there could be one vast tree of Porphyry in which only theology has access to some of the branches. Hence, with Christ, something new has emerged.[100] The semantics of the *via antiqua* can serve as a suitable vehicle of Christ the *novum*.

IX Conclusion

The distinction between law and gospel governs Luther's approach to philosophy. Nominalism and Realism are no longer alternatives for him because their conclusions must each be evaluated in light of the law/gospel distinction. Luther charts a new path beyond that philosophical debate in which universals as an ontological reality and not merely generalizations, as Realists contend, may prove to be appropriate in theology but his overall positioning of philosophy in relation to theology has a Nominalist contour. Philosophy is limited by the fact that it knows nothing of the incarnation and is not able to accommodate its truth; nor does philosophy have a sense of God's grace. But it does have its place when restricted to this-worldly matters. Even so, Luther values syllogistic reasoning and uses it in theology when it is accountable to theological grammar.

---

100 Bielfeldt waxes lyrically in his positive assessment of the role of philosophy for theology. »Just as old legalisms have been taken up in the grace of Christ's free justification, so too the old language of philosophy has been interrupted by the presence of something new. Just as the gospel is a new ingredient in the old mix of the law, so does the language that talks about the gospel possess a new ingredient in the old mix of philosophy. Just as the law cannot contain the gospel, so too does philosophical language not contain the good news about which theology speaks. The law, reason, and philosophy belong to God's left hand, while the gospel, faith, and theology concern His right. This intensionalist alternative fits well with the Lutheran notion of the infinite being available in the fine, for just as there is a real presence of Christ in the Lord's Supper, so too is there a ›real presence‹ of the deepest theological truths in human philosophical language. Just as God's presence is mediated through the earthly elements of the sacraments, so too is the presence of the nova lingua of theology mediated through the old language of philosophy. Just as everyday earthly elements are retained yet transformed sacramentally, so too is the everyday language of philosophy retained yet transformed in theology.« See Bielfeldt, Luther's Late Trinitarian Disputations (see n. 92), 114f.

Philosophy is no jump start which could impel us further along in the ladder of salvation. Instead, for Luther, philosophy becomes akin to law and can be affirmed as appropriate for temporal matters, though not for eternal ones. It can have a place in theology only as it is properly bathed. As such, it is most helpful in establishing doctrinal truth which is beholden to Christ who as the *new*, having in his resurrection emerged from sin and the consequences of sin, death refigures human relationship with creation, indeed allows us to accept our creatureliness under God and his goodness. Similar to other medieval thinkers, Luther denied philosophy a stance by which it could set the agenda for theology. More than anything, Luther would not want to see philosophy misused to limit or stymie an active, risen Christ through which God favors sinners and imputes to them his righteousness. But, Luther is ever vigilant that genuine theology faithful to the gospel employs rigorous logic, though only as faithful to the grammar of theology.

»The New Perspective on Paul« – eine Anfrage an die lutherische Paulusdeutung?[1]

Jens Schröter

I Einführende Bemerkungen

Die sachgemäße Interpretation der Theologie des Paulus gehört zu den zentralen Aufgaben der theologischen Wissenschaft. Das gilt nicht nur, weil sich die reformatorische Theologie in wichtigen Grundentscheidungen auf Paulus beruft, sondern auch, weil die in den Briefen des Paulus entwickelte Sicht auf die Offenbarung Gottes in Jesus Christus, einschließlich der daraus resultierenden Konsequenzen für Ethos und Gemeinschaftsleben der Glaubenden, von Beginn an eine grundlegende Rolle für die Gestaltwerdung des christlichen Glaubens gespielt hat. Die Interpretation der paulinischen Aussagen über Gott, Jesus Christus und den Menschen betrifft deshalb alle theologischen Disziplinen, weil dabei für die christliche Theologie Konstitutives zur Diskussion steht.

Für lutherische Theologie gilt das noch einmal in besonderer Weise, denn sie betrachtet die paulinische Aussage von der Rechtfertigung des Menschen allein durch den Glauben als Grundlage christlichen Glaubens überhaupt. In Martin Luthers Vorrede zu den Schmalkaldischen Artikeln von 1537 wird die Rechtfertigungslehre dementsprechend als »der erste und Häuptartikel« bezeichnet.[2] Im Jahr 1999 haben der Lutherische Welt-

---

1 Vortrag beim Lutherkongress in Helsinki am 9. August 2012. Die Vortragsform wurde für die Publikation weitgehend beibehalten, einige Anmerkungen wurden ergänzt. Für die Korrektur des Manuskripts danke ich meiner studentischen Mitarbeiterin Sophie Kottsieper.

2 BSELK, Göttingen [11]1992, 415. Vgl. auch WA 39,1; 205.

bund und der Päpstliche Rat zur Förderung der Einheit der Christen eine »Gemeinsame Erklärung zur Rechtfertigungslehre« verabschiedet,[3] in der eine weitreichende Übereinstimmung in dieser Frage konstatiert wird. Dies zeigt, dass die Rechtfertigung – jedenfalls aus der Sicht der offiziellen Vertreter dieser Kirchen – kein grundlegendes kontroverstheologisches Thema mehr ist. Vielmehr ist dort von einem »Konsens in Grundwahrheiten der Rechtfertigungslehre« die Rede, die darum nicht länger ein Grund für Lehrverurteilungen sei.[4] Sie gilt sogar als »ein unverzichtbares Kriterium, das die gesamte Lehre und Praxis der Kirche unablässig auf Christus hin orientieren will«.[5]

Vor diesem Hintergrund ist es umso bemerkenswerter, dass seit einiger Zeit, angestoßen durch die sogenannte »new perspective on Paul«, in der neutestamentlichen Wissenschaft eine intensive Diskussion über die Bedeutung der Rechtfertigungsaussagen in der paulinischen Theologie geführt wird. Diese Debatte ist inzwischen längst nicht mehr auf den exegetischen Bereich beschränkt. Vielmehr beteiligen sich daran auch Judaisten, Reformationshistoriker, systematische und praktische Theologen, was angesichts der Relevanz des Themas nicht verwundert.

Die »new perspective« hat sich vor allem in ihren Anfängen dezidiert als Alternative zur lutherischen Paulusdeutung verstanden, deren Unzulänglichkeiten sie korrigieren wollte. Programmatisch zum Ausdruck kommt das im Titel des von Michael Bachmann herausgegebenen Sammelbandes aus dem Jahr 2005 *Lutherische und neue Paulusperspektive*.[6] Diese Sicht wird aber vor allem in den grundlegenden Arbeiten dieser Richtung selbst deutlich. Eine wichtige Rolle spielt dabei die Überzeu-

---

3 Vgl. dazu B.J. HILBERATH/W. PANNENBERG (Hg.), Zur Zukunft der Ökumene. Die »Gemeinsame Erklärung zur Rechtfertigungslehre«, 1999. Der Wortlaut der Erklärung (kurz GE) findet sich a.a.O., 164–176. Die Erklärung ist von beiden Seiten auch online publiziert worden. Vgl. http://www.theology.de/religionen/oekumene/evangelischerkatholischerdialog/gemeinsameerklaerungzurrechtfertigungslehre.php. bzw. http://www.vatican.va/roman_curia/pontifical_councils/chrstuni/-documents/rc_pc_chrstuni_doc_31101999_cath-luth-joint-declaration_ge.html.

4 GE 5 und 40.

5 GE 18.

6 M. BACHMANN (Hg.), Lutherische und Neue Paulusperspektive. Beiträge zu einem Schlüsselproblem der gegenwärtigen exegetischen Diskussion (WUNT 182), 2005.

gung, hinter der paulinischen Opposition »Glaube versus Werke des Gesetzes« stehe ein negatives Stereotyp des antiken Judentums, das diesem in keiner Weise gerecht werde. Damit ist zugleich das Verhältnis von Christentum und Judentum tangiert. Die Wahrnehmung der tiefen Verwurzelung christlicher Theologie im Judentum der hellenistisch-römischen Zeit hat diesbezüglich in den vergangenen Jahrzehnten zu wichtigen Weichenstellungen in der neutestamentlichen Wissenschaft geführt, besonders in der Jesus- und der Paulusforschung. Die entsprechenden, im angelsächsischen Bereich angestoßenen Entwicklungen, die »third quest of the historical Jesus« und die »new perspective on Paul«, sind dabei nicht zuletzt aufgrund der Sensibilität für das christlich-jüdische Verhältnis nach der Shoa im deutschsprachigen Bereich auf große Akzeptanz gestoßen, haben freilich auch Anlass zu Kritik gegeben. Dass Jesus galiläischer Jude war und sein Wirken in diesem Kontext interpretiert werden muss, ist heute ebenso selbstverständlich wie die Feststellung, dass Paulus einen engagierten Diskurs mit Juden und Judenchristen seiner Zeit über die Offenbarung Gottes in Jesus Christus und die daraus resultierenden Konsequenzen geführt hat.[7] Unstrittig ist auch, dass christliche Äußerungen über das Judentum in ethischer Verantwortung vor der Geschichte, einschließlich seiner furchtbaren Verwerfungen in der Zeit des Nationalsozialismus, zu erfolgen haben. Deutlich ist aber auch, dass die philologische und historische Interpretation seiner Briefe die Grundlage jeder Darstellung der Theologie des Paulus und ihrer Rezeption in Theologie und Kirche bilden muss. Nur so ist dem christlich-jüdischen Gespräch tatsächlich gedient, das die Gemeinsamkeiten ebenso wie die Unterschiede in den Traditionen und Glaubensüberzeugungen nicht relativieren darf, sondern präzise beschreiben muss. Mit dieser hermeneutischen Vorbemerkung wende ich mich einem näheren Blick auf einige Aspekte der »new perspective on Paul« zu.

---

7 Zur Jesusforschung vgl. etwa W. Stegemann, Jesus und seine Zeit (Biblische Enzyklopädie 10), 2010, sowie J. Schröter, Jesus im Kontext. Die hermeneutische Relevanz der Frage nach dem historischen Jesus in der gegenwärtigen Diskussion (ThLZ 134, 2009, 905–928). Zu Paulus vgl. J. Frey, Das Judentum des Paulus (in: Paulus. Leben – Umwelt – Werk – Briefe, hg. v. O. Wischmeyer, 2006, 5–43).

II Facetten der »New Perspective on Paul«

Den Ausgangspunkt der »neuen Paulusperspektive« bilden die seit den sechziger Jahren des 20. Jahrhunderts von dem schwedischen Neutestamentler und späteren Bischof Krister Stendahl ausgegangenen Anstöße.[8] Die Diskussion über das Thema ist allerdings älter. Bereits an der Wende vom 19. zum 20. Jahrhundert hatten Vertreter der liberalen Paulusdeutung und der Religionsgeschichtlichen Schule, etwa Adolf Deißmann, Albert Schweitzer,[9] William Wrede[10] und Paul Wernle,[11] die Zentralstellung der Rechtfertigungslehre bestritten und stattdessen die Gemeinschaft mit Christus – mitunter auch als »Christusmystik« bezeichnet – als Zentrum der von Paulus entwickelten Erlösungsvorstellung betrachtet. Die Rechtfertigungslehre wurde dagegen als »Kampfeslehre«[12] oder »Nebenkrater […] im Hauptkrater der Erlösungslehre der Mystik des Seins in Christo«[13] bestimmt, die Paulus in Auseinandersetzung mit seinen judaisierenden Gegnern ausgebildet habe, um den Zugang der Heiden zum Heil in Christus zu begründen. Diese Ansätze, mit denen die lutherische Interpretation der paulinischen Theologie im 19. Jahrhundert schon einmal hinterfragt worden war, lassen sich deshalb als Vorläufer der »new perspective« auffassen.

---

8 K. STENDAHL, Paul and the Introspective Conscience of the West (in: Paul among Jews and Gentiles and other Essays, ed. by IDEM, 1987, 78–96 [zuerst 1963]); DERS., Final Account: Paul's Letter to the Romans, 1995.

9 A. SCHWEITZER, Die Mystik des Apostels Paulus, 1981 [zuerst 1930].

10 W. WREDE, Paulus (in: Das Paulusbild in der neueren deutschen Forschung [WdF 24], hg. v. K.H. RENGSTORF, 1964, 1–97 [zuerst 1904]).

11 P. WERNLE, Der Christ und die Sünde bei Paulus, 1897. Vgl. den Hinweis und das einschlägige Zitat bei M. WOLTER, Paulus. Ein Grundriss seiner Theologie, 2011, 341 f. Mit Wernle setzt sich R. BULTMANN in seinem ersten Aufsatz zu dieser Frage explizit auseinander: Das Problem der Ethik bei Paulus (ZNW 21, 1924, 123–140); wieder abgedruckt in: DERS., Exegetica. Aufsätze zur Erforschung des Neuen Testaments, ausgewählt, eingeleitet und herausgegeben von E. DINKLER, 1967, 36–54.

12 Wrede charakterisiert die Rechtfertigungslehre als eine »*Kampfeslehre* des Paulus«, die »nur aus seinem Lebenskampfe, seiner Auseinandersetzung mit dem Judentum und Judenchristentum verständlich [werde] und nur für diese gedacht«, jedoch von der Reformation zu Unrecht als »Zentralpunkt bei Paulus« behauptet worden sei (WREDE [s. Anm. 10], 67).

13 SCHWEITZER (s. Anm. 9), 220.

Stendahl kritisiert in seinem grundlegenden Aufsatz *Paul and the Introspective Conscience of the West* eine über Augustinus und Martin Luther vermittelte und bei Rudolf Bultmann neu zur Geltung gebrachte Tendenz, die Theologie des Paulus individuell verengt zu interpretieren. Paulus sei es jedoch bei der Rechtfertigung nicht um das individuelle Heil des einzelnen Menschen gegangen, sondern um das heilsgeschichtliche Problem des Verhältnisses von Juden und Heiden. Anders als Luther habe Paulus auch nicht die Frage nach einem gnädigen Gott umgetrieben, vielmehr hatte er, wie Stendahl mit Verweis auf Phil 3,6 betont, ein »robustes Gewissen«. Dementsprechend habe Paulus auch keine »Bekehrung« erlebt, sondern eine Berufung zur Verkündigung des Evangeliums unter den Heiden. Die Rechtfertigungslehre sei folglich keine Kritik am Gesetz als Heilsweg, sondern die Antwort auf die Frage, wie die Heiden Zugang zum Heil Gottes erhalten, ohne Juden werden zu müssen. Die Lösung des Paulus laute, dass es keinen Grund gebe, das jüdische Gesetz auch den Heiden aufzuerlegen, denn seine Funktion als »Aufseher auf Christus hin« (Gal 3,24) sei durch die Einlösung der Verheißungen an Abraham erfüllt. Die Rechtfertigungsaussagen seien demzufolge nicht als Aussagen über die Sündhaftigkeit und Erlösungsbedürftigkeit der Menschen, sondern als heilsgeschichtliche Überzeugung von der Erfüllung der allen Völkern geltenden Abrahamsverheißung zu verstehen.

Damit war eine von der lutherischen Theologie grundlegend abweichende Beurteilung der Reichweite der Rechtfertigungsaussagen sowie eine andere Stellung des Paulus zum Verhältnis von Israel und Kirche formuliert. Die Aussagen über das rechtfertigende Handeln Gottes seien nicht anthropologisch, sondern ekklesiologisch aufzufassen. Die Theologie des Paulus ziele darauf, einen Zugang zu Gott zu entwickeln, der den Heiden genauso möglich sei wie den Juden, keineswegs aber, den jüdischen Glauben hinter sich zu lassen. Die Opposition »Glaube versus Werke des Gesetzes« dürfe deshalb nicht von der konkreten historischen Konstellation abgelöst und als grundlegende Aussage über den Menschen, sein Gewissen und sein Heil, aufgefasst werden.

Etwas anders gelagert ist der Ansatz von Ed Parish Sanders. In seinem grundlegenden Werk *Paul and Palestinian Judaism*[14] kritisiert dieser –

---

14 E. P. SANDERS, Paul and Palestinian Judaism: A Comparison of Patterns of Religion, 1977

ähnlich wie bereits Stendahl –, dass die protestantische Paulusinterpretation Luthers Frage nach der Gerechtigkeit Gottes, die sich der Mensch nicht selbst verdienen könne, in die paulinische Theologie eingetragen habe. Dabei werde jedoch verkannt, dass Paulus keineswegs von dem Defizit her argumentiere, dass das Gesetz nicht gerecht machen könne. Vielmehr erweise sich das Gesetz erst aus der Perspektive der Christuserfahrung als überholt. Paulus sinne also nicht wie Luther vom Problem des nicht erfüllbaren Gesetzes her über eine Lösung nach, die er dann in der Gerechtigkeit allein aus Glauben finde, sondern denke genau umgekehrt »from solution to plight« – von der Lösung zum Dilemma. Die reformatorische Paulusinterpretation habe mit der Diastase von Gnade versus Werke dagegen ein Zerrbild des Judentums als »Gesetzesreligion« gezeichnet, das die polemischen Äußerungen Luthers über die Werkgerechtigkeit der spätmittelalterlichen Kirche in unhistorischer Weise auf die Auseinandersetzung des Paulus mit dem Judentum seiner Zeit projiziere.

In der jüdischen Religion sei das Gesetz kein Konglomerat von Vorschriften, die man erfüllen müsse, um in den Bund Gottes mit Israel *hineinzukommen*, sondern der *Inhalt* des Bundes, also das Zeichen der Zugehörigkeit zu Gott. Die Funktion des Gesetzes ist nach Sanders also nicht das »getting in«, sondern das »staying in«. In der Religion des Paulus habe sich das durch die Christusoffenbarung grundsätzlich verändert. Nunmehr sei die Teilhabe an Christus die Voraussetzung zur Erlangung des Heils, nicht mehr Erwählung, Bund oder Gesetz. Sanders spricht deshalb von zwei »Religionsstrukturen« (»patterns of religion«), der jüdischen und derjenigen des Paulus. Das Problem, das Paulus nach seiner Bekehrung mit dem Judentum gehabt habe, sei demnach nicht dessen Orientierung am Gesetz, sondern dass es die neue Offenbarung Gottes in Christus nicht erkenne, also kein Christentum sei.

Die Kritik von Sanders an dem in reformatorischer Theologie verbreiteten Zerrbild des Judentums ist eine wichtige Korrektur einer undifferenzierten Rede vom Gesetz als »Heilsweg« und dem Judentum als »Geset-

(dt.: Paulus und das palästinische Judentum. Ein Vergleich zweier Religionsstrukturen, 1985).

zesreligion«. Die Erforschung des antiken Judentums hat inzwischen deutlich gezeigt, dass die negative Beurteilung des Gesetzes in der Tat ein Merkmal lutherischer Paulusdeutung ist, das einer sorgfältigen Unterscheidung der historischen Kontexte bedarf, um nicht Luthers Kritik an der spätmittelalterlichen Kirche in unhistorischer Weise auf die Auseinandersetzung des Paulus mit dem antiken Judentum abzubilden.[15] Damit wird die Frage dringlich, in welcher Weise sich das, was Paulus mit den »Werken des Gesetzes« meint, hermeneutisch fruchtbar machen lässt, will man es nicht bei der Konstatierung des Befundes belassen, dass Paulus den Glauben an Jesus Christus dem jüdischen Glauben gegenübergestellt habe.

Das wäre jedoch schon deshalb wenig befriedigend, weil Sanders' Auffassung, das antike Judentum und die paulinische Theologie seien als zwei grundlegend verschiedene Religionsstrukturen zu verstehen, wenig überzeugend ist. Abgesehen davon, dass das antike Judentum kaum so einheitlich war, wie Sanders es darstellt, gerät dabei aus dem Blick, dass Paulus sich gerade um ein neues Verständnis der Schriften und Traditionen Israels und des Judentums bemüht und ihnen nicht ein anderes »Religionssystem« gegenübergestellt hat. Diese Kritik von Sanders Ansatz findet sich auch bei James Dunn in seinem 1983 zuerst erschienen Aufsatz *The New Perspective on Paul*, von dem sich die Bezeichnung der »neuen Paulusperspektive« herleitet.[16] Dunn argumentiert, dass Paulus *innerhalb* des Judentums seiner Zeit verstanden werden müsse, seine Theologie als Neuinterpretation zentraler jüdischer Überzeugungen zu verstehen sei. Die Kritik des Paulus am Gesetz habe deshalb auch keinen grundsätzlichen Charakter. Paulus kritisiere vielmehr, dass das Judentum das Gesetz als eine Institution verstehe, mit der es sich von den übrigen Völkern abgrenze, indem es dazu verwendet werde, die Grenzen des Judentums gegenüber den anderen Völkern zu befestigen. Paulus wende sich gegen

---

15 Exemplarisch verwiesen sei auf F. Avemarie, Tora und Leben. Untersuchungen zur Heilsbedeutung der Tora in der frühen rabbinischen Literatur (TSAJ 55), 1996, sowie auf L. Doering, Schabbat. Sabbathalacha und Sabbatpraxis im antiken Judentum und Urchristentum (TSAJ 78), 1999.

16 J.D.G. Dunn, The New Perspective on Paul (in: Ders., The New Perspective on Paul: Collected Essays [WUNT 185], 2005, 89–110).

diesen abgrenzenden Gebrauch des Gesetzes und ziele demgegenüber auf eine Öffnung des Judentums zu den anderen Völkern. Erst auf diese Weise werde die eigentliche Bedeutung des Gesetzes als Gottes Maßstab für das Leben der Menschen zur Geltung gebracht.[17]

Mit dem Ausdruck »Werke des Gesetzes« bezeichnet Paulus Dunn zufolge demnach auch nicht das jüdische Gesetz an sich, sondern diejenigen Teile mit einer abgrenzenden Funktion, nämlich Beschneidung, Reinheits- und Speisegebote sowie Sabbateinhaltung. Diese von Dunn als jüdische »identity markers« bezeichneten Rituale, die nach außen als Abgrenzungen, »boundary markers«, wirkten, seien bei Paulus mit dem Ausdruck ἔργα νόμου gemeint. Deshalb seien es im Galaterbrief auch genau diese Themen, um die der Streit zwischen Paulus und Petrus bzw. seinen judenchristlichen Gegnern ausgetragen wird. Das Argument des Paulus laute dabei, die Auffassung, mit dem Gesetz solle die exklusive Stellung Israels gegenüber den anderen Völkern gesichert werden, laufe dessen eigentlicher Intention zuwider, denn das Gesetz sei Gottes Weisung an alle Menschen, unabhängig davon ob sie Juden oder Heiden sind.[18]

Auch Dunn betont zu Recht, dass die Theologie des Paulus zunächst im Kontext des Judentums seiner Zeit interpretiert werden muss. Ein unreflektierter Gebrauch von Oppositionen wie »Glaube und Werke« oder »Gesetz und Evangelium« kann dagegen zu Fehlurteilen führen, die die Intention des Paulus verzerren. Paulus bezeichnet mit dem Ausdruck »Werke des Gesetzes« tatsächlich die Orientierung an den Identitätsmerkmalen des Judentums, die für den Glauben an Jesus Christus keine Voraussetzung mehr darstellen. Dagegen wäre es eine Verzeichnung, Paulus eine Kritik am angeblichen »Verdienstdenken« des Judentums zu unterstellen. Dies zeigt, dass klassische Begriffspaare der lutherischen Paulusinterpretation immer wieder der präzisen Auslegung anhand der paulinischen Texte bedürfen und sich diesen gegenüber nicht verselbständigen dürfen.

---

17 Vgl. dazu auch J.D.G. DUNN, The Theology of Paul the Apostle, 1998, 631–658.
18 Vgl. auch J.D.G. DUNN, Works of the Law and the Curse of the Law (Gal. 3.10–14) (in: The New Perspective on Paul, [s. Anm. 16], 111–130); DERS., Paul and the Torah: The Role and Function of the Law in the Theology of Paul the Apostle, a.a.O., 441–461.

Dunn betont ebenfalls zu Recht, dass die soziologischen Konstellationen der paulinischen Mission bedacht werden müssen. Beschneidung, Speisegebote und Sabbateinhaltung hatten für die Wahrung der Identität des Judentums, vornehmlich in der Diaspora, herausragende Bedeutung. Die Orientierung an diesen Ritualen hatte deshalb eine identitätsstabilisierende und zugleich abgrenzende Wirkung, denn die Tora bildete einen schützenden Zaun um das jüdische Volk, der es vor der Verunreinigung durch den Kontakt mit Heiden schützen sollte.[19]

Zusammenfassend zeigt sich: Der neuen Paulusperspektive ist daran gelegen, die Einbindung des Paulus in den jüdischen Diskurs seiner Zeit herauszustellen und sein Selbstverständnis als eines den Schriften und Traditionen Israels verpflichteten Juden zu betonen. Dass seine jüdische Herkunft die Sicht des Paulus auf das Christusgeschehen in maßgeblicher Weise geprägt hat, kann dabei nicht strittig sein. Paulus beruft sich an zentralen Stellen seiner Briefe auf die Schriften Israels, um die Bedeutung des Christusgeschehens darzulegen, etwa wenn er es im Horizont der Verheißungen Gottes an Abraham deutet und daraus die Einheit von Juden und Heiden in Christus herleitet. Ein weiterer wichtiger Aspekt ist die adäquate Erfassung des antiken Judentums, das nicht aus christlicher Sicht als »Werk-« oder »Gesetzesreligion« verzeichnet werden darf. Eine präzise Interpretation der Opposition von πίστις Ἰησοῦ Χριστοῦ und ἔργα νόμου ist demnach von grundlegender Bedeutung. Kritisiert Paulus mit dieser Opposition das Gesetz oder ein bestimmtes Verständnis des Gesetzes und was folgt daraus im Blick auf das Verhältnis der an Christus Glaubenden zum Judentum bzw. zu Israel? Schließlich ist zu klären, inwieweit die Kritik der »new perspective« an der Zentralstellung der Rechtfertigungslehre berechtigt ist. Kann diese tatsächlich auf das Problem der Heidenmission beschränkt werden oder hat sie grundlegendere Bedeutung für die paulinische Theologie? Mit diesen Fragen wende ich mich im Folgenden zwei zentralen Passagen des Galaterbriefes zu, um daran eine exegetische Antwort auf die genannten Fragen zu entwickeln.

19 Arist. 139.142.

III Der Entdeckungszusammenhang der Opposition »Gerechtigkeit aus Glauben, nicht aus Werken des Gesetzes« nach Gal 2,15–17

Die einschlägige Stelle für den Diskurs über die Rechtfertigung ist Galater 2,15–17. Paulus formuliert hier zum ersten Mal die Opposition von Glauben an Jesus Christus und Werken des Gesetzes im Blick auf die Gerechtsprechung des Menschen. Der Text bildet deshalb auch in dem genannten Aufsatz James Dunns den Ausgangspunkt.[20]

Der Passus ist eine Fortsetzung des Berichts des Paulus über den sogenannten »antiochenischen Zwischenfall«, bei dem er Kephas Heuchelei vorgeworfen hatte. Der Übergang zu den anschließenden, grundsätzlichen Reflexionen ist fließend, auf jeden Fall aber ist deutlich, dass die in V. 15 einsetzenden Ausführungen nicht mehr Bestandteil der Rede an Kephas sind, sondern die Grundlagen des Glaubens an Jesus Christus überhaupt darlegen.[21]

Paulus setzt dazu mit der aus jüdischer Perspektive formulierten Gegenüberstellung von »uns Juden« und »Sündern aus den Heiden« ein. Er schließt sich also mit den in V. 13 erwähnten Kephas, Barnabas und den »übrigen Juden« zusammen, um zunächst die gemeinsame Herkunft und das wesentliche Unterscheidungsmerkmal von den ἔθνη herauszustellen: Juden sind keine Sünder, denn sie haben, anders als die übrigen Völker, das Gesetz als die Weisung Gottes zum Leben. Daran schließt sich unmittelbar eine Aussage über ein »Wissen« an, das die Genannten offenbar ebenfalls miteinander teilen, nämlich: οὐ δικαιοῦται ἄνθρωπος ἐξ ἔργων νόμου ἐὰν μὴ διὰ πίστεως Ἰησοῦ Χριστοῦ. Es handelt sich dabei um eine Wendung, die Paulus nicht ad hoc formuliert, sondern die bereits älter ist und darum als Basis der Argumentation dient. Dafür spricht zunächst der Sachzusammenhang – Paulus führt den Satz als gemeinsame Überzeugung ein –, des weiteren das einleitende ὅτι, das sich als Zitateinleitung auffassen lässt, sodann der sentenzenartige Charakter des Satzes, der in

---

20 DUNN, New Perspective (s. Anm. 16), 95–107.
21 Vgl. H.-D. BETZ, Der Galaterbrief. Ein Kommentar zum Brief des Paulus an die Gemeinden in Galatien, 1988, 213–215. Betz bestimmt 2,15–21 als propositio, die der narratio folgt, ohne selbst Bestandteil von dieser zu sein.

Röm 3,28 noch einmal in variierter Form begegnet und dann verschiedene Rezeptionen im Neuen Testament erfahren hat.[22] Schließlich spricht für einen älteren Grundsatz, dass die Wendung in Spannung zu ihrem Kontext steht. Paulus formuliert als Konsequenz aus der genannten Überzeugung: καὶ ἡμεῖς εἰς Χριστὸν Ἰησοῦν ἐπιστεύσαμεν, ἵνα δικαιωθῶμεν ἐκ πίστεως Χριστοῦ καὶ οὐκ ἐξ ἔργων νόμου. Offenbar war der Satz also ursprünglich nicht auf Juden bezogen, sondern diente als theologische Begründung dafür, dass *Heiden* zum Glauben an Jesus Christus kommen können. Wenn Paulus ihn hier auch auf christusgläubige Juden bezieht, wendet er ihn offensichtlich auf einen Sachverhalt an, für den er ursprünglich nicht formuliert worden war, auf den er aber natürlich prinzipiell auch anwendbar ist. Das ist insofern eine entscheidende Weichenstellung, als damit das Sein in Christus gerade jenseits der Unterscheidung von Juden und Heiden bestimmt wird.

Der Grundsatz formuliert die Überzeugung, dass für die Gerechtsprechung des Menschen – ἄνθρωπος – der Glaube an Jesus Christus die einzige und hinreichende Voraussetzung ist. Die negative Wendung οὐκ ἐξ ἔργων νόμου grenzt dies von einer Auffassung ab, die die Bindung an das jüdische Gesetz als eine weitere, dazu gleichwertige Voraussetzung behauptet. Für die Herkunft des Satzes ist man damit auf einen Kontext verwiesen, in dem das Verhältnis von jüdischen Identitätsmerkmalen und Glauben an Jesus Christus bei Menschen, die diese nicht aufweisen, im Urchristentum virulent wurde und zu einer Klärung drängte. Dafür kommt im Prinzip nur eine Situation in Frage, nämlich diejenige in der Gemeinde von Antiochia, in der nach Apg 11,19f zum ersten Mal das Evangelium auch an Heiden verkündet wurde und zu der Paulus selbst in seiner Frühzeit gehörte. In dieser Gemeinde muss die Überzeugung ausgeprägt worden sein, dass der Glaube an Jesus Christus die Unterscheidung von Juden und Heiden aufhebt. Dem lassen sich andere Grundüberzeugungen an die Seite stellen, die ebenfalls aus Antiochia stammen könnten

---

22 Vgl. M. Theobald, Der Kanon von der Rechtfertigung (Gal 2,16; Röm 3,28). Eigentum des Paulus oder Gemeingut der Kirche? (in: Ders., Studien zum Römerbrief [WUNT 136], 2001, 164–225).

und die den genannten Grundsatz in einen breiteren Kontext stellen.[23] Dazu gehören:

1Kor 7,19: ἡ περιτομὴ οὐδέν ἐστιν καὶ ἡ ἀκροβυστία οὐδέν ἐστιν, ἀλλὰ τήρησις ἐντολῶν θεοῦ. (»Die Beschneidung ist nichts und die Unbeschnittenheit ist nichts, sondern die Bewahrung der Gebote Gottes.«)

1Kor 12,13: καὶ γὰρ ἐν ἑνὶ πνεύματι ἡμεῖς πάντες εἰς ἓν σῶμα ἐβαπτίσθημεν, εἴτε Ἰουδαῖοι εἴτε Ἕλληνες εἴτε δοῦλοι εἴτε ἐλεύθεροι, καὶ πάντες ἓν πνεῦμα ἐποτίσθημεν. (»Denn wir wurden alle in einem Geist in einen Leib getauft, seien es Juden oder Griechen, Sklaven oder Freie, und alle wurden mit einem Geist getränkt.«)

Gal 3,27f: ὅσοι γὰρ εἰς Χριστὸν ἐβαπτίσθητε, Χριστὸν ἐνεδύσασθε. οὐκ ἔνι Ἰουδαῖος οὐδὲ Ἕλλην, οὐκ ἔνι δοῦλος οὐδὲ ἐλεύθερος, οὐκ ἔνι ἄρσεν καὶ θῆλυ· πάντες γὰρ ὑμεῖς εἷς ἐστε ἐν Χριστῷ Ἰησοῦ. (»Die ihr nämlich auf Christus getauft wurdet, habt Christus angezogen. Da ist nicht mehr Jude und Grieche, nicht mehr Sklave und Freier, nicht mehr männlich und weiblich. Ihr seid nämlich alle einer in Christus Jesus.«)

Gal 5,6: ἐν γὰρ Χριστῷ Ἰησοῦ οὔτε περιτομή τι ἰσχύει οὔτε ἀκροβυστία ἀλλὰ πίστις δι᾽ ἀγάπης ἐνεργουμένη. (»In Christus Jesus gilt nämlich weder die Beschneidung noch die Unbeschnittenheit etwas, sondern der Glaube, der durch die Liebe wirksam wird.«)

Gal 6,15: οὔτε γὰρ περιτομή τί ἐστιν οὔτε ἀκροβυστία ἀλλὰ καινὴ κτίσις. (»Weder Beschneidung noch Unbeschnittenheit nämlich ist etwas, sondern neue Schöpfung.«)

Alle diese Sätze haben gemeinsam, dass sie den Unterschied von Juden und Heiden als in Jesus Christus aufgehoben bezeichnen. Diese Überzeugung hatte sich offenbar als Antwort auf die Frage herausgebildet, wie Juden und Heiden in einer Gemeinschaft zusammen leben können, deren gemeinsames Merkmal der Glaube an Jesus Christus ist. Beim sogenann-

---

23 Vgl. WOLTER (s. Anm. 11), 36.

ten Apostelkonzil war es in der Form akzeptiert worden, dass Heiden das jüdische Gesetz nicht aufzuerlegen sei. Es ist darum alles andere als ein Zufall, dass Paulus im Galaterbrief diese Vereinbarung als Argument sowohl gegen die Beschneidungsforderung seiner Gegner als auch gegen das Verhalten des Kephas ins Feld führt. Beides ist für ihn Verrat an dem einen Evangelium, das gemäß der Jerusalemer Vereinbarung an Juden und Heiden gleichermaßen auszurichten ist: als εὐαγγέλιον τῆς ἀκροβυστίας und εὐαγγέλιον τῆς περιτομῆς (Gal 2,7). Dass Petrus dieser Vereinbarung in Jerusalem ausdrücklich zugestimmt hatte, sich dann in Antiochia aber von der Tischgemeinschaft mit den Heidenchristen zurückzog, bezeichnet Paulus darum als »Heuchelei«.

Gleichwohl war die paulinische Interpretation keineswegs die einzige oder gar zwingend notwendige Folge aus dem antiochenischen Grundsatz.[24] Dieser beantwortete vielmehr zunächst nur die Frage, welche Voraussetzungen Heiden zu erfüllen haben, um in die Gemeinschaft der Glaubenden aufgenommen zu werden, nämlich: keine, außer dem Bekenntnis zu Jesus Christus, das durch die Taufe besiegelt wird. Die Frage nach Regeln für das Leben einer Gemeinschaft, zu der sowohl Heiden als auch Juden gehören, war damit indes keineswegs beantwortet. Diesbezüglich waren vielmehr unterschiedliche Optionen denkbar, wie die heftigen Kontroversen über diese Frage zeigen: Die galatischen Gegner des Paulus forderten die Integration der christusgläubigen Heiden ins Judentum durch die Beschneidung, akzeptierten also die Jerusalemer Vereinbarung, wenn sie sie kannten, nicht. Die in Antiochia aufgetretenen Jakobusleute haben sich offenbar an diese Vereinbarung gehalten und keine Beschneidungsforderung erhoben, jedoch darauf gedrungen, dass Juden ihrerseits auf die Bewahrung der Reinheit achten müssten und deshalb mit Heiden keine ungeregelte Tischgemeinschaft haben sollten. Paulus kennzeichnet diese Haltung, die offenbar auch Kephas übernommen hatte, in Gal 2,12 als ὑποστέλλειν und ἀφορίζειν. Das sogenannte Aposteldekret, das nach Apg 15,20 von Jakobus auf dem Jerusalemer Treffen ver-

---

24 Vgl. M. KONRADT, Zur Datierung des sogenannten antiochenischen Zwischenfalls (ZNW 102, 2011, 19–39), 24–28.

kündet wird, das aber eher eine nachträgliche Reaktion auf die in Antiochia entstandene Situation der Tischgemeinschaft von Juden- und Heidenchristen darstellen dürfte, könnte dabei den von Paulus in Gal 2,12 erwähnten Versuch der Jakobusleute darstellen, die antiochenische Praxis so zu regeln, dass sie für christusgläubige Juden akzeptabel war.[25] Paulus selbst dagegen forderte, die Aufgabe aller trennenden Vorschriften des Gesetzes konsequent zur theologischen Basis des Glaubens an Jesus Christus zu erklären und interpretierte die Frage der Tischgemeinschaft dementsprechend im Licht des in Gal 2,16 zitierten Grundsatzes.

Dieser Grundsatz beantwortete die Frage nach der konkreten Gestaltung des christlichen Glaubens für Juden und Heiden demnach keineswegs eindeutig, sondern barg vielmehr erhebliches Konfliktpotential in sich. Paulus interpretierte ihn in einer radikalen Weise, indem er ihn im Horizont der Jerusalemer Vereinbarung als Aufhebung aller trennenden Vorschriften deutete und als Argument gegen das Verhalten des Kephas in Antiochia ins Feld führte. Dass dies der spezifischen galatischen Situation geschuldet war und nicht pauschal auf die paulinische Gemeindeethik bezogen werden darf, zeigen die Ausführungen in Röm 14,1–15,13, wo Paulus das Beachten von Speisegeboten dem Maßstab der gegenseitigen Annahme und der Auferbauung der Gemeinde unterordnet.[26]

Die Anwendung des antiochenischen Grundsatzes auf christusgläubige Juden hat erhebliche Konsequenzen für die paulinische Theologie. Auch Juden sind, wie Paulus erläuternd fortfährt, zum Glauben gekommen, damit sie aus Glauben an Jesus Christus gerechtfertigt würden und nicht aus Werken des Gesetzes. Am Ende des Satzes nennt er dafür noch eine Begründung: ὅτι ἐξ ἔργων νόμου οὐ δικαιωθήσεται πᾶσα σάρξ. Damit spielt er auf Ps 143,2 (LXX 142,2) an: καὶ μὴ εἰσέλθῃς εἰς κρίσιν μετὰ τοῦ δούλου σου, ὅτι οὐ δικαιωθήσεται ἐνώπιόν σου πᾶς ζῶν. Paulus gibt dem Grundsatz dadurch eine schrifttheologische Begründung, die in diesem bereits durch die Formulierung angelegt ist, kein Mensch (ἄνθρωπος)

---

25 Vgl. J. Wehnert, Die Reinheit des »christlichen Gottesvolkes« aus Juden und Heiden. Studien zum historischen und theologischen Hintergrund des sogenannten Aposteldekrets (FRLANT 173), 1997, 129 f.

26 Röm 14,1–3; 15,1 f.

werde aus Werken des Gesetzes gerecht. Aus der Tatsache, dass auch »wir« Juden in Christus gerechtfertigt werden wollen, ergibt sich schließlich, dass »auch wir selbst« als Sünder angetroffen werden (2,17: εἰ δὲ ζητοῦντες δικαιωθῆναι ἐν Χριστῷ εὑρέθημεν καὶ αὐτοὶ ἁμαρτωλοί). Damit ist die Gegenüberstellung von Juden und »Sündern aus den Heiden« aus V. 15 aufgehoben. Anders gesagt: Paulus sieht die Tatsache, dass Juden wie Heiden vor Gott gleichgestellt und also auch Juden Sünder sind, in der Schrift selbst begründet. Das ist freilich keine allgemeine anthropologische Einsicht, sondern eine angesichts der Christusoffenbarung gewonnene Erkenntnis darüber, dass der in der Erwählung Israels gründende Unterschied von Juden und Heiden aufgehoben ist. Das wird in den ersten Kapiteln des Römerbriefs und auf eigene Weise noch einmal in der Beschreibung des Zwiespalts von Wollen und Tun in Röm 7 ausgeführt. Immer blickt Paulus von der Überzeugung der in Christus erlangten Gerechtigkeit her auf die Situation des Menschen vor und außer Christus, die die erwählungstheologisch begründete Vorrangstellung Israels zugunsten der Aufhebung des Unterschieds von Juden und Heiden hinter sich lässt. Es liegt auf der Hand, dass die Frage nach der Sonderstellung Israels für Paulus damit dringlich wird. Ihr wird sich Paulus in Römer 9–11 zuwenden und die Antwort entwickeln, dass die Rettung ganz Israels in Gottes geheimem Ratschluss verborgen liegt.[27]

IV Die »New Perspective« und Luthers Paulusdeutung

Die Vertreter der »new perspective« insistieren zu Recht darauf, dass die Gegenüberstellung von Glauben an Jesus Christus und Werken des Gesetzes zunächst aus ihrem konkreten Entstehungszusammenhang heraus verstanden werden muss. Es geht Paulus nicht um einen allgemeinen Gegensatz von Glauben und Werken im Blick auf die Rechtfertigung, etwa in dem Sinn, dass der Mensch nichts »leisten« solle oder sich die Gerechtigkeit nicht »verdienen« könne. Es geht Paulus bei dieser Alternative vielmehr sehr konkret um das Verhältnis von Juden und Heiden in Christus. Die hermeneutische Aufgabe besteht deshalb darin, die Opposi-

---

27 Röm 11,25–36.

tion von »Werken des Gesetzes« und »Glauben an Jesus Christus« vor diesem Hintergrund zu bestimmen und nicht unreflektiert jegliches Verständnis von »Werken« oder »Tun« in die paulinischen Texte hineinzulesen. Die »new perspective« hat damit eine wichtige Präzisierung formuliert, die die Theologie des Paulus hinsichtlich ihrer Entstehungsbedingungen zu erfassen verhilft. Dafür ist es nicht zuletzt von Bedeutung, die Kontrastierung von Werken des Gesetzes und Glauben an Jesus Christus im weiteren Kontext der oben genannten Basissätze zu lesen und sie im Gesamtzusammenhang der paulinischen Theologie zu interpretieren.

Im Blick auf das Verhältnis zur Paulusinterpretation Luthers ist zunächst festzuhalten, dass die »new perspective« – insbesondere James Dunn – eingeräumt hat, dass der Entdeckungszusammenhang der Rechtfertigungsaussagen des Paulus – eben die galatische Kontroverse – nicht bedeutet, dass deren Bedeutung darauf beschränkt sei. Die grundsätzliche Bedeutung der Aussage, dass kein Mensch ohne die rechtfertigende Gnade Gottes vor ihm bestehen kann, wird vielmehr auch von Dunn ausdrücklich anerkannt. Die Theologie des Paulus habe aber auch eine »korporative«, soziale Dimension, die nicht durch eine Überbetonung des individuellen Heils des einzelnen Menschen an den Rand gedrängt werden dürfe.[28] Gerade wenn man den oben genannten antiochenischen Grundsatz in den weiteren Kontext der Aufhebung der Unterschiede zwischen Juden und Heiden, Sklaven und Freien, männlich und weiblich stellt, wird deutlich, dass die paulinische Theologie nicht nur auf die Zueignung des Heils in Christus an den einzelnen Menschen zielt, sondern in gleicher Weise auf die Entstehung und das Leben von Gemeinschaften gerichtet ist, in denen der Glaube an Jesus Christus den alleinigen Maßstab für die Zugehörigkeit bildet. Das Herrenmahl als die Feier, in der die Gemeinde den erhöhten Herrn vergegenwärtigt und ihre Gemeinschaft mit ihm und

---

28 J. D. G. Dunn, The New Perspective: whence, what and whither? (in: The New Perspective on Paul, [s. Anm. 16], 1–88). Dunn betont dort mehrfach, dass er seine Paulusdeutung nicht als Gegensatz zur lutherischen oder generell reformatorischen Rechtfertigungslehre versteht (vgl. etwa a. a. O., 21.27.33.87). Allerdings sei die paulinische Rede von Gerechtigkeit und Werken des Gesetzes nicht auf die Gerechtsprechung des einzelnen Menschen beschränkt, sondern auf einen größeren sozialen und ethnischen Kontext bezogen.

untereinander durch die Teilhabe an dem einen Brot und dem einen Kelch symbolisch zum Ausdruck bringt, stellt dies eindrücklich vor Augen. Das Herrenmahl ist darum für Paulus keinesfalls nur Zueignung des Heils an den Einzelnen – »Christi Leib für dich gegeben« – sondern vor allem symbolischer Ausdruck der Gemeinschaft der Glaubenden als des einen, durch die Teilhabe an Christus konstituierten Leibes: »Mein Leib für euch«. Daran lässt sich die von der »new perspective« betonte soziale und ekklesiale Dimension der paulinischen Theologie verdeutlichen, die in der an Luther orientierten Auslegungsrichtung mitunter tatsächlich etwas in den Hintergrund tritt – bis hin zur Liturgie der Abendmahlsfeiern.

Zwei Konsequenzen seien zum Schluss angedeutet. Die Begründung einer gemeinsamen Identität von Heiden und Juden in Christus kann heute nicht mehr die theologische Pointe der Rechtfertigungsaussagen des Paulus sein und war es natürlich auch zu Augustins und Luthers Zeiten nicht mehr. Die grundlegende Bedeutung dieser Überzeugung liegt vielmehr darin, dass sie den Glauben an Jesus Christus zum alleinigen Kriterium für den Zugang zum Heil herausstellt und damit unterschiedliche Auffassungen zwischen den Konfessionen – etwa bezüglich der Eucharistie oder des Amtes – als nachgeordnete Aspekte erscheinen lässt. Zum zweiten zeigt sie, dass Paulus den Christusglauben als eine den Menschen in eine grundlegende neue Existenzweise stellende – ihn zu einer καινὴ κτίσις machende – Kraft auffasst. Der Weg dorthin vollzieht sich zwar heute in der Regel nicht mehr als Bekehrungsakt von einem alten zu einem neuen Leben, der zur Zeit des Paulus noch der Normalfall der Christusgläubigen war. Gleichwohl ist der Christusglaube auch jenseits dieses symbolischen Nachvollzugs von Tod und Auferweckung Jesu Christi eine grundlegende Bestimmung der menschlichen Existenz, die einen eigenen Sinnhorizont eröffnet und eine daraus resultierende ethische Orientierung vermittelt. Die paulinischen Aussagen über die Rechtfertigung aus Glauben erweisen sich damit als Grundlegung einer Wirklichkeitsdeutung aus der Sicht des christlichen Glaubens und seiner Entfaltung in gegenwärtigen Kontexten auf der Basis des Neuen Testaments.

Beyond juxtaposing Luther and the »New Perspective on Paul«

A common quest for the »other« way of giving?[1]

Bo Kristian Holm

I Introduction to an intricate matter

It would be no exaggeration to describe the relationship between Luther and Paul as rather intricate. Attempts have been made to clarify this relationship, but none of them has been successful in making the final clarification. It is the aim of this article to outline the problems connected to the role of Luther in the »New Perspective on Paul« and to propose another way of relating Paul and Luther, without neglecting the insights of the New Perspective by using the divine giving as link.

Luther has been a central figure in Pauline exegesis for the last 500 years, either positively as a motivator and collaborator or negatively as a chief opponent. Paul and Luther are, for obvious reasons, the two most central figures in Lutheran tradition, and studies on them have developed almost simultaneously, even in periods when awareness of the internal difference was prominent.

Studies on Paul – as well as on Luther – therefore proved to be direct ways into the intellectual history of modern Western Christianity. If Ritschl did influence Luther studies, as he surely did, he also, at the same time, influenced Pauline exegesis. If the discovery of Luther's lectures on

---

1 When I was revising this lecture for publication in Lutherjahrbuch, New Testament Scholar John M. G. Barclay generously allowed me to read some of the chapters from his forthcoming book on Paul and the gift, for which I am deeply grateful. This made me aware of additional material and helped me sharpen some of my points.

Romans was important for our understanding of Luther in the 20th century, it was almost equally important for our understanding of Paul.[2] If the Zeitgeist is anti-metaphysical and existential and concerned with hermeneutics, so are studies of both Luther and Paul.[3] If the Zeitgeist is sacramental and collectivistic, so is our understanding of Luther and Paul. If the Zeitgeist is critical towards the legacy from dialectical theology, so are readings of both Paul and Luther. From this perspective, it is no coincidence that the »New Perspective on Paul« and Finnish Luther studies developed almost simultaneously.[4]

The partner race of Pauline exegesis and Luther studies often presupposed that questions about what Paul said and meant, what Luther said and meant, and what a meaningful expression of Christianity would be today should not be treated as three distinct questions, but as one and the same. But this is not so. They have to remain three distinct questions, and before interrelating them, one should deal with them separately. That is why the relationship between Paul and Luther can never be exhaustively solved historically, but only theologically. This issue will be taken up below. First there is a brief survey of the role of Luther in the New Perspective.

Several introductions to the Luther-Paul-issue exist already,[5] which makes sheer repetition less relevant. My focus will instead be on some

---

2 One needs only refer to K. BARTH, Der Römerbrief, [2]1922, for a paradigmatic example.

3 The paradigmatic example is here G. EBELING, Die Anfänge von Luthers Hermeneutik (ZThK 48, 1951, 172–230).

4 An impression almost explicitly confirmed in R. SAARINEN, The Pauline Luther and the Law: Lutheran theology reengages in the study of Paul (Pro Ecclesia XV, No. 1, 2006, 64–86).

5 See, for example, the comprehensive study of S. WESTERHOLM, Perspectives old and new on Paul: The »Lutheran« Paul and his critics, 2004, and J.D.G. DUNN's lengthy introduction in his The New Perspective on Paul, [2]2008, 1–98, where Dunn confirms his own personal appreciation of Protestant theology and Luther's doctrine of justification without giving up his critique of »Lutheran misinterpretations« (Ibd. 89–95, see especially the discussion in the footnotes), arguing for a Luther complemented by Calvin (95). By this Dunn seems to mean a Protestant theology which pays more attention to the transformation of the human being as normally inherent in the understanding of forensic justification. See also the brief but instructive survey in M.E. BRINKMAN, Justification in

general characteristics of the current debate in an attempt to sketch an alternative way of coping with the Paul-Luther-divide, which takes both the historical and the theological perspectives into consideration.

II Judaism and Luther as »negative foils«

A general tendency in the New Perspective's criticism of the Lutheran Paul is the attack on the understanding of Judaism as the mere negative foil for the gospel of justification by faith alone. Another general tendency in relation to the role of Luther in the New Perspective is the use of Luther as the negative foil for the New Perspective's new and better understanding of Paul. As put by New Testament scholar Francis Watson, »in the [...] world of Pauline studies, ›Lutheran‹ is currently employed as a term of abuse«.[6] Luther is the paradigm prototype of the rival exegetical tradition, which surely *did* understand Second Temple Judaism almost parallel to the Roman Catholicism that Luther opposed and *did* find in Paul both a *simul* and a distinction between Law and Gospel that was not in Paul – at least not in Luther's version. Along these lines the following considerations are relying on the premise that the New Perspective did have a point in rejecting an exegesis too depending on Lutheran interpretations. It is beyond questioning that Luther was very much present in the »Lutheran« perspective on Paul. A single reference to a central question and its answer in Ernst Käsemann's work will suffice here. When he, for example, asks, »Who represents the Jewish nomism that Paul attacked?«

Ecumenical Dialogue: Central Aspects of Christian Soteriology in Debate, 1996, 57–78. For a detailed and very independent study, see V. STOLLE, Luther und Paulus. Die exegetischen und hermeneutischen Grundlagen der lutherischen Rechtfertigungslehre im Paulinismus Luthers (ABG 10), 2002. For a comprehensive assessment, see also K. HAACKER, Verdienste und Grenzen der ›neuen Perspektive‹ der Paulus-Auslegung (in: Lutherische und Neue Paulusperspektive. Beiträge zu einem Schlüsselproblem der gegenwärtigen exegetischen Diskussion [WUNT 182], hg. v. M. BACHMANN/J. WOYKE, 2005, 1–16). For a different and fresh opinion, arguing for a more Lutheran Paul, see SAARINEN, The Pauline Luther (see n. 4).

6 F. WATSON, Response: A response from Francis Watson (SJT 59, No. 4, 2006, 461–468), 461.

and answers that it is the community of pious people that made God's promise regarding their own privilege and God's law a means of their own self-sanctification, then Käsemann surely does not see Paul's but Luther's opponents in the Pauline corpus.[7]

Revisions were therefore very much needed, and one may look for a historical explanation for why exegetes from the Anglo-Saxon world were necessary in order to rediscover what had for a long period of time been accessible academic knowledge in works on ancient Judaism.[8] Such an explanation may include both theological and ideological reasons, but will not be elaborated further.[9]

But as the New Perspective had to revise the use of Second Temple Judaism as the negative foil for the Lutheran doctrine of justification, it is equally necessary to revise the use of Luther as the negative foil for the New Perspective. It is important to note (1) that a revision of the New Perspective's understanding of Second Temple Judaism, of Paul's relation hereto or of his use of paraenesis, a topic to which we will return later, is not necessarily implied in this second step of revision and (2) that bringing Luther's tendentious readings of Paul out in the open will not in itself clarify the Paul-Luther relationship. Further studies are very much needed.

III Luther in the New Perspective

It is commonly accepted, not least through the work of James D. G. Dunn, that the breakthrough of the New Perspective occurred with E. P. Sanders' seminal work *Paul and Palestinian Judaism.*[10] Here Sanders successfully

---

7 Cf. E. Käsemann, Rechtfertigung und Heilsgeschichte im Römerbrief (in: Ders., Paulinische Perspektiven, 1969, 108–139), 127f.

8 H. L. Strack/P. Billerbeck, Kommentar zum Neuen Testament aus Talmud und Midrasch, 1922ff; H.-J. Schoeps, Paulus. Die Theologie des Apostels im Lichte der jüdischen Religionsgeschichte, 1959.

9 See, however, Saarinen, The Pauline Luther (see n. 4), which at the end deals with the theological and ideological background for the breakthrough of the New Perspective. For a questioning of the »Newness« of the New Perspective see Notger Slenczka's article in the present volume.

10 E. P. Sanders, Paul and Palestinian Judaism: A Comparison of Patterns of Religion,

rectified the Weberian understanding of Judaism, which until then pervaded research on Second Temple Judaism.[11] This correction is accompanied by a harsh critique of the Lutheran tradition of Pauline exegesis. That the understanding of Luther that emerges from this work of Sanders is highly questionable has since been widely documented. Forensic justification was used by Sanders in a very narrow and fictional sense, allowing no dimension of change or transformation. And although exegetes like Sanders had no problems distinguishing between different kinds of forensic justification, or combining forensic justification with participation, this interpretational generosity was not transmitted to their understanding of forensic justification in a Lutheran context.[12] Sanders, explicitly and implicitly, made Luther a central character in the New Perspective, a positioning that his followers did not hesitate to keep. The traditional

---

1977; J.D.G. DUNN, The New Perspective on Paul (1983) (in: IDEM, Jesus, Paul and the Law, 1990, 183–214). See also H. HÜBNER: Pauli theologia proprium (NTS 26, 1980, 445–473), 448.

11 F. WEBER, System der altsynagogischen palästinischen Theologie aus Targum, Midrasch und Talmud, 1880. To Weber's dependence on a Lutheran realm of understanding, see, for example, T. LAATO, Paulus und das Judentum, 1991 and F. AVEMARIE, Tora und Leben. Untersuchungen zur Heilsbedeutung der Tora in der frühen rabbinischen Literatur (TSAJ 55), 1996, 11–23.

12 Cf. SANDERS, Paul (see n. 10), 492, n. 57, »The term ›forensic‹ is somewhat ambiguous, since it can refer to God's declaring one to be righteous (though he is not), a meaning conveyed by the term ›imputation‹ and the catch-phrase *simul justus et peccator*. This meaning arises from Luther's theology (see, for example, his *Commentary on Galatians*, ET, pp. 22–23.26.137 f.223–229), and it is a meaning which I do not find in Paul. Paul does use the term forensically in the sense of the acquittal of past transgressions (=forgiveness), and this is the sense referred to here.« Wilfried Härle's objection can here be made representative: W. HÄRLE, Paulus und Luther. Ein kritischer Blick auf die »New Perspective« (ZThK 103, 2006, 326–393): »Aber an *einem* Punkt besteht jedenfalls – entgegen dem Urteil von E.P. Sanders – vollständige Gemeinsamkeit zwischen Paulus und Luther: das ›paulinische‹ Sein in Christus und die ›lutherische‹ Anrechnung der Gerechtigkeit Christi sind nicht fiktiv, sondern *real* verstanden. Das schöpferische Wort, durch das Gott den Gottlosen durch den Glauben gerecht macht, ist nicht weniger wirkmächtig als das schöpferische Wort, durch das Gott dem, was nicht ist, ruft, daß es sei, und als das neuschaffende Wort, durch das Gott die Toten ins ewige Leben ruft (Röm 4,17).«

Lutheran exegesis represented a strong rhetorical position, but the attack on this tradition did not lack rhetorical strength either.

At the same time, Sanders was influenced by a clearly Christian,[13] if not Protestant, doctrine of grace in his reading of Second Temple Judaism. For example, his understanding of covenantal nomism implies an understanding of obedience where »obedience maintains one's position in the covenant, but [...] does not earn God's grace as such«.[14] For this reason, it has been criticised that Sanders' understanding of Palestinian Judaism was hard to distinguish from the traditional understanding of Paul' own religion. Later studies on Paul by Sanders show that there is hardly any difference between his understanding of what is known as covenantal nomism[15] and Paul, and he ends finding logical inconsistencies in Paul,[16] as also Heikki Räisänen did.[17] According to Räisänen, the reformers were right when finding an emphasis on divine grace in Paul, but in this question Paul is on the same line as the best of Jewish tradition.[18] Sanders and Räisänen illustrate that it is difficult to avoid at least some mirroring effect from one's opponent in strong controversies.

And in the eager of positioning, the New Perspective overlooked that even a Luther scholar and theologian like Gerhard Ebeling, paradigmatically representing the Lutheran Paul, comes very close to providing a pre-

---

13 As criticised by J. D. G. Dunn in DUNN Romans, 1988, lxvi with reference to M. D. HOOKER, Paul and Covenantal Nomism (1982) (in: EADEM, From Adam to Christ: Essays on Paul, 1990, 155–164). In a way this movement has been repeated in the work of Seth Schwartz, who in Judaism sees a society built on non-economic charity instead of competitive reciprocal relations, whereby he in Judaism's relation to Roman society finds a post-Kantian distinction between self-interested economic reciprocity and altruistic pure giving. S. SCHWARTZ, Were the Jews a Mediterranean Society? Reciprocity and Solidarity in Ancient Judaism, 2010. For a precise critique of Schwartz, see the forthcoming volume on Paul and the Gift from J. M. G. BARCLAY.

14 SANDERS, Paul (see n. 10), 420.

15 Cf. E. P. SANDERS, Judaism, Practice and Belief 63bce-66ce, 1992, 372–373.

16 E. P. SANDERS, Paul, the Law and the Jewish People, 1983.

17 H. RÄISÄNEN, Paul and the Law, 1983, 228: »In sum, I am not able to find in the relevant literature *any* conception of the law, which involves such inconsistencies or such arbitrariness as does Paul's.«

18 Ibd., 268.

cise description of the difference between Luther and Paul in his 1958 article on the law. The most significant difference for Ebeling is the way Luther makes a permanent situation of simultaneity out of a clear transition from one situation into another in Paul. Ebeling furthermore pointed to the tendency of weakening the original Pauline meaning in Luther's understanding.[19] According to Pannenberg, who dealt with the Luther-Paul problem in his Systematic Theology, this particular issue has led an almost miserable life in Lutheran Dogmatics.[20] However, to Pannenberg's conclusion has to be added that, in Ebeling's otherwise clear formulations, a tendency towards a certain reductionism can also be detected. It does not seem plausible, in the way Ebeling argues, that Luther is ignorant of a before and after regarding the life of a Christian. Pannenberg rightly points to Luther's understanding of baptism; at least his discussion with Latomus shows that baptism does play a crucial role in Luther's thinking, even if it is not always clearly expressed. The same is the case with Luther's revision of the ritual of baptism, which in 1526 surely reduced the number of ritual elements, but nevertheless kept the most crucial: the pre-baptismal cross signature and the post-baptismal clothing of the baptised in the christening gown, symbolising death and resurrection, respectively. It still, surely, remains a rather peculiar fact that Luther in his famous Preface to Romans only mentions baptism once, and when he does it, then in connection with the fulfilment of the baptism in the obedient taming of the body in the actual life of the Christian.[21] But even at this point, the

---

19 See G. EBELING, Erwägungen zur Lehre vom Gesetz (in: DERS., Wort und Glaube I, 1960, 255–293), 269–270: »Denn das ist doch, wenn man von der reformatorischen Lehre von Gesetz und Evangelium her an Paulus herantritt, die auffallendste Differenz: daß aus dem Nacheinander in einer einmaligen, nicht wieder rückgängig zu machenden Wende das reformatorische Schema ein eigentümlich gleichzeitigen Nebeneinander, sozusagen eine Wende in Permanenz gemacht hat, die in dem Verdacht steht, gar keine Wende zu sein.«

20 See W. PANNENBERG, Systematische Theologie Bd. III, 1993, 75–84.94–113, esp. p. 96.

21 WAB 7; 19,23–26, Vorrede auf die Epistel S. Pauli an die Roemer (1522): »Darumb wyr mit vns selbs genug zu schaffen vnser leben lang, das wyr vnsern leyb zemen, seyne luste todten vnd seyne gelidmas zwingen, das sie dem geyst gehorsam seyn vnd nicht den lusten, damit wyr dem tod vnd aufferstehen Christi gleych seyn, vnd vnsere tauffe volbringen.« WAB 7; 20,23–28 (1522/46): »Darumb haben wir mit vns selbs gnug zu

taming of the body is what distinguishes the baptised from the non-baptised and makes the paraenesis in Luther a pretty close functional equivalent to Pauline paraenesis. Such a reading would support Risto Saarinen's conclusion in his studies on the Pauline Luther. Saarinen finds in Luther an emphasis on the Christian life as a being in Christ, where the »justified person in his or her union with Christ can perform ›theological actions‹ in which good results are brought forth spontaneously, as the good fruit produced by a good tree«.[22]

Pauline paraenesis has over most of the last century remained a difficult subject, though not only for New Testament scholars. Luther research since Adolf Schlatter has used some time in clarifying the role of the law for the justified sinner.[23] A major tendency in contemporary exegesis emphasises the paraenetic sections, not as appendices but as the real aim of the Pauline letters and therefore seen as examples of the non-Lutheran Paul.[24] Also this view has to be nuanced. Luther has a positive

---

schaffen vnser leben lang, das wir vnsern Leib zemen, seine lueste toedten, vnd seine Gliedmas zwingen, das sie dem Geist gehorsam seien vnd nicht den luesten. Deutung der Tauffe. Damit wir dem Tod vnd aufferstehen Christi gleich sein, vnd vnser Tauffe volbringen (die auch den Tod der suenden vnd new Leben der gnaden bedeutet) Bis das wir gar rein von suenden, auch leiblich mit Christo aufferstehen, vnd ewiglich leben.«

22 SAARINEN, The Pauline Luther (see n. 4), 83. See also R. SAARINEN: How Luther got Paul right (Dialog 46, 2007, 170–173).

23 A. SCHLATTER, Luthers Deutung des Römerbriefes, 1917. Here Schlatter critisises Luther for reducing the meaning of justification and bypass a positive articulation of the Christian life. Schlatter's discussion was continued critically in P. ALTHAUS, Paulus und Luther über den Menschen, ²1952 and in W. JOEST, Gesetz und Freiheit. Das Problem des Tertius Usus legis bei Luther und die neutestamentliche Parainese, ³1961. In this book, Joest argues for an understanding of paraenesis, where the exhortations are connecting the resurrection with the actual life of the Christian (195–196). See also W. JOEST, Paulus und das lutherische Simul Iustus et Peccator (KuD 1, 1955, 269–320).

24 See, for example, the edited volume Early Christian Paraenesis, ed. by J. STARR and T. ENGBERG-PEDERSEN, 2004, although without reaching any final result. There is, however, a general tendency to see the paraenesis not as an appendix to the Pauline letters, but as the point to which the whole argumentation in the letters is directed. Paul's central concern is to make the communities live according to God's will. But again one might question whether this is the absolute opposite of Luther's view and whether one really can separate aims and medium in this way. In the end, the gospel in Luther is

166

use of paraenesis for the realisation of a life between human beings plea-
sant to God.[25]

We are, for such reasons, forced to conclude that Luther's theology
represents a multifaceted framework of interconnected thoughts, several
of which contradict each other *when* isolated. His understanding of the
Christian as a sinner *re vera* and justified *in spe* seems to exclude any kind
of difference between the baptised and the non-baptised (cf. WA 56; 347,12;
WA 39,1; 564,4) and surely does add something new to the Pauline texts.
Although many formulations in Luther can be balanced with other formulations,[26] and the difference between, for example, being a sinner *re vera*
and a justified *in spe* can be interpreted as a difference in visibility,[27]
Luther's formulations cannot always be praised for their clarity.[28] This, as

---

oriented towards bringing the sinner into the relationship where God's will will be done.
See also J. M. G. BARCLAY, Obeying the Truth: A Study of Paul's Ethics in Galatians, 1988.

25 In fact paraenesis also plays a central role in Luther. For different views on this matter,
supporting a paraenetic orientation in Luther, see P. ALTHAUS, Die Theologie Martin
Luthers, [7]1994, 238: »Luther gebraucht die Formel Melanchthons nicht, die dann von
der Konkordienformel, von der lutherischen Orthodoxie und der Theologie des 19. Jahrhunderts übernommen wurde: vom *tertius usus legis*. Aber der Sache nach findet dieser
sich auch bei ihm.« Oswald Bayer has emphasised Luther's »Haus-Tafel-Ethic«. See O.
BAYER, Nachfolge-Ethos und Haustafel-Ethos. Luthers seelsorgerliche Ethik (in: DERS.,
Freiheit als Antwort. Zur theologischen Ethik, 1995, 147–163). Also Saarinen argues in
favour of a positive fulfilment of the law by Luther, although not a third use, and in contrast to Paul with an anti-Pelagian emphasis. See SAARINEN, The Pauline Luther (see
n. 4), 78–81.

26 Cf., for example, WA 10,1,1; 377,1–4: »Eyn Christen mensch hatt durch seyne tauff und
glawben schon alle ding und wirt yhm geben allis auff eyn mal, on das erß nit auffge-
decht sihet, ßondern ym glawben yhm behallten wirt, umb dißes lebens willen, wilchs
nit ertragen mocht solcher gutter offenbaring.«

27 As by P. MANNS, Fides absoluta – Fides incarnata. Zur Rechtfertigungslehre Luthers im
großen Galater-Kommentar (in: Reformata Reformanda, FS für Hubert Jedin, hg. v. E.
ISERLOH/K. REPGEN, 1965, 265–312), 282–283; J. FORSBERG, Das Abrahambild in der Theologie Luthers. Pater fidei sanctissimus (VIEG 117), 1984, 91–98, and S. PEURA, Mehr als
ein Mensch. Die Vergöttlichung als Thema der Theologie Martin Luthers von 1513 bis
1519, 1990, 172f.

28 Therefore, Wilfried Härle's reservation remains valid. See HÄRLE (see n. 12), 390: »Es
stellt ein sprachliches und inhaltliches Problem dar, daß Luther immer wieder (z.B. WA
56; 347,12; WA 39,1; 564,4) sagt, die Christen seien ›re vera‹ Sünder, ›reputatione Dei‹

well as the differentiated ways by which Luther reads and uses Paul, has to be acknowledged.

IV Grace in the New Perspective

Post-Sandersian research on Paul leaves the distinct impression that the doctrine of grace was as profound in Second Temple Judaism as in Protestant theology. This, however, would imply that grace is a simple term that is easily understood. I am not convinced. Is grace really a concept that one can unambiguously operate with under all circumstances? Is it possible to understand Western theological and mental history at all without paying attention to the difficulties in reaching agreement about the nature of divine grace? In many cases, it is exactly the question of the nature of divine grace that is the motor of theological development, and the history of Christian theology shows abundant difficulties in conceptualising grace (Χάρις), not least in keeping it generous and excessive[29] – which in itself implies a certain perception of grace. If grace is the superabundant gift (as in Rom 5:17 and II Cor 9:14), then it cannot avoid the ambiguities otherwise connected to the gift. From an anthropological as well as philosophical perspective, gifts are from the outset ambivalent. And this ambivalence seems to make good and evil inseparable, as the good gift is often difficult to distinguish from the bad one.[30] A huge gift can be devastating

oder ›in spe‹ jedoch Gerechte. Dadurch *kann* der Eindruck entstehen, die Sünde sei *wirklich*, die Gerechtigkeit bloß *erdacht*. Dieses Mißverständnis ist bei Sanders anzutreffen, und es gibt bei Luther *Formulierungen*, durch die er dieses Mißverständnis mitzuverantworten hat. Die Einsicht, daß das, was Gott dem Sünder zuspricht und zurechnet, an Wirklichkeit der Realität *überlegen* ist, ist bei Luther jedoch stets vorauszusetzen und mitzudenken – auch dort, wo sie sprachlich nicht deutlich zum Ausdruck kommt.«

29 M. L. Frettlöh, Der Charme der gerechten Gabe. Motive einer Theologie und Ethik der Gabe am Beispiel der paulinischen Kollekte für Jerusalem (in: »Leget Anmut in das Geben.« Zum Verhältnis von Ökonomie und Theologie, hg. v. J. Ebach u.a. [Jabboq 1], 2001, 105–161).

30 In exemplary clarity, formulated by F. Viatte and R. Michael in the foreword to J. Starobinski, Largesse, trans. by J. M. Todd, 1997, vii: »This Story of the gift is a kind of double-entry bookkeeping: it has a light side and a dark side. Each of its stages is bur-

when no return is possible, and it also seems impossible to imagine a relationship without any kind of mutuality and exchange, even if the return is sheer gratitude.

Furthermore, we can understand Old Testament Judaism and its idea of the covenant without paying attention to the fact that several mediators are installed in Israel's history to make the chosen people live under divine grace: the Torah,[31] the prophets, the Temple, even Wisdom? All of them imply some dimension of divine presence on the human side of the covenant in order to make the human participants live up to their covenantal responsibilities under the grace of the covenant.

But it is one thing to argue, as Dunn does, that a concept of grace runs through the Old Testament, Second Temple Judaism as well as the Pauline Letters – Dunn believes he learned this from the Westminster Confession.[32] It is quite another thing to say that grace is always unambiguous and never insufficient. If grace really is grace, then there is something paradigmatically paradoxical about this concept. If grace is so self-evident, then all these variations that theological discussions have presented through the ages seem difficult to explain.

This point has been touched upon by scholars criticising the New Perspective for lacking a concise understanding of Pelagianism and Semi-Pelagianism.[33] I would argue in favour of a broadening of this issue, cover-

---

dened or cursed with the fundamental duality at work in the act of giving, where good has become inseparable from evil.«

31 For the role of the Torah, see, for example, AVEMARIE (see n. 11). Avemarie's description of the role of the Torah bears many similarities to Protestant ethics: »Die Tora ist nach rabbinischen Verständnis Mittel und Weg zum Leben, Mittlerin des Heils. Aber sie ist mehr als das. Israel hält sie, weil Gott sie gegeben hat und weil es sie liebt.« (AVEMARIE [see n. 11], 584).

32 J.D.G. DUNN, The New Perspective on Paul: Revised Edition, 2008, 19f: »from the Westminster Confession I early on learned that there is a single ›covenant of grace‹ running through both Testaments – ›not two covenants of grace differing in substance, but one and the same under various dispensations‹ – and that ›the justification of believers under the Old Testament was […] one and the same with the justification of believers under the New Testament‹.«

33 See T. GEORGE, Modernizing Luther, Domesticating Paul: Another Perspective (in: Justificaion and Variegated Nomism: Volume 2 – The Paradoxes of Paul, ed. by D.A. CAR-

ing the very concept of grace. In order to see the relation between Paul and Luther, a mere lexical comparison of the understanding of, for example, grace cannot be satisfying. What is needed is a reflection on the very nature of grace, which is a theological rather than lexical issue but, at the same time, implies that we interpret both Luther and Paul with regard to their own particular context. Such a procedure could end in a confirmation of central aspects in especially the New Perspective's understanding of Paul and, surely, of Judaism although, at the same time, criticising a loose use of theological terms and biased reading of the Lutheran tradition. Nevertheless, this would result in seeing the relation between Paul in the midst of Second Temple Judaism and Protestant theology as a continuation rather than as a rupture – a continuation specifically related to the struggle of understanding the nature of divine grace

V Sensus proprius *and* sensus ipsius *in dealing with Paul and Luther*

I cannot give a full explanation of the somewhat odd picture by which Luther is represented in the New Perspective, but I will attempt to point to some rather central aspects. There has been a tendency in the Lutheran tradition to read a certain *sensus proprius* into the texts of both Paul and Luther. Hermeneutically, it is impossible to get rid of all subjective elements in text interpretations. However, it seems that certain elements from Luther's theology can liberate themselves more or less from their original context and overshadow others. This has been the case with the two kingdoms doctrine versus the doctrine of three orders, the latter truly balancing the former. But it has also been the case with the doctrine of justification in its relation to other central elements in Luther's theology and with the distinction between law and gospel.

This gives reason for an ongoing examination of the role and context of the doctrine of justification. As the theologian Niels Henrik Gregersen

SON/P. T. O'BRIEN/M. A. SEIFRIED 2004, 437–463), 450, referring to P. F. M. ZAHL, Mistakes of the New Perspective on Paul (Themelios 27, No. 1, 2002, 5–11).

has argued, the doctrine of justification is not in itself, from a theological point of view, an object of belief.

> The saving power of Christ, and not a doctrine of justification, is what must be believed [...] a distinction must be made between a first-order address of the biblical message and the second-order theological reflection on this message.[34]

This theological statement converges with a methodical problem. The doctrine of justification has in the Lutheran tradition, and perhaps even by the reformers themselves, occasionally been emphasised so strongly that it has partly been neglecting the fact that the justification is not the primary frame of reference for the gospel's restoration of the God-human relationship. On the contrary, the doctrine of justification is embedded in a stronger framework of primary relationality, often expressed in social metaphors. By relocating the doctrine of justification within the framework of a full theology, it may be possible to at least partly solve the problem of the criteriological function of this key doctrine.[35]

The court metaphor has a long theological and biblical background, but a court room is not a total social fact, as Marcel Mauss and others have called gift-economy,[36] although Ebeling's understanding and use of the fundamental character of the *coram*-relation comes pretty close to depicting such a »total social fact«, although in existential attire.[37] The ideal court always serves the society outside the court room doors. In the same way, any understanding of the doctrine of justification that does not pay attention to its function in re-establishing the human fellowship with God through Christ and in the Holy Spirit runs the severe risks of reducing its meaning.[38] Too strong an emphasis on the forensic dimension of

---

34 N.H. GREGERSEN, Ten Theses on the Future of Lutheran Theology (in: The Gift of Grace: The Future of Lutheran Theology, ed. by IDEM et al., 2005, 1–16), 6.

35 An attempt to do so can be found in R. SAARINEN, Theology of Giving as a Comprehensive Lutheran Theology (in: Transformations of Luther's Theology: Historical and Contemporary Reflections, ed. by C. HELMER/B.K. HOLM [AKThG 32], 2011, 141–159).

36 M. MAUSS, The Gift: The Form and Reason for Exchange in Archais Societies, 1990, 78f.

37 G. EBELING, Luther. Einführung in sein Denken, 1964, 220–230.

38 As has been the case for those following what seems to be Melanchthon's reduction of the meaning of justification to its mere forensic dimension. For a brief discussion of this issue, see M.A. SEIFRIED, Paul's Uses of Righteousness Language Against Its Hellenistic

justification runs the risk of reducing faith to a life in front of God as opposed to a life with God – the latter seeming to preoccupy Paul the most – or to downplay the role of divine self-giving, which is also crucial to Paul.[39] As least as to the first point, New Testament scholars can rightly object to several too Lutheran readings. The question remains, however, whether Luther himself is adequately read in this juxtaposition. Some think so, others do not. Luther scholars from Helsinki are very reluctant, and so are Luther scholars who try to read Luther's theology as a theology of giving.[40]

Background (in: Justification [see n. 33], 39–74), 67–74; H. BLOCHER, Justification of the Ungodly (*Sola Fide*): Theological Reflections (in: Justification [see n. 33], 465–500), 490–499. The fact that one thereby runs the risk of reducing Melanchthon to a mere negative foil of the right Pauline-Lutheran understanding is yet another issue to be taken seriously. One might expect that close readings of Melanchthon may further nuance the debate.

39 The latter is even the case in Saarinen's use of Seneca in emphasising the role of the intention for understanding the gift as gift. See R. SAARINEN, Finnish Luther Studies: A Story and a Program (in: Engaging Luther: A (New) Theological Assessment, ed. by O.-P. VAINIO, 2010, 1–26), 17 f: »I am more inclined to grant God's merciful favor a conceptual primacy over the *donum*, the effective fruit. I believe that a gift can only be identified as gift if we know the intention of the giver. Thus divine mercy and benevolence in a way precedes divine gifts. At the same time, however, I interpret forgiveness in more effective terms than has been customary in Finnish research.« Although Saarinen adds important new aspects to the Finnish approach to Luther, it is nevertheless the question whether the emphasised focus on the intention of the giver is not in danger of reducing the gift-giving-relation to a single aspect by not downplaying the simultaneity of divine intention and divine self-giving. See also below.

40 Ibd.; R. SAARINEN, God and the Gift: An Ecumenical Theology of Giving, 2005; B.K. HOLM: Gabe und Geben bei Luther. Das Verhältnis zwischen Reziprozität und reformatorischer Rechtfertigungslehre (TBT 134), 2006; N.H. GREGERSEN, Radical Generosity and the Flow of Grace (in: Word – Gift – Being: Justification – Economy – Ontology, ed. by B. K. HOLM/P. WIDMANN [RPT 37], 2009, 117–144). An exemption is M. Seils, who at the Luther Congress in 1983 almost coined the term theology of giving, but in his recent work has been very critical of any attempt to include some kind of mutuality in divine giving. See M. SEILS, Die Sache Luthers (LuJ 52, 1985, 64–80); IDEM, Gabe und Geschenk. Eine Zugabe (in: Denkraum Katechismus. FS für Oswald Bayer, hg. v. J. VON LÜPKE/E. THAIDIGSMANN, 2009, 87–108).

VI Paul between covenant thinking and Roman gift-giving?

To focus on the social dimension of the Lutheran doctrine of justification is similar to the long tradition of locating Paul's understanding of justification in relation to issues related to sociality, as the New Testament scholar Nils Alstrup Dahl did several years before the New Perspective.[41] »Obviously«, Dahl states,

> the doctrine of justification is not primarily social; it is theological and soteriological. But the framework which Paul uses to locate the doctrine is social and historical rather than psychological and individualistic[42]

Dahl clearly points to the same individualistic reductionism in the Lutheran tradition that Krister Stendahl had in mind, and in this respect his reading is equally questionable.[43] On the other hand, Dahl provides a fruitful perspective, when extended beyond Dahl and his followers,[44] by ensuring that it does not merely focus on the social function and implica-

---

41 See N. A. DAHL, The Doctrine of Justification: Its Social Function and Implication (in: IDEM, Studies in Paul: Theology for the Early Christian Mission, 1977, 95–120). See also BRINKMAN (see n. 5), 69–72.

42 DAHL (see n. 41), 110.

43 K. Stendahl's idea of a specific introspective conscience in the Western world originating from Augustine just does not pay attention to the »introspective« character of many Old Testament Psalms. See K. STENDAHL: The Apostle Paul and the Introspective Conscience of the West (in: IDEM, Paul among Jews and Gentiles and other Essays, 1977, 78–96). On the other hand, it is by no means obvious that justification in Luther's theology could be equivocated with introspection. As P. Hinlicky has argued, justification in Luther is rather »extra-spection«. P. HINLICKY, Luther and the Beloved Community: A Path for Christian Theology after Christendom, 2010, 122.

44 See, for example, F. WATSON, Paul, Judaism, and the Gentiles: A Sociological Approach, 1986, 179: »Attention to the social context and function of Paul's arguments produces an interpretation of Paul in some respects very different from that which stems from the Lutheran tradition. For example, the fundamental antithesis between faith and works is not understood as primarily theological contrast between receiving grace as a free gift and earning it by one's own efforts, but as a sociological contrast between two different ways of life: ›faith‹, the way of life practiced in the Pauline congregations, marked by the abandonment of certain norms and beliefs of the surrounding society, and the adoption of new norms and beliefs; and ›works‹, the way of life of Jewish community sought to live in conformity with the law of Moses.«

tions of justification in a narrow sense, but also takes into consideration the social content of the doctrine itself and the social framework to which it belongs. Perhaps then the doctrine of justification in Luther can be regarded as nothing less than social in its core.[45]

One way to proceed would be to follow the trend in one branch of the New Perspective that relates Paul to Roman culture, placing him – like the New Testament scholar and expert in ancient philosophy Troels Engberg-Pedersen has done – between Jewish covenant thinking and Roman gift-giving relationships as described by Cicero and, especially, by Seneca in *De beneficiis*,[46] which means between two different understandings of

---

45 It is quite clear, as the Käsemann disciple H. Boers argued, that Paul did not understand the human being only »as an individual who stands existentially alone before the ultimate«, but as one who is also concerned with the human being as a »social being for whom engagement with others is constitutive for the meaning of life«. See H. Boers, The Justification of the Gentiles, 1994, 216. But the question that needs to be asked is: Whoever did so – apart from New Testament scholars in their description of their counter position? – See, for example, E. P. Sanders, Paul: A very short introduction, 2009, 77f: »The passive verb ›to be righteoused‹ in Paul's letters almost always means to be *changed*, to be *transferred* from one realm to another: from sin to obedience, from death to life, from being under the law to being under grace [...]. Luther saw the world and the Christian life quite differently. He was impressed by the fact that, though a Christian, he nevertheless felt himself to be a ›sinner‹: he suffered from guilt. Paul, however, did not have a guilty conscience.«

46 I will point especially to the work of T. Engberg-Pedersen, leaving aside, however, the whole question of Paul's »Stocism«. See T. Engberg-Pedersen, Gift-Giving and Friendship: Seneca and Paul in Romans 1–8 on the Logic of God's Χάρις and Its Human Response (HTR 101, No.1, 2008, 15–44); Idem, Om gavegivning hos Pierre Bourdieu, Seneca og Paulus (in: Historie og konstruktion, FS til N. P. Lemche, ed. by M. Müller/ T. L. Thompson, 2005, 129–142). The fact that we find Paul using the language of Roman gift-giving relations, as they are described by Seneca, does not in itself make Paul a Stoic, as Engberg-Pedersen argues; it does not preclude it either, though. See T. Engberg-Pedersen, Paul and the Stoics, 2000. – Further studies on Paul and the gift include J. M. G. Barclay's forthcoming volume on Paul and the gift and J. M. G. Barclay, Paul, the Gift and the Battle over Gentile Circumcision: Revisiting the Logic of Galatians (Australian Biblical Review 58, 2010, 36–56). See also J. R. Harrison, Paul's Language of Grace in its Graeco-Roman Context (WUNT II 172), 2003, who situates Paul in the context of Roman gift-giving, but, nevertheless, find in Paul a notion of a pure gift, which I find rather problematic (see below). For this discussion, see Engberg-Pedersen, Gift-Giving (see n. 46), 17, who also draws on unpublished material by J. M. G. Barclay and D. B. Mar-

---

the reciprocal structures building the base of society.[47] If we follow this line of reading, we may be able to see a connection between Paul and Luther. If Paul – as Engberg-Pedersen suggests – is using the Hellenistic and Roman gift-giving system to articulate how Judaic covenantal theology also includes the non-Jewish Christians,[48] then we seem to be rather close to a form of language uniting Paul and Luther across the Augustinian divide that introduced Pelagianism as a problem in need of a solution. What makes this possible is the fact that the reformers, Luther as well as Melanchthon, also used what we could call the gift-giving system of Seneca in describing the gift of grace and its consequences.[49]

tin. For the role of gift and exchange in New Testament in general, see O. DAVIDSEN: Give and Take: Narrative Exchange in the New Testament (web-publication: URL: http://pure. au.dk/portal/files/44152999/GT.OD.Part_One.Print.Open.pdf and http:// pure.au.dk/ portal/files/44153218/GT.OD.Part_Two.Print.Open.pdf). – From the point of view of systematic theology, M. Frettlöh has made some fine studies in gift exchange in Paul: M.L. FRETTLÖH, Und […] höchst anmutig sein das Danken. *Gabe*theologische und -ethische Perspektiven auf den Dank als *Ereignis* (NZSTh 47, 2005, 198–225); and FRETTLÖH, Charme (see n. 29).

47 See to this the forthcoming volume of J.M.G. BARCLAY on Paul and the Gift, where he offers a much more solid distinction between Old Testament Judaism and the Roman world than the dichotomised version found in the work of SCHWARTZ (see n. 13). The concept of the »pure« gift shows all signs of lack of terminological clarity as the pure gift can be found both in Paul, as by HARRISON (see n. 46), and in Second Temple Judaism, as by Schwartz. The fact that scholars have been able to find pure giving in both ancient Judaism, Paul and Luther could indicate that the concept is more connected to the semantic imagination of the reader or to his or her context than to the texts themselves.

48 Cf. ENGBERG-PEDERSEN, Gift-Giving (see n. 46), 27: »The background to the Christ event was set up in language that was covenantal rather than of the gift-giving sort. Then the notion of the gift was introduced in order to extend the covenantal language of God's justice, so as to explain the change from wrath to its opposite (the gift). Once it had been shown, by the end of chapter 4, how the original purpose of the covenant had been achieved through that change, the road was open to bring in even more elements from the gift-giving system.« – Jean Starobinski makes a converging connection between the idea of the covenant in OT and the gift-giving system of Roman culture, in general, and stoic philosophy, in particular, but without mentioning Paul. See STAROBINSKI (see n. 30), 64–71.

49 As in Luther's Anti-Latomus, WA 8; 105,36–198,31 and Melanchthon's understanding of

When Paul is read as a link between the covenant-thinking in Second Temple Judaism and Roman gift-giving, then Paul can be said to contribute to the formulation of a problem that theologians after him had to deal with – especially reading Paul in a new context formed at least partly by Paul himself. The primary link between Paul and Luther (or Melanchthon) then does not lie in Paul, but in the mental world that Paul contributed to create. This separation of Paul and Luther, however, has to be balanced by a new connection that could be provided by readings like Engberg-Pedersen's, though without reference to the consequences for the Paul-Luther debate. I will try to sketch these, thereby arguing that the relation between Paul and Luther has to be understood in relation to the world in front of the text, especially Paul's, dealing with the questions the text produces.

Considering some of the traditional crucial points in the debate, we may conclude that justification in Paul is not identical with the forgiveness of sins, and neither is that the case in Luther. The forgiveness of sins has its place in a large context of communication between God and human beings in a broad sense, involving some ideas of exchange of goods, acknowledgements, honours and benefits.

Using Seneca as a prototype of ancient gift-giving, it is possible to show how the same logic is used in two totally different settings. When the gift-giving system of ancient society, with its logic of benefits and recognition of the giver, is used both in Paul to integrate the pagan world in the salvation history and in Luther and Melanchthon to integrate the sinner in the renewed fellowship with God, overcoming the experience of divine wrath, then the understanding of similarities and differences could be nuanced, as could the sense of how the same thought model originated from basic social interaction.[50]

---

grace in P. MELANCHTHON, Loci communes 1521, übersetzt von H. G. PÖHLMANN, [2]1997, 200–204.

50 Risto Saarinen has argued in favour of using Seneca's *De beneficiis* as an interpretative tool in reading Luther and Melanchthon. See R. SAARINEN, Gunst und Gabe. Melanchthon, Luther und die existentielle Anwendung von Senecas »Über die Wohltaten« (in: Kein Anlass zur Verwerfung. Studien zur Hermeneutik des ökumenischen Gespräches. FS für Otto Hermann Pesch, hg. v. J. BROSSEDER/M. WRIEDT, 2007, 184–197).

According to Engberg-Pedersen, a Kantian reduction of the gift to a pure and unilateral action, implying no reciprocity or mutuality, has been preventing an accurate understanding of the gift. But if this is the case, Luther has to be placed on the same side of this Kantian demarcation line as Paul, which does not preclude that Luther at the same time in a certain sense is a precondition for Kant and modernity in identifying the sinner as the calculating self-centred egoist.[51]

The big issue here is whether Paul's thinking implies a distinction between divine and human initiative and action. New Testament scholar Francis Watson, who enrolled himself in the New Perspective with his book *Paul, Judaism, and the Gentiles: A Sociological Approach* from 1986 that made F. Chr. Baur's implicit Luther critique explicit,[52] has in his recent book distinguished between unconditional salvation, exclusively expressing divine agency, and conditional salvation, involving human agency.[53] This fundamental distinction, to which we shall return shortly,

---

51 Several authors have argued that the reformation implies a major shift in the understanding of gift-giving. See, for example, J.M.G. BARCLAY's forthcoming book and Y. LEV, Charity and Gift Giving in Medieval Islam (in: Charity and Giving in Monotheistic Religions, ed. by M. FRENKEL/Y. LEV, 2009, 235–264), 259: »The divorce of charity from its salvific and purifying associations was a development unique to Protestantism with no parallels in Judaism and Islam.«

52 See, for example, WATSON, Paul, Judaism (see n.44), 13: »Bultmann and other representatives of dialectical theology remain studiously silent about the fact that Baur persistently opposed Lutheran view of Paul's controversy with Judaism – the view which dialectical theology sought to revive. The idea that Paul's ›doctrine‹ might be closely related to his historical activity was implicitly rejected.« For a similar view, see D. BOYARIN, A Radical Jew. Paul and the Politics of Identity, 1994, who sees Paul as primarily a Jewish cultural critic. See also F.C. BAUR, Geschichte der christlichen Kirche vol 1, ³1863, 46–73.

53 F. WATSON, Paul and the Hermeneutics of Faith, 2004, 515–517. See also ibd., 8: »it is conceivable that, precisely within the covenant, future divine saving action might in some sense be conditional on faithful (though not sinless or graceless) observance of the law […]. If, for some Jews, law observance within the covenant was indeed a precondition of divine saving action, there is no longer any reason to deny that Paul *might* have contrasted this emphasis on certain modes of human action with an opposing emphasis on the radical priority of divine action« (italics by author). Watson himself declares that »it

makes Engberg-Pedersen label Watson's Paul just »Once More a Lutheran Paul?« – which is also the title of his review article of Watson's book;[54] although Watson himself assures that nothing could be further from his mind.

There are two significant and interrelated issues at stake here. Firstly, is it possible to operate with unconditional giving, as Barclay also does, without also operating with the idea of the pure gift? If so, Engberg-Pedersen's critique of Watson would be weakened. Secondly, is the distinction

---

is not part of my intention (conscious, subconscious, or whatever) to ›rehabilitate Luther‹« (ibd., 29).

54 T. ENGBERG-PEDERSEN, Article review: Once more a Lutheran Paul? (SJT 59, No. 4, 2006, 439–460), esp. 453–457. See also F. WATSON's reply: Response (see n. 6). According to Engberg-Pedersen the distinction between »faith« and »doing« or »working the law« is not, as Watson argues, the distinction between unconditionality (divine agency or saving action) and conditionality (human »salvific« action), but instead an ethnic one, as Sanders and his successors argued (ENGBERG-PEDERSEN, Lutheran Paul?, 457). Watson is helpful in demonstrating why Paul insisted on equal access for Gentiles as Gentiles, an answer that Sanders and his successors never gave. But according to Engberg-Pedersen, Watson blurs the fact that Paul in fact believed that in Christ one could find what was missing in the law: »the possibility of *fulfilling* the law in the quite concrete sense of actually doing God's will as expressed in the law« (ibd., 458). According to the general tendency within the New Perspective, this is one of the major points of divergence between Luther and Paul. As a consequence of his anthropology, Luther never taught an actual fulfilment of the law. A more careful reading of Luther, however, would show that this did not mean that believers never did fulfil the law. – Watson defends himself against accusations of having broken the exeget's code of good practice by imposing his own preconceptions on the text, distinguishing between divine and human agency in the following way: »I argue on exegetical ground (1) that this should not be understood (as it often has been) as entailing a maximal account of divine agency at the expense of human in the one case, and of human agency at the expense of divine in the other; and (2) that the relation of divine to human agency is nevertheless understood differently on the two sides of the antithesis. ›Faith‹ speaks of a communal life founded on and oriented towards the comprehensive reality of the divine saving action in Christ, of which it is the acknowledgement; ›works‹ speaks of a communal life oriented towards the Torah's prescriptions and prohibitions for the covenant people; and the relation of divine to human agency is understood differently within these two communal contexts.« Watson's objection shows how difficult it is to avoid *sensus proprius* when interpreting a text, even for those who most carefully try to avoid it. For both Paul and Luther scholars this remains a constant *memento*.

---

between unconditional and conditional giving to be avoided in relation to Paul or is it a necessary idea inherent in the Pauline writings? If the latter is the case, then Paul's idea of unconditional giving on the side of God is exactly what makes him break with the Jewish hierarchies, include pagans in the people of God etc. Then there is also a link to the breakdown of hierarchies in the Reformation which cannot be arbitrary.

The inclusion of the sinner in the renewed fellowship with God is not in Luther the pure reception of the pure gift since such a relation could never be understood as a fellowship and would instead reduce justified human beings to mere consumers, which is the permanent risk of exaggerating a pure forensic understanding.

A lot of issues, from social ethics to the Lord's Supper, have been disturbed by the idea of the pure, unilateral gift.[55] But the Lutheran idea of faith largely entails human acknowledgement of the divine giver, and this acknowledgement is precisely the gift that God seems to »want« from humans and is being given to him in the faith that God himself gives. From this perspective, Luther's theology can be read as a radicalisation of the divine-human giving in Paul; co-operation understood correctly is in one sense more important than the content in the act of giving, because in Luther's view humans cannot give anything that does not already belong to God – as is also reflected in Paul (Cf. II Cor 9: 8–11).[56] On the other hand,

---

55 W. Simon has shown how a careful and accurate reading of Luther's texts offers a new and nuanced interpretation of Luther's understanding of sacrifice in the Lord's Supper. See W. SIMON, Die Messopfertheologie Martin Luthers. Voraussetzungen, Genese, Gestalt und Rezeption (SMHR 22), 2003. See J. JOLKONEN, Eucharist (in: Engaging Luther [see n. 39], 108–137) for a »Finnish« reception of Simon's work.

56 See again FRETTLÖH, Charme (see n. 29), 37: »So sehr Paulus sich für ein möglichst hohes Spendenaufkommen einsetzt und auch bereits mit einer Fülle von Gaben rechnet ([II Cor] 8: 20) – entscheidender als die Höhe der Kollekte ist für ihn das ›Dass‹ der Kooperation.« – Following the argument of Frettlöh and her references to O. Bayer's »categorical gift« in particular, Paul and Luther can be said to reflect the fact that humans can fundamentally only give what they do not have. Here Frettlöh refers to B. WALDENFELS (see below n. 60) according to whom the act of giving remains more than the gift, and to Heidegger's concept of »Zu-Gabe« (ibd., 42). One could, however, also have referred to Seneca's understanding of the *beneficium* that remains after the gift has gone. Using the Roman understanding of *beneficium*, as described by Seneca, as a link between Paul

it would also be right to say that the content is the only thing that is really important, because what the human being is given to give is him- or herself in faith, as is the point in Luther's understanding of the three powers or virtues of faith in *On the Freedom of a Christian*.[57]

If we follow the line of »alternative giving« in Christ, then there is surely a bond between Luther and Paul, though not terminologically; both seem to operate with an alternative to earthly ways of giving.[58] No harmonisation, however, is forced upon neither Paul nor Luther, since relations of giving are as close to pure formal structures as one can get, and the specific content remains as historically defined as before.

In this transition of Christianity from the Jewish context through the Roman world to late medieval Christendom, the doctrine of justification

and Luther becomes even more obvious when one compares Bayer's understanding of the divine »Vorgabe« of food, or Luther's understanding of the totality of divine giving in the Small Catechism's explanation of the first article of faith. Also Seneca can operate with a kind of unconditional giving. See Seneca, De beneficiis, 4.5. The description of divine giving in this passage resembles Luther's commentary on the first article of faith in the Small Cathecism, ending with the clarification that all divine giving happens »without any merit or worthiness«. Some key element in the Reformation understanding of divine benevolence in creation and in Seneca's understanding of divine giving in *De beneficiis* are grounded in the same way of thinking, which is yet another argument for using Seneca as a link between Pauline and Lutheran theology. Luther is here not only bound to Senecan social logic, but also to a general tendency in Renaissance humanism, linking the giving God of the Old Testament to the Platonic demiurge and to the God benefactor of Stocism. See STAROBINSKI (see n. 30), 64. Starobinski overlooks, however, that the very idea of the all-giving God also plays a crucial role in Rom 1, although in a negative way. Paul's way of arguing is not that different from Seneca's way of convincing his reader that the gods give gifts through the created nature.

57 WA 7; 53,20–56,14. See B. K. HOLM, Wechsel ohnegleichen. Über die Grundstruktur der Rechtfertigung und Heiligung und das Austauschen von »Gaben« in Luther's »Tractatus de libertate christiana« (NZSTh 40, 1998, 182–196). See also SAARINEN, Finnish Luther (see n. 39), 24–26.

58 In this reading, the distinction between »nehmendes Geben« und »gebendes Nehmen«, which M. L. Frettlöh finds in Paul, converges with Bayer's understanding of the categorical gift in Luther. See O. BAYER, Schöpfungslehre als Rechtfertigungsontologie (in: Word – Gift – Being [see n. 40], 17–42), 20–25. See also B. K. HOLM, Der fröhliche Verkehr. Rechtfertigungslehre als Gabe-Theologie (in: Die Gabe. Ein »Urwort« der Theologie?, hg. v. V. HOFFMANN, 2009, 33–54).

became the vehicle for the continuation of the Pauline rearrangement of social and religious hierarchies, making the doctrine of justification the centre, which it was not in Paul. At the same time, this process opened for Reformation theology the possibility of new reductionisms that would further dissociate Lutheran tradition from Paul.

Both in Paul and in Luther, Christology is the motor, though not in the same way. Luther's theology does not depend exclusively on Paul, but also on John[59] – and in both Paul and John, Luther finds his Chalcedonian Christology confirmed. Paul's Christology is truly an intricate issue, but, notwithstanding some tendencies towards adoptianism, his understanding of the self-giving of God in Christ is one of the cornerstones of the subsequent Christological development.[60] The relation of divine grace to divine self-giving, however, is an issue where thorough scholarly work is still needed.

Finally, the relation between Paul and Luther is not an issue that can be solved by historical analysis alone. The element in Luther that brings him closer to Paul, as argued by Risto Saarinen, seems to be his Christology. This points to a tendency in 20th-century Lutheranism to downplay the role of Chalcedonian Christology in Luther's theology; this is often done by questioning the adequacy of the doctrine of *communicatio idiomatum* as the central doctrinal element.[61] But it is this very element that

---

59 To Luther's high estimation of the Gospel of John, see WADB 6; 10,29–34; WA 33; 200,9; WA 27; 528,8; WA 33; 166,3–5; 353,1. See also C. STANGE, Der johanneische Typus der Heilslehre Luthers im Verhältnis zur paulinischen Rechtfertigungslehre, 1949; J. ATKINSON, Luthers Einschätzung des Johannesevangelium (in: Lutherforschung heute, hg. v. V. Vajta, 1958, 49–56); J.D.K. SIGGINS, Martin Luther's Doctrine of Christ, 1970; M. LIENHARD, Martin Luthers christologische Zeugnis, 1980, 31–37.

60 Cf., for example, the very precise footnote in Magdalena L. Frettlöh's work with reference to B. WALDENFELS, Antwortregister, 1994, FRETTLÖH, Charme (see n.29), n. 11: »In der Menschwerdung wird die Selbsthingabe Gottes zu einem *nehmendem Geben*, also zur menschlich-geschöpflichen Art des Gebens, bei dem das Nehmen – so B. Waldenfels – ›kein *Ansichnehmen*, kein Bekommen oder Erhalten, sondern ein *Aufsichnehmen* und *Übernehmen*‹ (Antwortregister, 614) bedeutet.«

61 References to a sceptical attitude towards a Christology bound to ancient metaphysics are legio. For the central role of *communicatio idiomatum* in Luther's theology, see J.A. STEIGER, Die communicatio idiomatum als Achse und Motor der Theologie Luther. Der

combines Luther's forensic and transformative justification and associates him with the Protestant theology that Dunn asks for. At the same time, it would be rather futile and anachronistic to look for an explicit Chalcedonian Christology in Paul.

This leaves us with the problem that the link between Luther and Paul lies in the Christology that Paul – but not only Paul – builds a foundation for. This means that the connection between Luther and Paul depends on the tradition that Paul can only be said to be inaugurating. But it also means that a purely historical or exegetical solution is impossible to reach. Luther and Paul lived in two different worlds without any contact, despite a corpus of texts passed on through history from one to the other. Theologically, one should find inspiration in the History of Religions School, which, like Wilhelm Heitmüller, could argue that naturally Luther did differ from Paul, but he was closer to Jesus[62] – not by repeating Heitmüller, or Gottschick or Wernle,[63] but by stating that Luther continues a theological reflection on the meaning of the Christ event that Paul initiated, but did not finish.

The link between Luther and Paul thus constitutes the interrelatedness of divine-human gift-giving and its inter-human imitation that is based on structures present in the gift-giving relationship in Greek-Roman culture, but which was definitely further developed. In this transition, Seneca may function as a link between Luther and Paul. First and foremost, because the meaning of Luther's and Melanchthon's distinction between *favor dei* and *donum dei* lies pretty close to Seneca's distinction

»fröhliche Wechsel« als hermeneutischer Schlüssel zu Abendmahlslehre, Anthropologie, Seelsorge, Naturtheologie, Rhetorik und Humor (NZSTh 38, 1996, 1–28).

62 W. HEITMÜLLER, Luther Stellung in der Religionsgeschichte des Christentums (Marburger Akademische Reden 38), 1917. Heitmüller could even see Luther as the necessary correction to Paul: »Aber von einer Erneuerung kann auch hier nicht die Rede sein: der lutherischen Glaubensbegriff überragt den paulinischen bei weitem an Tiefe und Kraft.« And to quote another crucial formulation by Heitmüller: »Nein, Wiederherstellung oder auch nur Erneuerung des Paulinismus war Luthers Christentum nicht, es bedeutet vielmehr die Beseitigung wichtiger Elemente des paulinischen Christentum, der jeningen nämlich, welche die katholische Kirche *mitbegründet* haben.«

63 J. GOTTSCHICK, Paulinismus und Reformation (ZThK 6, 1897, 398–460); P WERNLE, Der Christ und die Sünde bei Paulus, 1897.

between the real *beneficium*, which lies in the intention of the giver, and the actual deed.[64] In the end it all depends on whether Paul can be said to articulate a transferal of convenantal thinking into the gift-giving system of the Greek-Roman world and thus create new ways of understanding divine and human giving.

At least three things become quite clear in reading works of the New Perspective with the eyes of a Luther scholar: Firstly, that exegetes in the New Perspective generally have had an unbecoming reductionist under-standing of Luther and the Lutheran tradition. Secondly, that Lutheran theology itself has contributed to this reductionism by, for example, its stereotypical understanding of non-Lutheran types of religion. Thirdly, that we need, on this background, to let Paul be Paul in his own right without relation to the late medieval discussion about workrighteousness and the role of penance. It is not necessary to see Luther directly in the Pauline letters in order to establish a clear connection. The vision of another, divine, way of giving that crosses or breaks with the world of human economies may be a link that bridges the historical gap between Paul and Luther and modern time without diminishing the distance in between. Relations of mutual giving are universal phenomena; grace, on the other hand, is theologically a much more complex term to be suffi-ciently grasped by a single author.

64 See SAARINEN, Gunst (see n. 50).

Die neue Paulusperspektive und die Lutherische Theologie

Notger Slenczka

These 1: Die Anhänger einer »New Perspective on Paul«[1] vertreten drei Thesen, die im Laufe der Theologiegeschichte des 19. Jahrhunderts, teilweise auch von lutherischen Theologen, bereits mehrfach vorgetragen wurden:

1.1. Nicht neu ist die These, dass die Rechtfertigungslehre nicht das Zentrum, sondern ein »Nebenkrater« der Theologie des Paulus sei – diese These wird bereits von William Wrede und bei Albert Schweitzer vertreten[2]: Paulus reflektiere lediglich eine bestimmte Situation, nämlich die

---

1 Aus der inzwischen uferlosen Literatur gebe ich hier nur wenige Titel an, auf die ich mich im folgenden beziehe; sie sind entweder grundlegend für die gesamte Debatte oder fassen sie zusammen: K. STENDAHL, The Apostle Paul and the Introspective Conscience of the West (HThR 56, 1963, 199–215); E. P. SANDERS, Paul and Palestinian Judaism: A Comparison of Patterns of Religion, 1977; J. D. G. DUNN, The New Perspective on Paul: Collected Essays (WUNT 185), 2007; M. BACHMANN (Hg.), Lutherische und Neue Paulusperspektive. Beiträge zu einem Schlüsselproblem der gegenwärtigen exegetischen Diskussion (WUNT 182), 2005; instruktiv daraus: K. HAAKER, Verdienste und Grenzen der »neuen Perspektive« der Paulus-Auslegung, 1–15; Vgl. auch das einschlägige Themenheft der ZNT 7,2 (2004); E. LOHSE, Theologie der Rechtfertigung im kritischen Disput – Zu einigen neuen Perspektiven in der Interpretation der Theologie des Apostels Paulus (GGA 249, 1979, 66–81).

2 Vgl. W. WREDE, Paulus, Tübingen ²1907; Wredes Feststellung, die Rechtfertigungslehre sei lediglich eine situativ bedingte polemische Lehre, ein »Nebenkrater« der Paulinischen Theologie, wird in der New Perspective kontrovers diskutiert und teilweise abgelehnt, vgl. nur J. D. G. DUNN, The Justice of God: A Renewed Perspective on Justification by Faith (in: Collected Essays, [s. Anm. 1], 187–205), 190; SANDERS (s. Anm. 1), 437; Zu Schweitzer vgl.: A. SCHWEITZER, Die Mystik des Apostels Paulus, 1930, zur Galatischen Kontroverse: 184–200; Gesetz und im »In Christus-Sein« angebrochene Eschatolo-

Infragestellung der Heidenmission und die von judenchristlicher Seite erhobene Forderung, dass die zur Kirche hinzutretenden Heiden zunächst zum Judentum konvertieren müssen.[3] Bereits in dieser Debatte wurde auch die These vertreten, dass im Zentrum der paulinischen Theologie nicht die Rechtfertigungslehre und die Diskussion über das Gesetz, sondern die »Christusmystik« des Apostels, nach der der Glaubende, der an Christus teil hat, eins ist mit Christus und Christus in ihm ist.[4] Einer der Initiatoren der New Perspective, Ed Parish Sanders, bezieht sich für seine Deutung des Zentrums der Soteriologie des Paulus ausdrücklich etwa auf Schweitzer.[5]

1.2. Auch die These, dass ursprünglich und eigentlich das palästinische Judentum den Bund einerseits und den Gesetzesgehorsam andererseits in ein unumkehrbares Verhältnis gestellt hat, ist nicht neu: Der Gesetzesgehorsam begründet nach den Vertretern der New Perspective nicht die Zugehörigkeit zum Bund, sondern der Bund geht jedem »Tun des Gesetzes« als gnädige Anordnung Gottes voraus – der covenantal nomism, nach dem das Tun des Gesetzes nicht das »getting in« begründet, sondern das

gie: 186–193; zum Verhältnis zur Rechtfertigungslehre und deren Unterordnung unter die »Christusmystik«: 201–221, bes. 214–221.

3 Etwa: J.D.G. Dunn, What was the Issue between Paul and »Those of the Circumcision«? (in: Collected Essays, [s. Anm. 1], 143–165); Ders., Justice (s. Anm. 2), 192–199. Bei Sanders ist die Fragestellung etwas anders: Ihm geht es nicht darum, die Identitäten zwischen dem palästinischen Judentum und Paulus herauszuarbeiten, sondern er zeichnet nach, dass Paulus und das palästinische Judentum zwei unterschiedliche »patterns« von Religion repräsentieren, die den unterschiedlichen Gebrauch der »dikaio«-Wurzel determinieren: Der jüdische Gebrauch ist am Phänomen des »staying in« orientiert, der paulinische am »getting in« – und die Probleme zwischen beiden Traditionen ergeben sich aufgrund dieser »pattern«-Verschiebung – vgl. 544f und Kontext: 543–556.

4 Schweitzer (s. Anm. 2), 214–221; vgl. nur: Sanders (s. Anm. 1), 453–472; in der gesamten Passage ordnet Sanders die soteriologische Begrifflichkeit des Paulus, unter der Voraussetzung, dass es um einen »transfer« geht, dieser Vorstellung zu, und zwar so, dass er die Versöhnungs-Terminologie, die nach seiner Ansicht in der Bultmannschule im Zentrum stand (453f), nun unter dem hermeneutischen Schlüssel einer »Partizipation an Christus« einordnet (472); vgl. auch 434–440 u. ö.; vgl. aber 492; vgl. auch Dunn, The New Perspective on Paul: whence, what, whither? (in: Collected Essays, [s. Anm. 1], 1–88), 83f, Anm. 354.

5 Freilich in einer im einzelnen höchst kritischen Auseinandersetzung: Sanders (s. Anm. 1), 453–492.543–556. Vgl. auch Dunn, The New Perspective (s. Anm. 4), 80–86.

»staying in«[6]. Diese These, die sich gegen die von vielen damaligen Neutestamentlern vertretene Degenerationsthese wendet – das intertestamentarische Judentum verliert den Sinn für die Zuordnung von Gnadenbund und Gesetz und betrachtet das Gesetz als Zugangsbedingung in den Bund[7] – geht unmittelbar oder mittelbar auf die Verhältnisbestimmung von Evangelium (Bund) und Gesetz bei Karl Barth zurück.[8] Damit wird erkennbar, dass die »New Perspective on Paul« keine Rückkehr zum unvoreingenommen wahrgenommenen Paulus ist, sondern die »New Perspective on Paul« ist selbst eine Option aus der Perspektive einer theologiegeschichtlich rezenten Alternative zur klassischen lutherischen Perspektive.[9]

1.3. Die Theologie Luthers, in der die Rechtfertigungslehre das Zentrum bildet, ist nicht deckungsgleich mit der Position des Paulus. Diese Feststellung ist in der Lutherischen Theologie des 20. Jahrhunderts längst anerkannt; es ist diskutiert worden, in welchem Sinne die Interpretation der Rechtfertigungslehre durch Luther dennoch ein Recht hat – zu verweisen ist hier, unter anderen, auf Paul Althaus, Wilfried Joest und Gerhard Ebeling.[10]

These 2: Bei E. P. Sanders gewinnt die unter 1.2. aufgeführte These die Gestalt, dass im palästinischen Judentum das Gesetz nicht die Funktion gehabt habe, den Bund Israels mit Gott zu konstituieren, sondern die Funktion, die gnadenhafte Bundeszugehörigkeit zu bewahren. Dem setze Paulus eine Soteriologie entgegen, die nicht an der Bewahrung einer Zugehörigkeit zum Bund, sondern am Übergang (transfer) in einen Heilsstatus orientiert sei, der für Heiden gleichermaßen wie für Juden an die Zugehö-

---

6 Vgl. Sanders (s. Anm. 1), 453–492; Definition des covenantal nomism: 75; vgl. 236.419–428, bes. 422f.

7 Vgl. Sanders (s. Anm. 1), 419f und den Überblick 1–12.

8 Vgl. nur: K. Barth, Evangelium und Gesetz (in: Gesetz und Evangelium, hg. v. E. Kinder u. a., 1968, 1–29).

9 Es wäre hochinteressant, die Wege des indirekten Einflusses der Barthschen Terminologie auf die New Perspective – die sich auch in der Zentralstellung des Bundesbegriffes etwa bei Dunn niederschlägt – zu verfolgen.

10 P. Althaus, Paulus und Luther über den Menschen: ein Vergleich, [4]1963; W. Joest, Gesetz und Freiheit. Das Problem des Tertius usus legis bei Luther und die neutestamentliche Parainese, 1951; G. Ebeling, Erwägungen zur Lehre vom Gesetz (in: Ders., Wort und Glaube, 1960, 255–293).

rigkeit zu Christus gebunden sei.[11] Damit tritt die im Glauben sich reali-
sierende und mit der Wiederkunft Christi vollendete Vereinigung mit
Christus ins Zentrum.[12] Der Widerspruch des Paulus gilt nicht den
»Gesetzeswerken« an sich, sondern dem Konzept eines von Christus
unabhängigen Bundes.[13] Das bedeutet: In der Auseinandersetzung des
Paulus mit seinen am Judentum festhaltenden Gegnern geht es nicht um
die Kritik an einer »Verdienstreligion«, die das zeitgenössische Judentum
in der Umgebung des Paulus auch nie vertreten habe; Sanders fasst das
Ergebnis seiner Studie folgendermaßen zusammen:

> our analysis of Rabbinic [...] literature did not reveal the kind of religion best character-
> ized as legalistic works-righteousness. But more important [...] is the observation that
> in any case that charge is not the heart of Paul's critique. [...] the basis for Paul's polemic
> against the law, and consequently against doing the law, was his exclusivist soteriology.
> Since salvation is only by Christ, the following of *any* other path is wrong. [...] the
> warning [against boasting] [...] is not against a self-righteousness which is based on the
> view that works earn merit before God. The warning is against boasting of the relation-
> ship to God which is evidenced by possession of the law[14].

Der Zusammenprall in Galatien ergibt sich nicht mit einer Ablehnung
von Werken oder aus der Erfahrung des Scheiterns am Gesetz, sondern
mit der Frage, wodurch der Bund mit Gott konstituiert ist: Durch die
Gabe des Gesetzes, oder durch die Teilhabe an Christus.[15]

These 3: Bei Dunn wird diese These dahingehend modifiziert,[16] dass es in
der im Galaterbrief dokumentierten Auseinandersetzung um die Frage
geht, ob die »identity marker« oder »boundary marker« des Judentums
(Reinheitsgebote und Beschneidung) unter den Bedingungen der Zugehörigkeit zu Christus verbindlich bleiben oder nicht.[17] Das bedeutet, dass
zwischen Paulus und seinen Gegnern die Feststellung, dass der Bund ein

11 Vgl. nur SANDERS (wie Anm. 1), 496f.548f.
12 Vgl. nur die Zusammenfassung aaO., 543–556.
13 AaO., 550.
14 Ebd.
15 Etwa aaO., 496f.
16 Zum Verhältnis zu Sanders vgl. nur DUNN, The New Perspective on Paul (in: Collected
   Essays, [s. Anm. 1], 89–110), 90–95; vgl. DUNN: The New Perspective (s. Anm. 4), 4–15.
17 DUNN, New Perspective (s. Anm. 16), 98–107, bes. 100.104.

Gnadenbund sei und die Werke auf die Gnade folgen, als Grundlage der Auseinandersetzung unstrittig ist.

> integral to the idea of the covenant itself, and of God's continued action to maintain it, is the profound recognition of God's initiative and grace in first establishing and then maintaining the covenant. Justification by faith is not a distinctively Christian teaching.[18]

Es ist nicht ganz verständlich, warum Dunn die »justification by faith« (und nicht die »justification by grace«) als das Judentum mit dem Christentum verbindende Lehre angibt – deutlich ist aber, dass Dunn sagen will, dass hier wie dort die Zugehörigkeit zum Bund in der Initiative Gottes begründet ist und jedem menschlichen Werk vorausgeht. In der Auseinandersetzung des Paulus mit seinen Gegnern in Galatien geht es darum, dass bei seinen Gegnern die identity marker eine Bedeutung erlangen, die sie für das Judentum nie hatten, nämlich eine konstitutive Funktion für die Zugehörigkeit zum Bund und damit eine Konkurrenzinstanz zur Initiative Gottes bzw. zum Glauben.[19]

These 4: Das würde bedeuten, dass die »Rechtfertigungslehre« des Paulus nicht in der Weise, wie Luther sie rezipierte, gegen eine Position gerichtet ist, die ein Gerechtwerden des Menschen aus dem Erwerb von Verdiensten verträte, sondern gegen eine Position, die von einem Vorzug des Judentums vor allen anderen Völkern ausgeht:

> Paul's new answer is that the advent of Christ had introduced the time of fulfilment, including the fulfilment of his purpose regarding the covenant. [...] God's eschatological purpose in making the covenant had been the blessing of the nations [...] now that the time of fulfilment had come, the covenant should no longer be conceived in nationalistic or racial [!] terms. No longer is it an exclusively Jewish *qua* Jewish privilege.[20]

Die Kritik des Paulus am Gesetz und an den »Werken des Gesetzes« richtet sich nach Dunn nicht gegen die ethischen Aspekte des Gesetzes, sondern ist strikt im Rahmen der antiochenischen bzw. galatischen Kontroverse zu verstehen: Es geht um den Stellenwert der »identity marker« oder »boundary marker« des Judentums (Beschneidung und Reinheitsge-

---

18 AaO., 98.
19 AaO., 104.
20 AaO., 104; vgl. 199 u. ö.

bote) und damit um die Frage, ob unter den Bedingungen des Gekommen-
seins Christi der Bund weiterhin an der Zugehörigkeit zum Judentum und
damit an einer ethnischen Kategorie hängt, oder ob der Bund nun durch
die Zugehörigkeit zu Christus (und so im Glauben) konstituiert ist.

> we should keep the precise limitations of Paul's distinction between faith in Christ and
> works of law before us. What he is concerned to exclude is he *racial* not the *ritual*
> expression of faith; it is *nationalism* which he denies not *activism*. [...] these works of
> the law [i.e. circumcision and ritual purity] had become identified as indices of Jewish-
> ness, as badges betokening race and nation [...] What Jesus has done [...], in Paul's under-
> standing, is to free the grace of God in justifying from its nationalistic restrictive clamps
> for a broader experience (beyond the circumcised Jew) and a fuller expression (beyond
> concern for ritual purity).[21]

Auch dies ist übrigens ein gerade in der deutschsprachigen Theologie des
18. und 19. Jhs. verbreitetes Muster, in der die Besonderheit des Christentums darin gesehen wurde, dass der zunächst national partikulare Bund
universalisiert werde.[22]

These 5: Das hat Folgen für die Frage, worum es in der Rechtfertigungslehre des Paulus eigentlich geht:

5.1. Nach Dunn geht es um das Abweisen des Anspruchs der judenchristlichen Gegner des Paulus, dass nur die Zugehörigkeit zum Judentum
die Zugehörigkeit zum Bund begründe.[23] Für Paulus sei mit dem Kommen
Christi eine neue heilsgeschichtliche Epoche eingetreten, in der der Bund
nicht mehr an der Zugehörigkeit zum alten Gottesvolk hänge, sondern für
Heiden ebenso wie für Juden an der Zugehörigkeit zu Christus. Die antiochenische und die daran anschließende Auseinandersetzung in Galatien
dreht sich, wie gesagt, um die Frage, ob das Christusgeschehen den Ein-
tritt der Heiden in den Gottesbund mit Israel bedeutet, oder dessen Erwei-
terung zu einem Bund, der Juden und Heiden ohne Unterschied einschließt. Erst dadurch, dass die Gegner des Paulus auf der unveränderten
heilsgeschichtlichen Prärogative des mit Israel geschlossenen Bundes
bestehen und die Übernahme der jüdischen identity-marker erwarten

---

21 AaO., 105.
22 Vgl. nur: A. Ritschl, Unterricht in der christlichen Religion, 1875, § 7.
23 Dunn, New Perspective (s. Anm. 16), 104f; Ders., Paul and Justification by Faith (in:
   Collected Essays, [s. Anm. 1], 361–374).

(Einhaltung der Reinheitsgebote und Beschneidung), werden diese »works of the law« zu Bedingungen des »getting in«, die sie nach dem Verständnis des palästinischen Judentums nie waren.

Damit gewinnt die Auseinandersetzung in Galatien ein heilsgeschichtliches Profil: Im Kontext des Verständnisses der Heidenmission durch die Gegner des Paulus erhalten die Beschneidung und das Einhalten der Reinheitsgebote den Charakter von Bundesbedingungen und werden zu Kriterien des »getting in«.[24]

Dunn führt dies ausdrücklich dahin weiter, dass die Rechtfertigungslehre eigentlich eine antinationalistische oder gar antirassistische Pointe habe:[25] Es geht in ihr um die Unabhängigkeit des Gottesverhältnisses von der Zugehörigkeit zu bestimmten Menschengruppen und damit um die Universalität des Heilswillens Gottes, der in seinem Handeln in Christus in den Israelbund die Heiden einschließt.

5.2. Das hat auf der anderen Seite zur Folge, dass Dunn sagen kann, dass das Gesetz als Verhaltensnorm und die Notwendigkeit eines die Zugehörigkeit zu Christus gestaltenden ethischen Lebens im Widerspruch gegen das Gesetz ursprünglich nicht intendiert ist. Vielmehr ist auch bei Paulus noch eine Position erkennbar (Gal 2,16), nach der der Zusammenhang von Bund und Gesetz nur christologisch präzisiert wird: »Rechtfertigung durch das Werk des Gesetzes gibt es nur im Glauben an Christus« (aber unter der Voraussetzung gibt es ihn[26]). Paulus radikalisiert nun diese Position in Gal 2,17 zu einer Antithese, in der er den Glauben an Christus an die Stelle der identity marker der Beschneidung und der kultischen Reinheit stellt:

> [in Gal 2,16] Paul pushes what began as a qualification on covenantal nomism into an outright antithesis. [...] in this verse faith in Jesus Messiah begins to emerge not simply as a *narrower* definition of the elect of God, but as an *alternative* definition of the elect of God.[27]

---

24 DUNN, New Perspective (s. Anm. 16), 102 f. u. ö.; vgl. SANDERS (s. Anm. 1), 548.496 f.

25 Etwa DUNN, New Perspective (s. Anm. 16), 104 f; DERS., Justice (s. Anm. 2), 199; DERS., Paul and Justification (s. Anm. 23), 364–374.

26 DUNN, New Perspective (s. Anm. 16), 102; vgl. aaO., 74–77; vgl. insgesamt: DUNN, Was Paul against the Law? The Law in Galatians and Romans: A Test-Case of Text in Context (in: Collected Essays, [s. Anm. 1], 259–277).

27 DUNN, New Perspective (s. Anm. 16), 103.

5.3. Das Problem bei Paulus ist nicht die Unfähigkeit zur Erfüllung des Gesetzes. Er geht in aller Selbstverständlichkeit davon aus, dass von den Christen ein den Anforderungen des Gesetzes entsprechendes Leben erwartet wird;[28] in diesem Sinne vertritt Paulus, wie das durchschnittliche Judentum seiner Zeit, einen covenantal nomism. Das bedeutet, dass die Lebensfrage des Paulus nicht, wie die Luthers, die Erfahrung des Scheiterns an der Forderung des Gesetzes war, sondern dass Paulus, wie Dunn klarstellt, ein relativ robustes Gewissen hatte, dem das Bewusstsein, das Gesetz erfüllen zu können, unproblematisch zur Verfügung stand.

These 6: Eine Auseinandersetzung mit der New Perspective könnte sich einerseits an der Frage nach danach orientieren, ob die Neuinterpretation der Theologie des Paulus gerecht wird. Das ist eine Frage für einen Neutestamentler.

Auf der anderen Seite könnte man die Frage stellen, ob denn die unter dem Vorzeichen der New Perspective vorgetragene Kritik an Luther und der Lutherischen Theologie diese oder die angeblich von Luther beeinflusste deutschsprachige Exegese wirklich trifft – das ist kein geeigneter Gegenstand für ein relativ kurzes Statement und auch eher ein Gegenstand für einen Kirchengeschichtler.

Drittens könnt man die Frage stellen, ob tatsächlich von einer Rezeption der Theologie des Paulus zu erwarten ist und verlangt werden kann, dass sie den Gehalt der paulinischen Theologie in der Gegenwart wiederholt. Wenn ich die Frage so stelle, lege ich eine negative Antwort nahe; zugleich stellt sich damit aber die zweite Frage: Wann und unter welchen Bedingungen kann eine solche nicht wiederholende Deutung der paulinischen Theologie den Anspruch erheben, angemessen zu sein?

Für James Dunn ist die Sache relativ klar: Er erhob in einem Vortrag in Berlin den Anspruch, dass die Bezeichnung »New Perspective« eigentlich die Sache nicht treffe, da diese theologische Position nicht neu sei, sondern zuerst von Paulus selbst vertreten worden sei.

Diese Behauptung lässt hermeneutisch schon darum zu wünschen übrig, weil damit implizit behauptet wird, dass es die Aufgabe der gegenwärtigen Theologie sei, das Selbstverständnis des Paulus zu wiederholen

---

28 Vgl. nur DUNN, New Perspective (s. Anm. 16), 104f; DERS., Justice (s. Anm. 2), 199.

und zur Geltung zu bringen. Allerdings zeigt bereits die Darstellung der »New Perspective«, dass diese Deutung selbst wenigstens einen Teil ihrer Plausibilität aus theologischen Vorentscheidungen zieht, die in theologischen und gesellschaftlichen Gegenwartsanliegen begründet sind – das gilt für die deutliche Grundierung der New Perspective durch die Barthsche Theologie ebenso wie für die von Sanders vorgetragene Kritik an einer individualistischen Soteriologie oder der Dunnschen Deutung des Paulus als Antipode eines Ethnizismus.[29] Wie im Ursprung der Leben Jesu-Frage, so ist auch hier die dem Anspruch nach methodisch exakte und vorurteilsfreie Rückfrage nach dem ursprünglichen Sinn geleitet von Gegenwartsinteressen, die gewiss andere als diejenigen Luthers sind, aber doch in derselben Weise die Lektüre leiten wie dessen Frage nach dem individuellen Heilsstand.

These 7: Für Luther werden die Briefe des Paulus zum Anlass eines Verständnisses der Bestimmung des Menschen.

Die entscheidende Differenz der Paulusdeutung Luthers zu der der Vertreter einer New Perspective liegt darin, dass Luther die Unterscheidung von Gesetz und Evangelium nicht heilsgeschichtlich fasst. Er versteht Paulus – gerade dessen These, dass er (Paulus) durch das Gesetz dem Gesetz gestorben sei – als einen Hinweis darauf, dass nicht eine heilsgeschichtliche Epoche durch eine andere abgelöst sei, sondern dass der Christ, indem er sich eins weiß mit Christus, durch diesen (und nicht durch sich selbst) so dem Gesetz stirbt, dass dieses nicht an sich, wohl aber über ihn keine Macht mehr hat. Der Wandel vollzieht sich nach Luther nicht als heilsgeschichtlicher Epochenwandel, sondern er vollzieht sich an der individuellen Existenz:

> Aber er spricht hier [Gal 2,19: Ich bin mit Christus gekreuzigt] [...] nicht vom Mitgekreuzigtwerden in der Form der Nachahmung oder des Vorbilds [...], sondern er spricht hier von jenem hohen Mitgekreuzigtwerden, durch die die Sünde, der Teufel, der Tod in Christus, nicht in mir, gekreuzigt werden. Hier tut Christus allein alles. Aber ich werde als Glaubender mit Christus durch den Glauben gekreuzigt, so daß sie [Sünde, Tod, Teufel] auch für mich tot und gekreuzigt sind.[30]

29 Dunn, The New Perspective (s. Anm. 4), 87; vgl. Dunn, Collected Essays (s. Anm. 1), 26.32f.140f.199 etc.pp.

30 M. Luther, Galaterkommentar 1535, WA 40,1; 280,25–281,20; Übers. N.Sl.

Das Christusgeschehen und das dort realisierte Ende des Gesetzes oder der Herrschaft der Sünde zielt also darauf ab, sich am individuellen Subjekt durchzusetzen und zu realisieren. Dies geschieht nach Luther so, dass der Mensch die ihm zugesprochene Person Jesu von Nazareth »ergreift« (apprehendit) und sich ihr entsprechend neu versteht:

> [So lebe nicht mehr ich] Hier zeigt er klar, wie er lebt und sagt, was die christliche Gerechtigkeit ist, die nämlich, durch die Christus in uns lebt, nicht diejenige, die in unserer Person ist. Daher: Wenn von der christlichen Gerechtigkeit gesprochen werden soll, muß die Person beiseite getan werden. Denn wenn ich auf die Person fixiert bin oder von ihr spreche, wird aus der Person, ob ich will oder nicht, ein Täter, der dem Gesetz unterworfen ist. Aber hier muß Christus und mein Gewissen ein Leib werden, so daß in meinem Blick nichts anderes bleibt als Christus, der gekreuzigt und auferstanden ist. [...] Der Glaube muß richtig gelehrt werden, dass du nämlich durch ihn mit Christus zusammengeklebt wirst, dass aus dir und ihm gleichsam eine Person wird [conglutineris Christo, ut ex te et ipso fiat quasi una persona], die nicht getrennt werden kann, sondern ihm beständig anhängt und sagt: Ich bin [wie] Christus; und umgekehrt sagt Christus: ich bin [wie] dieser Sünder, weil er an mir hängt und ich an ihm; verbunden sind wir nämlich durch den Glauben in ein Fleisch und Gebein [...] so, dass dieser Glaube Christus und mich enger verbindet als ein Ehemann seiner Frau verbunden ist.[31]

Genau dies ist der Vorgang der »Gerechtsprechung«: Es geht nicht einfach um ein Urteil über den Menschen, das ihn gegen die Faktizität seiner Sünde als gerecht beurteilt. Sondern es geht um die Zueignung der Person und des Lebens Jesu Christi, und das diesem Zuspruch entsprechende neue Selbstverständnis – vgl. im Zitat: dass der Mensch, indem er *sich* ansieht (in seinem Gewissen) nichts anders sieht als Christus: »Ich bin [wie] Christus«.

Das bedeutet, dass so weit die Vertreter der New Perspective ebenso wie übrigens die Vertreter der Finnischen Lutherschule zu Recht auf eine Verkürzung des Lutherverständnisses hinweisen: Auch bei Luther ist die Rechtfertigung nicht einfach ein Urteil Gottes über den glaubenden Sünder, sondern sie hat in der Tat, wie Sanders feststellt, mit dem Vorgang der Teilhabe an Christus zu tun. Diese Teilhabe an Christus ist aber, so liest Luther seinen Paulus, nicht eine Art mystischer Vereinigung mit Christus oder eine gegenständliche Gegenwart im Glaubenden, sondern diese Teil-

---

31 AaO., 285 f; Übers. N.Sl.

habe an Christus vollzieht sich in einem Zueignungsurteil und in der Folge in einem Glauben, der ein Selbsturteil ist: »Ich bin [wie] Christus«.

Von diesem Zentrum her versteht Luther nun, was Sünde und was Gnade – was gelingendes und was verlorenes Menschsein ist: Genau das »Sein im Glauben« ist die schöpfungsmäßige Bestimmung des Menschen: Er ist dazu bestimmt, im Glauben zu leben, das heißt: alles Gute von einem anderen her zu haben; und Sünde besteht in dem immer scheiternden Versuch, in sich selbst zu leben und von sich selbst her alles Gute zu haben.

These 8: Luthers hier nur angedeutete Interpretation des Paulus geht möglicherweise weit über die ursprünglichen Intentionen des Paulus hinaus – aber das ist nicht das Schlechteste, was man über diese Interpretation sagen kann.

8.1. Für Luther waren die Briefe des Paulus, die dessen Auseinandersetzung mit judenchristlichen Gegnern widerspiegeln (Gal, Röm, Phil), zunächst einmal eine Hilfe beim Bewältigen der individuellen Anfechtungserfahrung, in der ihm das »durch den Glauben, nicht durch die Werke« zunächst einmal Kategorien zur Deutung und Klärung seiner Situation bereitstellte. Er verstand dabei die Rechtfertigungslehre als die Anweisung, der Verzweiflung an sich selbst nicht zu widerstreben, sondern der darin gewiesenen Richtung in eine vertrauensvolle vollständige Abhängigkeit von Gott zu folgen. Insofern ist in der Tat die lutherische Paulusrezeption individualistisch und nicht an corporate identities orientiert[32] – aber genau dies gibt dieser Paulusrezeption gegenwartsorientierende Kraft.

8.2. Diese Lösung einer existentiellen Situation bestand darin, dass erst mit diesem Vertrauen die Gottheit Gottes anerkannt und der Mensch zu seiner Bestimmung gekommen ist:

> Er [der Glaube] gibt nämlich Gott die Ehre, über die hinaus ihm nichts Höheres zugewiesen werden kann. Gott die Ehre geben heißt: ihm zu glauben, ihn für wahrhaftig, weise, gerecht, barmherzig, allmächtig zu halten, kurz: ihn als den Ursprung und den Geber alles Guten anzuerkennen. Dies tut nicht die Vernunft, sondern der Glaube. Er fasst die Gottheit zusammen und ist, sozusagen, der Schöpfer der Gottheit, nicht in sei-

---

32 Vgl. etwa SANDERS (s. Anm. 1), 438 und die dann folgende Durchführung bis 515.

ner Substanz, sondern in uns [...] Keine Hoheit und Gottheit hat Gott, wo der Glaube nicht ist.[33]

Die anthropologischen Konsequenzen, die Luther daraus zog, gingen weit über Paulus und eine Paulusinterpretation hinaus: Sein Verständnis des Menschen als eines Wesens, das dazu bestimmt ist, nicht in sich selbst zu sein, sondern sich von einem anderen her und durch einen anderen zu verstehen. »Glaube« ist für Luther genau dieses »Sein und sich Verstehen im anderen« – dies ist eine durch Paulus angeregte, aber produktiv weit über ihn hinausgehende Erschließung der menschlichen Existenz.

8.3. Allerdings: Luthers Einsicht hängt nicht daran, dass sich seine Rechtfertigungsbotschaft mit einzelnen Paulusstellen belegen lässt, und sie fällt nicht damit, dass Paulus möglicherweise ursprünglich die Dinge etwas anders gesehen hat. Luther ist in einer Situation existentieller Bedrängnis – seiner Anfechtungserfahrung – der Text des Paulus zum Ursprung eines neuen Selbstverständnisses geworden: Dass es die Bestimmung des Menschen ist, nicht aus sich selbst zu leben, sondern in der schlechthinnigen Abhängigkeit von Gott. Diese in der Begegnung mit dem Paulustext entstandene Erkenntnis seiner selbst erschließt ihm die paulinischen Briefe; sie reden mit einer Stimme. Und mit derselben Stimme sprechen für ihn die Psalmen, die Johanneischen Schriften, und vor allem der Prophet Jeremia; und in allen findet Luther sich, seine Existenzfrage und die Anweisung zum angefochtenen Leben im rückhaltlosen Vertrauen wieder.

These 9: Der Umgang mit der paulinischen Theologie und mit den biblischen Texten insgesamt wird dann interessant und führt dann zu Einsichten, wenn sie gelesen werden unter Anleitung der Frage eines Menschen nach sich selbst. Das liegt daran, dass nur diese Frage – die »experientia« oder die »tentatio« im Sinne Luthers – der Bewegung entspricht, die die Briefe des Paulus umtreibt: Auch ihm geht es, insbesondere in den Korintherbriefen, um die Frage nach sich selbst, nach dem Wert der eigenen Per-

---

33 LUTHER, Galaterkommentar (s. Anm. 30), 360; dazu vgl. N. SLENCZKA, Fides creatrix divinitatis. Zu einer These Luthers und zugleich zum Verhältnis von Theologie und Glaube (in: Denkraum Katechismus. Festgabe für Oswald Bayer zum 70. Geburtstag, hg. v. J. VON LÜPKE u. a., 2009, 171–195).

son, dem *kauchasthai*. Das ist das Grundthema der Briefe an die Korinther, und die Grundeinsicht des Paulus ist die, dass er sich nicht im Blick auf sich selbst rühmen kann, sondern nur im Blick auf etwas, was außerhalb seiner selbst ist (1Kor 1,31 etc.), nämlich die Person Jesu, von deren Niedrigkeit sein Leben bestimmt ist.

Die »Rechtfertigungslehre« des Gal und des Röm ebenso wie des Phil sind die Anwendung dieser in den korinthischen Auseinandersetzungen gewonnenen Einsicht in das Wesen des Menschen und seiner außerhalb von ihm selbst begründeten Ehre auf das »Rühmen« dessen, der sich mit Bezug auf das Gesetz rühmt – und dabei ist es ganz gleichgültig, ob dieser Mensch, die Gegner des Paulus, sich ihrer Zugehörigkeit zum jüdischen Volk (so die New Perspective) oder ihres individuellen Gesetzesgehorsams und der darin liegenden Verdienste (so die traditionelle lutherische Theologie) rühmen: Es geht jeweils um den Versuch, von sich selbst her etwas zu sein, statt sich und das Verständnis seiner selbst in der Person Jesu Christi zu finden.

Luther hat in den Texten des Paulus diese Frage erfasst, die seiner eigenen Frage entsprach.

Vielleicht bleiben uns die Texte so fremd, weil uns diese Frage nach uns selbst nicht mehr umtreibt. Vielleicht ist eine Besinnung auf Luther auch ein Anlass, dieser Frage als grundlegender Frage des Menschseins wieder ansichtig zu werden.[34]

---

34 Vgl. dazu: N. SLENCZKA, Problemgeschichte der Christologie (in: Christologie [MJTh XXIII], hg. v. E. GRÄB-SCHMIDT u. a., 2011, 59–111); DERS., Entzweiung und Versöhnung. Das Phänomen des Gewissens und der Erlösung in Shakespeares »King Richard III.« als Hintergrund eines Verständnisses der »imputativen Rechtfertigung« bei Luther (KuD 50, 2004, 289–319); DERS., Das Kreuz mit dem Ich. Theologia crucis als Gestalt der Selbstdeutung (in: Kreuzestheologie – kontrovers und erhellend, hg. v. K. GRÜNWALDT u. a., 2007, 99–116); DERS., »Allein durch den Glauben« – Antwort auf die Frage eines mittelalterlichen Mönchs oder Angebot zum Umgang mit einem Problem jedes Menschen? (in: Luther und das monastische Erbe, hg. v. C. BULTMANN u. a., 2007, 291–315); DERS., Der endgültige Schrecken. Das Jüngste Gericht und die Angst in der Religion des Mittelalters (Das Mittelalter 12, 2007, 105–121); DERS., Gericht (in: Der Römerbrief als Vermächtnis an die Kirche, hg. v. C. BREYTENBACH, 2012, 161–176). Dazu: DERS., Die Rechtfertigung des Sünders (in: DERS., Der Tod Gottes und das Leben des Menschen. Glaubensbekenntnis und Lebensvollzug, 2003, 210–226).

The Early Modern Pastor between Ideal and Reality

Tarald Rasmussen

I The ministry in the Heinrichsagende

In the first Church Ordinance for the pastors of Albertine Saxony from 1539, there is an interesting preface stating the main characteristics of the new Protestant pastors – in contrast to the old Catholic priests. This ordinance, the socalled *Heinrichsagende*, was enforced by prince Heinrich, who succeeded his brother George as ruler in the Albertine part of Saxony that same year. Three years earlier, in 1536, he had allowed the city council in Freiberg, where he resided, to join the Reformation. Now, he wanted to take the opportunity to introduce the new religion in all of Albertine Saxony. Heinrich was a devout defender of Protestantism, and although his rule as prince was only to last for two years, he contributed in an important way to constructing the confessional profile of Saxonian Protestantism in the sixteenth century.[1] His Ordinance for the pastors – originally intended to be a just a preliminary regulation – continued to serve as official ordinance for Saxony for generations, and was reprinted several times until the early seventeenth century.[2]

---

[1] An overview of this part of Saxonian Reformation History is offered in G. WARTENBERG, Die Entstehung der sächsischen Landeskirche von 1539 bis 1559 (in: Das Jahrhundert der Reformation in Sachsen, hg. v. H. JUNGHANS, 2005, 69–92). See also G. WARTENBERG, Landesherrschaft und Reformation, 1988.

[2] The text is available online in a version of the Bayerische Staatsbibliothek: Kirchenordnunge zum anfang fur die Pfarherrn in Herzog Heinrichs zu Sachsen v. g. h. Fürstenthum, Sign.: 4 Liturg. 193, URN: urn:nbn:de:bvb: 12-bsb10164219–2, BVB-ID:BV001499727, Wit-

The most important practical tasks to be accomplished by a Lutheran pastor are prescribed by the main text of the Ordinance. These tasks include *Nottauf, Beichte, kranke Leute (berichten und trösten), Kirchenordnung in Städten und Dörfern, Segen von Bräutigam und Braut* and finally *Begräbnis der Todten.* In addition, the role of the pastor is defined in theological or ideological terms in the extensive preface, signed by six of the more influential church leaders of Saxony at the time: Justus Jonas, Justus Menius, Georgius Spalatinus, Johannes Weber, Caspar Cruciger and Fridericus Myconius.

In this Vorrede, the frome Gottfürchtige Pfarherr who have replaced the ungelerten Papisten are addressed:

> Und dieselbigen Gottfürchtigen und guten hertzen, die da recht erkennen, welch ein gros befelh, hohe ampt, trefflich, wichtig Titel das ist, wenn sich einer schreibt Seelhirt, Pfarher, in der stad NN in dem Dorff, und wie fur einen grossen Herrn und hohe Maiestet, die jenige tretten, die, wie Paulus sagt, fur Gottes augen, an Gottes stat predigen, leren, an Gottes stat die heiligen sacrament reichen, fur dem angesicht Christi und so vieler Engel, mit iren Pfarkindern beten, danck sagen, Psalmensingen etc.[3]

After having praised the dignity of the new Apostolic and Christian service and contrasting it to the idolatry of the papist Mass celebration, the text goes on:

> Denn es ist recht geredt, wie die Collect lautet (so die Papisten offt selbs gebraucht): Deus, cui seruire regnare est, Denn welcher Pfarher trewlich den namen und die gnade Christi prediget, die Tauff und Sacrament in rechtem brauch reichet, der ist freilich alle stunde ein gewaltig Siegman, ein König und Herrscher uber die grosse macht und schrecklichs Reich des Satans, der thut alle stunde dem Feind schaden, und vermehret das Reich Christi, wie auch der lxviii. Psalm, die Aposteln und Pfarher, Könige der Heerscharen nennet.
>
> Es ligt ein trew Seelsorger alle stunde zu felde, im heer des HErrn Zebaoth, bewacht, errettet, und schützt seine Pfarkinder, wider allerley list, verreterey, wider so starcken streit und sturm des Teufels, Und ist ein Pfarher oder Prediger ampt, nicht ein müssiggang oder schertzwesen, Wie denn Paulus Timotheum ein streiter und Kriegsmann Christi nennet, Aber davon wissen die Papisten eben so viel, als ein Kind.[4]

---

tenberg 1539 (http://www.bsbmuenchendigital.de/~web/web1016/bsb10164219/images/index.html?l=de&digID=bsb10164219&v=100&nav=0).

3 Heinrichsagende (see n. 2), ii.
4 Heinrichsagende (see n. 2), iii.

In the rhetoric of this preface, the Lutheran minister is first and foremost a warrior in Christ's army. In this capacity, he is a king and ruler (*ein gewaltig Siegmann, ein König und Herrscher*), representing Christ as the victor over Satan and his kingdom. »To serve God is to rule« (*Deus, cui seruire regnare est[5]*): this traditional dictum did not only apply to the ministers of the old regime. It also applies to the Protestant minister. He must be *en garde* at any moment, protecting his flock from the endless assaults of Satan. This task has been totally neglected by the papists and their priests, but will be taken care of now by the new ministers.

Closely connected to these statements about the Protestant minister, the text also talks about the *Pfarhe, the Kirch,* or the *Christlich Predigstühl*: the place or the function where the gospel is to be preached and the sacraments are to be administered. This function is to be taken care of everywhere now, in cities, villages and houses: »*da gibt es bald den heiligen Geist, da thut er bald den gantzen Himel auff, thut wunderwerck, gibt weisheit, Geist, zungen und sprachen*«. Whereas the papists neglected the presence and the continuous hard work of the priest in many cities and villages, the Protestant minister is to be present everywhere. No *Pfarhe* or *Christlich Predigstühl* without a minister. The ministry, the Pulpit and the kingdom of Heaven belonging to it may, according to the text, be called *eine Haushaltung* or *eine Oeconomia*: »*wie den die Schrift auch die Pfarher Oeconomos nennet, das ist, Haushalter uber die geistlichen und himlischen Schetze*«.

All orders of society are called upon to contribute to establishing the new ministries in every city and village: »*Und wahrlich, Adel, Ritterschafft, Stedte, Dörfer, die Christen sein wollen, sollten wissen, und recht erkennen, dass Pfarhen un Christlich Predigtstühl gross zu achten, und zu ehren sind.*« That is to say: ministries should not only be established, but also highly honoured.[6]

---

5 This phrase occurs (originally) in several medieval liturgical texts, *inter alia* in the postcommunion prayer for the *Missa pro pace* in the Gelasian Sacramentary. (*Deus auctor pacis et amator quem nosse uiuere, qui seruire regnare est…*). It is frequently quoted in sixteenth-century theological texts.

6 Heinrichsagende (see n. 2), v-vi.

It is evident that this preface goes quite far in praising not only the ministry of preaching the Gospel, but also the minister himself. There is, for instance, quite a distance between the rhetoric used to characterize the minister in Luthers preface to Melanchthon's *Unterricht der Visitatoren*, written ten years earlier, and also intended as an instruction for building up the church organization in Saxony, and this text from 1539. Where Luther has a main focus on the function of the ministry (»*Dann wer kan erzelen, wie nütz und not solch ampt in der Christenheyt sey*«[7]), the ordinance from 1539 has an additional focus on the minister as person. To the ministry belongs the minister, and both come together and are needed to open up to heaven on earth.

II Early Protestant Saxony and geistliches Sonderbewusstsein

Saxony was a Lutheran heartland, and offers an interesting case for discussing the Early Modern clergy. But even if one restricts oneself to Saxony and to the two or three first decades after the Reformation of Albertine Saxony, an overwhelming amount of interesting sources are available, many of which are now also digitally accessible to researchers on an open access basis.

My particular interest here is to try to say something more about the question of a *geistliches Sonderbewusstsein* which has been recognized as being present among the clergy in different parts of Germany, not least in the 1550s and 1560s, with a continuing influence at least until well into the seventeenth century[8]. It manifested itself very evidently also in the Lutheran heartlands of Saxony and Mitteldeutschland.

---

7 Quoted from M. LUTHER's preface to P. Melanchthon: Unterricht der Visitatoren an die Pfarrherrn im Kurfürstenthum zu Sachsen, version of the Bayerische Staatsbibliothek, Sign.: 4 Liturg. 193, urn:nbn:de:bvb: 12-bsb00025123–1, Nürnberg 1528 (VD16 M 2598) (http://dfgviewer.de/show/?set%5Bimage%5D=1&set%5Bzoom%5D=default&set%5Bdebug%5D=0&set%5Bdouble%5D=0&set%5Bmets%5D=http%3A%2F%2Fdaten.digitale-sammlungen.de%2F~db%2Fmets%2Fbsb00025123_mets.xml).

8 A resent important contribution is L. BERNDORFF, Die Prediger der Grafschaft Mansfeld. Eine Untersuchung zum geistlichen Sonderbewusstsein in der zweiten Hälfte des 16. Jahrhunderts, 2010.

Quite extensive research has been going on the last couple of decades into the roles and functions of the Early Modern Protestant minister. Most of this research has been undertaken by historians, describing and analyzing the social, political, legal, and ecclesiastical functions of this new profession.[9] Some of the observations and conclusions from this recent research can be summarized very briefly.

1. *Representing the authorities (Obrigkeit).* The Protestant clergy was no longer part of the Roman hierarchy. Instead, it was closely connected to the state and the *weltliches Regiment*, sometimes – at least in the case of the superintendents – even by oath. To this extent, it represented the *Obrigkeit*.

2. *Included in civil society.* At the same time, it was in a fundamentally new way integrated into the local community, first of all because the Lutheran pastors now had their own families, wives and children. It is true enough, as Susan Karant Nunn and others have pointed out, that for practical purposes this was not quite new, since many fifteenth-century priests also had their families, even though this was against the rules.[10] Still, the social role of the minister was redefined by the Reformation, and the clergy was integrated into civil society in new and closer ways. This was especially true for the first generation Protestant clergy, who were in these parts of Germany to a large extent recruited from craftsmen in the cities. Later on, a certain process of disintegration took place again, when the Protestant clergy to a greater degree was established as a self-recruiting group of civil servants.[11]

---

9 A major contribution in this field was L. SCHORN-SCHÜTTE, Evangelische Geistlichkeit in der Frühneuzeit. Deren Anteil an der Entfaltung frühmoderner Staatlichkeit und Gesellschaft. Dargestellt am Beispiel des Fürstentums Braunschweig-Wolfenbüttel, der Landgrafschaft Hessen-Kassel und der Stadt Braunschweig (QFRG 62), 1996. Among her later most relevant publications are S. DIXON/L. SCHORN-SCHÜTTE (ed.), The Protestant clergy of early modern Europe, 2003; L. SCHORN-SCHÜTTE (Hg.), Aspekte der politischen Kommunikation im Europa des 16. und 17. Jahrhunderts. Politische Theologe – Res Publica-Verständnis – Konsensgestütze Herrschaft (HZ.B. 39, 2004).

10 S.C. KARANT-NUNN, The Clergyman between the Cultures of State and Parish (in: The Protestant [see n. 9], 79–99).

11 BERNDORFF (see n. 8), 101.

3. *Representing Christ.* As we have seen in the preface to the *Heinrichsle-gende*, the clergy could also be regarded as a special part of the order of the *oeconomia*, representing and taking care of the heavenly goods within this context. This is an interesting statement. We are told here that the clergy – not as part of the Obrigkeit (*politia*), nor as a particular order of society (*ecclesia*), but as a specific part of civil society – had special responsibilities, representing the holy in society.

This last point touches upon the discussion about the so-called *geistliches Sonderbewusstsein* of the Protestant clergy. This concept has been introduced and developed not least by Luise Schorn-Schütte[12] and several of her pupils, and has served as a basis for defining the roles and functions of the clergy as something more than and other than an ordinary civil servant within the structure of the *Obrigkeit*. Much of the discussion concerning this *Sonderbewusstsein* has therefore had a focus on political questions, like the question of clerically initiated protests against the political rulers – which was also occurred in early Lutheran societies.

This *geistliches Sonderbewusstsein* is a quite complex phenomenon. It can be illustrated or exemplified by means of very diverse sources, and it can be interpreted in political, legal, cultural or more specifically religious terms. And it is not restricted to the subjective »Bewusstsein« of the clergy itself. It has to do with something closely integrated into the *role* and *the cultural function* of the early Lutheran clergy.[13]

I will look somewhat more closely at to the specifically *religious part* of this question. First, I will discuss one more specifically theological source which may contribute further to defining the religious role of the ministry in early Protestant Saxony, namely Erasmus Sarcerius' *Manuale*. Secondly, I will look at one specific priest who was active for a long time

---

12 SCHORN-SCHÜTTE, Evangelische Geistlichkeit (see n. 9), 449–452.

13 BERNDORFF (see n. 8) offers a fundamental discussion of this concept, 101–105, and applies it as an important analytical tool throughout his book. He also introduces the concept of *geistliches Amtsbewusstsein* (chapter 3, 147–195) in order to further specify the contents and functions of the *geistliches Sonderbewusstsein*. I will restrict myself here to the latter concept.

within the context defined by the *Heinrichsagende*, Anton Lauterbach in Pirna, in order to see how his memory was celebrated after his death. Both these discussions contribute to a further illumination of the religious function of the early Protestant clergy in Saxony. Indirectly, they may also be of relevance to the discussion about the *geistliches Sonderbewusstsein*, to which I will return at the end.

III The Pastorale of Erasmus Sarcerius

Sarcerius was born in Annaberg in Albertine Saxony in 1501. He was a student first in Leipzig and later probably also in Wittenberg, and served as priest at the Tomaskirche in Leipzig and later on as superintendent in Mansfeld.[14] After the death of Prince Moritz in 1553, he preached the funeral sermon. He died in Magdeburg in 1559, just a few months after arriving there as the minister in the Johanniskirche. In addition to these stations in Saxony and Mitteldeutschland, Sarcerius also spent a long time in the service of the count of Nassau-Dillenberg in Western Germany.

A considerable number of books and shorter texts survive from him, including the Pastorale oder Hirtenbuch, darin das gantz Ampt aller treuen Pastoren, Lehrer und Diener der Christlichen Kirchen beider ihr lehr unnd leben belangend beschrieben wird. This book was published for the first time in 1559, and reprinted several times after his death. Next to Niels Hemmingsen's Pastor sive Pastoris optimus vivendi agendique modus, which was published for the first time in 1565, this was the most influential handbook for pastors at the time.[15]

In the preface to the second edition of the book, edited by Sarcerius' son Wilhelm (who was also a pastor in Mansfeld/Eisleben)[16], it is stated

---

14 Sarcerius and his texts play an important role in BERNDORFF (see n. 8). See also S. RHEIN/ G. WARTENBERG, Reformatoren im Mansfelder Land. Erasmus Sarcerius und Cyriakus Spangenberg (Schriften der Lutherdenkstätten in Sachsen-Anhalt 4), 2006.

15 A. NELSON BURNETT has analyzed Sarcerius's *Pastorale* within the context of similar contemporary texts in her instructive article The Evolution of the Lutheran Pastors' Manual in the Sixteenth Century (Church History 73, 2004, 536–565).

16 The following quotations are all taken from the 1565 edition printed in Frankfurt, which is digitally available from the Herzog August Bibliothek Wolfenbüttel in the Post-Reformation Digital Library under: http://diglib.hab.de/drucke/68-2-quod-2f-1/start.htm.

PASTORALE

Oder Hirtenbuch/ vom Ampt/

Wesen/ vnd Disciplin der Pastorn/ vnd Kirchendie-
ner/ Vnd wie sie von jugend auff studieren sollen/vnd hernach
auch nützlich leren/ in jrem gantzen Kirchenampt/ in Lere vnd
Leben sich vnuerweislich verhalten/desgleichen in schwe-
ren/vnd vngewönlichen fellen erzeigen/welche sich
vmb/ vnd neben jrem Ampte teglich zutragen.
Dienstlich die ware Religion recht
anzustellen/da sie nicht ist/
vnd zuerhalten/
da sie ist.

Durch Eras. Sarcerium Annemontanum der alten
vnd löblichen Graffschafft Mansfelt Superint. geschrieben.

Image 1: Frontispiece *Pastorale*

that three different kinds of people carry the title of Minister: The first are the excellent ones, the second the mediocre and the third those unfit for the task, paying more attention to the benefits than to the duties of their ministry. This classification is interesting in itself, and particularly interesting is the way in which the first class of ministers, the best ones, are described in the text. These people are

> hohe, fürtreffliche, verstendige, und von Gott sonderliche erleuchte, begabte, unnd zu solchem Ampte geschickte Menner, welche Tag unnd Nacht sich im Gesetze des Herzen uben, Gott umb den rechten verstand desselbigen und umb den heiligen Geist embsig anruffen, und mit heilsamer Leere unnd fruchtbarlichem leben den leuten fürgehen und fürstehen, als im ersten alter der Welt Enos, Enoch, Nohah, Loth, Abraham, Melchisedech. Und im anderen Alter der Welt Moyses, Aaron, Helias, Eliseus unnd die lieben Propheten. Unnd im letzten theil der Welt die lieben Aposteln, Augustinus, Ambrosius, D. Luther seliger, Brentius, Cordatus Amassdorffius, Spangenbergius, Illyricus und andere Patres und trewe Leerer mehr gewesen sind und noch gefunden werden.[17]

The book is a huge handbook, intended to be used by superintendents as well as by other ministers, prescribing in detail most of the regular liturgical practices of the clergy.

Sarcerius reveals a particularly strong interest in treating the topic of Ordination of the so called Kirchendiener, – first and foremost ministers. The historian (and pupil of Schorn-Schütte) *Lothar Berndorff* has recently demonstrated how Sarcerius in his *Pastorale* as well as in other texts defines a quite strict, rigid and hierarchical order for the rule of the Protestant church. He draws heavily not only on Biblical sources, but also on Church Tradition, including councils and Church fathers, and even the *Decretum Gratiani* in order to support his construction of an ecclesiastical hierarchy.[18]

Within this hierarchy, the minister has a most prominent place. The role of the minister has roots back to the ministry of the Old covenant, going back to Levi and Moses. But at least as important are the Old Testament prophets and their words to the people of Israel.[19] The ministers are the prophets of the contemporary church, and one of their most important

---

17 http://diglib.hab.de/drucke/68–2-quod-2f-1/start.htm?image=00000004.
18 BERNDORFF (see n. 8), 150–158.
19 http://diglib.hab.de/drucke/68–2-quod-2f-1/start.htm?image=00000034.

tasks is to call the congregation to repentance. These Old Testament role models are still relevant, although they are renewed through Christ and his kingdom.

The dignity of the ministry is explained thoroughly in the chapter *Von der Hoheit, Wirdigkeit und nötigkeit des Kirchenampts*:

> So muss ja auch dass liebe Kirchenampt, ein hoch gross unnd wirdig Ampt sein, und dass auss folgenden ursachen, dass Gott hierzu seine sonderliche Gnad, Segen und gedeien gibt, dass es recht verwaltet wird, und dass dadurch frucht und nutz geschaffet. Denn solchs alles gibt Gott, und ist nicht Menschlicher kreffte und vermögens schuld. Und achtet nun Gott dass Kirchenampt also hoch, gross und wirdig, dass er i(h)m allein die ehre vorbehalten hat, dass er hierzu Segen und gedeien geben wil, dass es recht volzogen werde, und die Leute des, ewigen und zeitlichen nutzen haben mögen.[20]

In the first part of his book, Sarcerius discusses very carefully the question how to identify, raise and educate the best among the youth for service as ministers. The obligation to find the right people for this task rests on every Christian community. Parents in particular should share this responsibility and pay attention: maybe their children are suited for this task. It was (i. e. in pre-Reformation times) and still is a special honor to raise children who can serve God through the ministry:

> Daher viel Christlicher und Gottseliger Eltern zu allen zeiten, mit höchstem fleiss und ernst, ire Kinder dahin gezogen und gehalten, dass sie hernach dem Reich Christi haben dienen mögen, und in erweiterung desselbigen sich bearbeiten. Hierinnen auch unsere Voreltern (wiewol in grossem unverstande) an sich nichts haben erwinden lassen, welchen zugleich die höchste und grösste sorge für und für angehangen, damit sie ire Kinder zu Kirchendienern aufferzögen. Und ist solche sorg also hoch geachtet worden, dass man die Eltern dissfalls selig gepreiset hat. Und das nach dem gemeinen Sprichwort: Selig ist die Mutter, die einen Son zum Priester zeuhet.[21]

Within this context, the ordination is a big event. Here, the candidates chosen and educated for the ministry are introduced to the congregation, and reminded of the severe obligations, but also of the high rewards, connected to their work. They also are expected to live an exemplary life, suitable for imitation by the congregation. *Ir habt auch weiter verstanden, mit was Tugenden er in seinem leben sol gezieret und geschmücket sein,*

---

20 http://diglib.hab.de/drucke/68–2-quod-2f-1/start.htm?image=00000037.
21 http://diglib.hab.de/drucke/68–2-quod-2f-1/start.htm?image=00000008.

*euch zum Exempel der besserung und nachfolge. Und solch leben habt
ihr von ihm freundtlich zu fordern, ...* (if not, it has to be reported to the
superintendent).[22]

This, then, are some brief excerpts on the role of the minister, drawn
up in this famous handbook by the superintendent in Eisleben, where
Luther had died little more than ten years earlier. I cannot discuss here
the question of where and how Sarcerius differs from Luther (whom he
certainly and explicitly wants to follow) in his presentation and praise of
the Christian ministry. Rather, this text may serve to confirm some of the
theological and religious aspects of the *geistliches Sonderbewusstsein* of
precisely this generation of the German clergy.

And we see again, as we have seen in the *Heinrichsagende,* that the
ministry is praised as the highest and most important role in Christian
society, instituted by Christ himself, and defined within the solid context
of an ecclesiastical hierarchy supported with references to the councils,
the Church Fathers and even canon law. Within this framework, the good
minister will be supported by the Spirit of God, which is accessible in a
particular way precisely in the ministry. Here, he should not only preach
the gospel to congregation, but also live a life worthy of imitation by other
Christians.

This conclusion may be taken one step further by relating it to the frequently quoted article by Reinhard Schwarz from 1984, about *Sozialgeschichtliche und fundamentaltheologische Aspekte der protestantischen Drei-Stände-Lehre.*[23] In his third thesis in this article, Schwarz
stated:

22 http://diglib.hab.de/drucke/68-2-quod-2f-1/start.htm?image=00000035. In the Collect
   on the following page, the exemplarity of the minister, imitating Christ in words and
   deeds, is once again put forward as an example to be imitated by the congregation:
   »Barmhertziger Gott und Himmlischer Vatter, wir bitten dich [...], dass du diesem Ordi-
   nierten und bestettigtem Diener in seinem Ampt wöllcst hülff und beistand erzeigen,
   und im deinem heiligen Geist ubergeben, dass er das heilige Euangelium ohne forcht
   und schewe predige, [...] und zugleich nach dem Exempel deines lieben Sons, recht lehren und leben, dir zu lob, preiss und ehren, ihm selbt zum besten, und seinen Schäfflin
   zur seligen nachfolge, Amen«.
23 R. SCHWARZ, Ecclesia, oeconomia, politia: sozialgeschichtliche und fundamental-
   ethische Aspekte der protestantischen Drei-Stände-Theorie (in: Troeltsch-Studien 3:
   Protestantismus und Neuzeit, hg. v. H. RENZ/F. W. GRAF, 1984, 78–88).

Das soziale Ständegefüge erfährt in der protestantischen Gesellschaftsordnung eine sozialrechtliche Integration, da die Pfarrer dem weltlichen Recht unterstellt wurden. Auch die Funktion der Pfarrer wird durch die Reformation anders bestimmt: ihre höchste Aufgabe ist nicht mehr rein priesterlicher Gebetsdienst, sondern die Lehre.[24]

In the resolutiones to this thesis Schwarz went on to say:

Ein spezifisch priesterlich kultischer Gebetsdienst wurde ausgeschlossen; denn der protestantische Pfarrer betet mit der Gemeinde, und alle Glaubenden haben im Gebet gleichen Zugang zu Gott.[25]

Sarcerius' instructions for the ministry are not quite in accordance with this conclusion, at least not with the part about equal access to God. Here, the ministry is, according to Sarcerius, definitely not equal to other *Berufe* in society. It is something special, with a special access to the Spirit of God.

IV Remembering the outstanding ministers 1: *The Funeral Sermon on Erasmus Sarcerius*

I shall now take a look at another group of sources relevant to the topic discussed here: namely funeral sermons. First, I will say something about the sermon at Sarcerius' own funeral, which was held by his Magdeburg colleague *Johannes Wigand* in 1560.[26] How was Sarcerius represented here for the purposes of ecclesiastical memory?

One important strategy of Lutheran sixteenth-century funeral sermons was to connect the biography of the deceased to a specific Biblical person, in order as far as possible to retell the biography of the dead person in terms of a biblical biography.[27] Funeral sermons for ministers some-

---

24 Loc. cit., 80.
25 Loc. cit., 80.
26 Johannes Wigand, born in Mansfeld and known *inter alia* as one of the authors of the *Magdeburger Centurien*, was minister in Mansfeld since 1546 and superintendent in Magdeburg since 1553. The funeral sermon is digitally available from the SLUB, Dresden: http://digital.slubdresden.de/fileadmin/data/345763378/345763378_tif/jpegs/345763378.pdf.
27 C.N. Moore, Patterned Lives. The Lutheran Funeral Biography in Early Modern Ger-

times used Paul as a model, with conversion, fighting against idolatry and active preaching as important biographical elements. But Sarcerius is not mirrored in the image of Paul. Instead, Wigand has chosen an Old Testament text that is more closely connected to the pastoral ideals of the Old Testament prophets and holy men.

In addition to the quotation from Apoc. Xiiii on the front page of the sermon (*Selig sind die Todten, die in dem HErrn sterben*), he quotes Jes 57:1–2 as his main source for a biblical identification of the deceased (*Esaiæ am LVI. Cap.*):

> Der Gerechte kompt umb, und niemandt ist, der es zu hertzen neme, und heilige Leute werden auffgerafft, und niemandt achtet drauff. Denn die Gerechten werden weggerafft für dem Unglück, und die richtig für sich gewandelt haben, komen zu friede, und rugen in iren Kamern.[28]

This text summarizes the role of Sarcerius, and how he should be remembered: as a righteous and holy man, who died too early, in the midst of his endeavors. In particular, the specific historical context is important: Sarcerius was called to his work in a very special time of history, a time comparable to the era of the Apostles:

> Nach der Apostel zeit aber, halten viel gleubige, das kaumpt eine zeit auff Erden gewesen, da alle Artickel des Glaubens heller, reiner, deutlicher, und gewaltiger sein gelehret unnd geschrieben worden, als eben jtzt zu unserer zeit der Heimsuchung in Deudtschlandt, nun fast in die vierzig Jar, […] Auch sind nach der Apostel zeit nicht auff ein mal so viel hoher gelerter, trewer Lehrer und Schreiber in einem Lande erfunden worden, als diese zeit bey den Deudtschen, das beweiset das wreck, und sonderlich das es mit Bücher in Deudtscher, Hebraischer, Bohemischer, Polonischer, Denischer, Schwedischer und dergleichen Sprachen in Deutschlandt, von dem lieben Worte Gottes, unnd allen Artickeln des Glaubens, heuffig bissher geregnet und geschneiet hat. Nicht allein welche die alten für viel hundert Jahren gemacht, sondern man hat bisshierher in Deudschlant mit frembden Sprachen also geredt und geschrieben, und noch Gott lob, das man wol möchte sagen, dass Cicero mit der Lateinische sprache, Item die Hebraische und gantz Griechenlandt, so zu reden, in Deudtschlandt gezogen. Denn wo Gottes Wort angeht, und der heilige Geist wohnet, da geusset also die gaben der mancherleien

many, 2006. See also S. ANGEL, Preachers as Paul: Learning and Exemplarity in Lutheran Funeral Sermons, forthcoming 2013, in RefoRC Oslo Concference volume.

28 http://digital.slub-dresden.de/ppn345763378/5.

Sprachen, heuffig und uberflüssig aus, wie auch im Pfingstag uber die Apostel, und hernach uber andere mehr geschehen.[29]

The political aspects of Sarcerius' role as a holy man are also touched upon very explicitly in the text, expressing beyond any doubt the theological foundation for the *geistliches Sonderbewusstsein* in the interaction with political authorities:

> Gottes Wort [...] sagt: Durch mich herschen die Könige. Der Herr setzet Könige ein und abe. Item Gottes wort ehret die Obrigkeit mit dem Namen Gottes selber, und zeiget an, das sie Gottes Ordnung, Stathalter und Diener sein. Nun ist das Reich Gottes auff Erden, darinnen Gott selber durch sein Wort, eine Kirche oder Hauffen der Leute samlet und heiliget, vergebung der Sünden und ewiges Leben mitteilet, gar viel hoher und herlicher. Denn das Weltliche reich, ist gleich als eine Dinerin des Reichs Gottes, wie der ander Psalm leret: So lasset euch nun weisen ir Könige, und lasset euch züchtigen ir Richter auff Erden, dienet dem Herrn mit furcht.[30]

And further:

> Nun sind in diesem Geistlichen Reiche Gottes allhie auff Erden, die Lerer und Prediger, unsers lieben Gottes Diener und Knechte, welche an Gottes stat, sein Wort und willen (daran sie denn verbunden) den Menschen fürtragen, und die hochwirdigen Sacrament, nach Gottes einsetzung und ordnung reichen, und schreien, Thut Busse und gleubet dem Euangelio, Marci i. Und thut rechtschaffene früchte der Busse, Matth iii.[31]

V Remembering the outstanding ministers 2: The Epitaph and the Funeral Sermon on Anton Lauterbach (Pirna)

Another outstanding minister of the same generation, active in the same parts of Germany, was *Anton Lauterbach* in Pirna. He has been chosen as the second case here since he was one of the ministers recruited in the same year as the *Heinrichsagende* was published (1539) to help realize the aims and visions of this Ordinance throughout Albertine Saxony, and also since we have preserved not only his funeral sermon, but also a beautiful epitaph.

---

29 http://digital.slub-dresden.de/ppn345763378/15.
30 http://digital.slub-dresden.de/ppn345763378/8.
31 http://digital.slub-dresden.de/ppn345763378/10.

Lauterbach was born in 1502, one year after Sarcerius, and like Sarcerius, he also studied in Leipzig. He was there from 1517 to 1519, and then worked as a teacher in Freiberg in the early 1520s. In 1528, he came to Wittenberg for further studies and in order to join the Reformation movement. He lived there for five years, and for a long period he also lived in Luther's house.[32]

To Luther scholars, he is known as one of the secretaries who recorded Luther's lectures (Isaiah and the Song of Songs), Sermons (on John 6–8, 1531–32) and his Table Talk. Like Luther, he married a former nun (whom he learned to know in Luther's house), and several letters from Luther as well as from Melanchthon addressed to Lauterbach are still preserved. After his stay in Wittenberg, he was sent out to represent the Reformation Church, first as a deacon in Leising and in Wittenberg, and then as a Superintendent and pastor in Pirna.

He stayed there as the superintendent of the city for thirty years, until his death in 1569. Here he was responsible for finishing the beautiful *Marienkirche* in 1546, in accordance with Protestant iconographical ideals. This church was under construction when Lauterbach arrived in Pirna, and he put much effort into influencing the inner decorations according to the biblical teaching of the Lutheran movement.

Lauterbach also developed a local church ordinance for Pirna on the basis of the *Heinrichsagende*, differing from the latter most of all by prescribing a few more feast days, services and teaching obligations than the minimum mentioned in the *Heinrichsagende*.

Funeral sermon

Anton Lauterbach was buried on the 19th of July 1569, two days after his death. The Funeral Sermon was held by *Clemens Goldammer*, a Deacon at the Pirnaer Marienkirche, who had been working together with Lauterbach for several years.[33]

---

32 For a short introduction to the life and work of Lauterbach, see W. LECHNER, Anton Lauterbach. Pirnas Reformator. Freund Luthers, 2004.
33 The text is available at the ThULB in Jena under the signature 4 Theol.XXXV,24(6).

On the title page of the printed sermon one can read: Der Todt seiner Heiligen ist wert gehalten fur dem HERREN. (Ps 115 = 116: 15)

In the preface to his sermon, which Goldammer supplied for the printed version, he makes the following statement about Lauterbach as a Protestant hero:

> Sankt Paulus sagt zum Ephe. 4: Christus ist auffgefaren in die Höhe, und hat den Menschen Gaben gegeben. Und er hat etliche zu Aposteln gesetzt, etliche aber zu Propheten, etliche zu Euangelisten, etliche zu Hirten und Lerern, das die Heiligen zugerichtet werden zum Werck des Ampts, dadurch der Leib Christi erbawet werde, bis wir alle hinein komen zu einerley Glauben, und erkentnis des Sons Gottes. Aus diesen Worten ist klar, das der einige ware Hohepriester Jesus Christus, zu allen zeiten Diener seines Worts erweckt und sendet in die örter der Welt, do er im eine Kirche samlet, und das er selbst das Predigampt bestelt und erhelt.

And further:

> Also ists widerumb ein sonderlich tröstlich Zeugnis Gottes güte unnd Barmhertzigkeit, Wenn Gott einer Stadt oder Landt Christliche Lerer zuschickt, welche in Stedten und Dörffern die gemeine Christi mit reiner gesunder Lere weiden, unnd sie mit Gottseligen Exemplen bessern.[34]

Goldammer then goes on to prove how important this is by drawing the comparison between the ruler (Fürst) and the bishop: We all know, he says, what a great blessing of God it is to have worldly rulers who fear God and are wise, trustworthy and honest.

> ABer viel ein grosser Schatz ist es, wenn Gott christliche Bischoffe ins ministerium setzt, die für ire befohlene herd vleissig wachen, sie trewlich weiden, trösten, für dem verderbnis warnen, und wol zusehen, das nicht Wolffe einbrechen, die Herde zerstrewen und zerreissen.[35]

All this is written in order to introduce the funeral sermon about Pirna's first Protestant hero. And after talking about him in this way in the introduction, as a hero or a holy man to be *imitated*, most of the sermon itself is devoted to characterizing Lauterbach as a holy man to be *remembered*.

The key text is again precisely the same as in the funeral sermon for Sarcerius, from Isaiah 56 (57: 1–2):

34 Ibd., Aii, r-v.
35 Ibd., Aiii, r.

Der Gerechte kompt umb, und niemand ist, der es zu hertzen neme, und heilige leute werden auff geraffet, und niemandt achtet darauff. Denn die Gerechten werden wegge-raffet fur dem unglück, unnd die richtig fur sich gewandelt haben, kommen zum friede, und rugen in iren Kamern.

There is no need to identify Lauterbach further as a holy man. Everyone present in the funeral knows that. The question is: what does it mean, when God removes the really holy from a community or from society? According to Goldammer, it is first and foremost a signal for penitence/ Busse: *Das fromer Leute wegsterben, ein erinnerung und anzeigung sey, zukünfftiger straff und unglücks.*

Epitaph

Even more interesting than the funeral sermon is the epitaph. Restored in 2004, it stands at the left side of the main entrance just inside the church, close to the place where his grave was rediscovered in 1889. A first look at this epitaph shows that the deceased superintendent is present depicted as part of his family down left, half-way integrated into the biblical scene of the transfiguration of Christ, which is described in all the synoptic Gospels (e.g. Matthew 17). No fundamental distinction or border is drawn between Peter, James and John in the middle and Anton Lauterbach on the left side; they are all located in the same imaginary landscape looking up to Christ who reveals himself as divine light, with Moses and Elijah in conversation with Christ on his right and left hand. This landscape seems to have a greater resemblance to the steep mountains of the Saxonian Alps near Pirna than to the geography of the Holy Land. And while Peter says on a banner reaching up to Christ BONUM EST NOS HIC ESSE (*It is good for us to be here*), Lauterbach in a parallel banner says SIGNA LEGEM IN DISCIPULIS MEIS (*Write the Law on my disciples*). Above the whole scene are quoted the words from Matthew 17,5 HIC EST FILIUS MEUS DILECTUS IN QUO COMPLACUI. HUNC AUDITE. (*This is my beloved Son, in whom I am well pleased; hear ye him.*)

Lauterbach is not *quite* integrated into the biblical scene, though. He is also part of a family scene in the lower part of the image, together with his deceased first wife Agnes (who was probably a former nun of the same monastery as Luther's wife Catarina) and his two deceased daughters (next

Image 2: Epitaph Lauterbach

214

to the text in the middle of the image) and his deceased son in white behind him. All these are marked with crosses as signs of their status as dead. The last person, the woman with the black cap, has no such cross, and may either be his second wife – also named Agnes – who lived for a long time after his death, or his only child who reached adult age, a daughter who married in 1550.

Lauterbach is part of this family group. But his double identity, both as family man and as more distinctively integrated into the biblical scene as a colleague of Peter, James and John, is symbolized by his eyes. If one looks closely here (and one really has to go close to see it), it is difficult to escape the conclusion that his eyes are directed upwards, as is also the case with Peter and James. In this way, the superintendent and minister, in another way than his family, here takes part in the revelation of the divinity of Christ.

The inscription right in front of him confirms this interpretation:

GENS MIHI LAUTERBACHA
I come from the Lauterbach-family
PROFESSIO SACRA DOCERE
My profession was to teach sacred things
– LUTHERUS DOCTOR.
Luther was (my) teacher
SPES REQVIESQVE CHRISTUS
Christ is (my) hope and rest.
– QVAS PAVI VERBO CHRIST,
(The sheep) that I fed with the word of Christ
 QVAS FIDUS AMAVI. –
that I loved faithfully
INTER EAS PASTOR SUM TVMVLTATVS OVES –
Among those I, the pastor, am buried.
GAVDIA SPECTABO CELESTA, GAVDIA CHRISTI
I will see the joys of Heaven, the Joys of Christ
– MORTE ET PROFVSO SANGVINE PARTA MIHI.
given to me by [his] death and the blood that was shed

Around the frame: »Anno Domini 1539 25. Julii M. Antonius Lauterbach Pastor et Superatendens vocatus huic ecclesie, inservit Evangelio 1569. 18 Julii in Christo obdormivit in Pace et Quiescens.«

Image 3: Epitaph Lauterbach Detail

Small letters bottom lower part of frame: »Natus Anno Christi 1502 13. Januar: Vixit annos 67 Menses 7 Dies horas ferme 6. A creatore destinatos. Hiob 38.«

VI The religious aspects of the geistliches Sonderbewusstsein

In her interesting book on the clergy in Basel, Amy Nelson Burnett has reflected on the importance of paying attention to the phenomenon of *generations* in Reformation research. Especially when things change rapidly, the distinctions between generations become important.[36]

I have discussed the huge topic of the Early Modern clergy by talking primarily about one specific generation of prominent ministers in the core

---

36 A. Nelson Burnett, Teaching the Reformation: Ministers and their message in Basel, 1529–1629, 2006.

area of the Reformation. This generation includes Sarcerius and Lauterbach, but to a certain degree also the authors of the *Heinrichsagende*
(where Justus Jonas is generally held to have been the most influential).
They were all devout adherents of the Reformation, contributing to defining the profile of the Lutheran ministry in the second generation. They all
praise the ministry as the highest gift of God, and support it by arguments
and authorities which in some cases go well beyond the classical definitions of the ministry in the texts of Luther or Melanchthon or in the CA.

The *political* role envisaged for the good minister in these texts corre-
sponds quite well to the observations in recent historical research concerning a *geistliches Sonderbewusstsein* (Schorn-Schütte, Berndorff and
others) among parts of the German Lutheran clergy during the 1550s and
1560s.

But the *religious* aspects of this specific profile of a clerical identity in
this period deserve a closer inspection and further interpretation. One
interesting perspective to apply here is the history of *Christian sanctity*. It
may be a commonplace to suggest that certain Protestant pastors (and not
only Luther himself) took over some of the functions of Late Medieval
saints. But the texts (and the epitaph) we have been looking at give us the
opportunity to corroborate theories of this kind. The first-class priests
(according to Wilhelm Sarcerius' classification) were local or even regional
heroes, characterized by their *heroic deeds*: one of the main requirements
for acquiring status of sanctity in post-Tridentine Catholicism as well[37],
after the revision of procedures of canonization on the basis not least of
the experience with first-class saints like Teresa of Avila and Ignatius of
Loyola, where miracles played a minor role.

The holy life of the Lutheran first-class pastors was possible because
of their special access to the gifts of the Holy Spirit that were available-
available in the ministry. And these gifts not only contributed to the right
teaching of these men, they also contributed to their holy life. In the funeral sermons as well as in Sarcerius' handbook, these pastors were partly

---

37 For an overview, see the classical article by P. BURKE, How to be a Counter-Reformation
Saint, first printed (in: Religion and Society in Early Modern Europe, 1500–1800, ed. by
K. VAN GREYERZ, 1984, 45–55).

written into the religious roles of the Old Testament prophets and partly into the roles of the Apostles, and they were again and again characterized as holy men.

They were remembered in the funeral sermons through accounts that were not wholly unlike the Early Modern Catholic accounts of their Saints. And the epitaphs, which were so often put up in Lutheran churches in the late sixteenth and the seventeenth centuries and replaced the images and altars of the Medieval Saints, continued to take care of the religious function of remembering people of particular sanctity, even if no specific cultic activity was connected to these epitaphs.

The religious role and religious function of these early Lutheran pastors were not at all, then, restricted to teaching. This phenomenon goes well beyond the role of the Lehramt, although this is always also highly praised in the texts. In spite of the unquestioned theological priority attributed to the function of teaching in the Early Modern Lutheran ministry, the relationship between the Medieval and Early Protestant ministry seems to be rather more complex than the account given in the article of Schwarz from 1984, when he states that *der protestantische Pfarrer betet mit der Gemeinde, und alle Glaubenden haben im Gebet gleichen Zugang zu Gott.*[38] This is true about Luther, but does not seem to be a sufficient description of the generation of early Lutheran pastors at whom I have been looking today.

Two short remarks at the end: First about the generation question. According to the German historians who have studied the *geistliches Sonderbewusstsein,* this is not something which characterizes the Protestant clergy throughout the whole Early Modern period. Rather, it is a specific phenomenon of the late sixteenth and the early seventeenth centuries. In particular, it can be identified in the 1550s and the 1560s. Texts like the *Heinrichsagende* and the handbook of Sarcerius were in use and reprinted precisely in this same period. So, my contribution is restricted to illuminating this particular part of the history of the Early Modern Protestant clergy.

38 SCHWARZ (see n. 23).

Secondly: I was asked to deal with the question of *ideal and reality*. Have I escaped this challenge by restricting myself to talking only about ideals – in church law, in handbooks and in sermons? My answer would be that I have been talking about both at the same time. The official definition of a new role for the clergy is not only an ideal, it is also a social reality. The same is true about the memorial monuments that were revered in the communities. Even though they idealize the person to be remembered, these memories are, as such, important parts of the cultural reality of a society.

Luther between Theology and Cultural Studies

Pilgrim W. K. Lo

»Christian Dogmatics«, »Systematic Theology«, »Christian Thoughts« or »Christian Philosophy« – they are named differently, however the contents and subject matters are almost identical. There is no doubt that they are near-synonymous in seminary curriculum. In contrast to the USA and most Asian countries where »Systematic Theology« is widely used, the term »Christian Dogmatics« is commonly used in Germany and many other European countries, whereas universities in China are exclusively using the terms »Christian Thoughts« or »Christian Philosophy«. Which one might be considered the most proper theological expression does not really matter for the subject discussed in this paper. We do, however, have to note that the difference in the usage of those terms is related to theological concepts which are so much affected by culture and its context.

In the Prolegomena, or introductory session of a course, we would discuss with students the tension or conflict between »Christian Dogmatics« and »Contextual Theology«. Such conflict is rooted in their different emphases, in short, »Christian Dogmatics« primarily stresses the clear, authoritative teachings and the proper hermeneutics of the Church, whereas »Contextual Theology« puts the emphasis first and foremost on cultural, environmental, historical factors in theological development as well as the effect of theology on the context. The topic we are going to discuss today is »Luther between Theology and Cultural Studies«. The reason I consider this a valid topic for discussion is that over the past 400 years, ordinary people as well as those in the academic circles have considered Luther not merely a theologian but also a reformer. He is not an ordinary theologian, but a pioneer of the Protestant Church, the founder of the Lutheran teachings[1]; he is not an ordinary reformer, but a reformer who renewed the Church and brought the Western civilization to a new era. All these trigger our interests in studying how Luther's teachings impact the subtle connection between theology and culture.

I Theology and Cultural Studies

Moltmann has articulated a common opinion of many theologians. He said, »Theologie ist auch eine Kulturwissenschaft, aber sie geht darin nicht auf, denn ihr Gegenstand ›Gott‹ ist Gott und kann nicht ›als‹ etwas anderes gedacht werden.«[2]

For the purpose of clarity, it is necessary to reiterate that the word »theology« discussed here is the theology of Christian faith. This consensus in definition is decisive in Luther study. We may rephrase Moltmann's statement »Theologie ist auch eine Religionswissenschaft, aber sie geht darin nicht auf, denn ihr Gegenstand ›Gott‹ ist der uns in Christus geoffenbarte Gott.«

Hence, theology is different from cultural studies and religious studies which adopt a primarily humanistic orientation. Even though there is no question for us that Luther's reformation has brought remarkable impact to Western culture, yet he is not a scholar in cultural studies. His ultimate concern is the faith of the Christian Church. Therefore, the attempt to analyse Luther's impact on cultures purely through his cultural idea and concept is not the most appropriate approach for today's scholars in cultural study.

---

1 There are three documents by Luther recognised as Lutheran Confessions included in *The Book of Concord*. Moreover, according to the Constitution of the Lutheran World Federation all members are required to accept its Doctrinal Basis which states »The Lutheran World Federation confesses [...] the Small Catechism of Martin Luther, a pure exposition of the Word of God.«

2 J. MOLTMANN, Theologie als Kulturwissenschaft oder Theologie des Reiches Gottes? Zur Diskussion über die Funktion der Theologie heute (in: Denkraum Katechismus. Festgabe für Oswald Bayer zum 70. Geburtstag, hg. v. J. VON LÜPKE/E. THAIDIGSMANN, 2009, 527–539), 527.

In view of cultural studies, culture originates from humans. Thus there is only one kind of culture – human culture. Be it created consciously or not, it is uncertain. However, culture is surely a developed form of human existence, but not unchangeable. It keeps on changing and reforming over time as long as human history continues. A tribe, a nation or a society each has its unique culture. Yet, it is not easy to give each a definitive description, for they consist of various subcultures in themselves. Cultural studies do not neglect the impact of religion on human culture. Therefore, Luther has been perceived a man of the age in most cultural scholars' mind for what he has done during the Reformation is actually a counterculture movement which has successfully constructed a new culture.

Though theologians would not object to the notion »Culture is Human Culture«, yet they cannot agree that »human is the creator of culture«. This is essential to Luther for he thinks highly of the first Commandment – God is the Creator of all, and we should mark our minds to trust Him alone, to look to Him alone.[3] His submission to God's Word is the key to how he develops his theology and shapes the ministry of his reformation.[4] Thus, for Luther, it surely is heretical to say »human is the creator of culture«. However, the human is a crucial factor in forming culture, for ›he‹ is a co-creator[5] – a part-taker in God's creation according to God's perfect will. In this frame of reference, Luther's theology has cultural significance, and reversely, Luther gave human culture itself a theological meaning.

II Review of the Significance of Martin Luther

The attention of cultural studies on Luther focuses on his impact on culture, whereas theology is more interested in his contribution to Christian faith. Although the two approaches differ, they do not contradict, they

---

3 M. LUTHER, The Large Catechism (in: The Book of Concord: The Confessions of the Evangelical Lutheran Church, ed. by R. KOLB/T. J. WENGERT, 2000), 389.
4 LW 32,112 (WA 7; 838,7).
5 G. MÜLLER, Luther und die moderne Welt (in: DERS., Zwischen Reformation und Gegenwart II – Vorträge und Aufsätze, 1988, 77–79).

even complement one another. Luther, the venerable dead of five hundred years ago, still speaks to us today with his great work in theology and culture.[6]

Bernd Moeller observed that there is no one in the world like Luther who has been commemorated in numerous anniversaries year after year.[7] Though his saying is somewhat exaggerated, it still speaks out the minds of many Luther scholars. Furthermore, history shows how people over centuries continue to hold high esteem for Luther. Prior to being a subject for academic study, he has been commemorated publicly.[8] Since the beginning of last century with the emergence of a Luther-Renaissance, Luther studies have not only increased in scope and variety, but also triggered scholars' interest in the history of Luther research itself – the changes of Luther's image throughout history,[9] and differing interpretations of Luther's value and impact in different ages.[10] Some even suggest Luther a uniquely significant resource for postmodern theology.[11] All these proposals on Luther studies benefit us greatly with a better calibrated scale for today's research work.

For Lutheran churches, Luther's teaching is deemed to be authoritative.[12] His teachings on the doctrine of God, on preaching, on justification, on the doctrine of the church and on the means of grace constitute the

---

6 Martin Luther – Witness to Jesus Christ: A joint Statement of »Lutheran – Catholic Commission on Unity« of the Lutheran World Federation and Pontifical Council for Promoting Christian Unity, 1983, paragraph 1.

7 »Nichts und niemand auf der Welt hat bereits so viele Jubiläen erlebt wie Luther.« B. MOELLER, Luthers Erfolge (in: Luther-Rezeption. Kirchenhistorische Aufsätze zur Reformationsgeschichte, hg. v. J. SCHILLING, 2001, 270–284), 279.

8 H. MEDICK/P. SCHMIDT, Einleitung. Von der Lutherverehrung zur konfessionellen Lutherforschung und darüber hinaus (in: Luther zwischen den Kulturen. Zeitgenossenschaft – Weltwirkung, hg. v. DERS., 2004, 11–30), 16.

9 B. LOHSE, Wandlungen des Lutherbildes im Spiegel der Lutherjubiläen (in: Zugänge zu Luther, hg. v. H. FOERSTER, 1984, 96–108).

10 See n. 6, paragraph 2.

11 Such as K. A. KLEINHANS, Why Now? The Relevance of Luther in a Postmodern Age (Currents in Theology and Mission 24,6, 1997, 488–495), 488.

12 B. LOHSE, Luthers Bedeutung für die evangelische Kirche und Theologie (in: Luthers Sendung für Katholiken und Protestanten, hg. v. K. LEHMANN, 1982, 31–47), 32–36.

Lutheran confessions or the guideline for faith.[13] Scholars might hold differing views on some of Luther's theological issues, yet, none could deny the profound impact of Luther's teaching on the development of theology – especially the Word-centred Protestant theology and hermeneutics. Gerhard Müller further points out that the draft of the *Barmen Theological Declaration* is also influenced by Luther's theological thought, in particular the first and the fifth articles.[14]

After the Reformation, Roman Catholics not only regarded Luther as the black sheep that caused the division of the Church, but also decreed his teachings to be heretical.[15] Their study and position on Luther finally changed after four hundred years or so. The work *Die Reformation in Deutschland* (1939) by Joseph Lortz puts forth a view that differs from the previous Catholic tradition. He suggests Luther's reformation theology is still part of the Catholic, even though in the process of Reformation Luther had criticized or even rejected some of the official Catholic teachings of the time.[16] It is worth our attention that in the speech made by Cardinal Johannes Gerardus Maria Willebrands, the President of the Pontifical Council for Promoting Christian Unity, in 1970 at the 5th Assembly of the Lutheran World Federation, he expressed a new attitude on Luther held by the Vatican:

> Who [...] would still deny that Martin Luther was a deeply religious person who with honesty and dedication sought for the message of the gospel? Who would deny that in spite of the fact that he fought against the Roman Catholic Church and the Apostolic See – and for the sake of truth one must not remain silent about this – he retained a considerable part of the old Catholic faith? Indeed, is it not true that the Second Vatican Council has even implemented requests that were first expressed by Martin Luther, among others, and as a result of which many aspects of Christian faith and life now find better expression than they did before? To be able to say this in spite of all the differences is a reason for great joy and much hope.[17]

---

13 G. Müller, Martin Luther als Autorität für die lutherische Kirche (in: Luthers Sendung für Katholiken und Protestanten, [see n. 12], 48–70), 51–65.

14 G. Müller, Lutherische Theologie und die Barmer Theologische Erklärung (in: Zwischen Reformation und Gegenwart, [see n. 5], 127–131).

15 See n. 6, paragraph 2.

16 J. Lortz, Die Reformation in Deutschland, Bd. 1, 1982, 176.

17 See n. 6, paragraph 6.

Later, Joseph Lortz's student and successor Peter Manns even calls Luther ›Vater im Glauben‹ in his publications.[18]

In the area of cultural studies, Luther has been highly respected by many, especially in Germany. Prior to the Luther-Renaissance, apart from his great influence on pietism and early enlightenment, he was also a national hero in the heart of most German people.[19] His reformation works are grounded in various contextual factors, e.g. *The Freedom of a Christian* and *Address to the Christian Nobility of the German Nation* have become the theological foundation of German nationalism. A good example of this foundational status is the Wartburgfest in 1817. It was a festival to commemorate the Battle of Leipzig (Völkerschlacht bei Leipzig) where the German army defeated Napoléon Bonaparte. The Jenaer Burschenschaft invited 13 universities to hold the 4th anniversary in Wartburg and also concurrently to celebrate the 300th anniversary of the Reformation. The achievement of Luther's translation of the New Testament into German (in Wartburg) had made him the icon of counter-foreign culture;[20] likewise, he was lauded as a national hero at the Wartburgfest for opposing the Pope during the Reformation. In 1883, his 400th anniversary, Luther was given the name »Gründungsvater des deutschen Reichs«. Yet, it is beyond fairness to portray Luther as a national hero. Hartmut Lehmann's comment deserves our attention. He said all those past celebrations have politicized Luther thus making Luther a tool for political agendas.[21]

Undoubtedly, Luther, born and living in Germany, was a German! He cared not only for the Church, but also had a specific concern for those around him, – his neighbours, his fellow citizens, his countryfolk. That's the dynamic of his reformation which extends to the whole fabric of the life and culture of the German people. For this reason, Luther wrote German hymns, designed a German Mass, and translated the Bible into Ger-

---

18 The remarkable publications by J. Lortz are Martin Luther. Ketzer oder Vater im Glauben?, 1980 and Vater im Glauben. Studien zur Theologie Martin Luthers, 1988.

19 H. v. Treitschke, Deutsche Lebensbilder, 1927, 10.11.28f.

20 H. Münkler, Die Deutschen und ihre Mythen, 2008, 318.

21 H. Lehmann, Die Deutschen und ihr Luther (Frankfurter Allgemeine Zeitung, 16. Aug. 2008, Nr. 199, 7).

man. According to Bernhard Lohse, »Die Sprache unzähliger deutscher Dichter ist ohne Luthers Bibelübersetzung nicht vorstellbar«.[22] Thus the transformation of Latin culture to German culture could be said to be an integral part of Luther's reformation work.

Heinrich Heine highly commends the contribution Luther made for the German nation. He said,

> wie wir durch ihn (Luther) zur größten Denkfreiheit gelangt. Aber dieser Martin Luther gab uns nicht bloß die Freiheit der Bewegung, sondern auch das Mittel der Bewegung, dem Geist gab er nämlich einen Leib. Er gab dem Gedanken auch das Wort. Er schuf die deutsche Sprache. Dieses geschah, indem er die Bibel übersetzte.[23]

Did Luther create the German language? This is still very controversial. Martin Heidegger reminded us that »Die Sprache ist das Haus des Seins. In ihrer Behausung wohnt der Mensch«.[24] We cannot ignore the fact that Luther made a tremendous contribution in making German language popular, standardized and even nationalized. Language has a prominent effect on a nation's culture; therefore, we may conclude that from the linguistic aspect, Luther's work continues to provide immeasurable value for German society and culture.

III Luther and foreign Culture

There is a Chinese adage »Shēng yú sī, Zháng yú sī«[25] which is similar to English »Born and bred«. Some scholars credit Luther for his theological influence on liberating conscience and mind as a direct precursor to the Enlightenment.[26] His idea of Dreiständelehre or Berufskonzeption is the

---

22 LOHSE, Luthers Bedeutung (see n. 12), 35.

23 H. HEINE, Zur Geschichte der Religion und Philosophie in Deutschland (in: Werke und Briefe, Bd. 5, hg. v. H. KAUFMANN, 1961, 164–308), 207.

24 M. HEIDEGGER, Über den Humanismus, 1949, 5.

25 Literal translation: People who were born and grew up in a place have the typical character of the people who are living there.

26 K.-H. ZUR MÜHLEN, Wirkung und Rezeption (in: Luther Handbuch, hg. v. A. BEUTEL, 2005, 461–488), 475–477; E. SCHULIN, Die Luther-Auffassungen in der deutschen Geschichtsschreibung (in: Luthers Sendung, [see n. 13], 94–115), 98; KLEINHANS (see n. 11), 488; MÜLLER, Luther (see n. 5), 70.

foundation of modern capitalism.[27] Woven together, both the Enlightenment and capitalism have had a momentous impact on human culture across nations and countries, especially in Europe and in North America. Significantly, however, Luther is much more tightly bound to German culture than to others. He is not only part of German history, he belongs to its culture. Seen in this way, Luther's thought and reformation work are the crucial element that forms German culture. Because he was born and raised in Germany, he reformed the Church within the German context, and his reformation thus directly changed the trajectory of his people and their lives. It is unthinkable that a great man from another culture, such as from China or from Japan could have had the same effect in Germany.

The Goethe-Institute employed Alexander Grintsevich, a teacher in Russia to conduct research in Europe involving 13,000 participants. The study concluded on 2 May 2011 with results highlighted as below:[28]

The 1st question asks: Wer ist für Sie der/die bedeutendste Deutsche?
The Answer: Martin Luther is ranked 4th.

and the 7th question is: Welches ist das bedeutendste historische Ereignis, das Sie mit Deutschland verbinden?
The Answer ranked 3rd is: Reformation by Martin Luther.

When the New Millennium was about to start, similar research findings were reported in the USA:

1. Times Magazine 15 Oct 1992 listing Martin Luther among the list of the top ten figure of the age;

2. Both Life Magazine (1997 Autumn) and The History Channel today (June 2007) indicated that among the 100 most influential characters of the last Millennium, Martin Luther ranked the 3rd.

---

27 M. WEBER, Die protestantische Ethik und der Geist des Kapitalismus, [3]2010, Kap. 3.

28 http://alexandergrintsevich.wordpress.com/category/uber-die-deutsche-sprache-und-kultur/, 06.07.2012.

These results came as no surprise. The research was conducted in the context of Germany, Europe and the USA, which all hold a common element in their history, namely the legacy of the Reformation and the role of Christianity in their respective cultures. However, if the same study were done in Africa and Asia, the result could vary significantly. The reason is obvious. There is a huge gap of time and space between Martin Luther, a German of the 16th century, and people of Africa and Asia today, because we all understand that time and space are crucial in the formation of culture. To conclude in brief, while Luther stands as a prominent figure in the eyes of Europeans and Americans, he gains no echo from people of Africa and Asia. Therefore, the study on Luther in Africa and Asia is a subject which has not yet been well developed. For instance, if the International Congress for Luther Research is regarded as the most representative conference of Luther study, can we figure out how many participants are from Africa or Asia? Likewise, we can ask how many non-European or non-American are on the member list of the Luther Gesellschaft? In view of this, it is a big question: How significant is Luther's influence on the formation of culture in countries other than Europe and North America, diverse cultures in the continents of Africa and Asia, for example?

I have no objection to most scholars' comment that Luther is a Bible scholar, not a systematic theologian. However, with regards to the subject of discussion today, I am in agreement with Eric Gritsch that Luther is a contextual theologian.[29] We have to admit that Luther's theological teachings constitute the foundation of Lutheran doctrine; many of his works have become a core of study in systematic theology. We also notice that the construction of his theology, while deeply rooted in his biblical understanding, is continually influenced by an awareness of, and feedback from his context. Luther is not a pedant despite he buried himself in the library for theological study. Instead, he is a theologian in the midst of actual circumstances such as the plague and the peasant war. Because Luther is able to contextualize his theology in answering the questions of his time, his theology is, therefore, a contextual theology. Furthermore, through inter-

---

29 E. GRITSCH, The Cultural Context of Luther's Interpretation (Interpretation 37, 3, 1983, 266–276), 266.

action with and feedback from his context, Luther obtained public acceptance and support, thus, he was able to bring influence to the culture. Consider a different setting, if I were to put China forward as a subject of study for Luther, I am pretty sure that he would not have much interest. This is because China is not a Christian country nor does she have the issue of indulgences. Furthermore, Luther is a figure of the 16th century in Europe, his theology is not intended for China of the 21st century. In a parallel manner, neither does such a wide cultural distance provide much footing for Chinese to regard Luther and his work.

China is a multi-ethnic country shaped by more than five thousand years of cross cultural development. Despite the challenges of Imperialism and Colonialism over the past hundred years, China basically is still open to foreign cultures. China allowed universities established by missionaries to replace the imperial examination system[30] that had been exercised for more than a thousand years. In the early 20th century, foreign ideas exposed the weakness of the China Government. These new »alien« ideas fostered intellectuals and youngsters to reconsider Chinese tradition and culture, which led to the emergence of the New Culture Movement that advocated Western ideology – Mr. Dé (democracy) and Mr. Sài (science).[31] Since the set up of People's Republic of China, communism took hold of the whole of China at a speedy pace. From 1966 to 1976, the Great Proletarian Cultural Revolution replaced most Chinese tradition and culture with its own cultural forms. Under the influence of political ideology, China perceived Luther from the eyes of Marx and Lenin. On the one hand Luther is seen as a hero who liberated his people from slavery and as a pioneer of anti-capitalist revolution in Europe;[32] on the other hand, Luther is seen as a traitor to peasantry.[33]

---

30 The imperial examination was an examination system in Imperial China established during the Sui Dynasty in 605 which was designed to select the best administrative officials for the state's bureaucracy. In the Qing Dynasty the throne endorsed a memorial on 2 September 1905 which ordered that the imperial examination be discontinued.

31 The New Culture Movement of the mid 1910s and 1920s in China was led by Chén Dúxiù, Hú Shìh and Lǔ Xùn etc. who were disappointed with traditional Chinese culture and called for a new Chinese culture, advocated for democracy and science.

32 Lǐ Píngyè, Human Discovery (in Chinese), 1983, 201.205; Lóng Wénwǔ/Zhōu Róng,

Following the end of the Cultural Revolution Chinese started to rebuild their values. More and more intellectuals came to have a better understanding and new perspectives of Christian reformation. When Dēng Xiǎopíng advocated his economic reform in the 80s, Max Weber's work *Die Protestantische Ethik und der Geist des Kapitalismus* gained its popularity as the best-selling book in China. His work greatly inspired numerous intellectuals in considering the relationship between Christianity and Capitalism in economic development. Weber's analysis shows that Luther and Calvin's theology provides moral value to »diligent hard-working« hence affirming that »reasonable pursuit of money« constitutes theological meaning.[34] Such a conclusion has been widely accepted by the Chinese intellectuals, giving rise to the »cultural Christian«[35] phenomenon, and stimulating more and more interest in Luther.

The resolution on »Strengthening Theological Reconstruction« was voted through in churches of China in 1998. The objective of this resolution is to construct a theological system that is much more relevant to China's society and her culture. In other words, the aim is to eliminate the elements of ›Western Religion‹ in order that Christianity may find its place in China and her culture, and gain proper understanding and acceptance by the nation, so that the Chinese church may have her own theological system. For the past decade, the effort made was mainly driven by Bishop K.H. Ting's idea. He stressed that »»God is love‹ is the central message of the Bible.« As a Chinese Christian, one should know about this ›God is love‹ [...] He further said that,

Effects and Significances of Reformation in Europe: A cultural perspective (in Chinese) (Public Literature, 2009, No. 03, 98).

33 Sūn Lìxīn, Luther Research in the Contemporary theological Study of German Church History (in Chinese) (Journal of Literature, History and Philosophy, 1994, No. 01, 90).

34 Yáng Yànmíng, Factors determining the Rise of Capitalism of West Europe – interpreting Weber's *The Protestant Ethic and the Spirit* (in Chinese) (Journal of Héxī University, 2006, No. 03, 40f).

35 Cultural Christians in China are mostly intellectuals who are usually devoted to the study of great thinkers of Christian theology and refer to basic Christian ideas in their social criticisms, however they are not baptized and do not attend churches.

our church today has attached too much importance on Paul's letters [...] ›How Jesus Christ loves all men‹ as the message of the Gospel tells us ›how God loves all men‹. Therefore, I advocate reading the four gospels [...] The ideal Chinese church in my mind is [...] able to help believers to love our country and our church [...] The theological thinking of our church needs to be constructed and enhanced in order to make our church more human, rational and moral, to become the loved church of God and the God loving church.[36]

While certainly a pragmatic approach, what Bishop Ting advocates is of close concern to those who hold to Martin Luther's proposition of Justification by Faith. Ting criticises that the doctrine of justification by faith has no relevance to Chinese culture; it is even harmful for the future of Chinese church.[37] Therefore, the teaching must be tempered for the following reasons[38]:

1. It distorted the correct concept of God by teaching that God's love is given to believers only.

2. It abrogated the value of moral behavior by maintaining that the Gospel contains no morals, which is to say that the doctrine of justification by faith separates itself from good works.

3. It caused a rift between believers and unbelievers by claiming that the majority of humankind is bound for the eternal flames of hell regardless of their good morality, just because they are unbelievers. However all Christians are good in God's eyes, merely because they believe in Him.

---

36 Bishop K.H. TING, Theological Construction Entering a New Phase (in Chinese) (Tien-fen 9, 2003, 6f).
37 Loc. cit., 7.
38 OUYÁNG WÉNFĒNG, My Theological Reflections on Dilute ›Justification by Faith‹ (in Chinese) (Nanjing Theological Review 1, 2003, 130); K.H. TING, Tempering Justification by Faith (in: Heavenly Wind and Sweet Rain: K.H. Ting, the Leader of the Chinese Church [in Chinese], ed. by LIU HUAJUN, 2001), 289. See also P.W.K. LO, From Justification by Faith to Justification by Love? A Reflection on Theological Reconstruction in the Chinese Church (in: Glaube und Denken. Die Bedeutung der Theologie für die Gesellschaft, Festschrift für Hans Schwarz zum 65. Geburtstag, Sonderband 2004, hg. v. A.M. MADSEN, 2004, 277–287), 279f.

4. It caused serious political problems by asserting that believers like Hitler go to heaven, while unbelievers like Chairman Mao should go to hell because of his unbelief.

It is noteworthy that »Justification by Faith« is Luther's core belief as well as his theological ground, and it now faces great difficulty in the context of Chinese culture. When we review the history of Christianity in China, similar theological struggles have taken place, as we may recall the tremendous difficulties of cultural conflicts faced by the Protestant missions when they entered into China in the 19th century.[39] Now, when we talk about »Luther between Theology and Cultural Studies«, it is essential for us to take into consideration the consequences that may occur when two different cultures meet. To be more specific, when Luther's culture meets with China's, will they integrate with one another and form a new culture? Or will they exclude each other? Or will they counteract and exist as sub-culture? Or will one become dominant over the other? I believe the decisive factor lies in the inclusiveness and exclusiveness between the two cultures, that is to say: are they in contradiction or can they complement each other? Let's take China as an example again.

The Chinese Church considers itself to have stepped into the Post-denominational Era[40] – there are no denominations any more. This is also China's political position. The cause could be traced back to a hundred years ago when imperialism intruded China and the Protestant mission was regarded as its means. Therefore, the reconstruction of the Lutheran church would be viewed as the restoration of denominationalism and even imperialism, hence cultural intrusion – a taboo in China. Every denominational church or seminary is considered as portal of colonialism. That is the reason why seminaries and ministries in China are required to work under the three-self-principles – self-governance, self-support and self-propagation, as well as to conform to the socialism of the modern Chinese culture.

---

39 ZUǑ FÚRÓNG, Conflict and Integration of Cultures (in Chinese) (Study of Christianity 9, 2006, 346–349).

40 For more details of discussion on this topic see P. W. K. LO, Luther and the Post-denominational Era of China (Theology and Life 25, 2004).

Meanwhile, Chinese traditional culture puts much weight on livelihood and pragmatism. An idea has a much easier time gaining acceptance in China if it is practical in problem solving. A good example is the notion made by Deng Xiaoping during the economic reform: Regardless of its colour (black or white), the cat that can catch mice is a good cat. Therefore, we may say that the quick development of the Chinese church in the economic reform period is the effect of ridding herself of the historical burden, namely colonialism, and on the positive and practical side, the affirmation of her social contribution.[41]

IV A forward-looking Consideration

Was there once a phenomenon of »culture of Luther«? I wonder. If there truly existed one, it surely did not originate from Luther himself for he had not the slightest intent to create a »culture of Luther« or anything like it. He would not allow himself to be the focus for later generations, rather, what concerns him most is that Christ and His Gospel be fully and rightly preached and known. Luther considered his own teaching and theology as nothing compared to Christ. He wanted no Luther followers or so called Lutherans.[42] Furthermore, culture is collective. Thus »individual or personal culture« is impossible. However, for fostering the above discussion, a presupposition of a culture closely tied to Luther is made. Nevertheless, we still cannot call it »culture of Luther« but perhaps »Lutheran culture« instead. It is clear that the Lutheran church is not set up by Luther, but grounded in the Holy Scripture and bolstered by Luther's teachings and belief. Likewise, a »Lutheran culture« may originate from Luther but was not created by him. It is difficult to give full details of what Lutheran culture is. Nevertheless, if we are to propose a Lutheran culture, three elements are considered crucial:

---

41 P.W.K. Lo, Theology is Not Mere Sociology: A Theological Reflection on the Reception of Christian Religion in Mainland China (Dialog 43, 3, 2004, 159 f. 162–164).

42 The Preface to the Wittenberg Edition of his German writings (1539). LW 34,283–288 (WA 50; 654–661).

1. It must be in the spirit of Luther, i.e. its nature should be rooted in Luther's faith and theology, which is always firmly founded on the Word.

2. It must be a culture of Christian faith, i.e. it should be centred in Christ's salvation and revelation for the unity with other Christian circles.

3. There must be a successor for this culture for the continuity of Luther's spirit and to manifest the uniqueness of the group.

A temporally flourishing culture is not our concern. If a culture is to continue, it must possess a deep vitality, and this vitality must be organically intertwined with the essence of humanity. German thinkers of the 19th century »drew a sharp distinction between civilization, which involved mechanics, technology, and material factors, and culture, which involved values, ideals, and the higher intellectual artistic, moral qualities of a society«.[43] Such a distinction is not able to convince Samuel Huntington, yet he agrees that culture involves »values, norms, institutions, and modes of thinking to which successive generations in a given society have attached primary importance«.[44]

Should the study of theology make certain adaptations in the interest of making theology culturally effectual? My answer is yes! However, I could not agree to utterly subsume theology under the rubric of »cultural study«, hence losing its very nature or essence.[45] Therefore, when using the tools of cultural and social science research for understanding theology, one must consider the value of theology given to humanity, its unique method of thinking as well as its influence on human lives and social system. In other words the focus should be: How does theology influence people's values, thinking, lives and their social systems?

In regard to his teaching Luther confessed by saying »*Haec mea doctrina est, quae sinit deum esse deum*«.[46] We may see this clearly taught in

---

43 S. P. Huntington, The Clash of Civilizations and the Remaking of World Order, 1996, 41.
44 Ibd.
45 Jürgen Moltmann wrote a critique of such mistake. Moltmann (see n. 2), 534–539.
46 WA 17,1; 232,9–10.

his Catechism that we must trust in God since He is the Creator of all and the Saviour of human kind, and He is still working in the world that He created.[47] Thus, the God of Luther is the God and the Lord of culture. The development of culture should follow the good will of God in His creation. Diligently studying the Word is a must for knowing God and His will, yet Luther is also concerned with the pragmatic aspect of theology. He said »*theologia est practica, non speculativa*«.[48] Luther was opposed to the theology inherited from Aristotle which divides »theory« from »practice« and »meditation« from »acts«. Real theology should link them up, and this even happens in »the word of God and our experience«. Therefore, he advocates *sola autem experientia facit theologum*, such experience is the experience of life.[49]

The Lutherans are by nature the successors and agents who bridge between Luther of the 16th century and our modern world by living out the spirit of Luther. Today, Lutheran theologians should be cautious about the possible conflicts which can occur when Luther's theology enters certain specific cultural contexts. However, if we want to avoid those conflicts by discarding the essence of Luther's theology, we would fail to influence the world to turn to God. Luther will also be lost in the human culture. Michael Roth's comments are worth our attention. He said:

> Lutherische Theologie sucht ein Forum, das so konfliktreich ist wie das Leben selbst, um den Ort des Glaubens im Leben allererst zu verstehen. Gerade in einem solchen Forum wird sich die Kraft auch der theologischen Tradition erweisen, freilich nicht in dem Sinne, dass sie das Leben durch eine Welterklärungsformel zu erschließen vermag, sondern in dem Sinne, dass sie das Leben zu erschließen vermag, weil sie von den Erfahrungen des Lebens immer tiefer erschlossen wird.[50]

Martin Luther is not just a subject matter within theology and cultural studies, rather, through the Lutherans, Luther continues to stir up new ideas and new reforms in theology as well as in our many different cul-

---

47 The Creed in Luther's The Large Catechism and The Small Catechism.
48 WATR 2; 56,22.
49 WATR 1; 16,13.
50 M. ROTH, Was sucht lutherische Theologie bei den Kulturwissenschaften? Überlegungen zur Bedeutung des interdisziplinären Gesprächs für lutherische Theologie (in: Denkraum Katechismus [see n. 2], 507–526), 526.

tures and contexts. If Luther's theology rightly interprets the Gospel[51] his theology is not only significant for Lutherans, it has equal significance for believers of other denominations. There is no denying that the outstanding contributions Luther made to 16th century German society is significant and substantial, yet scholars of cultural studies seem not to admit a similar possibility of Luther's significance for the 21st century's society. Likewise, if Luther's reformation was made according to God's good will towards humans and in accordance with His provision of right values, thinking, a good livelihood and strong social systems, then Luther should be an important subject in cultural studies.

Who finds Luther's theology interesting for study? Needless to say – theologians. While they (theologians) should take into consideration the relationship between Luther's theology and culture, scholars of cultural studies should also uphold same significance of Luther's theology in their study. To take an allegoric approach, one could say the tie between Luther's theology and his cultural influence is like the relationship between a soul and its body. Acting as the embodiment of Luther's spirit and thought, Lutherans should be dutiful in fostering the manifestation of unity of theology and culture in the Lutheran heritage.

---

51 Such as his teaching of Justification by Faith or his Theology of the Cross.

Universitäten und Hochschulen des 21. Jahrhunderts als Erben der Bildungsreform Luthers – Schola Wittenbergensis: Freunde und Kollegen Luthers

Seminarleiter: Ricardo Rieth

Berichterstatter: Ricardo Rieth

Das Seminar befasste sich mit zwei Themeneinheiten. Die erste bezog sich auf die Diskussion über Universitäten und Hochschulen des 21. Jahrhunderts als Erben der Bildungsreform Luthers. Die Teilnehmer stellten sich zur Aufgabe, Texte zu identifizieren, zu diskutieren und auszulegen, in denen Luther über die Universität, ihre Funktion, Struktur, Fakultäten, Inhalte und Methoden mit dem Ziel handelte, seine Hauptreformvorschläge hervorzuheben. Außerdem wurde nach heutigen Erfahrungen mit Universitäten, Hochschulen und Seminaren gefragt, die sich bewusst auf Vorstellungen des Reformators beziehen, um Theorien und Praktiken neu zu denken. *Ernest L. Simmons, Jr.* fasste einige Hauptgedanken seines Buches *Lutheran higher education: an introduction* (1998) zusammen. Er stellte fest, dass für Luther die grundlegenden Ziele in der christlichen Erziehung die Erhaltung des Evangeliums und die Ausstattung des Priestertums aller Gläubigen für den Dienst in der Kirche und in der Welt waren. Ein direktes Ergebnis der Rechtfertigungslehre war die Förderung der öffentlichen Bildung. Das christliche Leben wird unmittelbar inmitten der Welt gelebt. Eine scharfe Linie zwischen dem Heiligen und dem Weltlichen darf für die lutherische Tradition nicht gezogen werden. Alle Dinge in der endlichen Welt können sich potenziell als Masken Gottes vorstellen und müssen daher in ständiger Beziehung zum Glauben gehalten werden. Es besteht eine Spannung in der Bildung, die sich in zwei Formen der Freiheit ausdrückt: die akademische und die christliche Freiheit.

237

Guy Erwin berichtete über die Lutherrezeption und die Förderung von Studien über Luther und die Reformation unter Studenten, Dozenten und Mitarbeitern an der California Lutheran University, einer 1959 gegründeten und heute der ELCA zugeordneten Hochschule. Die Begriffe Identität und Berufung wurden verwendet, um zwei Hauptfragen zu stellen: Welche Bedeutung hat eine Lutherische Universität an diesem Ort und in dieser Zeit? Wie können ihre Studenten ausgebildet werden, so dass bei ihnen ein Sinn für ihre Berufung in der Welt gepflegt wird? Die California Lutheran University wurde als vergleichsweise kleine, private, kirchlich bezogene und auf die *Liberal Arts* konzentrierte Hochschule beschrieben. Aus ihrer konfessionellen Tradition profilierte sich die Universität durch eine Kombination von gemeinschaftlichem Leben und Verantwortung, Freiheit und Pflicht zum Dienen.

Ricardo Rieth trug über Merkmale und Erfahrungen bezüglich der Lutherrezeption an der Universidade Luterana do Brasil, Canoas/ Brasilien, vor. Trotz ihrer vierzigjährigen Existenz und Präsenz in verschiedenen Teilen des Landes sind Kenntnisse über Luther und die Reformation bei ungefähr 95

Prozent der circa 50.000 immatrikulierten Studenten und der 2.000 Dozenten (2012) nicht oder nur marginal vorhanden. Die Vorlesung »Cultura Religiosa«, die verpflichtend in allen Studienrichtungen und Curricula angeboten wird, die Theologische Fakultät und unterschiedlichen Initiativen im Bereich des gottesdienstlichen Lebens und der Universitätsseelsorge geben Raum für eine Annäherung an Themen über und Impulse zu Luthers Erbe und das der Reformation.

Die zweite Seminareinheit bezog sich auf die Schola Wittenbergensis: Freunde und Kollegen Luthers. Damit widmeten sich die Teilnehmer den Arbeits- und Freundschaftsbeziehungen Luthers in doppelter Perspektive. Zum einen wurden diese Beziehungen im Zusammenhang mit der Wittenberger Universität in ihrer Kontinuität bzw. Diskontinuität über die gesamte Wittenberger Wirkungszeit Luthers dargestellt. Darüber hinaus wurde der Kreis der auswärtigen Reformatoren beschrieben, die in engem Kontakt mit Luther und seinem Umfeld die Wittenberger Reformation an ihren jeweiligen Wirkungsorten vorangetrieben hatten.

Thomas Hahn-Bruckart beschäftigte sich mit den Diffusionsprozessen innerhalb der frühen

Schola, die mit den Wittenberger Ereignissen während Luthers Wartburgaufenthalt einhergingen. Dabei ging es vor allem um die Frage, auf welche Weise die von Luther vollzogene Abgrenzung namentlich zu Karlstadt Gestalt gewann. Ausgangspunkt für die Überlegungen waren neuere Untersuchungen, die vor allem den Konstruktionscharakter eines kohärenten Phänomens »Wittenberger Bewegung« betonen und dieses als Ausdruck einer von Luther inaugurierten polemischen Historiographie sehen, die sich gegenüber anderen Deutungsmöglichkeiten schließlich durchsetzte. Gibt es für die späteren Überlieferungsphasen dieses Geschehenszusammenhangs durchaus entsprechenden Anhalt, stellt sich die Frage, wie früh dessen historiographische Konstruktion einsetzte. Die in der Literatur genannten Zeugnisse aus dem Umfeld der Rückkehr Luthers nach Wittenberg wurden im Seminar gemeinsam gelesen und diskutiert und ihre Inanspruchnahme für eine konstruktivistische Interpretation kritisch reflektiert.

Christian Winter widmete sich der Person Paul Ebers als einem wichtigen Vertreter der Schola Wittenbergensis. Im Mittelpunkt der Untersuchung standen Ebers Rolle in Wittenberg und Kursachsen nach Melanchthons Tod und die Frage, in welchem Maße Eber die Tätigkeitsfelder Melanchthons aufnahm und fortführte. Eber war seit 1560 Autor der theologischen und kirchenpolitischen Gutachten, die Kurfürst August von Sachsen in Auftrag gab. Ebers Tätigkeit war geprägt von der Positionierung Kursachsens in den innerprotestantischen Streitigkeiten. Schwerpunkte waren die Auseinandersetzungen in der Abendmahlsfrage (1560–1562), das Vorgehen gegen Kanzelpolemik (1565/66) und die vergeblichen Bemühungen um eine Verständigung mit den »Flacianern« im Altenburger Kolloquium (1568/69). Daneben standen Fragen der Universitäts- und Kirchenorganisation; vereinzelt fanden sich auch Ratschläge zu landes- und reichspolitischen Fragen (Thüringischer Krieg 1567). Es konnte gezeigt werden, wie stark gerade Eber den Einfluss der Schola Wittenbergensis auf die kursächsische Politik fortführte und prägte. Mit seiner auf Ausgleich und Vermittlung orientierten Haltung blieb Eber nahe bei Melanchthon. Eine Entspannung in den innerprotestantischen Konflikten konnte er damit allerdings nicht erreichen.

Die Verwendung von Autoritäten in den frühen Wittenberger Vorlesungen und Disputationen Martin Luthers

Seminarleiter: Volker Leppin

Berichterstatter: Matthias Mikoteit

Das Seminar zielte darauf ab, die Entwicklung Martin Luthers zum Reformator in seiner frühen Wittenberger Zeit anhand seiner Vorlesungen und Disputationen zu erforschen. Die leitende Frage dabei war, wie und wann sich sein Umgang mit den kirchlich anerkannten Autoritäten veränderte. Unter »Autoritäten« wurden durchgängig drei Kategorien von Textquellen begriffen, nämlich: *Sacrae literae*, *Ecclesiastici patres* und *Canones ac decretales Pontificiae* (vgl. WA 1; 529,33–530,1).

Die *Dictata super psalterium* aus den Jahren 1513–1515 waren die älteste Quelle aus Luthers früher Wittenberger Zeit, die im Seminar untersucht wurde. *Volker Gummelt* machte in seinem Referat darauf aufmerksam, dass Luther in den *Dictata* Augustin von allen Kirchenvätern am häufigsten benutzte und dass er biblische Auslegung zu dieser Zeit in großer Harmonie mit Kirchenväterauslegung betrieb. Die starke Betonung Au-

gustins durch Luther durfte nicht verwundern, ergab sie sich doch ohne weiteres aus dem Ordenszusammenhang, in dem er stand, und ohnehin aus dem größeren mittelalterlichen Traditionszusammenhang.

Stefano Leoni stellte dar, welch starken Entwicklungsschub im Denken Luthers die anschließende Römerbriefvorlesung von 1515–1516 mit sich brachte. Neu sei die systematische und respektvolle Bezugnahme auf die antipelagianischen Schriften Augustins gewesen und die damit zusammenhängende Ausbildung einer »augustinischen« Gnadenlehre als das Zentrum der christlichen Theologie – polemisch abgegrenzt gegen die »pelagianische« spätscholastische Theologie. Wenngleich die Mittel der philologischen Analyse nicht hinreichend seien, dränge sich schon allein wegen der Menge und der Kohärenz der Bezüge die Frage auf, ob nicht eigentlich die Lektüre der antipelagianischen Werke Augustins der

Anlass für den »reformatorischen Durchbruch« Luthers gewesen sein könnte. Festgehalten wurde, dass in der Römerbriefvorlesung die Bibelauslegung noch immer harmonisch mit der Kirchenväterauslegung verbunden war, sich aber beides gegen gewisse Grundannahmen, die Luther in seinem Kontext vorfand, zu wenden begann.

Die Disputation *De viribus et voluntate hominis sine gratia* im September 1516 bot Luther als dem Disputationsleiter die Gelegenheit, erstmalig mit dem während der Römerbriefvorlesung entwickelten theologischen Profil an die akademische Öffentlichkeit zu treten. Dass das Thesenwerk und wohl auch dessen Erläuterungen nicht von ihm, sondern von seinem Schüler Bartholomäus Bernhardi stammten, fiel nicht ins Gewicht, weil dieser ihm ganz ergeben war. *Matthias Mikoteit* betonte in seinem Vortrag, dass Luther und Bernhardi bei dieser Disputation nicht mit der Bibel – etwa mit Paulus –, sondern mit Augustin Furore gemacht hätten. Die Frage, ob der Sentenzenkommentar Gregor von Riminis bei der Abfassung der Thesen und Erläuterungen zu Hilfe genommen worden sei, wie es noch die neue Lateinisch-Deutsche Martin-Luther-Studienausgabe suggeriert (LDStA 1; 6,

Anm. 19), wurde von ihm ausgiebig erörtert und klar verneint. Der Text für die Disputation sei vermutlich in kritischer Distanz zum *Collectorium* Gabriel Biels entstanden.

Mit seinen Thesen *Contra scholasticam theologiam*, die Luther am 4. September 1517 disputieren ließ, verschärfte er den Angriff auf bestimmte vorherrschende Grundannahmen in der Theologie. *Ingo Klitzsch* bezeichnete in seinem Referat diese Disputation als einen Kristallisationspunkt multiperspektivischer Prozesse. Wie die Thesen bewiesen, habe Luther in der Auseinandersetzung mit Biel – wenn auch nur sehr selten – auf die für ihn »klassischen« Autoritäten Augustin und Bibel rekurriert. Zudem könne nicht zuletzt aufgrund der namentlichen Nennungen und sonstigen Hinweise in seinen Briefen aus den Jahren 1516/17 gesagt werden, dass er bei der Abfassung der Thesen Impulse aus der spätmittelalterlichen Mystik Johannes Taulers aufgenommen und sich zu zeitgenössischen Theologen – allen voran zu seinen einstigen Erfurter Lehrern, dann aber auch zu Erasmus und eventuell noch zu Johannes Eck – bewusst in Beziehung gesetzt habe.

Mit dem Kanonischen Recht beschäftigte sich Luther eingehender in den ersten Monaten des Jahres 1518. Sowohl die *Asterisci Lutheri adversus obeliscos Eccii* vom 23. März 1518 als auch seine *Resolutiones disputationum de indulgentiarum virtute*, die weitgehend bereits im Februar, in ihrer Endgestalt zwischen Februar und Mai 1518 entstanden sind, belegen das. *Christopher Voigt-Goy* referierte über Luthers differenziertes Verhältnis zur Autorität des Kanonischen Rechts, wie es in den *Resolutiones disputationum de indulgentiarum virtute* zutage trat. Alle Bezugnahmen darauf hätten dort etwas mit der Frage nach der Wirksamkeit des Ablasses für Verstorbene zu tun, die seit der von Sixtus IV. promulgierten Bulle *Salvator noster* aus dem Jahr 1476 diskutiert worden sei. Anders als seine Gegner im Ablassstreit habe Luther die wenigen einschlägigen Dekretalen zum Ablasswesen nicht etwa herangezogen, um die Bulle mit ihrer strittigen Äußerung zur Wirksamkeit des Ablasses »per modum suffragii« in den Horizont kirchlichen Rechts einzufügen, sondern, um jede Wirksamkeit eines Ablasses für Verstorbene zu bestreiten. Dementsprechend sei dann auch von Luther die Bulle *Salvator noster* als »neues Recht« strikt abgelehnt worden. Wenig später, nämlich am Vorabend der Leipziger Disputation, habe er sich bereits veranlasst gesehen, das Kanonische Recht *in toto* zu verwerfen.

Im Jahr 1519 begann Luther damit, die Autorität der Bibel in aller Öffentlichkeit differenziert zu betrachten. *Jason Lane* hob in seinem Vortrag hervor, dass Luther den Jakobusbrief zunächst ohne Kritik als biblische Autorität ausgelegt habe, wie es sich im *Sermo praescriptus praeposito in Litzka* – vom Referenten auf das Jahr 1516 datiert – und in der Römerbriefvorlesung zeige. Auch während der Leipziger Disputation vom 27. Juni bis 15. Juli 1519 habe er dem Protokoll zufolge mit dem Brief noch positiv argumentiert. In den im August 1519 veröffentlichten *Resolutiones* zu allen seinen Leipziger Thesen jedoch habe er dann in scharfer Reaktion auf Eck die apostolische Autorität des Briefes angezweifelt, ohne dass die gegnerische Partei daran Anstoß genommen hätte. Obwohl Luther den Brief nach 1519 als Ganzen heftig habe kritisieren können, weil dieser nicht Christus, sondern das Gesetz treibe, habe er an dessen formalen Autorität festgehalten und ihn deshalb in seinen späteren Predigten, Vorlesungen und Schriften sogar erstaunlich kraftvoll zur Geltung bringen können.

Von Anfang Dezember 1520 an

verfasste Luther die *Assertio omnium articulorum M. Lutheri per bullam Leonis X. novissimam damnatorum* – im Druck erschienen Mitte Januar 1521. Darin stellte er erstmals ganz programmatisch die Autorität der Bibel über alle anderen Autoritäten, gerade auch hinsichtlich der Schriftauslegung. Denn die Heilige Schrift sei »sui ipsius interpres« (WA 7; 97,23) und »per sui solius collationem« auszulegen (AaO., 99,20). *Jun Matsuura* wies in seinem Referat darauf hin, dass Luther seine exegetische Methode einer *collatio* innerbiblischer Sachverhalte schon bei der Leipziger Disputation 1519 beschrieben habe. Er habe dazu das Bild von den beiden *cherubim* auf der Bundeslade verwendet, deren entgegengesetzte Blicke sich in der Mitte treffen. Luthers hermeneutischer Grundsatz »scriptura sui ipsius interpres« sei darin begründet, dass nach ihm die biblischen *contraria* – wie Gesetz und Evangelium – durch ihre *collatio* notwendig auf ihr Zusammentreffen und -finden in Christus als der Mitte hinführen, wenn anders die Bibel eine Einheit und Ganzheit darstelle.

Dass Luther die Autorität der Bibel und die der Kirchenväter auf der theoretischen Ebene so klar abstufte, passte zu der Entwicklung, die auf der praktischen Ebene im Bereich seiner konkreten Schriftauslegung allenthalben sichtbar wurde. *Volker Gummelt* untersuchte in seinem bereits erwähnten Beitrag die Psalmenvorlesung Luthers von 1513–1515 und von 1519–1521 und auch die Bugenhagens von 1521–1524. Dabei konnte er belegen, dass Augustin jeweils die am häufigsten herangezogene altkirchliche Autorität war. Noch ab 1519/21 hätten Luther und Bugenhagen sich ihm anschließen können, wenn auch in größerer Selbständigkeit, als das zuvor bei Luther 1513–1515 vorgekommen sei.

Der von Luther angestoßene Diskurs über das Verständnis und die Auslegung der Autoritäten ereignete sich insofern unter einer günstigen Voraussetzung, als Verurteilungen durch theologische Fakultäten zwar zu erwarten, aber nicht mehr unbedingt zu fürchten waren. *Amy Nelson Burnett* verwies in ihrem Referat auf den so genannten Reuchlin-Streit seit 1510/11 um die jüdische Literatur. Zum ersten Mal sei das übliche akademische Verfahren der Lehrverurteilung, einen beschuldigten Theologen mit gelisteten Zitaten aus dessen Schriften zum Widerruf zu zwingen, anstatt eine freie wissenschaftliche Debatte zu initiieren, öffentlich diskreditiert worden. Dank des Einsatzes von Johannes Reuchlin und anderen philologisch gebildeten Humanisten sei dies auf eine nachhaltige Weise geschehen. Nachdem einige Lehrsätze Luthers durch die Löwener theologische Fakultät verurteilt worden waren, entsprach der Löwener Scholastiker Jacobus Latomus in gewisser Weise dem neuen Zeitgeist, als er sich daran machte, diese Sätze wissenschaftlich zu widerlegen. *Hannegreth Grundmann* behandelte in ihrem Vortrag die betreffende Vorlesung des Latomus, die er in den Sommerferien 1520 veranstaltete und deren Textfassung am 8. Mai 1521 unter dem Titel *Articulorum doctrinae fratris Martini Lutheri per theologos Louanienses damnator[um] Ratio ex sacris literis, & veteribus tractatoribus* in Löwen in den Druck ging. Latomus habe Luther ein durchgehend missbräuchliches Zitieren von Autoritäten nachweisen wollen. Jedoch sei sein akribischer Versuch, bei dem es schwerpunktmäßig darum gegangen sei, Augustin mit Augustin gegen Luther zu interpretieren, letztlich fehlgeschlagen, weil Luther längst schon auf der Grundlage einer ganz anderen Hermeneutik theologisch gedacht und argumentiert hätte.

Zum Diskussionsverlauf im Seminar gehörte ein Ausblick auf Luthers Ringen mit der Autoritätenproblematik in seiner späten Zeit ab 1539. Dieser wurde durch *Gury Schneider-Ludorff* eröffnet, die in ihrem Referat Luthers Positionierung in der Auseinandersetzung um die Doppelehe Philipps von Hessen erörterte. Der Landgraf habe Luther einerseits mit einer reformatorisch anmutenden Argumentation, die sich auf das Schriftprinzip gestützt hätte, konfrontiert, andererseits mit der Herausforderung, nach der Preisgabe des Kanonischen Rechts in zivilrechtlicher Hinsicht nun selbst Autorität geltend zu machen, sogar unter Missachtung des 1532 publizierten kaiserlichen Strafgesetzes *Carolina*, das im Fall der Bigamie die Todesstrafe vorsah. Luther habe es zwar abgelehnt, ein neues Eherecht zu proklamieren, habe es aber akzeptiert, – gemeinsam mit Philipp Melanchthon – zu einer zentralen Entscheidungsinstanz in einer privaten Angelegenheit mit hoher kirchenpolitischer Brisanz zu avancieren.

Luther, Preaching and the Reformation

Seminar Leader: Mary Jane Haemig

Reporter: Mary Jane Haemig

This seminar considered a variety of topics related to Luther and preaching in the 16th and 17th centuries. In »Early Lutheran Preaching on Mary Magdalene,« *Margaret Arnold* (Boston University, USA) surveyed Magdalene's place in evangelical piety, as taught by Luther and his followers in the first three generations of the Reformation. A study of Luther's teaching on the pericope of the anointing at Bethany reveals that he used Mary Magdalene to instruct believers that the love of the sinful woman of Luke 7 is the appropriate fruit of forgiveness. In Luther's comments on the resurrection narrative of John 20, he described her as an example of devotion to Christ and the proclamation of the Gospel. The postil sermons of Luther's followers, such as Johann Spangenberg and Anton Corvinus, repeat or expand these interpretations, addressing the question whether the priesthood of all believers entitles women to preach in the absence of a competent male preacher.

In »The postilla of Hans Tausen (1539): concepts of originality and theology,« *Rasmus H. C. Dreyer* (University of Copenhagen, Denmark) introduced the primary work of Danish reformer Hans Tausen (1494/98–1561). Tausen's postil of 1539 (*Winterdelen* [and] *Sommerdelen aff Postillen berid aff M. Hanss Tausen/Predickere ÿ Kiøbenhaffn*, Magdeburg: Hans Walther) was the first complete Danish postil and the first and finest collection of sermons from the Danish Reformation. The few scholarly works on it have considered it an original work by Tausen and have seen it as presenting a genuinely Lutheran theology. They have sought to prove the originality of the postil by comparing it with the parts of Luther's *Kirchenpostille* drafted by Luther himself. No one has compared Tausen's postil with Stephan Roth's contributions to Luther's postils or with Roth's many shortened versions of Luther's sermons. Dreyer demonstrated this new approach and substantiated it by examples and comparisons. Dreyer also asserted that the postil, when considered with other early writings by Tausen, indicates that Tausen's theology might not be genuinely Lutheran. Tausen's theological statements manifest a multi-faceted reformatory theology, typical of early non-Wittenbergian reformers in the German peripherals. Tausen's earliest writings and the postil support re-designating the so-called ›Danish Luther‹.

Sabine Hiebsch (Vrije Universiteit Amsterdam, Netherlands) presented on »Luther's use of *sermo humilis* in his sermons.« She explained that *sermo humilis* comes from and belongs to the same spectrum of tradition as figural interpretation. She also gave a short description of the history and development of *sermo humilis*. Hiebsch then emphasized that Luther's primary goal in his sermons was to reach the heart of his hearers and readers in order to evoke, nourish and strengthen their faith. He used *sermo humilis* to accomplish that. In *sermo humilis* the message, the messenger and the recipients of the message are always linked together. Before Luther could be a messenger, he had to be a listener, a recipient of the same message he later conveyed. Luther himself had to be touched in his heart by the humility of Christ on the Cross as found in the Scriptures. In the second part, Hiebsch read and dis-cussed excerpts from Luther's sermons to illustrate her explanations and to underline Erich Auerbachs's (1892–1957) opinion: »Luther hat die Überlieferung des *sermo humilis* aufs Genialste im Deutschen heimisch gemacht.«

Simo Heininen (University of Helsinki, Finland) discussed the first Finnish postil. Written by the bishop of Turku, Ericus Erici (c. 1550–1625), this postil, including 85 sermons on the Gospel lessons, was printed in two parts (Stockholm, 1621 and 1625). It comprised 1264 and 988 pages in quarto respectively. It remained the only postil in Finnish until the publication of the pietistic postil of Johan Wegelius in the 1740s. Ericus Erici wrote his postil for pastors and also for housefathers to read at home. He used as models contemporary German postils (for example, the postils of Johann Habermann and Nathanael Tilesius). His method was analytical. He made extensive use of quotations from the church fathers (for example, Augustine and Chrysostom) and »from the Holy Man Dr. Martinus Lutherus.« Some polemics are present but these are not as extensive as in German postils.

Allen Jorgenson (Waterloo Lutheran Seminary, Canada) examined Luther's *Sermon at the Dedi-*

cation of the Castle Church, Torgau (1544) (WA 49; 588–615). He explored how Luther developed a theology of place parallel to his notion of vocation. Native American theologian Vine Deloria Jr. has suggested that Christianity's landless nature betrays its Trojan horse character in service of imperialism: if Christianity can be at home anywhere, then everywhere can be its home. For Luther, as the Christian calling is to be in service of the neighbor, so the location of worship is ordered toward the good of the neighbor. Luther's theology of preaching presumes God's prevenient work and the divine voice behind the preacher's, both of which instill a measure of humility that counters what too many have experienced as Christianity's colonizing tendency.

Paul Robinson (Concordia Seminary St. Louis, USA) presented »Luther on Fighting the Turks: Crusade Sermons Inverted?« He asserted that model sermons for the crusades shed light on how Luther's audience would have read or heard his writings on war against the Turks. In particular, Luther's *Eine Heerpredigt wider den Türken* (1529) (WA 30,2; 160–197) inverted common themes of crusade sermons, including those related to scripture, papal authority, the holy land, martyrdom, and Christian suffering. Crusade sermons used the sufferings of Christians under Muslim rule as a rationale for the call to crusade and crusaders became God's sword to avenge these wrongs. In contrast, Luther assumed that Christians must suffer because Christ remains weak in the eyes of the world and saw the Turks as God's sword against Christendom. Reading the *Heerpredigt* in the context of crusade sermons suggests that Luther used juxtaposition rather than proposition to reject the idea of crusade.

Luther's Commentary on Galatians 1519

Seminar Leader: Anna Vind

Reporter: Anna Vind

The plan for the seminar was to read Luther's early *Commentary on Galatians* published in 1519, a book which for no apparent reason has drawn less attention than many of his other writings. The commentary is of great interest, because it has its roots in the early *Lectures on Paul* (1515–1518) and in the *Second Lecture on the Psalms* (1519–1521), at the same time that it points ahead and can be compared to the large *Commentary on Galatians* of 1531/1535.

The text sets the scene for a range of research themes which were formulated in the introductory statement describing the program of the seminar: First, Luther's interpretation of Paul; second, Luther's understanding of the relation between faith and works (these two were possible links to the contemporary discussion of the relation between the »New Perspective on Paul« and Luther research, which was treated in the context of a keynote lecture at the Congress); third, Luther's reformatory theology – breakthrough or development; and fourth, Luther's interpre-

tation of the fact that the peace and grace of God are hidden, invisible and incomprehensible (WA 2; 456,32–34; 457,3–4). The seminar welcomed both systematic and historical contributions with relation to the chosen text.

The working group counted eleven participants, including the seminar leader (*William J. Wright, Kirsten Diemer, Ilmari Karimies, Erik Hermann, Bernhard S. Erling, Ville Hassinen, Diane Bowers, Sasja Emilie Mathiasen, Ken Jones, Lauge O. Nielsen* and *Anna Vind*) and many wished to present papers. This informed shape and content of the discussions. Of the topics formulated in the introductory statement, number one and four were taken up in the presentations. Furthermore, Luther's concept of honor was brought into focus, adding new insights to the reading of the commentary.

Initially we went through the interpretation history of Paul's letter to the Galatians and especially the understanding of the law, looking at Pauline scholarship from the second century, where the emphasis on the connection between law and salvation history became central. An attempt at that time was made – and carried on throughout history, even though it was criticized by Augustine – to reduce Paul's negative statements about the law by limiting them to ceremonial law. Luther himself even applied this distinction between ceremonial law and the Decalogue in his *Dictata super Psalterium*: here, Gal 3:19–4:1 is seen as describing Old Testament times, and in general all distinctions and dichotomies are applied to the Old as opposed to the New Testament. Nevertheless, we observe a shift in Luther's thinking by the time of the lecture on Romans and the increasing influence of Augustine, a shift towards the distinction between *lex literae* and *lex spiritus* with reference to faith, which we find fully developed, for instance, in the commentary to Gal 3:24–25 (WA 2; 528,15–529,19 – even without explicit mention of the concepts *spiritus* and *literae*). Such an interpretation of the law was wholly new in Pauline interpretation history (*Erik Hermann*).

Touching upon the relationship between the commentary and *De libertate Christiana* with special focus on Luther's anthropological statements concerning the old and the new, the inner and the outer man (*Ken Jones*), the New Testament dimensions of the letter to the Galatians were also drawn up (*Bernhard S. Erling*) before we entered into four more specific presentations of Luther's interpretation.

Delving into Luther's interpretation of Gal 4, the story about Hagar and Sarah, we discussed the interpretation of the figure of Hagar with reference to contemporary literary-feminist exegesis (*Phyllis Trible*) and to different understandings of Luther's hermeneutics (*Gerhard Ebeling, James Preus, Kenneth Hagan*). In Genesis, as well as in Paul, the destiny of Hagar is hopeless and she is bound to represent law, slavery and sin. Luther continues this line of thought in his commentary, applying the difference between *lex literae* and *lex spiritus* to Hagar and Sarah in an allegorical interpretation: Hagar points to the Jews and all who trust in the law and work for justification, whereas Sarah is a picture of the true believer, God's free child of promise. Despite this quite negative use of the Hagar-figure, Luther seems to find another and more sympathetic place for Hagar in his later interpretation of Genesis

(1535–1545). Here, he sees her as an example of the sinner who repents and returns to God. Thus, as an example of the ungodly saint, or the damned but not abandoned church (*Diane Bowers*).

In the next two presentations, the focus shifted from Luther's biblical scholarship to the theme of ›invisibility‹ in the commentary. Going back to the *Dictata*, we looked for Luther's assertions on the nature of invisible things, finding numerous statements on the topic. We moved into a closer study of his understanding of sign and signified; temporality and eternity; creation and new-creation; visible, invisible and contrasting hidden realities; and finally of the Church and the believer as the center of it all. We observed the influence of Neo-Platonism present here, and set the reading up against the research results of former Luther scholars who focused on a more ›existential‹ interpretation (Gerhard Ebeling, Wilfried Joest). Lastly, the inquiry was applied to Luther's Galatians commentary, pointing to the fact that even though the more ›philosophical‹ ways of explaining the matter had decreased after 1516, the matter itself was still prominent in the interpretation of Paul (*Ilmari Karimies*).

With reference to specific parts of the Galatians commentary, we continued to develop the way in which Luther speaks of two kingdoms, the kingdom of grace versus the kingdom of glory, governed by God through faith and sight respectively. Again we discussed the fact that according to Luther man meets the world in two ways: through the senses and reason (the kingdom of the world) and through faith (the kingdom of grace). With his double anthropology divided between flesh and spirit he stands in this cleft – and the spiritual part of him, which through Christ's real presence in faith is truly the place for an ontological change of man (cf. the Finnish Luther research led by Tuomo Mannermaa), forms a hidden, incomprehensible, ›mysterious‹ reality here, which is hidden to the senses and reason but at the same time accessible through faith (*William J. Wright*).

At the end of the seminar, we heard a presentation of Luther's concept of honor with reference to Luther's statement *soli Dei honor et Gloria* in his German interpretation of the Lord's Prayer (1519). Taking honor to be a fundamentally relational concept describing man's relation to God and his neighbor, we defined honor here as a *gloria aliena* (not Luther's term!): an act of faith towards the other, in both an up-down perspective and sideways. Inseparably connected to this understanding of honor are shame and dishonor – and we sought to expound this in more detail on the basis of the Galatians commentary. Central is man's longing for false honor which takes the shape of his urge to boast of his own righteousness, and against this stands the foreign righteousness of Christ which serves as the true honor of Christians. True honor is to give credit to none but God, and thus to give Him what man owes Him – and in order to do this the Christian must be ashamed of himself and dishonored: a man without a name, without outer appearance, without a person (*Sasja Emilie Mathiasen*).

Winding up the seminar we found that we had touched upon a wide range of interesting topics and discussions which we could not sum up to some kind of mutually workable result, but which inspired each of us in our continuing work with Luther's theology.

Die Aufnahme Luthers und Melanchthons in der Schülergeneration: Memoria – theologische Synthese – Autoritätenkonflikte

Seminarleiter: Irene Dingel

Berichterstatter: Irene Dingel

Nach dem Tod Luthers und den einsetzenden innerprotestantischen Streitigkeiten, in die auch Melanchthon hineingeriet, sahen sich die Schüler der beiden großen Wittenberger vor der Aufgabe, ihre Theologie angesichts der gesellschaftlichen und politischen Herausforderungen neu zu formulieren. Dabei spielte die jeweils spezifisch gepflegte Memoria eine große Rolle. Sie konnte den Weg ebnen für eine theologische Synthese, aber auch auf Abgrenzung zielende Konfessionsbildungen stützen sowie Konkurrenzen und Autoritätenkonflikte auslösen. Diese rezeptionsgeschichtliche Perspektive lag dem

Seminar zugrunde. Leitend war die Frage danach, in welcher Weise die zweite Reformatorengeneration die Erinnerung an die großen Vorgänger pflegte, ob und wie man Luther und/oder Melanchthon in der Erinnerung stilisierte, ihnen Autorität zuschrieb und sie möglicherweise sogar gegeneinander ausspielte. Die damit einhergehende Konstruktion wie Dekonstruktion von Autorität in der Memoria lässt sich in den verschiedensten literarischen Gattungen verfolgen. Dies ermöglicht, klischeehaften Deutungsmustern auf die Spur zu kommen, die oft bis heute gepflegt werden.

Timothy Wengert (Die erste Luther-Biographie – Johannes Pollicarius über den Reformator [1547]) analysierte die *Historia de vita et actis reverendiss. Viri Lutheri*, die Johannes Pollicarius durch Kompilation unterschiedlicher Texte von verschiedenen Autoren im Jahre 1547 zusammengestellt hatte. Wengert konnte aufweisen, dass diese humanistische Form der Luther-Memoria bereits biographische Züge kultivierte, die noch stärker in den späteren Ausgaben des Werks (1554–1562) hervortraten. Die in dieser »Gedenkschrift« zu findenden Texte geben zudem Einblick in verschiedene Schichten der Lutherrezeption, die schon früh darauf

zielte, dem Reformator – wohl angesichts von Angriffen auf seine Person und Theologie – Autorität zuzuschreiben.

Irene Dingel (Das Bild Luthers und Melanchthons in den *Historiae der Augsburgischen Konfession*) stellte dar, wie die in der zweiten Hälfte des 16. Jahrhunderts mit dem Nürnberger Ratskonsulenten Christoph Herdesianus und dem Rostocker Theologieprofessor David Chytraeus einsetzende Bekenntnisgeschichtsschreibung die Autorität Luthers im Sinne konfessioneller Abgrenzung gezielt gegen diejenige Melanchthons ausspielte. Dazu wurden auf lutherischer Seite Typologien gebildet, die Luther als Friedfertigen, Selbstlosen, Seelsorger, heldenmütigen Bekenner und eigentlichen Urheber der Confessio Augustana stilisierten, während Melanchthon als der Vorsichtige und Sorgenvolle gezeichnet wurde. Dem setzte der Calvinismussympathisant Herdesianus ein Lutherbild entgegen, das den Reformator als streitbaren Provokateur und theologisch Wankelmütigen denunzierte.

Henning Jürgens (Luther-Biographie als Polemik bei Johannes Cochläus) stellte anhand der *Historia Martini Lutheri. Das ist / Kurtze Beschreibung seiner handlungen vnd*

252

Geschrifften (1549) die erste umfassende kontroverstheologische Stilisierung des Wittenberger Reformators vor, deren Wirkung bis in das katholische Lutherbild des 20. Jahrhunderts nachzuvollziehen ist. Luther wurde von Cochläus als Ehrgeizling, doppelzüngiger Heuchler und Lügner, Verfälscher der Bibel, politischer Aufrührer und Türkenfreund: schlicht als Ausgeburt des Teufels beschrieben, wobei sich der Autor zugleich selbst als Opponent Luthers in Szene setzte. Sein methodisches Vorgehen zielte darauf, Quellentreue und Überprüfbarkeit zu suggerieren. Zahlreiche Marginalien verweisen auf die benutzen Schriften, die Cochläus allerdings im Sinne des erstrebten Effekts sehr selektiv heranzog.

Diesem Focus auf die Historiographie stellte *Luka Ilić* (Die Vermittlung und Rezeption eines »Lutherbilds« in Flacius' Ausgaben von Luthers Werken) den Blick auf zeitgenössische Werkausgaben des Reformators zur Seite. Ilić konnte innerhalb der Gruppe der Anhänger des Matthias Flacius Illyricus eine Lutherrezeption nachweisen, deren theologische Perspektive von Flacius vorgegeben war. Luther war deshalb nicht nur der endzeitliche Prophet, sondern auch der mit Lehrautorität ausgestattete »prae-

ceptor noster«. Die spezifisch flacianische Luther-Memoria verlagerte im Zuge der Auseinandersetzungen um die Erbsünde den Fokus von der Person Luthers weg hin zur leitenden Funktion seiner Theologie. Lutherbild und Luthermemoria wirkten integrierend auf eine sich bildende Gruppe, die bereitwillig für ihre Theologie ins Exil ging.

Wie differenziert die Luther-Memoria in den Blick genommen werden muss, zeigte sich an dem Melanchthonschüler und Lutheranhänger Nikolaus Selnecker und seinen historischen *Orationes* und *Narrationes*. Ihn hatte *Vera von der Osten-Sacken* (Konfessionelle Aneignung und Stilisierung der Autorität Martin Luthers im Luthertum des späten 16. Jahrhunderts) als Beispiel gewählt. Eingebettet in eine Auseinandersetzung mit dem Karthäuser Laurentius Surius und dessen *Commentarius brevis* (1568) verteidigte Selnecker die Integrität Luthers. Dabei legte er Wert darauf, die theologische und persönliche Eintracht des Wittenberger Reformators mit seinem Freund und Gesinnungsgenossen Melanchthon herauszustellen. Gegen die von der Gegenseite aufgebaute Dämonisierung zielte Selnecker – so Osten-Sacken – auf eine »Normalisierung« der Luther-Memoria, die auf die al-

ten Topoi des endzeitlichen Propheten und Werkzeugs Gottes zurück-
griff.

Scott Hendrix (Luther und Melanchthon in der Perspektive Georg
Spalatins) wandte den Blick zurück
in die Frühzeit des Reformators, in
der noch keine spezifische Konstruktion eines Luther- oder Me-
lanchthonbildes auszumachen ist.
Weder die Luther- noch die Me-
lanchthon-Rezeption wurde entscheidend durch Spalatin beeinflusst, zumal seine *Annales* erst im
18. Jahrhundert gedruckt in die Öffentlichkeit kamen. Dagegen ist
dem kursächsischen Kanzler in seinem Einfluss auf die sächsischen
Kurfürsten eine nicht zu vernach-
lässigende Bedeutung zuzumessen.
Denn deren Wahrnehmung der Person Luthers und seiner Theologie
hat Spalatin, der einen intensiven
Briefwechsel mit dem Reformator
pflegte, entscheidend geprägt. Zugleich konnte Hendrix aufweisen,
wie selektiv neuere anglophone Lutherinterpretationen mit dieser reichen Quellenlage umgehen, um so
neue klischeehafte, aber publi-
kumswirksame Lutherbilder zu
konstruieren.

Mit dem Referat von *Naomichi
Masaki* (Luther-Memoria in Leichenpredigten) kam die Gattung
»Predigt« als Medium von Autori-
tätskonstruktionen in den Blick.
Die von ihm ausgewählten Leichenpredigten auf Luther (von Jonas, Coelius, Bugenhagen, Melanchthon) legten die Betonung auf
den Schriftausleger, den von Gott
in sein Amt gesetzten Prediger, den
Lehrer des Wortes Gottes in rechter
Unterscheidung von Gesetz und
Evangelium. Masaki stellte heraus,
dass die Leichenpredigten allesamt
dazu tendieren, Person und Inhalt
der Verkündigung stets miteinander zu verknüpfen, wobei die Genesisvorlesung als Ort wahrer reformatorischer Lehre in den Mittelpunkt rückte. Der rechtmäßig in
seinem Amt predigende Reformator wird als derjenige dargestellt,
der wie kein anderer auf Christus
hinweist und in exemplarischer
Weise *oratio*, *meditatio* und *tentatio* verkörpert.

Auch *Robert Kolb* (Melanchthon-Memoria in den Leichenreden
von 1560/61) zog *Orationes funeb-
ris* für die Frage nach Fremdwahr-
nehmung und Autoritätskonstruktion heran, wobei er den Blick auf
Melanchthon lenkte. Er führte vor,
wie sehr persönliche Erinnerungen
mit der Stilisierung der Person verbunden sein konnten und betonte,
dass die Leichenreden auf Melanchthon oft mehr Rückschlüsse auf
den jeweiligen Orator und dessen

theologische Position zuließen als auf den Verstorbenen. Wie ein roter Faden zog sich die Diskussion des Verhältnisses zwischen Melanchthon und Luther durch die Leichenreden. Man legte Wert darauf, deutlich zu machen, dass beide zusammen mit Bugenhagen, Jonas und Cruciger unter der CA eine reformatorische Einheit bildeten. Melanchthon kam dabei überwiegend als großer Gelehrter, als Bekenner des Glaubens und Lehrer in den Blick.

Mit dem Genre der biographischen Predigt, das der Joachimsthaler Pfarrer Johannes Mathesius in besonderer Weise pflegte, beschäftigte sich *Armin Kohnle* (Die Reformatoren neben Luther, besonders Melanchthon, in den Lutherpredigten des Johannes Mathesius). Er weitete die Fragestellung über Luther und Melanchthon hinausgehend auf den Wittenberger Reformatorenkreis aus. Indem Mathesius Luther die reformatorische Führungsrolle zusprach und ihn mit dem alttestamentlichen Mose gleichsetzte, degradierte er seine Kollegen und Zeitgenossen zu Mitläufern. Selbst Melanchthon, den Mathesius als treuen und fleißigen Professor beschrieb, stellte er bei aller aufrichtig empfundenen Bewunderung in den Schatten Luthers: ein Aaron neben Mose, verlängerter Arm des eigentlichen Helden, ohne eigenständigen theologischen Zugriff. Melanchthon konnte deshalb nur eine von Luther abgeleitete Autorität genießen, neben dem Grammatiker Bugenhagen, und dem Redner Jonas. Mit Karlstadt, Zwingli, Müntzer und Flacius kreierte Mathesius zudem negative Helden.

Den Abschluss des Seminars bildete das Referat von *Ulrich Michael Kremer* (Der Sieg des Melanchthonianismus an der Academia Julia infolge des Hoffmannschen Streits). Er schilderte den Konflikt zwischen dem Theologen Daniel Hoffmann und den in der Artes-Fakultät der Universität Helmstedt angesiedelten Gelehrten Cornelius Martini, Duncan Liddel, Owen Günther und Johannes Carelius. Hoffmann zog die Autorität Martin Luthers heran, um den seiner Ansicht nach verderblichen Einfluss der Philosophie auf die Theologie zu bannen. Dabei ging er bei weitem über die Positionen Luthers hinaus und dehnte so dessen Autorität auf Problemstellungen aus, mit denen dieser zu Lebzeiten nicht konfrontiert war. Die Tatsache, dass die Ratsstube unter dem braunschweigischen Kanzler Johann von Jagemann in den Streit hineingezogen wurde, gab ihm politische Dimension.

Die Abschlussdiskussion betonte, dass die in der Fremdperspektive auf Luther und Melanchthon genutzten Typologien zumeist von den beiden Reformatoren selbst geschaffen worden waren. Während sie in einer reichen Luther-Memoria kultiviert und in den theologischen Kontroversen jeweils situationsgebunden genutzt wurden, pflegten die Zeitgenossen kaum eine entsprechende Melanchthon-Memoria, auch wenn eine Melanchthon-Biographik durch Schüler und Freunde existiert. Auffällig ist, zu welchen Zwecken man die Luther-Memoria nutzte. Neben rein informatorischen Zielen stehen der pädagogische und seelsorgerliche Einsatz, aber auch die polemische und legitimatorische Instrumentalisierung von Erinnerungskultur und Autoritätskonstruktion.

Luther's Small Catechism

Seminar Leader: James Arne Nestingen

Reporters: Anna Marie Johnson and James Arne Nestingen

Shortly before the Luther Congress assembled, the original seminar leader withdrew. Consequently, with no previous planning in place and insufficient time to prepare papers, the seminar had to be arranged on the basis of oral reports concerning research already under way. *James Arne Nestingen*, professor emeritus Luther Seminary, St. Paul, Minnesota (USA), was asked to take over the lead. The members of the seminar were *Paolo Buss* (IELB seminary, Brazil), *Gordon Jenson* (Luther Seminary, Saskatoon, Canada), *Anna Marie Johnson* (Garrett Seminary, Evanston, USA), *John Pless* (Concordia Seminary, Fort Wayne, USA), *Wilhelm Weber* (Lutheran Seminary, Pretoria, South Africa) and *Hans Weirsma* (Augsburg College, Minneapolis, USA).

The *Small Catechism* was not written for academic purposes, but to serve families in the instruction of their children in the home. Thus, while there has been important scholarship devoted to the catechism, most work with it involves study of its use in Christian education. The seminar approached Luther and catechesis from a number of angles, but shared the common conviction that Luther's catechism and catechetical writings were an overlooked and under-valued aspect of his thought. In many ways, each of the presentations given showed the centrality of catechetical issues in Luther's theology.

Nestingen led off the seminar with a report on the current state of catechetical studies. There are two main types: investigations of the *Small Catechism* as a primary resource in Christian education programs and academic study. Lutheran churches in Europe and in the various countries to which Lutherans have immigrated have commonly produced studies of the *Small Catechism* primarily for religious purposes. These introductions have reflected the theological movements influential in the churches: orthodoxy, pietism and rationalism. Johan Michael Reu of Wartburg Seminary in Dubuque, USA, published a classic German-American treatment, *Luther's Small Catechism*. In the 1970s, Nestingen and Gerhard O. Forde wrote *Free to Be: A Handbook to Luther's Small Catechism*, which was widely used in parish instruction. More recently,

the Church of Finland has published several smaller volumes for congregational use.

The most important scholarly work on the *Small Catechism* was published by Herbert Girgensohn in two volumes in the USA, *Teaching Luther's Catechism*, tr. J. Doberstein, 1959; and most importantly by A. Peters, *Kommentar zu Luthers Katechismen*, 5 volumes, 1990–1994. Peter's definitive treatment has been translated into English by Thomas Trotter and published by Concordia Publishing House, St. Louis.

Matti Poutiainen of the Cathedral Parish in Helsinki reported on use of the *Small Catechism* in Christian education programs throughout Finland. Ninety per cent of Finnish 15-year-olds participate in classes; 77% become church members. Using PowerPoint, Dr. Poutiainen demonstrated how the chief parts of the catechism are set up in sets of triangles to invite students into further reflection. He also distributed copies of the literature produced for this purpose.

In the presentation by *Gordon Jensen*, he examined how Christian piety as taught through catechesis was shaped by the order of the traditional parts of the catechism in the 16th century: The Apostles' Creed, the Decalogue, and the Lord's Prayer. He compared three late medieval catechisms; the first by Dietrich Kolde, who first published *A Fruitful Mirror* or *Small Handbook for Christians* in 1470; *The King's Primer*, attributed to Thomas Cranmer, and also known as *A Necessary Doctrine and Erudition for Any Christian Man*, published in 1543; and Martin Luther's *Small Catechism*, first published in 1529. The order in which the Creed, Lord's Prayer and Decalogue were placed in catechisms was shown to make a difference in understanding the goal and focus of the Christian life. For example, the Kolde catechism placed the Decalogue third, intending it to be a ›guide to living‹ while Luther placed it first, as a part of self-evaluation. Similarly, the placement of the Lord's Prayer might determine whether prayer and worship was seen as the core of the Christian life, as structured in the *King's Primer*, or as a spiritual tool to be used in preparation for living that life, enabling one to follow the requirements of the Decalogue. The *King's Primer* also helped shape the emphasis on worship and prayer, which is at the heart of the *Book of Common Prayer*. It was concluded that each of these catechisms arranged the parts of the catechism in a particular order to foster and shape the piety of the people.

Hans Wiersma presented a report on his work, drawing on Luther's catechism as a resource for modern college students. Wiersma sees the catechism as a rich source of Christian formation for the particular challenges of today's young adults. The radical questioning of inherited faith that often accompanies the college years includes a desire to explore the fundamental tenets of Christianity. Luther's treatment of the commandments, the creed, prayer and the sacraments can not only inform young adults on these topics, but they also offer thematic emphases that resonate with the concerns of emerging adults. The commandments can help them probe the issues of legalism and hypocrisy versus Spirit-led, consistent faith; the creed can be an opportunity to explore the question of certainty; the treatment of prayer is a way to frame questions of free will, fate and the role of humanity in the vast universe. Luther's treatment of sacraments also offers hope in their emphasis on God's promises, which can speak powerfully to the openness and uncertainty of the early adult years. Luther's insistence that every Christian has a God-given vocation can help assure young adults that their lives have meaning beyond the judgments of their society.

A presentation by *Paolo Buss* detailed the project underway in Brazil to translate Luther's works into Portuguese. Despite centuries of Lutherans living in Brazil, Portuguese translations did not begin until the 1980s because most pastors and many lay people before then could read German. The first Portuguese Book of Concord appeared in 1980; the first volume of Luther's works in Portuguese was published in 1983. Currently, 11 volumes are in print out of the 17 volumes planned under the editorship of Ricardo Rieth. The current translation of Luther's *Small Catechism* into Portuguese includes the explanations added to the English version in the nineteenth century by Heinrich Christian Schwann.

John Pless introduced his forthcoming book, which is aimed at pastors and presents Luther as a practical theologian. Pless notes that Luther's protest began with a pastoral concern over the use of indulgences. Throughout Luther's life, he framed his theology in practical terms; the Law-Gospel Distinction, the Theology of the Cross, and Luther's approach to the Bible all show that Luther constructed his theology out of faith and in order to teach the faith. Luther's catechism came out of the observation that lay people did not know the rudiments of Christian faith, and in it, he intended to provide a hermeneutic for both pastor and congregants. In the chief parts of the catechism, we can see Luther's pastoral bent. The first commandment orients pastoral care to focus on how God is being loved and feared in each situation. The table of duties and the daily prayers Luther suggests also orient faith toward its enactment in daily life. Finally, Pless detailed the ways in which Luther used Scripture in pastoral care situations to address anxiety, doubt and despair. Luther's written sources of consolation span the full range of life experiences, from poverty to persecution to death, and Luther's responses show that his theology is inherently practical.

Anna Marie Johnson presented her research on Luther's earliest devotional works. During the early years of Luther's controversy with Rome, 1518–1520, he wrote many sermons and treatises on practical matters. These works were usually written at his initiative, and as the conflict progressed, he composed them in German instead of Latin. The sheer number of devotional works shows that Luther had a practical, catechetical bent from the earliest years of his reform movement. These works also show the practical, pastoral nature of his theological conflict with Rome. Throughout these writings, Luther emphasizes that humans cannot earn merit before God but instead must learn to trust in God's grace. His recommendations for reform-

ing Christian practices center on this concern for works-righteousness and promoting faith in God's promises. In some cases, Luther advises the abolition of certain religious practices, but often he aims to reshape practices or to change the way they are understood. Reading these sources alongside the accounts of Luther's conflict with Rome shows the pastoral reasons for Luther's protest.

Pietas et Eruditio. Concepts of Education in Reformation Theology

Seminar Leader: Markus Wriedt

Reporter: Markus Wriedt

A total of eleven scholars took advantage of the seminar chaired by *Markus Wriedt*, Goethe University Frankfurt am Main. He suggested to discuss the following perspectives: One of the main features of the Wittenberg Reformation was a thorough reform of education and schooling. Though not exclusively initiated by Luther, his programmatic writings became widespread and were practically completed by Melanchthon and a large number of

their friends and students. Their writings could serve as springboard for the examination of practical reforms in schools and universities. It was planned to have short presentations, source readings and panel discussions on various topics of the Wittenberg Reformation and its School Reform. The leading question of the investigation was the quest for a specific evangelical reform in comparison with other reform attempts (Humanists, Catholic Reform, etc.). We also investigated some predecessors and successors. Because of the reactions of the seminar participants, a focus was put on questions of continuities and discontinuities between Luther's attempts of educational reform and late medieval proposals of Gerson, Ockham and others, as well as its contemporary reception in global perspective. Although this wide range focus was endangered by a certain arbitrariness, it turned out that the inner coherence of the seminar was given by the reformers' sources as we dealt with them and the question for a specific confessional quality of Christian education.

After an introduction into current research on Lutheran education in the early 16th century given by Markus Wriedt on the basis of his studies, *Vesa Hirvonen*, a Finish Luther scholar and medievalist, turned his interest on the reception of Ockham in the reformers educational writings. He gave special attention to the question of childhood and children's education which presented an interesting counterpart to the modern conviction that the exploration of »childhood« did not happen before Pietistic reform attempts in the 18th century (e.g. August Hermann Francke). However,

Hirvonen showed that there are tendencies toward a more differentiated picture in the writings of the 13th and 14th centuries.

Thomas Appelqvist, a Swedish Lutheran and systematic theologian, focused on the question of Law and Gospel in Luther's treatises on evangelical school reform. No wonder that this pattern is certainly given in the Wittenberg reformer's writings. However, Appelqvist sketched out several specific articulations of this main feature of Luther's theology of the cross within the theological foundation of his educational reform attempts.

Jeffrey Janes, Church historian from the Methodist Theological School in Ohio (USA), introduced some astonishing insights in the development of early modern cartography as part of the curriculum in liberal arts education in Protestant schools. Far away from modern understanding of science as a neutral, non-denominational field of expertise he was able to show the influence of confessional convictions even within world and territory maps of the 16th and 17th centuries.

Louis Reith, librarian and theologian from Georgetown University in Washington D.C. (USA), introduced a confessional model of princely education from the late 16th century court in Württemberg. As always the question arose how many elements of the reform treatise did come from humanist sources and what decisively emerged from confessional Lutheran convictions. His introduction led to an intense discussion of modern research, e.g. the relation between Humanist and Lutheran reform, the methods of intertextual references as given in the sources, and much more.

The question of Luther reception in the second half of the 16th century, »the Age of Confessionalism« as many scholars refer to it, was continued by two papers presented by *Robert Rosin* and *Gerhard Bode* from Concordia Seminary St. Louis, Missouri (USA). Both presented printed material found in the Herzog August Bibliothek in Wolfenbüttel. Rosin referred to Andreas Neidecker, a Catholic who served in upper Franconia, later studied in Cologne and Freiburg, and finally returned to Bamberg. His treatise *Vermanung Christlicher Aufrichtung der Schulen* from 1543 shows many parallels to Luther's writings and his admonition to educate the youth. He obviously faced similar problems as

Luther did, and opted for educating children as a long term engagement which certainly pays off. As such, his treatise is an emphatic plea for patience. Gerhard Bode turned his focus on Conrad Dietrich and his advice for Lutheran education in early Lutheran Orthodoxy. It was clearly shown how much the influence of Aristotle came back and how little the position of Peter Ramus was accepted. Bode's interpretation shed new light on the development of confessional orthodoxy and its impact on schooling and university training.

David Hockenberry, historian from Columbus, Ohio (USA) and veteran member of the school of Harold Grimm, introduced a wide dimensioned survey on the reception of Luther's educational reform attempts from the 16th to the 20th century. Interestingly enough, it covered not only the wide range of reception and interpretation through the centuries but also the different and diverse accentuation of his theological foundations. Several aspects reaching from the theological acceptance of his newly revealed message of redemption, over a certain humanist understanding, up to practical advises and source material were presented. His contribution was continued but slightly modified by the paper of *Duane Larson*, Lutheran Professor of Systematic Theology from Iowa (USA). His emphasis was to identify the *non-literal* and *affective* (thus strengthening *pietas*) ways by which Luther was communicated in his own and the succeeding generation. In turn, he argued how consonant 17th century »affective« Lutheran catechesis is with today's prevailing »postmodern« consciousness in higher education, especially given the new emphasis on »practices« so prominent in American graduate theological education.

With this paper the seminar discussion finally turned to questions of contemporary education and theology's place in it. Fascinating and certainly cross-cultural was the presentation of *Yuan-Wei Liao*, Professor of History and Theology from China Evangelical Seminary in Taipei, Taiwan. He introduced the majority of western educated and socialized members of the seminar to a completely different world and gave some very deep insights into the problem of enculturation. However, it was thrilling to see where the subjects of intercultural discourse had been anticipated in Luther's writings and how they have been received in modern China.

Each presentation was followed by extended Questions and Answers sections in which both, the interdisciplinary talk between historians and theologians, and the cross cultural comparison of Luther reception in the Western world and China could be discussed in many perspectives. *Markus Hein*, theologian from Leipzig University, presented some parts of his investigation of Luther reception in Hungary and with this rounded up the multi-dimensional picture.

The seminar in its great variety and diversity served as a marvelous example of academic exchange at the International Luther Congress. It did not focus on a certain result. Talks, discussions, the learning from each other were a major outcome and result. More academically spoken, it served as a model of postmodern Luther research in a diverse, if not fragmented world in which Christendom and theology are no longer self-evident terms of experience. As much as the presentations varied and showed diverse case studies, they still led back to the two keywords of the Seminar Title: *pietas* and *eruditio* – piety and erudition. As Melanchthon argued in 1543, there is a necessary, indestructible conjunction between these two poles of Christian education, ecclesiastical and secular welfare, and individual safety. The seminar gave a brilliant example to the everlasting truth of this nearly 500 year old Wittenberg treatise and its contemporary importance.

The Impact of Luther's Hymns

Seminar Leader: Christopher Boyd Brown

Reporter: Christopher Boyd Brown

The seminar sought to explore the theology, influence, and social and liturgical location of Luther's *geistliche Lieder*. Selected hymns and prefaces by Luther and others were circulated in advance as common reading. The seminar began with a discussion of Luther's *Nun freut euch lieben Christen g'mein*, noting its form as proclamation of God's work in dramatic form (rather than as direct address to God or bare dogmatic summary). Its close theological relationship with the theology of the bound will in the *Heidelberg Disputation* and the *De servo arbitrio*, as well as the affective differences in presentation in hymnic form were explored.

Rose Guok Swee-Choo (University of Western Australia) presented from her doctoral research on the role of emotion in Luther's theology of music (as *domina et gubernatrix affectuum humanorum*) and its implications for liturgy in the contemporary church. Luther's emphasis on the affective power of music was related to his own struggles with depression and the development of his understanding of justification. The alternatives in interpretation presented by modern and early modern psychology (e.g., Melanchthon) were discussed by the seminar.

Sarah Hinlicky Wilson (Institute for Ecumenical Research, Strasbourg) presented her work on Luther's 1523 *Märtyrerlied, Ein neues Lied wir heben an*, exploring the question of its relation to the Anabaptist martyr-hymn tradition and the possibilities it raises for evangelical veneration of the saints, particularly in connection with Melanchthon's proposals and Luther's *Vom Bruder Henrico*. The seminar discussed the theology of martyrdom and the word in the hymn and made comparisons with other forms of Lutheran sanctoral literature.

Jeannine Olson (Rhode Island College) offered comparisons between the tradition of the Genevan Psalter and the Lutheran hymn tradition. Noting obvious differences in musical practice, the seminar discussed whether or not emphases on praise and proclamation respectively characterized the Reformed and Lutheran theology of song.

Christopher Brown (Boston University, USA) presented on the schoolmistress Magdalena Heymair as a self-conscious imitator of Luther in theology and in hymn-writing. Her engagement with the Gnesio-Lutheran controversies, self-presentation, and support from Lutheran clergy were explored as one sample of the influence of Luther's hymns and example on the following generations.

Scott A. Moore (Universität Erfurt) presented on his work with the renovations, especially of the font, at Luther's baptismal church in Eisleben. In this connection, the seminar focused in its final discussion of Luther's catechetical hymns on *Christ unser Herr zum Jordan kam* and its depiction of the relationship between word, sign and sight, and faith, pointing to the simultaneous theological depth and clarity of Luther's hymns and their continuing richness as a resource for modern liturgy and thological reflection.

Luther's Critical Concept of Church

Seminar Leader: Kirsten Busch Nielsen

Reporter: Kirsten Busch Nielsen

In Luther's early writings (1520–1523) on church and ministry, an understanding of church is put forward which is both critical and »upbuilding,« complex and simple. Departing from an analysis of selected key passages of these texts, it was the aim of the seminar *Luther's Critical Concept of Church* to discuss issues which seem crucial to any contemporary Lutheran »theory of the church.« Participants were invited to propose relevant Luther texts for discussion and to present papers on the subject of the seminar.

On August 6, *Christine Põder* (Aarhus/Tallinn) gave a paper on »Karl Barth's reception of Luther in his *Epistle to the Romans* with particular reference to the critical concept of religion and of the church.« Through the discussion recurring issues were the differences between the early and the later theology of both Luther and Barth. Repeatedly, the negative rhetoric of the *Epistle to the Romans* was questioned as to how the transition from negativity to the positive communication should be reflected and, more generally, as to its fundamental theological capacity in the long run – thereby recognizing the fact that Barth eventually had to take leave of it and find another mode of doing theology. The affinity to the early Luther which Christine Põder demonstrated in the presentation was discussed in some detail, and one participant pointed to the existence of a particularly radical reformed church that, rejecting Barth's theology, had a certain affinity to the early Luther. In the further discussion, the participants particularly questioned critically the overall radicalism of Barth's *Epistle to the Romans* which was to a certain extent attributed to the historical situation and, particularly, to the German intellectuals supporting the war policy of Germany at the beginning of the First World War. The consequent eschatology and the affinity to mysticism were commented on. Finally, a participant pointed out the similarity between Barth and the theologians of the Swedish Luther renaissance which, contrary to the German Luther renaissance, would not interpret Luther extensively but rather use him as inspiration and authority for their own theology.

In the second session, on August 7, *Carl Axel Aurelius* (Lund/Copenhagen) under the heading »Luther's Understanding of *ecclesia abscondita*« presented a paper examining Luther's use of different characteristics when speaking of the church such as *invisibilis, abscondita* and *spiritualis*. Carl Axel Aurelius chose examples from Luther's early exegetical and polemical writings, not the least *Operationes in psalmos*. He stressed that these characteristics have their biblical setting. It means that for example Luther's talk about the hidden church (*ecclesia abscondita*) has to be seen in the light of his exploration of the 9th psalm of the

Book of Psalms. These early writings of Luther also present an understanding of the *notae ecclesiae* which later on was further developed in the writings *Von den Konciliis und Kirchen* and *Widder Hans Worst*. The discussion of the paper in the seminar dealt mainly with the meaning and the function of these signs or *notae*. Aurelius underlined the pastoral concern of Luther when developing his teaching on the *notae* as the answer to a question raised by »ein armer irriger Mensch.«

On August 8, *Kirsten Busch Nielsen* (Copenhagen) gave a paper on »Communio in Luther's 1519-sermon *Von dem hochwürdigen Sakrament des heiligen wahren Leichnams Christi* and in Dietrich Bonhoeffer's *Sanctorum Communio* (1927/1930).« A thematic move was taken from invisibility and hiddenness of the church in the previous discussions to the church as *communio*/»community« in this session. This move was motivated by the wish to investigate whether the critical interpretation of church which the notions invisibility and hiddenness in Luther's writings express is also part of Luther's interpretation of the church as *communio*. Kirsten Busch Nielsen briefly outlined the role of Luther's theology in Bonhoeffer's writings. Drawing upon both Oswald Bayer and Joachim von Soosten she further showed in detail how the understanding of Christian community in the 1519-sermon is taken up by Bonhoeffer in one of the key chapters of *Sanctorum Communio*. What mostly inspired the young Bonhoeffer in his much debated »ecclesiological maximalism« thus was exactly the debated ecclesiology (and theology of sacraments) of the young Luther. The discussion dealt with the possibility of developing ecclesiology in a Lutheran context without giving up the difficult idea of the church as community. The participants particularly focused on Bonhoeffer's use of *notae* (as effective, heuristic and critical) and further unfolded the idea of vicarious representation.

In the final session, which took place on August 9, *Josef Freitag* (Erfurt) introduced a discussion of *Von Konziliis und Kirchen* (1539). For a start, he contextualized the text posing the leading questions, firstly regarding the concept of councils, questioning how the council could be enforced having no actual authority, and, secondly, how, then, unity of the church could be achieved, thereby pointing to the ecumenical significance of the text.

The discussion dwelt mainly on the meaning of the *notae ecclesiae*, being the subject of the chosen text excerpt. Particularly, the point was emphasized that the *notae* obviously were not regarded as criteria which the church had to meet in order to be church, but rather as means of sanctification (»heuptstück Christlicher heiligung« thus substituting the debated sacramental terminology), as well as means of recognition – they are heuristic, as one participant pointed out, but they are not offering any security, being subject to eschatological reservation. Finally the participants discussed at some length the seventh sign of the cross, marking the transition of the signs of the church to the works of love. Particularly the notion of self-sacrifice was questioned. On one hand, it might be significant in the case of e.g. political resistance against totalitarianism. On the other hand, it might take the shape of self-imposed or meaningless suffering. It was concluded that the cross as a sign would (in contrast to self-chosen sacrifice) essentially be marked by absence of self-righteousness.

Philosophical Psychology in Luther's Theology

Seminar Leader: Pekka Kärkkäinen

Reporter: Pekka Kärkkäinen

Throughout his career Luther showed a thorough acquaintance with the academic psychology of his time. This acquaintance sometimes expressed itself in his harsh criticism of scholastic applications of Aristotle's *De anima* in theology. During the last years of Luther's career, however, psychology was incorporated again into the curriculum of the University of Wittenberg. The main idea of the Helsinki seminar was to read and discuss some of Luther's texts in comparison with texts on philosophical psychology found in certain natural philosophy treatises written by Luther's colleagues in Wittenberg.

The seminar sessions were based on discussions of particular themes and source texts related to them. The texts were distributed to the participants beforehand. They included Luther's texts from the 1530s and 1540s, which were compared to texts from natural philosophy in Wittenberg, namely *Epitome de anima* by Johann Bernhardi of Feldkirch (Johannes Velcurio, 1490–1534), written circa 1532–34, and *Commentarius de anima* (1540) and *Liber de anima* (1553) by Philip Melanchthon. Nearly all of the discussed texts were English translations, but Latin originals were also available during the seminar sessions.

The first task of the discussions was to compare the definition of the human soul found in Melanchthon and Bernhardi with Luther's definitions of the human being in the *Disputation Concerning the Human Being* (*Disputatio de homine*, 1536). The discussions soon spread to various issues concerning the human soul, such as moral psychology, the immortality of the soul, and so on. A considerable part of the discourse centered on Luther's view of the effect of original sin on human mental capabilities. The exact nature of the effect of the Fall, and respectively, the effect of justifying grace in healing the wounds caused by original sin, were felt to be extremely difficult to discern in Luther's

text, as well as the texts of his more philosophical colleagues in Wittenberg.

The second theme was the image of the Triune God in human being. Luther's commentary on Gen 1:26–27 from the *Lectures on Genesis* was discussed, although it was noted during the discussions that on the question of similitude Luther's interpretation of Gen 5:1 found later in the same work actually provides more new insights. Luther's critical tone regarding certain traditional interpretations of the Augustinian doctrine of *imago Trinitatis* was presented in its broad historical context, and the lines of continuity in Luther's and Melanchthon's notion of the knowledge and the love of God were pointed out. Although Melanchthon has more to say about the doctrine concerning the image of the Trinity, the main theme of his exposition follows to a considerable degree Luther's teaching: the image of God is to be found in the powers of the soul only after the light of grace illuminates them.

The theme of the next session was the immortality of the soul. Luther's views were briefly outlined since this time no specific reading was provided beforehand. The discussion took its starting point from

Melanchthon's *Liber de anima*. Unlike Luther, Melanchthon is known for his approval of the philosophical argumentation for the immortality of the human soul, but the difference between the two reformers does not seem that sharp. Melanchthon is obviously more sympathetic than Luther to the idea that Aristotle also was basically teaching the immortality of the soul, although for Melanchthon the main philosophers to provide arguments here are Plato, Xenophon and Cicero. In this respect, Johannes Bernhardi seems to still follow Luther's views, despite his overall strongly Aristotelian outlook. Finally, Melanchthon still holds that the philosophical arguments for the immortality of the soul are inconclusive and that the Word of God is the main source of certainty about these matters. The discussion in the seminar also raised questions concerning dualism with respect to the intellectual soul/spirit and body in Melanchthon's and Luther's views of the human being. Furthermore, Luther's unusual ontological views were discussed, in particular the problem of the continuity of individual identity after death.

The final theme of the seminar was conscience, or in general, the psychology of making ethical judgements. Luther's reference to the function of the Aristotelian practical syllogism in his *Lectures on Paul's Letter to Titus* (WA 27) from as late as 1527 provided an interesting parallel to Bernhardi's and Melanchthon's later expositions on conscience and related powers of the soul. These expositions show that despite Luther's criticism of medieval theories of moral psychology, which were often used in forming the philosophical basis for the doctrines of grace, similar theories were still current, although in modified forms, among the early Lutheran reformers in Wittenberg. Themes raised during this final session included, among others, Melanchthon's and Luther's views on the possibility of knowing good within the framework of natural righteousness and the different functions of knowledge of natural law on the one hand, and the preaching of the law on the other. Here it was recalled that in discussing the immortality of the soul, Melanchthon refers to a certain internal punishment for sins in the form of sadness produced by a bad conscience, which seems to be a phenomenon largely independent of external impulses, such as preaching of the law.

Luther als Bibelausleger

Seminarleiter: Christoph Burger

Berichterstatter: Christoph Burger

Aufgrund der von den Teilnehmern und Teilnehmerinnen angebotenen Referate lag der Akzent der gemeinsamen Arbeit auf Luthers Exegese von Psalmen und biblischen Cantica. Als besonders bereichernd erwiesen sich die ganz unterschiedlichen theologischen Prägungen, die in den Referaten und Diskussionen zur Sprache kamen.

Johannes Schilling (Kiel) behandelte Luthers Auslegung von Psalm 23, die Georg Rörer 1536 herausgab, im Rahmen seiner Psalmenauslegungen seit 1513/15. Bemerkenswert sind einige Momente der Kontinuität der Auslegung, aber auch eine zunehmende Konzentration der Deutung von Gottes Wohltaten für den Menschen in Gestalt seines Wortes. Insgesamt erweist sich die Auslegung als Transformation akademischer Theologie für eine breitere Leserschaft. Welcher Anteil Rörer dabei zukommt, wird sich im einzelnen nicht klären lassen.

Christoph Burger (Amsterdam) stellte »Luthers Deutung des Redens von Gottes Wirken mit seinem ›Arm‹ in seiner Auslegung des Magnifikat (Lk 1,46b–55), ein Ergebnis seiner Psalmenexegese« dar. Er erinnerte eingangs daran, dass der Reformator voraussetzt, dass Gott die Welt regiere; dass nur ein glaubender Mensch angemessen verstehen könne, wie Gott auf verborgene Weise handelt; dass es sinnvoll sei, zum Verständnis einer Bibelstelle Aussagen aus einem anderen biblischen Buch heranzuziehen und dass die Heilige Schrift kein unnötiges Wort enthalte, weswegen es denn in allen Fällen, in denen das gleiche zweimal gesagt werde, auf den tieferen Sinn zu achten gelte. Im Anschluss an Wilhelm Maurer wies er auf Luthers Unterscheidung zwischen Gottes offenkundigem und seinem verborgenen Handeln sowohl in Luthers beiden frühen Psalmenvorlesungen als auch in der Auslegung des Magnifikat hin.

Hans-Martin Kirn (Kampen/Groningen) sprach über »Targumrezeption bei Martin Luther – eine Spurensuche«. Die Rezeption des Targum (*translatio Chaldaica*) bzw. der Targumim als sprachlicher Monumente und Hilfsmittel für Bibelexegese und -übersetzung, Apologetik und Polemik lässt sich auch bei Luther im Rahmen der für die christliche Hebraistik zunehmend wichtigen Auseinandersetzung mit den rabbinischen Traditionsquellen feststellen. Zwar waren Luther sprachlich und theologisch engere Grenzen gesetzt als den Straßburger, Basler und Zürcher Exegeten, doch finden sich Spuren der Rezeption in wichtigen Diskursen, etwa zur Frage des Verhältnisses von *res* und *verba* in der Übersetzungspraxis oder in der Frage des alttestamentlich-prophetischen Christuszeugnisses. Dabei blieben die spätmittelalterlichen indirekten Rezeptionswege dominant (Nikolaus von Lyra, Paulus von Burgos, später Porchetus de Salvaticis), teilweise vermittelt durch Johannes Reuchlins *Rudimenta* und – im Falle der frühen Psalmenexegese – durch Faber Stapulensis.

Austra Reinis (Springfield, USA) führte aus, dass Luther in Bezug auf das Buch Jona lehrte, dass Christen sich in Jona wiedererkennen sollten, der ja sowohl ein Geheiligter gewesen sei als auch ein großer Sünder. Sie sollten darauf vertrauen, dass Gott ihnen ebenso barmherzig sein werde, wenn sie mit der Bitte um Vergebung zu ihm schrien, wie er Jona barmherzig gewesen sei, als dieser seine große Sünde bekannte. Luthers Interpretation brach mit

der patristischen Tradition, in der Autoren versucht hatten, Jona zu entschuldigen. Seine neue Weise der Deutung fand dann ihren Weg in den Predigten über das Buch Jona von Michael Helding (1506–1561), dem letzten katholischen Bischof des sächsischen Merseburg.

Rune Söderlund (Lund) referierte über »Luther als Ausleger des Hohen Liedes«. In seiner 1539 gedruckten Auslegung des Hohen Liedes schreibt Luther, es läge am nächsten, dieses Bibelbuch so zu deuten, dass es von dem weltlichen Regiment Salomos handle. Dieser *scopus* solle deswegen überall im Text beachtet werden. Luther hat sich auch, gemäß 2 Tim 3,16–17, in seiner Auslegung darum bemüht, sowohl Vermahnung als auch Trost zu vermitteln. Insbesondere beschäftigt er sich mit den Anfechtungen, die ein frommer Fürst erleiden muss, und mit dem Trost in diesen Anfechtungen. Die Erfahrung von Trübsal und Trost könne für einen Fürsten eine Hilfe sein, das Hohe Lied zu verstehen. Luther betont, dass gewisse Aussagen in der Schrift nur aus der Perspektive des Glaubens verstanden werden können, wie zum Beispiel die, dass ein Reich als schön und sicher gepriesen werden kann, obwohl es zugleich von Fehlern und Schwachheit geprägt ist.

Christopher Croghan und *Sarah Stenson* (Sioux Falls, USA) referierten gemeinsam über »Luther und Calvin« und über »Luthers Deutung der Opferung Isaaks«. Der erstgenannte Beitrag konzentrierte sich erstens darauf, welche Rolle die Ausbildung, die Luther und Calvin genossen hatten, dabei spielte, wie sie bei der Auslegung der Heiligen Schrift methodisch vorgingen und zweitens darauf, aufgrund welcher fundamentaler Annahmen sie diese Methoden anwandten. Calvin versuchte, die historische Grenze zwischen der Zeit, in der die biblischen Schriften geschrieben wurden, und seiner eigenen Zeit durch Logik und Rhetorik zu überbrücken, um deren Wahrheit zu erweisen. Luthers Verständnis des *verbum reale* ist grundlegend für seine Auslegung der Heiligen Schrift, weil diese für ihn das lebendige Wort ist, das dem Hörer begegnet, seine Existenz begründet und dem Hörer Glauben schenkt. Luthers Deutung der Opferung Isaaks verdeutlicht, auf welche Weise er in seiner Exegese der Heiligen Schrift philosophische Methoden heranzog. Kennzeichnend ist Luthers Unterscheidung zwischen dem ›wer‹ und dem ›was‹. Konzentriert sich der Ausleger auf das ›wer‹, dann trifft er auf Gottes Wort in der Gestalt von Befehl oder Verheißung, auf die Sache selbst, das wirkende Wort (*verbum efficax*).

Luther and the Old Testament

Seminar Leaders: Brooks Schramm and Kirsi Stjerna

Reporters: Brooks Schramm and Kirsi Stjerna

Though it is commonplace to say, with H. Bornkamm, that Luther »Christianized the OT thoroughly,« the influence that the OT itself had on Luther's own personal faith and theology is perhaps less appreciated. The seminar invited papers seeking to reassess the influence of the OT on Luther's theology, as well as Luther's own unique understanding of the OT as a whole.

Brooks Schramm presented on »Luther on Jacob and the Election of Israel: the Coercion of the OT on Luther's Understanding of God (and of the Jews).« He noted the double-edged character of Luther's thinking on election. On the one hand, the Jewish claim to be the children of Abraham and thus the chosen people of God was something against which Luther contended throughout his career. On the other, the doctrine of election itself was at the center of Luther's own theology. Luther never opposed chosenness as such, but he did oppose Jewish chosenness based upon natural descent. The double-edged character of Luther's thinking on election comes into clear focus in his discussions of the meaning of the name »Israel.« He understood God's *in utero* choice of Jacob over Esau as the definitive statement regarding the nature of God and the way in which God works in the world. The chief function of the story of the conception and birth of Jacob and Esau is to prove the claim that apart from the election of God, natural birth is useless before God – even for Abraham, Isaac, and Jacob. Luther makes Jacob's natural descent from Abraham and Sarah, Isaac and Rebecca, actually irrelevant, in that in his interpretation of Gen 25:23 he defines *populus Dei* in a completely spiritual manner. In so doing, he simultaneously establishes the theological principle that what makes the people of God the

people of God has always been the same. Luther is thus not a traditional supersessionist, rather his understanding of *populus Dei* as a wholly spiritual reality makes him a suprasessionist, in the sense that for him the true Jew has always been a *de facto* Christian.

In »Luther and ›Proper‹ Philological Interpretation in *On the Last Words of David* (1543),« *Stephen Burnett* discussed this late work of Luther's, written as the final installment of a three-part series of polemics against German Jewry in 1543. Luther's calculated use of anti-Jewish polemic in the book was not directed against Jews but rather against Christian Hebraists who deferred too willingly to the authority of Jewish scholars. As in *Bondage of the Will* (1525), Luther asserted that a knowledge of the »subject matter« (*res*) of the Bible was essential for complete understanding of the biblical text, and since Jewish interpreters rejected Jesus the Messiah, the subject of the OT, their interpretations of individual passages were to a greater or lesser extent flawed. Luther expounded II Sam 23:1–7, translating the Hebrew text into German and then emphasizing places in the passage that he believed referred to the Triune God and to Jesus the Messiah. Mere philological interpretation of the passage, such as one finds in S. Münster, was inadequate, and Münster's reticence in identifying Christian teaching in the OT mirrored the rabbis and their blindness to the »subject matter«. By emphasizing the theological distance between Jew and Christian, rabbi and Christian Hebraist, Luther hoped to »strengthen« the faith of Christian Hebraists, by warning them that those who uncritically followed the Jews in biblical interpretation were in danger of becoming »thieves of truth« themselves. Here, Luther was more worried about Jewish »lies« and their impact upon Christian interpretations of the Bible than flesh and blood Jews.

In his recent dissertation, *Is Evil Inevitable for Creation and Human Life? – Studies on Martin Luther's Biblical Interpretation*, *Jussi Koivisto* argued that the inevitability of evil in its various forms is an attribute that can be added to Luther's theology of evil. In his seminar paper, »Luther on the Inevitability of Evil,« Koivisto presented two examples of the inevitability of evil in Luther's interpretation of Gen 3. Example 1) »The Serpent Possessed by the Devil,« demonstrated that there exists an ancient, medieval, and early modern exegetical tradition regarding Gen 3, which modern biblical scholarship has been unaware of or reluctant to refer to. According to this tradition, the serpent mentioned in Gen 3 was possessed. Luther shared this view, and his personal contribution to this tradition was the clarification of the »logic« behind this odd-sounding conception. According to Luther, the serpent became the victim of the Devil, who possessed it and used it for his evil wiles. Because the serpent became a victim, it can be said that evil (inevitably) took over the serpent. Luther in fact called the Devil the architect (*architectum*) of the whole deceitful event. Example 2, »The Fall,« suggested that Luther's interpretation of Gen 3 differs substantially from Catholic tradition. For Luther, the »poison« of the serpent possessed by the Devil takes over a human being through God's secret permission. By this »poison« Luther meant the original sin which took over the first woman through the corrupting words of the serpent. Catholic tradition depicts the human being as much more of an autonomous subject in the Fall.

David Whitford, drawing from his *The Curse of Ham in the Early Modern Era*, examined »The Curse of Ham in Luther's Sermons on Gen

9« and argued that Luther's approach changed over time. In his 1519 sermons, Luther emerges as a preacher who is conversant with medieval traditions of the text while simultaneously feeling free to set aside part of that tradition. He ignores the common medieval question regarding whether Noah sinned when he became drunk. With the tradition, Luther reads the condemnation of Ham who saw his father naked as an allegorical condemnation of the Jews, for just as the Jews mocked Christ so Ham mocked Noah. With a new Protestant reorientation to the text, Luther's later 1523 sermon condemns Noah's drunken behavior as entirely sinful and considers the fallen Ham as a dire warning to those who mock or deride their parents, and to Christians who could fall just as the »perfect man« Ham fell. Luther passes over in silence any message of mocking the Jews, emphasizing rather the Reformation tenets of *sola fide* and *sola gratia* as well as his understanding of the theology of the cross. Whitford reminded of the importance of Gen 9 and the condemnation to slavery of Canaan, Ham's son, as an ideological and theological defense for African slavery and then American segregation.

Kristen Kvam presented on »Luther, the Psalms, and the Communion of Saints: Gleanings in the Twenty-First Century for a Christian Theological Commentary.« She argued that the influence of the OT on Luther's theology and personal faith is clearly seen in his longstanding, deep immersion in the Psalms. Kvam examined one facet of the importance of the Psalms for Luther's theology by offering a close reading of Luther's *Preface to the Psalter* (1545/1528). She contended that Luther's praises for the significance of the Psalms crescendo even as his descriptions of their texture acquire complexity. Through this double movement, Luther calls upon Christians to be nurtured by the piety of the Psalms and come to recognize their own inclusion in the *communio sanctorum*. Luther's *Preface* gives evidence of his »Christianizing« of the OT, but the Christological theme, in actuality, receives scant attention. Luther's concentration instead is upon the ways that the Psalms provide examples of how saints have spoken to God, and have done so with joy as well as sorrow. He frequently compares the virtues of the Psalms to the legends of the saints, praising the former for how it offers access to »real, living, active saints,« and contrasting this to the »silent« and

»half dead« saints of the legends. Luther values that the saints not only speak and pray in the Psalms; they also »lay out their heart,« speaking to God both from the storms and sorrows of their lives as well as from positions of joy and thanksgiving. By expressing both fear and thanksgiving, the Psalms teach Christians that they too are included in the *communio sanctorum*.

Kerstin Wimmer's »A Repressed Lament« began with the claim that lament awakens hope and strengthens compassion and solidarity. She then raised the question: what happens when lament is repressed at the expense of praise and joy? Luther points to the paramount importance of verbalizing every situation before God, and he considers a silent human being to be »half-dead.« For Luther, the way to encounter God's grace anew is by living through situations of despair and of God's absence, while bringing these traumatic deep-death experiences before God. The ongoing movement from lament to joy constitutes the non-solitary journey of baptism, from death to life anew. Luther's intention from the beginning was to encourage people to verbalize their fear and pain, joy and thanksgiving, *coram Deo*. His concern also included communication with ordinary people, to provide them with resources for their God-talk. Noteworthy is that in Luther's introduction to *The Seven Penitential Psalms*, nothing is said about penitence. In his following exposition the emphasis is on the perpetual journey from death to life, and thus his concern was to elucidate the significance of lament. Even if lament, crying out against suffering or the absence of meaning, is an unknown way, it must be vocalized. Luther's encouragement to become loud-voiced in situations of pain and loss derives from his confidence in the dialogue. In lamentation, a hope resides. But the journey toward hope includes a descent into the abyss, not knowing the way any further. Luther highlights *The Seven Penitential Psalms* as encouragement to learn that trusting God is also to question God. With Luther, therefore, it can be said that self-knowledge as well as solidarity require lamentation.

Kirsi Stjerna offered »Observations on Luther's Passionate and Assiduous Reading of the OT«. First, Luther reads thc OT with an uncompromisingly Christ-centric premise and with misinformed anti-Jewish faith convictions that permeate his theology. As demonstrated in *Martin Luther, the Bible, and the Jewish People: A Reader* (Fortress Press, 2012), co-authored with B. Schramm, Luther's dismissal of Jewish exegesis and conversation partners compromises his biblical hermeneutics and celebrated arguments on salvation. At the same time, Luther's abiding love of the texts and especially the matriarchs and patriarchs fundamentally shape his faith. His piety and theological convictions are inseparable, and both are rooted in his devouring of the OT. Second, Luther consistently reads into OT texts his chief revelation about justification and original sin as faith issues. This affords him the opportunity to interpret the Fall-story in Gen 3 in less misogynist and sex-phobic ways than one might expect from a medieval exegete. Identifying the first disobedience as a matter of the will when the human heart lost trust in God, and not as the *culpa* of the body or the first woman, Luther grieves over the post-Fall distorted (mis)awareness that makes human beings experience as shameful their most divine, original state: nudity and sexuality. In gender relations and »in the nude« human beings know what it means to live as *simul iustus et peccator*. Third, future re-exploration of Luther's interpretation of the OT as a source for his theology will do well to embrace the input of gender studies and Jewish scholarship and to address issues pertaining to unnecessarily male-centric and Christ-centric readings of the Hebrew texts.

Luther Reception in Asia and Africa

Seminar Leader: Miikka Ruokanen

Reporter: Miikka Ruokanen

The participants of this seminar were: *Michael Albrecht, Armin Buchholz, Chen Yongtao, Jin-Seop Eom, Paulos Huang, Kathryn Kleinhans, Gregory Miller, Kenneth Mtata, Miikka Ruokanen, Carolyn Schneider, William Schumacher, Jane Strohl, Wang Aiming* and *Karl Weber*. Half of the fourteen participants of the seminar presented a paper. The sessions were filled with lively, sometimes even enthusiastic discussions.

Jin-Seop Eom gave a paper on »Luther in Korea.« *Paulos Huang* and *Miikka Ruokanen* both offered separate papers on »Luther and China.« *Armin Buchholz* spoke on »Luther in the Chinese Context of Taiwan.« *Michael Albrecht* presented a paper on »Confessional Lutheranism Encounters Pentecostalism in India.« *Kenneth Mtata's* presentation was on »The Holy Spirit and Luther Reception in Africa.« *Jane Strohl* spoke on »The Lutheran Church in Rwanda.«

I The Potential of Luther's Theology for Asia

The person and theology of Martin Luther in many ways inspire many non-Western Christians. Luther is seen as the founding father of Protestantism at large, not only of Lutheranism; he belongs to all the Protestants, not only the Lutherans. Consequently, his theology is somewhat influential in all Protestant churches, not only in the Lutheran churches.

The »four *solae*« of Luther's theology are highly appreciated, for instance, in Korea and China. They are a healthy counterbalance against the persistent anthropocentrism of Asian religious thinking, against the trends of the so-called prosperity gospel, and against all kinds of legalistic tendencies so typical in many Asian churches. The Asian Christians willingly refer to Luther when defending the doctrine of grace, the idea of the justification of the sinner by grace and through faith alone. They also regard Luther's distinction between law and gospel as crucially important.

Jin-Seop Eom summarized the relevance of Luther's theology for East Asia:

> Luther's theology of the cross can be a corrective to the theology of prosperity; his principles of *sola fide* and *sola gratia* to Calvinistic legalism; his understanding of a Christian being simultaneously justified and sinner to the Methodist notion of perfectionist sanctification; his principle of *sola scriptura* to the Full Gospel Church's enthusiasm and mysticism; his law and gospel dialectic to the fundamentalist view of Scripture in general; his ecclesiology and sacramental theology to the low view of church and sacraments; his evangelical liturgy to simplistic worship; his doctrine of two kingdoms to the mixture of religion and politics, etc.

Many Asian theologians see an especially strong point of contact between Luther's theological paradoxes and the East Asian view of reality. East Asian philosophies and religions emphasize the harmony of the opposites, one reality with two mutually indispensable and inseparable aspects, such as the simultaneity of *yin* and *yang*. Similarly, the backbone of Luther's theology consists of the idea of *simul*, the simultaneity of the opposites. Luther and the East may meet as they reflect on the meaning of reality.

In spite of the great potential of Luther's theology for Asia, it is a fact that Luther is overshadowed by Jean Calvin and even by John Wesley in most Asian churches. Their theology has been influenced more by the Calvinistic/Reformed tradition than the Lutheran theological heritage. In addition, Asian Lutheran churches normally are very small and often divided among themselves to several small independent synods – this weakens the impact of Lutheran theology.

II Luther on Chinese Soil

The Chinese Protestant church, the fastest growing church in the world, identifies herself as a »post-denominational« church. After the Communist revolution, all of the about 70 Protestant denominations were compelled to become united in the 1950's. Still today, this church is exploring and seeking her true theological nature; in this process the theologies of both Luther and Calvin seem to play an important role.

It seems that Calvin is dominating the theological development of the non-registered church communities (the so-called house churches), whereas in the registered churches, under the leadership of the Three-Self Patriotic Movement and the China Christian Council, Luther and Calvin seem to have an equally important influence. The strict discipline and stern atmosphere of Calvinism, creating something completely »other« in regard to the current fluctuating society, has a special appeal to Christian intellectuals of non-registered churches.

Interestingly, not only the theological heritage of Luther but also his personality has inspired Asian Christians. Korean Protestants, who are predominantly Calvinists, see Luther as a symbolic figure expressing the power of reforming various spheres of life. They also appreciate Luther who »prayed three hours a day.« The Bible-loving Chinese Christians see Luther as a model of a good pastor and preacher who concentrated both his theological thinking and his pastoral work on the truthful exposition of Scripture. Luther is seen as »a man of the Bible« emphasizing the authority of God's word. Because many non-Western churches lack trained pastors, the role of lay leadership is crucially important. Consequently, Luther's teaching on the common ministry of all believers is highly appreciated.

In today's secular academic circles of Mainland China, Luther has a high regard as model of a »revolutionary« modern man. In many textbooks, he is included among the one hundred most influential persons of human history. In spite of Luther's failure to support the German peasants' revolution, he is seen as a reformer who served the interests of the people, opposing the feudal »tyranny« of the pope, the emperor, and the privileged nobility. He worked for the freedom and equality of all people and created a popular education system.

Among Luther's works, his treatise *The Freedom of a Christian* is most loved by both Chinese scholars and Christians. They feel that the idea of maximal inner personal freedom combined with complete loyalty in the service of the people expresses a core concept of traditional Chinese ethics. As China became a leading economic power in the world, secular Chinese scholars are deeply interested in the connection between the development of Western capitalism and Protestant ethics; Max Weber is carefully studied in Chinese universities.

III India and Africa

Some of the theological concerns in the Indian and African contexts are similar to those arising in the East Asian context, but there are differences, too. In India, the Lutheran identity is not very strong: Many Lutherans have a »dual membership« in the sense that they attend the Lutheran service on Sunday morning and then go to Pentecostal meetings afterwards. Many Lutheran pastors in India have never even seen Luther's *Small Catechism*! Well over half of the Christians in India are Pentecostals, a situation which challenges all other denominations. Indian Pentecostals respect Luther as a significant Christian leader, though they hardly understand the core of his theology.

Similar to the Indian situation, understanding and experiencing the reality of the Holy Spirit plays a central role in the growth of Christianity in Africa. Due to the influence of the context, i.e. traditional African religions and culture, pneumatology and healing are top issues of African Christian spirituality.

A leading Lutheran theologian, Manas Buthelezi is engaging Reformation tradition from the African perspective trying to reformulate it. Emphasis of the Holy Spirit is combined with insights from liberation theology. As a Lutheran theologian, Buthelezi uses the Bible as the basis of discussion; while as a contextual theologian, he begins with his personal experience and the experiences of his church members. He is unwilling to relinquish the ministry of the Holy Spirit to the Pentecostals, he reclaims it as a genuinely Lutheran heritage. In doing so, he needs to recover teachings on sanctification which he thinks have been marginalized because of the unbalanced appropriation of justification.

IV Luther Research in Non-Western Countries

In spite of the deep interest in Luther among the non-Western Protestants, scholarly Luther research can – according to our knowledge – only be found in Korea, Japan, China, and some Latin American countries (though we had no representatives from Japan or Latin America in this seminar). The most important challenge here is the language barrier: the inability to read Luther in original German and Latin. Most of the research is based on English translations. Also, access to international research materials is very limited.

The Lutheran Confessions, parts of Luther's works, as well as some well-known Western pieces of research on Luther have been translated into Korean, Chinese, and Japanese languages. For instance, a new Chinese series of *Luther's Works* has begun to appear in Shanghai, but even this is based on the American edition of Luther's works. In China, secular scholars in universities do research on Luther, whereas in theological seminaries, there is an interest but a lack of capacity to study Luther. In Korea, 172 Master's theses during the period of 2001–2010 were related to Martin Luther. An ecumenical Korean Luther Study Society was founded in 2008.

It is obvious that a further development of academic scholarship in Luther research as well as Reformation studies in general is urgently needed in non-Western countries, where already two thirds of all the Christians of the world are living.

Disciplined Freedom, or Free versus Slave? Recuperating Luther for Feminist Theology in an Age of Terror

Seminar Leader: Else Marie Wiberg Pedersen

Reporter: Else Marie Wiberg Pedersen

The seminar had as its goal to find ways of recuperating Luther for feminist theology by taking its point of departure in Luther's *On the Freedom of a Christian*.[1] Hence, its focus was not historical, but theological, addressing the question of Lutheran theology in the 21st century, especially how Lutheran theology can be critiqued and corrected by an engagement with feminist theology challenging also some of the taboos.

With the paper »Reading Luther's *On the Freedom of a Christian* in the 21st century,« *Else Marie Wiberg Pedersen* introduced the theme of the seminar and Luther's treatise through an overview of its dual-dialectical structure. In *Freedom of a Christian*, Luther in the tradition from Paul to Bernard of Clairvaux uses the dialectics of the human double nature of inner (the justified human being where God's gift, faith, operates with Christ as gift) and outer (the sinful human being where human love should operate with Christ as example) being. Luther uses different relational metaphors for the two natures (mirroring Christ's two natures). The nuptial metaphor pictures the sharing of grace between Christ and humans as *imago Dei*[2] in a three-dimensional giving and receiving: a physical dimension, bride and groom becoming one flesh (Eph

[1] Luther wrote the treatise in Latin for Pope Leo, *De libertate christiana,* but also composed a text in German, *Von der Freiheit eines Christenmenschen.* These are different on several points, but are found in a sequel in WA 7; 20–28 (the Latin) and 39–73 (the German), and in Clemens 2;10ff; as parallel texts in StA 2; 263–309. For an English translation of the Latin, see LW 31,333–377; of both the Latin and the German, see Woolf, Reformation Writings of Martin Luther, 1952. It should be noted that some words in the original versions may gain other meanings in English such as the term *Mensch* in German and *homo* in Latin, which, when translated into *man* in English, is often misread as *male* though the meaning is *human being.*

[2] The human being as *imago Dei* is absent in the German version.

283

5: 26–32); a grace-economical dimension, the sinless groom, Christ as both God and human (*homo*, not *vir*!), sharing sin and justice with the sinful bride (*homo*, not *mulier*!) (Hos 2: 19 ff); and a social dimension, groom and bride belonging to each other (Songs 2: 16).[3]

Expounding the relation between the outer human being and God, Luther shifts to the child-parent metaphor, transitioning from the »dogmatic« to the »ethical« domain, from the creational-anthropological aspect of the human being as *imago Dei* to the soteriological-Christological aspect of God in Christ being *similitudo hominis*. Both concur in a circulation of love, from God to the individual human to the inter-human, lifting up the interrelatedness of otherness.

Jone Salomonsen posed the question of how the text can be read in light of acts of terror perpetrated by Christians, focusing on the act of terror in Norway on 22 July 2011 by the radical right-wing Anders Behring Breivik. Envisioning himself as a Christian crusader, he went on a political mission and killed 77 people, mainly young Social Democrats.

Arnfridur Gudmundsdottir focused on the question whether Luther's idea of the priesthood of all believers through baptism as a foundation for his critique of the distinction between spiritual and worldly people, launched in his Reformation writings of 1520, really made a difference for women. Luther's idea of the priesthood as responsibility toward the neighbor and his rejection of an ontological distinction between lay and ordained in *The Babylonian Captivity of the Church* opened avenues to women, yet they remained subjected to a patriarchal understanding of gender roles and were silenced both then and in most history books. She concluded that Luther's radical notion of baptism as the true ordination of all believers was only partially *in re*, while truly *in spe* as the foretaste of an eschatological future. Women were free, but they remained slaves to the patriarchal understanding of their freedom.

In her paper »Luther's Nuptial Imagery Revisited – Erotic Union of Business Exchange?« *Elisabeth Gerle* discussed two feminist readings of Luther's use of the nuptial metaphor. With their focus on

---

3 The reference to Songs 2: 16 is absent in the German version.

fluidity, hybridity, and queer features of his employment of the metaphor both Wiberg Pedersen and
Kleinhans offer readings that de-
construct the Luther reception's
gender hierarchical reading, while
emphasizing its meaning of inti-
mate relationship. She concluded
that such fluid readings could serve
as an ecumenical resource as well
as a resource for contemporary
ethics in creating space for multiple forms of affective relationships.

Sini Mikkola discussed in her
paper »Gendered Sexuality in Marriage in Luther's Anthropology in
the Treatise *Estate of Marriage*
(1522)« the focal points concerning
sexuality in Luther's thoughts in
the early 1520s, exemplified by *The
Estate of Marriage*.[4] She stated that
Luther differed from tradition in
his view on sexual desire, in his terminology »shameful desire« originating from the fall, as he tied this
solely to male bodies, though he
saw the sexual act as part of the human creational situation, though
without desire. The fallen and gendered life thus had to be controlled
within marriage. Though it is clear
that Luther problematized sexually
cold wives on the one hand and cas-
trates on the other as not fulfilling

the creational order of life either
through lack of will or lack of mas-
culinity, she concluded that the
picture of Luther's view on sexuality seems to be gendered, male
sexuality being bound to lust and
female to self-control. But given
the fact that the still celibate
Luther is defending marriage in
this treatise and holding other
thoughts on sexuality, his view on
the matter is rather more complex
than this one text reveals.

Mary Streufert redressed in her
paper Paul's proclamation of justification by grace through faith, understood by Luther as the antithesis
of the law according to his freedom
treatise. Using the criticism by B.
Kahl and Popez of a forensic understanding of Galatians, she contended that this understanding of
justification builds on a combative
hierarchical binary between Self
and Other, true of much Lutheran
theology following a patriarchal
pattern of gender construction as in
the United States, but not congru-
ent with Paul's and Luther's own
understanding of justification by
faith as a new law, love as self-
othering as opposed to Roman imperial law or the Roman curia. She
concluded that Paul is a gender

---

4 WA 10,2; 275–304.

transgressor preaching a theology of »one-an(d)-otherness,« just as Luther propagates transgressing boundaries by alienation of the Self into the place of the Other.

Marit Trelstad continued in her paper »Terror begins at Home: Luther and the ›terrifying and killing‹ Law« by addressing Luther's understanding of the law as driving us to Christ. Exploring connections between terror, domestic violence, Luther and law, she challenged and corrected Luther in his law-gospel dynamic and pointed to the fact that he himself had a critical view on his freedom treatise, e.g. in his *First Disputation Against the Antinomians*, where he expounds on the two functions of the law, the theological use being both descriptive and performative. While the descriptive is neutral, she found the performative function – where God pulls down the self-satisfied – abusive and terrorizing. In order to avoid abusive images of God as justification of domestic violence and terror, she concluded by suggesting to place God's love and grace before the law.

Åste Dokka focused on Luther's anthropology and the constitution of the subject in contrast to postmodernity's subject theory of no pre-discursive subjects (Foucault) or gender theories on de-stabilizing the gendered subject (Butler). Based on his *Large Catechism*, she proposed to see Luther's idea of relational anthropology and continual creation as resonating with the idea of a fluid subject in constant mediation between relations, situations and other factors. A person's subject is constituted every day by way of the God relation and the inter-human relation; both communal and social relations are constantly processed.

Finally, by focusing on Christ's love for the harlot, *Christine Helmer* laid out a project for reading Luther's freedom treatise through a new angle of the agape-tradition, and to use it as a starting-point for exploring theological method in relation to its subject matter that integrates love and truth. She assessed love in the epistemological and theological terms of the love of the subject matter and love for the other, both loves grounding three aspects of truth: coherence, correspondence and comprehensiveness. She stated that since neither love nor doctrinal truth are perfect in time, theology must be developed in a happy exchange that deals with difference and involves God and others in relationship.

Luther in the Ibero-American World

Seminar Leader: Andrew Wilson

Reporter: Andrew Wilson

Our seminar explored certain Spanish reforming movements that were repressed after Luther's excommunication, the use of Luther as archheretic in counter-Reformation art of Mexico and Peru, and contemporary *resourcement* of Luther's marginality for minority theologies. We suggest mysticism as a promising research topic that could avoid worn polemics and focus on historical thought and practice.

I Poorly received

Ibero-America received Luther as a heretic and knew him only enough to inoculate a pure Catholic body from a foreign disease. The diagnosis of healthy (Catholic-Iberian) and infected (Lutheran-foreign) bodies gained racial overtones, as in Menéndez Pelayo, *Historia de los heterodoxos españoles*, 1978 [1880], vol. I, p. 47: »La lengua española no se forma decir herejes.« The association of Spanish blood with orthodoxy was strong in Ibero-America. Clerics and bishops still now tend to be *ladino*; indigenous populations tend toward Protestantism.

Ibero-America's theology was forged in counter-Reformation. Only after Vatican II was Luther widely studied. Anticlerical 19th century governments hoped Protestant immigrants would bolster their nations' technical expertise and democratic spirit. Today, Luther sits well amongst Ibero-America's intellectual elite as a hero of conscience, a courageous voice against hegemony.

It is easy to forget the many reforms of religious life that flourished in Spain before Luther, only to be rejected as »Lutheran« heresy. Franciscan regent and cardinal Ximénez de Cisneros patronized a new humanist university at Alcalá de Henares, like Wittenberg specialized in languages and philology. It produced the Complutensian Polyglot Bible, six columns of Hebrew, Greek, Latin, Syriac, Aramaic and Coptic. It dwarfed Erasmus's 1516 edition in erudition, but was beyond anybody but Spain's *converso* minority. Five hundred of the initial six hundred exemplars went down with their ship on the voyage to Rome, and it was largely forgotten. But just as his reforms gained ground, Luther came along; the Inquisition vigorously stamped out Erasmus and associated humanism.

Illuminism popularized types of monastic contemplation, but apart from the cloister these roused suspicions. These »mystics« contacted God directly through the Holy Spirit with private prayer and bible study. Luther was a mystic of similar ideas who promoted the mystical *Theologica Germanica* and approved Bernard of Clairvaux. As with humanism, after Luther was excommunicated, the Inquisition raised its vigilance. Books were much more closely regulated, foreign travel and trade much more suspicious.

Spain's reformers took to the road, visiting Basel, Strasbourg, Mainz, Geneva, and even Wittenberg. Francisco de Enzinas went from Alcalá to Wittenberg to perfect his Greek under Melanchthon then presented his translation of the New Testament to Emperor Charles in Antwerp, 1539. Other exiles worked to bring the Reformation back to Spain. From Geneva, Juan Pérez de Pineda translated and smuggled hot books. Safe in Italy, Juan Valdés limited the sacraments to three, emphasized the Bible, and rejected priestly celibacy;

passages of his *Alfabeto Cristiano* may have been taken from Luther's *Large Catechism*.

The 1540s and 1550s saw conventicles grow around star preachers; in Seville, Constantino Ponce de la Fuente argued for justification by faith and three sacraments (as Luther). Perhaps he got these ideas from Melanchthon, or Erasmus. His work was burned with him (in effigy) in Valladolid's 1558–1559 *autó de fé* as »Lutheran,« but was used unawares in the New World under the name of bishop Zumárraga, and later inspired the Jesuits (!) in Brazil and Goa.

II Images of Luther

Alicia Mayer expanded on her work, *Lutero en el Paraíso* (2005) that Luther found a role in the New World as whipping boy. Images of the arch-heretic appear throughout Mexico and Peru. In Mexico City's cathedral, Cristóbal de Villalpando paints Luther straight behind the apse, writhing in pain as the chariot of orthodoxy rolls over him; a similar scene hangs with the Carmelites in Celaya: Luther is found among a float of heretics and schismatics – also Calvin, Sabellius, and Faustus – being rowed away from the boat of orthodoxy by devils. In the church of Guanajuato Miguel Cabrera paints Luther as a Turk with demonic fangs, pierced by the pricks of own writing quills (alongside Calvin, Pelagius, and Arius). The Virgin of Guadelupe protected Mexico against Luther: Andrés Lopez depicts lightning shooting from a host that floats above the chalice born by the virgin, bouncing off a copy of the Gospels only to strike Luther dead with lightning.

III Luther, Outsider

Vitor Westhelle presented the *resourcement* of Luther by Latin American theologians, beginning by emphasizing Wittenberg for the backwater it was. Questionable doctrines were critiqued, and a new piety for common people was formed not in a great city but from the very margins of the world. Lutherans of Latin America are (and ought to be) driven by their marginality to receive the Reformation in this broad setting, and take more account of Luther's own social teaching against usury, poor relief, and his reformulation of good works as directed toward the neighbor.

As an example of this, *Justin Eller* presented the Lutheran church in Bolivia which is to 98% indigenous and very poor. They are inspired to resist constant pressure to abandon their traditional culture by receiving Luther's adaptation of local traditions, notably music, for catechesis and worship.

The subject of Luther in Ibero-America is large and elusive. Future research could profitably be directed at the spiritual roots of the Reformation in certain strains of late-medieval piety present also in Iberia, in better comprehending Luther's reception as heretic in Latin American letters and arts, and creative application of the contextual theology of the Reformation.

The Legacy of Swedish Luther Renaissance

Seminar Leader: Roger Jensen

Reporter: Roger Jensen

The goal of the seminar was to discuss distinctive features of the twentieth century Swedish Luther Renaissance and its legacy for contemporary Swedish Luther research. The participants presented short papers focusing on historical and theological aspects. These aspects were explored in a comparative way in discussing the parallel development in the German Luther Renaissance.

Roger Jensen led the first seminar session by both providing a larger framework for use in the seminar discussions and discussing the methodological approach of Gustaf Wingren. In this framework, Jensen especially discussed the notion of vocation related to modernization and enlightenment, and the challenges this development meant to theology. The notion of privatization, the separation of public from private spheres, was exemplified in the debate, and different positions on Luther's understanding of vocation were presented. Jensen argued that Kantian philosophy was in many ways a precondition for this development in representing an epistemological framework for the understanding of the teaching of the two realms on modern premises. Jensen pointed further to the influence of neo-Kantian epistemology in the Luther research of the 20th century.

One of the main differences from the German Luther Renaissance, according to Jensen, was the special focus on *God acting in history*. Yet, Jensen argued that the neo-Kantian influence in epistemology was also present in the Swedish Luther Renaissance, notably in Anders Nygren. Exactly this aspect was criticized by Gustaf Wingren, so Jensen. Contrary to the conceptual focus of Nygren and the motif research, Wingren sought a way of making the concrete, tangible and empirical the starting point of theology. In seeking an alternative way, Wingren developed what he called *a double phenomenological orientation* in theology, combining creational theology with the kerygmatic approach – a position that avoided the pitfalls that came to characterize much of the German Luther Renaissance marked by neo-Kantian epistemology.

Maria Erling of Gettysburg Seminary discussed the various ways that Swedish perspectives on Luther's theology were transmitted to America in the wake of World War II. Particularly important was the need to salvage Luther's reputation after the capitulation of large parts of the German church to Nazism. Furthermore, Swedish Lutherans in the United States were interested in using Luther to promote their own goal of healing divisions among various branches of Lutherans. An essential transmitter of Luther's theology to America was Edgar Carlson. Another key source was the visit to post-war Scandinavia by Carl Rasmussen to solicit manuscripts for Muhlenberg Press for possible translations.

Critical discussions in the seminar centered on the nature of Rasmussen's work and the interpretive lens he used to ask questions of his subjects. Which theologians were visited and which books merited translation? Also, Rasmussen's idiosyncratic style raises issues for the historian about accuracy of transcription.

Karin Johannesson of Uppsala University presented a paper on the Swedish theologian Arvid Runestam and his views on sanctification. Johannesson's desire was to take the present day »subjective turn« and the interest in spirituality seriously and to understand and shape it through the filter of the Lutheran theological tradition. Such a discussion naturally points in the direction of the meaning of sanctification and she enlisted Runestam to assist her with this project. Johannesson noted how Runestam identifies Luther's *Bondage of the Will* as an unavoidable challenge for any meaningful exposition of a Lutheran theology; he also used the turn of the German philosopher Wilhelm Windelband to help explicate the various relationships between psychological and moral freedom in the human subject.

In the following discussion, it was pointed out that Runestam's interpretation of Luther might grant the human subject a degree of freedom never suggested by the reformer. The further conversation included Runestam's use of Windelband to help explain the freedom of the will in a modern context. It was noted that Windelband was pre-Freudian in his analysis of the will and that this meant his work

was unduly influenced by the optimism of the Enlightenment and a
neo-Kantian epistemology.

Leif Svensson from Umeå University presented a critical note on
the two kingdoms doctrine in the
Swedish Luther Renaissance. In his
paper, Svensson analyzes studies
by Einar Billing, Gustaf Törnvall,
Gustaf Wingren and Per Frostin in
order to highlight and problematize
what he sees as the »Troeltschian«
nature of the Swedish two kingdoms interpretations, especially: a)
the understanding of the church as
a spiritual entity (Christian life is
all about an inner community with
God), b) the reduction of Christian
ethics to an inner spiritual sphere
of dispositions, and c) a conserva-
tive stress on obedience to authority.

Critical discussions in the
seminar focused on the question to
what degree the Swedish two kingdom interpretations are subject to
Ernst Troeltsch's criticism of
Lutheran ethics. The development
of Troeltsch's critique by e.g. John
Howard Yoder and Alasdair MacIn-
tyre was suggested to be an important challenge for contemporary
Lutheran theology.

Thomas Girmalm from Umeå
University presented a text discussing Gustaf Wingren's theory of
preaching as it emerges in his book
on preaching (G. WINGREN, Predikan: En principiell studie, 1949).
Girmalm examines how Wingren
brings the human and Christian together by using the notion of *communicatio ideomatum*, and how
this methodological approach
marks what came to be the hall-
mark of the theology of Wingren,
combining creational and kerygmatic theology. The book *Predikan*
represented a clash with the methods of Lundensian theology, i.e. the
motif research, and with Anders
Nygren. The bringing together of
preaching *and* theology was criticized for being non-academic, but
denotes the practical turn in Wingren's theology and the making of
the phenomena of preaching into
the starting point of theological
work.

The following discussion
pointed to how a new reading of
the book *Predikan* can lead to new
insights regarding Wingren's theological aim of bringing the divine
and the human together, namely
through a theology of incarnation
and Christology – aspects neglected
in the later Wingren-reception. The
further discussion focused on *the
problem of universality* in Wingren
regarding his understanding of the
Word, the preaching, the preacher

and the congregation, i.e. the lack of emphasis on contextuality and diversity.

Mark D. Tranvik from Augsburg College presented a paper on Luther and Wingren on baptism. In providing an overview of Luther's understanding of baptism, Tranvik argued that Wingren builds on the early church fathers and Luther. The overall goal of Tranvik was to promote a baptismal language and baptismal theology that focuses on the relationship *faith and daily life.* – Baptism for Luther is, so Tranvik, neither »just the sacrament of infancy« nor an initiation rite, rather, baptism spans the entire life of the believer. According to Wingren, man is through baptism restored in Christ, recapitulated, brought back into proper relationship with creation, neighbor and God; in baptism, man truly becomes man. Yet, the »true and proper baptism for all humanity« is the death and resurrection of Christ, the reversing of the life-death pattern set by Adam; hence all the believer ever receives is a renewal and continuation of baptism. There were some questions raised concerning the bearing of the Luther-Wingren connection. It was argued that the understanding of baptism in Wingren seems to be drawn more from Irenaeus, hence the language of recapitulation and becoming man, and not that closely from Luther.

Sola Scriptura

Seminar Leader: Friederike Nüssel

Reporters: H. Ashley Hall and Friederike Nüssel

While the *sola scriptura* principle is widely regarded as an essential element of Luther's thought and Lutheran theology, it has gone through several transformations in the history of Lutheran thinking. The goal of the seminar was to identify and reflect some crucial steps in this development and to discuss possible ways of re-thinking the way in which the principal role of the Bible could be defined today consistent with Lutheran thought.

The seminar participants included *Lubomir Batka* (Comenius-

University Bratislava, Slovakia), *H. Ashley Hall* (Creighton University, Nebraska, USA), *Anne Käfer* (Evangelical Church in Germany, Germany), *Friederike Nüssel* (Heidelberg University, Germany), *Steffen Kjeldgaard-Petersen* (Copenhagen, Denmark), and *Jens Schröter* (Humboldt-University Berlin, Germany).

First, the group studied some crucial passages from Luther's *De servo arbitrio*. Therein, Luther elaborates some central aspects of his hermeneutical approach to the Bible. Of particular concern was the *claritas scripturae* and the key idea that obscure and difficult passages in the Bible which cannot be clarified through philological exegesis need to be interpreted in the light of Jesus Christ as the center of the Bible. In his controversy with Erasmus, Luther argues that the Bible is a clear and sufficient source to develop an understanding of the human condition and the need for salvation in Christ. Both constitute the clear testimony of Scripture. The group asked whether this necessarily involves the *sola scriptura* principle and the complete exclusion of church tradition, especially the writings of the church fathers. An article by Timothy Wengert (T. J. WENGERT, A Note on *Sola Scriptura* in Martin Luther's

Writings, in: Luther-Bulletin, vol. 20, 2011, 21–31) was particularly helpful. Through a word study of Luther's works, Wengert demonstrates that Luther only rarely uses the phrase *sola scriptura*, and when he does so, it is often to deny that Scripture alone (Scripture *qua* Scripture) is sufficient. Instead, Luther's primary interest is to find Christ within Scripture as well as within the better tradition of the Church's theology and preaching. This generated a lot of conversation about whether and to what extent *sola scriptura* might nonetheless be implicit in Luther's understanding of authority.

Next, the group turned to the Lutheran theologians of the 17th century with particular examination of the locus *de scriptura sacra* in the works of Johann Gerhard and others. Here, we find a marked development. In these teachings, the *sola scriptura* principle was now both formulated in a strictly exclusive sense (i.e. relative to other authorities), and also informed by the particular doctrine of verbal inspiration. The reasons for this development were manifold. On the one hand, Lutherans faced challenges from the Council of Trent and its teaching on Scripture and tradition; and on the other, they faced challenges from radical reformers and eclectic ways of using Scripture. Still another development was noted in the following century. In examining the works of Lutheran theologian Johann Franz Buddeus, who taught in Jena at the beginning of the 18th century, we noted that the argumentative weight of the idea of verbal inspiration was reduced. At the same time, Buddeus articulates the differentiation between exegetical and dogmatic readings of Scripture. According to Buddeus, the task of dogmatic theology is to identify those articles in the Bible necessary for salvation. For Buddeus, the *fundamentum in re* expressed in the Bible is God's reconciling activity through his new covenant in Christ. Buddeus thus systematically integrates Reformed federal theology into his Lutheran account of faith. Biblical theology is necessary only to clarify difficult passages in the Bible on a philological and syntactical level. For this reason, it has a methodological responsibility distinct from dogmatic theology.

For a prominent example of a post-Enlightenment revision of the article concerning Scripture, we then discussed Friedrich Schleiermacher's *Glaubenslehre*. In his account of Scripture, Schleiermacher reflects a rationalist critique of the Bible. The same is found in the ground-breaking research of Johann Salomo Semler's *Abhandlung von freier Untersuchung des Kanons* (1771). Schleiermacher transfers the doctrine of Scripture from the prolegomena to the ecclesiological section of his dogmatics. As a result, he indicates that the inspired authority of the Bible is an expression of faith resulting from an encounter with the Bible primarily from within the Christian community. Moreover, Schleiermacher discusses the canonical character of the biblical writings. For him, the authority of the apostolic writings is based upon their account of the experience of Jesus, their account of his ultimate concern for God, and their witness as inspired through the Holy Spirit. For Schleiermacher, it is important that the early witness of the Apostles was pure. The sense for the truly apostolic witness is a gift of the Holy Spirit, which is deepened and promulgated in the course of the church's history. Hence, Schleiermacher, like Luther, stresses the role of the Spirit together with the salvific experience of Christ as the ground for the authority of the Bible. Yet, he does not defend *sola scriptura* in the exclusive manner of Lutheran Orthodoxy. This is because, for Schleiermacher, the immediate source for Protestant theology is in the interpretation of the biblical witness in the confessional writings of the Reformation.

In the modern ecumenical movement of the 20th century, the issue of Scripture and tradition has become a major topic. Lutheran and Roman Catholic theologians have explored the fact that the canon itself was defined through a process of tradition. For a Lutheran perspective on this development, the group discussed an article by WILFRIED HÄRLE, Tradition und Schrift als Thema des interkonfessionellen Dialogs heute aus evangelischer Sicht (in: Kircheneinheit und Weltverantwortung. Festschrift für Peter Neuner, hg. v. C. BÖTTIGHEIMER/H. FILSER, 2006, 617–632). For Härle, the development of the canon involved the distinction between canonical and non-canonical tradition. While the identification of canonical writings was dependent on a process in which oral and written tradition played a decisive role, Härle affirms with Karl Barth that the authority of the biblical canon has emerged within the church through the work of the Spirit. Hence, Scripture is the normative source in comparison with all non-

canonical tradition, although tradition may help to deepen exegesis. Thus, the critical perspective on tradition, which we found in the Reformation and especially in the post-Reformation era, is changed.

Today, however, it is no longer sufficient to reflect upon the relationship between Scripture and tradition in an effort to describe the canonical character of the Bible. Rather, it is necessary to defend and explain both (i) the impact of God's revelation as witnessed in the Bible for a systematic understanding of the world as God's creation and (ii) the claim of the existence of God as the ultimate and all-determining reality. This was pointed out by Wolfhart Pannenberg in an early article on the crisis of the *sola scriptura* principle (Die Krise des Schriftprinzips (1962) [in: Grundfragen systematischer Theologie, hg. v. DERS., ²1971, 11–21]). Theology, therefore, has the task to demonstrate the rationality of Christian faith in dialogue with other disciplines. For Pannenberg, it is impossible to defend the normative role of Scripture in the academy today without first giving a systematic justification for why Scripture offers a plausible perspective on the world. This is how, as a modern Lutheran theologian, Pannenberg transforms the principle of *sola scriptura*. In our discussion we agreed that this kind of theological approach would meet the concerns of confessional Lutheran theology of the 17th and 18th centuries in their distinction between and combination of natural and revealed theology. Moreover, this insight is a recovery of Luther's insistence on finding and proclaiming Christ within the Scriptures, a commission that preserves the authority of Scripture relative to the person and benefits of Christ proclaimed and understood *pro nobis*.

Glaube und Vernunft bei Luther

Seminarleiter: Hans-Peter Großhans

Berichterstatter: Michael Plathow

Der aspektreiche und disparate Themenkomplex »Glaube und Vernunft bei Luther« erwies in unserer Seminararbeit seine Multiperspektivität, die sich bei dem existenziell denkenden Frömmigkeitstheologen M. Luther nicht ohne weiteres systematisieren lässt. Textorientiert wandten sich die aus Finnland, Dänemark und Deutschland kommenden Wissenschaftler dem Thema in verschiedenen Lutherschriften zu. Die situative Verortung und die unterschiedlichen Genera der Primärtexte reflektierend, verlieh gerade das theologische Unterscheiden, ohne zu trennen, von *Gesetz und Evangelium* als konstitutiver und kriteriologischer Zugang Klarheit für den Themenkomplex.

In der Spannbreite von einerseits Luthers kritischen Äußerungen über die »Hure Vernunft« (WA 51; 126,7.32; WA 18; 164,25–27) und seiner konfessorischen Berufung auf den Schrift- und eben auch den Vernunftbeweis vor dem Reichstag zu Worms (WA 7; 838,4) wurden folgende Quellentexte interpretiert und diskutiert:

1. *Disputatio de homine* (1536) in: WA 39; 175–177 nach: G. EBELING, Lutherstudien Bd 2. Disputatio de homine I, 1977, 15–24 mit einer Einführung durch *Michael Plathow*: nec eo ipsa ratio novit a priori, sed tantum a posteriori.

Nicht aus sich – wie These 10 feststellt – vermag die Vernunft ihr Wesen zu bestimmen (a priori); erst aus den Wirkungen (a posteriori) wird sie als *optimum et divinum quiddam* und als *inventrix et gubernatrix* der Wissenschaften erkannt (T 4. 5), als *sol coram mundo* (T 8). In der Beziehung *coram deo* – wie Luther unter Hilfenahme des Aristotelischen Vier-causa-Schemas verdeutlicht (T 12–16) – vermag sie nichts (T 11); werkgerecht und selbstrechtfertigend dient sie sich vielmehr in der spätscholastischen Glaubenslehre dem *Gesetz* an (T 26–31). Der Glaube, *fiducia*, ist es, der, heilsgeschichtlich entfaltet, konzentriert mit Röm 3,26 im Rechtfertigungsgeschehen, der die Fülle der Weisheit erschließt (T 20. 32). Der Glaube lässt die Vernunft als *omnium rerum res et caput* mit der Begrenzung auf Zeit und Raum (T 4. 8. 18. 19. 35) unter die Macht der Sünde gestellt (T 22. 24. 34), dennoch in ihrer Würde von Gott erhalten, erscheinen in der Ambivalenz von *rationis regna* und *schema mundi* (T 40): die Vernunft coram mundo ist nach dem Schöpfungsauftrag (T 7) zu gebrauchen (*uti*) als das, wozu sie bei der Unterscheidung von Gottes Handeln und menschlichem Tun bestimmt ist (1Kor 7,3); nicht soll sie, sich selbst verabsolutierend, als *regnum mundi* Gott (*frui*) die Ehre nehmen wollen.

2. *In epistolam S. Pauli ad Galatas Commentarius* (1531) 1535 zu Gal 3,6, in: WA 40,1; 359–373 mit Einführung durch *Hans-Peter Großhans*.

Das hermeneutische Unterscheiden, ohne zu trennen, von Gesetz und Evangelium ist es, das, wie Paulus exemplarisch mit Abraham zeigt, erschließt: *Der Glaube ohne Werke des Gesetzes rechtfertigt*. In diesen Verstehenszusammenhang zeichnet Luther ein, dass die Vernunft als Repräsentantin selbstrechtfertigender Werke sich gleichsam als *Feindin Gottes* erweist (363,25; 365,18f), die, *geopfert*, Gott allein die Ehre geben lässt (363,11f). Der Glaube ändert den Existenzgrund, weil die fremde Gerechtigkeit Gottes im Werden von *simul peccator et iustus* in der Weise vervollkommnet wird, dass Gott dem Geschenk des *Glaubens im Herzen* die Gerechtigkeit um Christi willen zurechnet (364,12–14; 370,19–21).

Für praktisch ausgerichtete Themen und Konkretionen wurden folgende Texte analysiert und diskutiert:

3. *De votis monasticis Lutheri iudicium* (1521), in: WA 8; 629–641 mit M. Luther, Freiheit und Lebensgestaltung, hrsg. u. übers. K.-H. ZUR MÜHLEN, 1983, 156–174.

Apologetisch und polemisch

weist Luther mit der Distinktion von *Gesetz und Evangelium* nach, dass die Mönchsgelübde nicht nur der Gerechtigkeit allein aus Gnade widersprechen, sondern auch im Gegensatz zur natürlichen Vernunft, *ratio naturalis*, des allgemeinen Naturrechts stehen (630,2–5).

4. Präsentation von *Andreas Pawlas: Glaube und wirtschaftliche Vernunft bei Luther.*

Bei der Relationalität der menschlichen Person (Gewissen) *coram deo* und *coram mundo* ist die ökonomische Vernunft mit ihrem Benutzen Aristotelischer Denkformen und Begriffe (ausgleichende Gerechtigkeit, Billigkeit) dem *usus civilis legis* des weltlichen Regiments Gottes zuzuordnen. Luthers klare Ablehnung des Wuchers im Kontext der damaligen agrarischen Gesellschaft wusste zugleich um die Ausnahmen des Zinskaufes, Notwuchers und Schaderechts. Das Kriterium der vernünftigen Billigkeit verbindet sich mit dem christlichen Motiv der Nächstenliebe: nicht für mich, um des andern (Armen, Witwe, Waise u.a.) willen; dem entgegengesetzt ist die Habsucht als Wirkung der *vom Teufel besessenen Vernunft* (WATR 1; 192,15–19). Die durch den Glauben *erleuchtete* Vernunft ist es, die ihre Eigentlichkeit im Auf-

trag Gottes für Friede, Gerechtigkeit, Barmherzigkeit offen legt.

5. *Vernunft und Klarheit der Schrift* in der Einleitung von *De servo arbitrio* (1525) in: WA 18; 606–609 (bzw. ab 600); 653.

Für das theologische Schriftverständnis unterscheidet Luther – anders als der skeptische Erasmus von Rotterdam – zwischen *claritas externa* und *claritas interna*. Den Predigern, die im öffentlichen Dienst stehen, werden – gegen schwärmerischen Spiritualismus und buchstäblichen Fundamentalismus – mit vernünftigen philologischen Methoden im Blick auf Christus als *Mitte der Schrift* die dunklen Textstellen von den hellen her klar und die *res* und die *summa* der Theologie zugänglich. Exegetische Unkenntnis, Missbrauch der Schrift und vor allem die *Finsternis des Herzens* bringen mit sich die Nichtzugänglichkeit der *claritas interna*. Diese schenkt allen Glaubenden der heilige Geist persönlich als *Kenntnis des Herzens* im *Sinn des Herrn*.

Zusammenfassend lassen sich für den aspektreichen und disparaten Themenkomplex folgende Leitlinien aufzeigen:

A) Luther weiß – bei aller Kritik – um die segensreichen Wirkungen der natürlichen Vernunft in den begrenzten Lebenswelten und in den zeitlichen Wissenschaften und Künsten. Luther weiß um das gegenseitig bereichernde, kritische und konstruktive Verhältnis von Glaube und Vernunft. Das ist in unserer Zeit nach der Aufklärung zu betonen gegen die verschiedenen Formen des biblizistischen, naturalistischen und szientistischen Fundamentalismus.

B) Luther erkennt im Licht des Evangeliums mit hamartiologischem Realismus die Widersprüche und die Diskrepanzen der Vernunft-Wirkungen *coram mundo*:

Einerseits ist die Vernunft durch den Schöpfungsauftrag auch nach dem Sündenfall kooperativ hineingenommen in den *usus civilis legis* göttlicher Erhaltung der Menschenwelt, Leben fördernd und Zukunft erschließend. Andererseits droht die Vernunft, unter der Macht der Sünde durch gesetzliche Selbstverabsolutierung als Unvernunft missbraucht und pervertiert, Leben zu zerstören und Zukunft zu verschließen, worüber im Streit zwischen Glaube und Unglaube um die Wirklichkeit der Widerspruch und die Kritik des *usus theologicus legis* von Wort und Glaube ergeht. *Ratio* und *iustificatio* sind wie Gesetz und Evangelium einander zugeordnet als Entsprechung und Widerspruch.

C) In praktischen, handlungstheoretischen Prozessen benutzt (*uti*) Luther konstruktiv die rationale Urteilskraft (z. B. Disputationen), die kritisch philologisch-exegetische Methode zur Vertiefung theologischen Verstehens (*Geist und Buchstabe*) und naturrechtliche und philosophische Denkformen (*causa-Schema*) in der auf das Wohl der konkreten Menschen (Arme, Notleidende u. a.) bezogenen Sozialethik (*Billigkeit* u. a.) mit dem *Gebot der Nächstenliebe*. Der Glaube führt die Vernunft durch rationale hermeneutische Prozesse in *Entsprechung und Widerspruch* »zum bade«, d. h. als Weisheit der Theologie durch den Weg vernünftiger Urteils- und Entscheidungsfindung.

D) *Coram deo*, d. h. für das Heil durch Gottes Gnade in der Rechtfertigung der Sünders, vermag die Vernunft nichts. Unter der Macht der Sünde und im Sog des Unglaubens steht sie, selbstrechtfertigend und werkgerecht pervertiert, unter dem *usus theologicus legis* Gottes, des Gottes, dem allein die Ehre (*frui*) zukommt und der im Zum-Wort-Kommen seine Existenz in Gericht und Gnade erweist, wie der Glaube bekennt.

E) Das *Evangelium* lässt die im Glauben befreite und *erleuchtete*

Vernunft philologischen Schriftverständnisses die *Sache* und die *Summe* der Glaubenswissenschaft vertiefen und schafft als *verbum creatrix divinitatis* das in Zeit und Ewigkeit geltende Einverständnis mit der persönlichen Rechtfertigung allein aus Gnade um Christi willen durch den Glauben.

A Postmodern Luther? *Enarrationes in Genesin* in Conversation with Philosophical and Theological Reconsiderations

Seminar Leaders: Paul R. Hinlicky and Mickey L. Mattox

Reporter: Phillip Anderas

This seminar engaged Luther's *Enarrationes in Genesin* (1535–1545) along roughly two lines of inquiry: (1) How might the postmodern turn open up new avenues for research into the historical Luther's thought? (2) How might Luther's thought contribute to a constructive post-modern theology?

Mark Mattes addressed the theme of faith and reason. Luther praised reason highly within the sphere of its earthly competence. He also held that, when schooled by the grammar of faith, reason could become a fit servant of public inquiry into theological truth. Left untutored, however, reason tends to transgress its proper bounds (e.g. *in articulo iustificationis*). Luther therefore shied from strategies of correlation and analogy that sought commensurability between faith and reason. Instead, he favored a kind of scripturally-ruled Dionysian apophaticism that endured the contradictions of reason in order to celebrate the joyful paradoxes of the Gospel. As neither rationalist nor irrationalist, Luther charts a path for theologians seeking to ground their work, not in the eccentricities of experience, but in the objectivity of the Word.

Jennifer Hockenbery Dragseth compared Augustinc and Luther on various loci suggested by their respective exegeses of Genesis 1–2, e.g. Augustine's more contemplative orientation toward eternity versus Luther's historical timefulness; simultaneous versus successive theories of creation; allegorical versus literal-historical hermeneutics; and, decisively, the aspiration for spiritual ascent *ex mundo* characteristic of Platonism's metaphysical axiology of The Good versus the this-worldliness of faithful life in *oeconomia et politia* issuing from the sheer imputation of goodness bestowed in justification. In this last instance, the contrast between Augustine's philosophical essentialism and Luther's proto-existentialism emerges as the underlying explanation of their respective differences.

Dennis Bielfeldt argued that, in Luther's theology of creation, God acted causally to create all that is out of nothing. Previous scholarship has allowed its own modern assumptions about causality and ontology to obscure Luther's basic continuity with late medieval semantic and metaphysical theory. Johannes Schwanke,[1] for example, argues that Luther's *creatio ex nihilo* should be interpreted not primarily in the theoretical terms of ontological causality, but rather as expressive of the existential relationship of absolute dependence (*schlechthinnige Abhängigkeit*) obtaining between creature and Creator. On the basis of close textual analysis of the *Enarrationes*,[2] Bielfeldt demonstrates that in fact Luther was a realist who believed God created causally, and suggests that it is this real causal relation that forms the prior ontological condition for the creature's *Gefühl* of absolute dependence upon God.

Kjell Ove Nilsson reflected on Luther's understanding of the *mandatum dei* in its intrinsic relatedness to the human person. For Luther, abstract metaphysical thought about either the divine or the human is impossible, for to be human means to exist under God's will and to receive one's total existence from God. God's *mandatum* is his creative Word, the very principle of life, through which humans are rightly related to God and the world. Since its *raison d'être* is the mystery of the human created to live in indissoluble communion with God, its content is not re-

---

1 J. SCHWANKE, Creatio ex nihilo. Luthers Lehre von der Schöpfung aus dem Nichts in der großen Genesisvorlesung (1535–45), 2004.

2 E.g. WA 42; 8,31–33; 13,16–19; 37,16–22.

ceived as discrete and manipulable data (whether by *lex naturae* rationalistically construed, or by *lex scripta* in a fundamentalist sense) but discovered and experienced as an existential factor suffusing and forming everyday human life.

Knut Alfsvåg brought insights from Luther's exegesis of the story of the Tower of Babel to bear on the incredulity toward meta-narrative and predilection for alterity characteristic of postmodernity. Luther regarded linguistic difference as the result of the divine punishment of human self-glorification recounted in Genesis 11. Because he thought language structured and constituted reality rather than merely reflecting it, this loss of linguistic unity was for Luther an especially baneful happening in human history. For linguistic conflict leads to political and ecclesial division, and inexorably so: apart, that is, from the hope of humanity's restoration to holy harmony through the Evangelical and Pentecostal *nova lingua* spoken by Jesus Christ. Whereas postmodernity's celebration of difference is ultimately self-defeating – for difference itself becomes a universal concept (»Alterity«), no less totalizing than the classical or modern predecessors which it means to dethrone – Luther's deeply suggestive presen-

tation of Christ's *nova lingua* – as unifying truth that coexists with cultural and linguistic difference without being conquered by it – secures the very goal, or receives the very gift, that postmodernity strives vainly to attain.

Mickey Mattox re-examined Luther's interpretation of Abraham's unique role in history as the *gubernator tertii millenarii* in light of the Reformer's apocalypticism. For Luther, Abraham is not only a choice case study in the doctrines of election and justification, but an eschatological gatekeeper of a radically new age in the history of the unfolding of the Promise. His singularity as *gubernator* consists in his receiving the *nova promissio* that the Messiah will descend from his own flesh. This promise is confirmed in his encounter with Melchizedek, the »King of Righteousness,« in whom Abraham glimpses the eschatological kingdom and eternal priesthood of Jesus Christ. Reading Abraham in this way afforded Luther the occasion to interpret his own position in the last days of an earth grown old. If the fierceness and assuredness of Luther's apocalyptically-charged polemic gives reason to pause, his admirable determination to situate his own life within the overarching context of eschatological origins and ends challenges an earth grown purposeless and bored.

Jeffrey Silcock mined Luther's exegesis of the story of Jacob's Ladder for resources with which to revise modern metaphysical assumptions. Following medieval precedent, Luther explains that the ladder signifies literally the incarnation of God's Son, allegorically the union of Christ and the believer by faith, and spiritually the worshipping Church gathered around Word and Sacrament as the *porta coeli* on earth. Particularly this latter, earthly localizing of God's presence, strikes the modern ear as downright untoward, predisposed as it is to privilege inwardness and downplay external things as (at best) mere starting points for more elevated forms of spirituality. But with the help of Luther's theological exegesis and Johann Georg Hamann's (1730–1788) genuinely Lutheran philosophy, the post-modern thinker can begin to re-imagine a robustly scriptural and sacramental ontology that welcomes the *perichoresis* of spiritual and material reality.

Phillip Anderas explored Luther's theology of holiness on the basis of his exegesis of Jacob's *summa tentatio* at the Ford Jabbok in Genesis 32. Luther states expressly that Jacob's sanctification involves the death of the stubborn remnants of his »old Adam« in temptation. But when considered in light of the Reformer's proto-logical anthropology, it becomes clear that Jacob's triumphant victory over God by faith entails nothing less than his restoration to the natural holiness enjoyed originally by Adam before the Fall. According to Luther, God's *donum Spiritus et fidei* finds in Jacob a vitiated shadow of what Adam was created to be, and restores him *per contraria* to that act which is his nature's perfection: that is, to faith's eucharistic sacrifice, offered to the praise of God's glory by a redeemed and deified heart radiant with drunken joy in God.

Paul Hinlicky discussed Luther's reconsideration of God's power, wisdom, and goodness in regard to his theodicy of faith, as epitomized in the story of Joseph. Luther did not criticize *ratio*'s fleshly metaphysical speculation because it grasps nothing true at all about divine attributes, but because it cannot grasp these very truths truly (like a cow staring at a new door). A new theological subjectivity, fluent in the *nova lingua* of the Spirit, must come into being in order for Joseph to hold on to a practical knowledge of God's power, wisdom, and goodness amidst affliction and suffering. When Joseph is abandoned by the Spirit into the world's cruel hands but remains steadfast through the »patiency« of faith, he is in fact created anew by God in true righteousness and holiness, conformed to the image of Christ. Only thus does he come to know in truth the fiery (and complex) furnace of the Holy Trinity's power, wisdom, and love.

Ralf Wüstenberg assayed traces of Luther's thought in the political ethics of Dietrich Bonhoeffer (1906–1945). Bonhoeffer follows Luther in articulating a »theology of distinctions,« e.g. worldly-spiritual, preservation-redemption, office-person. On the other hand, he also follows Luther, though not the Lutheranism of his days, in resisting any clean break between the worldly and the spiritual; for God's preservation of the world is ordered to its redemption. But Bonhoeffer does maintain a certain openness in his reinterpretation of Luther's doctrine of the two kingdoms via his distinction between ultimate and penultimate things. For Bonhoeffer, it is possible to see ultimate things *within* the penultimate, that is, to recognize signs of Christ's forgiveness within the scope of the political.

Perhaps it is fitting that no single master-narrative united the themes of the seminar. That said, the working thesis that sees in postmodernity an opportune moment for reappraising Luther's thought was generally well received. The more spirited conversations tended to come back to divergent responses to a basic question: ought the theologian take advantage of the postmodern situation to *retrieve* a substantially pre-modern theology? Or instead, should he or she *revise* traditional positions in novel directions? Of course, an assuredly correct answer to that question is ultimately eschatological.

Martin Luther's and Philip Melanchthon's Aristotle

Seminar Leader: Theodor Dieter

Reporter: Theodor Dieter

In recent years, several studies have contributed to overcoming widespread stereotypes concerning Luther's relation to philosophy and »Aristotle.« They do not start with a contemporary understanding of Aristotelian philosophy but ask what Luther had in mind when he used the name »Aristotle.« These analyses of his conflicts with and his reception of »Aristotle« allow for deeper insights into both Luther's theology and the positions to which he referred. A rapidly increasing interest in philosophical problems within Protestant theology has allowed for dealing with the philosophical contents and debates in Reformation theology with fewer prejudices than before. The fact that Melanchthon often commented on Aristotelian texts and made positive use of the ideas of this philosopher is now seen in a more open-minded way. It seems remarkable that Luther and Melanchthon worked side by side while having such different attitudes towards »Aristotle.« The intention of this seminar was to present new insights into Luther's and Melanchthon's views of »Aristotle.« The participants reported on their respective research. Topics were very different in terms of content and methodology.

Theodor Dieter (Strasbourg) elaborated on Luther's famous saying: »Non enim, ut Aristoteles putat, iusta agendo iusti efficimur, sed iusti […] fiendo et essendo operamur iusta.« This has often been taken in order to identify the basic difference between Aristotle's and Luther's ontology. But Luther himself became aware that Aristotle spoke only about civil righteousness, while for scholastics like Gabriel Biel morally good acts gained significance for salvation through the *pactum Dei* (*facienti quod in se est* …). Only through this theological reception could the Aristotelian concept of becoming just receive a soteriological meaning. In fact, the decisive point was the understanding of human freedom. But Luther would not have needed to deny this claim; it would have been enough to emphasize that a morally good act is something quite different from fulfilling the law of God in a theological sense. After the condemnations of 1277 in Paris, the concept of human freedom was further developed but as a criticism of an alleged Aristotelian tradition of necessitarianism. Luther could find that understanding of freedom (critical of Aristotle) in commentaries on the *Nicomachean Ethics* (e.g. Buridan's). Thus Luther criticized an anti-Aristotelian concept of freedom as if it was Aristotle's own view.

Timothy Dost (Clayton) pointed to Luther's critique of Aristotle in the theological theses of the *Heidelberg Disputation*. He emphasized that Luther used scholastic techniques in order to criticize Aristotelizing scholastics while he himself was prone to employ Renaissance humanism and presented himself as being less critical of Plato.

In order to define Luther's and Agricola's understanding of the relation between law and gospel in the Antinomian controversy, *Annelise Eeman* (Chicago) made use of the Aristotelian terms »correlative« (for Luther) and »contradictory« (for Agricola). In her dissertation she elaborates that for Luther law and gospel require each other and only together form a whole or, as she says, a co-constitutive, dynamic system.

Markus Matthias (Amsterdam) developed the thesis that Luther's understanding of *experientia* can be understood with respect to and to a certain degree in line with Aristotle's concept of *experientia*. In the latter, *experientia* has a mediating role between the many individual occurrences and the respective common concepts, while in Luther's concept doctrinal truth gains or increases its certainty by being applied to concrete situations of life. In addition, Luther often appeals to *experientia* in order to falsify a certain claim, e.g. that human beings by their own power are able to love God above all. From early on, Luther understood theology as a form of »practical« knowledge as it was later seen in Lutheran Orthodoxy.

Matti Nikkanen (Helsinki) reported about his dissertation project *Ecclesia, oeconomia, politia. Eine Untersuchung zur Ideengeschichte der altlutherischen Dreiständelehre.* This study investigates whether there was an Aristotelian-Lutheran political or social doctrine in the 16th and 17th centuries that can be traced back to Luther's and Melanchthon's interpretation of Aristotle. Nikkanen presented Aristotle's theory of *polis* with reference to his metaphysics and compared it with Luther's social theory as it can be found in his Genesis lectures, identifying both structural analogies and differences. This suggests that Luther's theory of the three estates may have depended on Aristotle's social thought.

How are we to understand the phenomenon, notion, and function of »conscience?« *Claudia Welz* (Copenhagen) investigated this question by comparing two influential approaches, namely Martin Luther's and Martin Heidegger's. Both of them connect the movements of volition, emotion, and cognition taking place in conscience with Aristotle's notion of *phrónêsis*. If conscience can be seen as a sphere of intentionality, of moving willingly, of being-moved passionately, and of understanding oneself as being in union or division with oneself, conscience conditions human action in one way or another – but what does this imply for the ethical significance of conscience in relation to its soteriological and ontological meaning?

Robert von Friedeburg (Rotterdam) dealt with *Melanchthon's Aristotle: His 1531/32 Comment on Book V of Aristotle's Nicomachean Ethics*. Under the title *De iustitia particularis*, Melanchthon introduces the distinction between natural and positive law that cannot be found in Aristotle's text. In addition, he provides a detailed catalogue of six natural laws so that it became a law code (»Rechtsregel,« M. Schmoeckel) as foundation of any positive law. The understanding that natural law is inscribed as *notitiae* in our souls gains increasing significance for Melanchthon in the course of time.

Mads Jensen (London) argued that existing scholarship has missed Melanchthon's central objective in writing the 1530 *Commentarii in aliquot politicos libros Aristotelis*. Rather than merely criticizing peasants and radical preachers, Melanchthon sought to refute the Ockhamist political thought of Gabriel Biel and John Mair. Using Aristotle's naturalism within the theological framework of the political order as ordained by God, Melanchthon criticized the conventionalist account of the Ockhamists, specifically the arguments underlying the case for popular sovereignty or the power of the community over the ruler. Instead, he forwarded a theory of politics and constitutional monarchy grounded in natural law with the ruler as the representative of God.

John A. Maxfield (Edmonton) analyzed Melanchthon's preface to the first volume of Luther's *Lectures on Genesis*, 1544 (WA 44; XIV-XX). He interpreted Melanchthon's use of philosophy as follows: Plato, Aristotle, and other philosophers from the ancient world are not viewed as authorities, in natural philosophy any more than in theology, but rather are ancient witnesses who thought about the existence and nature of God in relation to creation. Different from the scholastics was that Melanchthon was not focusing on reconciling various ancient authorities with Scripture through the method of the *quaestio*, but rather simply cites their ideas, often with criticism, as he presents a view based on the Bible and emphasizes the centrality of the Bible for understanding God and man.

Joar Haga (Oslo) investigated Melanchthon's treatment of immortality in his 1540 commentary on Aristotle's psychology. This entailed a different attitude towards the Greek philosopher than his Wittenberg colleague, Martin Luther had. While two decades earlier Luther had accused Aristotle of being responsible for the corruption of theology, Melanchthon had a far more friendly approach to Aristotle, except concerning the understanding of the soul's immortality. From Cicero, Melanchthon adopted the concept of *endelechia* as a fitting description for the soul as the form of the body. The reason for leaving Aristotle's *entelechia* lies in the possibility of removing the soul from the corruptible body. Being closely related to the concepts of potentiality and actuality, *entelechia* was not easy to combine with the Christian understanding of the soul's capacity of an afterlife, formulated in the doctrine of the resurrection. It tied the soul to the physical body. With the Neoplatonic concept of *endelechia* from Cicero, however, Melanchthon can claim that the soul is not merely the form of the body. It adds a notion of perpetual motion, describing the soul as a process which is not accomplished in this life but only in heaven. Thus, Melanchthon rescues the Aristotelian doctrine of the soul from its pagan materialism. He is not primarily interested in the exegesis of Aristotle's text, but uses it as a starting point for his own Neoplatonic position informed by Christian theology.

Luther – Katholik und Reformer?!

Seminarleiter: Wolfgang Thönissen und Augustinus Sander OSB

Berichterstatter: Wolfgang Thönissen und Augustinus Sander OSB

I Zusammenfassung

Wolfgang Thönissen gab einen einführenden Überblick über die katholische Lutherforschung des 20. Jahrhunderts und präsentierte den derzeitigen Stand des katholisch-lutherischen Dialogs. *Augustinus Sander OSB* stellte seinen Ansatz der konfessorisch-katholischen Lutherinterpretation vor und verdeutlichte diesen am Beispiel der eucharistischen Realpräsenz, des diözesanen Bischofsamtes und des Kirchenverständnisses im frühen Luthertum. Am Seminar nahmen teil *Kaarlo Arffman, Oswald Bayer, Juhani Forsberg, Günter Frank, Eero Huovinen, Tomi Karttunen, Jonathan Mumme, Simo Peura* und *Stefan Rhein.*

II Überblick über die katholische Lutherforschung des 20. Jahrhunderts vorgetragen von Wolfgang Thönissen

Die katholische Lutherforschung des 20. Jahrhunderts verdankt sich dem neuerwachten Interesse katholischer Theologen an reformationsgeschichtlicher Forschung seit der zweiten Hälfte des 19. Jahrhunderts. Die Auseinandersetzung des deutschen Katholizismus folgte dem Bestreben der katholischen Bevölkerung im protestantisch geprägten deutschen Reich, durch die Gründung historischer Institute und die Aufnahme gründlicher historischer Quellenarbeit die vor- und nachreformationsgeschichtliche Forschung von der Hypothek einer einseitigen antirömischen Geschichtsschreibung zu befreien. Nachdem der junge Bonner Privatdozent Dr. Joseph Greving 1906 durch die Gründung der *Reformationsgeschichtlichen Studien und Texte* sich dem »Begriff« der Reformation zugewandt hatte, gelang der Durchbruch für die katholische Lutherforschung im 20. Jahrhundert durch die Arbeiten von Joseph Lortz und Adolf Herte. Lortz prägte durch sein mehrfach aufgelegtes Buch über *Die Reformation in Deutschland* (1939/40) gegen anfänglich nicht geringe innerkatholische Widerstände das katholische Lutherbild wie kein anderer durch die Ausarbeitung der These vom katholischen Luther. Lortzens Schüler Peter Manns suchte Luther als Vater im Glauben zu verstehen, wobei Luther die Wahrheit im Glauben in für die Kirche unannehmbar erscheinende Formulierungen gekleidet habe. Adolf Herte, dem eine größere Öffentlichkeit versagt blieb, konnte hingegen durch mühevolle historische Kleinarbeiten aufzeigen, dass die katholische Lutherliteratur über vier Jh.e bis in die Neuzeit hinein durch die Kommentare des Johannes Cochläus, eines zeitgenössischen Gegners Luthers und Berater des Herzogs Georg von Sachsen, geprägt war, der Luther als abgefallenen Mönch, als Zerstörer der Kircheneinheit, als Sittenverderber und Häretiker charakterisiert hatte; Urteile, wie sie in der Bulle Papst Leos X. *Exsurge Domini* von 1520 und in der Exkommunikations-Bulle *Decet Romanum Pontificem* von 1521 vorgeprägt waren. Die katholische Lutherforschung vom Bann solch einseitiger Lutherkommentare und -biographien zu befreien, ist die Leistung dieser ersten kritisch-wohlwollenden Auseinandersetzungen mit Luthers Persönlichkeit.

Der neueren Lutherforschung seit den 1970er Jahren mit Otto Hermann Pesch gelingt es auf dem Weg einer systematisch arbeitenden Kontroverstheologie, exemplarisch durchgeführt am nicht historisch zu verstehenden Gespräch zwischen den konfessionellen Exponenten Thomas von Aquin und Martin Luther, in der unvermittelten Konfrontation der Denkformen die zunächst unentdeckt gebliebene Komplementarität ihrer Theologien aufzudecken. Die typologisch-hermeneutische Methodik der systematisch arbeitenden Luther- und reformationsgeschichtlichen Forschung erweiterte Vinzenz Pfnür um die Frage nach der Bedeutung der Rechtfertigungslehre der Confessio Augustana für die Frage nach dem »eigentlich Reformatorischen«. Früchte trug diese weit über ein Jahrhundert sich erstreckende Forschungsarbeit in zweierlei Hinsicht. Zwar kommt in den Texten des Zweiten Vatikanischen Konzils der Name Martin Luthers nicht vor, doch ist unbestreitbar, dass dieses Konzil einige zentrale Einsichten seiner Theologie aufgenommen und verarbeitet hat, so u. a. die Hochschätzung und Verehrung der Heiligen Schrift im Leben der Kirche, die Wiederentdeckung des allgemeinen Priestertums, das Verständnis des kirchlichen Amtes als Dienst, die Erneuerungsbedürftigkeit der Kirche. Diese implizite Verständigung mit

Luther ermöglichte dann im Zusammenhang mit der Anerkennung seines Reformwillens eine neue Bewertung seiner Katholizität, wie sie insbesondere in den Äußerungen von Johannes Kardinal Willebrands und Papst Johannes Paul II. zu finden sind. Die Wiederentdeckung dieser beiden zentralen Charakteristika seiner Person und Theologie führt zu einer neuen ökumenischen Verständigung über Luther als »Zeuge des Evangeliums«.

III Konfessorisch-katholische Lutherinterpretation vorgetragen von Augustinus Sander OSB

Das Reformanliegen Luthers und der Wittenberger Reformbewegung ist vom Ansatz her nicht konfessionell, sondern konfessorisch ausgerichtet. D.h.: Der von Luther und dem frühen Luthertum eingenommene *status confessionis* bleibt zunächst innerkatholisch verortet, zielt aber nicht von vornherein auf die Konstituierung einer eigenständigen Konfessionskirche. Für die Quelleninterpretation bedeutet dies: Das konfessorische Profil ersetzt nicht den bisherigen katholisch-ekklesialen Kontext; es setzt ihn, wo er nicht ausdrücklich in Frage gestellt wird, vielmehr ganz selbstverständlich voraus.

Die Wittenberger Reformbewegung konstatiert die Reform-Bedürftigkeit der katholischen Kirche unter der Voraussetzung ihrer prinzipiellen Reform-Fähigkeit. Kontinuität und Erneuerung bedeuten hier keine Gegensätze, sondern bilden die notwendigen Pole konfessorischer Katholizität.

Nun kann freilich nicht geleugnet werden, dass die konfessorische Bedeutung der Wittenberger Reformtheologie in der Folgezeit unterschiedlich rezipiert wird und zunächst eine konfessionalisierende Transformation erfährt. Im Prozess der Konfessionsbildung wird der »*confessor*« Martin Luther zum Kirchengründer und die ursprünglich innerkatholisch verortete »*confessio*« – insbesondere die Confessio Augustana – zur Gründungsurkunde einer eigenständigen lutherischen Kirche, anders formuliert: Dem Bekenntnis wächst eine neue Bedeutung zu; es ist nicht mehr länger Zeugnis für die konfessorische Katholizität der Wittenberger Reformbewegung, sondern wird zum Dokument konfessionskirchlicher Identität und Partikularität.[1]

---

1 »Ab 1586 erscheint ›lutherische Kirche‹ in Württemberg und Kursachsen als Bez[eich-

Von diesem konfessionalisierten Luthertum, das, trotz aller Frontstellung gegenüber Rom, in Theologie und Liturgie weiterhin durchaus katholische Züge tragen konnte, sie im Blick auf das Reformiertentum mitunter auch kultivierte, ist noch einmal das protestantisierte[2] zu unterscheiden. Wurde im konfessionellen Luthertum das Bekenntnis in seiner konfessorischen Katholizität zwar auf gewisse Weise eingeschränkt, so wird es im kritischen Protestantismus nun selbst zum Gegenstand der Kritik. Unter Luthertum versteht man dann nur mehr eine Richtung innerhalb eines insgesamt profiliert antikatholischen Protestantismus. In Folge der protestantischen Unionen des 19. Jahrhunderts verlieren reformiert-lutherische Lehrunterschiede als Schulmeinungen ihren kirchentrennenden Charakter, wobei die dem protestantischen Prinzip widersprechenden Inkonsequenzen Luthers, etwa in der Sakramentologie, der Amtstheologie und der Ekklesiologie, gerne als biographisch bedingte, nicht überwundene »katholische Restbestände« eingeordnet werden.

Die konfessionalisierende und die protestantisierende Transformation der ursprünglich konfessorisch-vorkonfessionellen Wittenberger Reformtheologie sind nicht einfach nur als einander ablösende rezeptionsgeschichtliche Perioden aufzufassen. Vielmehr wird man für das heutige Luthertum die faktische Gleichzeitigkeit unterschiedlicher Rezeptionsweisen festhalten können sowie u. U. die Bildung gemeinsamer inhaltlicher Schnittmengen trotz verschiedener theologischer Ansätze.

Mag die vorkonfessionelle konfessorisch-katholische Lutherinterpretation angesichts bestehender Konfessionskirchen historisch überholt sein, theologisch ist ihre transkonfessionelle Bedeutung – und damit ihre ökumenische Relevanz – noch längst nicht eingeholt.

---

nung] der Kirche, die sich auf Luthers ›reine Lehre des Evangeliums‹ beruft« (A. Birmelé, Art. Luthertum [LThK³ 6, 2006, 1143–1149], 1143).

2 Reinhard Frieling weist darauf hin, dass »v[or] a[llem] bewußte Lutheraner im Begriff P[rotestantismus] eine verschwommene unierte od[er] ökum[enische] Konfessionsbez[eichnung] [sehen], die sich mit ihrer luth[erischen] Identität nicht deckt« (R. Frieling, Art. Protestantismus I. Begriff [LThK³ 8, 2006, 655 f], 655).

Buchbesprechungen

THOMAS KAUFMANN: Der Anfang der Reformation. Studien zur Kontextualität der Theologie, Publizistik und Inszenierung Luthers und der reformatorischen Bewegung. Tübingen: Mohr Siebeck, 2012. XVIII, 676 S. m. Abb. (Spätmittelalter, Humanismus, Reformation / Studies in the Late Middle Ages, Humanism and the Reformation; 67)

Der Beginn der reformatorischen Bewegung stellt die Forschung stets vor die Frage: Wie konnte aus Luthers Ablass- und Romkritik die Reformation werden? Die Erklärungsversuche sind zahlreich und setzen – je nach Sichtweise – mit Luthers Biographie und Theologie, mit den zeitgenössischen Reformtendenzen in Wissenschaft, Kirche und Gesellschaft oder den dominierenden Verbreitungsmedien Predigt und Flugschriften an. Von diesen am Inhalt oder Medium orientierten historiografischen Interpretationskonzepten der Reformation und ihrer Einheit hebt sich der Ansatz einer »Kontextuellen Reformation« ab, den Thomas Kaufmann im ersten Kapitel (1–27) des vorliegenden Werkes entfaltet. Wie bereits in seinem 2009 erschienenen grundsoliden Werk »Geschichte der Reformation« erprobt, setzt der Göttinger Kirchenhistoriker bei den individuellen und sozialen Reformationsak-

teuren sowie deren Strategien und Aneignungspraktiken an.

Gegenüber dem sich nicht nur im angloamerikanischen Forschungskontext verbreitenden pluralen Sprachgebrauch der Reformation*en* folgt K. einem Verständnis von Reformation, das sich dem »Konzept der in sich pluralen, gleichwohl einen spezifischen und einheitlichen historischen Zusammenhang bildenden, untereinander mannigfach vernetzten territorialen, lokalen, regionalen und nationalen Veränderungsprozesse als *der* Reformation« (3) verpflichtet sieht. Weil sich insbesondere in der Frühzeit höchst komplexe Interaktionen zwischen diesen Entwicklungssträngen abspielten, erscheint für K. die Reformation als ein »dynamischer Prozess literarisch-publizistischer bzw. aktional-inszenatorischer Interaktionen, der wesentlich von häufig kaum mehr sichtbar zu machenden Mobilitätsmomenten bestimmt und geprägt« (ebd.) war. Mit dem Begriff der »Kontextuellen Reformation« sucht K. diesen auf Kommunikationsnetzwerken und Mobilitätsstrukturen basierenden Interaktionsprozess zwischen lokalen, regionalen, territorialen und nationalen sowie sozialen und sprachlichen Kontexten zu verdichten, durch den sich die reformatorische Bewegung und »schließlich ›die Reformation‹ in der Vielfalt ihrer spezifischen Aneignungs- und Auslegungsgestalten« (5) formte.

Diesen theoretischen, »einer konsequenten Historisierung« seines Gegenstandes verpflichteten Ansatz (18) entfaltet K. in drei Teilen. Während sich der erste Teil unter dem Stichwort »Traditionskonstruktionen« verschiedenen Momenten der Aneignung reformatorischen Gedankengutes und Konstruktionen von Tradition zuwendet, geht es im zweiten Teil unter der Überschrift »Kommunikationsdynamiken« um »die frühreformatorische Dynamisierung der Kommunikation mit publizistischen und disputatorischen Mitteln« (26). Der dritte Abschnitt wendet sich schließlich den innerreformatorischen »Lehrbildungen und Identitätsentwürfe[n]« zu. Unter diesen drei Leitkategorien versammelt K. insgesamt 15 Aufsätze, von denen fünf – mit den einführenden Prolegomena sechs – hier erstmals veröffentlicht werden. Die übrigen, bereits an anderer Stelle publizierten Beiträge sind größtenteils sorgfältig überarbeitet und durch neuere Literatur ergänzt worden, so dass hier mehr als ein rein thematischer Sammelband vorliegt.

Im ersten Teil (29–163) werden vier Themenfelder verhandelt: »Häresiologie« (Jan Hus und die reformatorische Bewegung), »Bibeltheologie« (Vorreformatorische Laienbibel und reformatorisches Evangelium), »Religionshermeneutik« (Spätmittelalterliche und reformatorische Wahrnehmung des Islams) und – hier neu – »Politiktheorie« (Theokratische Konzeptionen in der spätmittelalterlichen Reformliteratur und in der Radikalen Reformation).

Der m. E. innovativste Teil bildet der zweite Abschnitt (165–434), welcher schon allein von der quantitativen Gestalt her am umfänglichsten ausfällt und größtenteils Erstpublikationen enthält. Überzeugend erörtert K. in dem als »Ausgangsszenario«

(166–184) titulierten Eingangskapitel »Luthers 95 Thesen in ihrem historischen Zusammenhang«, indem er sie konsequent kontextuell verortet. Das Konzept einer »Kontextuellen Reformation« gewinnt gerade in diesem und in den folgenden Kapiteln an Plausibilität. Die Themen reichen von »Aktionale[n] Aneignungen« (Die studentische Reformation) über »Stilisierungen« (Die Heroisierung Luthers in Wort und Bild), »Argumentative Impressionen« (Bucers Bericht von der Heidelberger Disputation) bis hin zur »Publizistische[n] Mobilisierung« (Anonyme Flugschriften der frühen Reformation). Für den Lutherforscher bilden K.s Ausführungen zur Heroisierung Luthers in der frühen Reformation eine anregende Fundgrube. Durch zahlreiche Bildbeispiele verdeutlicht, skizziert K., wie Luther als »martyriumsbereiter Kämpfer gegen viele Feinde« zum Helden wird (329). Parallel zu dieser Entwicklung beobachtet K. bei Humanisten und schweizerisch-südwestdeutschen Reformatoren von Anfang an Tendenzen einer »Entheroisierung im Sinne einer Kontextualisierung und Historisierung« (ebd.), betont aber zugleich, dass die Heroisierungen bzw. Entheroisierungen in eine Vielzahl reformatorischer Strategien einzuordnen sind und z. T. in einer unvermittelten Spannung zu theologischen Grundaussagen Luthers stehen. Die Thesen, dass mit Beginn der innerreformatorischen Abendmahlsdebatte im Herbst 1524 und mit dem Bauernkrieg »eine tiefgreifende Veränderung in der Bewertung Luthers« (331) erfolgte und dass die Zukunft »nicht dem heroisierten, sondern dem monumentalisierten Luther« (ebd.) gehörte, wären wert, vertieft zu werden.

Im dritten Teil (435–605) versammelt K. verschiedenartige Beiträge zur reformatorischen Lehre und Lebenswelt, welche folgende Themen verhandeln: »Theologisch-philosophische Rationalität« (Die Ehre der Hure. Zum vernünftigen Gottesgedanken in der Reformation), »Integrale Existenz« (Lehre und Leben in der sog. Radikalen Reformation der frühen 1520er Jahre), »Ekklesiologische Revolution« (Das Priestertum der Glaubenden in der frühreformatorischen Publizistik – Wittenberger und Basler Beispiele), »Reformation der Lebenswelt« (Luthers Ehetheologie), »Personale Identitätskonstruktionen« (›Erfahrungsmuster‹ in der frühen Reformation) sowie »Fragmentarische Existenz« (Der »alte« und der »junge« Luther als theologisches Problem).

In ihrer Materialfülle, die z.T. durch den Abdruck einzelner Quellen bereichert wird, und in ihrer Gedankendichte sind K.s Reformationsstudien allesamt anregend und der kontextuell-interdisziplinären Lutherforschung höchst förderlich. Ein umfangreiches Personen-, Orts- und Sachregister rundet ein gewichtiges Werk ab, das der Erforschung der Reformation neue Perspektiven eröffnet.

Jena   Christopher Spehr

BIRGIT STOLT: »Laßt uns fröhlich springen!« Gefühlswelt und Gefühlsnavigierung in Luthers Reformationsarbeit. Eine kognitive Emotionalitätsanalyse auf philologischer Basis. Berlin: Weidler Buchverlag, 2012. 350 S. m. Abb. (Studium Litterarum; 21)

Luthers Sprache ist eine emotionale Sprache, die zu Herzen geht und vom Herzen handelt. Sie kann sowohl frohe Stimmungen hervorrufen, als auch durch finstere Ausdrücke Momente des Fürchtens erzeugen. Sensibilisiert für den Facettenreichtum der lateinischen wie deutschen Sprache, ge-

schult am Lehr- und Lebensbuch der Psalmen und ausgestattet mit begnadeter Kreativität wirkte Luther sprachschöpfend in seinen Schriften, insbesondere beim Dolmetschen der Bibel.

Die Stockholmer Germanistin und Lutherforscherin Birgit Stolt, welche u.a. in dem Buch »Martin Luthers Rhetorik des Herzens« (2000) die Herzensdimension der Luthersprache eindrücklich herausarbeitete (siehe LuJ 69, 149f), wendet sich in ihrem neusten Werk programmatisch der Gefühlswelt in Luthers Reformationsarbeit zu. Dabei greift sie Impulse der seit mehreren Jahrzehnten tätigen Emotionalitätswissenschaft auf und macht sie für die Lutherforschung fruchtbar.

In charmanter und gut lesbarer Weise entfaltet S. diese spezifische Akzentuierung in zwei Teilen, die auch unabhängig voneinander rezipierbar sind. Während sie im ersten Teil (11–142) die Gefühlswelt Luthers durch die Erkenntnisse der gegenwärtigen Emotionalitätsforschung interpretiert, pointiert S. diese Beobachtungen im zweiten Teil (143–341) anhand konkreter Fallstudien zu Luthers Bibelübersetzung. Weil die in elf Kapiteln gegliederten Studien des zweiten Teils zwischen 1980 und 2002 bereits an anderen Orten publiziert wurden, kann auf eine vertiefende Vorstellung hier verzichtet werden. Gleichwohl bieten die Fallstudien nicht nur eine übersichtliche Zusammenstellung provokanter Titel wie »Hier irrt der Lutherforscher« (147) und programmatischer Texte wie »Kulturbarrieren als Verständnisproblem« (159), sondern ermöglichen auch eine Zusammenschau gewichtiger Beiträge aus der Feder der renommierten Germanistin. Für den von der EKD beauftragten Lenkungsausschuss zur »Durchsicht der Lutherbibel« samt seinen exegetischen Arbeitsgruppen, welche an einer 2017 abgeschlossenen neuen Fassung der Lutherbibel arbeiten, sollten S.s Untersuchungen zur Pflichtlektüre gehören.

Der erste Teil widmet sich der Emotionalitätsarbeit Luthers. Ausgehend von der spätmittelalterlich-ikonographischen Darstellung Gottes, der mit Pfeilen auf die Sünder schießt, und Marias, die den Sündern unter ihrem die Pfeile abwehrenden Schutzmantel Geborgenheit bietet, richtet S. ihre Aufmerksamkeit auf den Gefühlswandel Luthers – vom richtenden zum gnädigen Gott. Dieses veränderte Gottes- und Christusbild habe einen grundstürzenden Wechsel bei Luther und seinen Anhängern für den Prozess der Reformation hervorgerufen: »Es galt, das ›Grundgefühl ›Angst‹ durch ein ›Grundgefühl ›vertrauensvolle Liebe‹ zu ersetzen.« (14). Von den gegenwärtigen Emotionalitätsforschungen Martha Nussbaums und Monika Schwarz-Friesels her akzentuiert S. die Frage nach dem Umgang mit Emotionen (»the navigation of feeling«) (17) und plädiert aus sprachwissenschaftlicher Perspektive für eine »emotive Wende« in der Lutherforschung (18).

Was S. hierunter versteht, erläutert sie am Begriff des Herzens, das für Luther stets die Gesamtpersönlichkeit – bestehend aus »intellectus et affectus« – meint und die enge Verbindung zwischen Gedanken und Gefühlen hervorhebt. Nicht ohne Grund sei daher das Herz der Sitz des Glaubens. »Affectus« umfasse näherhin den gesamten Gefühlsbereich, welcher folglich von S. durch das Begriffsfeld »Emotion, Affekt, Gefühl« erschlossen wird. Hilfreich ist in diesem Zusammenhang die methodische Beobachtung, dass Gefühlswörtern eine »doppelseitige Semantik« aneignet (44). Sie können, wie das Wort »unglücklich«, sowohl kognitive Sach- bzw. Umstandsbezeichnungen als auch emotive Gefühlsbezeichnungen ausdrücken und quasi als zwei Seiten einer »Wortmünze« gelten (45). Erst der Kontext

ermögliche eine genauere Konnotation, was nicht zuletzt bei der Interpretation von Luthers Schriften beachtet werden sollte.

Im Blick auf die spätmittelalterliche Gefühlswelt Luthers, die – so betont S. zurecht – unserer nicht vergleichbar ist, wird an Luthers Teufelsvorstellung erinnert, die »eine reiche Quelle für intensive Emotionen kriegerischer und feindseliger Art« bildete (46). Gerade das Bewusstsein des kosmischen Kampfes verleihe Luthers Dasein jene intensiv erlebte Dramatik, die eine Vielzahl von Gefühlen auslöste.

Nach den orientierenden Ausführungen des ersten Kapitels (17–51) wird im zweiten Kapitel (52–108) den Grundgefühlen der Religion, einerseits der Angst/Furcht unter der Überschrift »Pathos: Höllenangst und Gottesfurcht« (53), andererseits der Liebe/Freude unter dem Titel »Ethos: Freude, Liebe, Trost« (93) nachgegangen. Ohne Rücksicht auf systematisch-theologische Lutherinterpretationen, welche die unzeitgemäße Teufelsthematik nur zu gern ausklammern oder in den Bereich der Psychologie verweisen, betont S., Luther habe als Urheber der Angst stets den Teufel identifiziert. Als wirksamste Waffen gegen das durch den Teufel An-ge-fochten-sein gelten Luther das Wort Gottes sowie die Fröhlichkeit, die Musik und die Verachtung. Aufgrund des lateinischen Gebrauchs erkennt S. bei Luther eine eindeutige Unterscheidung zwischen dem Wortfeld »Angst« (pressura, angustia, tristitia, tribulatio u.a.) und »Furcht« (timor). Luther selbst habe »timor« nie mit »Angst« übersetzt, sondern das Wort »Angst« vorwiegend als Zustand einer bedrängnisvollen Lage (Drangsal) gebraucht und damit bei der »Wortmünze« das Schwergewicht auf die Situationsseite (eng) gelegt. Heute habe sich für »Angst« die reine Gefühlsbedeutung etabliert und somit die Konnotation auf die andere Seite verlagert.

Aufgrund ihrer Untersuchung gelangt S. zu dem Ergebnis, dass die Unterscheidung zwischen Furcht und Angst im Lateinischen angelegt und als Lehnbedeutung übernommen sei, so dass »Angst« nicht spezifisch für das Deutsche sei. Ein durch Luthers Schriften konstituiertes kulturelles Konstrukt eines deutschen Angst-Konzeptes sei daher nicht haltbar (90).

Dass die Freude als Grundgefühl christlicher Existenz gilt, überrascht den Lutherforscher nicht. Eindrücklich ist schließlich das dritte Kapitel (109–142), in dem die Katechismusformel »Fürchten, Lieben und Vertrauen« als »strategische Emotionsarbeit« entfaltet wird. Den philologisch-emotiven Mehrwert dieser insgesamt anregenden Untersuchungen schmälern weder die mancherlei Redundanzen, noch die leider nur selektiv wahrgenommenen Forschungsbeiträge (warum wird Gerhard Ebelings Buch »Luthers Seelsorge« [1997] nicht rezipiert?) oder die fehlenden Register. Es steht zu wünschen, dass die künftige Luther- und Reformationsforschung S.s Ansatz aufgreift und weiterführt.

Jena   Christopher Spehr

MARTIN LUTHERS TISCHREDEN: Neuansätze der Forschung, hg. v. Katharina Bärenfänger, Volker Leppin u. Stefan Michel. Tübingen: Mohr Siebeck, 2013. VIII, 263 S. (Spätmittelalter, Humanismus, Reformation / Studies in the Late Middle Ages, Humanism and the Reformation; 71)

Neben den Schriften (einschließlich der Vorlesungen und Predigten), dem Briefwechsel und der Deutschen Bibel bilden die Tischreden Martin Luthers innerhalb der maßgeblichen Kritischen Ausgabe seiner Werke (»Weimarer Ausgabe«) eine eigene, sechs Bände umfassende Abteilung, die zwischen 1912 und 1921 erschienen ist. Seitdem hat die Fachwelt mannigfache überlieferungsgeschichtliche, editionstechnische und philologisch-hermeneutische Schwierigkeiten, die sich damit verbinden, entdeckt und erörtert. Eine dem Stand und Problembewusstsein der aktuellen Forschung gemäße, umfassende Neuedition dieser Quellentexte stellt eine ebenso drängende wie herausfordernde Aufgabe reformationsgeschichtlicher Spurensicherung dar. Am 20. April 2010 widmete sich auf dem Alten Schloss zu Dornburg ein offenbar nur eintägiges Arbeitsgespräch zum Thema »Luthers Tischreden als historische Quelle und editorische Aufgabe« diesem Gegenstand. Die Beiträge des vorliegenden Bandes entstanden, wie es im »Vorwort« etwas undeutlich heißt, »im Zuge der ausgesprochen intensiven Gespräche« dieser Zusammenkunft.

Einleitend bietet *Helmar Junghans*, der wenige Wochen nach jenem Arbeitsgespräch überraschend verstarb, zu Luthers Tischreden eine kenntnisreiche »Geschichte ihrer Ausgaben und Editionen« (7–19). Sie führt von der durch Johann Aurifaber 1566 besorgten Ausgabe, die bereits durch handfeste Gestaltungs- und Deutungsabsichten gekennzeichnet ist und von der ein breiter, nachhaltiger Einfluss ausging, über etliche spätere Ausgaben und die namentlich von Ernst Kroker verantwortete Edition innerhalb der »Weimarer Ausgabe« bis zu den jüngsten, über den deutschen Sprachraum hinausreichenden Präsentationen der Tischreden Luthers.

Das erste Kapitel (allerdings ist die Kapitelgliederung nur im Inhaltsverzeichnis, jedoch nicht im Fortgang des Bandes ausgewiesen) eröffnet erstaunliche »hermeneutisch-methodische Erwägungen« der Jenaer

Promovendin *Katharina Bärenfänger* »Zum Umgang mit Luthers Tischreden« (21–45). Was auch immer sie mit der mehrfach erhobenen Forderung gemeint haben könnte, man müsse sich hinsichtlich der »Sache und Intention Luthers selbst« auf »die Suche nach *regulativen Ideen*« (39 u. ö.; Hervorhebung von mir) begeben, scheint die von Immanuel Kant gesetzte transzendentalphilosophische Ursprungsbedeutung des Ausdrucks (vgl. etwa KrV B 710–714) offenkundig zu ignorieren. Und wenn Bärenfänger von der theologiehistorischen Rekonstruktion einer Tischrede nicht allein in das »historisch rekonstruierbare Selbstverständnis« des Tischredners vordringen, sondern von dort aus dann auch eine »theologische Applikation auf das [!] Existenzverständnis der Gegenwart« und ineins damit die »Gewinnung konkreter ethischer Handlungskriterien« (44) leisten will, fühlt man sich unversehens in das existentialhermeneutische Laboratorium der 1950er Jahre zurückversetzt.

Für seinen gehaltvollen Beitrag »Erinnerungssplitter« (47–61) gibt *Volker Leppin* zwar an, sich an den Erwägungen von Bärenfänger orientieren zu wollen (47, Anm. 2), kommt darauf in der Durchführung dann aber aus guten Gründen nicht mehr, jedenfalls nicht erkennbar zurück. Vielmehr zeigt er in der subtilen, exemplarischen Analyse der »Erinnerungssplitter« zu Luthers Widerstand gegen Predigtamt und Promotion, zum Prädestinationsratschlag von Staupitz sowie zum sog. Turmerlebnis, wie massiv die Tischredenüberlieferung von heilsgeschichtlichen Konstruktionen, theologischen Überlagerungen und anekdotischen Zuspitzungen durchwoben ist, so dass sie vornehmlich als »ein Dokument der Luther-Memoria« (61) in Betracht kommt, ohne dadurch ihre unverzichtbare, aber problematische Bedeutung »als Quelle für die biographische Lutherforschung« (61) einzubüßen.

Im Kapitel »Gattungsfragen« rekapituliert *Barbara Müller* »Die Tradition der Tischgespräche von der Antike bis in die Renaissance« (63–78) und gewinnt daraus starke Gründe, die Tischreden Luthers als Varianten der Apophthegmata-Literatur aufzufassen und zu interpretieren. Am Beispiel von »Philipp Melanchthons Exempla« (79–94) führt *Alexander Bartmuß* einen analogen, von der Forschung eher vernachlässigten Niederschlag der »Wittenberger Gruppenidentität« (79) vor. Mit seiner »Irdisches Kampfmittel und göttliche Vorsehung« überschriebenen Analyse »Zur Bedeutung der Fabel in den Tischreden Luthers« (95–111) kommt der promovierende Germanist *Jörg Zimmer* zu erhellenden literaturgeschichtlichen Einsichten.

Im Zentrum des Bandes – forma externa est forma interna – stehen zwei Beiträge des Marburger Kirchenhistorikers *Wolf-Friedrich Schäufele*. Zunächst bietet er einen konzisen Abriss »Zur handschriftlichen Überlieferung der Tischreden Martin Luthers und ihrer Edition« (113–125). Er mündet in die Annonce von vier Mängeln, die in der Tischredenedition Krokers (WAT 1–6) aus heutiger Sicht zu konstatieren seien. So beruhte die Ausgabe der Weimarana lediglich auf rund 40 Handschriften, wogegen heute bereits 110 Handschriften bekannt seien. Ferner habe Kroker »ein hoch spekulatives Bild der Handschriftenüberlieferung erzeugt« (124), das falsche Gewissheiten suggeriere und dadurch eine unbefangene Arbeit am Text nachhaltig erschwere. Zudem habe Kroker die vorfindlichen Überlieferungseinheiten zugunsten eigener Ordnungsgestaltung aufgelöst und somit den Blick dafür verstellt, dass etwa die Sammlung Aurifabers »eine schlechte Quelle für die *vox Lutheri* sein mag, aber eine hervorragende Quelle für die Luther-Memoria der Gnesiolutheraner darstellt« (124). Der vierte Punkt, den Schäufele anführt, indiziert allerdings weniger einen Mangel der Kroker-Ausgabe, bietet vielmehr den entscheidenden Hinweis für eine künftig zu leistende Editionsarbeit. Die dabei markierte doppelte Zielsetzung, wonach einerseits der Gesamtzusammenhang der wichtigsten Handschriften originalgetreu dargeboten, andererseits »die Atomisierung der Tischredenüberlieferung [...] konsequent fortgeführt« (124) werden sollte, verliere insofern den Anschein eines unvereinbaren Widerspruchs, als sich »mit Hilfe moderner EDV-gestützter Editionstechnik [...] beides unschwer kombinieren« (125) lasse. Damit scheint tatsächlich der beste, ja der einzig gangbare Weg einer zeitgemäßen Präsentation von Luthers Tischreden gewiesen zu sein. In einem gesonderten Beitrag erstellt Schäufele sodann eine umfassende, detaillierte »Beständeübersicht zur handschriftlichen Überlieferung der Tischreden Martin Luthers« (127–180), die zwar immer noch auf Vervollständigung angewiesen und angelegt ist, sich aber schon jetzt als das entscheidende Hilfsmittel aller weiterführenden Überlegungen ausweisen dürfte.

Exemplarische, jeweils hoch gelehrte Hinweise zur Quellenerschließung, denen meist eine kleine Edition bislang unbekannter Lutherzeugnisse beigefügt ist, geben *Ernst Koch*, der die »Tischredenüberlieferung in der Wissenschaftlichen Bibliothek Dessau« (181–189) aufschlüsselt, ferner *Daniel Gehrt* zur »Handschriftensammlung der Forschungsbibliothek Gotha« (191–219) und *Stefan Michel* zur »Thematische[n] Bearbeitung der Tischreden Martin Luthers durch Georg Rörer« (221–240). Nach den von *Thomas Wilhelmi* knapp angestellten »Vorüberlegungen zu einer möglichen Edition von Luthers Tischreden« (241–247) emp-

fiehlt *Margrit Glaser* in ihrem fachkundigen und engagierten Beitrag »Zur Editionsphilologie« (249–258) einen beherzten »Sprung in die digitale Editorik« (249), da doch »im Zeitalter des Internets [...] eine kollaborative Online-Edition« (258) der Tischredenüberlieferung am ehesten als sinnvoll, aussichtsreich und praktikabel erscheine.

So wurde, alles in allem, ein vielfach anregender Band produziert. Leider weist er nicht wenige Schreib- und Satzfehler, vereinzelt sogar eine korrumpierte Textgestalt auf (besonders gravierend 194). Bedauerlicherweise hat das Inhaltsverzeichnis allein die mitunter blumigen, aber kaum sachhaltigen Obertitel der Beiträge aufgeführt, deren sprechende Untertitel hingegen durchweg verschwiegen. Der stattliche Umfang des Bandes legt nahe, dass die darin versammelten Studien kaum den Verlauf jenes eintägigen Arbeitsgesprächs dokumentieren, sondern, jedenfalls in der vorliegenden Gestalt, erst im Nachgang entstanden sind. Insofern hätte eine sorgfältige Redaktion vielleicht darauf achten können, dass die Editionsgeschichte der Tischreden Luthers nicht mehrfach referiert und die Initialleistung Aurifabers von 1566 nicht in fast jedem Beitrag erwähnt und kritisch gewürdigt wird.

Indessen hat der Band die Notwendigkeit einer digitalen Neuausgabe der Tischreden eindrücklich untermauert. Ein gigantisches Editionsprojekt zeichnet sich ab, und während die von Kroker vor 100 Jahren besorgte Ausgabe noch »ohne jede Projektförderung« (15) hergestellt wurde, dürfte die Erfolgsaussicht des aktuellen Projekts in erster Linie von der Gewährung einer kaum weniger gigantischen Sachbeihilfe abhängen.

Münster   Albrecht Beutel

LEHREN UND LERNEN IM ZEITALTER DER RE-
FORMATION. Methoden und Funktionen, hg.
v. Gerlinde Huber-Rebenich. Tübingen:
Mohr Siebeck, 2012. XI, 263 S. (Spätmittelalter, Humanismus, Reformation / Studies in
the Late Middle Ages, Humanism and the
Reformation; 68)

Die Durchsetzung eines neuen Bildungs-
ideals gehört zu den wesentlichen Zielset-
zungen der Reformation. Trotz der breiten
Forschung zum Bildungswesen jener Zeit
bleibt es eine weiterhin berechtigte Frage,
was das Spezifikum des protestantischen
Erziehungsprogramms ausmacht und welche Ausprägungen es zeitigte. Beide Fragen
können nicht durch jene Pauschalurteile
beantwortet werden, die Reformation habe
entweder bloß die humanistischen Bil-
dungsziele modifiziert oder habe sich lediglich auf die katechetische Unterweisung
des Glaubens auf der Grundlage der Bibel
konzentriert.

Der Vielfalt des Bildungstransfers widmete sich die Tagung »Lehren und Lernen
im Zeitalter der Reformation«, die im
Herbst 2009 in der Forschungsbibliothek
Gotha stattfand und deren Ergebnisse nun
in einem Tagungsband veröffentlicht worden sind. Der Band umfasst elf Beiträge von
Referenten aus verschiedenen Disziplinen.

In einer gegenwartsorientierten Lektüre von Luthers Schulschriften diskutiert
Ralf Koerrenz (Pädagogik) das hermeneutische Vorverständnis hinsichtlich der Frage
nach den Lehr- und Lernmethoden im Zeitalter der Reformation. Aus strukturanalyti-
scher Sicht warnt er vor Engführungen des
Verständnisses von »Schule«. Schule erhält
ihr Gepräge nicht allein durch die direk-
ten pädagogischen Steuerungsmechanis-
men (Lehrpläne, Lehrende), sondern auch
durch die indirekten Mechanismen (Archi-
tektur der Schulgebäude, Organisations-

strukturen, Einrichtung der Räume). Insofern ist Schule nicht nur ein Ort der Kultur-
vermittlung, sondern selbst Ausdruck des
kulturellen Standards einer jeden Epoche. Je-
nen systemischen Blick entdeckt Koerrenz
nun auch in den Schulschriften Luthers. Er
macht dies fest an Luthers Hervorhebung
der Funktion von Schule als Garant von Kul-
turvermittlung, seiner Warnung, die Förderung der Schulen aus ökonomischer Kurz-
sichtigkeit zu vernachlässigen, und seinen
Aufforderungen, die Schulträgerschaft in
den Verantwortlichkeitsbereich des weltlichen Regiments zu verlagern, Bibliotheken
einzurichten, eine Stipendienstruktur für
die Ärmsten aufzubauen und eine zwangs-
freie Lernatmosphäre zu schaffen.

Einen Einblick in den Mikrokosmos
der klösterlichen Bildungswelt gibt *Harald
Müller* (Geschichte) anhand der Briefkorres-
pondenz des Benediktiners Nikolaus Ellenborg (1481–1543) aus Ottobeuren. In einer
Art Fernunterricht über die Klostermauern
hinweg (33) empfiehlt Ellenborg den Nonnen des Zisterzienserklosters Heggbach deren Sprachkompetenz im Lateinischen zu
steigern, indem er auf die Bedeutung der
Epistolographie hinweist. Da es keine La-
teinlehrer vor Ort gab, gibt er den Nonnen
den Rat, sich autodidaktisch weiterzubil-
den, indem sie sich im Verfassen lateinischer Briefe üben sollen.

Michael Rupp (Germanistik) untersucht die der lateinischen Sprache gewid-
meten Unterrichtswerke des Frühhumanis-
ten Paulus Niavis (ca. 1460–1514). Vonseiten
der Forschung wurde dieser mit dem Ver-
dikt belegt, sein eigenes Sprachvermögen
erreiche bei weitem nicht das Niveau eines
Cicero oder Quintilian. Niavis repräsentiere
durch ein solches Auseinanderklaffen von
Anspruch und Realität die erste Generation
von Verfassern humanistischer Schülerge-
sprächsbücher. Rupp gelingt es, diese For-

schungsmeinung über Niavis zu revidieren, indem er aufzeigt, dass er in seinen szenischen Dialogen bewusst verschiedene Sprachniveaus einsetzt. Damit richtet er seine Schulbücher nach den alltagspraktischen Anforderungen der Lernenden aus, in denen sie sich im Umgang mit der lateinischen Sprache zu bewähren haben – von der Unterhaltung in der Mensa bis hin zum Verfolgen geschliffener Reden eines Rektors an der Universität. Ziel ist eine flexibel gemachte *eloquentia* zu erlangen, die es ermöglicht, sich je nach Situation fehlerfrei und gewandt ausdrücken zu können.

Die für den Lateinunterricht wirkungsmächtige Textsammlung der frühen Neuzeit – die *Opuscula aliqot* von Erasmus (1514) – untersucht *Michael Baldzuhn* (Germanistik). In seiner kenntnisreichen Untersuchung hebt er hervor, dass sich das Werk noch zwischen kollektiver Nutzung im Rahmen des Unterrichts und individueller Nutzung in Form eines Thesaurus kritisch redigierter Texte bewegt (74). Durch das Aufkommen der Drucklegung von Lehrbüchern verändert sich die Lernweise, da die Erstellung eigener Abschriften durch Diktat des Lehrers als erste Form der Aneignung entfällt und sich nun im Übergang vom Mittelalter zur Neuzeit Textreproduktion und eigentlicher Unterricht ausdifferenzieren (77).

Walther Ludwig (Klassische Philologie) analysiert die didaktischen Methoden des naturphilosophischen Einführungswerk *Initia doctrinae physicae* (1549) von Melanchthon. Die Konzentration auf das Wesentliche in einer sprachlichen Klarheit gepaart mit rückschauenden Zusammenfassungen und illustrativen Erläuterungen komplexer Zusammenhänge machen die Besonderheit der Lehrweise Melanchthons aus, die Ludwig hervorhebt, allerdings ohne den Erweis durch den Vergleich mit ähnlichen Einlei-

tungswerken anderer Autoren vorzunehmen.

Auf den Wandel des Disputationswesens zu Beginn der Reformation in Wittenberg und in Zürich weist der Beitrag von *Volker Leppin* (Theologie) hin. Besonderes Merkmal ist die Einbeziehung der Öffentlichkeit. Zwar gibt es auch Vorläufer unter den mittelalterlichen Disputationen, die einen öffentlichen Charakter annahmen; jedoch kommt es erst mit Beginn der Reformation zu einer besonderen Dynamik, woraus die Bewegung ihre »enorme Schlagkraft« (116) zog. Hierbei unterscheidet Leppin vier Stufen im Umgang mit Disputationen, die sich phasenweise zeitlich überlappen: Von der »affirmativen Lehrmitteilung« neuer Lehren hin zur »Entscheidung über fragliche Wahrheiten«, in der die kirchliche Hierarchie bewusst eingebunden wird und sich zu einem öffentlichen Häresieverfahren steigert, über die »Propagierung« als Mittel zur demonstrativen Durchsetzung protestantischer Überzeugungen hin zur »demonstrativen Durchsetzungsstrategie« als Instrument zur gezielten Etablierung der reformatorischen Bewegung in den Städten.

Im Zusammenhang der Entwicklung von Melanchthons ›Loci‹ vom didaktischen Hilfsmittel in seinen ersten Auflagen hin zur frühen Form evangelischer Dogmatik widmet sich *Thomas Töpfer* (Geschichte) der Rezeptionsgeschichte jenes Werkes im Kontext der Auseinandersetzung um das Erbe Melanchthons nach 1560 mit Augenmerk auf die Wittenberger Universitätsordnung des Jahres 1588 und zeigt hierbei auf, wie deutlich sich die konfessionspolitischen Entscheidungen des Landesherrn auf den universitären Lehrbetrieb in Wittenberg und Leipzig auswirkten.

In seiner gelehrten Untersuchung dokumentiert *Daniel Gehrt* (Geschichte) die Entstehung, Inhalt und Rezeption der

Schrift *Das Kleine Corpus Doctrinae* (Erstdruck 1564) von Matthäus Judex, dem Mitverfasser der *Magdeburger Zenturien*. Gedacht als Ergänzung zum *Kleinen Katechismus* Luthers diente es als Schul- und Bekenntnisbuch der Gnesiolutheraner für die Elementarbildung mit einer breiten Wirkung in Mitteleuropa bis hin zum Ende des 17. Jahrhunderts.

Zwei Beiträge stammen von *Franz Körndle* (Musikwissenschaft). Der eine gibt Einblick in fünf musikspezifische Vokabularien, die sich aus Glossarien entwickelten und zu den Frühformen musikalischer Wörterbücher zählen. Der andere Beitrag ergänzt die spärlichen Kenntnisse zu Musikstücken und Chören in Schuldramen des Jesuitenordens zur Zeit der Gegenreformation. Bedauerlicherweise zieht Körndle aus seinen Erkenntnissen keine Schlussfolgerungen für das Thema des Tagungsbandes.

Christel Meier (Mittel- und Neulatein) weist schließlich auf das didaktische Potential des Theaters in den Erziehungsdramen der frühen Neuzeit hin (229), die vorwiegend in protestantischen Schulen und katholischen Ordensschulen aufgeführt und dementsprechend von Pädagogen verfasst wurden. Neben der Moralerziehung bezweckten sie auch eine bessere Sprachbeherrschung des Lateinischen.

Freilich kann ein solcher Tagungsband keine geschlossene Bildungsgeschichte der Reformation bieten. Vielmehr lenkt jener den Blick auf verschiedene Gesichtspunkte, die es bei der Aufarbeitung des Gesamtkomplexes zu beachten gilt. Gleichwohl wäre die Bündelung der Ergebnisse in Form eines Nachwortes wünschenswert gewesen.

Naumburg   Roland M. Lehmann

MEDIALITÄT, UNMITTELBARKEIT, PRÄSENZ. Die Nähe des Heils im Verständnis der Reformation, hg. v. Johanna Haberer u. Berndt Hamm. Tübingen: Mohr Siebeck, 2012. X, 390 S. (Spätmittelalter, Humanismus, Reformation / Studies in the Late Middle Ages, Humanism and the Reformation; 70)

Wenn man ein anderes Bild von reformatorischer Theologie und Frömmigkeit zeichnen will, als dies z. B. der nationalprotestantische Historismus des 19. Jahrhunderts in heroisierender Weise getan hat, muss man sich einerseits weiterer Quellen bedienen, die über den engeren Zirkel z. B. Luthers hinausgehen, und andererseits versuchen, diese methodisch schärfer zu fassen. In vorbildlicher wie weitere Forschungen anregender Weise führt dies der hier vorzustellende Band mit seinen 19 höchst unterschiedlichen Beiträgen vor, die auf eine interdisziplinäre Tagung vom Herbst 2010 in Erlangen zurück gehen. Die kirchenhistorisch, mediävistisch, literaturwissenschaftlich und kunstgeschichtlich ausgerichteten Beiträge versuchen, dem bunten Bild des Spätmittelalters im Übergang zur Neuzeit in durchaus differenzierten Deutungen Rechnung zu tragen.

Den Rahmen für die Ausführungen gaben die beiden Herausgeber *Johanna Haberer* und *Berndt Hamm* vor: Ziel ist es, die Darstellung der Reformation nicht »zu stark vom Spätmittelalter« abzukoppeln, die auftretende »Medienvielfalt« stärker wahrzunehmen und sich nicht nur auf Druckwerke wie Flugblätter zu beschränken sowie die auf Medialität einwirkende religiöse Kraft stärker herauszuarbeiten (VI). Damit wird das Konzept »Medienereignis Reformation« von Berndt Hamm weiterentwickelt. Leitfrage ist dabei (VII): »Wie thematisiert die Reformation in ihren verschiedenen Protagonisten, Strömungen und

Phasen das spannungsreiche Verhältnis von unmittelbarer Präsenz und medialer Vermittlung, um der traditionellen Kirche des Mittelalters eine genuin christliche Wirklichkeit von Gnaden- und Heilsnähe entgegenzusetzen?« Auftretende Konfliktlinien und vom Mittelalter her weiterwirkende Strömungen sollten in dieser Frageperspektive nicht ausgeklammert werden. Aus medientheoretischer Sicht schärft deshalb *Johanna Haberer* (Erlangen) in ihrem Eröffnungsbeitrag die Grundannahmen des Tagungsbandes nochmals methodisch. Als neue – freilich noch näher zu diskutierende – Kategorie schlägt sie »Aufmerksamkeit« vor, um die zeitgenössischen Wahrnehmungsprozesse medialer Einwirkungen zu umschreiben. Martin Luther sollte jedoch (5, Anm. 9) nicht als Verfasser des gegen ihn gerichteten Wormser Edikts angegeben werden.

Ein Block allgemeiner Vorfragen steht zu Beginn des Bandes: Häufig wird behauptet, die Reformation sei sinnen- oder leibfeindlich gewesen. *Thomas Kaufmann* (Göttingen) geht dieser These in Auseinandersetzung mit Quellen von Luther, Müntzer, Hans Hut und Ludwig Hätzer nach und kommt zu einem ganz anderen Ergebnis: Gerade die Feier des Abendmahls im Spätmittelalter »trägt Züge einer signifikanten Entsinnlichung des Sakraments« (42); Wort und Sakrament, die reformatorischen Weisen der Heilsaneignung, sind evident sinnlich; die lutherische – anders als die reformierte – Reformation führte zu einer »Versinnlichung des Christentums«; »Vertreter [...] einer radikalen Reformation« billigten »dem Leiden als sinnlicher Aneignungsform des Heils eine zentrale Bedeutung zu« (43).

Berndt Hamm (Erlangen) verfolgt »Augustins Auffassung von der Unmittelbarkeit des göttlichen Gnadenwirkens« über seine Transformationen im Mittelalter (Bonaventura, Hugo von St. Viktor, Johannes Tauler u. a.) bis zur divergenten Rezeption in der Reformation durch Luther, Zwingli und Müntzer u. a. Medienhistorisch höchst differenziert stellt *Marcus Sandl* (Zürich) die überraschende, aber lohnende Frage nach der Präsenz reformatorischer Ereignisse angesichts der Fülle von Flugschriften und anderer reformatorischer Medien. Medien in Wort und Bild sorgten für die Verbreitung reformatorischer Ereignisse (wie dem Bekenntnis Luthers vor dem Kaiser auf dem Wormser Reichstag 1521), die so eine gewisse »Anwesenheit« entstehen ließen, die wiederum die Glaubwürdigkeit von Luthers Schriften unterstrich. In der Reformation wurden Medien des Heils nicht einfach nur reduziert, wie man landläufig annehmen könnte. *Gudrun Litz* (Ulm) weist darauf hin, dass es eine sehr wohl gestufte Hierarchie der Medien (z. B. Bibel, Predigt, Lied, Abendmahl etc.) gab, so dass sie statt Reduktion lieber von »Depotenzierung« sprechen möchte, was die »Umwertung« deutlicher herausstellt.

Ein Mittelteil der Aufsatzsammlung geht nun einzelnen Medien nach: *Sven Grosse* (Basel) untersucht die unterschiedlichen Auffassungen der »Medialität der Bibel« bei Luther, Karlstadt und Sebastian Franck. Die Unterschiede in Marienpredigten Bernhard von Clairvauxs, Hugo von St. Viktors, Jean Gersons im Vergleich zu Luther, Zwingli, Bullinger, Calvin analysiert *Christoph Burger* (Amsterdam). Auf die Inszenierung reformatorischer Inhalte durch Inschriften im Kirchenraum macht *Christine Magin* (Greifswald) an Beispielen zu fünf Epitaphen für lutherische Geistliche aus Goslar (1547, 1585), Lübeck (1544), Jena (1561) und Greifswald (1595) sowie an drei Kanzeln aus der Lübecker Marienkirche (1534), Greifswald (1587) und Esperstedt

(1612) aufmerksam. *Sabine Griese* (Leipzig) erforscht eine Übersetzung eines Andachts- und Gebetbuchs von Thomas von Kempen auf die Frage literarischer Andachtsstrategien hin. Die Vermittlung von Gnadenvorstellung durch lutherische Altäre ist das Thema des Beitrags von *Susanne Wegmann* (Halle-Wittenberg). Dass das Heil im »Totengedenken und Stiftungswesen« eine zentrale Rolle spielt, demonstriert *Gury Schneider-Ludorff* (Neuendettelsau) mit ihren Beobachtungen an reformatorischen Epitaphen. »Gottes Nähe und Allmacht« sind natürlich besonders Themen für Menschen, die des Trostes bedürfen, wie auch *Matthieu Arnold* (Straßburg) anhand von Briefen Luthers und Bucers herausstellt. Heilsvermittlung spielt in den Vorstellungen des theologischen Amtes immer wieder einer Rolle, was *Wolfgang Simon* (Erlangen) an den »reformatorischen Modi des Amts« an den Beispielen Luthers, Zwinglis und Calvins bearbeitet. Dass Leiden ein »Gnadenmedium« sein kann, stellt *Ronald K. Rittgers* (Valparaiso) am Beispiel einer Flugschrift Lazarus Spenglers fest. *Reinhold Friedrich* (Erlangen) weist nach, dass durch Bildung auch »Heilsvergegenwärtigung«, freilich auf intellektueller Ebene, geschieht.

Nach der Konzeption der Herausgeber kommen im letzten Teil des Bandes grundsätzliche Perspektiven zum Tragen: Aus literaturwissenschaftlicher Sicht geht *Susanne Köbele* (Zürich) »Spielräumen« in heilsgeschichtlicher Rede bei Meister Eckhart und Sebastian Franck nach, wobei sie auf die Unterschiede im Gebrauch von Metaphern und metaphysischen Bildern verweist. Die drei abschließenden Beiträge nähern sich aus kirchenhistorischer Sicht dem Thema: So zeigt *Volker Leppin* (Tübingen) detailreich »spätmittelalterliche Wege der Immediatisierung« auf, die auf die »reformatorische Entwicklung Martin Luthers« Einfluss ausübten. Dazu zählen Tendenzen der Verinnerlichung bei Meister Eckhart oder Johannes Tauler, die allerdings bei Luther in einem allmählichen Prozess transformiert werden. Dass Luthers Aufruf in der Adelsschrift, Reformen zu fördern bzw. Verantwortung für die »Kommunikation des Evangeliums« zu übernehmen, im Rahmen spätmittelalterlicher Traditionen erklärt werden kann, ist bekannt; wie aber dieses reformatorische Konzept diskutiert wurde, zeigt *Andreas Zecherle* (Erlangen) am Beispiel eines täuferischen Gutachtens von 1530 aus Nürnberg und den dazu eingereichten Entgegnungen. *Martin Ohst* (Wuppertal) nimmt den Leser schließlich auf eine theologisch tiefsinnige relecture von Luthers Römerbriefvorlesung aus dem Jahr 1515/16 (WA 56) unter dem Gesichtspunkt »Gottes Nähe und Gottes Ferne« mit. Luthers Ringen und verschränktes Denken dieser beiden Pole, das noch frei ist von späteren rechtfertigungstheologischen Festschreibungen, tritt so deutlich zu Tage.

Ein Personen- und ein Sachregister erleichtern die gezielte Benutzung des vorzüglichen Bandes, der vom Medienereignis Reformation – zwischen Spätmittelalter und Neuzeit – ein deutlicheres Bild gezeichnet hat, als dies bisher zur Verfügung stand. Weitere Vertiefungen auf dieser Grundlage wären zu wünschen.

Jena   Stefan Michel

Melanchthons Briefwechsel Band T 11: Texte 2866–3126 (1542), bearb. v. Matthias Dall'Asta, Heidi Hein, Simone Kurz u. Christine Mundhenk. Stuttgart-Bad Cannstatt: Frommann-Holzboog, 2010. 414 S.

MELANCHTHONS BRIEFWECHSEL BAND T 12:
Texte 3127–3420a (1543), bearb. v. Matthias
Dall'Asta, Heidi Hein u. Christine Mund-
henk. Stuttgart-Bad Cannstatt: Frommann-
Holzboog, 2011. 533 S.

Über Rang und Bedeutung der Ausgabe von
Melanchthons Briefwechsel muss man,
auch und gerade nach dem erfolgreichen
Übergang in die nächste Generation, nicht
mehr rechten. Beachtlich und erfreulich ist
überdies, dass in jedem Jahr ein Band
erscheint, und zwar in gleichbleibender
hoher Qualität. Das Glück der Tüchtigen
möge dem Unternehmen und seinen Mitarbeiterinnen und Mitarbeitern erhalten bleiben.

Das Vorwort der neuen Herausgeberin
Christine Mundhenk zu T 11 berichtet vom
Übergang in der Herausgeberschaft von
Heinz Scheible auf die Leiterin der Melanch-
thon-Forschungsstelle, so dass Leitung der
Forschungsstelle und Herausgeberschaft
von MBW wieder in einer Hand liegen.
Heinz Scheible, der in 33 Jahren seit 1977 22
Bände als Herausgeber betreut hat, bleibt
dem Unternehmen nicht nur gewogen, sondern mit Rat und Tat – vor allem im Amt des
Korrekturlesers – verbunden. Die Bearbeitung der Stücke ist einzelnen Editoren über-
tragen; als Gesamtbände sind die Bücher
nun Gemeinschaftsleistungen des Editoren-
teams, das sich auch als solches versteht.

Nach den aufregenden Jahren 1540 und 1541
mit der Doppelehe des Landgrafen Philipp
von Hessen und den Religionsgesprächen in
Hagenau und Regensburg war 1542 ein eher
ruhiges Jahr. Das belegt auch das Itinerar
(vgl. MBW 10, 515–525). Auch der Umfang
von M.s Korrespondenz dieses Jahres ist ge-
ringer als in anderen Jahren – 271 Stücke
(incl. der Vorreden, Gutachten etc.) auf 363
Druckseiten.

Der Inhalt ist, wie nicht anders zu erwarten, vielfältig. Eindrucksvoll ist schon
der erste Brief des Jahres, in dem M. sich für
die Zwickauer Schule und ihre mehr als ca.
600 Schüler einsetzt. Mehrfach geht es, etwa
im Briefwechsel mit dem hessischen Landgrafen, der auch hier einen Ausgleich sucht,
um Schwenckfeld und seine Christologie
(2870, 2885, 2892, 2906, 2912) – M. spricht von
»ungereimten absurditates« (2912) in
Schwenckfelds Vorstellungen. Auch die
Doppelehe hat noch ihre Nachwirkungen.
Zahlreich sind die Empfehlungsschreiben
für Wittenberger Studenten und andere Personen, die bei M. vorstellig geworden waren:
Da bittet er seine Briefpartner, den Betreffenden eine Pfarrstelle zu vermitteln oder eine
Aufgabe als Lehrer (3073, 3119a u. a.) – über
einen ehemaligen Mönch heißt es: »Mores
et ingenium non improbo, sed literas in illo
genere vitae [nämlich der vita monastica]
non didicerunt« (S. 307, 5 f.). Universitätsge-
schichtlich von Interesse sind Ausführungen über Promotionsgebühren (2967) und der
Studienplan für einen Spanier (3123), alltags-
geschichtlich der Weinkauf (2884). Die Be-
förderung eines Briefes Philipps von Hessen
mit der Ermahnung zum Frieden wird mit
»Cito Cito Cito Cito Citissime« überschrie-
ben (2934; S. 132). Unter den Vorreden zu eigenen und fremden Werken (2973, 3070) ragt
die Vorrede zu den »Heubtartikeln« von
1542 hervor (2921; vgl. auch 2999).

In den hitzigen Aktivitäten zur Befrie-
dung der Würzener Fehde schreibt M. mehrfach an einem Tag (2935 f), auch für Luther,
der nur unterschreibt (2937). Einmal ist M.
sogar nur der Schreiber eines Briefes (2944).
Zu den Vorgängen in Nordhausen (3042,
3068) sollte auf Ernst Kochs beispielhafte
Reformationsgeschichte der Stadt hinge-
wiesen werden (E. Koch, Geschichte der Reformation in der Reichsstadt Nordhausen
am Harz. Nordhausen 2010).

Immer wieder einmal geht es im Briefwechsel um die rechte Praxis und das rechte Verständnis von Taufe (2995) und Abendmahl; sei es, dass in Jena mit Wein getauft wurde und die Frage der Gültigkeit dieser Taufe verhandelt wird (3111), sei es, wie es mit der Elevation der Hostie zu halten sei (2996). Besonders bemerkenswert ist die breite Überlieferung eines Abendmahlsgutachtens (3119).

Die regsten Korrespondenzen mit weltlichen Herrschern in diesem Jahr 1542 sind die mit Kurfürst Johann Friedrich von Sachen (11 Schreiben an M., 7 von ihm), Herzog Albrecht von Preußen (7:3) und Landgraf Philipp von Hessen (5:11). M.s persönlich wichtigste Adressaten bleiben Joachim Camerarius mit 33, Veit Dietrich mit 17, Spalatin mit acht und Hieronymus Baumgartner mit fünf Briefen, die M. an sie gerichtet hat. Wie im Falle Luthers, freilich nicht ganz so extrem, ist auch bei M. die Überlieferung ungleich – seine eigenen Briefe sind wesentlich breiter erhalten (und ggf. auch im Autograph bewahrt) als die an M. gerichteten Schreiben. Durch die Nachweise fehlender Briefe im Apparat Q erhält man einen Eindruck davon, wie viele Schreiben nicht mehr erhalten sind. Justus Jonas erhält einen »lachrymans« geschriebenen Trostbrief zum Tode seiner Frau (3115).

Auch dieser Band ist das Ergebnis sorgfältigster Arbeit. Fehler gibt es so gut wie nicht; nur muss es in den Kopfzeilen von 2964 und 2969 statt »1542« [1542] heißen. Nicht ganz leicht verständlich sind die Wiedergaben der Präsentationsvermerke im Kopf der Stücke. Sie werden unter 2892, 2912 u.ö. folgendermaßen notiert: »Presen.^te« Dass diese Notiz als »[literae] presentatae« zu verstehen ist, ist nicht allen Lesern und Benutzern von MBW offenkundig.

Wie inzwischen gewohnt pünktlich ist auch MBW.T 12 erschienen. Er enthält 311 Stücke; 32 von ihnen waren bisher nicht oder nur in Auszügen bekannt. MBW 3410 stammt nicht von M., sondern von Caspar Cruciger, wurde aber an seiner Stelle belassen, um die Zählung nicht zu stören. – Zwei Winzigkeiten: S. 218 im Regest lies: ungedruckte (so richtig S. 199); S. 432 lies: WAB 10 … Nr. 3941. – In 3373 ist »Fürstenberg« nicht identifiziert; in Frage kommen Fürstenberg in Waldeck, in Westfalen und an der Weser. – Ob es in 3405, S. 472,4 aufsatz (statt: aussatz) heißen könnte?

Die wichtigsten Adressaten von M.s Schreiben bleiben auch in diesem Jahr Joachim Camerarius mit 22, Veit Dietrich mit 19 und Hieronymus Baumgartner mit acht erhaltenen Briefen; auch die Korrespondenz mit Nikolaus Medler (10 Briefe an ihn) ist 1543 besonders lebhaft. Wiederum sind verschollene (3133, 3147, 3212) oder nicht auffindbare (3209) Autographen zu beklagen.

Einen Schwerpunkt des Jahres 1543 bilden Briefe zur (gescheiterten) Kölner Reformation. Der erste Brief aus Bonn datiert vom 5. Mai, der letzte – nach einer Pause – vom 25. Juli 1543. Immer wieder präsent ist die »Türkengefahr«, die M. sogar in einen Zusammenhang mit der Dogmatisierung der Transsubstantiationslehre bringt: An Herzog Albrecht von Preußen schreibt er: »Was grösser abgötterey auß dem bepstlichen decret von der transsubstantiation gevolget, werden alle menschen nach der ufferstehung sehen, so Christus den greulichen irthumb uffdecken und straffen wirt. Ich gedenck auch offt, das der Turck furnemlich zu straff dieses puncten verhenget. Denn die Othomanni haben eben die zeit angefangen zu regirn, da zu Rhom im concilio Lateransensi der artikel von der transsubstantiation beschlossen« (3170.2, S. 94,17–23).

Gelegentlich gibt es noch immer Nachzuckungen der Doppelehe des Landgrafen Philipp. Daneben enthält der Band wiederum wichtige Vorreden, etwa zu M.s *Danielkommentar* (3131) und zu den *Loci theologici* (3419), einen griechischen Brief von Antonios Eparchos (3179), aber auch einen Brief M.s an seinen Sohn Philipp (3243) sowie einen Brief seines Bruders Georg Schwartzerdt, der aus Bretten von Kriegshandlungen berichtet (3316a). Gegenüber Johannes Brenz setzt M. sich für Anton Bodenstein, einen Neffen Karlstadts ein (3401).

Einen Hinweis auf M.s immense Korrespondenz, die ihn einen großen Teil seiner Arbeitszeit (und auch seiner Nächte) kostete, findet sich in einem Brief an Leonhard Crispinus in Homberg/Efze (3189): Dies sei der zehnte (und kürzeste) Brief an diesem Tag. Ich möchte daher erwägen, die Nummer 3190 vor 3189 zu setzen. Auch am 9. und 23. Mai schrieb M. jeweils fünf erhaltene Briefe (3240–3244; 3249–3253).

Zahlreiche Schreiben bieten einen Einblick in das Alltagsleben: In Wittenberg gibt es ein Überangebot an Häusern, die sich nicht leicht verkaufen lassen (3158), Veit Dietrich datiert einen Brief nach seinem Geburtstag (3395), M. sogar vier Briefe am 27. September (3321–3324), »uff welchen [Tag] vor 3831 iarn die arca Nohe nach der sindflus erstlich still gestanden. Also woll der ewige got itzund auch seiner kirchen ruge geben« (3321; S. 338,38–40 und die folgenden entsprechenden Briefschlüsse).

Die menschlich anrührendsten Briefe sind zwei Trostbriefe an das Ehepaar Georg und Agnes Aemilius in Siegen zum Tode ihrer Tochter – der Brief an den Mann lateinisch, jener an die Frau auf Deutsch geschrieben (3284, 3285) –; man denkt dabei an Luthers Trostbriefe an Jonas von Stockhausen und seine Ehefrau vom 27.11.1532 (WA.B 6, Nr. 1974f). Noch stärker aber berührt den Leser Justus Jonas' Bericht vom Sterben sei-

ner Frau, in welchem der Witwer die letzten Worte der Sterbenden wiedergibt: »Her doctor, ich brecht euch gern ein frucht; ich weis, ir habt kinder lieb. Weintt nicht, es gefelt dem hern Christo also woll. Ich danck euch aller treu. Hab ich euch zu zeiten vorzornt, vergebt mirs. Ir habt – eins wortts macht – wol mich gehalten, her« (3135; S. 40f,14–18). So starb die Ehefrau eines Reformators.

Kiel   Johannes Schilling

GEORG RÖRER (1492–1557). Der Chronist der Wittenberger Reformation, hg. v. Stefan Michel u. Christian Speer. Leipzig: Evangelische Verlagsanstalt, 2012. 338 S. m. Abb. (Leucorea-Studien zur Geschichte der Reformation und der Lutherischen Orthodoxie; 15)

Georg Rörer war keinesfalls nur der einfache Stenograph Luthers – so viel dürfte mittlerweile der interessierten Öffentlichkeit klar geworden sein. Der von Stefan Michel und Christian Speer verantwortete Sammelband vertieft diese Einsicht, festigt sie und erweitert das Spektrum der Möglichkeiten, Rörer als wichtigen Teil der Wittenberger Reformation wahrzunehmen. Entstanden ist der Band aus einer Tagung 2010: »Gedächtnis der Reformation: die Aufarbeitung der Sammlung Georg Rörers (1492–1557) im transdisziplinären Wissenschaftsdiskurs«. Sie bildete einen Zielpunkt des Projektes zur digitalen Aufarbeitung und »Tiefenerschließung« (7) der Sammlung Rörers, die in der Thüringer Universitäts- und Landesbibliothek Jena verwahrt wird. Diese ist nunmehr der Wissenschaft und Öffentlichkeit in einer wunderbar zugänglichen Form präsentiert. Darüber hinaus ergibt sich so eine erneute Beschäftigung mit den Rörer-Beständen, die weiterhin sicher Neues bereithalten und die reformationsgeschichtliche Forschung um neue Erkenntnisse bereichern wird.

Der Titel des Bandes ist ein wenig irreführend: Erstens geht es nicht nur um Rörer, zweitens geht es nicht nur um seine Rolle als »Chronist«. Es versammelt sich vielmehr eine teils disparate Vielzahl von Beiträgen, die Orte, Themen und Tätigkeiten, die sich – direkt oder indirekt – mit Rörer verknüpfen lassen, behandeln. In drei Blöcken werden die Beiträge gesammelt: Der erste widmet sich den Universitäten Jena und Wittenberg als »Räume[n] oder Institutionen der Erinnerung«. Ein zweiter Block kreist um Rörer selbst in seinen unterschiedlichen Tätigkeiten als Sammler, Theologe und Korrektor sowie um seine Sammlung. Der dritte Block schließlich thematisiert explizit, was in der Diskussion um Rörers Rolle in der Reformation schon immer implizit mitschwang: die Frage um die Autorität Luthers und das wahre Erbe der Reformation.

Eröffnet wird der Band von einem umfangreichen, innerhalb des Bandes als grundlegend zu bezeichnenden Aufsatz von *Stefan Michel*, der sich – als Ertrag des o. g. Projektes – der Person und Sammlung Rörers umfangreich, differenziert und äußerst kenntnisreich widmet. Neben der Biographie Rörers erhält der Leser einen Einblick in die Dynamik der Wittenberger Reformatorengruppe. Auch wenn Rörer theologisch weiter schwer zu fassen bleibt, wurde er jedenfalls in die Streitigkeiten besonders nach Luthers Tod hineingezogen. Rörers Sammlung (eine Übersicht findet sich auf den Seiten 52–58) lässt sich als Produkt einer gezielten Sammlertätigkeit (33) bezeichnen, die sich allerdings nicht auf Luther be-

schränkte, was in der Rezeption meist vernachlässigt wurde (48). Später schälte sich das Ziel, Quellen für künftige Zeiten zu erhalten, deutlich heraus. So wurde die Sammlung in den Streit um das authentische Erbe Luthers hineingezogen (42), sie wurde gar zur »Staatssammlung« (44) der Ernestiner. Hier muss deutlich zwischen der Intention Rörers und dem Geschick der Sammlung bzw. ihrer Rezeption in den nächsten Jahrhunderten unterschieden werden.

Der Person und Sammlung Rörers widmet sich vertiefend der zweite Themenblock mit acht Beiträgen. *Hellmut Zschoch* macht es anhand der Predigtnachschriften Rörers plausibel, dass sich Luther seiner eigenen Postillen in der Vorbereitung bediente. *Anneliese Bieber-Wallmann* untersucht detailliert die Predigten Bugenhagens in Rörers Sammlung. Nachschriften Rörers, Stephan Roths und Bugenhagens eigene *Indices* lassen sich hier ins Verhältnis setzen. *Johannes Schilling* bietet mit »Auditor, Scriba, Autor und Editor. Luthers Werk(e) in Rörers Händen« einen würdigenden Querschnitt der Arbeitsleistungen Rörers für die Reformation. *Stefan Michel* ergänzt seinen ersten Beitrag um eine Darstellung der Tätigkeit Rörers als »Korrektor der Bibel«. Rörer hatte großen Anteil an Revision und Druck der Lutherbibel, seine Bemühungen wurden aber nach Luthers Tod durch das Bestreben beeinträchtigt, unverfälscht Luther wiederzugeben: Dem musste die gewissenhafte, korrigierende Arbeit Rörers zum Opfer fallen. *Konrad Amann* widmet sich den notizhaften Spuren Rörers in den Druckwerken der Bibliothek, von denen er sich Einblicke in Rörers Arbeitsweise verspricht. Hier lassen sich Ansätze zur Klärung der Frage nach den Eingriffen Rörers in der Herausgabe der Lutherwerke vermuten. *Alexander Bartmuß* stellt sich denn auch den überlieferungshistorischen und editorischen Problemen anhand der Tischreden Luthers und den *Dicta* Melanchthons. Dabei erweisen sich die überlieferungshistorischen Unsicherheiten teilweise als recht groß. Ob deshalb wirklich eine Revision der Tischreden ansteht, sei dahingestellt. *Joachim Ott* schildert kenntnisreich das Geschick der Rörersammlung in Jena. Die Lektüre lässt erahnen, wie wertvoll die Arbeit des Projektes war, diese Sammlung zu erschließen und aufzubereiten. Nicht nur die Sammlung, auch Rörer selbst war einer wechselhaften und teilweise entstellenden Rezeption in der reformationshistorischen Forschung ausgesetzt, wie *Christian Speer* eindrücklich zeigt.

Flankiert werden diese Beiträge durch Aufsätze zur Universitätsgeschichte im ersten Themenblock: Rörer wurde zur wichtigen Figur für die Universitäten Wittenberg und dann besonders Jena in ihrem Wettstreit um das wahre Erbe Luthers. *Sabine Wefers* stellt einen Vergleich der Universitätsgründungen in Jena und Wittenberg an. *Uwe Schirmer* untersucht die Möglichkeiten, die Praxis und die Bedeutung der finanziellen Absicherung der Universitäten Leipzig, Wittenberg und Jena im Vergleich. Näher am Thema ist *Joachim Bauer*, wenn er die Gründung der Universität Jena als Ausgangspunkt korporativer Erinnerungskultur, deren Teil auch Rörer wurde, untersucht.

Ein abschließender Block widmet sich den Rörer zum Schicksal gewordenen Diskussionen und Streitigkeiten um die Autorität und das Erbe Luthers. *Volker Leppin* untersucht die von ihm als »Monumentalisierung« bezeichnete Sonderstellung Luthers in der Reformation. *Johannes Hund* schlägt in seinem Beitrag Schneisen in das Dickicht der Frage nach der Bedeutung Luthers in den nachinterimistischen Streitkreisen in der Wittenberger Reformation, die sich als Identitätsfindung begreifen lassen. *Berndt Hamm* weitet den Blick auf eine im Gefälle »Reform – Reformation – Konfession« zu begreifende Gesamtentwicklung der Neuformation aus den Potentialen des Mittelalters. In diese gezeichneten großflächigen Entwicklungen lässt sich Rörers Geschick eintragen und könnte so zu mehr Tiefenschärfe beitragen.

Insgesamt lässt sich der Band auch als Beitrag zur Klärung des wirklichen Vorgehens, der Wege, Personen und Motive der Wittenberger Reformation verstehen. Rörer ist Teil dieser Bewegung, Teil der Frage nach dem Erbe der Reformation, Teil des Problems, »die« Wittenberger Reformation historiographisch redlich abzubilden und lebendig zu halten, und Teil der Erkenntnis, dass sie ein Gruppenphänomen war. Der Forschung ist weiterhin aufgegeben, sich kritisch mit Rörer und seiner Sammlung auseinanderzusetzen und das hier gezeichnete Bild seiner Person sowie Grundfragen möglicher Reformationserinnerung weiter zu differenzieren.

Münster   Christoph T. Nooke

WILHELM LÖHE. Erbe und Vision: ILoeS Loehe Theological Conference II, Neuendettelsau, 22. bis 26. Juli 2008, hg. v. Dietrich Blaufuß. Gütersloh: Gütersloher Verlagshaus, 2009. 381 S. m. 1 Beil. (Die Lutherische Kirche – Geschichte und Gestalten; 26)

Wilhelm Löhe gehört zu den Gestalten des 19. Jahrhunderts, deren Profil wenig fraglich zu sein scheint: Er ist der konfessionelle Lutheraner par excellence. In der TRE wird er sowohl unter »Konfessionalismus« als auch unter »Neuluthertum« als wichtiger Vertreter genannt. Daneben verbinden sich typische Reizwörter mit seinem Namen: kirchliches Amt, Abendmahl, konfessionelle Mission, und nicht zuletzt denkt man bei Löhe an Neuendettelsau.

Wenn ein Name die immer gleichen Assoziationen hervorruft, dann müssen diese nicht unbedingt falsch sein – im Gegenteil: meistens haben sie durchaus Anhalt an der Wirklichkeit. Gleichwohl wird das Bild dadurch verengt und der Vielschichtigkeit einer Persönlichkeit nicht mehr gerecht. Darum ist es gut, wenn die vertrauten Bilder immer wieder hinterfragt und neu koloriert werden. Das geschieht in dem von *Dietrich Blaufuß* herausgegebenen Tagungsband. Er präsentiert der Öffentlichkeit die Referate der im 200. Geburtsjahr veranstalteten Tagung der »International Loehe Society« und der »Gesellschaft für Innere und Äußere Mission im Sinne der lutherischen Kirche e.V.«. Gemeinsam mit der Wilhelm Löhe-Studienausgabe legt der Band Zeugnis von der neueren Löheforschung ab. Er weist sogleich voraus auf ein geplantes »Löhe Handbuch« (23), in dem der gesamte derzeitige Forschungsstand zusammengetragen werden soll. Doch das ist noch Zukunftsmusik.

Der Untertitel des vorliegenden Bandes signalisiert, dass die Beiträge von einem »Miteinander von historischer Rekonstruktion und Gegenwartsorientierung« (17) geprägt sind. Freilich überwieg die Thematisierung des Erbes. Inwieweit Löhes Gedanken auch heute noch als visionär gelten können und einen »Aufbruch aus Tradition« (14) ermöglichen, wird eher am Rande erwähnt. Doch werden Löhes Auffassungen in den Referaten durchweg mit Sympathie vorgetragen, kritische Töne finden sich demgegenüber selten – der Herausgeber begründet das in der Einleitung mit dem »Erwartungsvorschuß« (15), den die Referenten der Tagung, größtenteils selbst »Löhe-Er-

ben«, ihrem Forschungsgegenstand entgegenbringen. Man könnte auch von einer »Hermeneutik des Einverständnisses« sprechen.

Die Tagungsbeiträge lagern sich an die Themenbereiche an, die man üblicherweise mit Löhe in Verbindung bringt: Auf der einen Seite werden Kirche, Amt, Bekenntnis und Gottesdienst thematisiert, auf der anderen Seite nimmt die Frage nach Löhes Einfluss in Nordamerika und anderen Teilen der Welt einen großen Raum ein. Daneben spielt sein diakonisches Profil eine Rolle. Was man allerdings vermisst, sind Beiträge über Löhes praktische Tätigkeit und sein Wirken in Neuendettelsau.

Um mit Löhe »weltweit« zu beginnen: Löhes Bruch mit den Lutheranern der Missouri Synode prägt mehrere Beiträge. Besonders instruktiv ist der Beitrag von *Craig L. Nessan* »Wilhelm Löhe und die Iowa Synode«, der anhand von Löhes Missionskorrespondenz zeigt, dass Löhe bei der Unterstützung der Iowa Synode andere Wege wählte als bei seinem ersten Versuch in Michigan (v. a. 289 f). Genauere Informationen über die Ursprünge der Iowa Synode bietet *Martin J. Lohrmann* »A Monument to American Intolerance«, der die Trennung der von Löhe geprägten Lutheraner auf den amerikanischen Kontext zurückführt, in dem Theologumena des deutschen Lutheraners in einem neuen Licht erscheinen mussten. Dabei wird die Fähigkeit der Iowa Synode, theologisch offene Fragen stehen zu lassen und gleichwohl Gemeinschaft leben zu können, hervorgehoben. Dass Löhe trotz der Auseinandersetzungen nicht dauerhaft eine persona non grata unter den Missouri-Lutheranern blieb, belegt der Aufsatz von *John T. Pless* »The Lively Use of Loehe«. Er stellt Kenneth Korby als »a faithful disciple and an able interpreter« (126) Löhes vor, der das Löheerbe unter den Angehörigen der

Missouri-Synode neu zur Geltung gebracht habe.

Zwei weitere Referate befassen sich mit Löhes Internationalität im weiteren Sinne: *Christian Weber* stellt seinen Beitrag unter den verheißungsvollen Titel »Löhe im Kongo« und vergleicht auf gewagte Weise die Verhältnisse im Kongo mit denen im Europa des 19. Jahrhunderts. Abgesehen davon bietet er aber einen guten Einblick in Löhes Missionstheologie und zeigt als einer der wenigen Beiträge, wie sich Visionen aus der Löhelektüre – »Löhe im Kongo gelesen« (78) – ergeben können. Dass Löhes Einfluss weit über seinen Tod hinaus wirksam war, zeigt die Darstellung von *Dean Zweck* »The Influence of Wilhelm Löhe/Neuendettelsau on the Lutheran Church in Australia« über die Beziehung der lutherischen Kirche Australiens zu Löhe und Neuendettelsau. Dabei weist er sowohl die Neuendettelsauer Traditionslinien als auch das über Nordamerika wirksame Löheerbe nach (314f). Im Fokus des Beitrags steht der in Neuendettelsau ausgebildete Johann Flierl, der zunächst unter den Aborigines in Australien und später in Neuguinea tätig war. Löhes Gedankengut wird darüber hinaus das Verdienst zugeschrieben, die Einheit der lutherischen Kirche in Australien bewirkt zu haben – in erster Linie ist dies freilich dem Löheinterpret Hermann Sasse zu verdanken (322–324).

Dem diakonischen Erbe widmen sich drei Referate: Kurz und knapp behandelt *Hans Schwarz* »Wilhelm Löhe zu sozialen Fragen seiner Zeit«. Dabei kommt bereits Löhes distanziertes Verhältnis zu Wichern in den Blick, das von *Jürgen Albert* im Aufsatz »Löhe und Wichern« ausführlicher besprochen wird. Albert führt die unterschiedlichen Konzeptionen von Innerer Mission in einleuchtender Weise auf den Umstand zurück, dass Wichern die Diakonie an die Taufe und Löhe die Diakonie an das Abendmahl gebunden habe (256). *Theodor Strohm* »Wilhelm Löhes Verständnis der Diakonie der Kirche und die Wirklichkeit der Diakonie heute« behandelt Löhes Verständnis der Diakonie und geht dabei insbesondere auf die Stellung des diakonischen Amtes ein.

Mit dem Stichwort »Amt« kommen die Themen in den Blick, die den größten Raum in dem Tagungsband einnehmen: Amt, Kirche, Bekenntnis. Die Beiträge bemühen sich in diesem Bereich um eine Revision des herkömmlichen Löhebildes. Zu Recht wird die Frage gestellt, ob und inwiefern Löhe als Konfessionalist zu bezeichnen ist. *Dietrich Blaufuß* weist in seinem – leider etwas aphoristischen – Referat »Extra Lutheranismum nulla salus?« überzeugend nach, dass Löhe zwar »einem konfessorischen Luthertum« zuzuordnen sei, aber »eine konfessionalistische Fixierung« nicht zulasse (169). *Wolfhart Schlichting* geht in dieselbe Richtung, wenn er in seiner sehr klaren Darstellung »Kirche – Bekenntnis – Pluralität bei Wilhelm Löhe« betont, dass Löhe immer wieder für Überraschungen gut sei (133). Er konstatiert vor allem in der Amtslehre eine Distanz zu den Reformatoren, die auch Löhe selbst nicht verborgen geblieben sei (142). *Klaus Raschzok* rekonstruiert in seinem Beitrag »Das geistliche Amt nach Wilhelm Löhe« dessen Ämterlehre aus praktisch-theologischer Sicht, indem er die Metaphern untersucht, mit denen in Löhes Werk das geistliche Amt beschrieben wird. Die Betonung der göttlichen Stiftung des Amtes sei demnach keineswegs hierarchisch, sondern als differenzierte Zuordnung von Amt und Gemeinde zu verstehen (94 u. ö.; mit deutlichem Bezug auf Friedrich Hebarts Darstellung). Auch *Rudolf Kellers* Beitrag »Kirche im Sinn des lutherischen Bekenntnisses« bemüht sich um Revisionen des Löhebildes. Er bringt Löhes Vorstellungen von einer freien Kirche mit dessen Verbindungen zu den »freikirchlichen Lutheranern« in Preußen und andernorts in Zusammenhang – eine Verbindung, die »in Bayern [...] gerne verschwiegen« werde (189).

Deutlich wird in jedem Fall: Löhes Rekurs auf das Bekenntnis ist von einem reformorientierten, modernisierenden Impetus getragen. Dies wiederum weist auf Löhes Herkunft aus der Erweckungsbewegung hin. Sowohl die »Hoffnung besserer Zeiten« (127) als auch die Beziehungen zu den schlesischen Lutheranern entstammen dieser Wurzel. Damit aber wird eine Frage virulent, auf die man bei der Behandlung der konfessionellen Theologie immer wieder stößt: Inwiefern bleibt die konfessionelle Theologie auf Dauer ein Kind der Erweckungsbewegung? *Lothar Vogel* verfolgt Löhes Weg »[v]on der Erweckung zur Wiederentdeckung der Konfession« und weist dabei den Einfluss Berliner Theologen nach (236). *Jobst Reller* hebt in dem Beitrag »Bekehrung und geistlicher Durchbruch bei Löhe« hervor, welche Bedeutung die Entdeckung der Lehre von der Rechtfertigung des Sünders für den geistlichen Werdegang Löhes spielte. Offen bleibt jedoch, inwiefern auch der spätere Löhe noch Erweckungstheologe ist. Nach Meinung des Herausgebers der Werke Löhes, Klaus Ganzert, war Löhe kein Erweckter (vgl. 199). Diese Sicht, die ein Entweder-Oder von Erweckungs- und konfessioneller Theologie postuliert, wird in dem vorliegenden Tagungsband – m. E. zu Recht – korrigiert, indem Löhe bewusst als »Theologe [...] der Erweckungsbewegung« (17; vgl. 157) verstanden wird. Auch Löhes oft zitiertes, wenn auch unsicher überlieferter Diktum, er habe eine »apostolisch-episkopale Brüderkirche« (129; 265) erstrebt, spricht dafür. Man wird gut daran tun, wenn man den Übergang von der Erweckungs- zur konfessionellen Bewegung

nicht so sehr als Bruch denn vielmehr als organische Weiterentwicklung und Ausdifferenzierung zu interpretieren versucht.

In das Zentrum des Löheschen Denkens führen die beiden eröffnenden Aufsätze, die den Gottesdienst zum Thema haben. *Manfred Seitz'* Beitrag »Gottesdienst und liturgische Sprache bei Wilhelm Löhe« plädiert dafür, den Reichtum liturgischer Sprache sowie den Reichtum der Agenden zu entdecken und verdeutlicht dies u. a. an Löhes Bemühungen um eine erneuerte Agende. *Thomas H. Schattauer* belegt in seiner Untersuchung »Reclaiming the Christian Assembly as *Communio*«, dass die Bezeichnung des Abendmahlsgottesdienstes als »Communio« für Löhe fundamental war. Indem die »Communio« auf den frühen Luther zurückgreife, betone sie ein Element, das in der lutherischen Tradition verloren gegangen sei. Sie unterstreiche das Bemühen Löhes, die Kirche als eine »distinctive and responsive community« (64) wiederzugewinnen.

Der Tagungsband wird durch einen sehr umfangreichen Anhang abgerundet, der neben Registern auch einen Überblick über die in dem Band verwendete Löhequellen und die benutzte Löheliteratur bietet; außerdem werden im Abkürzungsverzeichnis bibliographische Angaben korrigiert (331–333). Die Beiträge wurden sehr sorgfältig redigiert, was sich nicht zuletzt in der Ergänzung fehlender Nachweise zeigt (109, Anm. 71); nur wenig Tippfehler blieben stehen.

Das Buch ist geeignet, gängig Löhebilder in Bewegung zu bringen und zu präzisieren. Insofern stellt es tatsächlich einen »Meilenstein« (11) dar. Ihm ist eine breite Rezeption – auch außerhalb der Löhe Society – zu wünschen.

Herrenberg   Matthias A. Deuschle

Lutherbibliographie 2013

Bearbeitet von Michael Beyer

Ständige Mitarbeiter

Professor Dr. Knut Alfsvåg, Stavanger (Norwegen); Professor Dr. Matthieu Arnold, Strasbourg (Frankreich); Professor Dr. Lubomir Batka, Bratislava (Slowakei); Professor em. Dr. Christoph Burger, Amsterdam (Niederlande); Professor Dr. Zoltán Csepregi, Budapest (Ungarn); Professor Dr. Jin-Seop Eom, Kyunggi-do (Südkorea); Pfarrer Dr. Emanuele Fiume, Roma (Italien); Professor Dr. Pilgrim Lo, Hong Kong, China; Kaisu Leinonen Th.M., Helsinki (Finnland); Professor Dr. Ricardo W. Rieth, São Leopoldo (Brasilien); Professor Dr. Maurice E. Schild, Adelaide (Australien); Librarian Rose Trupiano, Milwaukee, WI (USA); cand. theol. Lars Vangslev, København (Dänemark); Professor Dr. Jos E. Vercruysse, Antwerpen (Belgien) und Dr. Martin Wernisch, Praha (Tschechien).

Die »Lutherbibliographie« wird seit 2011 unter der Bezeichnung »LuB-online« als ein gemeinsames Projekt weiterentwickelt. Partner des Projekts sind seitens der Universität Leipzig die Theologische Fakultät, Institut für Kirchengeschichte: Abt. Spätmittelalter und Reformation und die Fakultät für Mathematik und Informatik, Institut für Informatik, Betriebliche Informationssysteme. Weitere Partner sind die Luther-Gesellschaft. e. V., Lutherstadt Wittenberg, sowie die Stiftung Luthergedenkstätten in Sachsen-Anhalt, Lutherstadt Wittenberg. »LuB-online« dient der Erarbeitung der jeweils aktuellen LuB für das LuJ und soll zukünftig alle Titel der Lutherbibibliographie seit ihren Anfängen öffentlich zugänglich machen.

ABKÜRZUNGSVERZEICHNIS

1 Verlage und Verlagsorte

ADVA	Akademische Druck- und Verlagsanstalt
AnA	Ann Arbor, MI
B	Berlin
BL	Basel
BP	Budapest
BR	Bratislava
CV	Calwer Verlag
DA	Darmstadt
dtv	Deutscher Taschenbuch Verlag
EPV	Evangelischer Presseverband
EVA	Evangelische Verlagsanstalt
EVW	Evangelisches Verlagswerk
F	Frankfurt, Main
FR	Freiburg im Breisgau
GÖ	Göttingen
GÜ	Gütersloh
GVH	Gütersloher Verlagshaus
HD	Heidelberg
HH	Hamburg
L	Leipzig
LO	London
LVH	Lutherisches Verlagshaus
M	München

MEES	A Magyarországi Evangélikus Egyház Sajtóosztálya
MP	Minneapolis, MN
MRES	A Magyarországi Református Egyház Zsinati Irodájának Sajtóosztálya
MS	Münster
MZ	Mainz
NK	Neukirchen-Vluyn
NV	Neukirchener Verlag
NY	New York, NY
P	Paris
PB	Paderborn
Phil	Philadelphia, PA
PO	Portland, OR
PR	Praha
PUF	Presses Universitaires de France
PWN	Pánstwowe Wydawníctwo Naukowe
Q&M	Quelle & Meyer
S	Stuttgart
SAV	Slovenská Akadémia Vied
SH	Stockholm
StL	Saint Louis, MO
TÜ	Tübingen
UMI	University Microfilm International
V&R	Vandenhoeck & Ruprecht
W	Wien
WB	Wissenschaftliche Buchgesellschaft
WZ	Warszawa
ZH	Zürich

2 Zeitschriften, Jahrbücher

AEKHN	Amtsblatt der Evang. Kirche in Hessen und Nassau (Darmstadt)
AG	Amt und Gemeinde (Wien)
AGB	Archiv für Geschichte des Buchwesens (Frankfurt, Main)
AKultG	Archiv für Kulturgeschichte (Münster; Köln)
ALW	Archiv für Liturgiewissenschaft (Regensburg)
ARG	Archiv für Reformationsgeschichte (Gütersloh)
ARGBL	ARG: Beiheft Literaturbericht (Gütersloh)
BEDS	Beiträge zur Erforschung der deutschen Sprache (Leipzig)
BGDS	Beiträge zur Geschichte der deutschen Sprache und Literatur (Tübingen)
BlPfKG	Blätter für pfälzische Kirchengeschichte und religiöse Volkskunde (Otterbach)
BlWKG	Blätter für württembergische Kirchengeschichte (Stuttgart)
BPF	Bulletin de la Societé de l'Histoire du Protestantisme Fançais (Paris)
BW	Die Bibel in der Welt (Stuttgart)
CA	CA: Confessio Augustana (Oberursel)
ChH	Church history (Chicago, IL)
CJ	Concordia journal (St. Louis, MO)
CL	Cirkevné listy (Bratislava)
Cath	Catholica (Münster)
CThQ	Concordia theological quarterly (Fort Wayne, IN)
CTM	Currents in theology and mission (Chicago, IL)
DLZ	Deutsche Literaturzeitung (Berlin)
DPfBl	Deutsches Pfarrerblatt (Essen)

DTT	Dansk teologisk tidsskrift (København)
EÉ	Evangélikus Élet (Budapest)
EHSch	Europäische Hochschulschriften: Reihe …
EN	Evangélikus Naptár az … èvre (Budapest)
EP	Evanjelickì Posol spod Tatier (Liptovsky Mikuláš)
EThR	Etudes théologiques et religieuses (Montpellier)
EvD	Die Evangelische Diaspora (Leipzig)
EvTh	Evangelische Theologie (München)
GTB	Gütersloher Taschenbücher [Siebenstern]
GuJ	Gutenberg-Jahrbuch (Mainz)
GWU	Geschichte in Wissenschaft und Unterricht (Offenburg)
HCh	Herbergen der Christenheit (Leipzig)
He	Helikon (Budapest)
HThR	The Harvard theological review (Cambridge, MA)
HZ	Historische Zeitschrift (München)
IL	Igreja Luterana (Porto Alegre)
ITK	Irodalomtörténeti Közlemények (Budapest)
JBrKG	Jahrbuch für Berlin-Brandenburgische Kirchengeschichte (Berlin)
JEH	Journal of ecclesiastical history (London)
JHKV	Jahrbuch der Hessischen Kirchengeschichtlichen Vereinigung (Darmstadt)
JLH	Jahrbuch für Liturgik und Hymnologie (Kassel)
JNKG	Jahrbuch der Gesellschaft für Niedersächsische Kirchengeschichte (Blomberg/Lippe)
JGPrÖ	Jahrbuch für Geschichte des Protestantismus in Österreich (Wien)
JWKG	Jahrbuch für Westfälische Kirchengeschichte (Lengerich/Westf.)
KÅ	Kyrkohistorisk Årsskrift (Uppsala)
KD	Kerygma und Dogma (Göttingen)
KI	Keresztýen igaszag (Budapest)
KR	Křestanská revue (Praha)
LF	Listy filologické (Praha)
LK	Luthersk kirketidende (Oslo)
LP	Lelkipásztor (Budapest)
LQ	Lutheran quarterly N. S. (Milwaukee, WI)
LR	Lutherische Rundschau (Stuttgart)
LThJ	Lutheran theological journal (Adelaide, South Australia)
LThK	Lutherische Theologie und Kirche (Oberursel)
Lu	Luther: Zeitschrift der Luther-Gesellschaft (Göttingen)
LuB	Lutherbibliographie
LuBu	Luther-Bulletin (Kampen)
LuD	Luther digest (St. Louis, MO)
LuJ	Lutherjahrbuch (Göttingen)
MD	Materialdienst des Konfessionskundlichen Institutes (Bensheim)
MEKGR	Monatshefte für evangelische Kirchengeschichte des Rheinlandes (Köln)
MKSz	Magyar Könyvszemle (Budapest)
NAKG	Nederlands archief voor kerkgeschiedenis (Leiden)
NELKB	Nachrichten der Evangelisch-Lutherischen Kirche in Bayern (München)
NTT	Norsk teologisk tidsskrift (Oslo)
NZSTh	Neue Zeitschrift für systematische Theologie und Religionsphilosophie (Berlin)
ODR	Ortodoxia: Revista Patriarhiei Romine (Bucureşti)
ORP	Odrodzenie reformacja w Polsce (Warszawa)
PBl	Pastoralblätter (Stuttgart)
PL	Positions luthériennes (Paris)
Pro	Protestantesimo (Roma)

PTh	Pastoraltheologie (Göttingen)
RE	Református Egyház (Budapest)
RHE	Revue d'histoire ecclésiastique (Louvain)
RHPhR	Revue d'histoire et de philosophie religieuses (Strasbourg))
RL	Reformátusok Lapja (Budapest)
RoJKG	Rottenburger Jahrbuch für Kirchengeschichte (Sigmaringen)
RSz	Református szemle (Kolozsvár, RO)
RuYu	Ru-tu yun-ku (Syngal bei Seoul)
RW	Rondom het woord (Hilversum)
SCJ	The sixteenth century journal (Kirksville, MO)
STK	Svensk theologisk kvartalskrift (Lund)
StZ	Stimmen der Zeit (Freiburg im Breisgau)
TA	Teologinen aikakauskirja / Teologisk tidskrifst (Helsinki)
TE	Teológia (Budapest)
ThLZ	Theologische Literaturzeitung (Leipzig)
ThPh	Theologie und Philosophie (Freiburg im Breisgau)
ThR	Theologische Rundschau (Tübingen)
ThRe	Theologische Revue (Münster)
ThSz	Theológiai szemle (Budapest)
ThZ	Theologische Zeitschrift (Basel)
TTK	Tidsskrift for teologi og kirke (Oslo)
US	Una sancata (München)
Vi	Világosság (Budapest)
VIEG	Veröffentlichungen des Instituts für Europäische Geschichte Mainz
ZBKG	Zeitschrift für bayerische Kirchengeschichte (Nürnberg)
ZEvE	Zeitschrift für evangelische Ethik (Gütersloh)
ZEvKR	Zeitschrift für evangelisches Kirchenrecht (Tübingen)
ZHF	Zeitschrift für historische Forschung (Berlin)
ZKG	Zeitschrift für Kirchengeschichte (Stuttgart)
ZKTh	Zeitschrift für katholische Theologie (Wien)
ZRGG	Zeitschrift für Religions- und Geistesgeschichte (Köln)
ZSRG	Zeitschrift der Savigny-Stiftung für Rechtsgeschichte: Kanonistische Abteilung (Wien; K'ln)
ZThK	Zeitschrift für Theologie und Kirche (Tübingen)
ZW	Zeitwende (Gütersloh)
Zw	Zwingliana (Zürich)
ZZ	Zeitzeichen (Berlin)

3 Umfang der Ausführungen über Luther

L"	Luther wird wiederholt gestreift.
L 2–7	Luther wird auf diesen Seiten ausführlich behandelt.
L 2–7+"	Luther wird auf diesen Seiten ausführlich behandelt und sonst wiederholt gestreift.
L*	Die Arbeit konnte nicht eingesehen werden.

SAMMELSCHRIFTEN

01 **Die Anfänge des protestantischen Kirchenbaus im 16. Jahrhundert:** Tagung des Vereins für Kirchengeschichte der Kirchenprovinz Sachsen Osterwieck 14.–15. September 2007/ hrsg. vom Verein für Kirchengeschichte der Kirchenprovinz Sachsen; Redaktion: Christina Neuß; Michael Scholz. Magdeburg: Verein für Kirchenge-

schichte der Kirchenprovinz Sachsen, 2010. 135 S.: Ill. (Schriften des Vereins für Kirchengeschichte der Kirchenprovinz Sachsen; 3) – Siehe Nr. 74 f. 207. 405.

02 **Anhalt/** hrsg. vom Landeskirchenrat der Evang. Landeskirche Anhalts; Johannes Killyen. L: EVA, 2013. 81 S.: Ill. (Orte der Reformation: Journal; 5) – Siehe, Nr. 68. 330. 416. 427 f.

03 **Anmut und Sprachgewalt:** zur Zukunft der Lutherbibel; Beiträge der Jenaer Tagung 2012/ hrsg. von Corinna Dahlgrün; Jens Haustein. S: Deutsche Bibelgesellschaft, 2013. 320 S. – Siehe Nr. 159. 161 f. 164. 172. 178. 180. 183–185. 187. 462.

04 **Der Augsburger Religionsfrieden 1555:** wissenschaftliches Symposium aus Anlaß des 450. Jahrestages des Friedensschlusses, Augsburg 21. bis 25. September 2005/ hrsg. von Heinz Schilling; Heribert Smolinsky. [GÜ]: GVH, 2007. VII, 486 S. (Schriften des Vereins für Reformationsgeschichte; 206) – Siehe Nr. 355. 493. 497.

05 Baur, Jörg: **Lutherische Gestalten – heterodoxe Orthodoxien:** historisch-systematische Studien/ hrsg. von Thomas Kaufmann. TÜ: Mohr Siebeck, 2010. X, 379 S. – Siehe Nr. 413. 463. 485. 543.

06 **Die Luther-Bibel von 1534:** vollständiger Nachdruck. Verkleinerter Nachdruck [der Ausgabe 2002] auf der Grundlage des Exemplars der Stiftung Weimarer Klassik, Herzogin Anna Amalia Bibliothek/ Projektleitung: Petra Lamers-Schütze. Redaktion und Lektorat: Juliane Steinbrecher. 2 Bde., 1 Begleitbd. Köln: Taschen, 2012. [1824] S.: Ill. & Beilage (Begleitbd./ Stephan Füssel). – Siehe Nr. 16 f. 173. [Vgl. LuB 2002, Nr. 051]

07 **Das Bild des neuen Glaubens:** das Cranach-Retabel in der Schneeberger St. Wolfgangskirche/ hrsg. von Thomas Pöpper; Susanne Wegmann. Regensburg: Schnell + Steiner, 2011. 227, [48] S.: Farbtaf. – Siehe Nr. 400. 403 f. 407 f. 410. 412.

08 **Briefkultur:** Texte und Interpretationen – von Martin Luther bis Thomas Bernhard/ hrsg. von Jörg Schuster; Jochen Strobel. B; Boston, MA: De Gruyter, 2013. XXIV, 409 S.: Ill. – Siehe Nr. 18. 179.

09 **Dialog über Luther und Müntzer:** zwanzig Expertengespräche zwischen kirchlichen und marxistischen Reformationshistori-

kern der DDR (1981–1990); eine Dokumentation/ hrsg. von Joachim Heise; Christa Stache; unter Mitarbeit von Johannes Gruhn. B: Evang. Zentralarchiv: Gesellschaft zur Förderung Vergleichender Staat-Kirche-Forschung, 2011. 429 S. (Veröffentlichungen des Evang. Zentralarchivs in Berlin; 10) – Siehe Nr. 566 f. 570. 644.

010 **Donauwellen:** zum Protestantismus in der Mitte Europas; Festschrift für Karl W. Schwarz/ hrsg. von Michael Bünker; Ernst Hofhansl; Raoul Kneucker. [W]: EPV in Österreich, 2012. 622 S.: Ill., Kt. – Siehe Nr. 225. 399. 446. 455. 572. 599.

011 **Das ernestinische Wittenberg:** Stadt und Bewohner/ im Auftrag der Stiftung Leucorea hrsg. von Heiner Lück ... 2 Bde.: Textband. Bildband. Petersberg: Imhof, 2013. 426; 186 S.: Ill. & Beilage (1 Faltkt.). (Wittenberg-Forschungen; 2 1/2) – Siehe Nr. 47. 50 f. 56. 73. 87. 156. 220. 308. 328.

012 Eyjólfsson, Sigurjón Árni: **Anfechtung und Nachfolge:** Luther und lutherische Theologie von Island aus betrachtet. Helsinki: Luther-Agricola-Gesellschaft, 2012. 304 S. (Schriften der Luther-Agricola-Gesellschaft; 64) – Siehe Nr. 139. 149. 166–169. 209. 466. 558 f. 585.

013 **Geschichte Mitteldeutschlands:** deutsche Lebensläufe aus 2000 Jahren; Gesichter, Geschichten, Geheimnisse/ hrsg. von Winifred König; Claudia Schreiner. Begleitbuch zur Fernsehserie »Geschichte Mitteldeutschlands« des Mitteldeutschen Rundfunks (MDR). Reichenbach: Bild und Heimat, 2010. 287 S.: Ill. – Siehe Nr. 91. 360.

014 **Gott – Götter – Götzen:** XIV. Europäischer Kongress für Theologie (11.–15. September 2011 in Zürich)/ hrsg. von Christoph Schwöbel. L: EVA, 2013. 960 S. (Veröffentlichungen der Wissenschaftlichen Gesellschaft für Theologie; 38) – Siehe Nr. 111. 174. 269. 457. 571. 600.

015 **Handbook of theological education in world Christianity:** theological perspectives – regional surveys – ecumenical trends/ hrsg. von Dietrich Werner. Oxford: Regnum Books International, 2010. XXIX, 759 S.: Ill. (Regnum studies in global Christianity) – Siehe Nr. 574. 575. 581.

016 **Heidelberg und die Kurpfalz/** hrsg. von Christoph Strohm unter Mitarb. von Albert de Lange; Johannes Ehmann. L: EVA,

2013. 96 S.: Ill. (Orte der Reformation: Journal; 6) – Siehe LuB 2013, Nr. 52. 326. 430.

017 Des **Himmels Fundgrube:** Chemnitz und das sächsisch-böhmische Gebirge im 15. Jahrhundert/ hrsg. für das Schloßbergmuseum Chemnitz von Uwe Fiedler; Hendrik Thoß; Enno Bünz. Ausstellung, 3. Oktober 2012 bis 20. Januar 2013; ein Gemeinschaftsprojekt Kunstsammlungen Chemnitz, Schloßbergmuseum, Lehrstuhl für Europäische Geschichte an der Technischen Universität Chemnitz, Lehrstuhl für Sächsische Landesgeschichte an der Universität Leipzig. Chemnitz: Kunstsammlungen Chemnitz, Schloßbergmuseum: Edition Mobilis, 2012. 352 S.: Ill. – Siehe Nr. 43. 262. 398.

018 **Katechismen der Reformationszeit:** Beiträge des Theologischen Arbeitskreises für Reformationsgeschichtliche Forschung der Union Evangelischer Kirchen in der Evangelischen Kirche in Deutschland zum Thema Katechismen/ Textbearbeitung: Michael Beyer; hrsg. vom Gemeinschaftswerk der Evang. Publizistik (GEP); Redakteur: Peter Bosse-Brekenfeld. F: Gemeinschaftswerk der Evangelischen Publizistik, 2012. 49 S. (epd-dokumentation; 39 [2012]). – Siehe Nr. 221. 263. 431. 451. 522. 538.

019 **Kirkens bekjennelse i historisk og aktuelt perspektiv:** festskrift til Kjell Olav Sannes (Das Bekenntnis der Kirche in historischer und aktueller Perspektive: Festschrift für Kjell Olav Sannes)/ hrsg von Torleiv Austad; Tormod Engelsviken; Lars Østnor. Trondheim: Tapir, 2010. 278 S. – Siehe Nr. 129. 182. 218. 606.

020 **Konfessionelle Ambiguität:** Uneindeutigkeit und Verstellung als religiöse Praxis in der Frühen Neuzeit/ hrsg. von Andreas Pietsch; Barbara Stollberg-Rilinger. [GÜ]: GVH, 2013. 379 S.: Ill. (Schriften des Vereins für Reformationsgeschichte; 214) – Siehe Nr. 515. 524.

021 **Konstruktion von Geschichte:** Jubelrede – Predigt – protestantische Historiographie/ hrsg. von Klaus Tanner unter Mitarb. von Sebastian Kranich; Annina Ligniez; Christian Muth; Silvio Reichelt. L: EVA, 2012. 378 S.: Ill. (Leucorea-Studien zur Geschichte der Reformation und der Luth. Orthodoxie; 18) – Siehe Nr. 243. 474. 491. 512. 525. 536. 544-547. 552 f. 555.

022 **Kryptoradikalität in der Frühneuzeit/** hrsg. von Günter Mühlpfordt; Ulman Weiß. S: Steiner, 2009. 386 S. (Friedenstein-Forschungen; 5) – Siehe Nr. 304. 357. 359. 365. 367. 371. 450. 513. 518. 539-541.

023 **Lehren und Lernen im Zeitalter der Reformation:** Methoden und Funktionen/ hrsg. von Gerlinde Huber-Rebenich. TÜ: Mohr Siebeck, 2012. XI, 263 S. (Spätmittelalter, Humanismus, Reformation; 68) – Siehe Nr. 222–224. 317. 332. 495.

024 **Luther, reformaatio ja kirja = Luther, the Reformation, and the book/** Redaktion: Tuija Laine. Ausstellung der Finnischen Nationalbibliothek, 7. Juni – 10. Oktober 2012. Helsinki: Suomalainen teologinen kirjallisuusseura: Suomen kirkkohistoriallinen seura, 2012. 209 S.: Ill. (Suomen Kirkkohistoriallisen Seuran toimituksia; 220) (Suomalaisen Teologisen Kirjallisuusseuran Julkaisuja; 272) – Siehe Nr. 64. 439-442. 449. 453 f. 475 f. 481. 507-510. 653 f.

025 **Lutherjahrbuch:** Organ der internationalen Lutherforschung. 79. Jahrgang/im Auftrag der Luther-Gesellschaft hrsg. von Albrecht Beutel. GÖ: V&, 2012. 391 S.: Ill. – Siehe Nr. 88. 116. 216. 270. 294. 402. 526. 643. 649. 655.

026 **Martin Bucer zwischen den Reichstagen von Augsburg (1530) und Regensburg (1532):** Beiträge zu einer Geographie, Theologie und Prosopographie der Reformation/ hrsg. von Wolfgang Simon. TÜ: Mohr Siebeck, 2011. IX, 273 S. (Spätmittelalter, Humanismus, Reformation; 55) – Siehe Nr. 375. 381. 383.

027 **Martin Luthers Tischreden:** Neuansätze der Forschung/ hrsg. von Katharina Bärenfänger; Volker Leppin; Stefan Michel. TÜ: Mohr Siebeck, 2013. VIII, 263 S. (Spätmittelalter, Humanismus, Reformation; 71) – Siehe Nr. 1-3. 5-7. 9 f. 12. 14. 204. 266. 295. 321.

028 **Matija Vlačić Ilirik [III]:** zbornik radova s Trećeg međunarodnog znanstvenog skupa »Matija Vlačić Ilirik« Labin, 22.–24. travnja 2010 = Beiträge der dritten internationalen Konferenz zu Matthias Flacius Illyricus, Labin/Kroatien, 2010 = Proceedings of the Third International Conference on Matthias Flacius Illyricus, Labin/Croatia, 2010/ hrsg. von Marina Miladinov in Zsarb. mit Luka Ilić. Labin: Grad Labin, 2012. 420 S. – Siehe Nr. 4. 487. 498. 502. 504. 506.

029 **Medialität, Unmittelbarkeit, Präsenz:** die Nähe des Heils im Verständnis der Reformation/ hrsg. von Johanna Haberer; Berndt Hamm. TÜ: Mohr Siebeck, 2012. X, 390 S.: Ill. (Spätmittelalter, Humanismus, Reformation; 70) – Siehe Nr. 107. 112. 140. 142. 158. 175. 219. 228. 236. 260f. 264. 279. 291. 401. 406. 411.

030 **Die Merseburger Fürstengruft:** Geschichte – Zeremoniell – Restaurierung/ hrsg. von Ulrike Wendland; Elisabeth Rüber-Schütte; Redaktion: Markus Cottin ... Petersberg: Imhof, 2013. 607 S.: Ill. (Landesamt für Denkmalpflege und Archäologie, Sachsen-Anhalt: Arbeitsberichte; 11) (Schriftenreihe der Vereinigten Domstifter zu Merseburg und Naumburg und des Kollegiatstifts Zeitz; 6) – Siehe Nr. 225. 399. 489. 517. 534.

031 **Profil und Abgrenzung – Luthers (vergessenes?) Vermächtnis:** 475 Jahre Schmalkaldische Artikel; Beiträge des Historisch-Theologischen Symposions Schmalkalden, 21. bis 23. Juni 2012/ hrsg. im Auftrag der Evang. Kirche von Kurhessen-Waldeck von Jürgen Römer. Kassel: Evang. Medienverband, 2013. 169 S.: Ill. (Monograhiae Hassiae; 27) – Siehe Nr. 120f. 123. 288. 293. 349. 582. 588. 598. 602. 616.

032 **Reformation erinnern:** eine theologische Vertiefung im Horizont der Ökumene/ hrsg. von Martin Heimbucher. NK: NV, 2013. 159 S. (Evang. Impulse; 4) – Siehe Nr. 145. 256.

033 **Reformation und Musik/** Kirchenamt der Evang. Kirche in Deutschland (EKD); Jochen Arnold ...; Redaktion: Klaus-Martin Bresgott; Reinhard Mawick; Vorwort: Nikolaus Schneider. B: Medialis, 2012. 80 S.: Ill. (Das EKD-Magazin zum Themenjahr der Lutherdekade; 4: Reformation und Musik) (500 Jahre Reformation – Luther 2017) – Siehe Nr. 205. 214. 473.

034 **Religion und Naturwissenschaften im 16. und 17. Jahrhundert/** hrsg. von Kaspar von Greyerz ... GÜ: GVH, 2010. 342 S. (Schriften des Vereins für Reformationsgeschichte; 210) – Siehe Nr. 163. 231f. 301. 334. 511. 520f.

035 **Schatten der Reformation:** der lange Weg zur Toleranz/ hrsg. vom Kirchenamt der Evang. Kirche in Deutschland (EKD): Thies Gundlach ... F: Hansisches Druck- und Verlagshaus, 2012. 80 S.: Ill. (Das EKD-Magazin zum Themenjahr der Lutherdekade; [5]: Reformation und Toleranz) (500 Jahre Reformation – Luther 2017) [Auch als elektronische Ressource: <http://www.kirche-im-aufbruch.ekd.de/downloads/Tole[-]ranzmagazin_einzeln_neu.pdf>] – Siehe Nr. 244. 361. 584. 587. 589. 611.

036 **Schmalkalden/** hrsg. von Jürgen Römer; Redaktion: Hedwig Gafga. L: EVA, 2013. 81 S.: Ill. (Orte der Reformation: Journal; 7) – Siehe Nr. 71f. 426. 429.

037 **Der späte Bugenhagen/** hrsg. von Irene Dingel; Stefan Rhein. L: EVA, 2011. 256 S.: Ill. (Schriften der Stiftung Luthergedenkstätten in Sachsen-Anhalt; 13) – Siehe Nr. 296. 300. 302f. 307. 310-316. 320. 325.

038 Stolt, Birgit: **»Laßt uns fröhlich springen!«:** Gefühlswelt und Gefühlsnavigierung in Luthers Reformationsarbeit. B: Weidler, 2012. 350 S.: Ill. (Studium litterarum; 21) – Siehe Nr. 147. 188-198.

039 **Thomaskirche Leipzig/** hrsg. von Martin Petzoldt. 2., überarbeitete Aufl. von »St. Thomas zu Leipzig« (2000). L: EVA, 2012. 198 S.: Ill. – Siehe Nr. 66. 425.

040 **»Vidimus enim stellam eius ...«:** konferenciakötet (Konferenzband)/ hrsg. von László Szávay. BP: Károli Gáspár Református Egyetem: L'Harmattan, 2011. 563 S.: Ill. (Károli Könyvek: Tanulmánykötet) – Siehe Nr. 486. 615.

041 **Wege von Trennungen und Versöhnungen:** ein Themenheft der Evangelisch-Lutherischen Landeskirche Sachsens zum Jahr der Lutherdekade »Reformation und Toleranz«/ hrsg. von der Evang.-Luth. Landeskirche Sachsens, AG zum Themenjahr »Reformation und Toleranz«; Michael Seimer; Vorwort: Jochen Bohl. Dresden: endstrichlos, 2013. 37, [7] S.: Ill. (500 Jahre Reformation – Luther 2017) – Siehe Nr. 385. 392. 580.

042 Wengert, Timothy J.: **Philip Melanchthon, speaker of the Reformation:** Wittenberg's other reformer. Farnham, Surrey; Burlington, VT: Ashgate, 2010. XVI, [294], 9 S. (Variorum collected studies series; CS963) – Siehe Nr. 137. 33-345. 356.

043 **Das Wesen des Christentums/** hrsg. von Jan Rohls; Gunther Wenz; Ludwig Mödl. GÖ: V&R unipress, 2003. 368 S.: Ill. (Münchener theol. Forschungen; 1) – Siehe Nr. 132. 255.

044 **A zsoltár a régi magyar irodalomban:** a Csurgón 2007. május 24–27-én tartott konferencia előadásai (Der Psalm in der alten ungar. Literatur: Vorträge der in Csurgó 24.–27. Mai 2007 gehaltenen Konferenz)/ hrsg. von Éva Petrőczi; András Szabó. BP: Károli Gáspár Református Egyetem: L'Harmattan, 2011. 356 S.: Ill. (Károli Könyvek: Tanulmánykötet) – Siehe Nr. 437. 482. 492.

A QUELLEN

1 Quellenkunde

1 Bärenfänger, Katharina; Leppin, Volker, Michel, Stefan: **Luthers Tischreden von der Bestandssicherung zu neuen Perspektiven.** In: 027, 2–6.

2 Bärenfänger, Katharina: **Zum Umgang mit Luthers Tischreden:** hermeneutisch-methodische Erwägungen anhand von Luthers Aussagen über Kind und Kindheit in den Tischreden. In: 027, 21–45.

3 **Beständeübersicht zur handschriftlichen Überlieferung der Tischreden Martin Luthers/** bearb. von Wolf-Friedrich Schäufele. In: 027, 127–180.

4 Jembrih, Alojz; Runjak, Tamara: **»Flaciana« u Knjižnici HAZU u Zagrebu** (»Flaciana« in der HAZU-Bibliothek in Zagreb). In: 028, 378–410.

5 Gehrt, Daniel: **Tischreden in der Handschriftensammlung der Forschungsbibliothek Gotha.** In: 027, 191–219.

6 Glaser, Margit: **Zur Editionsphilologie:** Möglichkeiten einer Neuedition von Luthers Tischreden im 21. Jahrhundert. In: 027, 249–258.

7 Junghans, Helmar: **Luthers Tischreden:** Geschichte ihrer Ausgaben und Editionen. In: 027, 7–19.

8 Kadelbach, Ada: **Das »Achtliederbuch«** vom Jahre »1523/1524«: zu unserer Faksimile-Beilage. Jahrbuch für Liturgik und Hymnologie 50 (2011), 30–34.

9 Koch, Ernst: **Zur Tischredenüberlieferung in der Wissenschaftlichen Bibliothek Dessau.** In: 027, 181–189.

10 Leppin, Volker: **Gedankensplitter:** zur Problematik der Tischreden als Quelle von Luthers Biographie. In: 027, 47–61.

11 Möncke, Gisela: **Editionsnachtrag zu einer Flugschrift über Luther in Worms.** ARG 103 (2012), 273–280: abstract. – Siehe LuB 1991, Nr. 27.

12 Schäufele, Wolf-Friedrich: **Zur handschriftlichen Überlieferung der Tischreden Martin Luthers und ihrer Edition.** In: 027, 113–125.

13 Wennemuth, Udo: **Wertvolle Neuzugänge in Archiv und Bibliothek:** seltener Lutherdruck. Jahrbuch für badische Kirchen- und Religionsgeschichte 6 (2012), 331 f: Ill.

14 Wilhelmi, Thomas: **Vorüberlegungen zu einer möglichen Edition von Luthers Tischreden.** In: 027, 241–247.

15 Zwanepol, Klaas: **De »tools« van de Lutherstudie** (Hilfsmittel zum Lutherstudium). LuBu 20 (Kampen 2011), 32–50.

2 Wissenschaftliche Ausgaben und Übersetzungen der Werke Luthers sowie der biographischen Quellen

16 **Biblia das ist, die gantze Heilige Schrifft Deudsch. Mart. Luth. Wittemberg.** Teil 1: **Das Alte Testament.** Nachdruck der Ausgabe Wittenberg, 1534. Köln: Taschen, 2012. [815] S.: Ill. – In: Nr. 06.

17 **Biblia das ist, die gantze Heilige Schrifft Deudsch. Mart. Luth. Wittemberg.** Teil 2: **[Die Propheten alle Deutsch. Apokryphen].** Das Neue Testament. Nachdruck der Ausgabe Wittenberg, 1534. Köln: Taschen, 2012. [860] S.: Ill. – In: Nr. 06.

18 [Luther, Martin]: **Martin Luther an den Erzbischof von Mainz und Magdeburg, Albrecht von Brandenburg, 31. Oktober 1517** (*Briefe – WABr, Nr. 48*). In: 08, 1–6.

19 Luther, Martin: **Deutsch-deutsche Studien-**

ausgabe/ hrsg. von Johannes Schilling mit Albrecht Beutel; Dietrich Korsch; Notger Slenczka; Hellmut Zschoch. Bd. 1. **Glaube und Leben**/ hrsg. von Dietrich Korsch. L: EVA, 2012. XVII, 676 S.

20 Luther, Martin: **Treatise on good works** (*Von den guten Werken* <engl.>)/ übers. und eingel. von Scott H. Hendrix. MP: Fortress, 2012. VII, 136 S.: Ill., Kt. (Luther study edition)

21 Luther, Martin: **Van der fryheyt eynes Christen mynschen:** niederdeutsche Fassung des Traktats »Von der Freiheit eines Christenmenschen« (Wittenberg: Melchior Lotter d. J., 1523); Festschrift für Heinrich Kröger zum 80. Geburtstag. Faksimile der Ausgabe Wittenberg, Lotter, 1523/ hrsg. und transkribiert von Walter Sauer; mit ei-

nem Vorwort von Bernd Jörg Diebner. Neckarsteinach: Tintenfaß, 2012. 56 S. (De Kennung: Beiheft; 19)

22 [Luther, Martin]: **Dem gestrengen vnd vhesten Hans Metsch / Heubtman zu Wittemberg / meinem günstigen herrn vnd guten freunde** (*Vorrede zu Justus Menius: Oeconomia Christiana*), 35–42. In: LuB 2013, Nr. 128.

23 [Luther, Martin] Lutero, Martin: **Contra el papado de Roma, fundado por el diablo & Imagen del papado** (*Wider das Papsttum zur Rom, vom Teufel gestiftet* <span.>. *Abbildung des Papsttums* <span.>)/ eingel., übers. und komm. von Gabriel Tomás. Barcelona: Publidisa [de Sevilla], 2012. XXX, 130 S. (Colección sola fides; 1)

3 **Volkstümliche Ausgaben und Übersetzungen der Werke Luthers sowie der biographischen Quellen**

a) Auswahl aus dem Gesamtwerk

24 [Luther, Martin]: **»... sich auf die Dinge in der Welt einrichten«:** Martin Luther: über Moral und Ethik des weltlichen Handelns/ hrsg. von Sylvia Weigelt. Erfurt: Landeszentrale für Politische Bildung Thüringens, 2011. 125 S. (Quellen zur Geschichte Thüringens; 38)

b) Einzelschriften und Teile von ihnen

25 **Die große HörBibel:** die Bibel nach Martin Luther; Altes und Neues Testament. Tonträger. Ungekürzter und unv. Text; in der rev. Übersetzung von 1984; in szenischer Lesung/ Sprecherinnen und Sprecher: Christian Brückner; Michael Mendl; Walter Kreye ... Regie: Philipp Schepmann. S: Deutsche Bibelgesellschaft, 2007. 8 CDs (MP3).

26 **Die Bibel kompakt:** in 120 Hörminuten durch die Heilige Schrift. Tonträger. Szenische Lesung aus der Großen HörBibel; die Bibel nach der Übers. Martin Luthers, rev. Fassung 1984/ Sprecher: Otto Mellies ... Textauswahl: Bertram Salzmann; Regie: Philipp Schepmann. S: Deutsche Bibelgesellschaft, 2009. 2 CDs.

27 **Die Bibel: oder die ganze Heilige Schrift des Alten und Neuen Testaments.** Rev. Fassung der deutschen Übersetzung Martin Luthers (1912). Elektronische Ressource, Kindle Edition. Interaktives Inhaltsverzeichnis; Lutherbiographie. Altenmünster: Jazzybee Verlag Jürgen Beck, 2012. 3573 S. (3505 KB).

28 Luther, Martin: **An den christlichen Adel deutscher Nation von des christlichen Standes Besserung.** Berliner Ausgabe, 2013. Vollst., durchges. Neusatz mit einer Biographie des Autors bearb. und eingerichtet von Michael Holzinger. Textgrundlage: Weimarer Ausgabe, Abt. Schriften. Bd. 6. North Charleston, USA: CreateSpace, 2013. 72 S. (Edition Holzinger)

29 [Luther, Martin]: **Bol'šoj katehizis d-ra Martina Lûtera** (*Deutsch [Großer] Katechismus* <russ.>)/ bearb. und hrsg. von Markku Särelä; russ. Übersetzung von Andreâ A. Nikitina. Lahti: STKL, 2012. 296 S.

30 Luther, Martin: **Die 95 Thesen** (*Disputatio pro declaratione virtutis indulgentiarum* <dt.>). Elektronische Ressource. Erw. Ausgabe. Altenmünster: Jazzybee, 2012.

31 Luther, Martin: **Kranich und Wolf** (*Etliche Fabeln* <neuhochdt.>). In: Mit Geschichten durchs Jahr: ein literarischer Kalender mit

344

365 Geschichten/ ausgewählt von Daniel Kampa. ZH: Diogenes, 2011, 130. (Diogenes-Taschenbuch; 24155)

32 **Frau Musica spricht …:** Chorbuch Reformation (*Geistliche Lieder*)/ hrsg. von der Evangelischen Kirche in Deutschland (EKD); zsgest. von Klaus-Martin Bresgott. Kassel [u. a.]: Bärenreiter, 2011. VIII, 396 S.: Noten. (500 Jahre Reformation – Luther 2017)

33 **Kirche klingt:** 77 Lieder für das Kirchenjahr (*Geistliche Lieder*)/ Geleitwort: Jochen Arnold; Vorwort: Klaus-Martin Bresgott. Hannover: LVH, 2011. 319 S. (Gemeinsam Gottesdienst gestalten; 19)

34 [Luther, Martin]: »**Nun freut euch, lieben Christen g'mein!**«: Liedpredigt zu EG 341 am Sonntag Kantate, 6. Mai 2012 (*Geistliche Lieder: Nun freut euch …*)/ von Reinhard Brandt. Lu 84 (2013), 2–7.

35 [Luther, Martin]: **Eine Lutherpredigt zum Gleichnis vom Sämann** (*Hauspostille, Luk 8, 4–15*)/ Anmerkung von Sieghard Mühlmann. Mitteilungsblatt des Fördervereins Versöhnungskirche Leipzig-Gohlis 5 (2013) Nr. 1, 16 f.

36 [Luther, Martin]: **Kratkij katehizis d-ra Martina Lûtera i Hristianskoe učenie** (Dr. Martin Luthers *Kleiner Katechismus*; Die Christliche Lehre <russ.>)/ bearb. und hrsg. von Markku Särelä; russ. Übersetzung von Andreâ A. Nikitina; Ill.: Kimmo Pälikkö. Lahti: STKL, 2012. 160 S.

37 [Luther, Martin]: **Luthers Testament/** hrsg. von den Mitarb. des Evang.-Luth. Landesmuseums. BP: Evangélikus Országos Múzeum, [2012]. 11 S.: Ill.

38 [Luther, Martin]: **Luther's last will** (*Luthers Testament* <engl.>)/ hrsg. von den Mitarb. des Evang.-Luth. Landesmuseums. BP: Evangélikus Országos Múzeum, [2012]. 11 S.: Ill.

39 [Luther, Martin]: **Luther Márton végrendelete** (*Luthers Testament* <ungar.>)/ hrsg. von den Mitarb. des Evang.-Luth. Landesmuseums. BP: Evangélikus Országos Múzeum, [2012]. 11 S.: Ill.

40 [Luther, Martin]: **Von wahrem Glauben und sichtbaren Werken:** Luthers »Sermon von dem unrechten Mammon« von 1522 (*Ein Sermon vom unrechten Mammon [Auszug]* <neuhochdt.>)/ bearb. von Arne Dembeck. Lu 83 (2012), 128–132.

41 **Die Psalmen:** Hymnen, Lieder und Gebete; nach der Übers. von Martin Luther (*Psalter* <neuhochdt.>). Köln: Anaconda, 2013. 208 S.

4 Ausstellungen, Bilder, Bildbiographien, Denkmäler, Lutherstätten

42 **Aber ein Christ schmeckt oder sieht den Tod nicht:** Berichte über Luthers Tod; Luther über den Tod/ hrsg. von Jochen Birkenmeier; Christian Philipsen. Publikation der Stiftung Luthergedenkstätten in Sachsen-Anhalt anlässlich der Eröffnung der neuen Dauerausstellung »Luthers letzter Weg« in »Luthers Sterbehaus«, Lutherstadt Eisleben. L: PögeDruck, 2013. 66 S.

43 **Auswahlkatalog** [Chemnitz]: Skulpturen, Tafelbilder, Grafiken, Kunsthandwerk, Militaria, Urkunden, Handschriften, Inkunabeln. In: 017, 271–339: Ill. L 284.

44 Birkenmeier, Jochen: **Luthers letzter Weg:** ein Rundgang durch Luthers Sterbehaus/ Stiftung Luthergedenkstätten in Sachsen-Anhalt; Konzeption: Jochen Birkenmeier; Christian Philipsen; Florian Trott; Vorwort: Stefan Rhein. Potsdam: Rüss, 2013. 96 S.: Ill.

45 Dieckmann, Christoph: **Martini Himmelfahrt:** Luthers Sterbehaus in Eisleben gehört zum Unesco-Welterbe – nach aufwendiger Renovierung wird es am 1. Februar neu eröffnet. Die Zeit 68 (2013) Nr. 6 (31. Januar), 18: Ill.

46 **Eilenburg:** ein frühes Zentrum der Reformation/ Projektgruppe »Eilenburg zur Reformationszeit« in Zsarb. mit dem Stadtmuseum Eilenburg; Martin-Rinckart-Gemeinde Eilenburg. [Eilenburg]: CARLI-medien, [2012]. 15 S.: Ill., Kt.

47 Frase, Isabelle: **Das Collegium Augusteum – Zur Baugeschichte während der Universitätsnutzung.** In: 011 1, 239–253; 2, 127–144: Ill.

48 **Glaubwürdig bleiben:** 500 Jahre protestantisches Abenteuer; Katalog zur Kärntner Landesausstellung 2011 in Fresach/ hrsg. von Alexander Hanisch-Wolfram; Wilhelm

Wadl. Klagenfurt am Wörthersee: Evang. Diözesanmuseum, 2011. 240 S.: Ill. [Vgl. LuB 2013, Nr. 438]

49 **Heimatskunde von Mansfeld und Umgegend:** ein Lern- und Lesebuch für die Schulen/ bearb. von Gustav Walther. Reprint der 2., orthograph. und inhaltlich umgest. Aufl. Mansfeld, 1881/ mit einem Vorwort hrsg. von Matthias Paul. Mansfeld-Lutherstadt: Das ev. Kirchspiel Mansfeld-Lutherstadt, 2012. [8], 95 S. L 12 f+".

50 Hennen, Insa Christiane: **Reformation und Stadtentwicklung – Einwohner und Nachbarschaften.** In: 011 1, 33–76; 2, 21–28: Ill.

51 Hennen, Insa Christiane: **Der Wittenberger Schulbau von 1564 bis 1567 im städtebaulich-historischen Kontext.** In: 011 1, 175–186; 2, 97–104: Ill.

52 Hepp, Frieder: **Auf den Spuren der Reformation:** Was hat der Dicke Turm des Heidelberger Schlosses mit Martin Luther zu tun? In: 016, 15–25: Ill.

53 Hummel, Günter: **Die beiden Bildnisse von Luther und Melanchthon.** In: Die Salvatorkirche von Weißbach/ hrsg. von der Altenburger Akademie, Evang. Erwachsenenbildung; Texte von Hans-Jürgen Beyer …; Redaktion: Günter Hummel. Altenburg; Langenweißbach; Neumark: Beier & Beran, 2003, 17 f. [27 (Ill.)]. (Der kleine sakrale Kunstführer; 7)

54 König, Siglind: **Die Bilderdecke der Löbnitzer Kirche:** nachreformatorische biblische Bilder/ mit Fotografien von Hartmut König; hrsg. vom Förderverein zur Erhaltung der evang. Kirchen im Kirchspiel Löbnitz. L: EVA, 2012. 131 S.: Ill. L 32.

55 Krüger, Jürgen; Wallraff, Martin: **Luthers Rom:** die Ewige Stadt in der Renaissance. DA: Primus, 2010. 174 S.: Ill., Kt. – Rez.: Kruse, Jens-Martin: Lu 83 (2012), 179 f.

56 Ludwig, Ulrike: **»das sie beisammen fridtlich, zuchtick und stille leben« – Die Bewohner der Wittenberger Kollegien in der Frühen Neuzeit.** In: 011 1, 213–237; 2, 123–126: Ill.

57 **Lutherstadt Wittenberg:** vivre l'histoire au present …/ hrsg. von Wittenberg Information; Texte: S. Gruhl … Wittenberg: Elbe-Druckerei, s.a. [28] S.: Ill., 1 Faltkt.

58 **Lutherweg:** ein Rundgang durch Zwickau/ hrsg. von der Stadtverwaltung Zwickau; Redaktion: Stadtverwaltung – Kulturamt;

Texte: Stadtarchiv Zwickau … [Zwickau]: Druckerei Zschiesche, s.a. 1 Faltbl.: Stadtkt., Ill. (Luther in Zwickau)

59 **Lutherweg in Sachsen-Anhalt/** hrsg. von der Lutherweg-Gesellschaft e.V. beim Regionalen Tourismusverband »Tourismus-Region Wittenberg« e.V.; Gesamtredaktion: Elke Witt. 1. Aufl. Wernigerode: Kamarys Druck, 2007. 1 Faltbl.: Ill., Kt.

60 **Lutherweg in Sachsen-Anhalt/** hrsg. von der Lutherweg-Gesellschaft e.V. beim Regionalen Tourismusverband »Tourismus-Region Wittenberg« e.V.; Gesamtredaktion: Elke Witt. 2. Aufl. Wernigerode: Kamarys Druck, 2008. 1 Faltbl.: Ill., Kt.

61 **Lutherweg in Sachsen-Anhalt/** hrsg. von der Lutherweg-Gesellschaft e.V. beim Regionalen Tourismusverband »Tourismus-Region Wittenberg« e.V.; Gesamtredaktion: Elke Witt. 3. Aufl. Wernigerode: Kamarys Druck, 2009. 1 Faltbl.: Ill., Kt.

62 Mühlmann, Sieghard: **Bericht von der Studienfahrt zu Max Alfred Brumme.** Mitteilungsblatt des Fördervereins Versöhnungskirche Leipzig-Gohlis 3 (2011) Nr. 4, 14–17: Ill. L 16.

63 **Musée Maison de Luther:** visite de l'exposition/ Texte: Martin Treu; Bildredaktion: Petra Grabowski; Gabi Protzmann. Aschersleben: Mahnert, s.a. [34] S.: Ill. (Stiftung Luthergedenkstätten in Sachsen-Anhalt)

64 **Näyttelyluettelo:** Luther, reformaatio ja kirja/Exhibition catalogue: Luther, the Reformation and the book/ bearb. von Simo Heininen; Tuija Laine. In: 024, 152–206. Ill.

65 [Paffrath, Arno]: **Der Gekreuzigte umarmt die beiden vor ihm knienden und betenden Kreuzestheologen Bernhard von Clairvaux (1090–1153) und Martin Luther (1483–1546):** Gedanken von Arno Paffrath zur Bronzeplastik im Altenberger Dom […]/ Gemeinschaft Evang. Zisterzienser-Erben in Deutschland. Internetressource. Heilsbronn: Medienservice, s.a. 1 S.: Ill. – <http://www.evangelische-zisterzienser-erben.de/Erlaeuterungen_Logo.pdf> – Abb. siehe <http://www.pilger-portal.de/index.php?id=111>.

66 Petzoldt, Martin: **Kunstwerke** [Leipzig: St. Thomas]. In: 039, 49–67: Ill.

67 Petzoldt, Martin: **Leuchtende Erinnerung:** die Fenster der Thomaskirche Leipzig/ mit einem Beitrag von Christian Wolff. Deut-

68 Prasse, Matthias: **Bekenntnis im Wandel:** in Zerbst predigte Martin Luther bereits 1522. In: 02, 48–51: Ill.

69 **Der Reformationsaltar:** Lucas Cranach der Ältere, Lucas Cranach der Jüngere – Stadtkirche St. Marien, Lutherstadt Wittenberg/ Albrecht Steinwachs; Jürgen M. Pietsch. Spröda: Edition Akanthus, 2011. 59 S.: Ill. (Schätze Mitteldeutschlands; 1)

70 Reinitzer, Heimo: **Tapetum concordiae:** Peter Heymans Bildteppich für Philipp I. von Pommern und die Tradition der von Mose getragenen Kanzeln. B; Boston, MA: de Gruyter, 2012. 379 S.: Ill. (Abhandlungen der Akademie der Wissenschaften in Hamburg; 1)

71 Römer, Jürgen; Liebaug, Ralf: **Auf Luthers Spuren durch Schmalkalden.** In: 036, 12–19: Ill.

72 Römer, Jürgen; Werner, Bertl: **Glanzvolle Treffen, bittere Trennungen:** berühmte Persönlichkeiten prägten die Ereignisse, in denen Schmalkalden europäische Geschichte schrieb. In: 036, 28–31: Ill.

73 Rothe, Vicky: **Wittenberger Buchgewerbe und -handel im 16. Jahrhundert.** In: 011 1, 77–90; 2, 29–32.

74 Rüger, Reinhard: **Die Marktkirche zu Hal-** le: der Neubau im Spannungsfeld der Reformation. In: 01, 41–52: Ill.

75 Seehase, Hans: **Pfarrkirchen der Reformationszeit in der Renaissance in Mitteldeutschland.** In: 01, 21–39: Ill.

76 Thümmel, Rainer: **Luthers Glocken in Rom:** das Schilling-Geläut der Ev.-Luth. Christuskirche/ hrsg. im Auftrag der Ev.-Luth. Kirchengemeinde Rom. Karlsruhe: arte factum, 2010. 43 S.: Ill.

77 Treu, Martin: **»… von daher bin ich«:** Martin Luther und der Bergbau im Mansfelder Land; Rundgang durch die Ausstellung [in Martin Luthers Sterbehaus Eisleben vom 25. März bis 12. November 2000]. Lutherstadt Eisleben: Stiftung Luthergedenkstätten in Sachsen-Anhalt, 2000. 96 S.: Ill. (Stiftung Luthergedenkstätten in Sachsen-Anhalt: Heft; 7)

78 Treu, Martin: **»Von daher bin ich«** – Martin Luther und Eisleben: ein Rundgang durch die Ausstellung im Geburtshaus. Wittenberg: Stiftung Luthergedenkstätten in Sachsen-Anhalt, 2007. 112 S.: Ill.

79 **Wittenberg – Dessau – Wörlitz:** die Unesco-Welterbestätten/ von Michael Pantenius. 2., verb., aktualisierte und neu gestaltete Aufl. Halle (Saale): Mitteldeutscher Verlag, 2010.

B DARSTELLUNGEN

1 Biographische Darstellungen

a) Das gesamte Leben Luthers

80 Diwald, Hellmut: **Luther:** eine Biographie. Lizenz des Verlages Lübbe, Bergisch Gladbach. Bergisch Gladbach: LiCo, [2005]. 461 S.

81 Diwald, Hellmut: **Martin Luther.** Curie, Eve: **Marie Curie.** Krockow, Christian Graf von: **Friedrich der Große.** S; ZH; W: Reader's Digest Deutschland, Schweiz, Österreich, 2010. 461 S.: Ill. (Menschen, die die Welt bewegten)

82 Schilling, Heinz: **Martin Luther:** ein Rebell in einer Zeit des Umbruchs; eine Biographie. M: Beck, 2012. 714 S.: Ill., Kt. – Rez.: Rublack, Ulinka: Die Zeit 67 (2012) Nr. 1 (27. Dezember), 49: Ill.

83 Schilling, Heinz: **Martin Luther:** ein Rebell in einer Zeit des Umbruchs; eine Biographie. 2., durchges. Aufl. M: Beck, 2013. 714 S.: Ill., Kt.

84 Wallmann, Johannes: **Kirchengeschichte Deutschlands seit der Reformation.** 7., durchges. Aufl. TÜ: Mohr Siebeck, 2012. XIII, 351 S. (UTB; 1355: Theologie)

85 Zitelmann, Arnulf: **»Widerrufen kann ich**

nicht«: die Lebensgeschichte des Martin Luther. 5. Nachdruck. Weinheim; Basel: Beltz & Gelberg, 2009. 203 S.

b) Einzelne Lebenphasen und Lebensdaten

86 Birkenmeier, Jochen: »**Wo Luther fror**«: die »kalte Stelle« und der Tod des Reformators. Lu 84 (2013), 8–14: Ill.

87 Bünz, Enno: **Wittenberg 1519**: was ein Reisender von der Stadt wahrgenommen hat, und was nicht; mit einer Teiledition der Aufzeichnungen Hans Herzheimers. In: 011 1, 9–24; 2, 15–18: Ill.

88 Mennecke, Ute: **Luther als Junker Jörg.** LuJ 79 (2012), 63–99: Ill.

c) Familie

89 Alderliesten, A[rthur]: **Vader en zoon Luther**: Hans herinnerde zijn vader vermoedelijk als warm, streng en hartelijk (Vater und Sohn: Hans erinnerte seinen Vater vermutlich als warm, streng und herzlich). Protestants Nederland 78 (Rotterdam 2012), 215–217: Ill.

90 Ellrich, Hartmut: **Die Frauen der Reformatoren.** Petersberg: Imhof, 2012. 80 S.: Ill.

91 Hohmann, Lew: **Katharina von Bora:** die Lutherin. In: 013, 78–95: Ill.

92 Luther, Peter: »**Hier stehe ich, ich kann nicht anders**«: Geschichte einer deutschen Familie. [Ebersdorf]: [Web-Site-Verlag], 2007. 313 S.: Ill.

d) Volkstümliche Darstellungen seines Lebens und Werkes, Schulbücher, Lexikonartikel

93 Hesse, Helge: **Hier stehe ich, ich kann nicht anders:** in 80 Sätzen durch die Welt-

geschichte. F: Eichborn, 2006. 368 S. L 105–110.

94 Hesse, Helge: **Hier stehe ich, ich kann nicht anders:** in 80 Sätzen durch die Weltgeschichte. Ungekürzte Taschenbuchausgabe. M; ZH: Piper, 2008. 367 S. L 105–110. (Piper; 5127)

95 Hesse, Helge: **Hier stehe ich, ich kann nicht anders:** in 80 Sätzen durch die Weltgeschichte. Ungekürzte Lizenzausgabe. [Rheda-Wiedenbrück; GÜ]: RM-Buch-und-Medien-Vertrieb, 2009. 368 S. L 105–110. (Club-Taschenbuch)

96 Hesse, Helge: **CD WISSEN – Hier stehe ich, ich kann nicht anders:** in 80 Sätzen durch die Weltgeschichte/ gelesen von Marina Köhler; Michael Schwarzmaier. Tonträger. M: Audio Media, 2011. 12 CDs (ca. 860 Minuten).

97 **Impuls Reformation:** Akteure, Projekte, Materialien; Bildungsimpulse der Reformation/ Träger: Theologisch-Pädagogisches Institut der Ev.-Luth. Landeskirche Sachsens in Moritzburg. Moritzburg: Theologisch-Pädagogisches Institut, s.a. – <http://www.impuls-reformation.de/>.

98 **Martin Luther und die Gemeinde/** hrsg. von Gottfried Orth. Norderstedt: Agentur des Rauhen Hauses, 2013. 96 S. & Beilage (1 CD-ROM). (Gemeindearbeit praktisch)

99 Strauchenbruch, Elke: **Luthers Wittenberg.** L: EVA, 2013. 247 S.: Ill.

100 Wermke, Michael; Leppin, Volker: **Lutherisch – was ist das?:** eine Unterrichtseinheit für die Sekundarstufe I. GÖ: V&R, 2011. 63 S.: Ill. (Martin Luther – Leben, Werk und Wirken) [Auch als elektronische Ressource]. – Rez.: Basse, Michael: Lu 84 (2013), 66f.

2 Luthers Theologie und einzelne Seiten seines reformatorischen Wirkens

a) Gesamtdarstellungen seiner Theologie

101 Barth, Hans-Martin: **The theology of Martin Luther:** a critical assessment (Die Theologie M. Luthers: eine kritische Würdigung <engl.>)/ übers. von Linda M. Maloney. MP: Fortress, 2012. X, 547 S.

102 Meding, Wichmann von: **Luthers Lehre:**

Doctrina Christiana zwischen Methodus Religionis und Gloria Dei. Teil 1: **Ihre historische und literarische Gestalt.** F; B; Bern; Bruxelles; NY; Oxford; W: Lang, 2012. 440 S.: Ill.

103 Paulson, Steven D.: **Lutheran theology.** LO

[u. a.]: T & T Clark, 2011. VII, 293 S. (Doing theology) – Rez.: Zwanepol, Klaas: LuBu 20 (2011), 53–56.

b) Gott, Schöpfung, Mensch

104 Alfsvåg, Knut: **Cusanus and Luther on human liberty.** NZSTh 54 (2012), 66–80.

105 Alfsvåg, Knut: **Negativ teologi hos Martin Luther** (Negative Theologie bei Martin Luther). Over alt 21 (Son 2009), 91–100.

106 Alfsvåg, Knut: **On the unexpectedness of salvation in Maximus, Cusanus and Luther.** LQ 26 (2012), 271–294.

107 Arnold, Matthieu: **Gottes Nähe und Gottes Allmacht in den Briefen Martin Luthers und Martin Bucers.** In: 029, 225–235.

108 Helenius, Timo: **Ilman teologiaa:** ilman käsite Martti Lutherin metafysiikassa (Theologie der Luft: der Begriff der Luft in der Metaphysik Martin Luthers). Alue ja ympäristö 41 (Helsinki 2012), 96–107.

109 Koivisto, Jussi: **Is evil inevitable for creation and human life?:** studies on Martin Luther's biblical interpretation. [Helsinki], 2012. 223 S. (Internetquelle). – Helsinki, Univ., Theol. Fak., Diss., 2012.

110 Korsch, Dietrich: **De onvrijheid van de wil en de vrijheid voor God** (Die Unfreiheit des Willens und die Freiheit vor Gott). LuBu 20 (2011), 5–20.

111 Ohst, Martin: **Atheismus – ein Begriff im Spannungsfeld der Konfessionen.** In: 014, 83–105. L 85–92+".

112 Ohst, Martin: **Gottes Nähe und Gottes Ferne in der Theologie Martin Luthers.** In: 029, 359–376.

113 Zwanepol, Klaas: **Spreken over God:** een Lutherse bijdrage (Über Gott reden: ein luth. Beitrag). In: Protestantse bronnen over God (Protestantische Quellen über Gott)/ hrsg. von de Protestantse Kerk in Nederland; Redaktion: J[akobus] M[aarten] van 't Kruis. Zoetermeer: Boekencentrum, 2011, 53–69.

c) Christus

114 Alfsvåg, Knut: **What no mind has conceived:** on the significance of Christological apophaticism. Leuven: Peeters, 2010. X, 358 S. (Studies in philosophical theology; 45)

115 Kolb, Robert: **Luther's theology of the cross fifteen years after Heidelberg:** lectures on the Psalms of ascent. JEH 61 (2010), 69–85.

116 Plathow, Michael: **Kreuz und Rose:** ihre Symbolik in Goethes Dichtung, in Hegels Philosophie und in Luthers Kreuzestheologie für die Beziehung von Glaube und Vernunft. LuJ 79 (2012), 139–157.

d) Kirche, Kirchenrecht, Bekenntnisse

117 Heckel, Johannes: **Lex charitatis:** a juristic disquisition on law in the theology of Martin Luther (Lex charitatis <engl.>)/ nach der 2. Aufl. übers. und hrsg. von Gottfried G. Krodel in Verb. mit Henning F. Falkenstein; Jack A. Hiller; Vorwort: Martin Heckel. Grand Rapids, MI; Cambridge, UK: Eerdmans, 2010. XXIII, 566 S. (Emory University studies in law and religion) – Rez.: Wriedt, Markus: ARGBL 40 (2011), 27.

118 Heckel, Martin: **Luthers Traktat »Von der Freiheit eines Christenmenschen« als Markstein des Kirchen- und Staatskirchenrechts.** ZThK 109 (2012), 122–152.

119 Jachmann, Tobias: **Die Auseinandersetzung Luthers mit Rom über die Kirche:** anhand der Schriften Martin Luthers: »Von den Conciliis und Kirchen« (1539) und »Wider Hans Worst« (1541): Vordiplomarbeit. Elektronische Ressource; print on demand. s. l. GRIN; Norderstedt: Books on Demand, 2008. 25 S.

120 Kleffmann, Tom: **Zur systematischen Relevanz der Schmalkaldischen Artikel:** Gibt es einen prinzipiellen Lehrgegensatz und lässt sich über ihn streiten? In: 031, 139–149.

121 Korsch, Dietrich: **Konfession zwischen Konstruktion und Konfrontation:** zur Situation des Bekennens in Luthers Schmalkaldischen Artikeln. In: 031, 79–91.

122 Lehmann, Kai: **»Ewig geschieden und widereinander«:** Martin Luthers Schmalkaldische Artikel sind eine scharfe Streitschrift gegen die Papstkirche und bis heute Glaubensgrundlage lutherischer Kirchen weltweit. In: 036, 40 f: Ill.

123 Nüssel, Friederike: **Was eint? Was trennt?:** zur Bedeutung der Schmalkaldischen Artikel für die Formierung der Wittenberger Reformation. In: 031, 93–103.

124 Véghelyi, Antal: **Luther az egyház ismerte-**

tőjeleiről I (Luther über die Kennzeichen der Kirche I). KI 96 (2012), Heft 4, 4–6.

125 Véghelyi, Antal: **Luther az egyház ismertetőjeleiről II** (Luther über die Kennzeichen der Kirche II). KI 97 (2013), Heft 1, 5 f.

126 Zschoch, Hellmut: **Kirchenordnung der Freiheit:** die presbyterial-synodale Ordnung im Wandel politischer Konstellationen. MEKGR 60 (2011), 115–133. L".

e) Sakramente, Beichte, Ehe

127 Amberg, Joel Van: **A real presence:** religious and social dynamics of the eucharistic conflicts in early modern Augsburg, 1520–1530. Leiden; Boston: Brill, 2012. VII, 270 S. (Studies in the history of Christian traditions; 158) – Zugl.: Tucson, AZ, University of Arizona, PhD, 2004. [Auch als Online-Ressource]. [Vgl. LuB 2006, Nr. 290]

128 **Ehe und Familie im Geist des Luthertums/** hrsg. von Ute Gause; Stephanie Scholz. L: EVA, 2012. 144 S. (Historisch-theol. Genderforschung; 6) – Siehe LuB 2013, Nr. 22.

129 Ellefsen, Kenneth: **Luthersk dåpsteologi i spenningen mellom dåp og omvendelse** (Luth. Tauftheologie in der Spannung zwischen Taufe und Buße). In: 019, 87–98.

130 Henkel, Mathias: **Hatte Martin Luther eine muttersprachliche Vorlage für das »Sintflutgebet«?:** eine kritische Replik auf eine These von Walter Dürig. JLH 49 (2010), 29–38.

131 Margraf, Erik: **Die Hochzeitspredigt der Frühen Neuzeit:** mit einer Bibliographie der selbständig erschienenen Hochzeitspredigtdrucke der Herzog August Bibliothek Wolfenbüttel, der Staats- und Stadtbibliothek Augsburg und der Universitätsbibliothek Augsburg. M: Utz, 2007. IX, 660 S.: Ill. (Geschichtswissenschaften; 16) – Zugl.: Augsburg, Univ., Diss., 2005. – Rez.: Kümper, Hiram: Schweizerische Zeitschrift für Religions- und Kulturgeschichte 102 (2008), 464–466.

132 Rohls, Jan: **Mensch versus Gott – die Entzauberung des christologischen Dogmas.** In: 043, 231–257.

133 Véghelyi, Antal: **A félreértett Luther: bűnbánat – keresztség – úrvacsora** (Der missverstandene Luther: Buße – Taufe – Abendmahl). KI 97 (2013), Heft 1, 20–32.

134 Véghelyi, Antal: **Luther a gyónásról** (Luther über die Beichte). KI 95 (2012), Heft 3, 2–6.

135 Véghelyi, Antal: **Luther a keresztségről:** »Baptisatus sum« (Luther über die Taufe: »Baptisatus sum«). KI 94 (2012), Heft 2, 3–7.

136 Véghelyi, Antal: **Luther az úrvacsoráról** (Luther über das Abendmahl). KI 93 (2012), Heft 1, 4–7.

137 Wengert, Timothy J.: **Luther and Melanchthon on consecrated communion wine (Eisleben 1542–43).** (2001). In: 042, [Text] VIII, 24–42.

138 Wolff, Jens: »**Das ist mein Leib«:** die Poesie des Abendmahls nach Martin Luther. LuBu 18 (2009), 44–58.

f) Amt, Seelsorge, Diakonie, Gemeinde, allgemeines Priestertum

139 Eyjólfsson, Sigurjón Árni: **Der Pastor als Diener des Staates und der Kirche:** Untersuchung zum Verhältnis von Staat und Kirche in Island. (1995). In: 012, 13–34.

140 Rittgers, Ronald K.: »**Got neher machen«:** das Gnadenmedium des Leidens am Beispiel der Flugschrift Lazarus Spenglers »Eine tröstliche christliche Anweisung und Arznei in allen Widerwärtigkeiten« (1521). In: 029, 255–269.

141 Rittgers, Ronald K.: **Pastoral care as Protestant mission:** ministry to the sick and suffering in evangelical church ordinances. ARG 103 (2012), 149–181: Zusammenfassung.

142 Simon, Wolfgang: **Reformatorische Modi des Amtes.** In: 029, 237–253.

g) Gnade, Glaube, Rechtfertigung, Werke

143 Arffman, Kaarlo: **Luterilaisen reformaation vaikutus moraaliin** (Bedeutung der luth. Reformation für die Moral). Internetressource. Teologia.fi. 28.5.2013. 1 S. – <http://www.teologia.fi/artikkelit/etiikka/737-luterilaisen-reformaation-vaikutus-moraaliin>.

144 Friedrich, Sören: **Luther und die Gnade:** eine Betrachtung des Gnadenverständnisses im Kontext der reformatorischen Wende. HH: Bachelor + Master, 2013. 61 S. (Staatsexamensarbeit) – Zugl.: F, Univ., Staatsexamensarbeit, 2012. [Auch als Online-Ressource]

145 Konradt, Matthias: **Luthers reformatori-sche Entdeckung – Eine Relektüre aus exe-getischer Sicht.** In: 032, 13–41.

146 Stegmann, Andreas: **Luthers Auffassung vom christlichen Leben.** 2 Bände. B, 2011. – B, Humboldt-Univ., Theol. Fak., Habil., 2011. 324 S.; S. 325–643.

147 Stolt, Birgit: **Joy, love and trust:** basic ingre-dients in Martin Luther's theology of the faith of the heart. (2002). In: 038, 323–339.

148 Vind, Anna: »**God's peace exceeds the power of the senses, that is, it is incompre-hensible except in faith**«: an interpretation of Luther's concept of sin and faith. LuBu 19 (2010), 17–39.

h) Sozialethik, politische Ethik, Geschichte

149 Eyjólfsson, Sigurjón Árni: »**So gebt dem Kaiser, was des Kaisers ist, und Gott, was Gottes ist!**« (**Mt 22:21**): die Lehre Luthers von den zwei Reichen. In: 012, 204–225.

150 Füllsack, Manfred: **Arbeit.** W: Facultas, 2009. 118 S. L 55f. (Grundbegriffe der euro-päischen Geistesgeschichte) (UTB; 3235: Profile)

151 Kovács, György: **Protestantizmus és kapi-talizmus:** magyar gazdaság- és eszmetörté-neti tanulságok (Protestantismus und Kapi-talismus: Lehren aus der ungar. Wirt-schafts- und Ideengeschichte). Szeged: Ethelbert Stauffer Teológiai Kutatóintézet, 2011. 251 S.

152 Ligniez, Annina: **Das Wittenbergische Zion:** Konstruktion von Heilsgeschichte in frühneuzeitlichen Jubelpredigten. L: EVA, 2012. 336 S.: Ill. (Schriften der Stiftung Luthergedenkstätten in Sachsen-Anhalt; 15) – Zugl.: Halle (Saale), Univ., Theol. Fak., Diss., 2011.

153 Rentto, Juha-Pekka: **Laillinen esivalta – puhdas valtio- ja oikeusoppi Lutherin mu-kaan** (Staat, Recht und Obrigkeit – Luthers reine Lehre). Lakimies 110 (Helsinki 2012), 677–698.

154 Rentto, Juha-Pekka: **Luther, laki ja valtio** (Luther, Recht und Staat). Internetressour-ce. Edilex 15.10.2012. 7 S. (PDF): <http://www.edilex.fi/lakikirjasto/9072.pdf>.

155 Richter, Susan: **Fürstentestamente der Frü-hen Neuzeit:** politische Programme und Medien intergenereller Kommunika-tion. GÖ: V&R, 2009. 541 S. L 300 f+". (Schriftenreihe der Historischen Kommis-sion bei der Bayerischen Akademie der Wissenschaften; 80)

156 Scheliha, Arnulf von: **Protestantische Ethik des Politischen.** TÜ: Mohr Siebeck, 2013. XI, 422 S. L 20–32+".

157 Vainio, Olli-Pekka: **Lutherin poliittisesta teologiasta** (Über die politische Theolo-gie Luthers). Internetressource. Edilex 25.07.2012. 9 S. (PDF): <http://www.edilex.fi/lakikirjasto/8956.pdf>.

158 Zecherle, Andreas: **Die Verantwortung der Obrigkeit für die Kommunikation des Evangeliums aus der Sicht Luthers und sei-ner Anhänger:** Aspekte der frühen Diskus-sion im Spannungsfeld von Immediatisie-rung und Remediatisierung. In: 029, 339–358.

i) Gottes Wort, Bibel, Predigt, Sprache

159 Kähler, Christoph: **Zur Durchsicht der Lu-therbibel.** In: 03, 9–15.

160 Bell, Theo M. M. A. C.: **Humanity is a mic-rocosm:** Adam and Eve in Luther's Lectures on Genesis (1535–45). In: Out of paradise: Eve and Adam and their interpreters/ hrsg. von Bob Becking; Susanne Hennecke. Shef-field: Sheffied Phoenix, 2011, 67–89. (Heb-rew Bible monographs; 30)

161 Beutel, Albrecht: »**Es ist mein testament und mein dolmetschung, und sol mein bleiben unnd sein**«: Bemerkungen zur theologischen und sprachlichen Klassizität der Luther-Bibel. In: 03, 17–37.

162 Brödel, Christfried: **Durch Sprache das Le-ben formen.** In: 03, 97–108.

163 Chassagnette, Axelle: **Geographia sacra:** usages confessionels de la cartographie bib-lique au XVIe siècle. In: 034, 102–122: Ill.

164 Cramer, Thomas: **Wider die Verständlich-keit um jeden Preis:** eine Invective In: 03, 123–130.

165 Crüsemann, Frank: **Reformatorische Im-pulse aus der hebräischen Bibel.** Begegnun-gen: Zeitschrift für Kirche und Judentum 95 (2012) Heft 3, 13–22.

166 Eyjólfsson, Sigurjón Árni: **Anfechtung und Glaube:** der Traum Jakobs aus der Sicht der systematischen Theologie. In: 012, 257–278.

167 Eyjólfsson, Sigurjón Árni: **Luther und Ja-kobs Kampf.** In: 012, 226–255.

351

168 Eyjólfsson, Sigurjón Árni: **Luthers Ausle-gung des Gleichnisses vom barmherzigen Samariter (Lk 10: 23–37)**. In: 012, 181–203.

169 Eyjólfsson, Sigurjón Árni: **Überblick über die Bewertung von Luthers Predigten in der Forschung.** (2004). In: 012, 160–180.

170 Fabiny, Tibor: **Luther az 51. zsoltárról** (Luther über den Psalm 51). KI 95 (2012), Heft 3, 20–33.

171 Fabiny, Tibor: **Uralkodónak szánt tükör:** Luther Magnificat-kommentárja (Ein Fürstenspiegel: Luthers Magnificatauslegung). Credo 18 (BP 2012) Heft 3/4, 26–33.

172 Freytag, Hartmut: ἄτινα ἐστιν ἀλληγορού-μενα »**Die Worte bedeuten etwas**« (Gal 4, 24) **und** ταῦτα δέ τυπικῶς συνέβαινεν ἐκεί-νοις »**Solches alles wiederfuhr ihnen zum Vorbilde**« (1 Kor 10, 11): Allegorica und Typologica in deutschen Übersetzungen des Novum Testamentum Graece. In: 03, 109–121.

173 Füssel, Stephan: **Das Buch der Bücher:** die Luther-Bibel von 1534; eine kulturhistorische Einführung. 64 S.: Ill. – In: 06.

174 Grözinger, Albrecht: **Der eigene und der wahre Gott:** praktisch-theologische Kriterien der Rede von Gott. In: 014, 179–186.

175 Grosse, Sven: **Fundamentalkommunika-tion – Luther, Karlstadt und Sebastian Franck im Disput über die Medialität der Bibel.** In: 029, 99–116.

176 Keller, Andreas: **Frühe Neuzeit:** das rhetorische Zeitalter. B: Akademie, 2008. 231 S.: Ill. (Akademie-Studienbücher: Literaturwissenschaft) [Auch als Online-Ressource] – Rez.: Galle, Christoph: BlPfKG 77 (2010), 393–396; Ebernburg-Hefte 44 (2010), 123–126.

177 Kolb, Robert: **Luther's recollections of Erfurt:** the use of anecdotes for the edification of his hearers. LuBu 19 (Kampen), 6–16.

178 Lüpke, Johannes von: **Sprachgebrauch und Norm:** Luthers theologische Grammatik in Grundzügen. In: 03, 69–83.

179 Mennecke, Ute: **Von der Kunst, demuts-voll einen kühnen Brief zu schreiben.** In: 08, 7–18.

180 Michelsen, Uwe: **Luther öffentlich:** Professor, Prediger und Publizist – oder: Zwischen Kanzel, Katheder und Kachelofen. In: 03, 85–95.

181 Reents, Christine; Melchior, Christoph: **Die Geschichte der Kinder- und Schulbibel:** evangelisch – katholisch – jüdisch/ Vorworte: Thomas Schlag; Werner Simon. GÖ: V&R unipress, 2011. 676 S.: Ill. (Arbeiten zur Religionspädagogik; 48) – Rez.: Zschoch, Hellmut: Lu 83 (2012), 189–191.

182 Sandnes, Karl Olav: **Paulus og Luther – to alen av same stykke?** (Paulus und Luther – zwei Ellen vom gleichen Stück?). In: 019, 27–38.

183 Schrader, Hans-Jürgen: **Zwischen verbaler Aura und Umgangsdeutsch:** zur Sprachgestalt der Lutherbibel und der Problematik ihrer Revision. In: 03, 145–180.

184 Seyferth, Sebastian: **Wie viel »September-testament« steckt noch in der Lutherbibel von heute?:** ein Übersetzungsvergleich aus germanistischer Perspektive zwischen den Versionen von 1522 und 1984. In: 03, 181–199.

185 Slenczka, Notger: **Die Lutherbibel zwischen Buchstabe und Geist:** Überlegungen zur hermeneutischen Funktion der Bibelübersetzung. In: 03, 53–67.

186 Söderlund, R[une]: **Luther als Ausleger des Hohenliedes.** LuBu 21 (2012), 5–12.

187 Spehr, Christopher: **Luther als Dolmetscher:** Notizen zur Wittenberger Bibelübersetzung. In: 03, 39–52.

188 Stolt, Birgit: **Bibelübersetzung – ihre philologische Genauigkeit und Verständlichkeit.** (1980). In: 038, 175–192.

189 Stolt, Birgit: **Biblische Erzählweise vor und seit Luther – sakralsprachlich – volks-sprachlich – umgangssprachlich?** (1982). In: 038, 211–228.

190 Stolt, Birgit: **Hier irrt der Lutherforscher:** zur ausschlaggebenden Bedeutung kritischer Texteditionen. (1983). In: 038, 147–157.

191 Stolt, Birgit: **Kulturbarrieren als Verständnisproblem.** (1988). In: 038, 159–174.

192 Stolt, Birgit: »**Laßt uns fröhlich springen!**«: Gefühlswelt und Gefühlsnavigierung in Luthers Reformationsarbeit; eine kognitive Emotionalitätsanalyse auf philologischer Basis. In: 038, 13–142.

193 Stolt, Birgit: **Lieblichkeit und Zier, Unge-stüm und Donner:** Martin Luther im Spiegel seiner Sprache. (1989). In: 038, 229–250.

194 Stolt, Birgit: **Luther, die Bibel und das menschliche Herz:** Stil- und Übersetzungsprobleme der Luther-Bibel damals und heute. (1983/84). In: 038, 193–210.

352

195 Stolt, Birgit: »**Mit fröhlichem springenden Geist**«: ethnolinguistische und sprachhistorische Notizen zu Ausdrücken für »Freude« in Martin Luthers Bibelübersetzung. (1994). In: 038, 299–306.

196 Stolt, Birgit: **Revisionen und Rückrevisionen des Luther-NT aus rhetorisch-stilistischer Sicht.** (1988). In: 038, 275–297.

197 Stolt, Birgit: »**... und fühl's im Herzen ...**«: Luthers Bibelübersetzung aus der Sicht neuerer Sprach- und Übersetzungswissenschaft. (2001). In: 038, 251–273.

198 Stolt, Birgit: **Vorwürfe als Trost?**: zum officium consolandi in Luthers Coburg-Briefen. (1998). In: 038, 307–321.

199 Véghelyi, Antal: **A prédikáló Luther I** (Luther als Prediger I). KI 95 (2012), Heft 3, 34–41.

200 Véghelyi, Antal: **A prédikáló Luther II** (Luther als Prediger II). KI 96 (2012), Heft 4, 33–39.

201 Wengert, Timothy J.: **A note on »sola Scriptura« in Martin Luther's writings.** LuBu 20 (2011), 21–31.

202 **Wörterbuch der philosophischen Begriffe**/ begr. von Friedrich Kirchner; Carl Michaëlis; fortges. von Johannes Hoffmeister; vollständig neu hrsg. von Arnim Regenbogen; Uwe Meyer. Sonderausgabe. HH: Meiner, 2006. X, 895 S. L". (Philosophische Bibliothek; 500)

203 **Wörterbuch der philosophischen Begriffe**/ begr. von Friedrich Kirchner; Carl Michaëlis; fortges. von Johannes Hoffmeister; vollständig neu hrsg. von Arnim Regenbogen; Uwe Meyer. HH: Meiner, 2013. X, 895 S. L". (Philosophische Bibliothek; 500)

204 Zimmer, Jörg: **Irdisches Kampfmittel und göttliche Vorsehung:** zur Bedeutung der Fabel in den Tischreden Luthers. In: 027, 95–111.

k) Gottesdienst, Gebet, Spiritualität, Kirchenlied, Musik

205 Arnold, Jochen: **Ton der Tiefe:** Musik als Gabe Gottes und Trost des Herzens, als Zeugnis von Christus, als Seufzen des Geistes und Botin des Evangeliums. In: 033, 11–15: Ill.

206 Bubmann, Peter **Schöpfungsklang und Christuslied:** Hildegard von Bingen und Martin Luther teilten die Hingabe an die Musik. ZZ 13 (2012) Heft 12, 44–46: Ill.

207 Delang, Steffen: **Die Schlosskapelle in Torgau – der erste protestantische Kirchenbau?** In: 01, 91–116: Ill.

208 Ellsel, Reinhard: **Lieder der Reformation:** aktuell ausgelegt. Bielefeld: Luther-Verlag, 2013. 128 S.

209 Eyjólfsson, Sigurjón Árni: **Luther lehrt uns das Beten.** In: 012, 143–159.

210 Hafenscher, Károly: **Az imádkozó Luther** (Luther als Beter). KI 97 (2013), Heft 1, 10–19.

211 Hafenscher, Károly: **Az istentisztelet teológiája Luthernél:** Die Theologie des Gottesdienstes bei Luther; egy elfeledett könyv ismertetése (Darstellung eines vergessenen Buches). KI 94 (2012), Heft 2, 11–19.

212 Mentes, Katalin: **A lutheri tanok hatása az európai zenében:** szakdolgozat (Luthers theologische Wirkung in der europäischen Musik). Diplomarbeit. BP: KGRE BTK, 2012. 78 S.: Ill.

213 Naumann, Bettina: **Heilige Orte und heilige Zeiten?:** Kirchenräume und Kirchenjahr. L: EVA, 2013. 114 S.: Ill. L". (Theologie für die Gemeinde)

214 Schaede, Stephan: **Vater der Lieder:** mit dem Dichter Luther begann die Singebewegung der Reformation. In: 033, 8–10: Ill.

215 Schilling, Johannes: »**Musicam semper amavi« – »Die Musik habe ich allezeit liebgehabt**«: Martin Luther, Johann Walter und die Anfänge evangelischer Kirchenmusik. Lu 83 (2012), 133–144.

216 Spehr, Christopher: **Der Gottesdienst bei Martin Luther:** Facetten eines theologischen Grundbegriffs. LuJ 79 (2012), 9–37.

217 Thust, Karl Christian: **Die Lieder der Evangelischen Gesangbuchs.** Band 1: **Kirchenjahr und Gottesdienst (EG 1–269).** Kassel; BL; LO; NY; PR: Bärenreiter, 2012. 484 S.

l) Katechismus, Konfirmation, Schule, Universität

218 Alfsvåg, Knut: **Hovedtrekk ved menneskesynet i Luthers Lille katekisme** (Hauptzüge der Anthropologie in Luthers Kleinem Katechismus). In: 019, 123–132.

219 Friedrich, Reinhold: **Heilsvergegenwärtigung durch Bildung:** Schule, Unterricht und Katechismus. In: 029, 271–283.

220 Gornig, Antje J.: **Das Wittenberger Schulwesen vor der Reformation.** In: 011 1, 157–173; 2, 91–96: Ill.

221 Jørgensen, Ninna: Katechetische Vermittlung bei Martin Luther, 14–22.

222 Koerrenz, Ralf: **Schule als strukturelles Arrangement:** eine gegenwartsorientierte Lektüre von Luthers Schulschriften. In: 023, 1–19.

223 Leppin, Volker: **Disputationen als Medium der Theologie- und Kirchenreform in der Reformation:** zur Transformation eines akademischen Mediums. In: 023, 115–125.

224 Meier, Christel: **Lehren »in lebendigen Bildern«:** zum pädagogischen Impetus des frühneuzeitlichen Theaters; ein Projektbericht. In: 023, 227–248. L 237.

225 Miklas, Helene: **Die Reformation, das steirische Schulwesen und Kapfenberg.** In: 010, 449–461. L 449–451.

226 Wennemuth, Heike; Wennemuth, Udo: **Heidelberger Katechismus und Katechismuslied als Ausdruck gesungenen Glaubens.** Jahrbuch für badische Kirchen- und Religionsgeschichte 6 (2012), 151–166: Ill. L 152–154.

m) Weitere Einzelprobleme

227 Anttila, Miikka: **Lutherin estetiikka** (Luthers Ästhetik). TA 117 (2012), 53–61.

228 Burger, Christoph: **Spätmittelalterliche und reformatorische Marienpredigten.** In: 029, 117–128.

229 Cavallotto, Stefano: **Santi nella Riforma:** da Erasmo a Luter (Heilige in der Reformation). Roma: Viella, 2009. 431 S.: Ill. (Sacro, santo: N.S.; 12) – Rez.: Vercruysse, Jos E.: Cristianesimo nella storia 33 (2012), 294–297.

230 Domröse, Sonja: **Frauen der Reformationszeit:** gelehrt, mutig und glaubensfest. GÖ: V&R, 2010. 157 S.: Ill. L 133–144L".

3 Beurteilung der Persönlichkeit und ihres Werkes

239 Braun, Eberhard; Heine, Felix; Opolka, Uwe: **Politische Philosophie:** ein Lesebuch; Texte, Analysen, Kommentare. Neuausgabe. Reinbek bei HH: Rowohlt-Taschenbuch, 2008. 505 S.: Ill.L 133–144. (rororo; 55700: Rowohlts Enzyklopädie)

240 Bultmann, Christoph: **Trost finden und**

231 Greyerz, Kaspar von: **Religion und Wissenschaft im 16. und 17. Jahrhundert:** eine Einführung. In: 034, 9–31.

232 Hammond, Mitchell Lewis: »**Ora Deum, & Medico tribuas locum**«: medicine in the Theology of Martin Luther and Philipp Melanchthon. In: 034, 33–50.

233 Heal, Bridget: **The cult of the Virgin Mary in early modern Germany:** Protestant and Catholic piety, 1500–1648. Cambridge [u.a.]: Cambridge University, 2007. XVI, 338 S.: Ill. (Past and present publications) – Rez.: Scheer, Monique: Schweizerische Zeitschrift für Religions- und Kulturgeschichte 102 (2008), 453–456.

234 Heal, Bridget: **The cult of the Virgin Mary in early modern Germany:** Protestant and Catholic piety, 1500–1648. Nachdruck. Cambridge [u.a.]: Cambridge University, 2009. XVI, 338 S.: Ill. (Past and present publications)

235 Ittzés, Gábor: **Üdvképek, szentségek és szentek közössége:** teológiai súlypontok Luther meghalásra felkészítő sermójában (Gemeinschaft von Heilsbildern, Sakramenten und Heiligen: theol. Schwerpunkte in Luthers Sermon von der Bereitung zum Sterben). RSz 105 (2012) Heft 2, 148–165.

236 Litz, Gudrun: **Die Depotenzierung traditioneller Gnaden- und Heilsmedien.** In: 029, 87–97. L".

237 Metz, Detlef: **Das protestantische Drama:** evangelisches geistliches Theater in der Reformationszeit und im konfessionellen Zeitalter. Köln: Böhlau, 2013. 884 S. – Zugl.: TÜ, Univ., Habil., 2011.

238 Schildhammer, Georg: **Glück.** W: Facultas, 2009. 119 S.: L 63f. (Grundbegriffe der europäischen Geistesgeschichte) (UTB; 3236: Profile)

Recht haben: eine Erinnerung an Luther aus Anlass der Thüringer Bachwochen 2012. Lu 83 (2012), 145–160.

241 Carlyle, Thomas: **On heroes, hero-worship and the heroic in history.** Reprint. Gloucester: Dodo, 2007. 196 S.

242 Carlyle, Thomas: **Helden und Heldenver-**

ehrung (On Heroes, hero-worship and the heroic in history <dt.>)/ übers. von Egon Friedell. Neue Ausgabe. F: Edition Flaschenpost, 2012. 180 S.

243 Fuchs, Thomas: **Reformation als Erinnerungsrevolution:** Erinnerungsstrategien der reformatorischen Bewegung. In: 021, 15–27.

244 Gundlach, Thies: **Verdunkelter Christus:** mühsam erkämpften Aufklärer Toleranz gegen die verfasste Kirche; der lange Schatten der Reformation – Überlegungen zum Themenjahr. In: 035, 4–6.

245 Leppin, Volker: **Luther als Mensch entdecken:** warum es der Reformator nicht verdient hat, auf seinem Sockel festgenagelt zu bleiben. ZZ 14 (2013) Heft 5, 12–14: Ill.

246 Lütz, Manfred: **Hätte Luther ihn doch nur verstanden!:** gemalte Reformation; Michelangelos Deckengemälde der Sixtinischen Kapelle wird fünfhundert Jahre alt; als es entstand, war Martin Luther in Rom […]. Frankfurter Allgemeine Zeitung [64] (2012) Nr.254 (31. Oktober), 29: Ill.

247 **Luther ohne Mythos:** das Böse im Reformator; Hubertus Mynarek stellt sein neues Buch vor; Lesung & Diskussion; Aufnahme vom 18.03.2012 im Rahmen der Leipziger Buchmesse/ Hubertus Mynarek. Tonträger: Hörbuch. 1. Aufl. FR: Ahriman, 2012. 2 CD (ca. 111 Minuten) & 1 Beilage.

248 Mynarek, Hubertus: **Luther ohne Mythos:** das Böse im Reformator. 1. Aufl.. FR: Ahriman, 2012. 115 S. (Reihe: Unerwünschte Bücher zur Kirchen- und Religionsgeschichte; 13)

249 Rebe, Bernd: **Die geschönte Reformation:** warum Martin Luther uns kein Vorbild mehr sein kann; ein Beitrag zur Lutherdekade. Marburg: Tectum, 2012. 108 S.

250 Rebe, Bernd: **Die geschönte Reformation:** warum Martin Luther uns kein Vorbild

251 Roper, Lyndal: **Der feiste Doktor:** Luther, sein Körper und seine Biographen/ aus dem Englischen von Karin Wördemann. GÖ: Wallstein, 2012. 78 S.: Ill. (Historische Geisteswissenschaften; 3) – auch als E-book: <https://wallstein-verlag.e-bookshelf.de>. – Rez.: Rublack, Ulinka: Die Zeit 67 (2012) Nr. 1 (27. Dezember), 49: Ill.

252 Rublack, Ulinka: **Der ganze Luther.** Die Zeit 67 (2012) Nr. 1 (27. Dezember), 49: Ill. – Rezension zu LuB 2013, Nr.82. 251.

253 Russell, Bertrand: **History of the Western philosophy.** Neue Ausgabe. Nachdruck der Ausgabe LO, 2004. LO [u.a.]: Routledge, 2010. XI, 778 S. L".

254 Russell, Bertrand: **Philosophie des Abendlandes:** ihr Zusammenhang mit der politischen und der sozialen Entwicklung (History of the Western philosophy <dt.>)/ aus dem Engl. von Elisabeth Fischer-Wernecke … ZH: Europa, 2012. 855 S. L".

255 Schilling, Heinz: **Die Konfessionalisierung des lateinischen Christentums und das Werden des frühmodernen Europa – Modernisierung durch Differenzierung, Integration und Abgrenzung.** In: 043, 209–229.

256 Schilling, Johannes: **Die Reformation – »Segen« oder »Katastrophe«?** In: 032, 42–66.

257 Stekeler-Weithofer, Pirmin: **Philosophiegeschichte.** B; NY: de Gruyter, 2006. VIII, 279 S. L". (Grundthemen Philosophie) [Auch als E-Book verfügbar]

258 Zitelmann, Arnulf: **Die Geschichte der Christen:** erzählt von Arnulf Zitelmann. Weinheim; BL: Beltz & Gelberg, 2009. 255 S.: Ill. L 183–186L". (Gulliver; 5532)

4 Luthers Beziehungen zu früheren Strömungen, Gruppen, Persönlichkeiten und Ereignissen

259 Alfsvåg, Knut: **Luther as a reader of Dionysius the Areopagite.** Studia theologica: Nordic journal of theology 65 (Oslo 2011), Nr.2, 101–114.

260 Hamm, Berndt: **Augustins Auffassung von der Unmittelbarkeit des göttlichen Gna-** denwirkens und die reformatorische Medialitätsproblematik. In: 029, 45–64.

261 Kaufmann, Thomas: **Die Sinn- und Leiblichkeit der Heilsaneignung im späten Mittelalter und in der Reformation.** In: 029, 11–43.

262 Kohnle, Armin: **Martin Luther, Johannes Hus und die hussitische Tradition in Sachsen.** In: 017, 175–187: Ill.

263 Leppin, Volker: **Katechismen im späten Mittelalter.** In: 018, 5–13.

264 Leppin, Volker: **Spätmittelalterliche Wege der Immediatisierung und ihre Bedeutung für die reformatorische Entwicklung Martin Luthers.** In: 029, 307–337.

265 Lopes Pereira, Jairzinho: **Augustine of Hippo and Martin Luther on original sin and justification of the sinner.** Helsinki: Unigrafia, 2012. IX, 411 S. – Zugl.: Helsinki, Univ., Diss., 2012.

266 Müller, Barbara: **Die Tradition der Tischgespräche von der Antike bis in die Renaissance.** In: 027, 63–78.

267 Schwarz, Reinhard: **Die Stiftung der christlichen Religion und Kirche durch Jesus Christus:** nach der Matthäus-Auslegung des Nikolaus von Lyra. In LuB 2011, Nr. 040, 471–492. L 480f.

268 Seidel, Thomas A.: **Die heilige Elisabeth in Erfurt.** In: Die heilige Elisabeth in Erfurt: eine historische und sakralkünstlerische Spurensuche/ hrsg. von Lothar Schmelz; Thomas A. Seidel. Erfurt: Gesellschaft für Thüringische Kirchengeschichte: Evang. Augustinerkloster zu Erfurt, 2007, 9–25: Ill. (Beiträge zur Thüringischen Kirchengeschichte: N. F.; 3)

269 Stengel, Friedemann: **Kulturtransfer am Vorabend der Reformation:** Überlegungen zum Verhältnis zwischen Reformation und hermetisch-neuplatonisch-kabbalistischen Rezeptionen in der Renaissance. In: 014, 491–509.

270 Tetz, Martin: **Zum Psalterverständnis bei Athanasius und Luther.** LuJ 79 (2012), 39–61.

271 Thiede, Werner: **Braut und Bräutigam:** zwei Grundmodelle europäischer Mystik – und was aus ihnen entstand. ZZ 13 (2012) Heft 12, 22–24: Ill.

5 Beziehungen zwischen Luther und gleichzeitigen Strömungen, Gruppen, Persönlichkeiten und Ereignissen

a) Allgemein

272 **Atlas zur Geschichte und Landeskunde von Sachsen/** hrsg. von der Philologisch-historischen Klasse der Sächsischen Akademie der Wissenschaften zu Leipzig in Verbindung mit dem Staatsbetrieb Geobasisinformation und Vermessung Sachsen … Wissenschaftliche Gesamtleitung/Redaktionskommission: Karlheinz Blaschke … Beiheft zur Karte C III 1: **Die wettinischen Länder von der Leipziger Teilung 1485 bis zum Naumburger Vertrag 1554/** von Karlheinz Blaschke. L: Sächsische Akademie der Wissenschaften zu Leipzig; Dresden: Staatsbetrieb Geobasisinformation und Vermessung Sachsen, 2010. 50 S.: Karten.

273 **Atlas zur Geschichte und Landeskunde von Sachsen/** hrsg. von der Philologisch-historischen Klasse der Sächsischen Akademie der Wissenschaften zu Leipzig in Verbindung mit dem Staatsbetrieb Geobasisinformation und Vermessung Sachsen … Karte C III 1: **Die wettinischen Länder von der Leipziger Teilung 1485 bis zum Naum-** burger Vertrag 1554/ von Karlheinz Blaschke unter Mitarbeit von Jana Moser. [L: Sächsische Akademie der Wissenschaften; Dresden: Geobasisinformation und Vermessung Sachsen], 2011. 1 Karte.

274 **Atlas zur Geschichte und Landeskunde von Sachsen/** hrsg. von dem Staatsbetrieb Geobasisinformation und Vermessung Sachsen unter Mitwirkung der Hochschule für Technik und Wirtschaft Dresden … Wissenschaftliche Gesamtleitung/Redaktionskommission: Karlheinz Blaschke … Beiheft zur Karte E II 3: **Die Reformation in Mitteldeutschland 1517–1559:** Menschen – Orte – Ereignisse/ von Karlheinz Blaschke; Christian Winter. Dresden: Staatsbetrieb Geobasisinformation und Vermessung Sachsen, 2011. 24 S.: Karten.

275 **Atlas zur Geschichte und Landeskunde von Sachsen/** hrsg. von dem Staatsbetrieb Geobasisinformation und Vermessung Sachsen unter Mitwirkung der Hochschule für Technik und Wirtschaft Dresden …

Karte E II 3: **Die Reformation in Mittel-deutschland** 1517–1559/ von Karlheinz Blaschke; Christian Winter; Kartographie: Gregor Seidel; Tobias Große. [Dresden: Geobasisinformation und Vermessung Sachsen], 2012. 1 Karte.

276 Blickle, Peter **Das alte Europa:** vom Hochmittelalter bis zur Moderne. M: Beck, 2008. 320 S.: Ill.

277 **Einführung in die Geschichte des Christentums/** von Franz Xaver Bischof; Thomas Bremer; Giancarlo Collet; Alfons Fürst. FR; BL; W: Herder, 2012. 636 S.: Ill.

278 Füllgrabe, Jörg: **Luther twitterte anders.** Literaturkritik.de: Rezensionsforum für Literatur und für Kulturwissenschaften 14 (2012), 257–260. – Rez. zu LuB 2013, Nr. 290.

279 Haberer, Johanna: **Distribution – Partizipation – Individualisierung:** grundsätzliche Beobachtungen zum Mediengeschehen des 16. Jahrhunderts in der Perspektive moderner Medienentwicklung. In: 029, 1–10.

280 Hinrichs, Ernst: **Von der Reformation bis zum Westfälischen Frieden (Ende 15. Jahrhundert bis 1648).** In: Kleine deutsche Geschichte/ von Ulf Dirlmeier … Aktual. und erg. Ausgabe. S: Reclam, 2006, 113–186.

281 Hinrichs, Ernst: **Von der Reformation bis zum Westfälischen Frieden (Ende 15. Jahrhundert bis 1648).** In: Kleine deutsche Geschichte/ von Ulf Dirlmeier … Nachdruck der aktual. und erg. Ausgabe S, 2006. S: Reclam, 2007, 113–186. (Reclams Universal-Bibliothek; 17054)

282 Hinrichs, Ernst: **Von der Reformation bis zum Westfälischen Frieden (Ende 15. Jahrhundert bis 1648).** In: Kleine deutsche Geschichte/ von Ulf Dirlmeier … Nachdruck der aktual. und erg. Ausgabe S, 2006. S: Reclam, 2009, 113–186. (Reclams Universal-Bibliothek; 17054)

283 Kaufmann, Thomas: **Der Anfang der Reformation:** Studien zur Kontextualität der Theologie, Publizistik und Inszenierung Luthers und der reformatorischen Bewegung. TÜ: Mohr Siebeck, 2012. XVIII, 676 S.: Ill. (Spätmittelalter, Humanismus, Reformation; 67)

284 Kommer, Dorothee: **Frauen verfassen reformatorische Flugschriften:** Studien zu von Frauen verfassten Flugschriften der frühen Reformationszeit (1523–1534/1557) und der in ihnen vertretenen Sicht von Geistlichkeit. TÜ, 2010. 334 Bl. – TÜ, Univ., Evang.-Theol. Fak., Diss., 2012.

285 Kommer, Dorothee: **Reformatorische Flugschriften von Frauen:** Flugschriftenautorinnen der frühen Reformationszeit und ihre Sicht von Geistlichkeit. L: EVA, 2013. 420 S. (Arbeiten zur Kirchen- und Theologiegeschichte; 40) – Zugl.: TÜ, Univ., Evang.-Theol. Fak., Diss., 2012, unter dem Titel: »Frauen verfassen reformatorische Flugschriften«.

286 Leppin, Volker: **Die Reformation.** DA: WB, 2013. 136 S. (Geschichte kompakt)

287 Oberman, Heiko A.: **Zwei Reformationen:** Luther und Calvin – Alte und Neue Welt (The two Reformations <dt.>)/ aus dem Engl. von Christian Wiese; durchges. und mit einem Nachwort von Manfred Schulze. Elektronische Ressource. one loco: Ciando: PeP eBooks, 2009. 320 S. (514 KB).

288 Ortmann, Volkmar: **Zwischen Profil und Konzil:** die Schmalkaldischen Artikel im Kontext der Religionsgespräche. In: 031, 43–55.

289 Rychlak, Gabor: **Hexenfieber im Erzgebirge:** die Annaberger Krankheit 1712–1720. Elektronische Ressource. MZ, 2009. 451 S.: Ill. (PDF). L 239–254L" – MZ, Univ., Fachbereich 05 Philosophie und Philologie, Diss., 2009. – Siehe: <http://ubm.opus.hbz-nrw.de/volltexte/2009/2159/pdf/diss.pdf>.

290 Sandl, Marcus: **Medialität und Ereignis:** eine Zeitgeschichte der Reformation. ZH: Chronos, 2011. 596 S.: Ill. (Medienwandel, Medienwechsel, Medienwissen; 18) – Teilw. zugl. Konstanz, Univ., Habil., 2008. – Rez.: Blickle, Peter: HZ 295 (2012), 778–780; siehe auch LuB 2013, Nr. 278. 292.

291 Sandl, Marcus: **Sinn und Präsenz in der frühen Reformation.** In: 029, 65–85.

292 Tschopp, Silvia Serena: **(K)eine neue Mediengeschichte der Reformation.** Internationales Archiv für Sozialgeschichte der deutschen Literatur 37 (2012), 462–475. – Rez. zu LuB 2013, Nr. 290.

293 Zur Nieden, Burkhard: **Schmalkaldische Artikel und Schmalkaldischer Bund aus historischer Sicht.** In: 031, 35–41.

b) Wittenberger Freunde, Philipp Melanchthon

294 Ahuis, Ferdinand: **Johannes Bugenhagen und England.** LuJ 79 (2012), 159–182: Ill.

295 Bartmuß, Alexander: **Martin Luthers Tischreden und die Wittenberger Gruppenidentität:** Philipp Melanchthons Exempla. In: 027, 79–94.

296 Bergholz, Thomas: **Reich Gottes und Kirchenordnung:** Johannes Bugenhagens kirchenordnendes Wirken als Ausdruck seiner Ekklesiologie und Zwei-Reiche-Lehre. In: 037, 139–150.

297 Degen, Daniel: **Das Lied »Es ist das Heil uns kommen her« von Paulus Speratus.** JLH 49 (2010), 135–162.

298 Fuchs, Thorsten: **Philipp Melanchthon als neulateinischer Dichter in der Zeit der Reformation.** TÜ: Narr, 2008. 428 S.: Ill. (Neo-Latina; 14)

299 Greschat, Martin: **Christlicher Glaube und Freiheit im Verständnis Melanchthons.** Jahrbuch für badische Kirchen- und Religionsgeschichte 5 (2011), 57–67.

300 Gummelt, Volker: **Johannes Bugenhagens Kommentar- und Exegesepraxis:** ein Überblick. In: 037, 109–116.

301 Gunnoe, Charles D., Jr.: **German Protestantism and astrology:** the debate between Thomas Erastus and the Melanchthon circle. In: 034, 86–101.

302 Hasse, Hans-Peter: **Bugenhagen und der Schmalkaldische Krieg.** In: 037, 197–217.

303 Hennen, Insa Christiane: **Bugenhagens Haus.** In: 037, 35–61: Ill.

304 Hoyer, Siegfried: **Simon Haferitz – Prediger zwischen Luther und Müntzer.** In: 022, 85–96.

305 Jung, Martin H.: **Kirchengeschichte.** GÖ: V&R, 2010. 300 S. (Grundwissen Christentum; 3)

306 Jung, Martin H.: **Melanchthon és kora** (Philipp Melanchthon und seine Zeit <ungar.>). BP: Kálvin, 2012. 172 S.

307 Kohnle, Armin: **Johannes Bugenhagen und das Interim.** In: 037, 219–227.

308 Kohnle, Armin: **Die Wittenberger Theologische Fakultät in der Reformationszeit:** Probleme – Themen – Perspektiven. In: 011 1, 201–211; 2, 119–122: Ill.

309 Kuropka, Nicole: **Melanchthon.** E-Book-Ausgabe. S: UTB, 2010. 143 S.: Ill. (UTB; 3417: Profile)

310 Lausten, Martin Schwarz: **Bugenhagen und Dänemark.** In: 037, 229–240.

311 Leppin, Volker: **Bugenhagen auf der Kanzel:** Beobachtungen zu Predigten der zwanziger Jahre. In: 037, 127–137.

312 Loehr, Johanna: **»... jetzt, da dein Leben vollbracht ist, lebst du auf dem Gipfel des Himmelspols ...«:** Melanchthons Gedicht auf Bugenhagen. In: 037, 95–106.

313 Lohrmann, Martin: **Bugenhagens Jonas-Kommentar.** In: 037, 117–126.

314 Lorentzen, Tim: **Theologie und Ökonomie in Bugenhagens Fürsorgekonzept.** In: 037, 151–174.

315 Lück, Heiner: **»Recht« und »Gesetz« in den Kirchenordnungen Johannes Bugenhagens.** In: 037, 177–195.

316 Ludwig, Ulrike: **Die Leichenpredigt von Johannes Bugenhagen auf Martin Luther 1546.** In: 037, 75–93.

317 Ludwig, Walther: **Art und Zweck der Lehrmethode Melanchthons:** Beobachtungen anlässlich der ersten Übersetzung seiner »Initia doctrinae physicae«. In: 023, 91–113.

318 [Melanchthon, Philipp]: **Melanchthon deutsch/** begr. von Michael Beyer; Stefan Rhein; Günther Wartenberg †. Band 4: **Melanchthon, die Universität und ihre Fakultäten/** hrsg. von Michael Beyer; Armin Kohnle; Volker Leppin; unter Mitarbeit von Christiane Domtera; Annika Schmidt. L: EVA, 2012. 383 S.

319 [Melanchthon, Philipp]: **Melanchthons Briefwechsel:** kritische und kommentierte Gesamtausgabe/ im Auftrag der Heidelberger Akademie der Wissenschaften hrsg. von Christine Mundhenk. Band T 13: **Texte 3421–3779 (1544)/** bearb. von Matthias Dall'Asta; Heidi Hein; Christine Mundhenk. S-Bad Cannstatt: Frommann-Holzboog, 2012. 631 S.

320 Michel, Stefan: **»... mein lieber Schwager ...«:** Johannes Bugenhagen und Georg Rörer in ihren familiären und theologischen Beziehungen. In: 037, 63–73: Ill.

321 Michel, Stefan: **Thematische Bearbeitungen der Tischreden Martin Luthers durch Georg Rörer (1492–1557):** Beobachtungen zu Überlieferung und Funktion In: 027, 221–240.

322 Mischok, Volker: **Aegidius Faber und die**

Anfänge der Reformation in Schwerin. Mecklenburgia sacra: Jahrbuch für mecklenburgische Kirchengeschichte 12 (2009), 116–144.

323 Plath, Uwe: **Philipp Melanchthon und Lüneburg.** Jahrbuch der Gesellschaft für niedersächsische Kirchengeschichte 109 (2011), 43–74: Ill.

324 Rajhman, Jože; Voglar, Dušan: **Melanchthon in Trubar** (Melanchthon und Trubar). Stati inu obstati: revija za vprašanja protestantizma 11/12 (Ljubljana 2010), 220–228

325 Rhein, Stefan: **Bugenhagen und Wittenberg:** eine Spurensuche. In: 037, 11–33: Ill.

326 Scheible, Heinz: **Philipp Melanchthon und Heidelberg:** eine lebenslange Liebe. In: 016, 30–33: Ill.

327 Schmidt, Bernward: **Briefe Philipp Melanchthons und Caspar Peucers im Archiv der Römischen Inquisition.** ARG 103 (2012), 281–292: abstract.

328 Speer, Christian: **Georg Rörer (1492–1557) in Wittenberg und Jena – Versuch einer lokalen und sozialen Verortung:** zugleich ein Beitrag über Möglichkeiten und Grenzen der Stadtbuchforschung. In: 011 1, 255–264; 2, 145 f: Ill.

329 Sternhagen, Eick: **Ethik und Drama bei Melanchthon.** MS, 2006. V, 264 S. – MS, Univ., Philos. Fak., Diss., 2006. [Zugänglich als freie Online-Ressource: <http://d-nb.info/983438056/34>].

330 Stoye, Angela: **Schon zu Lebzeiten »der Gottselige«:** als Reformationsfürst ging Georg III. von Anhalt in die Geschichte ein. In: 02, 30 f: Ill.

331 Strohm, Christoph: **Das Melanchthon-Bild Dietrich Bonhoeffers.** Jahrbuch für badische Kirchen- und Religionsgeschichte 6 (2012), 27–39.

332 Töpfer, Thomas: **Philipp Melanchthons »Loci communes«:** Systematisierung, Vermittlung und Rezeption gelehrten Wissens zwischen Humanismus, Reformation und Konfessionspolitik (1521–1590). In: 023, 127–147.

333 Treu, Martin: **Philipp Melanchthon:** Leben – Werk – Wirkung; Begleitheft zur Ausstellung im Melanchthonhaus/ Bildredaktion: Petra Gröschl; Einleitung: Stefan Rhein. Wittenberg: Stiftung Luthergedenkstätten in Sachsen-Anhalt, 2013. 80 S.: Ill.

334 Wels, Volkhard: **Melanchthons Anthropologie zwischen Theologie, Medizin und Astrologie.** In: 034, 51–85.

335 Wengert, Timothy J.: **Beyond stereotypes:** the real Philip Melanchthon. (1999). In: 042, [Text] I, S. 9–31.

336 Wengert, Timothy J.: **The day Philip Melanchthon got mad.** (1991). In: 042, [Text] VII, S. 419–433.

337 Wengert, Timothy J.: **Famous last words:** the final epistolary exchange between Erasmus of Rotterdam and Philipp Melanchthon. (2005). In: 042, [Text] XII, 18–38.

338 Wengert, Timothy J.: **Melanchthon and Luther / Luther and Melanchthon.** (1999). In: 042, [Text] X, 55–88.

339 Wengert, Timothy J.: **»Not by nature ›Philoneikos‹«:** Philip Melanchthon's initial reactions to the Augsburg interim. (2007). In: 042, [Text] XIII, 33–49.

340 Wengert, Timothy J.: **Philip Melanchthon and a Christian politics.** (2003). In: 042, [Text] IX, 29–62.

341 Wengert, Timothy J.: **Philip Melanchthon and Augustine of Hippo.** (2008). In: 042, [Text] IV, S. 249–267.

342 Wengert, Timothy J.: **Philip Melanchthon on time and history in the Reformation.** (2005). In: 042, [Text] V, S. 9–33.

343 Wengert, Timothy J.: **Philip Melanchthon's 1522 Annotations on Romans and the Lutheran origins of rhetorical criticism.** (1996). In: 042, [Text] II, 118–140.

344 Wengert, Timothy J.: **»Qui vigilantissimis oculis veterum omnium commentarios excusserit«:** Philip Melanchthon's patristic exegesis. (1999). In: 042, [Text] III, 115–134.

345 Wengert, Timothy J.: **»We will feast together in haeven forever«:** the epistolary friendship of John Calvin and Philipp Melanchthon. (1999). In: 042, [Text] XI, 19–44.

c) Altgläubige

346 **Akten und Briefe zur Kirchenpolitik Herzog Georgs von Sachsen.** Bd. 4: 1535–1539/ hrsg. von Heiko Jadatz; Christian Winter. Köln; Weimar; W: Böhlau, 2012. 808 S.

347 Dietrich, Stephanie-Thalia: **Martin Luthers Papstkritik im Spiegel der Flugblätter:** »Wider das Bapstum zu Rom vom Teuffel gestifft« und die »Abbildung des Bapstums«: Studienarbeit. Elektronische Ressource. s. l. GRIN, 2011. 26 S. (PDF).

348 Fuhrmann, Horst: **Die Päpste:** von Petrus zu Benedikt XVI. 4., aktual. und erw. Aufl. in der Beck'schen Reihe. M: Beck, 2012. 330 S.: Ill. L". (Beck'sche Reihe; 1590)

349 Leppin, Volker: **Das Papstbild der Schmalkaldischen Artikel.** In: 031, 57–78.

350 Schlageter, Johannes: **Die sächsischen Franziskaner und ihre theologische Auseinandersetzung mit der frühen deutschen Reformation.** MS: Aschendorff, 2012. VI, 395 S. (Franziskanische Forschungen; 52)

351 Schubert, Anselm: **Das Lachen der Ketzer:** zur Selbstinszenierung der frühen Reformation. ZThK 108 (2011), 405–430.

352 Vercruysse, Jos E.: **Jakobus Latomus en een vergeten boekje** (Jakobus Latomus und ein verschollenes Büchlein). LuBu 21 (2012), 17–31.

d) Humanisten

353 Mertens, Dieter: **Jakob Wimpheling als zentrale Gestalt des oberrheinischen Humanismus.** Jahrbuch für badische Kirchen- und Religionsgeschichte 6 (2012), 49–72: Ill.

354 Recki, Birgit: **Freiheit.** W: Facultas, 2009. 119 S. L 24–28L". (Grundbegriffe der europäischen Geistesgeschichte) (UTB; 3233: Profile)

355 Walter, Peter: **Humanismus, Toleranz und individuelle Religionsfreiheit:** Erasmus und sein Umkreis. In: 04, 105–126.

356 Wengert, Timothy J.: **Philip Melanchthon's contribution to Luther's debate with Erasmus over the bondage of the will.** (2004). In: 042, [Text] VI, S. 110–124.

e) Thomas Müntzer und Bauernkrieg

357 Bräuer, Siegfried: **Thomas Müntzer und die Zensur.** In: 022, 39–65.

358 **Ein heller Schein:** die andere Seite der einen Wirklichkeit; ein Gespräch mit Gerhard Wehr über die Mystik/ Gesprächsführung: Helmut Kremers. ZZ 13 (2012) Heft 12, 35–31: Ill.

359 Heyer, Andreas; Saage, Richard: **Utopie oder Chiliasmus?:** zur Idee der Radikalität bei Thomas Morus und Thomas Müntzer. In: 022, 67–84.

360 Schmidt, Matthias: **Thomas Müntzer:** »der Satan von Allstedt«. In: 013, 62–77: Ill.

361 Schorlemmer, Friedrich: **Der blutige Kampf um den neuen Glauben.** In: 035, 18–20.

362 Vogler, Günter: **Thomas Müntzer in einer Bildergeschichte:** eine kulturhistorische Dokumentation. GÜ: GVH, 2010. 135 S.: Ill. (Schriften des Vereins für Reformationsgeschichte; 211)

363 Vogler, Günter: **Thomas Müntzer in einer Bildergeschichte:** eine kulturhistorische Dokumentation. Lizenzausgabe. Mühlhausen: Thomas-Müntzer-Gesellschaft, 2010. 135 S.: Ill. (Thomas-Müntzer-Gesellschaft: Veröffentlichungen; 13)

364 Vogler, Günter: **Thomas Müntzer – Irrweg oder Alternative?:** Plädoyer für eine andere Sicht. ARG 103 (2012), 11–40: abstract.

f) »Schwärmer« und Täufer

365 Bubenheimer, Ulrich: **Martin Luthers Invocavitpredigten und die Entstehung religiöser Devianz im Luthertum:** die Prediger der Wittenberger Bewegung 1521/1522 und Karlstadts Entwicklung zum Kryptoradikalen. In: 022, 17–37.

366 Burnett, Amy Nelson: **Karlstadt and the origins of the Eucharistic controversy:** a study in the circulation of ideas. Oxford; NY: Oxford University, 2011. XVIII, 234 S. (Oxford studies in historical theology) – Rez.: Bürki, Silvianne: Zw 39 (2012), 157–161.

367 Dejung, Christoph: **Zur Frage der Kryptoradikalität in Bezug auf Sebastian Francks Ulmer »Declaration«.** In: 022, 106–139.

368 Kühlmann, Wilhelm: **Sebastian Franck (1499–1542) – Geistfrömmigkeit und Protest.** Jahrbuch für badische Kirchen- und Religionsgeschichte 6 (2012), 73–90: Ill.

369 Trelenberg, Jörg: **Luther und die Bestrafung der Täufer.** ZThK 110 (2013), 22–49.

370 Waite, Gary K.: **Eradicating the devil's minions:** anabaptists and witches in Reformation Europe, 1525–1600. Toronto; LO: University of Toronto, 2007. XVI, 319, [12] S.: Ill., Kt. – Rez.: Tremp, Kathrin Utz: Schweizerische Zeitschrift für Religions- und Kulturgeschichte 102 (2008), 457–459.

371 Wollgast, Siegfried: **Kryptoradikalität in Sebastian Francks »Guldin Arch« und »Das verbüthschiert Buch«.** In: 022, 141–161. L".

g) Schweizer und Oberdeutsche

372 Balke, W[illem]: **Calvijn over de heilige doop:** de doop teruggebracht tot het zuivere terrein van Woord, Geest en geloof (Calvin über die heilige Taufe: die Taufe zurückgebracht zum reinen Bereich von Wort, Geist und Glaube). Protestants Nederland 78 (Rotterdam 2012), 281–283.

373 Bryner, Erich: **Die Reformation in Schaffhausen und ihre Besonderheiten.** Zw 39 (2012), 79–92.

374 [Bucer, Martin]: **Martin Bucers Deutsche Schriften/** im Auftrag der Heidelberger Akademie der Wissenschaften hrsg. von Christoph Strohm. Bd. 15: **Schriften zur Reichsreligionspolitik der Jahre** 1543/1546/ bearb. von Susanne Haaf unter Mitarb. von Albert de Lange. GÜ: Kaiser GVH, 2011. 650 S.: Faks. (Bucer, Martin: Opera omnia: series 1, Deutsche Schriften; 15)

375 Buckwalter, Stephen E.: **Die Entwicklung einer eigenen Position:** Bucer und die innerprotestantische Abendmahlskontroverse bis zum Tod Zwingiis und Oekolampads. In: 026, 98–107.

376 Bundi, Martin: **Zur Dynamik der frühen Reformbewegung in Graubünden:** staats-, kirchen und privatrechtliche Erlasse des Dreibündestaates 1523–1526. Zw 38 (2011), 1–34.

377 Bundi, Martin: **Zur Führungsrolle des Grauen Bundes und der Stadt Ilanz in der frühen Reformbewegung Graubündens.** Zw 39 (2012), 23–50. L 37.

378 Christ-von Wedel, Christine: **Das Buch der Bücher popularisieren:** der Bübelübersetzer Leo Jud und sein biblisches Erbauungsbuch »Vom lyden Christi« (1534). Zw 38 (2011), 35–52.

379 Greschat, Martin: **Martin Bucer:** egy reformátor és a kor, amelyben élt (Martin Bucer: ein Reformator und seine Zeit <ungar.>). BP: Kálvin, 2011. 334 S.: Ill.

380 Grimmsmann, Damaris: **Heinrich Bullingers Deutung der Türkengefahr und des Islam.** ARG 103 (2012), 64–91: abstract.

381 Mundhenk, Christine: **Die Beziehung Bucers zu Luther und Melanchthon.** In: 026, 205–216.

382 Oberman, Heiko A.: **John Calvin and the Reformation of the refugees/** eingel. von Peter A. Dykema. Genéve: Droz, 2009. (Travaux d'humanisme et Renaissance; 464) – Rez.: Balserak, Jon: Zw 38 (2011), 243–245.

383 Simon, Wolfgang: **Die Überschreitung der Grenze:** Bucers Annahme der Confessio Augustana und deren Apologie. In: 026, 108–124.

384 Zimmermann, Ulrich: **Martin Bucers Schrift über die Kindertaufe von** 1533: Übersetzung und Erklärungen. Jahrbuch für badische Kirchen- und Religionsgeschichte 6 (2012), 275–313. L".

h) Juden

385 Arndt, Timotheus: **Seiten der Reformation.** In: 041, 8: Ill.

386 Brumlik, Micha: **Martin Luther und die Juden – eine politologische Betrachtung.** Begegnungen: Zeitschrift für Kirche und Judentum 95 (2012) Heft 3, 23–30.

387 Gamm, Hans-Jochen: **Das Judentum:** eine Einführung. Nachdruck der aktual. Ausgabe F; NY, 1998. B; MS: Lit, 2011. 180 S. L".

388 Homolka, Walter: **Überwinder des Mittelalters:** wie liberale deutsche Juden Martin Luther und sein Werk bewertet haben. ZZ 14 (2013) Heft 4, 14–17: Ill.

389 Jung, Martin H.: **Christen und Juden:** die Geschichte ihrer Beziehungen. DA: WB, 2008. 302 S. – Rez.: Wagner, Wolfgang: BlWKG 110 (2010), 412–415.

390 Kaplan, Debra: **Sharing conversations:** a Jewish polemic against Martin Luther. ARG 103 (2012), 41–63: Zusammenfassung.

391 Matthias, Markus: **Marteen Luthers theologie – antisemitisch?:** enkele theologiehistorisch en historische notities bij en Nederlandse discussie (Martin Luthers Theologie – antisemitisch? einige theologiehistorische und historische Notizen zu einer Diskussion in den Niederlanden). LuBu 21 (2012), 32–59.

392 Steinhäuser, Martin: **Antijudaismus bei Martin Luther:** Konfirmanden/-innen erkunden eine Grenze der Toleranz. In: 041, 30 f: Ill. [Unterrichtsmaterial als Online-Ressource: <http://www.impuls-reformation.de/_script/dbDetail_material.asp?mm=0&list=1161,0,250,83&bUrl=de/reformation_materialien.asp>]

393 Süss, René: **Luther, een sympathieke potentaat** (Luther, ein sympathischer Potentat). Amsterdam: Bibliotheca Theologica

Formicae, 2012. 392 S.: Ill. – Rez.: Matthias, Markus: LuBu 21 (2012), 60–63.

i) Künstler, Kunst, Bilderfrage

394 Beyer, Franz-Heinrich: **Geheiligte Räume:** Theologie, Geschichte und Symbolik des Kirchengebäudes. 2., durchges. Aufl. DA: WB, 2009. 231 S.: Ill. L 182–184L".

395 Beyer, Franz-Heinrich: **Geheiligte Räume:** Theologie, Geschichte und Symbolik des Kirchengebäudes. 3. Aufl.; unveränd. Nachdruck der 2., durchges. Aufl. DA: WB, 2011. 231 S.: Ill. [Auch als Online-Ausgabe (eBook; PDF). s. l.: eblib, 2012.]

396 **Dürer to Veronese:** sixteenth century paintings in the National Gallery/ hrsg. von Jill Dunkerton; Susan Foister; Nicholas Penny. Taschenbuchausgabe. New Haven, CT; LO: Yale University; LO: National Gallery, [2002]. XI, 317 S.: Ill., Kt. L".

397 Fleck, Miriam Verena: **Ein tröstlich gemelde:** die Glaubensallegorie »Gesetz und Gnade« in Europa zwischen Spätmittelalter und Früher Neuzeit. Korb: Didymos, 2010. 680, [136] S.: Ill. (Studien zur Kunstgeschichte des Mittelalters und der Frühen Neuzeit; 5) – Zugl. aktual., ergänzte und überarb. Fassung von B, Freie Univ., Diss., 2006 unter dem Titel: »Gesetz und Gnade – Entstehung und Rezeption eines Bildthemas«. – Rez.: Packeiser, Thomas: sehepunkte: Rezensionsjournal für die Geschichtswissenschaften 12 (2012), Nr. 9 [15.09.2012] – <http://www.sehepunkte.de/2012/09/18409.html>.

398 Kühne, Hartmut: **Frommes Spektakel:** liturgische Inszenierungen am Ende des Mittelalters im Chemnitzer Raum. In: 017, 216–233: Ill.

399 Kunde, Claudia: **Wettinische Begräbniskultur vom 16. bis zum 18. Jahrhundert.** In: 030, 11–76: Ill.

400 Lagaude, Jenny: **Das verlorene Pfingstbild des Schneeberger Retabels im Spiegel der Theologie Luthers.** In: 07, 137–148: Ill.

401 Magin, Christine: **Soli Deo gloria?:** inschriftliche Medien der Reformationszeit. In: 029, 129–165.

402 Michael, Angelika: **Luther und die Bilder:** von Bildern, die man sieht, und solchen, die man nicht sieht. LuJ 79 (2012), 101–137.

403 Packeiser, Thomas: **Wo bleibt Schneeberg auf dem Schneeberger Retabel?** In: 07, 163–185: Ill.

404 Schlie, Heike: **Das Holz des Lebensbaumes, des Kreuzes und des Altarretabels:** die Cranach'sche Neufassung einer sakramentalen Bildgattung In: 07, 101–117: Ill.

405 Schmidt, Frank: **Der lutherische Kirchenbau im 16. und 17. Jahrhundert.** In: 01, 9–19.

406 Schneider-Ludorff, Gury: **Reformatorische Epitaphkultur:** Vergegenwärtigung des Heils im Totengedenken und Stiftungswesen. In: 029, 213 223.

407 Slenczka, Ruth: **Lutherische Landesherren am Altar:** das Schneeberger Fürstenretabel von Lucas Cranach als protestantisches Initialwerk. In: 07, 119–136: Ill.

408 Tacke, Andreas: **»ich het euch vil zuschreiben, hab aber vil zuschaffen«:** Cranach der Ältere als »Parallel Entrepreneur«; Auftragslage und Marktstrategien im Kontext des Schneeberger Altars von 1539. In: 07, 71–84.

409 Unger, Corona: **Barocke Emporenmalerei in Dorfkirchen des Herzogtums Sachsen-Gotha:** Bedeutung, Entstehung und Gestaltung/ mit einem Geleitwort von Peter Poscharsky; Redaktion: Stefan Michel. Weimar: Gesellschaft für Thüringische Kirchengeschichte, 2006. 159 S.: Ill. L 47–50L". (Beiträge zur Thüringischen Kirchengeschichte: Neue Folge; 2)

410 Wegmann, Susanne: **Die Öffnung zum Glauben:** Lucas Cranachs Schneeberger Retabel und das Konzept seiner Wandlung. In: 07, 87–100: Ill.

411 Wegmann, Susanne: **Die Sichtbarkeit der Gnade:** Bildtheorie und Gnadenvermittlung auf den lutherischen Altären. In: 029, 187–211.

412 Wiemers, Michael: **Die Rettung der Frommen:** Überlegungen zur Lot-Ikonographie. In: 07, 149–162: Ill.

j) Territorien und Orte innerhalb des Deutschen Reiches

413 Baur, Jörg: **Johannes Brenz:** ein schwäbischer Meisterdenker auf den Spuren Luthers. (2000). In: 05, 18–46.

414 Brecht, Martin: **Adam Weiß:** der Crailsheimer Reformator/ mit Beiträgen von Winfried Dalferth und Folker Förtsch. Crailsheim: Baier, 2011. 58 S.: Ill. (Historische

Schriftenreihe der Stadt Crailsheim; 10) – Rez.: Huber, Wolfgang: ZBKG 80 (2011), 541.

415 Bunners, Michael: **Der Landtag an der Sagsdorfer Brücke von 1549 – ein Konzil? – der Reformator Gerd Oemcke.** Mecklenburgia sacra: Jahrbuch für mecklenburgische Kirchengeschichte 12 (2009), 61–75: Ill.

416 Detmers, Achim: **Fürsten zwischen Glaube und Vernunft:** Einblicke in die wechselhafte Konfessionsgeschichte Anhalts. In: 02, 26–29: Ill.

417 Ehmer, Hermann: **Die Reformation in Schwaben.** Leinfelden-Echterdingen: DRW, 2010. 242 S.: Ill. (Bibliothek schwäbischer Geschichte; 2)

418 **Die Geschichte der Reformation in Zwickau:** von den Anfängen bis zu ihrer Durchsetzung. Zwickau: Stadtverwaltung Zwickau – Kulturamt, s.a. 1 Faltbl.: Ill. (Luther in Zwickau)

419 Hauschild, Wolf-Dieter: »**Suchet der Stadt Bestes**«: neun Jahrhunderte Staat und Kirche in der Hansestadt Lübeck/ hrsg. von Antjekathrin Graßmann; Andreas Kurschat. Lübeck: Schmidt-Römhild, 2011. 312 S. – Rez.: Huber, Wolfgang: ZBKG 80 (2011), 539–541.

420 Jadatz, Heiko: **1547:** der Schmalkaldische Krieg und die Wittenberger Kapitulation. In: Zäsuren sächsischer Geschichte/ hrsg. von Reinhardt Eigenwill. Beucha; Markkleeberg: Sax, 2010, 95–121: Ill.

421 Jürgens, Klaus: **Das Zeitalter der Reformation im Lande Braunschweig.** In: Von der Taufe der Sachsen zur Kirche in Niedersachsen: Geschichte der Evangelisch-lutherischen Landeskirche in Braunschweig/ hrsg. von Friedrich Weber … Braunschweig: Appelhans, 2010, 129–179.

422 Kaufmann, Thomas: **Der »Schriftaltar« in der Spitalkirche zu Dinkelsbühl – ein Zeugnis lutherischer Konfessionskultur.** ARG 103 (2012), 117–148: Ill.: abstract.

423 Kawerau, Gustav: **Caspar Guttel:** ein Lebensbild aus Luthers Freundeskreise. (1882). Whitefish, MT: Kessinger 2010. 110 S. (Kessinger legacy reprints)

424 Koch, Ernst: **Im Auftrag des Kurfürsten:** Dienstreisen des Gothaer Superintendenten Friedrich Mykonius. In: »Hinaus ins Weite …«: Reisen Thüringer Protestanten/ hrsg. von Susanne Böhm, Miriam Rieger.

Erfurt: Gesellschaft für Thüringische Kirchengeschichte, 2010, 11–33: Ill. (Beiträge zur Thüringischen Kirchengeschichte: Neue Folge; 4)

425 Koch, Ernst: **Reformation, Kryptocalvinismus und Dreißigjähriger Krieg.** In: 039, 129–136: Ill.

426 Lehmann, Kai: **Balthasar Wilhelm:** der Reformator Schmalkaldens. In: 036, 27: Ill.

427 Preckel, Günter: »**Weit überlegen den Papisten**«: die Entwicklung der Reformation in der Muldestadt Dessau. In: 02, 45–47: Ill.

428 Preckel, Günter: **Wolfgang der Bekenner:** ein streitbarer Fürst und treuer Anhänger Luthers. In: 02, 32 f: Ill.

429 Römer, Jürgen: **Der Kampf für den rechten Glauben – und um die Macht:** im Schmalkaldischen Bund schlossen sich die evangelischen Territorien und Städte zusammen […] In: 036, 36–39: Ill.

430 Strohm, Christoph: **Reformatorische Anfänge:** von Luther bis Ottheinrich. In: 016, 34–37: Ill.

431 Weismann, Christoph: **Welches Glaubens bist du? – Der Katechismus des Johannes Brenz zwischen Wittenberg und Heidelberg.** In: 018, 28–36.

432 Wolgast, Eike: **Der lange Weg zur obrigkeitlichen Reformation im Herzogtum Mecklenburg:** Herzog Heinrich V. und Herzog Johann Albrecht I. Mecklenburgia sacra: Jahrbuch für mecklenburgische Kirchengeschichte 12 (2009), 39–59.

k) Länder und Orte außerhalb des Deutschen Reiches

433 Appel, Sabine: **Heinrich VIII.:** der König und sein Gewissen; eine Biographie. Originalausgabe. M: Beck, 2012. 318 S.: Ill. (Beck'sche Reihe; 6056)

434 Balserak, Jon: »**We need teachers today, not prophets**«: Peter Martyr Vermigli's exposition of prophecy. ARG 103 (2012), 92–116: Zusammenfassung.

435 Bryner, Erich: **Theologische Motive in der Bibelübersetzung von Primus Truber.** In LuB 2013, Nr. 501, 73–81.

436 Campi, Emidio: **The Reformation in Croatia and the »Beneficio di Cristo«.** In LuB 2013, Nr. 501, 39–51.

437 Ecsedi, Zsuzsanna: **Luther zsoltárparafrázisai és a 16–17. század magyar zsoltárdalla-**

mai (Luthers Psalmparaphrasen und die ungarischen Psalmtöne des 16.–17. Jh.). In: 044, 113–123.

438 **Glaubwürdig bleiben:** 500 Jahre protestantisches Abenteuer; wissenschaftlicher Begleitband zur Kärntner Landesausstellung 2011 in Fresach/ hrsg. von Wilhelm Wadl. Klagenfurt am Wörthersee: Verlag des Geschichtsvereines für Kärnten, 2011. 544 S.: Ill.. Kt. (Archiv für vaterländische Geschichte und Topographie; 101) [Vgl. LuB 2013, Nr. 48]

439 Heininen, Simo: **Reformaatio Suomessa** (Reformation in Finnland). In: 024, 17–23: Ill.

440 Heininen, Simo: **Reformation in Finland** (Reformaatio Suomessa <engl.>). In: 024, 25–30: Ill.

441 Heininen, Simo: **Reformaation riemujuhlat Suomessa** (Reformationsfeiern in Finnland). In: 024, 115–120: Ill.

442 Heininen, Simo: **Reformation celebrations in Finland** (Reformaation riemujuhlat Suomessa <engl.>). In: 024, 123–130: Ill.

443 Hiebsch, S[abine]: **Luther en de Bijbel:** Antwerpen een belangrijke schakel in verspreiding van Luthers theologie (Luther und die Bibel: Antwerpen als wichtige Schaltstelle für die Verbreitung von Luthers Theologie). Protestants Nederland 78 (Rotterdam 2012), 217–220.

444 Imre, Mihály: **Az isteni és emberi szó párbeszéde:** tanulmányok a 16–18. századi protestantizmus irodalmáról (Dialog des göttlichen und menschlichen Wortes: Studien über die protestantische Literatur des 16.–18. Jh.). Sárospatak: Hernád, 2012. 444 S. (Nemzet, egyház, művelődés; 7)

445 Kinczler, Irén: **Képek a magyarországi evangélikus egyház történetéből:** egyháztörténeti füzetek gyűjteménye (Bilder aus der Geschichte der Evang.-Luth. Kirche in Ungarn: kirchengeschichtliche Heftsammlung). Piliscsaba: Fébé, 2011. [266] S.: Ill.

446 Klátik, Miloš: **Leonhard Stöckel, 1510 – Juni 1560:** ein Persönlichkeitsprofil. In: 010, 319–332.

447 Lausten, Martin Schwarz: **Reformationen i Danmark.** 3., überarb. Aufl. Frederiksberg: Anis, 2011. 264 S. [Vergl. LuB 1989, Nr. 774; LuB 2004, Nr. 1164]

448 Lausten, Martin Schwarz: **Die Reformation in Dänemark** (Reformationen i Danmark

<dt.>]/ aus dem Dän. übers. von Lise Miller Tönnies; hrsg. von Johannes Schilling. GÜ: GVH, 2008. 200 S.: Ill. (Schriften des Vereins für Reformationsgeschichte; 208)

449 Lavery, Jason: **The Swedish kingdom in Europe's age of reform** 1523–1611. In: 024, 9–14: Ill.

450 Lundbak, Henrik: **Crypto-radicalism or latent radicalism?:** the cases of the Danish towns Copenhagen and Malmö. In: 022, 97–106.

451 Müller, Andreas: **Katechismen in Ungarn und Siebenbürgen im 16. Jahrhundert.** In: 018, 23–27.

452 Őze, Sandor: **Reformation und Grenzgebiete:** zur Verbreitung der Reformation in den ungarisch besiedelten Gebieten. BP: METEM: Historia Ecclesiastica Hungarica Alapítvány; L: Universitätsverlag, 2011. 330 S.: Ill., Kt.

453 Perälä, Anna: **Suomen reformaatioajan kirjallisuuden kuvitus** (Illustrationen in der Literatur der finnischen Reformationszeit). In: 024, 33–41: Ill.

454 Perälä, Anna: **Illustrations in Finnish Reformation-era literature** (Suomen reformaatioajan kirjallisuuden kuvitus <engl.>). In: 024, 43–51: Ill.

455 Petritsch, Ernst D.: **»Der Türk« – der lutherischen Glück ...?** In: 010, 335–347.

456 Ritoókné Szalay, Ágnes: **Kutak:** tanulmányok a XV-XVI. századi magyarországi művelődés köréből (Brunnen: Studien zur Bildung in Ungarn des 15. und16. Jh.). BP: Balassi, 2012. 398 S.: Ill. (Humanizmus és reformáció; 33)

457 Siddiqui, Mona: **God, gods, idols:** Muslim and Christian perspectives on divine unity in revelation. In: 014, 140–154. L 143f.

458 Szabó, András: **A rejtőzködő bibliafordító:** Károlyi Gáspár (Gáspár Károlyi: der sich verbergende Bibelübersetzer). BP: Kálvin, 2012. 162 S.: Ill.

459 Tózsa-Rigó, Attila: **A reformáció hatásai a polgári végrendelkezés gyakorlatában pozsonyi és bécsi források példáján** (Wirkungen der Reformation in der bürgerlichen Testamentspraxis, dargestellt an Pressburger und Wiener Quellen). Egyháztörténeti szemle 13 (Miskolc 2012), Heft 4, 39–57.

460 Vinkler, Jonatan: **Primož Trubar in »nepravoverne« smeri reformacije v slovenskem slovstvu 16. stoletja: prekščevalci** (Primus

Truber und unorthodoxe Strömungen der Reformation in der slovenische Literatur

des 16. Jahrhunderts: Wiedertäufer). In: LuB 2013, Nr. 501, 99–108: summary.

6 Luthers Wirkung auf spätere Strömungen, Gruppen, Persönlichkeiten und Ereignisse

a) Allgemein

461 Alfsvåg, Knut: **Luthersk spiritualitet:** om lære og liv i den éne, kristne kirke (Lutherische Spiritualität: Lehre und Leben in der einen christlichen Kirche). Dansk tidsskrift for teologi og kirke 40 (Århus 2013), 42–56.

462 Anderegg, Johannes: **Aufs Maul geschaut?:** Überlegungen zum Einfluss Luthers auf die deutsche Literatur. In: 03, 131–144.

463 Baur, Jörg: **Der reformatorisch-lutherische Rechtfertigungsglaube angesichts der Herausforderung durch das neuzeitliche Selbstbewußtsein.** (2000). In: 05, 351–362.

464 Brakelmann, Günter: **Martin Luther:** Beiträge zu seinem Verständnis. Kamen: Spenner, 2012. 308 S. (Schriften der Hans-Ehrenberg-Gesellschaft; 19)

465 Eichel, Christine: **Das deutsche Pfarrhaus:** Hort des Geistes und der Macht. Originalausgabe. © Köln: Lübbe, 2012; B: Quadriga, 2012. 367 S. – auch als E-book: <www.quadrigaverlag.de>.

466 Eyjólfsson, Sigurjón Árni: **Luther als Gefangener der Interpretationsgeschichte.** (2004). In: 012, 59–72.

467 Fafié, G[erard]: **Iets over het wezen van het Lutheranisme** (Einiges zum Wesen des Luthertums). Documentatieblad Lutherse kerkgeschiedenis 39 (Haarlem 2011), 2–15: Ill.

468 Groß, Reiner: **Geschichte Sachsens.** 4., erw. und aktual. Aufl. Sonderausgabe der Sächsischen Landeszentrale für politische Bildung. L: Edition Leipzig; Dresden: Landeszentrale für Politische Bildung, 2007. 336 S.: Ill., Kt.

469 Groß, Reiner: **Geschichte Sachsens.** 5., erw. und aktual. Aufl. Sonderausgabe der Sächsischen Landeszentrale für Politische Bildung. Le: Edition Leipzig; Dresden: Sächsische Landeszentrale für Politische Bildung, 2012. 343 S.: Ill., Kt.

470 Heckel, Martin: **Die zwiespältigen Rechtswirkungen der lutherischen Reformation durch das Wort.** ZThK 108 (2011), 202–224.

471 Kaufmann, Thomas: **Reformationsgedenken in der Frühen Neuzeit:** Bemerkungen zum 16. bis 18. Jahrhundert. ZThK 107 (2010), 285–324.

472 Kaufmann, Thomas: **Vertreiben, aber nicht töten:** Luthers Umgang mit Abweichlern war ein Impuls für allgemeine Toleranz. ZZ 14 (2013) Heft 4, 24–26: Ill.

473 **Komponisten:** Boten der Reformation/ Clara Rempe; Christoph Wolff … In: 033, 24–33: Ill. L".

474 Kranich, Sebastian: **Einleitung** [Konstruktion von Geschichte]. In: 021, 9–14.

475 Laine, Tuija: **Lutherin suomenkieliset käännökset ja niiden julkaiseminen** (Finnische Übersetzungen und Ausgaben von Luthertexten). In: 024, 101–106: Ill.

476 Laine, Tuija: **Finnish translations and publication of Luther's texts** (Lutherin suomenkieliset käännökset ja niiden julkaiseminen <engl.>). In: 024, 109–113: Ill.

477 Lehmann, Hartmut: **Luthergedächtnis** 1817 **bis** 2017. GÖ; Bristol, CT: V&R, 2012. 328 S. (Ref500 academic studies; 8) – Rez.: Käßmann, Margot: ZZ 14 (2013) Heft 5, 63.

478 Mjaaland, Marius Timmann: **Does modernity begin with Luther?:** the origin and topology of self-consciousness according to Reiner Schürmann.. Studia theologica: Nordic journal of theology 63 (Oslo 2009) Nr. 1, 42–66.

479 Noordwijk, Bernard van: **Lutherse kerkgeschiedenis te voet:** Asterdam-(Oud)-West (Luth. Kirchengeschichte zu Fuß: Amsterdam-[Ost]-West). Documentatieblad Lutherse kerkgeschiedenis 39 (Haarlem 2011), 16–28: Ill.

480 Steinmetz, David C.: **Taking the long view:** Christian theology in historical perspective. Oxford; NY: Oxford University, 2011. IX, 187 S. – Rez.: Vind, Anna: ThLZ 138 (2013), 59–61.

481 Sundkvist, Bernice: **Det lutherska arvet i finländskt gudstjänstliv** (Das luth. Erbe im

finnischen gottesdienstlichen Leben). In: 024, 91–98: Ill.

b) Orthodoxie und Gegenreformation

482 Ács, Pál: »**Én fiam vagy, Dávid ...**«: a historikus értelmezés korlátai a 2. zsoltár unitárius fordításában (»Du bist mein Sohn, David ...«: Grenzen der historischen Auslegung in der antitrinitarischen Übersetzung von Psalm 2). In: 044, 61–75.

483 **Antitrinitarische Streitigkeiten:** die tritheistische Phase (1560–1568)/ hrsg. von Irene Dingel; zsgest. und bearb. von Kęstutis Daugirdas. GÖ: V&R, 2013. IX, 622 S. (Controversia et confessio; 9) [Auch als Online-Ausgabe]

484 **Der Augsburger Religionsfrieden 1555:** wissenschaftliches Symposium aus Anlaß des 450. Jahrestages des Friedensschlusses, Augsburg 21. bis 25. September 2005/ hrsg. von Heinz Schilling; Heribert Smolinsky. MS: Aschendorff, 2008. VII, 486 S. (Reformationsgeschichtliche Studien und Texte; 150) [Vergl. LuB 2013, Nr. 04 mit Nr. 413. 463. 485. 543.

485 Baur, Jörg: **Die Helmstedter Lesart des Rechtfertigungsartikels und deren rechtgläubige Kritiker:** eine Untersuchung zur Genese des »synkretistischen Streites«. (2003). In: 05, 69–123.

486 Blázy, Árpád: **Simon Griner – Grynaeus – és Buda,** 1521–1523 (Simon Grynaeus und Ofen). In: 040, 39–46.

487 Bollbuck, Harald: **Die Magdeburger Zenturien – Entstehung und Arbeitstechnik eines kirchenhistorischen Unternehmens.** In: 028, 248–278.

488 Bos, G[errit]: **Het decreet over de rechtvaardiging:** twee invloedrijke scholen hadden invloed tijdens concilie van Trent (Das Dekret über die Rechtfertigung: zwei einflußreiche Schulen hatten Einfluss während des Konzils von Trient). Protestants Nederland 77 (Rotterdam 2011), 214–216.

489 Brandtner, Ellinor: **Von der Konservierung des Glaubensbekenntnisses zur Darstellung des Herrscheramtes:** die Prunksärge der Merseburger Herzöge. In: 030, 207–230: Ill. L 213.

490 Brinkmann, Inga: **Grabdenkmäler, Grablegen und Begräbniswesen des lutherischen Adels:** adelige Funeralrepräsentation im Spannungsfeld von Kontinuität und Wandel im 16. und beginnenden 17. Jahrhundert B: Deutscher Kunstverlag, 2010. 432 S.: Ill., Kt. (Kunstwissenschaftliche Studien; 163) – Zugl.: B, Freie Univ., Diss., 2008.

491 Cordes, Harm: **Ernst Salomon Cyprian als Chronist des Reformationsjubiläums von 1717.** In: 021, 89–103.

492 Cziczka, Katalin: **Egy lipcsei zsoltáros magyarországi hatása** (Wirkung eines Leipziger Psalmdichters [Nikolaus Selnecker] in Ungarn). In: 044, 93–102.

493 Dingel, Irene: **Augsburger Religionsfrieden und »Augsburger Konfessionsverwandtschaft« – konfessionelle Lesarten.** In: 04, 157–176.

494 Ehmann, Johannes: **Der Heidelberger Katechismus (1563).** Jahrbuch für badische Kirchen- und Religionsgeschichte 6 (2012), 125–150: Ill. L".

495 Gehrt, Daniel: »**Zum besseren vnd gründtlicheren verstandt des Catechismi Lutheri**«: das »Kleine Corpus Doctrinae« des Matthäus Judex. In: 023, 149–199.

496 Himmighöfer, Traudel: **Der reformierte Theologe David Pareus (1548–1622) und sein Bibelwerk.** BlPfKG 77 (2010) 45–55.

497 Hoffmann, Carl A.: **Die Reichsstädte und der Augsburger Religionsfrieden.** In: 04, 297–320. L 313 f.

498 Ilić, Luka: »**Der heilige Mann und thewre held**«: Flacius' view of Luther. In: 028, 294–314.

499 Ilić, Luka: **Theologian of sin and grace:** the process of radicalization in the theology of Matthias Flacius Illyricus. Phil, 2012. IV, 324 S. – Phil, The Lutheran Theological Seminary, PhD, 2012.

500 Illg, Thomas: **Ein anderer Mensch werden:** Johann Arndts Verständnis der imitatio Christi als Anleitung zu einem wahren Christentum. GÖ: V&R unipress, 2011. 329 S. (Studien zur Kirchengeschichte Niedersachsens; 44) – Zugl.: HH, Univ., theol. Diss., 2010. – Rez.: Deuper, Christian: JNKG 109 (2011), 203–206.

501 **Jeziki, identitete, pripadnosti med središči in obrobji:** v počastitev 500. obletnice rojstva Primoža Trubarja (Sprachen, Identitäten, Zugehörigkeiten zwischen Zentren und Radgebieten: zu Ehren des 500. Geburtstages von Primus Truber)/ hrsg. von Kozma Ahačić; Petra Testen. Tagung Ljubl-

jana, 5.–8. Juni 2008. Ljubljana: Založba ZRC, 2011. 317 S.: Ill. – Siehe LuB 2013, Nr. 435 f. 460.

502 Jürgens, Henning P.: **Der Konflikt zwischen Matthias Flacius und Philipp Melanchthon in der Sicht des Johannes Cochläus:** die Schrift »De excvsatione Philippi Melanthonis, adversus clamores Flacij Illyrici«. In: 028, 214–238.

503 Kohnle, Armin: **Die Kurpfalz als calvinistisches Territorium im Reich des 16. Jahrhunderts.** BlPfKG 77 (2010), 11–25.

504 Kolb, Robert: **Matthias Flacius' Glossa compendiaria:** the Wittenberg way of exegesis in its second generation. In: 028, 72–89.

505 **Konversion und Konfession in der frühen Neuzeit/** hrsg. von Ute Lotz-Heumann; Jan-Friedrich Mißfelder; Matthias Pohlig. [GÜ]: GVH, 2007. 563 S.: Ill. L". (Schriften des Vereins für Reformationsgeschichte; 205)

506 Kordić, Ivan: **Vlačićeva teološka antropologija** (Die theologische Anthropologie des Flacius). In: 028, 21–47: Zusammenfassung.

507 Laine, Esko M.: **Vääristikö lukemaan pakottaminen luterilaisuuden?:** lukukontrollin vaiheet Suomessa (Verzerrte die Pflichtlektüre das Luthertum: Kirche, Literatur und Sozialkontrolle in Finnland von der Reformationszeit bis zur luth. Orthodoxie). In: 024, 73–79: Ill.

508 Laine, Esko M.: **Did mandatory literacy distort Lutheranism?:** the church, literacy, and social control in Finland from the Reformation era to the age of Lutheran orthodoxy (Vääristikö lukemaan pakottaminen luterilaisuuden?: lukukontrollin vaiheet Suomessa <engl.>). In: 024, 81–89: Ill.

509 Laine, Tuija: **Kirkon ja kansanopetuksen kirjat uuden ajan alussa** (Finnische religiöse Elementarbücher aus dem 16. und 17. Jahrhundert). In: 024, 53–61: Ill.

510 Laine, Tuija: **Finnish primary religious books from the sixteenth and seventeenth centuries** (Kirkon ja kansanopetuksen kirjat uuden ajan alussa <engl.>). In: 024, 63–71: Ill.

511 Laube, Stefan: **Wissenswelten sinnlicher Frömmigkeit:** theatrale Antriebsmomente in der Naturanschauung von Bernard Palissy und Jacob Böhme. In: 034, 217–236.

512 Ligniez, Annina: **Legitimation durch Ge-**

513 schichte: das erste Reformationsjubiläum 1617 in Wittenberg. In: 021, 53–66.

513 Looß, Sigrid: **Zum Menschenbild des Kryptoradikalen Valentin Weigel:** seine Schrift »Vom Leben Christi«, 205–215. L 214.

514 Maaser, Michael: **Humanismus und Landesherrschaft:** Herzog Julius (1528–1589) und die Universität Helmstedt. S: Steiner, 2010. 222 S. (Frankfurter historische Abhandlungen; 46: Geschichte) – Zugl.: F, Univ., phil. Diss., 2002. – Rez.: Mager, Inge: JNKG 109 (2011), 197 f.

515 Macha, Jürgen: **Konfessionelle Differenzen auf dem Feld der Sprache?:** sprachhistorische Befunde zur Frühen Neuzeit. In: 020, 99–117. L".

516 Mager, Inge: »**Allein den Betern kann es noch gelingen«:** Johann Balthasar Schupps Erklärung der Litanei. JLH 50 (2011), 150–162.

517 Mai, Bernhard: **Die Gruftanlagen Mitteldeutschlands:** Erfahrungen und Eindrücke aus zwei Jahrzehnten denkmalpflegerischer Praxis. In: 030, 373–380: Ill. L 374.

518 Mai, Klaus-Rüdiger: **Frühneuzeitliche Geheimbünde als Kryptoradikalität?** In: 022, 217–227.

519 Matthias, Markus: **Zur Auseinandersetzung um Martin Luthers »De servo arbitrio« im 16. Jahrhundert.** LuBu 19 (2010), 40–67.

520 Mehl, Édouard: **La science capitale:** Johann Valentin Andreae et les mathématiques. In: 034, 198–216.

521 Methuen, Charlotte: **To delineate the divinity of the creator:** the search for Platonism in late sixteenth-century Tübingen. In: 034, 186–197.

522 Mühling, Andreas: **Anmerkungen zur reformierten Katechismusbildung.** In: 018, 37–41.

523 Mühling, Andreas: **Das theologische Umfeld der Duisburger Synode von 1610.** MEKGR 60 (2011), 103–114. L".

524 Pohlig, Matthias: **Wahrheit als Lüge – oder:** Schloss der Augsburger Religionsfrieden den Calvinismus aus? In: 020, 142–169.

525 Reichelt, Silvio: **Die Universität als Instrument der Konfessionalisierung:** die akademische Reformationsjubelfeier in Straßburg 1617. In: 021, 67–87.

526 Reinis, Austra: **Catechism and »Querelle des Femmes« (1556–1689):** Lutheran »Haus-**

367

tafel« sermons as contributions to the debate about women. LuJ 79 (2012), 183–209.

527 Rose, Alexander: **Der Reformation im Amt Peine eine Gestalt geben:** die Kirchenordnung 1561 – Superintendent Eilhard Segebode. Peine: Selbstverlag [Rose, Burgkamp 57], 2011. 52, Q 44 S.: Ill., Noten. – Rez.: Scharbau, Friedrich-Otto: JNKG 109 (2011), 244–246.

528 Rowlands, Alison: **»Ein verschlagener Geist«:** Vorstellungen des Teufels in den Hexenprozessen der Reichsstadt Rothenburg ob der Tauber. ARG 103 (2012), 211–236: abstract. L 217 f.

529 Schultze, Harald: **Reinhard Bake und die Magdeburger Pastoren im Dreißigjährigen Krieg.** In: Konfession, Krieg und Katastrophe: Magdeburgs Geschick im Dreißigjährigen Krieg; Tagung des Vereins für Kirchengeschichte der Kirchenprovinz Sachsen Magdeburg 9.–10. Mai 2005/ hrsg. vom Verein für Kirchengeschichte der Kirchenprovinz Sachsen; Redaktion: Margit Scholz; Christina Neuß. Magdeburg: Verein für Kirchengeschichte der Kirchenprovinz Sachsen, 2006. 111 S.: Ill. (Schriften des Vereins für Kirchengeschichte der Kirchenprovinz Sachsen; 1), 25–42: Ill. L 37 f.

530 Selderhuis, H[erman] J.: **Luther is gereformeerd:** het Reformatiejubileum van 1617 in de strijd tussen Lutheranen en Gereformeerden (Luther ist reformiert: das Reformationsjubiläum von 1617 im Streit zwischen Lutheranern und Reformierten [Teil 3]). Protestants Nederland 78 (Rotterdam 2012), 227–229.

531 Selderhuis, H[erman] J.: **Uitgangspunt is breedte Reformatie:** het Reformatiejubileum van 1617 in de strijd tussen Lutheranen en Gereformeerden (Ausgangspunkt ist die Breite der Reformation: das Reformationsjubiläum von 1617 im Streit zwischen Lutheranern und Reformierten [Teil 2]). Protestants Nederland 78 (Rotterdam 2012), 193–196.

532 Selderhuis, H[erman] J.: **Van wie is de Reformatie?:** het Reformatiejubileum van 1617 in de strijd tussen Lutheranen en Gereformeerden (Wem gehört die Reformation?: das Reformationsjubiläum von 1617 im Streit zwischen Lutheranern und Reformierten [Teil 1]). Protestants Nederland 78 (Rotterdam 2012), 160–162.

533 Slenczka, Björn: **Das Wormser Schisma der Augsburger Konfessionsverwandten von 1557:** protestantische Konfessionspolitik und Theologie im Zusammenhang des zweiten Wormser Religionsgesprächs. TÜ: Mohr Siebeck, 2010. XVIII, 545 S. (Beiträge zur historischen Theologie; 155) – Zugl.: Überarb. Fassung von: B, Humboldt-Univ., theol. Diss., 2008. – Rez.: Keller, Rudolf: ZBKG 80 (2011), 523 f.

534 Slenczka, Björn: **Das Wormser Schisma der Augsburger Konfessionsverwandten von 1557:** protestantische Konfessionspolitik und Theologie im Zusammenhang des zweiten Wormser Religionsgesprächs. Elektronische Ressource. TÜ: Mohr Siebeck, 2012. XVIII, 545 S. (Beiträge zur historischen Theologie; 155)

535 Spangenberg, Cyriacus: **Doctor Martin Luther als Treckejunge:** eine Bergmannspredigt/ mit einem Vorwort, Spangenbergs 22 Predigten über Luther betreffend hrsg. von Heinrich Rembde. Reprint der 1. Ausgabe Eisleben, 1887 hrsg. vom Ev. Kirchspiel Mansfeld-Lutherstadt; Vorwort: Matthias Paul. Mansfeld-Lutherstadt: Das ev. Kirchspiel Mansfeld-Lutherstadt, 2012. [6], XXIII, 64 S.

536 Straßberger, Andres: **Die Leichenpredigten auf die Herzöge von Sachsen-Merseburg.** In: 030, 287–326: Ill. L".

537 **Theologie im Dialog:** Georg Calixt (1586–1656) als Wegbereiter der Ökumene; Beiträge eines Studientags zum 350. Todestag am 30. Oktober 2006 im Predigerseminar Braunschweig/ von Inge Mager; Wolfgang Sommer, Christoph Böttigheimer; Martin Friedrich; hrsg. vom Landeskirchenamt Wolfenbüttel. Wolfenbüttel: Ev.-Luth. Landeskirche in Braunschweig, Landeskirchenamt, Landeskirchliches Archiv, 2007. 87 S.: Ill. L". (Quellen und Beiträge zur Geschichte der Evang.-Luth. Landeskirche in Braunschweig; 17)

538 Töpfer, Thomas: **Zwischen bildungskultureller Vorbildwirkung und politischer Legitimitätsstiftung:** die Universität Wittenberg in der lutherischen Bildungslandschaft der zweiten Hälfte des 16. Jahrhunderts. In: 021, 29–52.

539 Wagner-Peterson, Boris: **Zacharias Ursinus und seine katechetischen Arbeiten.** BlPfKG 77 (2010), 26–43.

540 Walter, Peter: **Der Catechismus Romanus – Seine Entstehung und seine Stellung im Rahmen der Katechismen des 16. Jahrhunderts.** In: 018, 42–49. L 47 f.

541 Weigelt, Horst: **Martin Johns »Kurtzer Bericht von den Schwenkfeldern« – ein Beitrag zur Erinnerungskultur.** In: 022, 247–265. L 253 f.

542 Weiß, Ulman: Zur Kommunikation von Kryptoradikalen. In: 022, 349–369. L".

543 Weißmann, Robert: **Kryptoradikale Ansätze und Emanzipation im Werk des Jenaer Polyhistors Michael Neander.** In: 022, 181–204. L".

544 Witt, Christian: **Protestantes – Protestierende – Protestanten:** zum Werden eines Integrationsbegriffs in der theologischen Literatur des 16. und 17. Jahrhunderts. MEKGR 60 (2011), 205–224.

c) Pietismus und Aufklärung

545 Baur, Jörg: **Martin Luther im Urteil Goethes.** (1996). In: 05, 3–17.

546 Drese, Claudia: **»Es ist nicht genug, dass wir uns der durch Lutherum geschehenen Reformation rühmen ...«:** zur Geschichtsanschauung im kirchlichen Pietismus. In: 021, 105–116: Ill.

547 Fleischer, Dirk: **Protestantische Kirchengeschichtsschreibung im Zeitalter der Aufklärung.** In: 021, 117–139. L".

548 Flügel, Wolfgang: **Das Beste aus zwei Welten:** Geschichtskonstrukte lutherischer Pastoren im Pennsylvania des 18. Jahrhunderts. In: 021, 179–211. L".

549 Römmelt, Stefan W.: **Kalter Konfessions-Krieg auf Kanzel und Katheder?:** die 200-Jahrfeiern des Augsburger Religionsfriedens von 1755 an den Universitäten Wittenberg, Leipzig und Halle. In: 021, 142–177: Ill. L".

550 Vogt, Peter: **Die Liturgik der Herrnhuter Brüdergemeine.** BlWKG 110 (2010), 201–217: Ill. L 203 f.

551 Wennemuth, Udo: **Religiöse Einheitsbestrebungen und Aufklärung im Gesangbuch der Kurpfalz.** Jahrbuch für badische Kirchen- und Religionsgeschichte 5 (2011), 87–116: Faks. L 89–94L".

d) 19. und 20. Jahrhundert bis 1917

552 Eyjólfsson, Sigurjón Árni: **Lutherdeutung in Island um 1900.** Lu 84 (2013), 15–27.

553 Harnack, Adolf von: **Das Wesen des Christentums:** sechzehn Vorlesungen vor Studierenden aller Fakultäten im Wintersemester 1899/1900 an der Universität Berlin gehalten von Adolf v. Harnack/ hrsg. von Claus-Dieter Osthövener. 3., erneut durchges. Aufl. TÜ: Mohr Siebeck, 2012. VIII, 327 S. L 152–165L".

554 Hund, Johannes: **Das Augustana-Jubiläum von 1830 als Kulminationspunkt der Ausbildung moderner theologischer Positionen während der Vormärzzeit.** In: 021, 237–253

555 Muth, Christian: **Schüler und Dolmetscher des Propheten?:** Grundlinien protestantischer Erinnerung an Melanchthon und Calvin bei ihren Jubiläen 1897 und 1909. In: 021, 321–345.

556 Wendebourg, Dorothea: **Die Reformationsjubiläen des 19. Jahrhunderts.** ZThK 108 (2011), 270–335.

557 Wischmeyer, Johannes: **Reformation als Epoche und Strukturmoment:** Protestantismustheorie und Historismus bei Karl von Hase und der Jenaer freisinnigen Theologie. In: 021, 277–306: Ill.

558 Zahl, Simeon: **Pneumatology and theology of the cross in the preaching of Christoph Friedrich Blumhardt:** the Holy Spirit between Wittenberg and Azusa Street. LO: T & T Clark, 2010. X, 206 S. (T & T Clark studies in systematic theology; 7) – Rez.: Ising, Dieter: BlWKG 111 (2011), 367–369.

e) 1918–1996

559 Alderliesten, A[rthur]: **500 jaar Luther in de DDR:** herdenking heeft een correctieve, zo niet heilzame, uitwerking gehad (500 Jahre Luther in der DDR: das Gedenken hat eine korrektive, wenn nicht sogar heilsame Auswirkung gehabt). Protestants Nederland 77 (Rotterdam 2011), 207–209: Ill.

560 Eyjólfsson, Sigurjón Árni: **Rechtfertigung, Mystik, Neue Schöpfung:** mystische Elemente in der Theologie Werner Elerts. (1992). In: 012, 122–140.

561 Eyjólfsson, Sigurjón Árni: **Der verborgene Gott in der Theologie Werner Elerts.** (2000). In: 012, 75–97.

562 Fischer, André: **Zwischen Zeugnis und Zeitgeist:** die politische Theologie von Paul Althaus in der Weimarer Republik. GÖ: V&R, 2012. 800 S. (Arbeiten zur kirchlichen Zeitgeschichte: Reihe B, Darstellungen; 55) – Zugl.: Erlangen-Nürnberg, Univ., Fachbereich Theologie, Diss., 2010/2011. [Auch als E-book].

563 Fitschen, Klaus: **Reformator ohne Hammer?:** protestantische Irritationen auf dem Weg zum Reformationsjubiläum 1967. Lu 83 (2012), 161–166.

564 Hammann, Konrad: **Rudolf Bultmann:** eine Biographie. TÜ: Mohr Siebeck, 2009. XI, 582 S.: Ill.

565 Hammann, Konrad: **Rudolf Bultmann:** eine Biographie. 2., durchges. Aufl. TÜ: Mohr Siebeck, 2009. XI, 582 S.: Ill.

566 Hammann, Konrad: **Rudolf Bultmann:** eine Biographie. 3., erneut durchges. und erg. Aufl. TÜ: Mohr Siebeck, 2012. XIV, 584 S.: Ill.

567 Hammann, Konrad: **Rudolf Bultmann:** a biography (Rudolf Bultmann <engl.>)/ übers. von Philip E. Devenish. Salem, OR: Polebridge, 2013. XI, 611 S.

568 **Interview mit Adolf Laube/** geführt von Joachim Heise. In: 09, 259–280.

569 **Interview mit Siegfried Bräuer/** geführt von Joachim Heise. In: 09, 281–303.

570 Jasper, Gotthard: **Paul Althaus (1888–1966):** Professor, Prediger und Patriot in seiner Zeit. GÖ: V&R, 2013. 430 S.: Ill. auf Tafeln. [Auch als E-book].

571 Jehle, Frank: **Fritz Blanke – Lehrer und Forscher.** Zw 39 (2012), 131–144.

572 Laube, Adolf: **Akademische Forschung und Kooperationsbeziehungen am Beispiel der Reformation.** (2001). In: 09, 358–384.

573 Leonhardt, Rochus: **Äquidistanz als Götzendienst?:** Überlegungen zur politischen Ethik im deutschen Nachkriegsprotestantismus. In: 014, 656–674.

574 Rampler, Herbert: **»Kannst du wissen, was aus dem winzigen Pflänzchen werden wird …«** – Anmerkungen zu Friedrich Ulrichs Lutherbuch und Nachlass. In: 010, 463–474.

7 Luthers Gestalt und Lehre in der Gegenwart

575 **Auf dem Weg zum Reformationsjubiläum 2017:** warum wir feiern; Wort der Kirchenleitung der Evangelisch-Lutherischen Landeskirche Sachsens/ hrsg. von der Kirchenleitung der Evan.-Luth. Landeskirche Sachsens. [Dresden]: Evang.-Luth. Landeskirche Sachsens, 2013. 7 S. (500 Jahre Reformation – Luther 2017)

576 Beintker, Michael: **The study of Protestant theology in Europe.** In: 015, 557–562.

577 Bloomquist, Karen L.; Sinaga, Martin L.: **Theological education in Lutheran churches.** In: 015, 652–661.

578 Brandt, Reinhard: **Luther, Lübeck und die Musik:** Seminar der Luther-Gesellschaft in Lübeck, 4.–6. Mai 2012. Lu 83 (2012), 175–178.

579 Brink, G[ijsbert] van den; Kooi, C[ornelis] van der: **Christelijke dogmatiek:** een inleiding (Christliche Dogmatik: eine Einleitung). 1.–3. Aufl. Zoetermeer, Netherlands: Boekencentrum, 2012. 722 S. – Rez.: Matthias, Markus: LuBu 21 (2012), 63–65.

580 Brown, Christopher Boyd: **In memoriam:** Gottfried G. Krodel (1931–2011), North American editor 1988–1998. ARG 103 (2012), 307–309.

581 Deeg, Alexander: **Auf der Spur des Wortes und der Worte:** das »Zentrum für evangelische Predigtkultur« in Wittenberg. Thema: Gottesdienst 31 (2010), 18–23.

582 Deeg, Alexander: **Toleranz, Liebe und der Ruf zur Buße:** Predigtmeditation über Matthäus 7, 21–23. In: 041, 34–37.

583 Dehn, Ulrich; Werner, Dietrich: **Protestant theological education in Germany and the role of religious studies, missiology and ecumenics.** In: 015, 577–583.

584 Dicke, Klaus: **ewig geschieden und widereinander?:** die Schmalkaldischen Artikel heute in ökumenischer Perspektive. In: 031, 121–138.

585 Dieckmann, Christoph: **Eine feste Burg:** das protestantische Pfarrhaus ist ein deutscher Mythos […] Die Zeit 68 (2013) Nr. 12 (14. März), Beilage »Zeitmagazin«, 16–27: Ill.

586 Eißler, Friedemann; Käfer, Anne: **Nur nicht vereinnahmen!** In: 035, 42–44.

370

587 Eyjólfsson, Sigurjón Árni: **Bischof, Kirchenrat, Kirchenkonferenz:** die Aufgaben der isländischen Kirchenleitung. (2000). In: 012, 35–58. L 54.

588 Fafié, T[hedorus] A[rnoldus]: **De geschiedenis van de SLUB:** Stichting Lutherse Uitgiverij en Boekhandel 1973–2011 (Die Geschichte der Luth. Verlags- und Buchhandelsstiftung 1973–2011). Documentatieblad Lutherse kerkgeschiedenis 39 (Haarlem 2011), 28–40: Ill.

589 Fleischman-Bisten, Walter: **Die Stiefkinder der Reformation:** Dulden heißt beleidigen […]; zehn Thesen und Fakten zur innerevangelischen Intoleranz. In: 035, 14–17: Ill.

590 Freitag, Josef: **Rückfragen an die Schmalkaldischen Artikel und eine ökumenisch-katholische Lektüre heute.** In: 031, 105–119.

591 Göring-Eckardt, Katrin: **Wie viel Religion verträgt die Demokratie.** In: 035, 26f.

592 Gräb-Schmidt, Elisabeth: **Die Bedeutung reformatorischer Einsichten für die ethische Urteilsbildung der Gegenwart.** ZThK 107 (2010), 479–504.

593 Härle, Wilfried: **Ethik.** B; NY, NY: De Gruyter, 2011. XVI, 522 S. L". (De-Gruyter-Studium)

594 Härle, Wilfried: **Warum Gott?:** für Menschen, die mehr wissen wollen. L: EVA, 2013. 305 S. (Theologie für die Gemeinde)

595 Hobson, Theo: **Faith.** Durham: Acumen, 2009. V, 138 S. L". (The art of living series)

596 Hobson, Theo: **Glaube:** eine Urgewalt verstehen (Faith <dt.>)/ aus dem Engl. von Gabriele Stein. FR; BL; W: Herder, 2012. 200 S. L". – Rez.: Wandel, Jürgen: ZZ 13 (2012) Heft 12, 65.

597 **In memoriam [Karl-Heinz zur Mühlen]/** Redaktion. Lu 83 (2012), 174.

598 Jüngel, Eberhard: **Das Evangelium von der Rechtfertigung des Gottlosen als Zentrum des christlichen Glaubens:** eine theologische Studie in ökumenischer Absicht. 6. Aufl. TÜ: Mohr Siebeck, 2011. XXI, 244 S.

599 Jütte, Kathrin: **Auf ein Wort zu 2017:** Timmendorfer Strand: unterschiedliche Perspektiven auf das Reformationsjubiläum. ZZ 13 (2012) Heft 12, 50f.: Ill.

600 Kasparick, Siegfried: **Christsein heute:** 475 Schmalkaldische Artikel. In: 031, 17–33.

601 Kišš, Igor: **Ethik der Liebe Jesu und ihr erforderlicher Einfluss auf die heutige Gesellschaft:** einige Thesen zur politischen Ethik Jesu. In: 010, 255–267. L 261.

602 Kuhlmann, Helga: **Gott oder Götze?:** zum Modus des Umgangs mit der Frage nach der Identität Gottes im interreligiösen Dialog. In: 014, 569–584. L 570f.

603 Leonhardt, Rochus: **Beschneidung der Religionsfreiheit?:** zur Aktualität von Luthers politischer Ethik. Leqach: Mitteilungen und Beiträge der Forschungsstelle Judentum 11 (2013), 67–85.

604 Lugazia, Faith K.: **The relevance of »Smalkald articles« in the Tanzanian context:** a Lutheran view. In: 031, 151–160.

605 Mawick, Gudrun: **Reformation und Musik 2012.** Thema: Gottesdienst 34 (2011), 4–6.

606 **»Niemand darf verloren gehen!«:** evangelisches Plädoyer für mehr Bildungsgerechtigkeit; 3. Tagung der 11. Synode der Evangelischen Kirche in Deutschland, 7. bis 10. November 2010 in Hannover/ hrsg. vom Kirchenamt der Evang. Kirche in Deutschland (EKD) im Auftrag des Präsidiums der 11. Synode der EKD; Vorwort: Karin Göring-Eckardt; Texte: Rolf Bade … F: Gemeinschaftswerk der Evang. Publizistik, 2010. 46 S. (epd-dokumentation; 49 [2010])

607 **»Niemand darf verloren gehen!«:** evangelisches Plädoyer für mehr Bildungsgerechtigkeit; **Lesebuch** zum Schwerpunktthema der 3. Tagung der 11. Synode der Evangelischen Kirche in Deutschland (EKD) vom 7. bis 10. November 2010 in Hannover/ hrsg. vom Kirchenamt der Evang. Kirche in Deutschland; Comenius-Institut: Evang. Arbeitsstätte für Erziehungswissenschaft; Redaktion: Rolf Bade … MS: Comenius-Institut; Hannover: Kirchenamt der EKD, 2010. 121 S. L 8. 11–13.

608 Østnor, Lars: **Katekismens etikk i dagens samfunn** (Katechismusethik in unserer heutigen Gesellschaft). In: 019, 135–148.

609 Peters, Frank: **Taufgedächtnis für alle Tage:** liturgische Anknüpfungen. Thema: Gottesdienst 33 (2011), 26–37.

610 Rendtorff, Trutz: **Ethik:** Grundelemente, Methodologie und Konkretionen eincr ethischen Theologie. 3., durchges. Aufl./ hrsg. von Reiner Anselm; Stephan Schleissing. TÜ: Mohr Siebeck, 2011. XXII, 587 S. L".

611 Reuss, András: **Mária a mai evangélikus teológiában** (Maria in der heutigen evang.-

371

luth. Theologie). Credo 18 (BP 2012) Heft 3/ 4, 14–25.

612 Rößler, Martin: **Psalter und Harfe, wacht auf:** Liedpredigten. S: CV, 2009. 223 S. – Rez.: Schendel, Gunther: BlWKG 110 (2010), 456–458.

613 Scheliha, Arnulf von: **Lästiger Nahbereich:** Die Kirchen sollten die Gesellschaft einladend gestalten; stattdessen verschenken sie Möglichkeiten, ein Vorbild für Toleranz zu sein. In: 035, 30–33.

614 Schwöbel, Christoph: **Evangelische Pointe:** Wer den eigenen Glauben als Geschenk erfährt, kann den Glauben anderer tolerieren. ZZ 14 (2013) Heft 4, 27–29: Ill.

615 Skottene, Ragnar: **Herlighet uten kors?:** »trosbevegelsens« grunnlagstenkning i lys av Martin Luthers theologia crucis (Herrlichkeit ohne Kreuz?: die Bewegung von Wort und Glaube als grundlegender Gedanke im Hinblick auf Martin Luthers theologia crucis). TK 81 (Oslo 2010), 41–59.

616 Szentpétery, Péter: **Prőhle Károly** (1911–2005). Vallástudományi szemle 8 (BP 2012), Heft 2, 145–158.

617 Szerdi, András: **A reformátorok imádságról szóló tanítása és mai jelentősége – a »Mi Atyánk« megszólításról szóló tanítás** (Die reformatorische Lehre über das Gebet und deren Bedeutung für heute – Lehre über die Anrede »Vater unser«). In: 040, 452–459.

618 Ulrich, Gerhard: **Predigt im Festgottesdienst »475 Jahre Schmalkaldische Artikel«:** 24. Juni 2012, Stadtkirche St. Georg Schmalkalden. In: 031, 161–166.

619 Véghelyi, Antal: **Luther Formula missae-jének bemutatója a zuglói evangélikus templomban** (Aufführung von Luthers Formula missae in der evang.-luth. Kirche in Zugló). Magyar Egyházzene 18 (BP 2011) Heft 1, 91 f.

620 Winkler, Eberhard: **Luther aktuell – Reformation heute.** L: EVA, 2013. 296 S.

621 Zimmerling, Peter: **Ein glühender Ofen voll Liebe:** Mystik als Gegenwart und Zukunft des Christentums. ZZ 13 (2012) Heft 12, 28–31: Ill.

622 Zschoch, Hellmut: **Abendmahl ist Essen und Trinken – nicht Tunken:** gegen das Vordringen der Intinctio in die evangelische Abendmahlspraxis. Thema: Gottesdienst 35 (2012), 4–10.

623 Zschoch, Hellmut: **Abendmahl ist Essen und Trinken – nicht Tunken:** gegen das Vordringen der Intinctio in die evangelische Abendmahlspraxis. Geringfügig überarb. Fassung. Lu 83 (2012), 167–173.

8 Romane, Schauspiele, Filme, Tonträger, Varia

624 **24 Adventstage mit Martin Luther:** Türchenkalender/ hrsg. von Margot Käßmann. 2. Aufl. F: Hansisches Druck- und Verlagshaus, 2011. 24 S. (edition chrismon)

625 **Boten:** Reformation und Musik; Motetten und Choräle/ Johann Walter; Heinrich Schütz; Johann Sebastian Bach ...; Athesinus Consort Berlin; Idee, Konzeption, Leitung: Klaus-Martin Bresgott. F: Hansisches Druck- und Verlagshaus, 2011. 1 CD. (edition chrismon)

626 **Bruder Martinus:** Martin-Luther-Musical/ Komponist: Siegfried Fietz. Greifenstein (Wetzlar): Abakus-Musik, 2012. 1 CD.

627 **Bruder Martinus:** Martin-Luther-Musical/ Musik: Siegfried Fietz; Texte: Jürgen Werth. Notenausgabe, Lieder- und Textheft. Greifenstein (Wetzlar): Abakus-Musik, 2012. 27 S. & Beilage (1 Playback-CD)

628 **Chrismon spezial:** das evangelische Magazin zum Reformationstag 2012; Hier stehe ich!; er kann nicht anders: Martin Luther .../ im Auftrag der Evang. Kirche in Deutschland (EKD) hrsg. von Johannes Friedrich ... Redaktionsleitung: Arnd Brummer; Ursula Ott. F: Hansisches Druck- und Verlagshaus, 2012. 28 S.: Ill.

629 **Hier stehe ich, ich kann nicht anders:** Luthers Leben in deftigen Anekdoten, von ihm selbst erzählt/ Heinz Drewniok; Text, Regie, Produktion: Mario Süßenguth. Tonträger. B: Eulenspiegel-Das-Neue-Berlin-Verlags-Gesellschaft, 2008. 1 CD. (Ohreule)

630 Jäckel, Karin: **Die Frau des Reformators:** das Leben der Katharina von Bora; historischer Roman. 4. Aufl. Reinbek bei HH: Rowohlt-Taschenbuch, 2007. 604 S. (rororo; 23946)

631 Jäckel, Karin: **Die Frau des Reformators:** das Leben der Katharina von Bora; historischer Roman. 5. Aufl. Reinbek bei HH: Rowohlt-Taschenbuch, 2009. 604 S. (rororo; 23946)

632 Jacobs, Birte: **Geheimsache Luther:** historischer Roman. Karlsruhe: Der Kleine Buch-Verlag, 2012. 317 S.: Kt.

633 Leibrock, Felix: **Lutherleben:** ein Reformations-Roman. Petersberg: Imhof, 2011. 192 S.

634 Leibrock, Felix: **Luthers Kreuzfahrt:** Roman. Petersberg: Imhof, 2012. 207 S.

635 Lienhard, Friedrich: **Luther auf der Wartburg:** Schauspiel in fünf Aufzügen. Nachdruck der Originalausgabe S, 1906. PB: Salzwasser Verlag, 2013. VI, 115 S.

636 **Luther:** er veränderte die Welt für immer/ Darsteller: Joseph Fiennes; Alfred Molina; Jonathan Firth ... Drehbuch: Camille Thomasson; Bart Gavigan. Regie: Eric Till. Farbfilm in dt. und engl. Sprache; dt. Untertitel. HH: Warner Home Video, 2010. 1 DVD-Video (118 Minuten; Zeittafel »Luthers Leben«).

637 **Luther:** er veränderte die Welt für immer/ Darsteller: Joseph Fiennes; Alfred Molina; Jonathan Firth ... Drehbuch: Camille Thomasson; Bart Gavigan. Regie: Eric Till. Farbfilm in dt. und engl. Sprache; dt. Untertitel. HH: Universal Pictures Germany, 2010. 1 DVD-Video (121 Minuten; Zeittafel »Luthers Leben«).

638 Schlicht, Friedrich Viktor: **2 Päpste + Martin Luther = 2012:** ein mystischer Countdown? Norderstedt: Books on Demand, 2012. 44 S. [Auch als Online-Ressource]

639 Simon, Eckehard: **Fastnachtspiele inszenieren die Reformation:** Luthers Kampf gegen Rom als populäre Bewegung in Fastnachtspielzeugnissen, 1521–1525. In: Fastnachtspiele: weltliches Schauspiel in literarischen und kulturellen Kontexten/ hrsg. von Klaus Ridder. Tübingen: Niemeyer, 2009, 115–135.

640 Stetter, Moritz: **Luther.** [Bildergeschichte]. GÜ: GVH, 2011. 112 S.: Ill. (graphic novel)

641 Stetter, Moritz: **Luther.** [Bildergeschichte]. Elekronische Ressource. GÜ: E-Books der Verlagsgruppe Random House, 2013. 112 S.: Ill. (graphic novel)

642 Vogt, Fabian: **2017 – die neue Reformation.** [Roman]. Asslar: adeo, 2012. 347 S. [Auch als Online-Ressource]

643 Zimmer, Anja: **Auf dass wir klug werden:** das Leben der Herzogin Elisabeth zu Sachsen; Roman. Laubach: Frauenzimmer-Verlag, 2011. 513 S.: Ill.

644 Zimmer, Anja: **Auf dass wir klug werden:** das Leben der Herzogin Elisabeth zu Sachsen; Roman. Online-Ressource. Laubach: Frauenzimmer-Verlag, 2013. 513 S.: Ill.

C FORSCHUNGSBERICHTE, SAMMELREZENSIONEN, BIBLIOGRAPHIEN

645 **Bibliographie zur Ethik Martin Luthers/** zsgest. von Andreas Stegmann. LuJ 79 (2012), 305–342.

646 Bräuer, Siegfried: **Martin Luther in marxistischer Sicht von 1945 bis zum Beginn der achtziger Jahre.** (1983). In: 09, 307–357.

647 Bräuer, Siegfried: **Der TARF** [Theol. Arbeitskreis für Reformationsgeschichtliche Forschung]: von seiner »spontanen« Entstehung bis zum Anfang der siebziger Jahre. HCh 34/35 (2010/2011), 231–255.

648 Buchholz, Armin: **Luther-Tischreden auf Chinesisch:** im theologischen Gespräch mit chinesischen Akademikern über Luthers Relevanz im heutigen China. Lu 84 (2013), 28–47.

649 Burger, Christoph: **Een verslag van het XIIe Internationale Congres voor Lutheronderzoek in Helsinki (5–11 augustus 2012)** (Ein Bericht vom 12. Internationalen Kongress für Lutherforschung in Helsinki [5.–11. August 2012]). LuBu 21 (2012), 13–16.

650 Lapp, Michael: »**Das Kreuz Christi und das Heil des Menschen**«: Seminar der Luther-Gesellschaft vom 21. bis 23. September 2012 in Wittenberg. Lu 84 (2013), 48–51.

651 **Lutherbibliographie** 2012/ bearb. von Michael Beyer mit Matthieu Arnold ... LuJ 79 (2012), 345–391.

652 **Luther-Courier:** Informationen der Luther-Akademie Sondershausen-Ratzeburg/ hrsg. von der Luther-Akademie Sondershausen-

Ratzeburg; Rainer Rausch. Nr. 4. Sine loco, [2012]. 11 S.: Ill.

653 Rhein, Stefan: **Melanchthon 2010: von Bret-ten nach Wittenberg.** Jahrbuch für badische Kirchen- und Religionsgeschichte 5 (2011), 237–254.

654 Saarinen, Risto: **Luther-tutkimuksen kah-destoista maailmankongressi Helsingissä** (12. Internationaler Kongress für Lutherfor-schung in Helsinki). TA 117 (2012), 491–495.

655 Saarinen, Risto: **Suomalaiset Lutherin tul-**

656 Saarinen, Risto: **The study of Luther in Fin-land** (Suomalaiset Lutherin tulkitsijoina <engl.>). In: 024, 143–151: Ill.

657 Stegmann, Andreas: **Die Geschichte der Er-forschung von Martin Luthers Ethik.** LuJ 79 (2012), 211–303.

658 Wolgast, Eike: **Reformation im Plural und im Singular:** zwei neue Darstellungen der Reformationszeit von Thomas A. Brady und Thomas Kaufmann. ARG 103 (2012), 293–306. – Rez. zu LuB 2010, Nr. 474. 478.

kitsijoina (Lutherforschung in Finland). In: 024, 133–140: Ill.

NACHTRÄGLICHE REZENSIONEN

LuB 2003

571 Burkhardt, Johannes. – Huber, Wolfgang: ZBKG 80 (2011), 518f.

706 Volkmar, Christoph. – Ebert, Immo: ZBKG 80 (2011), 541f.

LuB 2004

1261 Kleinöder-Strobel, Susanne. – Reuter, Do-rothea: BlWKG 110 (2010), 423.

LuB 2005

927 Krüger, Thilo. – Molitor, Kurt: BlPfKG 77 (2010), 238–240.

LuB 2007

982 Kaufmann, Thomas. – Haag, Norbert: BlWKG 110 (2010), 419–421.

1030 Cordes, Harm. – Hohenberger, Thomas: ZBKG 80 (2011), 530–534.

LuB 2008

042 Luther und das monastische Erbe. – Schil-ling, Johannes: Lu 84 (2013), 52f.

145 Luther für zwischendurch. – Rieske, Uwe: Lu 83 (2012), 184f.

584/5 Melanchthons Briefwechsel T 4 I/II. – Treu, Martin: HCh 34/35 (2010/2011), 284f.

LuB 2009

598 Melanchthons Briefwechsel T 9. – Keller, Rudolf: ZBKG 79 (2010), 189–191.

622 Volkmar, Christoph. – Haag, Norbert: BlWKG 110 (2010), 483–485; Kohnle, Armin: Lu 83 (2012), 186–188.

LuB 2010

021 Humanismus ... – Jung, Martin H.: BlWKG 110 (2010), 395–397.

043 Scheible, Heinz. – Hans, Friedhelm: BlPfKG 77 (2010), 236 f; Jung, Martin H.: BlWKG 110 (2010), 458–461.

17 Luther, Martin. – Burger, Christoph: LuBu 20 (2011), 51–53; Kaufmann, Thomas: ARGBL 40 (2011), 25f.

21 Die Neustadter Bibel ... – Stüber, Gabriele: BlPfKG 77 (2010), 226–228.

474 Brady, Th. A. – Wolgast, Eike: ARG 103 (2012), 293–306; vgl. LuB 2013, Nr. 658.

478 Kaufmann, Th. – Wolgast, Eike: ARG 103 (2012), 293–306; vgl. LuB 2013, Nr. 658.

482 Lexutt, Athina. – Haug-Moritz, Gabriele: BlWKG 111 (2011), 309 f; Mähling, Patrik: BlPfKG 77 (2010), 403–405; Ebernburg-Hefte 44 (2010), 133–135.

492 Scheib, Otto. – Spehr, Christopher: ThLZ 138 (2013), 197–199.

530 Kuropka, Nicole. – Schwab, Eckart: MEKGR 60 (2011), 440–442.

LuB 2011

014 Franz Lau ... – Huber, Wolfgang: ZBKG 80 (2011), 548–550.

018 Johannes Bugenhagen ... – Brunk, Yvonne: Lu 83 (2012), 185 f.

036 Primus Truber. – Wennemuth, Udo: Jahrbuch für badische Kirchen- und Religionsgeschichte 6 (2012), 341 f.

115 Strauchenbruch, Elke. – Hein, Markus: Lu 83 (2012), 181 f.

174 Kandler, Karl-Hermann. – Brandt, Reinhard: Lu 83 (2012), 191 f.

180 Spehr, Christopher. – Arnold, Matthieu: http://www.perspectivia.net/content/publikationen/francia/francia-recensio/2012–2/FN/spehr_arnold

486 Greschat, Martin. – Mähling, Patrik: BlPfKG 77 (2010), 405–408; Ebernburg-Hefte 44 (2010), 135–138.

531 Melanchthon deutsch III. – Wennemuth, Udo: Jahrbuch für badische Kirchen- und Religionsgeschichte 6 (2012), 336–338.

606 Bucer, Martin. – Buckwalter, Stephen: ZBKG 79 (2010), 188 f.

615 Greschat, Martin. – Landgraf, Michael: BlPfKG 77 (2010), 237 f.

912 Jaspert, Bernd. – Mohr, Rudolf: MEKGR 60 (2011), 427 f.

LuB 2012

03 Auf Luthers Spuren unterwegs. – Wolf, G. Ph.: ZBKG 80 (2011), 592 f.

06 Davon ich singen und sagen will. – Enk, Jens-Peter: Lu 84 (2013), 62.

010 Georg Rörer ... – Stegmann, Andreas: ThLZ 138 (2013), 195–197.

013 Helmar Junghans ... – Haendler, Gert: ThLZ 138 (2013), 193–195; Leppin, Volker: Lu 84 (2013), 67 f.

022 Nürnberg. – Wolf, Gerhard Philipp: ZBKG 80 (2011), 591 f.

84 Luther, Martin. – Kuropka, Nicole: Lu 83 (2012), 180 f.

192 Koerrenz, Marita. – Basse, Michael: Lu 84 (2013), 66 f.

193 Krasselt-Maier, Judith. – Basse, Michael: Lu 84 (2013), 66 f.

217 Saarinen, Risto. – Kümper, Hiram: Lu 84 (2013), 60–62.

235 Kolb, Robert – Wenz, Gunter: ThLZ 138 (2013), 57–59.

299 Steiger, Johann Anselm. – Otte, Hans: JNKG 109 (2011), 195–197.

343 Steiger, Johann Anselm. – Nooke, Christoph T.: Lu 84 (2013), 55 f

344 Strauchenbruch, Elke. – Dembek, Arne: Lu 84 (2013), 54 f.

490 Gritsch, Eric W. – Barth, Hans-Martin: Lu 83 (2012), 182–184.

493 Kaufmann, Thomas. – Leppin, Volker: Lu 84 (2013), 53 f.

516 Hohenberger, Thomas. – Dienst, Karl: BlPfKG 77 (2010), 401–403; Ebernburg-Hefte 44 (2010), 131–133.

521 Münchow, Christoph. – Beyer, Michael: Lu 84 (2013), 58 f.

632 Küllmer, Björn – Schneider, Thomas Martin: Lu 83 (2012), 188 f.

716 Wipfler, Esther P. – Quaas, Anne Kathrin: Lu 84 (2013), 64–66.

378

Bugenhagens Reformatorische Schriften

Anneliese Bieber-Wallmann (Hg.)
Johannes Bugenhagen
Reformatorische Schriften
(1515/16–1524)
Bearbeitet von Wolf-Dieter Hauschild und
Anneliese Bieber-Wallmann
Johannes Bugenhagen. Werke, Band 1,1.
2013. XLIII, 935 Seiten, mit 19 Abb., Leinen
ISBN 978-3-525-55441-8
auch als eBook erhältlich

Mit dieser Edition lateinischer, frühneuhochdeutscher und niederdeutscher Texte dokumentiert Anneliese Bieber-Wallmann erstmals Bugenhagens literarischen Beitrag zur Verbreitung der Reformation. Die frühesten Schriften zeigen, wie stark Johannes Bugenhagen zunächst vom Humanismus beeinflusst war. In Pommern bemühte er sich um eine Verbesserung des Lateinunterrichts und eine Reform der Frömmigkeit nach biblischen Gesichtspunkten. Aus der Zeit in Wittenberg ab 1521 stammen Flugschriften mit einfachen Darstellungen der reformatorischen Lehre sowie Ausschnitte aus exegetischen Vorlesungen, mit denen Bugenhagen die evangelische Frömmigkeit nachhaltig prägte.

Editionsplan Reformatorische Schriften:

Band 2 (1525–1527), 2014

Band 3 (1528–1529), 2018

Band 4 (1531–1556), 2024

www.v-r.de

Refo 500 Academic Studies

Band 12: R. Ward Holder (Hg.)
Calvin and Luther:
The Continuing Relationship

2013. 235 Seiten, gebunden
ISBN 978-3-525-55057-1
auch als eBook erhältlich

Karl Barth's argument continues to be representative of a generally accepted modern view that Calvinism and Lutheranism are complete separate, opposing movements and theologies. And yet, in many ways the movements built on the teaching of Luther and Calvin developed in relationship and resonance with one another. Despite this fact, very few scholars have explicitly considered the relationship between Calvin and Luther. Through the articles of this volume we begin to see the possibility of a rapprochement between Calvin and Luther as sources, though not as historical figures.

www.v-r.de

Refo 500 Academic Studies

Band 11: Silvio Reichelt

**Der Erlebnisraum
Lutherstadt Wittenberg**

Genese, Entwicklung und Bestand eines
protestantischen Erinnerungsortes

2013. 448 Seiten mit 61 Abbildungen, gebunden
ISBN 978-3-525-55054-0
auch als eBook erhältlich

Silvio Reichelt untersucht den in Wittenberg gepflegten Umgang mit dem reformationsgeschichtlichen Erbe der Stadt unter den Bedingungen von fünf verschiedenen politischen Systemen. Reichelt zeigt, wie Wittenberg als historischer Raum des Wissens, politischer Raum der Ideologie und sakraler Raum des Glaubens Erinnerung leiten, kanalisieren und kodieren konnte. Deutlich wird dabei, dass historische Erinnerung die Vergangenheit nicht einfach rekonstruiert, sondern sich vielmehr als permanenter Überschreibungsprozess charakterisieren lässt. Bewohner und Besucher machen sich mittels Erinnerung ein »Bild« von der Vergangenheit.

www.v-r.de

Reformed Historical Theology

Vol 23: Herman J. Selderhuis/ Martin Leiner/
Volker Leppin (Hg.)

**Calvinismus in den Auseinanderset-
zungen des frühen konfessionellen
Zeitalters**

2013. 196 Seiten, gebunden
ISBN 978-3-525-55050-2
auch als eBook erhältlich

Das Calvin-Jahr 2009 gehörte zu den wichtigsten Ereignissen im Vorfeld des großen
Reformationsjubiläums: Eindrücklich wies es darauf hin, was die Reformation alles
ist: international, ökumenisch, facettenreich – und mehr als nur ein Martin Luther
mit Umfeld. In den Beiträgen dieses Bandes steht das Moment der Auseinandersetzung des Luthertums mit dem entstehenden Calvinismus im Vordergrund, sowohl
in historischer als auch in systematisch-theologischer Perspektive. In den Beiträgen melden sich bekannte Fachleute zu Wort: Irene Dingel, Matthias Freudenberg,
Wim Janse, Robert Kolb, Martin Leiner, Volker Leppin und Herman Selderhuis.

www.v-r.de